INTERVIEWING
Strategy, Techniques, and Tactics

Advisory Editor in Sociology

Charles M. Bonjean

The University of Texas at Austin

INTERVIEWING
Strategy, Techniques, and Tactics

Fourth Edition

Raymond L. Gorden
Antioch College

The Dorsey Press
Chicago, Illinois 60604

ISBN 0-256-03407-9

Library of Congress Catalog Card No. 86–81819

Printed in the United States of America

1 2 3 4 5 6 7 8 9 0 K 4 3 2 1 0 9 8 7

To Charlotte, Gregory, and Karen

Preface

The treatment of interviewing in this fourth edition should be useful to people who want to improve their interviewing performance and to anyone responsible for training people to interview more effectively. The concepts, tools, and activities presented here are essential to practitioners in human relations professions such as social work, teaching, business management, public administration, nursing, counseling, law enforcement, and journalism. They will also serve people doing basic field research in social anthropology, social psychology, and sociology.

The major focus of the book is the information-gathering interview as distinct from the therapeutic or persuasive interview. The text does cover the principles of therapeutic and persuasive communication as they apply to the collection of information.

This is not a cookbook of do's and don'ts for narrowly defined situations. My aim is to help anyone develop a more sophisticated, deep, varied, and flexible approach to the problems that may arise when one human being seeks information from another in a face-to-face encounter.

To be able to interview people successfully in a wide variety of situations and professional settings requires three basic ingredients, which this book provides. First, it introduces readers to the *theoretical concepts* that explain the ways communication is inhibited or facilitated in an interview. The concepts make clear the vital relationships between three factors: the type of information sought, the role of the interviewer, and the role of the respondent in the larger social context. Second, the text describes and illustrates three sets of *practical tools* called strategies, techniques, and tactics that the interviewer can use to minimize the inhibitors and to maximize the facilitators of communication. Third, it designs a set of *experiences* to enhance sensitivities, insights, and skills needed to apply the tools to a variety of concrete situations.

The theoretical concepts are presented in Chapters 1 through 6. The tools are separated into three types: *strategies* (Chapters 7 through 12), *techniques* (Chapters 13 and 14), and *tactics* (Chapters 15 through 17). The *experiences* are provided throughout the book in the form of ten laboratory problems, eight critical analysis assignments, and one field assignment. All of these assignments are in the text. In addition, instructors will find thirteen multiple-choice tests in the *Instructor's Manual*.

Chapters 18 through 25 illustrate the application (and misapplication) of strategies, techniques, and tactics in eight professional settings: social work, employee appraisal, teaching, mass media impact assessment, nursing, counseling, journalism, and police interrogation. Each setting provides a pair of dialogues. The first illustrates an interviewer making mistakes typical of that setting; the second illustrates a much more effective interview. Within each pair the setting and objectives are the same. Critical analysis questions after each pair of interviews ask readers to compare the strengths and weaknesses of the two interviews.

An unusual feature of this book is that it not only provides a creative mix of theory, tools, and experience, but also provides a pretest and posttest to validly and reliably measure the amount of improvement in the students' insights and sensitivities to interviewing problems and solutions. Twenty years of classroom use has shown that 99 percent of the students show improvement after reading the book and doing many of the assignments. Also, 75 percent of the students at Antioch College had a higher posttest score than the highest pretest score in their class. The construction and use of these tests is described in the *Instructor's Manual*.

The *Instructor's Manual* contains all materials and procedures needed by the instructor to carry out, evaluate, and discuss the assignments. For each of the ten laboratory problems the *Instructor's Manual* lists the materials and facilities needed (if they are not provided in the text), describes the central purpose of the assignment, estimates the amount of time required for students to complete each phase of the problem, gives model solutions, provides forms for obtaining and summarizing students' answers, and makes suggestions for discussion procedures. Sample forms, which can be photocopied, are provided to facilitate both the students' and the instructor's work. The *Instructor's Manual* also suggests ways of selecting which critical analysis problems to assign, and provides model answers for all questions.

For thirteen of the twenty-six chapters, the *Instructor's Manual* provides multiple-choice tests, answer forms, correct answers, and procedures for scoring. All materials are in $8\frac{1}{2} \times 11$ format to be xeroxed directly from the manual. Finally, the *Instructor's Manual* provides the procedure and scoring forms to be used in comparing the students' performance on the pretest and posttest.

It is neither possible nor desirable to require all of the activities in this text in a single course. The activities are therefore flexible enough to suit the background of the students and the objectives of the course. For example, many of the laboratory problems are arranged in stages so that the instructor can choose which stages to require. Six of the ten laboratory problems have alternative multiple-choice tests, which require less inductive analysis than do the laboratory problems.

The general objective of the book is not to make a polished interviewer, but to raise people's skill and insight, and to broaden the range of tools with which they are familiar, so that they can continue to grow on their own. The procedure of *self-guided practice* is described in Chapter 26, "Focal Skills in Interviewing."

Among the groups of persons who have had a vital place in the experiences that led me to write and revise this book are the Disaster Study Team at the National Opinion Research Center; the interviewers on the Youth Study Project and the Social Cohesion Study in Dayton, Ohio; the Colombian interviewers on the Cross-Cultural Communication Project in Bogotá, Colombia; the management interviewers of the Illinois Bell Telephone Company and the Toledo Edison Company; the trainees of the Michigan State Nursing Association; the recruits at Navy Instructional Technology Development Center; the outreach staff of the SCOPE Community Action Agency; the staff at the Sunrise Comprehensive Care Center in Dayton, Ohio; and the interviewing crews on several opinion and attitude surveys.

I also want to acknowledge the help and advice of several individuals. Dr. Lawrence Atherton, San Diego Mesa College, helped design the figures. Eugenie Eddie, RN, gave advice on the nursing interview; Patricia Day Malone, school psychologist, helped with the teacher–parent interview setting; Cheryl McHenry of WHIO–TV critiqued the journalistic interview; and Charles J. Gift, polygraph expert of the Dayton Police Department, provided suggestions on the police interrogation chapter.

The most prominent in providing criticism and suggestions for this fourth edition were Susan Florio-Ruane, of Michigan State University; Bruce London, of Florida Atlantic University; and Richard Schuster, of Virginia Polytechnic Institution and State University. They were very helpful in pointing out weaknesses, omissions, and lack of clarity as well as in supporting the book's strengths. Needless to say, any remaining shortcomings are the responsibility of the author. I am particularly indebted to my wife, Charlotte Gilson Gorden, who helped with the final drafts of the manuscript in all four editions.

The students at Antioch College have also been important to the life of this text. Over a period of years they have shown a keen interest in learning to interview and in applying their skills in their work–study program jobs. They have helped me develop materials and demonstrate the effectiveness of a broad systematic approach to interviewer training.

Raymond L. Gorden

Contents

AN OVERVIEW

Chapter One

Interviewing in Perspective

To the uninitiated, interviewing is "just talking to people!" Perhaps this deceptively simple appearance accounts for the historically recent advent of systematic attempts to analyze and experiment with the interaction between interviewer and respondent. Since the dawn of civilization, human survival in organized groups has depended upon the ability to ask a question and get an answer. Even though a certain amount of confusion, distortion, incompleteness, and outright lying has always occurred in this communication dyad, there was always enough success to keep society functioning. Even ancient civilizations did systematic interviewing to obtain a crude census, but it is likely that more systematic analysis of the communication process has been done in the last thirty years than in the preceding centuries.

USES OF INTERVIEWING

Often the word *interviewing* evokes images of a person taking a census, doing a sample opinion poll, interviewing prospective employees—all done in some setting in which the person's major activity is interviewing.

Many people—in addition to these full-time interviewers—have a vital need for interviewing skills. Dozens of occupations depend upon the interview as a major source of information needed to carry out their central task. A police officer investigating an auto accident, a teacher having a conference with a parent, a nurse talking with a patient, a lawyer getting information from a client, a dermatologist taking a medical history, a detective talking with witnesses at the scene of a crime, an oral historian collecting the memoirs of a statesman, or a parent trying to discover why a child has a stomachache are all using interviewing.

This omnipresence of the interview is reflected in the social science literature dealing with information-gathering methods. Highly specialized books and articles abound dealing with specific types of respondents.

For example, Milford describes the difficulties of interviewing associates of legendary figures.[1] Jacobson gives an example of the field problem involved in eliciting information from delegates who are attending international assemblies, a problem that is complicated by cross-cultural communication barriers.[2] Even the Supreme Court has been invaded by interviewers.[3] Urban Protestant ministers have been the focus of interviews to determine their relationship to the changing problems of the urban scene.[4] The elderly have been a target of study for many years and are sometimes viewed as a special type of respondent.[5] Engle gives pointers on how to interview medical patients.[6]

Sometimes the focus is on a particular type of interviewer rather than respondent. For example, Oblinger's book is aimed at oral historians,[7] and Kreider produced a book specifically for military officers.[8] Umiker, in one of the most recent and perhaps most specialized books, shows medical laboratory supervisors how to carry out interviews with prospective laboratory technicians.[9] In short, all types of people do interviewing and are interviewed for myriad purposes.

This explosive growth in the variety of uses of the interview as a tool in the study of individuals, groups, organizations, and institutions makes it highly desirable to seek some basic underlying principles and sensitizing concepts that can be applied in a variety of interviewing settings. This book is an attempt to provide general principles and tools for maximizing the flow of valid and relevant information in any situation

[1]Nancy Milford, "The Golden Dreams of Zelda Fitzgerald," *Harper's Magazine*, January 1969, pp. 46–53.

[2]Harold K. Jacobson, "Deriving Data from Delegates to International Assemblies: A Research Note," *International Organization*, 21 (1967), pp. 592–613.

[3]David Grey, "Interviewing at the (Supreme) Court," *Public Opinion Quarterly*, 31 (1967), pp. 285–89.

[4]W. C. Kloetzle et al., "Guide for Interviewing the Minister and Selected Key Members of the Congregation of the Urban Church Effectiveness Study," *Social Compass*, 9 (1962), pp. 387–402.

[5]J. Zelan, "Interviewing the Aged," *Public Opinion Quarterly*, 33 (1969), pp. 420–24.

[6]George L. Engle and W. L. Morgan, Jr., *Interviewing the Patient* (New York: W. B. Saunders, 1973).

[7]Carl Oblinger, *Interviewing the People of Pennsylvania: A Conceptual Guide to Oral History* (Philadelphia: Pennsylvania History and Museums, 1981).

[8]Paul T. Kreider, *Interviewing Handbook for Military Officers* (San Anselmo, Calif.: KCE Publishers, 1981).

[9]William O. Umiker, *Interviewing Skills for Laboratory Supervisors* (New York: Medical Economics, 1983).

where one person is trying to obtain information from another. Although the emphasis is on general principles, Part 4, "Professional Settings of the Interview," illustrates the application of these basic principles by giving good and bad examples of interviews taken from eight professional settings: social work, employee appraisal, parent-teacher conferences, the mass media impact evaluation, nursing, counseling, and police interrogation. Surprising similarities exist between such apparently opposite types of interviews as counseling and police interrogation. Presenting both the general principles and specific applications shows that there may be more difference between one type of social work interview and another than between a social work interview and a journalistic interview. Thus, looking at the diversity shows the value of a general frame of reference that will sensitize the interviewer to the underlying problems and solutions regardless of the specific setting.

INTERVIEWING RELATED TO OTHER METHODS

There are many methods used to collect information about human behavior. Regardless of the form of the data collected, how it is recorded, or the purpose for which it is used, it is collected by three elementary forms of human activity: *empathy, participation*, and *observation*.

In this context empathy refers to feeling with another person or understanding how he or she *feels* about something. Participation means *doing* something with people in their regular ongoing activity. This participatory role furnishes a vantage point from which either to observe another's activity (including verbal) or to introspectively note one's thoughts and feelings related to the situation in which the activity is taking place. Observation means not only visual perception but *any sensory perception* of external cues which help us understand human behavior.

From these three activities all of the methods for studying human behavior (such as the interview, questionnaire, pure observation, participant-observation, and nonreactive methods) are derived. Within this framework, interviewing is seen as one specific form of empathizing, participating, and observing which takes place between two people.[10]

---

[10]In this context the questionnaire is seen not so much as a unique data-gathering method but simply as a technique for extending the interview in which the researcher participates by constructing the questionnaire. The researcher's observation is restricted to noting the written responses on the questionnaire unless he or she is present while the respondent is filling it out. Then the researcher can participate more fully by clarifying questions, motivating the respondent to complete the questionnaire, encouraging the respondent to give full answers. Also if the researcher is present, his or her observation function can be expanded to include noting nonverbal behavior as the respondent fills out the questionnaire.

The interviewer's participation takes the form of determining the setting or social context in which the interview takes place and asking questions or presenting other stimuli to elicit information from the respondent. The observation consists of noting not only the content of the verbal message but also the tone of voice, facial expressions, and body movements. Empathy is involved in anticipating probable reactions to questions and in sensing how the respondent felt about events he or she is relating.

Personal Documents

The use of personal documents such as diaries or letters involves the observation of verbal behavior elicited by someone other than the researcher. The use of such spontaneous documents has both advantages and disadvantages over direct eliciting of information via the interview; however it is not our task to compare the relative merits of these different sources of information but to show how they involve the same or different basic activities. Two classical treatments of the use of personal documents have been done by Allport[11] and by Gottschalk et al.[12]

One of the most monumental uses of personal letters was in the classic work by William I. Thomas and Florian Znaniecki in their study of *The Polish Peasant in Europe and America.* Personal documents were used to demonstrate processes of acculturation and assimilation of the Polish immigrants to the United States. Although the study came under severe criticism as a case of proof-by-example (in which there is no evidence that either a representative sample or negative cases have been sought) it is still clearly an excellent exploratory study giving insights, discovering new relationships, and suggesting hypotheses to be tested by more logically rigorous methods.

It is sometimes suggested that many types of spontaneous documents such as diaries[13] and confessions[14] should be suspect because of

---

[11]Gordon W. Allport, *The Use of Personal Documents in Psychological Science* (New York: Social Science Research Council, 1942).

[12]Louis Gottschalk, Clyde Kluckhohn, and Robert Angell, *The Use of Personal Documents in History, Anthropology and Sociology* (New York: Social Science Research Council, 1947).

[13]For example, *A Young Girl's Diary* (translated in 1921 by E. and C. Paul from the German version which Hug-Helmuth claimed to be the unedited diary of a young girl, demonstrating her psychosexual development) was referred to by Freud as a "gem," but was later discovered to be a fraud.

[14]St. Augustine, in his *Confessions, Book X*, even gives his reason for writing the confessions: "As to what I now am while I am writing my Confessions, there are many who desire to know—both people who know me personally, and people who do not, but have heard from me or about me. Yet they have not

the possible bias introduced by the fact that very few people, and therefore unusual people, write such things. Either they may have unique experiences to write about or they may have special motivations leading them to deceive rather than to enlighten the researcher. This problem of possible falsification is not unique to spontaneous personal documents; it is also a problem in the use of the interview and the questionnaire.

Personal documents may be completely spontaneous, as in the case of some diaries or the same type of information elicited by the life-history interview; the latter has some advantages of historical perspective but some disadvantages in loss of detail over time. A classic example of this is Sutherland's interviewing of a professional thief to learn how professional thieves operated in relationship to each other, to lawyers, to judges, to police, to their families, and to society in general.[15] Sutherland obtained the information by having the thief write on certain topics, and then having seven hours of discussion per week, for twelve weeks. The thief was paid a small weekly wage for his work from funds provided by the Social Science Research Committee of the University of Chicago. Much of the information was of the type a professional in any field might write in a diary, but it was guided and stimulated by the researcher's participation.

Another study in the same life-history category produced an autobiography of a drug addict.[16] Howard Becker, a sociologist with an interest in playing jazz piano, got acquainted with Janet and her husband who played in the band. Janet came to the Beckers' house frequently to talk with the Beckers about mutual acquaintances of the jazz world. She was persuaded to tell her life story and to make a series of tape recordings. She was paid a small amount for these sessions. She needed the money but also hoped to have an opportunity to become an author. Her attendance at the appointed sessions was sometimes irregular because of the need to steal and evade police to raise the price of a "fix." The result is a case study of a personality being molded by a series of forces in a large American city, a rare personal account from the addict's point of view on how she got "hooked."

Becker's role was at times that of an interviewer engaging in an unstructured give-and-take, but the interviewer had other roles in the jazz world, giving him a special link to the respondent. His role was a combination of that of an interviewer and a participant-observer.

---

their ear to my heart, where I am, what I am. They wish, therefore, to hear from my own confession what I am inwardly where they cannot pierce with eye or ear or mind."

[15]Edwin H. Sutherland, *The Professional Thief* (Chicago: University of Chicago Press, 1956).

[16]Helen McGill Hughes, ed., *The Fantastic Lodge: The Autobiography of a Drug Addict* (Greenwich, Conn.: Fawcett Publications, 1971).

Although the informal series of interviews or discussions can blend into the participant-observer role, it is helpful to think of the pure type of participant-observation as something clearly different from the pure-type interview.

Participant-Observation

Participant-observation differs from the interview in that the research situation involves more than two interacting participants, and the researcher participates in some role other than that of interviewer. One of the major problems of the participant-observation method is to find some role in the group, community, or organization which the researcher can successfully play and which will provide access to those people and situations he or she must observe to accomplish the objectives of the study.

This problem of getting a role inside the group has been solved in many distinctly different situations. Respectable suburbia was studied by Gans by simply deciding to study the community in which he lived.[17] His participant roles as property owner, taxpayer, parent, and neighbor were readily accessible, but there were still problems of maneuvering into the right position at the right time to observe and hear what was relevant to his study of Levittown.

In contrast to this setting is Liebow's study of lives in the black ghetto in Washington, D.C., in which he focused on the family, friendship, and work life of the black underemployed man.[18] Liebow, being a white stranger in a black ghetto, was met with suspicion at first, but after helping with the legal defense of a man accused of killing his wife, he became accepted as someone who wanted to help.

In another study of the black ghetto, Hannerz gives a fascinating account of the challenges and problems in explaining who he is and what he wants to black residents of a Washington, D.C., ghetto.[19]

In some instances participant-observer methods have given rise to controversy concerning ethics, particularly in the study of secret societies or any groups hostile to outsiders. Many political sects, religious sects, and social movements have the attitude that "if you are not for us, you are against us," and only the true believers are allowed access to the group. In these cases the researchers must either quit trying to understand these groups, or they must enter in some acceptable role such as a "believer" or at least a "potential recruit." This ethical problem of simulating a role is seen in the controversy over the study by Festinger et al.

---

[17]Herbert Gans, *The Levittowners* (New York: Pantheon, 1967).

[18]Elliot Liebow, *Tally's Corner* (Boston: Little, Brown, 1967).

[19]Ulf Hannerz, *Soulside: Inquiries into Ghetto Culture and Community* (New York: Columbia University Press, 1969).

of a group predicting the destruction of the world on a certain date in the near future.[20] The research team posed as traveling businessmen who had learned of the group's activities and were interested in learning more. Their description of the group's reaction to the failure of their prophecy is interesting and useful to the understanding of human behavior, and the participation of the research team did no harm to the members of the group studied, but the ethics of playing a false role is still controversial.

The fact that it is possible for a participant-observer to study deviant groups' behavior without playing a false undercover role is demonstrated by Humphreys' study of homosexuals, including their sexual activities in restrooms known as "tearooms."[21] His roles in the homosexual community included being a "lookout" at the "tearooms" to warn of any possible intrusion upon their privacy and being an "advocate" in organizing homosexuals to protect themselves against police harassment, blackmail, and discrimination.

One of the apparent dilemmas of participant-observation is that if the researcher does not succeed in getting into the group in an acceptable role, he or she cannot get the opportunity to observe; but the researcher who is fully accepted as an equal member of the group is in danger of losing the objectivity needed to carry out valid observations and interpretations. This problem is dramatically illustrated in the account by Reiss of a large-scale study of the police in several cities.[22] The researchers were so thoroughly assimilated into the police that observers playing the role of plainclothesmen threatened suspects with nightsticks. According to Reiss the majority of the participant-observers became pro-police.

This problem of finding an intermediate position between being an objective outsider with no opportunity to observe and being an insider whose participation has rendered the observer incapable of objective observation is central to the method of participant-observation. It has been solved in several ways. The observer may assume *marginal* roles, like "potential recruit" or "friend of the cause," which provide the opportunity to observe but do not require the types of participation liable to totally assimilate the observer. Another solution is to train the researcher to observe carefully and report his or her own feelings, attitudes, and beliefs as they change during the time that the researcher is being assimilated into the group. Another strategy appropriate in some cases is the

---

[20]Leon Festinger, Henry Riecken, and Stanley Schachter, *When Prophecy Fails* (New York: Harper & Row, 1956).

[21]Laud Humphreys, *The Tearoom Trade*, rev. ed. (Chicago: Aldine Publishing, 1975).

[22]Albert J. Reiss, Jr., "Stuff and Nonsense about Social Surveys and Observations," in *Institutions and the Person*, ed. Howard S. Becker et al. (Chicago: Aldine Publishing, 1968).

substitution of pure observation or nonparticipant observation. In this case, of course, there is no opportunity to ask questions, to stimulate discussion, or to manipulate the situation experimentally.

Pure observation has little relationship to interviewing in that it does not provide a context for either formal or informal interviewing, which participant-observation does provide. For this reason it will not be dealt with separately. However, the following section points out how certain unobtrusive measures can combine the values of pure observation with the values of participation without requiring the researcher's direct participation.

Unobtrusive Measures

The term *unobtrusive measure* has developed in reference to types of observation which remove the observer from any direct interaction with the people involved in the behavior he or she is studying. Webb et al. have given an overview with examples of unobtrusive measures.[23] Such methods include *hidden observation* or photography; *trace examination* that deals with examining the physical effects of human behavior, such as the wearing down of the stone steps in a Mayan pyramid; or *examination of documents* such as marriage licenses, auto registrations, and newspapers; or *contrived observations*. It is this last category which is of particular interest here because it combines the advantage of not being observed (a disadvantage of pure observation) with the advantage of being able to participate by providing certain stimuli to those in the situation being observed.

The researcher participates *indirectly* by contriving the situation to include certain stimuli designed to elicit action toward some object. Instead of having to directly ask people, for example, their attitudes toward certain organizations like the American Legion and the Communist Party, the observer contrives to have them demonstrate their attitudes by action. One way of doing this is by the "lost letter technique" described by Milgram.[24] In this study, stamped letters addressed to different organizations were dropped about the city. Then an observer recorded whether the "lost letter" was left on the sidewalk, picked up and destroyed, or picked up and mailed. It was assumed that the differences in behavior reflect differences in attitude toward the organizations to whom the letters are addressed.

---

[23]Eugene J. Webb, Donald T. Campbell, Richard D. Schwartz, and Lee Sechrest, *Nonreactive Measures in the Social Sciences*, 2nd ed. (Boston: Houghton Mifflin, 1981).

[24]Stanley Milgram, "The Lost Letter Technique," *Psychology Today* 3 (1969), pp. 30–33.

With imagination, researchers can contrive other situations requiring a choice of alternative actions by those to be observed.

Relative Value of Methods

There is much literature devoted to studies and experiments on the relative value of interview, questionnaire, pure observation, empathy, and participant-observation. Some studies show that one method was more valid and other studies show that another method was more valid. Gradually, the question has shifted from "Which method is most valid?" to "Which method is best for what purpose under what circumstances?"

Interviewing is most valuable when we are interested in knowing people's beliefs, attitudes, values, knowledge, or any other subjective orientations or mental content. Whether the interview is more valuable than the questionnaire depends upon the degree to which we know exactly what we want to know and what the possible range of answers might be. The exploratory values of the unstructured interview are impossible to attain in a questionnaire where there is no opportunity to formulate new questions or probe for clarifications.

Observation is often superior to the interview in situations where we are asking the respondent to report his or her own overt actions in the past but where the respondent's memory may be faulty or where the respondent may want to hide the real nature of certain actions from the interviewer. In this case an observer who is either unseen or not defined as such by the observed can get more reliable information. On the other hand, observation of isolated physical actions is often very difficult to interpret unless we know the person's intent or motivation.

Participant-observation has many of the advantages of pure observation while allowing the researcher to intervene in a meaningful way in the ongoing action under observation. In comparison with pure observation, it has one disadvantage: the researcher, as participant, may have unintended effects upon the behavior of the observed.

Personal documents present an advantage since they often have already been accumulated, and they cannot be biased by the researcher because he or she was not involved in eliciting the information. However, since the researcher was not present to guide the response, to ask additional questions, or to probe for further elaboration or clarification, much of the information in a diary, letter, or confession will be irrelevant to the problem being studied, and much of the relevant information the person could have furnished is missing. Historians must often wish that they could interview certain historical figures to find out what really happened or why these figures did what they did in a particular situation.

One strong recommendation made more and more often in studies of comparative method is that we cease quibbling over which method is the best, use methods to fit the purposes or conditions of the study, and use multiple methods whenever possible. This use of multiple methods, each to cross-check or supplement the others, is often referred to as *triangulation.*

Triangulation

Often the nature of the problem under investigation demands a multimethod approach because the various methods give totally different kinds of information that can supplement each other, because we do not know how to interpret some of the information unless we can couple it with other information, or because we need a cross-check to verify the validity of our observations.

For instance, we may want to supplement our analysis of certain public speeches made by a congressman by interviewing him and by reading biographical material about him. By combining these sources we would be better able to predict how he will vote on a specific issue in Congress than by using any one source alone.

Community studies must triangulate information from public records, personal documents, newspapers, direct interviews with the focal persons, interviews with others about the focal persons, participant-observation, and pure observation merely to obtain the many types of information needed to cover the complex phenomenon we call a community. Experimental studies, naturalistic communities studies, and statistical surveys can be fruitfully combined in many instances. The general topic of triangulation is clarified by detailed examples of comparative studies by Denzin.[25]

All of these methods of gathering information in the social sciences are influenced by the profound fact that empathy enters into not only the way we participate or observe as part of the information-gathering activity but also into the way we interpret and analyze the information and in the application of the results to future situations. Only the scientist studying human behavior is a part of the phenomenon being studied. This unique relationship between the observer and the observed in the social sciences has both its advantages and disadvantages, which the following section will now try to describe.

Empathy

The concept of empathy, under various names, is found in the literature of philosophy, anthropology, sociology, and psychology. George Herbert Mead used the phrase "taking the role of the other," and Max Weber

---

[25]Norman K. Denzin, ed., "Triangulation: A Case for Methodological Evaluation and Combination," pt. 12 in *Sociological Methods: A Sourcebook* (Chicago: Aldine Publishing, 1970).

discussed what he called the *verstehende* method. Charles H. Cooley used the term *sympathetic introspection*, while Freud and others speak of *empathy, identification*, and *rapport*. Anthropologists have often dealt with the problem of understanding the meaning behind overt acts of people in a culture foreign to the observer. They might use the term *rapport, insight*, or *understanding*. All of these concepts overlap in their meaning and involve to some extent what we mean by empathy. Empathy is defined as the process by which one person is able to imaginatively place himself or herself in another's role and situation in order to understand the other's feelings, point of view, attitudes, and tendencies to act in a given situation. In essence, empathy is the ability to correctly answer the question, "How would I feel or act in the situation if I were in his place?"

Some reject this method as being too subjective. They argue that it is useless because it is based upon an *if* proposition which may be untrue. Others have too much faith in empathy and rely upon it in situations where it is not dependable. We prefer to turn away from the question, "Is it or is it not reliable?" to the more fruitful question, "Under what conditions is it valid or invalid?"

In general terms, a person's ability to successfully empathize with another person in a situation depends upon:

1.   The degree to which this person's knowledge of the other's situation is complete and accurate.

2.   The extent to which this person has experienced the same situation, or the degree to which he can imaginatively construct such a situation from elements of several similar situations.

3.   The degree to which this person accurately observes and remembers his own experiences.

Let us assume that one person's observation and inferences regarding the other's situation are complete and accurate. Then we can ask how the probable validity of empathic prediction varies with the probability that the observer has had an experience similar to the one observed. This probability generally corresponds to the degree of universality of the behavior to be predicted. We can think of all forms of behavior and experience as ranging on a continuum from the most to the least universal.

Most				*Least*
universal				*universal*
Biological	Human	Cultural	Role	Personal
behavior	behavior	behavior	behavior	behavior

Biological behavior includes those biological attributes which *all* members of the *homo sapiens* species share. For example, all people are born, must eat, and must eliminate waste material from the body. All people have sexual impulses, are startled by loud, unexpected noises, become fatigued, and must finally die. These are all necessary aspects of the human biological nature, regardless of the amount or type of interaction with other human beings.

Human behavior signifies those characteristics of behavior which all human beings share as a result of interaction with other human beings. In contrast to biological behavior, which is inherited, human nature must be learned in social interaction. Therefore, characteristics of behavior such as the use of language, self-consciousness, conscience, and sentiments (such as love, hate, embarrassment, or the desire for recognition) are acquired, but are universal to mankind.

Cultural behavior encompasses those aspects of behavior that are common to a particular group of people, but which distinguish them from another group. This would include such aspects as the particular *content* of the conscience rather than the mere possession of a conscience. Similarly, culture determines the *particular* language spoken by a group as distinguished from the more general characteristic of having a language. It includes all the folkways, mores, values, ideologies, and attitudes which distinguish one group from another and which all members of each group normally hold in common.

Role behavior includes those actions which depend upon a particular *role* played in a culture group. Therefore, this aspect of behavior varies within a culture group, depending upon the role or combination of roles played by a person. A corollary to this is that the range of role behavior within a culture group depends upon the complexity of the social organization (role structure) in that group. The differences between the behavior of a father and a mother toward their child are essentially differences in role.

Personal behavior indicates those characteristics of behavior which may vary from person to person while playing the same role in the same culture. Here we are intentionally avoiding the concept of personality as the "total behavior pattern of an individual," sometimes used in anthropology, sociology, and psychology, because our scheme is intended to bring into sharp focus the varying degrees of universality of behavior forms. Our definition includes such things as individual tastes, preferences, basic personality traits such as optimism or pessimism, and feelings of security or insecurity.

This scheme suggests that one person cannot empathize with all people in all situations with equal success. The empathizer can be limited by the degree of universality of the situation and by his or her own experience. Thus, if the behavior to be understood is at the biological or the human behavior level, the empathizer need not be from the same culture or have the same role in society as the person to whom the empathy is directed. However, if the behavior is at the cultural or role level, the person attempting to empathize may fail miserably in the attempt unless he or she has participated in the same culture or the same role.

This is not to suggest that anyone can empathize with others at the biological or human behavior level. That has been proved untrue. But if the person attempting to empathize at this level is not successful, it is not for the lack of common experience, but rather because that person does not perceive the other as being human in the same sense as the person attempting the empathizing is human. In other words, he or she does not appreciate the other's circumstances or is unaware of what his or her own reactions would be in the same circumstances.

Not only would we expect a person with a wider fund of experiences to empathize more successfully, but we would also expect a person who accurately observes and remembers his or her own behavior to have more success. We have all encountered individuals who have difficulty understanding or predicting the behavior of others mainly because they miscalculate how they themselves would behave under the same conditions.

A person's ability to empathize may also be distorted by a tendency to see only the "good" aspect of reality. All human beings tend to do this to some extent, but there are wide variations in people's ability to see themselves or others objectively when what they see does not correspond with what they would like to see.

The following situations illustrate some of the values and limitations of empathy. Agreement will vary greatly, but the situations will demonstrate some of the strengths and weaknesses of the method.

Situation 1. Samu lived in the crescent-shaped clearing in the palm grove. His thatched hut was near the coral reef on the island of Baikta. Although he was only ten years old, he proudly assisted his father who, like most of the inhabitants of the island, was a fisherman. These preliterate people had never seen a movie nor heard a radio. The island was a battleground between the Americans and the Japanese for about three days in 1945. These soldiers were the last foreigners on the island. The fastest transportation on the island was the dugout canoe with outrigger pontoons and no sails. Samu's father was proud of his skill in launching and paddling a canoe in the heavy surf when they went fishing each day. None of the islanders had been farther than Choru Island about sixty miles away.

Samu had never seen a white man until a boat arrived in the lagoon with the technical staff of the movie "Coral Sands." In Samu's words, "My father told me that they were not a war party like the last white men he had seen, but that they wanted to make a story which the white man called a 'movie.' They talked to my father and asked whether they could take me with them for several weeks to an island about 285 miles east of Baikta. No one lives on the island because no fruit trees grow there. They said that I was just the right size for the movie. One of them spoke our language, but it was difficult to understand his words. He told my father that if I would stay for six weeks or more he would give my father a new fishing net. That is something my father would like very much. They had no room for any of my relatives on their boat and they needed a boy just my size."

In this case what would the father's reaction be?

Discussion. If we look at this situation more abstractly, we see a father being asked to let his ten-year-old son leave home with strangers. They would be taking the boy to an uninhabited island almost five times as far away as any of his acquaintances had traveled in their lives. Furthermore, all but one would speak only a foreign language, and that one person showed only a crude knowledge of the native language and was difficult to understand. In effect, the father was being asked to entrust his son to strangers with no more compensation than the *promise* of a fishing net. The boy would be among strangers who spoke a foreign language and ate strange food. None of his relatives would be with him.

In the primitive culture, where kinship ties are extremely strong, a ten-year-old boy is an important asset in helping his father, and his absence would upset the family's usual division of labor. Samu's people had never heard a radio, seen a movie, or read any books which might have given them knowledge beyond the traditional folklore of the tribe. Therefore, little motivation could be attached to appearing in a movie. Furthermore, it is improbable that the earlier battle between the Americans and Japanese would make the father remember Americans as kind, predictable people.

Considering these factors, we are almost certain that the father would refuse the offer. The ten anthropologists and sociologists who were consulted agreed unanimously.

Untrained interviewers gave various reasons for believing that Samu's father would accept the offer: "The father is proud of his son and would like to have him in a movie." "The father realized that these men were different from the other white men he had seen." "The father knew that the white men would not harm Samu." "The islanders would be honored that Samu was chosen." "The father would want to give Samu an opportunity that he himself had never had." "There's not enough information." "There's no information about this particular culture telling how they react to strangers."

The "reasons" above reflect a failure of empathy due to the great divergence in cultural backgrounds. The person from a more affluent and complex culture tends to *project* images, values, and assumptions from his or her own culture in attempting to understand the motives and reactions of a person in a less affluent and less complex culture. In this case an assumption, for example that the father would be proud to have

Samu in a movie, is incorrect for that culture. Short of actually experiencing and internalizing the other person's culture, the only hope for increasing a person's ability to predict the behavior of people in another culture is to have some abstract theoretical framework that allows a situation in one culture to be translated into its equivalent meaning in another culture.

Situation 2. A friend has offered Bob, a student at College X, free transportation and lodging for a weekend of skiing. If they go, it will be impossible for Bob to return to campus in time to attend his Monday morning philosophy class. Although college regulations do not require obtaining permission to miss classes, Bob feels that he should find out from the professor how to make up anything he might miss in the Monday session. He goes to the professor's office and says:

Bob: Hello, Dr. Belden! Could I speak to you for a minute?

Dr. Belden: Surely.

Bob: I was just wondering if anything important will be going on in class on Monday?

Dr. Belden: Why do you ask?

Bob: (Enthusiastically) Well, to be frank, I have a chance to take a skiing trip this weekend, and I wanted to find out if I would be missing anything.

What is likely to be Dr. Belden's reaction in this situation?

Discussion. This situation is a matter of two points of view associated with two complementary roles in an institutional setting. In general, professors feel that they work hard to transform the raw material they find in freshmen into educated human beings. They usually do not enter a field unless they think it is important, and their egos are intimately involved with that field. Under these conditions, the student, who has been wondering if "anything important" would go on in class Monday, implies with his choice of words that there have been days when nothing important occurred.

Even though the professor responds with a civil "Why do you ask?" he certainly has not been flattered by the student's question. Nor is the student's answer gratifying. Instead of asking how he can make up what he will miss, he asks whether he will miss anything.

For these reasons, it seems that the professor would react with a negative feeling. This hypothesis has been substantiated by the responses of a small sample of college professors teaching where class attendance is not required. None of them reacted favorably. Two said they would have no special reaction, and the remaining nineteen said they would react unfavorably.

Several typical reasons were offered by untrained observers who thought the professor would react positively: "The professor will probably be impressed by the student's interest in making up the work." "The student didn't have to make any excuses since permission to miss class is not required." "The professor would admire the student's honesty. After all he could have used the 'sick aunt' excuse."

These types of replies simply show an observer's inability to empathize with the professor's role in the student-teacher relationship, and their complete identification with the student causes them to marvel at Bob's honesty.

The ability to empathize is an integral part of the interviewing process. An interviewer who is incapable of empathizing with the respondent has little success. Differences between individual interviewers' abilities to empathize are more striking when the general style of interviewing is less structured and when the topic of the interview contains more ego-involved material for the respondent. This is true because the nonscheduled interview gives more freedom to the interviewer to select the content, form, and sequence of questions. The interviewer is freer either to make more errors or to take advantage of opportunities not available in a highly scheduled interview.

It is the interviewer's ability to empathize which allows him or her to select techniques and tactics most appropriate to the circumstances. Without this basic skill, the interviewer who has learned several specific techniques cannot use them effectively when faced with the respondent but can only proceed in either a mechanical fashion or a way that satisfies the ego. Neither course will produce best results.

Although empathic predictions are sometimes incorrect, the interviewer must constantly *try* to empathize in order to utilize observations of self and of the respondent as a guide to effectively modifying behavior during the interview.

This possibility of error makes it necessary for the interviewer to treat a prediction of the respondent's behavior as a tentative hypothesis to be modified by subsequent observations. Thus, the interviewer, through the use of empathy and observation, constantly revises predictions of the respondent's behavior and adjusts the interviewing behavior accordingly.

An interviewer also should be aware of his or her strengths and limitations in empathic observation in order to judge which types of interviews can be handled effectively. For example, a social worker whose background was anti-Catholic might have great difficulty empathizing with a Catholic's feeling on the socialist state or on contraception. Or a young sociology student doing a community study might find that his

Protestant background interferes with his appreciation of an older Jewish woman's feelings about anti-Semitism in the community. A personnel interviewer in a large industry might not be able to empathize with the employee's untrusting attitude toward the company's in-service education program.

There are possible problems in the use of empathy sometimes referred to as *over-rapport*. This term is used to warn interviewers of dangers in interviewing someone too like themselves with whom they can empathize readily. One danger is that the interviewer empathically senses the painfulness of certain types of questions and is reluctant to ask them. A related danger lies in not asking the question because it would "seem silly" to the respondent since the answer is assumed to be obvious. These two dangers are greater for the lone-wolf researcher than for researchers on a team in which interview results may be challenged.

A third danger of over-rapport occurs even when the needed question is asked, but the interviewer, assuming the answer in advance, may fail to notice and probe the subtle differences between the answer expected and the one actually received.

Another less obvious disadvantage of over-rapport may occur even though the appropriate question is asked and the interviewer notes deviations from assumptions or does not assume the answer in advance. It can be impossible for anyone but the interviewer and the respondent to interpret the answer meaningfully: The larger outside audience cannot understand the answer, yet the interviewer does not see the need to probe for the hidden assumptions necessary to interpret the answer correctly. This may happen when the interviewer and respondent share one culture or subculture and the audience for whom the information is intended is from a different culture or subculture.

The author found many examples of this problem when he was directing a study of the cultural barriers to communication between North Americans and Colombians in Bogotá. The approach was to study situations in which Colombians and Americans interacted to discover miscommunication due to differences in cultural background other than language. Realizing that the etiquette barrier would prevent Colombians from frankly telling an American interviewer what they thought of the American guests, the author used Colombian interviewers to interview the Colombians and American interviewers to interview the Americans about the same interaction situation.

When the American director of the project listened to the tape-recorded interviews, he found many examples of answers from Colombian respondents that seemed to be meaningful to the Colombian interviewer who saw no need to probe further; but the answers were meaningless to an American. For example, the American sojourners (students and Peace Corp trainees) reported to the American interviewer that, when they stood in line at the bank teller's window to cash a check, the Colombian bank customers in the same line did not wait their turn for service. Instead, the Colombian customers cut in front of the Americans and gave their checks to the teller before the Americans had a chance to receive their cash. The Americans concluded from this that Colombians were rude. A mutual hostility began to develop between the Americans and the Colombian customers of the bank. To discover whether or not this conflict was caused by miscommunication, a Colombian interviewer was sent to interview the tellers at the bank where about 200 American Peace Corps trainees cashed their checks every two weeks. The assignment was to discover the Colombians' views of the Americans and to look for any possible misunderstandings that could be corrected. A portion of the interview follows:

Interviewer: Do any *norteamericanos* come to this bank?

Respondent: Yes, many of them now since the Peace Corps has come to Colombia.

I: What kind of people are they?

R: They are young and many wear beards—and they dress like peasants and are rude. At least many of them are rude!

I: How are they rude?

R: Well, when they come in to cash their checks they come to my window, hand me their checks and just stand there blocking the way and won't move until they get their money. This makes a lot of the customers angry because the *norteamericanos* are so rude.

I: Yes, I see what you mean; that is very rude!

Although the American project director learned from this that the Colombians also see the Americans as rude, he still could not understand why standing in front of the teller's window until receiving the cash, as is done in American banks, would be considered rude. So the director interviewed the Colombian interviewer as follows:

I: Señora Vasquez, I was very interested in listening to your interview with the teller at the Banco Commercial Antioqueno. But there is one thing I didn't understand. Why did it make the other customers angry when the American stood at the window until he got his cash?

R: Standing there is rude because they already had their turn and were blocking the way so that others couldn't get to the teller.

I: What are they supposed to do?

R: Just like in any bank; it is the same at this local bank.

I: But I don't understand exactly what the customer is supposed to do to get a check cashed.

R: You just give your check to the teller and then get away from the window so someone else can have their turn giving their check to the teller.

I: But where does the customer get the cash?

R: The teller will give it to him.

I: The same teller?

R: Yes.

I: But *when* does this happen?

R: As soon as he has the cash, the teller will call the customer's name, and then the customer comes back to the window for the cash.

I: Now I think I understand. First the customer gives the check to the teller and then leaves the window so other customers can give their checks to the teller; then the first customer waits until the teller calls his name and goes back for the cash.

R: Right. That's the only efficient way to work it!

Why "that is the only efficient way to work it" becomes clear when we understand how the Colombian banking system works. In their system the teller does not have cash to give out. The teller's function is to check the customer's identification and to pass the check along to various other people depending on the type of the account. A bookkeeper must first check the balance in the account and (if there is a sufficient amount) send the cash with the customer's name back to the teller and deduct this amount from the balance shown in the statement for that account. This system makes overdrafts impossible. This process may require only ninety seconds for some checks and five minutes for others. Therefore the cash does not become available to the teller in the same sequence that checks were received from the customers. Under these circumstances a person with the type of check requiring five minutes to clear should not stand in front of the window for five minutes preventing other transactions that could have been completed in this time.

In this illustration it took the insider with empathy to get a frank response from the respondent, but it also took an outsider to interview the interviewer in order to discover the complete meaning of the frank response.

In summary, it is clear that empathy is very useful because it sensitizes the interviewer to possible inhibitors; it helps the interviewer to select the best methods to minimize these inhibitors; in many cases it produces the sympathetic understanding needed to facilitate frank responses; and it allows the interviewer to use the most appropriate wording of questions and the most sensitive approach in probing. On the other hand, empathy becomes over-rapport when it makes the interviewer unwilling to ask certain questions, when it leads the interviewer to assume the answer in advance, and when it blinds the interviewer to the need to probe in a way that will make silent assumptions explicit. Retaining the advantages of empathy while avoiding the disadvantages of over-rapport can be done either by using the insider-outsider team as in the Colombian example, or by carefully training the insider in the objectives of the study and in the nature of the larger culture to which the results of the study must be communicated.

INTERVIEWING COMPARED WITH ORDINARY CONVERSATION

Just as interviewing cannot be divorced from other methods of gaining understanding of human behavior, neither can it be separated from the basic skills of ordinary conversation. Any two-way conversation involves many of the same skills and insights needed for successful interviewing. The main difference is in the *central purpose* of interviewing as opposed to other forms of conversation.

There is a tendency for those faced with the problems of obtaining information on human behavior to vacillate between two views: that interviewing is just talking to people in a spontaneous sociable way or that it is a magical and mysterious formula which allows the interviewer to put away all of his common sense, knowledge, insight, and intuition. People with the latter view tend to follow a single "technique" with a slavish rigidity. During the process of training interviewers in industrial, governmental, and educational settings, it is common to hear that "here, we use the _____ technique of interviewing." This blank is filled in with such words as "permissive," "nondirective," "focused," "understanding-listening," "supportive," "depth," "structured," "unstructured," "free-wheeling," "subjective," "expressive," "spontaneous," "projective," "phenomenological," "indirect," "transactional," or "psychiatric." The remarkable thing is that the same technique is often used for divergent types of interviewing situations and at all points within a particular interview.

Experience in interviewing, training others to interview, and doing research on interviewing methods, shows that no single approach, style, or technique of interviewing is adequate except within narrow limits. The interviewer should strive to use an increasingly wide range of techniques and should have the ability to adapt flexibly to the purposes of the interview and the requirements of the specific situation.

The interviewer should realize the wide range of functions of ordinary conversation and how they relate to interviewing. If this is not done in a self-conscious way, the interviewer may be limited by habits acquired in previous forms of conversation or may be reluctant to use insights or skills learned previously, for fear that they are not "techniques" but merely "common sense."

Whenever two or more human beings are conversing, several social-psychological types of communication may prevail, one at a time or in combination. These types may be delineated according to their purpose.

Expression

One of the most common functions of conversation is the joy of self-expression. One or both of the conversationalists may be fulfilling the need to express ideas, feelings, attitudes, or moods. One person may assume that the other is listening in fascination when in reality the other person's expression is in response to his or her own thoughts, which are being organized for the next assault. This illusion of an audience is important to the person doing the expressing. Such a conversation may be quite satisfying to both participants even though neither has the slightest idea of what the other has said. Of course there are times when one person's eagerness for self-expression interferes with the other's opportunity for the same.

This urge for spontaneous expression can be a vital asset in interviewing, provided that once it has been encouraged in the respondent, it can (*a*) then be directed by the interviewer toward the information-gathering objectives of the interview and (*b*) the interviewer does not give in to the urge for self-expression.

One of the common errors made by the novice interviewer is to yield to the temptation to impress the respondent with his or her own knowledge of the subject of the interview. This form of expression runs the risk of threatening the respondent, who will then tend to guard responses rather than to express thoughts and feelings frankly. It should not be inferred from this that it is always undesirable for the respondent to express ideas not directly relevant. On the contrary, it is often vital to the respondent's morale. Neither should it be assumed that any spontaneous expression of feeling by the interviewer is detrimental to the success of the interview. However, the interviewer must keep both his or her own and the respondent's urge for expression within bounds by constantly asking, "How will this effect the completeness and accuracy of the information I seek?" This self-discipline distinguishes the interviewer from the conversationalist.

Persuasion

To a certain extent, the concepts of expression and of persuasion over-lap in that both involve the expression of feelings and ideas. Expression includes only those cases where the speaker is not concerned with con-vincing the other person. The speaker merely wants an opportunity to express ideas and feelings spontaneously. Persuasion is behavior which may or may not be spontaneous but which is essentially aimed at con-vincing the other person.

There are times when persuasive conversation is an integral part of the information-gathering process. In certain types of survey work one of the chief problems is to "sell" the potential respondent on the impor-tance of the study, to persuade the respondent that he or she is of vital interest, or that the information will be kept anonymous.

There are many situations in which an interviewer's urge to per-suade the respondent may endanger the interview. In extreme cases, yielding to this urge has sent the interviewer to jail. For example, the so-ciology department in a graduate school was studying racial tensions in an area that was between an all-black area and an all-white residential area. One of the graduate student interviewers felt strongly about the injustices of the violence against blacks who moved into the white resi-dential area. During interviews, this student interviewer could not resist the temptation of admonishing the respondents for their social values and for their superstitions about race. Respondents began to react de-fensively and aggressively, and a rumor began to circulate that a "bunch of Communists" were going from house to house "stirring up trouble." One respondent then called the police, informing them that a Commu-nist was molesting his wife, and the police took the interviewer to jail. This dramatically illustrates a situation in which the role of the informa-tion-gatherer and the role of reformer could not be mixed.

More frequently, the interviewer's urge to persuade results in gath-ering distorted information. Tape-recorded interviews have provided the following examples: a minister could not resist the opportunity to "convert" disaster victims during the interview; a social worker could not separate her therapeutic function from giving the client advice; and an opinion pollster unconsciously and subtly influenced the respondent by the context and wording of the questions used. Only by the system-atic analysis of tape-recorded interviews can these subtle manifestations of the persuasive urge be demonstrated.

Therapy

In ordinary conversation with a friend, a person often expresses ideas and feelings to release emotional tension. This release is called *catharsis* and is encouraged by the psychiatrist or clinical psychologist in therapeutic interviews.

The permissive atmosphere and spontaneous give-and-take involved in certain types of social science interviews may also have a therapeutic effect on the respondent by fulfilling the need for catharsis. However, the interviewer should not delve into the respondent's inner conflicts if these conflicts are not connected to the information that is sought. In some cases, the respondent will feel resentful later if the interviewer has "allowed" the respondent to talk of irrelevant matters in seeking catharsis. This is a particular danger when the attempt for catharsis is unsuccessful and when the interviewer needs to establish a continuing relationship with the respondent or with acquaintances of the respondent.

There are many times when the information sought is closely related to the respondent's inner conflicts and tensions. This was frequently the case in interviews with disaster victims. Many times it was obvious to the interviewer that the respondent was suffering from guilt feelings about his behavior in the disaster. For example, a mayor of a small town felt guilty because he had been unable to direct the rescue operations and had become confused "just like anyone else." A mother felt guilty because she had let the tornado jerk her baby from her arms while her husband had kept the other child safely. And a husband felt guilty because, when the storm struck his house, he was talking with a waitress rather than eating supper at home with his wife.

In a study of industrial personnel, the interviewer might detect an employee's guilt feelings about stealing certain supplies from the employer. The interviewer might note that a management person feels guilty that he teaches honesty in his Sunday School class but keeps two sets of records on production efficiency.

The social scientist, primarily concerned with collecting valid information, sometimes finds it necessary to play a therapeutic role temporarily to get the desired information. Other times the social scientist feels a moral obligation to do what is possible therapeutically if he or she is qualified to do so. More often, however, the interviewer finds that some therapy results without any special effort.

Often the sensitive interviewer is concerned with the ethics of dabbling in therapy while obtaining information. This cannot altogether be avoided. Anyone who speaks to another person giving sympathetic understanding or creating a permissive nonjudgmental atmosphere is likely to encourage cathartic release in the other person. This is true whether the two people involved in the conversation are just good friends or whether the conversation takes place in the confessional or on the psychoanalyst's couch. In trying to obtain valid information it is often necessary for the person studying human behavior to offer just such an atmosphere.

Ritual

Another common form of conversation might be called ritualistic. It is merely a form of verbal behavior which has no real significance other than to provide the security in interpersonal relations which comes with having certain forms of verbal behavior acceptable in all instances of a certain type of occasion. These empty forms may provide little real information. The person who says "Good morning!" is not trying to persuade nor to give information which characterizes the particular morning. Occasionally, situations are confusing because a question is asked but the responding person does not know whether the question calls for objective information or for a ritualistic answer. For example, in the hospital when the nurse says, "How are you this morning?" the patient doesn't know whether to say, "I have a bad headache," or to say, "Fine, thanks, and how are you?"

In interviewing, we must learn to detect ritualistic answers by the respondent and also learn to avoid giving them ourselves. For example, a common error appears when the respondent says, "You know what I mean!" and the unwary interviewer unthinkingly responds as he or she would in an ordinary conversation with, "Uh huh," when the interviewer does not actually understand what the respondent has in mind. To obtain more accurate information, it would be much better to say, "I'm not sure I know exactly what you mean. Could you tell me a little more about it?"

In general, this ritualistic function of conversation has little use in gathering information. The interviewer must merely be aware of the danger of engaging in such ritualistic conversation and then confusing the results with valid information.

Information

A fifth function of conversation is to exchange information. Although the previous four functions have a peripheral place in the type of interview we are dealing with, the exchange of information is the central purpose of the interview. The word exchange reminds us that in the interview the flow of information must be two-way. Too frequently, an interviewer becomes so concerned with the information to be obtained, and with interpreting what the respondent says, that he or she forgets to be equally concerned with communicating to the respondent the type of information needed. The interviewer must also communicate the appropriate attitude toward the respondent and toward the information to motivate the respondent to continue to give relevant information.

The exchange of information is not found only in interviews. Two excavators discussing possible ways to avoid a cave-in, two scientists engaged in a discussion of a common problem, a teacher leading a discussion, or two criminals planning a bank robbery—all are participating in an exchange of information. Two characteristics often distinguish an interview from the other situations just mentioned. Often the problem about which the interviewer is seeking information is not equally important to the respondent; hence there might be certain motivational problems. Also, interviewers often deal with a wide variety of types of people in obtaining a wide variety of types of information; because of this diversity there may be an initial communication barrier between interviewer and respondent which does not exist between two people whose activities bring them into regular contact.

This lack of an equal stake in the problem and of a habitual channel of communication between the interviewer and respondent puts the burden of overcoming these barriers on the interviewer, who must translate the problem to a level of concreteness clearly understood by the respondent and must learn the vocabulary familiar to the respondent. The interviewer must be sensitive to the important difference between the conceptual information that is needed and the concrete questions that must be asked in order to obtain the information. For example, it is hopeless for an anthropologist to try to explain to a tribesman that he would like his help in a structural-functional analysis of the kinship system of the tribe. It is equally difficult to explain to a disaster victim that you are interested in the process of progressive redefinition of the situation in the first few minutes of the crisis period and its relationship to adaptive behavior and psychosomatic illness during and after the crisis. Less obviously, it is expecting far too much to ask a college freshman, "Why did you come to this college rather than to some other one?"

In studies where the investigator will have many contacts with the respondent, it becomes more possible to build up a rational sharing relationship, even where the cultural backgrounds of the interviewer and the respondent may be quite different. For example, Whyte found that his informants were becoming sophisticated in their observations and in the way they thought about them as a result of a process of progressive sharing and mutual education.[26] However, in studies involving only one contact between the interviewer and respondent, rarely do we find a respondent with whom we can discuss the problem directly in common theoretical terms.

Many interviews may involve the functions of expression, persuasion, therapy, and even a minimum of ritual; but the interviewer must

---

[26]William F. Whyte, *Street Corner Society: The Social Structure of an Italian Slum* (Chicago: University of Chicago Press, Third edition revised and expanded, 1981).

keep in mind that these four functions (whether they are found in the behavior of the interviewer or the respondent) must be subordinated to the main function of exchanging information. This does not mean that the interviewer should hesitate to use any mode or type of communication that aids in the free flow of relevant information.

Preceding sections of this chapter have shown some of the relationships between interviewing and other general methods of obtaining information about human behavior such as empathy, participation, and observation. These sections have also focused more closely on the relationship between various functions of conversation and the central function of the information-gathering interview. The discussion now will be concerned only with the information-gathering interview, looking at its various styles and objectives.

But before you go to the next chapter, you should think about the discussion questions and do Laboratory Problem 1 lest you have gotten the impression that learning to interview is a spectator sport!

DISCUSSION QUESTIONS

1. Think of situations in which empathy, participation, and observation would be useful in an interview.

2. What are the advantages and disadvantages of using personal documents in research? Think of a situation in which you might use personal documents profitably.

3. What are some of the difficulties in using participant-observation? What are some of the advantages? Think of a situation in which you might choose this method.

4. Think of some situations in which people are using interviewing to obtain information but do not define themselves as interviewers.

5. How would you predict a person's ability to empathize successfully in a given situation? Illustrate with specific examples.

6. Give an example of situations in which each of the functions of ordinary conversation might be used in interviewing.

Selected Readings

These books deal either with methods other than interviewing or with interviewing in the context of participant-observation.

Allport, Gordon W. *The Use of Personal Documents in Psychological Science.*
New York: Social Science Research Council, 1951.
Deals with diaries, letters, case studies, and other documents in the scientific study of human behavior and makes a basic plea to the psychologist to avoid dealing in abstractions not connected to everyday behavior.

Bruyn, S. T. *The Human Perspective in Sociology: The Methodology of Participant Observation.* New York: Irvington Publishers, 1985 reprint.
A fairly systematic treatment of participant-observation methods and techniques.

Denzin, Norman K., ed. "Triangulation: A Case for Methodological Evaluation and Combination," pt. 12 in *Sociological Methods: A Sourcebook.* Chicago: Aldine Publishing, 1970, pp. 471–525.
Shows the need for both methodological and theoretical "triangulation" as a means for achieving greater validity in conclusions about human behavior.

Festinger, Leon, et al. *When Prophecy Fails.* New York: Harper & Row, 1956.
A fascinating example of the use of team participant observation of a religious sect awaiting the end of the world on a specific date in the near future. Raises both methodological and ethical issues.

Gottschalk, Louis, et al. *The Use of Personal Documents in History, Anthropology and Sociology.* New York: Social Science Research Council, 1951.
The methods of utilizing personal documents are treated separately for each of the fields. The contexts of these fields are preserved as they give many illustrations of research using personal documents. This is a classic in the field.

Hughes, Helen M., ed. *The Fantastic Lodge: The Autobiography of a Drug Addict.* Greenwich, Conn.: Fawcett Publications, 1971.
An example of a "personal document" in the form of an autobiography stimulated by the writer's interaction with a sociologist. The young woman came to the Beckers' house to tell her story, which was recorded on tape.

McCall, George J., and J. L. Simmons. *Issues in Participant Observation.* Reading, Mass.: Addison-Wesley Publishing, 1969.
A collection of views on the strengths and weaknesses of participant-observation and conditions for its relative success or failure.

Webb, Eugene J., et al. *Nonreactive Measures in the Social Sciences.* 2nd ed. Boston: Houghton Mifflin, 1981.
Nonreactive methods are those that do not involve direct interaction between the researcher and the people being studied. This includes the measurement of physical erosion and accretion, governmental and other records, and simple observation.

LABORATORY PROBLEM 1

Critique of Telephone Company Interview

This first laboratory problem gives you the opportunity to critically analyze the performance of another interviewer. Your success in this will depend to some extent upon the degree to which you can imaginatively put yourself in the role of the interviewer and clearly understand both the interviewer's objectives and the setting in which he or she is operating. Of course playing the role of the interviewer also involves being sensitive to the respondent's probable reaction to what the interviewer does or fails to do. To get the most out of this experience carefully follow the procedure below.

PROCEDURE

Preparation. Before writing your critique (which can probably be done in two or three typewritten pages) you must carefully prepare with the following steps.

1. Note the nature of Parts A and B of the written critique as described below.

2. Carefully read the description of the telephone company's study from which the interview script was taken. Note the setting of the study, the general purposes, and the specific information objectives of the interview.

3. Read the script of the interview up to the interviewer's fifth question (*I-5*) then write Part A of your critique (described below).

4. Now read the entire script only once, writing the critique of each of the twenty specified questions as you go along. This is Part B of your critique (described below).

NATURE OF THE CRITIQUE

A. Strategy errors. By strategy errors we mean errors in the way the interview situation is set up: the time, place, selection of the respondent, selection of the interviewer, how the interviewer approaches the respondent, how the interviewer explains the situation, or any aspect of the interview setting which might help or hinder the flow of relevant and valid information.

This part of your critique should be written after you read up to *I-5* in the script and before you go on to read the remainder of the interview. Simply say what was wrong, if anything, with what was done or with what was not done up to this point. This part of your report should be only a few succinct statements.

B. Errors in tactics and techniques. This category includes everything the interviewer says or does not say which affects the relevance, completeness, and validity of the information given by the respondent. What the interviewer says and how it is said should be viewed in terms of the probable effect upon the respondent.

Twenty only. You are to comment on only twenty of the interviewer's questions. These are indicated by the numbers 1 through 20 in the margin. This sample of the interviewer's behavior was selected to avoid unnecessary repetition in your critique and yet provide a representative portion of this interviewer's behavior.

Context. Comment on each of the questions before going on to the next. When judging the adequacy of the question, keep in mind the context in which it appears. The context in this case includes everything that precedes the question, including the silence, but *not* what follows that particular question.

Diagnosis and treatment. Each of the twenty critiques should include the number of the question you are analyzing followed by (*a*) your diagnosis of what was wrong with it and (*b*) your suggested treatment in the form of a concrete example of what the interviewer should have done instead. If no improvement is needed, say so, and go on to the next question. Here is a sample of one of the twenty critiques.

I–49:   *a.* The interviewer should have probed instead of accepting the superficial answer.

   b. "That's very interesting. Could you explain that a little more?"

The number I–49 in the above example is furnished in the script. Note that the silences of one second or longer are indicated in parentheses. The silence immediately preceding each question is considered to be part of the interviewer's behavior connected to the question, since the interviewer determines the length of the silence before breaking it with a question.

Now that you can visualize the form of the critique you are to do, carefully read and think about the study as described below. You must understand the setting of the study, its general purposes, and the specific information objectives of the interviews in order to do a valid critique of each of the twenty points.

DESCRIPTION OF THE STUDY

The company's purposes. The central purpose of the study from which this interview has been taken was to evaluate management's efforts to influence the employee's attitudes and beliefs. A telephone company decided to launch an employee information program in which management would explain to the 40,000 employees the company's need for an increase in the telephone rates. Management felt that the first task was to sell the employees on the need for the rate increase and to hope that the employees would carry the campaign to the public through contacts with their families, friends, and telephone subscribers. It was considered important to influence general public opinion because the company expected the main opposition to the rate increase to come from the lawyers for many of the larger cities in the state at the request of politicians, who then could point to their "record" of opposition to the "big monopolies" for its vote-getting appeal.

Information was gathered and summarized in attractive pamphlets containing tables, charts, and graphs; a movie was produced using employees as actors; all the employees met with management in small discussion groups where the materials were presented and discussed. There was considerable variation in the way in which the discussion was handled and the way in which the materials were used from one meeting to another, depending upon the particular manager leading the group.

The basic ideas in the company's rate-information program included the following:

1. Telephone services, in order to be efficient, must constitute a monopoly in any one geographical area.

2. To protect the consumer against the company's taking unfair advantage of its monopoly position, the government grants the company a charter to operate only as long as it charges a "fair and reasonable" price for its services.

3. The state commerce commission is the governmental agency set up to protect the consumer and must determine whether the company is in fact charging a "fair and reasonable" price.

4. The calculation of a reasonable price should take into consideration not only the percent return on the investment but also the need to pay greater dividends to stockholders during prosperity in order to compete with more prosperous industries for the investor's money.

5. The telephone company is more vulnerable to financial recessions than other utilities because people are more likely to give up telephone service than gas, water, or electricity. Therefore, during times of prosperity it must accumulate an emergency fund to protect it against such times.

6. The increased efficiency of service due to the accelerating trend in installation of dial phones and other automation is offset by the fact that phone service, unlike other utilities, becomes more costly as a larger number of subscribers is included in any local-call area. This is due to the fact that a potential electrical connection must be made between each phone and every other one in the system. The cost would be much higher if it were not for efficiency.

7. The cost of telephone service has not risen nearly as much as prices in general since World War II. Therefore, a rate increase would not be unfair to the consumer. The company, too, is a victim of inflation since it must now pay more for materials and labor.

Specific information objectives of the interview. In order to evaluate the effectiveness of the rate-information program the company set up the following criteria of effectiveness:

1. The amount of relevant *information* the employee retains. (Here relevant is defined as being related to points one through seven in the company's purposes section.)

2. The general *attitude* of the employee toward the way in which the materials were presented in the *group* meeting.

3. The degree of *conviction* or faith the employee has in the correctness of the company's arguments.

4. The willingness of the employee to *influence* others to see the company's point of view.

Strategy used in the study. A random sample of employees to be interviewed was selected from the payroll lists. The interviews were done by management people about three months after the small group meetings had been held. In no case did a manager interview any of his own subordinates or anyone in his own department. All interviewers introduced themselves as working for the Employee Information Department and explained that this was a staff department which has no supervisory jurisdiction over employees. The interviews were done on company time in any office or conference room where complete privacy was available.

The interviews were all tape-recorded so that the interviewer could devote his full attention to the respondent. Later the information was transcribed by the interviewer who selected out relevant verbatim excerpts and organized them into a report under the four main headings shown above. Neither the respondent's name nor that of his supervisor was known by the interviewer. Therefore, all reports were anonymous. Most of the summary report consisted of statistical tables and verbatim excerpts to illustrate the meaning of the categories used in the tables.

In each case the employee was sent to the interview room by the immediate supervisor who was supposed to explain the nature of the interview. All of the supervisors had been told that the interview would take from one to three hours. Since the aim of the study was to detect any *lasting* effect of the information program, employees were intentionally not notified until the day of the interviewing so that they would not be tempted to refresh their memories by rereading some of the materials they had forgotten.

The Interview Script

The following is a detailed report of the events from the time the employee arrived at the interviewing room. The employee enters the room with a questioning look on her face and the interviewer rises to greet her. He does not know how much she has been told about the interview by her supervisor. He begins . . .

I-1: How do you do! I'm Mr. Anderson, but you do not need to tell me your name since everything you tell me is supposed to be anonymous. (1)[27] We want you to feel free to say anything you have on your mind.
R-1: That's okay with me! (Smiling) (2)

---

[27]The numbers in parentheses represent the number of seconds of silence.

1 **I-2:** How much have you already been told about this interview? (1)

R-2: Not much . . . (3) just that someone wanted to talk to me about the meetings we had a couple of months ago. They didn't say who it was or why. (2)

I-3: I see. Well, I'm working for the Employee Information Department which is interested in what the employees think about the rate-information meetings and how they were handled. (1)

R-3: Gee, that was a long time ago. I can't remember a thing about how well the meeting went! (1)

2 **I-4:** Won't you just try? I'm sure you must remember something about it . . . (2) . . . there are things you probably remember much longer than that. (1)

R-4: Well, of course I remember something but nothing of any great importance. (2)

Read only to this point before writing Part A of your critique.

I-5: Just tell me in your own words what happened at the meeting. (2)

R-5: Uh . . .

I-6: You know just how it started and all that. (3)

R-6: We just went to the conference room and there was some man I had not seen before. He just gave us the facts about the situation. (1)

3 **I-7:** He just gave the facts? (2)

R-7: Yes, he didn't preach at us or anything. He asked if there were any questions . . . (1) . . . just listened. I don't think there was anything very complicated. (2)

I-8: You felt that it was not very complicated. (1)

R-8: Yes . . . there were a few questions asked about the proposed suburban rates but outside that nothing was said. (1)

4 **I-9:** Do you feel that the leader was well-informed? (2)

R-9: Yes, he knew what he was talking about. He had all the facts. (1)

I-10: Did he hand out any materials to read? (3)

R-10: Oh yes, we had pamphlets with very nice charts and pictures. They were very well done and must have cost quite a bit of money.

I-11: You feel they cost quite a bit of money.

R-11: That's right. (3)

I-12: Did they show you a movie?

R-12: Yes. (1)

5 **I-13:** Did you think it was a good movie considering it was made by amateurs? (1)

R–13:   Yes, it was very interesting. It was good to see a movie for a change with amateur actors. They were people just like me and my own friends in real life. It was sort of matter-of-fact. People were bored and not too brilliant or beautiful. I got a bang out of that . . . (5) . . . I guess we're all amateurs at heart and we like to know that others are too. I understand that all the actors are employees. I can believe that even if I didn't recognize any of them. After all there are over 40,000 employees and I know only about twenty of them. I guess there are some disadvantages to working for such a large outfit. A girlfriend of mine works in the bookkeeping department. This was not her first job. She had worked in an office before where she had her own desk and a private room and could bring in a few flowers now and then to brighten up the place. It was her own room. She almost quit the first day when she saw that her desk was one of about forty in a large room and they all looked exactly alike. She felt like one of a herd. (1)

6 I–14:   How did you feel about the meeting in general?
R–14:   Oh, it was fine. (1)
I–15:   Does that mean that you liked it? (2)
R–15:   Sure (giggling), if I hadn't been in the meeting I would have been at the switchboard. (3) It was good to take a break and get away from it all. The meeting lasted, I guess, a couple of hours. (1)

7 I–16:   But outside of that, was there anything good about the meeting?
R–16:   Of course. Like I said, it was very informative. (2) I learned a lot of facts. It was packed with facts and figures. Most of them I had never heard before. (2)

8 I–17:   Were you with the company the last time they asked for a rate increase?
R–17:   No.

9 I–18:   Why do you supppose we gave all this information to the employees this time before we file for a rate increase? (4)
R–18:   I can't understand why they want to know how people think unless it is just for their own satisfaction or to see how people will take it. I guess they think, this is my humble opinion, that if the people are accepting it maybe the Commerce Commission would accept it too. (2) They want to see if it holds water. (2)

10 I–19:   Do you feel you learned something new at the meeting or in reading the pamphlets? (1)
R–19:   Like I said, I learned a lot of facts and figures.
I–20:   For example . . .
R–20:   Well, they said that there was inflation which made everything cost more and that the company was in a pretty bad way.

They also showed how if the rates were increased they would also give additional service and also put in more dial phones. (1)

I–21:   Anything else you can remember?

R–21:   That's about all (2) it was a long time ago.

11   **I–22:**   Some say that since we are now making 6.7 percent profit on our investment we should not ask for a rate increase now. Do you agree with this? (3)

R–22:   I think that they should be allowed to make more than 6 percent but assuming that what they said in the book (pamphlet) is true, that they look in pretty bad shape. (2) But you wonder how could a business like this that is so well established (2) and almost as valuable as your public utilities like water, gas, electric, (1) how could they be in such a tough spot. (4) Their operating expenses can't cost that much compared to the business they do. I think that more people have phones today than they ever had before and the communities are building up so rapidly, I can't see where they are in such poor shape financially. (2)

12   **I–23:**   Would you say the company is government regulated? (2)

R–23:   That means that the government has the power to freeze your job, or make the company comply with their rules of secrecy and stuff like that. They have the power with the telephone company, which is very vital in the national defense, to do things or come in and suggest doing things in their way. There is no other way the government can regulate the company. (1)

13   **I–24:**   Would you say that the company is a monopoly? (1) If it were, how could the subscriber be protected against having to pay unfair rates for telephone service? (3)

R–24:   Well, it is true like Western Electric or AT&T. But it has to be that way. Something that is a utility has to be *one* as far as I can see. It would be impossible for bookkeeping purposes too. And how about the poles? Who would use them, or would there be two sets? It's just like any other utility . . . you can't get your gas or water somewhere else. (2) I think the people benefit by the monopoly because it is cheaper. (1)

I–25:   You feel that a monopoly is good for the people.

R–25:   Yes! Don't you think so too? (1)

I–26:   (Smiling) I guess I would logically have to say 'yes.' What stops us from raising the telephone rates higher and higher if we have a monopoly?

R–26:   They might raise the rates but they lose a lot of business in doing so. People can only take so much and they'll see through it. Coffee is a good example. The price went up so high that people quit drinking it and drank other things like tea instead. In the case of the

telephone, when you have a choice between eating or having a telephone, you'll eat and get rid of the telephone. That's the way. . . .
R–27:   So the only thing that stops the rates from going up is the threat of the subscribers getting rid of the phone.
R–27:   That's the only thing I can see.

14   R–28:   Do you think it is a good thing that we have to obtain the permission of the Commerce Commission before getting a rate increase? (3)
R–28:   Yes, that is a good thing. (2) I think that is the way it should be.
I–29:   Is it true that the more subscribers the company has the more profit it can make? (2)
R–29:   Maybe they don't always make more money at the time when they are expanding and getting more subscribers, but later on that equipment pays for itself and I would think that they would make more profit in time. (2) Isn't that true?

15   I–30:   I suppose you might be right, but doesn't the company claim that growing doesn't increase its profits?
R–30:   To me that's silly because . . . well, in the first place just let a lot of people pull out their phones and they'd be complaining that business is falling off. They'd naturally have to get rid of some of their help and then they would probably complain that business wasn't what it used to be and they'd be contradicting what they said. I mean in any business when you grow that is your benefit. Don't you agree with this? (2)
I–31:   You would like to know if I agree with you.
R–31:   That's right. (1)

16   I–32:   I don't really know the answer to that question. It sounds like it would make sense to most people. (1) Do you feel that the telephone company needs to make higher profits than other utilities like gas and water? Should we make more or less than the Edison Electric is making at the present time? (3) What factors determine this, such as the effects of inflation, deflation, the rate of dividends paid by competitive business or anything like that? (2)
R–32:   I don't see any reason why the telephone company should make any higher profits than any public utility (2) but this depends on what you mean by *profit*. You have to figure in the higher cost of living, (3) the cost of putting new equipment where the old stuff wears out, convenient and efficient, to improve the service. The telephone company has to give service, it isn't just like putting in the water mains and letting the individual pay for connecting to it and for all the plumbing in the house. The telephone company supplies *all* of the equipment and on top of that they need all the operators

and all the bookkeeping to put the calls through and keep track of the charges that have to be made. I think the telephone company has more expenses to pay. (2) It should make higher profits than the gas or electric company.

I-33: Does the company need to pay higher dividends to stockholders in good times than in a depression? (2)

R-33: It should because it makes more money in good times than in bad so it should pass along the profit to the shareholders. That's only right . . .

I-34: But is it *really* necessary for the company to pay higher dividends?

R-34: Higher than what?

I-35: Higher than during a depression.

R-35: Well, I'd say that it was necessary, yes.

I-36: Why is that? (2)

R-36: It's just the nature of economics—if you don't pay the people, there is less buying power and the situation would just be worse.

17 **I-37:** Pay who, the stockholders? Does a monopoly have to compete for stockholders? Or can they just pay any dividend they want? (2)

R-37: I guess they would have to pay the stockholders good dividends or they would put their money in some other company. So I guess you could say that even a monopoly has to compete for stockholders. (2)

I-38: When all things are considered, do you actually feel that the company needs a raise in rates? (2)

R-38: I don't really know. Since I have a 50 percent concession on my phone bill it would be easy for me to say the rates should be raised but what about the other people who have to pay the full rate because they are not employees of the company. You should maybe ask them what they think.

I-39: That would be a good idea, but right now I am interested in what you think. (3)

R-39: What bothers me is this whole program. They have been putting out pamphlets and everything. What good does it do? (2) It wouldn't make any difference whether people said they weren't for it. That wouldn't stop them from getting a raise, would it? Because no one wants to pay more, let's face it. And all this stuff about asking your opinion . . . (1) but when it comes down to it they may ask fifty people what they think and if they need this raise, I mean if they really need it, they will still raise the prices even if fifty people say "no."

I-40: Then you feel that this whole thing is sort of a fake.

R–40:   Well, I . . .

1–41:   I mean you don't really believe the information that has been given out on the rate increase.

R–41:   I wouldn't say that exactly. They have all the facts so what can you say. There it is in the book complete with charts and pictures. But the poor working man could put his facts before them and say, "I pay so much for this and so much for that and I'm not getting a raise, I can't afford it." (3)

18 I–42:   Has anyone ever asked you about the rate increase? I mean anyone outside the company, (2) family, friends, neighbors or people you see on the way to and from work? (3)

R–42:   When it comes out in the papers and people know you are working for the telephone company, they always blame it on you because you're getting a raise. Or they think, well . . . not that you are to blame but it kind of aggravates them. (2)

I–43:   Did anyone ever talk to you about it or did you ever bring up the subject yourself with anyone at all? (2)

R–43:   I really don't talk to people about it much.

I–44:   Did you talk to your family about it? (1)

R–44:   I don't know if I brought the pamphlet on inflation home or not because we covered everything in it and it wouldn't make very interesting reading to anyone at home. When I explained to others what was told to us, they thought that it didn't hold much water because people today are using their phones more than ever and the equipment and telephones are built to last a lot longer. But they say in the pamphlet that every four years a phone is put in a house, but all the people I have talked to have had their phones for years.

19 I–45:   Then how many people would you say you have talked to about the rate increase? (3)

R–45:   I guess when it comes right down to it, I only mentioned it to my mother. (2)

I–46:   Is there anything else you would like to say about the rate information program to round out the picture?

R–46:   I don't think so. (3)

20 I–47:   Well, thank you for your help.

Chapter Two

Interview Types
and Objectives

A review of the growing number of books on interviewing shows that some are written for specific use and others for general use. Both types have their legitimate place in methodology. The reader, however, must avoid the tendency to overgeneralize. Often the book clearly warns the reader that any generalizations made in the form of "do's and don'ts" should be kept within the context of the specific purpose and setting which is assumed. Sometimes the title clearly specifies that the book is written for interviewers connected with a particular organization's functions. For example, a handbook of one polling organization makes it clear that the suggestions hold only on the assumption that most interviews are done to obtain information on opinions, beliefs, and attitudes rather than on objective verifiable facts.[1] Also, the polling function assumes that the respondents will be a random sample of some population, usually interviewed in the home, and that the interviewer will use a highly structured interview schedule (guide or questionnaire).

Sometimes the title of the book may not give warning that it deals with a highly specialized type of interview. For example, Polansky's excellent book deals mainly with the therapeutic interview.[2] Instead of dealing with a random sample of the U.S. population at their own residences, the respondents were usually those who found their way into the office of a social worker, psychiatrist, or clinical psychologist. In this case a more helpful subtitle might be "Theory for the Psychotherapeutic Interview" rather than "Theory of *the* Interview." The point is

---

[1]National Opinion Research Center, *Interviewing for NORC* (Denver, Colo.: National Opinion Research Center, 1947).

[2]Norman A. Polansky, *Ego Psychology and Communication: Theory for the Interview* (New York: Atherton Press, 1973).

that we must be careful not to generalize from what is effective in one specific setting to all interviewing.

Specialized treatments of interviewing can be classified into three kinds: those that focus on the type of *respondent*, on the type of *interviewer*, and on the type of interview *function*.[3] The respondent-focused books deal with types of respondents such as children, adolescents, the aged, elites, or foreign students.

The interviewer-specialized treatments usually focus on a particular profession or role of the interviewer, such as managers, ethnographers, journalists, police, lawyers or social workers.

The function-specialized treatments focus on some basic function of interviewing, such as the focused interview, the diagnostic interview, the depth interview, the problem-solving interview, the helping interview, or the job-seeking interview.

Usually such function-specialized treatments view the particular purpose as something other than, or in addition to, information gathering. The purpose might be to persuade, to educate, to arrive at agreement, to solve a problem, to give therapy, or simply to build goodwill. Gaining information in this case is seen as a means to some end in relationship to the respondent. The success of the interview, nevertheless, depends on general methods and skills used to motivate the respondent to provide information necessary to the specific purpose.

THE RATIONALE FOR STUDYING
INTERVIEW TECHNIQUES

Since the information-gathering function is common to all types of interviewing, this book will focus on this function and will avoid both the respondent-specialized approach and the interviewer-specialized approach. Successful information-gathering requires three dimensions of mastery. First, the interviewer must understand *concepts* about the nature of communication in the interview. Toward this end, eight *inhibitors* of communication are described in Chapter 5, and eight *facilitators* of communication in Chapter 6.

Second, the interviewer must have a set of *tools* that can be used to minimize the inhibitors and maximize the facilitators of communication. Three kits of social-psychological tools are offered: strategies, techniques, and tactics. *Strategy* refers to decisions that the interviewer makes or fails to make before the interview actually begins and that can

---

[3]See Selected Readings for a listing of books dealing with specific types of interviews.

determine which inhibitors and facilitators are brought into play. Strategy includes such things as deciding who would be the best respondent, who would be the best interviewer, when the interview should be done, where it should be done, and how to explain the situation to the respondent. These are dealt with in Chapters 7 through 12.

Techniques are the various ways in which a particular question can be put. This includes the verbal techniques of providing contextual statements, selecting appropriate vocabulary, deciding between using narrow- or broad-scope questions, deciding between having open-ended or structured answers, and deciding when to use loaded questions versus neutral ones. These are dealt with in Chapter 13. There are also nonverbal techniques, such as the use of silence, the pacing of speech, the tone of voice, the use of interpersonal space and gestures, that affect the flow of information. These are dealt with in Chapter 14.

Tactics are those decisions the interviewer must make about the chronological order of topics, subtopics, questions, and probes. Some of these decisions are part of the advance planning and some are made on the spot in the give-and-take of the interview process. Tactics are described in detail in Chapters 15, 16, and 17.

Learning a wide variety of tools (strategies, techniques, and tactics) will not necessarily allow the interviewer to increase the flow of relevant information by minimizing the inhibitors and maximizing the facilitators. In order to successfully apply the concepts and the tools the interviewer must have certain basic *skills*.

Skills, the third dimension of mastery, includes such things as *wording* the question, *listening* to the respondent, *observing* the respondent's nonverbal behavior, *remembering* what the respondent has said, taking *probe notes*, *judging* the relevance, validity, and completeness of the response, and *probing* to improve the quality of the information given. These skills are dealt with in Chapter 26.

Although the book begins by dealing with each dimension of communication separately, it also illustrates their simultaneous application to a variety of interview settings presented in Part 6, Professional Settings of the Interview, where there are detailed interview transcripts and analyses for eight different professional settings: social work, employee appraisal, parent-teacher conference, mass media impact research, nursing, journalism, and police interrogation. Thus, the book is not restricted to a single specialized use of the interview, and it shows the application of the basic principles to a variety of concrete interview situations.

Even though the book's central focus is on the function of information-gathering, the reader will note that at times it deals with methods of persuasion or therapy when these are necessary to increase the flow of needed information.

DIMENSIONS OF INTERVIEW STYLES

Standardized and Nonstandardized Interviews

One dimension of a typology of interviews is the dichotomy between standardized and nonstandardized interviews. To understand the difference, we must conceive the interview as *one of a set* of interviews gathering information bearing on the same problem. If all of the interviews in a set seek the *same* information, it is a *standardized* interview. Obviously a public opinion poll must use the standardized interview so that quantitative statements may be made about how many or what percent of the sample responded in a certain way to a given question. To do this every person must be asked the same questions.

In contrast there are sets of interviews that are *nonstandardized* because the nature of the study requires that we ask each person *different* questions. This might be the case if we were studying sources of inefficiency in a police department. We might ask the police chief whether the salary offered is high enough to attract people with the best qualifications; we might ask the radio dispatcher whether there are enough incoming lines; and we might ask the patrolman how far he usually has to travel to respond to a call. In some settings, such as case management or police interrogation, the interviewing is mainly nonstandardized, since the interviewer cannot know in advance the questions needed.

In some complex studies the interview may consist of a standardized set of questions asked of all respondents regardless of their role, another set of questions asked only of people in a certain category, and additional questions formulated on the spot to take advantage of a particular respondent's role or experience in a situation.

Scheduled and Nonscheduled Interviews

Another dimension of a typology of interviews is the dichotomy between *scheduled* and *nonscheduled* interviews. Even in cases where it is necessary to obtain the same information from all of the respondents, each interview may or may not be identical in the *sequence* in which the questions are asked, the *number* of questions asked, and the *wording* of the questions. In a completely scheduled interview all of these variables are fixed, while in the nonscheduled interview they are flexible. In certain circumstances information can be obtained more validly and more quickly by not adhering to a fixed sequence or by not asking every detailed question directly. For example, in studying people's behavior in a community-wide disaster, we were able to obtain answers to over 200 specific questions by asking only eight or ten general questions and letting each respondent tell his or her story of the disaster. Needless to say the answers to the specific questions were not given in the same order as they appeared on the interview schedule. Experience with disaster interviews showed that it was not advisable to interrupt the free-association flow of emotional experiences by asking many very specific questions. In this case the interview schedule contained all of the detailed questions merely as a check list to remind the interviewer which questions had been answered at any particular point in the interview.

In some studies the interviews are unstandardized or unscheduled only in the initial exploratory phase of the study until it is learned which questions are relevant, how they should be worded, and the order in which they should be asked. Then after the exploratory phase it is possible to design either a scheduled or nonscheduled interview procedure to collect the needed information. In some cases the exploratory experience indicates that one method is best for one portion of the information, and the other method is best for the remainder of the information.

An interview may be scheduled in varying degrees depending on how many aspects are specified. A schedule may specify (*a*) the content of questions related to the central problem, (*b*) the exact wording of the question, (*c*) any context to be supplied with each question, and (*d*) the answer categories, if any, which are to be used. In the case of the completely scheduled interview, these decisions are made by the person who designs the interview schedule; in nonscheduled interviews, the interviewer makes these decisions. To illustrate control of interview style by a schedule, let us look at a completely nonscheduled interview, a moderately scheduled interview, and a highly scheduled interview, all concerned with the same interview topic.

Assume that we wish to discover types of conflict between parents and children and their relationship to juvenile crime. We interview a sample of children who are known to have committed no crimes and a group who have been known to commit several typical juvenile crimes.

The Nonscheduled Interview

Instructions to the interviewer: Discover the kinds of conflicts that the child has had with the parents. Conflicts should include disagreements, tensions due to past, present, or potential disagreements, outright arguments, and physical conflicts. Be alert for as many categories and examples of conflicts and tensions as possible.

The Moderately Scheduled Interview

Instructions to the interviewer: Your task is to discover as many specific kinds of conflicts and tensions between child and parent as possible. The more *concrete* and detailed the account of each type of conflict the better. Although there are twelve areas of possible conflict which we want to explore (listed in Question three below), you should not mention any area until after you have asked the first two questions in the order indicated. The first question takes an indirect approach, giving you time to build up rapport with the respondent and to demonstrate a nonjudgmental attitude toward teenagers who have conflicts with their parents.

1. What sorts of problems do teenagers you know have in getting along with their parents?
   (Possible probes: Do they always agree with their parents? Do any of your friends have "problem parents"? What other kinds of disagreements do they have?)

2. What sorts of disagreements do you have with your parents?
   (Possible probes: Do they cause you any problems? In what ways do they try to restrict you? Do you always agree with them on everything? Do they like the same things you do? Do they try to get you to do some things you don't like? Do they ever bore you? Make you mad? Do they understand you? etc.)

3. Have you ever had any disagreements with either of your parents over:
   a. Using the family car.
   b. Friends of the same sex.
   c. Dating.
   d. School (homework, grades, activities).
   e. Religion (church, beliefs, etc.).
   f. Political views.
   g. Working for pay outside the home.
   h. Allowances.
   i. Smoking.
   j. Drinking.
   k. Eating habits.
   l. Household chores.

The Highly Scheduled Interview

Interviewer's explanation to the teenage respondent: We are interested in the kinds of problems teenagers have with their parents. We need to know how many teenagers have which kinds of conflicts with their parents and whether they are just mild disagreements or serious fights. We have a checklist here (see Figure 2–1) of some of the kinds of things that happen. Would you think about your own situation and put a check to show which conflicts you, personally, have had and about how often they have happened. Be sure to put a check in every row. If you have never had such a conflict then put the check in the first column where it says "never."

    (*Hand him the first card dealing with conflicts over the use of the automobile, saying,* "If you don't understand any of those things listed or have some other things you would like to mention about how you disagree with your parents over the automobile let me know and we'll talk about it.") (*When the respondent finishes checking all rows, hand him card number 2 saying,* "Here is a

FIGURE 2–1   **Checklist of disagreements**

Automobile	Never	Only once	More than once	Many times
1. Wanting to learn to drive				
2. Getting a driver's license				
3. Wanting to use the family car				
4. What you used the car for				
5. The way you drive it				
6. Using it too much				
7. Keeping the car clean				
8. Putting gas or oil in the car				
9. Repairing the car				
10. Driving someone else's car				
11. Wanting to own a car				
12. The way you drive your own car				
13. What you use your car for				
14. Other				

list of types of conflicts teenagers have with their parents over their friends of the same sex. Do the same with this as you did with the last list.")

The first of the three interview examples given does not provide any specific questions to be asked, but merely states the problem, leaving to the interviewer the choice of techniques. In the second kind of interview, specific questions related to the central problem are provided. The order of the three basic questions is indicated and for questions 1 and 2 some possible probes are suggested but are not mandatory. Question 3 is followed by a list of various areas of possible conflict which should be covered by the interviewer, but neither the actual wording of the questions nor the answer categories are supplied. The third interview example shows how the information designated by question 3a in the second example is obtained by completely scheduled interviewing, in which not only the exact wording of the questions and their sequence is given but the answers are also structured qualitatively and quantitatively.

As is implied in the examples above, an interview may be scheduled to a consistent degree throughout its total length, or certain portions of it may be more completely scheduled than others. The degree of scheduling of any portion of an interview depends upon the purpose to be achieved. This will be discussed in detail later. At the moment another dimension of style will be defined.

Topic Control

Just as the previous dimensions dealt with the degree to which the interviewer's behavior is determined by an outside source, the schedule, topic control deals with the degree to which the interviewer allows his behavior to be controlled by another outside source, the respondent.

Topic control is the extent to which the interviewer controls the topic of discussion and so takes the initiative in directing the course of the interview. It is helpful to think of the area of discussion as having (*a*) a central focus and (*b*) a certain scope with the boundaries more or less defined. Thus, the amount of topic control exercised by the interviewer depends upon the extent to which the interviewer takes the initiative in either shifting the central focus of the discussion or changing the scope of the topic. At one extreme, the respondent leads while the interviewer merely listens and shows interest in anything the respondent wishes to say, and at the other, the interviewer abruptly changes the central focus and scope of the discussion, even if doing so will interrupt the respondent's trend of thought.

With the basic dimensions of interviewing style defined, the next section of this chapter will describe the two basic objectives of interviewing—discovery and measurement—in order to relate them to the dimensions of style.

BASIC OBJECTIVES OF INTERVIEWING

Discovery Objectives

Discovery indicates gaining new consciousness of certain qualitative aspects of the problem. The problem is viewed broadly to include both substantive and methodological aspects of the interview. This will become clearer as the specific discovery functions are described.

Locating special informants. In many types of surveys and community studies where the informants are not all selected by random sampling, a rough-and-ready pilot study is done to locate a certain type of informant. Often there is no need to interview all informants of this class, but several must be located because they have had certain relevant experiences. In this case, the only reason for interviewing more than once is to obtain a more detailed account of the event and to cross-check the accuracy of the informant's observations.

In this type of situation, the interviewer, often a stranger in the community, does not know whether the first contact person is one or several steps removed from the type of person needed for the interview. The first informant may be the type of person the interviewer is trying to locate, may know someone who is, or may know someone who knows someone who is. This informant may or may not wish to help find the type of person the interviewer seeks. An interviewer studying the conditions that contribute toward peaceful integration of public schools would probably have to do a long series of interviews leading to the persons involved in bombing the local school board office.

Focusing of the problem. It is helpful to think of any study as involving four interrelated levels: first, focusing the problem; second, deciding upon definite types of information relevant to the problem; third, formulating specific questions to be asked in order to obtain relevant information; and fourth, deciding upon the strategy, techniques, and tactics to be used in obtaining answers to the questions. Often it becomes apparent in the early exploratory field work that the problem must be focused more clearly on some specific manifestation of the more general problem being studied.

For example, in a study of intergenerational conflict a few exploratory interviews indicated that most of the conflict which either adults or children could report was within their own family. Therefore, the investigator decided to focus on parent-child conflict. Further nonscheduled interviews with college students indicated that there was a sudden reduction in parent-child conflict when the children went away to college. This narrowed the focus to high school students living at home. Deeper nonscheduled interviewing showed that it was very difficult to obtain accurate information about conflicts which occurred more than a year in the past. Earlier conflicts were either forgotten or so vaguely remembered that the teenager was unable to give complete information or tended to dismiss the whole thing as "just kid stuff" not worthy of discussion. So the quest was further restricted to an analysis of conflicts occurring within the past year. Thus, in this study the nonscheduled interview was used to focus the problem.

Discovering, defining, and testing categories. Often the researcher begins a study with certain general ideas of the questions we want to ask, but with little knowledge of categories appropriate for the answers. For example, in a study of the layman's misconceptions of science we first needed to discover the layman's images of science. This necessitated a set of categories within which the images could be arranged. Since the problem called for classifying the images into two dimensions, we devised a tentative a priori set of categories which were to be tested in exploratory interviews. The first a priori dimension was called "areas of science" and included the physical, biological, and social sciences. The second dimension was called "aspects of science" and included the purposes, methods, and results of science. Although this system of cross-categorization was relevant to the problem, it was not clear that all the images or misconceptions people could have would fit into this system.

Therefore, using the categories in the exploratory interviewing was avoided by using a very broad open-ended question followed by a series of neutral probes.[4] The opening question was, "What comes to your mind when you think of science?" This would be followed by such neutral probes as, "That's interesting!" "Tell me a little more about that." "I see, now why do you feel that way?" etc. The respondent was allowed to free associate as much as possible and very little topic control was used by the interviewer. These interviews were tape-recorded and the content of the responses was analyzed to determine whether the a priori categories were sufficient or whether they would need some modification. Certain types of statements made by the respondents were considered very relevant to the problem but did not fall into the a priori categories. In the dimension of "areas of science" we found that we needed a fourth category, and in the dimension of "aspects of science" we found we needed two additional categories. Thus, in this case, the nonscheduled interview was used to determine the clarity and adequacy of a set of categories.

Once a system of categories is worked out, it sometimes appears to be "obvious" and therefore possible to have been decided in an a priori fashion. In some cases, the system appears to be unnecessarily complex, or the definitions seem either too loose or too detailed. The only criteria by which to judge any set of categories arrived at by any method are (a) how relevant the categories are to the problem at hand, (b) whether the categories include the full-range of relevant responses, and (c) how reliably the information can be classified by using the system.

Determining range of response. "Range" refers to quantitative variations in response, in contrast to qualitative categories. To illustrate, in a community study of a village in an underdeveloped area, the interviewer wanted an interview schedule in which to check the appropriate class interval representing a family's cash income per year. As an American, the interviewer would have very little idea of the range needed. Should the item on income run from $25 to $200 per year, $100 to $1,000 per year, or $500 to $5,000 per year? In some cases, studies of income have already been done so that exploratory interviewing is not necessary. However, sometimes nothing is published on the problem, or only mean or median figures are given, with no range. Here the nonscheduled interview can determine the range of responses.

---

[4]A "neutral" probe is one which indicates that the interviewer would like more information on the topic about which the respondent has been speaking, but it does not restrict the scope of the topic because no specific information is requested (for example: "Tell me more about that." "That's very interesting. Could you say more about that?").

Determining best sequence of questions. In many interviews there is a natural order in which the various subtopics seem to flow. In some studies the natural flow will follow the same sequence for nearly all respondents. In other cases, it will vary depending upon the type of respondent. For example, Schatzman and Strauss found that this pattern varied with social class.[5] In some cases, the order of the topics will be different for each individual. The best way to discover the natural order of topics and the degree to which a given order is either general or individualized is to interview a small sample, exerting *minimal topic control*. Each respondent is thus allowed to follow his or her own inclinations. If a given sequence of topics is found to be general, it is then feasible to use a more scheduled interview. The more individualized the pattern appears, the freer should be the topic sequence in the interview schedule.

Exploratory interviews sometimes show that information obtained early in the interview is not valid because a "warm up" period is needed. This gives the respondent time for unhurried reflection and free association. In the interview it is often best to begin by discussing related events which occurred prior to those which are of central interest to the interviewer. For example, in the study of the effectiveness of an employee information program referred to in laboratory problem 1, the main point was to discover (*a*) the amount of factual information absorbed by the employee, (*b*) the employee's general attitude toward the information meetings, (*c*) the degree to which the employee believed the information he or she was given, and (*d*) the degree to which the employee passed the information on to other people.

Since the interview took place many days after the meetings, it was necessary to start with a question which was in itself irrelevant; but since it focused on a time immediately before the events in which the interviewer was interested, it stimulated the respondent's memory and initiated a trend of thought leading to the central focus of the interview. The interview was opened with the question, "How did you first hear about the information meeting?" This was followed by, "What happened at the meeting?" These two questions usually laid a good foundation for obtaining information regarding the respondent's attitudes toward the meeting. The information obtained was probably more valid than it would have been if the first question had been, "How did you like the information meeting you attended last week?" This question asked abruptly before the respondent had an opportunity to "relive" the experience would tend to elicit a response like, "Oh, it was nice," or "I don't really remember much about it."

---

[5]Leonard Schatzman and Anselm Strauss, "Social Class and Mode of Communication," *American Journal of Sociology* 60, no. 4 (1955), pp. 329–38.

Similarly, in his study to determine why people bought "Brand X" automobiles, the author found that the respondent could talk more spontaneously about his first purchase of a "Brand X" if a thoughtful, permissive atmosphere was established. The interviewer started with "When did you first drive a car?" and later, "When did you first own a car?" This helped establish a reminiscent mood, sometimes quite nostalgic, which always led smoothly into more recent car-buying episodes. By the time the more recent events were reached, the respondent was becoming aware of changes in his own tastes and motivations in car buying as well as certain consistent patterns. All this provided not only a stimulus to the memory, but also a general *context*, enabling the interviewer to make inferences and pose more searching questions.

Discovering special vocabularies. Every social group has its own special vocabulary, or *universe of discourse*, which is often not clearly intelligible to outsiders. We are seldom aware of this universe of discourse in our own group unless it is consciously learned as a defense mechanism against the outsider, as is done by professional groups in medicine, education, arts, crafts, and the underworld.

The plumber might complain about the philosophy professor using a lot of "big words," while the plumber himself has a vocabulary equally confusing for the professor. Often these jargons distinguish the initiated from the uninitiated. A person not only has to have the "right ideas," but must also express them in a particular way to be recognized by the group.

These universes of discourse are not always merely a protective jargon, but often provide a type of shorthand or code which may be more efficient and accurate than ordinary language. Special vocabularies are not only associated with professions and occupations but also with certain social strata and geographical regions.

The nonscheduled interview with minimal topic control is needed to discover these special vocabularies. By carefully listening to the modes of expression the respondent uses to talk about certain topics, the interviewer learns which words can be used in phrasing questions for a more scheduled interview.

Detecting inhibitors and facilitators of communication. Later we will deal in detail with a theoretical framework outlining certain types of inhibitors and facilitators of communication in the interview situation. Now we will merely illustrate the need for using nonscheduled interviewing as an aid in mapping out possible trouble spots in the interview, as well as possible "spontaneity producers" which might be brought into play. Experience shows us that attempts to empathize with an imaginary respondent to predict his reactions to certain questions sometimes fail completely. Our empathic hunches should be tested in a few exploratory nonscheduled interviews.

As an example, a social worker was interviewing Puerto Ricans in New York to determine the need for aid to dependent children. Three items of information were necessary to estimate the future budget requirements of certain social welfare agencies: whether the woman of the house was married, how many children she had, and the ages of the children. The social worker assumed that the best order of questioning would be as follows:

1. Are you single, married, widowed, separated?

2. (If ever married) How many children do you have?

3. What are the ages of your children?

She had assumed that the first question should precede the second, because a woman would be embarrassed if she first answered she had three children and then was asked whether she was married. To avoid this embarrassment, it was assumed that the respondent with children would falsely report that she was married even if she were not. In this case, however, the interviewer's own cultural values prevented her from empathizing correctly with the respondent.

During a few exploratory interviews the interviewer discovered that there was a large percentage of couples with children who were not legally married. However, these couples did *not* have guilt feelings. If they lied about their marital state, it was usually to avoid embarrassing the interviewer. The longer the common-law couple had been in the United States, the more they were likely to lie about their marital state to those outside the Puerto Rican community. On the basis of this experience, the interviewer decided to reschedule the sequence and phrasing of questions as follows:

1. How old is your oldest child? The next? The next? etc.

2. Are you married, living common-law, or alone?

This order of questioning indicated to the respondent that the interviewer realized there was no necessary connection between having children and being legally married. If, in addition, the interviewer's attitude was not one of condemnation or shock, the respondent was assured that the interviewer "understood" the situation.

The nonscheduled interview frequently uncovers unexpected inhibitors or shows that expected inhibitors are not actually present under the conditions of the interview.

In order to understand why people are willing to talk about some things and very reluctant to talk about others, we must be free to explore many avenues of information in addition to those immediately relevant to the subject of the interview. We need to know:

1. How the respondent interprets the interview situation.

2. How we can influence his definition of the interview situation.

3. What "meaning" the information signifies for the respondent in terms of his own ego or social status.

4. What the respondent can gain by talking to the interviewer.

Sometimes this type of information is obtained through skillful non-scheduled interviewing and sometimes it is stumbled upon by accident. The use of the nonscheduled exploratory interview should considerably increase the probability of obtaining this needed information since, unlike the highly scheduled interview, it does not rule out accidental findings which might be relevant.

Measurement Objectives

It is possible to combine the objectives of discovery and measurement in the same interview; but as more emphasis is placed upon one objective, the other must be subordinated. What style is best for the purpose of measurement? Generally, the scheduled interview, with high topic control, is more efficient and effective in obtaining uniform coverage, precision, and reliability of measurement. The measurement is likely to be valid if the interview schedule has been constructed on the basis of results from skillful nonscheduled interviews.

Although the scheduled interview where the measurement objective predominates is used more, there are several situations in which the nonscheduled interview would be capable of more valid measurements if done by a skilled interviewer. This would be true in several types of interview situations where communication barriers would arise if the strictly scheduled interview were used.

One of these situations would be where the *universe of discourse* varies so greatly from respondent to respondent that the interviewer must vary the wording of questions and sequence of probes to fit the understanding of the particular respondent. This might be the case in dealing with topics like toilet training of children, sex behavior among teen-agers and adults, and other topics dealing with private spheres of experience.

The nonscheduled interview is also needed where communication on the topic is inhibited by the respondent's *fading memory.* The interviewer must be free to exercise low topic control and to vary the sequence of questions, thus allowing the respondent to follow the natural paths of free association. To further stimulate the memory, the interviewer must be free to probe particular vague points in the story. Also, the interviewer must be free to create a mood of thoughtful reminiscence and to return to the same topic several times. In this case, a skilled interviewer can be more effective by freely devising tactics as the interview progresses.

There are other barriers to communication which can be surmounted best by a skilled interviewer unhindered by a schedule. The next chapter deals with eight inhibitors of communication, at least four of which can be handled better by skilled nonscheduled interviewing. They are forgetting, chronological confusion, inferential confusion, and unconscious experience.

A basically different situation in which the nonscheduled interview might be more practical for measurement purposes occurs where the measurement is simple and the respondents so few that the construction of a schedule is not necessary or efficient to validly and reliably rank the respondents on the variable being measured.

In deciding whether a scheduled or nonscheduled interview should be used, one argument advanced is that the nonscheduled interview is dangerous because the interviewer is free to bias the responses. This is true if unskilled, careless, or dishonest interviewers are used. However, bias can also be built into the interview schedule itself, offering the doubtful virtue of uniformity to the bias. We must be careful not to simply trade one source of bias for another. Neither should neatness of the interview schedule, efficiency of coding, or reliability of response be confused with the more important criterion—validity of the information.

It is sometimes argued that the scheduled interview is usually more reliable and *therefore* more valid than the nonscheduled interview. This reasoning is not necessarily correct. It can be demonstrated that it is possible to have perfect reliability, in that the same or different interviewers obtain precisely the same answers from the same respondent on two different occasions, yet despite this reliability, the validity of the information may be very low.

In cases where the purpose of the interview is to obtain accounts of deviant behavior, but where the situation or the interviewing methods jeopardize the respondent if he or she reports the deviant behavior, we can expect the reliability to be high and the validity low. For example, if a manager of a department store used an interview or a questionnaire to ask, "Do you often steal from the company?" the answer would be a simple "no" even if the respondents were reinterviewed. Thus, we could reliably depend upon the falsehood being repeated.

This validity-reliability conflict would also be found when the interview seeks information considered by the respondent as a competitive secret. In this case, the most ironclad guarantee of anonymity for the respondent is of little value, since the object of the secrecy is to prevent the information from getting to a competitor. This situation is found, for example, in governmental secrecy where the object is to keep the information from a competing or hostile nation and in industrial secrecy where the purpose is to avoid leaks to competing corporations. It is interesting that in both of these situations a system develops in which each institution tries to obtain the secrets of its competitors. Thus, it is to be expected that the naïve interviewer who asked an employee of the automotive industry questions about the next year's model of his company's automobile, or who asked a member of the State Department what the next move was to be in disarmament negotiations, would not obtain valid information except for the occasional straightforward response, "That is a secret."

A third situation, much more frequently encountered by interviewers, is that in which the information sought has faded from the respondent's memory so that the images that are recalled are confused, amorphous, or ambiguous. If the situation in which this interview takes place, or the methods used, tend to suggest a plausible or socially acceptable answer, the bias will be in that direction and will persist upon repeated interviewing under the same conditions.

These three examples do not exhaust the types of validity-reliability conflicts which can result from the inhibitors of communication described in detail later. Here, we merely wanted to point out that validity and reliability do not necessarily go hand in hand, nor are they necessarily related to whether a scheduled or nonscheduled interview is used.

Both the scheduled and the nonscheduled interview may be reliable or unreliable, valid or invalid, depending on the conditions and purposes. The nonscheduled interview may suffer from bias due to freedom permitted unskilled interviewers. Likewise, the scheduled interview may have a built-in bias which prevents the best interviewer from obtaining valid information. One type of error may be no better than the other.

SUMMARY

Interviewing can be seen in four different perspectives. First, it can be seen as one of the most basic modes of collecting data on human behavior along with the other basic modes of empathizing, participating, and observing. All of these basic modes are intertwined and are included to some extent in the nonscheduled interview which, therefore, provides an excellent focus for learning basic skills for studying human behavior.

Second, in comparing the interview with ordinary conversation we note that interviewing may include several possible functions of ordinary conversation, but these must be judiciously subordinated to the central purpose of gathering information. Habitual patterns of conversation must be modified in order to maximize the flow of relevant information in the interview.

Third, in viewing the different types of interviewing we see that one of the most important distinctions is in the amount of freedom allowed in the interview. The interviewer's freedom is controlled by the degree to which the interview schedule is structured in all dimensions. The respondent's freedom is inversely related to the amount of topic control used by the interviewer within the bounds of the interview schedule. In the highly structured interview, topic control decisions by the interviewer are limited to probing for elaboration or clarification of the immediately preceding response, but in the nonscheduled interview the interviewer has considerable latitude in his use of topic control.

Fourth, interviewing has two basically different functions—discovery and measurement. Discovery must always precede measurement. The nonscheduled interview is more effective for discovery, and the scheduled interview for measurement. Both the scheduled and nonscheduled interview may be used reliably or unreliably, validly or invalidly, depending on the purposes and conditions.

To develop the skills and insights needed for good nonscheduled interviewing or for building good interview schedules for use by less skillful interviewers, a person must be free to make decisions and to then evaluate the results of his or her performance. In order to use this freedom fruitfully a person must be guided by some diagnostic concepts regarding the problems of communication in the interview. He or she must be aware of a variety of interviewing strategies, techniques, and tactics available to solve or prevent these communication problems.

DISCUSSION QUESTIONS

1. What is validity? How is it tested?

2. What is reliability?

3. Is it possible to have perfect reliability and low validity at the same time? How?

4. How is it possible to draw valid conclusions from biased information?

5. Describe situations in which a nonscheduled, a moderately scheduled, and a highly scheduled interview should be used.

6. Try to think of situations in which each of the seven discovery objectives would be important.

7. What is an interview guide and what is its purpose?

8. What are the advantages and disadvantages of the interview compared to the questionnaire?

Selected Readings

Allen, Jeffrey. *How to Turn an Interview into a Job Offer.* New York: Simon and Schuster, 1983.
    Provides techniques and tactics for the job seeker to use the employment interview to his or her advantage in obtaining a job.

Banaka, William H. *Training in Depth Interview.* New York: Harper & Row, 1971.
    Deals with the techniques and tactics of getting beneath the initial superficial responses and overcoming the barriers of egothreat and forgetting.

Benjamin, Alfred. *The Helping Interview.* 3rd ed. Boston: Houghton Mifflin, 1981.
    Deals mainly with the counseling interview. One of the better books on the conditions, stages, and forms of interaction in the interview. Gives many examples of the helping interview.

Beveridge, Wilbert E. *Problem-Solving Interviews.* London: Allen & Unwin, 1968.
    Deals mainly with the tactics of interviewing to help identify problems and explore alternative solutions.

Bradburn, Norman M., et al. *Improving Interview Method and Questionnaire Design.* San Francisco: Jossey-Bass, 1979.
    A comparison of four survey techniques (face-to-face, telephone, self-administered, and randomized response) to determine which produce the most truthful responses to threatening questions.

Broughton, Irv. *The Art of Interviewing for Television, Radio and Film.* Blue Ridge Summit, Penna.: TAB Books, Inc., 1981.
    Deals with how to prepare for an interview, types of questions, types of respondents, legal aspects and technical aspects of the interview. Gives specific techniques for handling the sound aspects of the interview. Features one hundred pages of transcripts of actual interviews.

Burdock, E. I., and A. S. Hardesty. *Structured Clinical Interview Manual.* New York: Springer-Verlag, 1969.
    A carefully constructed, highly standardized interview, with a convenient recording format for the assessment of psychopathology. The manual includes both an interview transcription and an inventory of 179 verbal and nonverbal behavior items for the interviewer to observe in scoring six dimensions of psychopathology.

Cannell, C. F., and R. L. Kahn. "Interviewing," in *The Handbook of Social Psychology,* 2d ed., vol. 2, ed. G. Lindzey and E. Aronson. Reading, Mass.: Addison-Wesley, 1968, pp. 526–95.

A review of opinions in the field and research on the use of the information-gathering interview for *opinion surveying* and other social-psychological research. Reviews empirical findings related to the conditions for successful interviewing, and for the selection and training of interviewers.

Cormier, William H., and L. Sherilyn Cormier. *Interviewing Strategies for Helpers.* 2nd ed. Monterey, Calif.: Brooks-Cole Publishing, 1985.

Deals with skills and techniques needed for four major stages of the helping process: relationship development, assessment and goal setting, strategy selection and implementation, and evaluation and termination. Rich with structured learning activities and feedback exercises.

Dexter, Lewis A. *Elite and Specialized Interviewing.* Evanston, Ill.: Northwestern University Press, 1970.

Application of interviewing to the study of political elites in and out of office. Contains a thirty-page bibliography on the topic.

Downs, Cal W., G. Paul Smeyak, and Martin Ernest. *Professional Interviewing.* New York: Harper & Row, 1980.

Part I deals with the general theory of interviewing. Part II deals with interviewing in various management settings: selection, appraisal, counseling, disciplining, and exit interviews. Part III deals with the types of interviews used in the mass media: journalistic, broadcast and news conferences. Part IV deals with interviews in the research setting: survey interviews, telephone interviews, group interviews and organizational diagnosis.

Ianuzzi, John N. *Cross Examination: The Mosaic Art.* Englewood Cliffs, N.J.: Prentice-Hall, 1982.

Discusses the problems encountered by the trial lawyer in cross examining witnesses. Particular emphasis on the tactics that can be helpful in getting the truth out of hostile witnesses.

Inbau, Fred E., and John E. Reid. *Criminal Interrogations and Confessions.* Baltimore, Md.: Williams and Wilkins, 1985.

Presents the problems of obtaining confessions that will stand up in court and offers techniques, tactics and strategies of interrogating and recording the responses to minimize these problems.

Kastenbaum, R., and S. Sherwood. *VIRO: A New Scale for Assessing the Interview Behavior of Elderly People, Proceedings of the 20th Annual Meeting of the Gerontological Society, 1967.*

Presents a detailed procedure for quantitatively measuring various dimensions of the aging process on the basis of an interview with an elderly person.

Mahler, Walter R. *How Effective Executives Interview.* Homewood, Ill.: Dow Jones-Irwin, 1983.

Deals with the philosophy and aims of executive interviewing, with emphasis on the nonroutine interview situations.

Merton, Robert K. *The Focused Interview: A Manual of Problems and Procedures.* New York: Free Press, 1956, reprint 1981.

A classic on the assessment of people's reactions to mass media or any other stimulus situation where (*a*) the exact nature of the stimulus situation is known, (*b*) the interviewer has been able to analyze the stimulus situation and hypothesize the respondent's reaction, (c) the stimulus content of the situation provides the framework for the interview schedule, and (d) the interviewer focuses on the respondent's subjective experiences to ascertain his definition of the situation.

Pascal, Gerald R. *The Practical Art of Diagnostic Interviewing,* Homewood, Ill.: Dorsey Press, 1983.
Shows how to elicit information from the respondent to be used in the diagnostic process.

Rich, J. *Interviewing Children and Adolescents.* New York: Macmillan, 1968.
Deals with the problems of adults interviewing younger children and adolescents and makes suggestions on certain tactics and techniques that can be used to minimize these problems.

Schulman, Evaline D. *Intervention in Human Services: A Guide to Skills and Knowledge.* 3rd ed. St. Louis: C. V. Mosby Co., 1982.
Written to integrate didactic with skill training of undergraduates in mental health technical programs. Rich in verbatim examples and exercises. Provides a broad theoretical framework of intervention as well as interviewing skills and tactics.

Spradley, James P. *The Ethnographic Interview.* New York: Holt, Rinehart & Winston, 1983.
Describes the objective and field procedures used by the ethnologist in studying different kinds of communities and cultures.

Part II

THE INTERVIEW AS COMMUNICATION IN SOCIETY

Chapter Three

The Social Context of
the Interview

Successful interviewing is not the routine application of mechanical techniques. People do not respond, like Pavlov's dog, in a direct stimulus-response fashion. As stimuli, the interviewer's questions do not elicit predictable knee-jerk responses. In human affairs the respondent's *understanding* of a question as well as the *willingness* and *ability* to answer it depend to a large extent upon the larger social context of the conversation. It depends on who asks who what question, when, where, and why. It is important to establish this larger context of the interview situation lest we myopically focus on the techniques of the interaction and forget that the *relationship* between interviewer and respondent is determined to a great extent by how their roles fit into the larger society, and that this relationship tends to either inhibit or facilitate the flow of certain types of information.

The methods used to improve this relationship will be dealt with as *strategy* in Part 3, as *techniques* in Part 4, and as *tactics* in Part 5 of this book.

A CONTEXTUAL MODEL

Figure 3-1 attempts to conceptualize visually the social context of the interview. Note that C in the center represents the communication process we are trying to facilitate.

This communication process depends upon the relationships among three factors in the interview situation: the *interviewer*, the *respondent*, and the *questions* asked. This relationship between interviewer, respondent, and question can be controlled by the interviewer's behavior to a limited extent after the interview has begun. Much of this relationship is determined *before* the interaction between the interviewer and a particular respondent begins. These predetermined relationships

FIGURE 3-1   Social context of the interview

include such things as the time and place of the interview, the sponsoring organization, the combinations of interviewer and respondent, the potential threat of failure to preserve the respondent's anonymity, or the respondent's ability to understand the potential value of the study for which the interview is being done.

All of these social-psychological factors determine the *definition of the situation* by both the interviewer and the respondent. Although there is little the interviewer can do about many of these factors *after* the interview has begun, there is much that can be done in planning the interview situation in advance. This phase of planning is dealt with later under the heading of strategy and consists of such decisions as selecting respondents who are the most able and willing to give relevant information, selecting interviewers with the best relationship to the respondent, choosing the most appropriate time and place for the interview, giving respondents the most acceptable explanation of the purpose and sponsorship of the interview, and promising the appropriate safeguards of anonymity when needed.

In making strategy decisions we must consider the probable effects on the meaning of the situation as viewed by the respondent. To know this we must know how the intrasituational factors in the interview (information, interviewer, respondent) are connected to the extrasituational factors relating the interview to the larger society, community, or culture.

IMPLICATIONS OF THE MODEL

There are several important practical considerations that can be derived from the social context model that can help in planning any study using interviewing. Here we will describe some of the most important.

Consider the problem as primary. Since we can assume there is a wide variety of possible strategies, techniques, and tactics to be used in data collection, we should make no final choices of method until *after* we have clearly specified the problem and the precise information relevant to it.

There is no rational way, for example, to decide whether to use white or black interviewers until we know what information the interviewer will be seeking and from whom. Even if the information sought could be obtained only from black respondents, this does not automatically tell us whether we should use white or black interviewers, because some information a black respondent might relate would be as freely given to a white as to a black interviewer, while other information would not. An experiment done by Shuman, for example, in a northern city after the urban riots of 1967 clearly showed that certain kinds of information on racial discrimination, blacks' living conditions, and personal background was given as freely to white as to black interviewers, but information on militant black protest and blacks' hostility toward whites was given less freely to white interviewers.[1]

Consider the triadic relationship as fundamental. The interrelationships between the nature of the *information* sought, the nature of the *respondent*, and the nature of the *interviewer* is the fundamental *unit* of analysis in the interview process.

This model assumes that it is impossible to say how the relationship between a certain type of respondent and the interviewer would affect the information flow unless we know what kind of information we want to make flow. Similarly, we cannot say that a particular respondent will or will not be willing to give certain types of information unless we know to whom the respondent is expected to give that information. Also, we cannot predict whether a particular kind of interviewer is the right one to ask a particular question unless we know to whom that interviewer must pose that question. This triadic relationship is demonstrated in the Shuman study where the white interviewers could get one type of information much better than another type. Thus, if the nature of the problem restricts us to one kind of respondent, we must select

---

[1] H. Shuman and J. M. Converse, "Effect of Black and White Interviewers on Black Responses in 1968," *Public Opinion Quarterly* 35 (1971), pp. 44–68.

interviewers to fit the other elements of the triad. If the nature of the interview restricts us to one type of interviewer, then we must take care to select the type of respondent willing to give the required information to that type of interviewer. Clearly, we cannot consider these elements in isolation one at a time, but must view the interaction among the three elements as a unit.

The basic notion of the triadic relationship (that we can maximize the flow of valid information only by having the optimum combination of interviewer and respondent in view of the type of information sought) may in some cases preclude the possibility of obtaining valid data by using a fixed team of interviewers to interview a random sample of respondents. This typical survey strategy may or may not be valid depending on the type of information sought.

In a *public* opinion poll, for example, the failure to match interviewer and respondent may be harmless because the opinion sought is one that will be willingly declared in public and therefore will not require a special type of person as the interviewer.

On the other hand if we seek *private* opinion, it becomes much more important to match the interviewer and respondent. This may be very difficult or even impossible to do with a small, fixed team of interviewers.

Sometimes there is a way out of this dilemma even when we seek sensitive private opinion. Instead of blindly assigning members of a random sample of respondents to any member of a preexisting team of interviewers, we can sometimes first obtain some publicly accessible information about each respondent. Depending on the topic, such things as race, age, sex, political affiliation, occupation, or educational level might indicate the best interviewer for that respondent. The respondents could then be matched with different interviewers on the existing team. There may be a residual group of respondents for whom there is no matching interviewer; in that case additional interviewers would need to be recruited. This would increase the cost of the survey.

Any organization with a small, fixed team of interviewers is not able to interview a random sample from any population on any topic with equal validity. For some populations and some topics it is necessary to recruit different interviewers. In cases where variations on the traditional survey are called for, the cost is higher, and there is a temptation to ignore the invalidity of the traditional method. The real question becomes "Should we do a cheap, invalid study; a more expensive, valid study; or no study at all?"

Classify needed information. Do not assume that there is one best way to obtain all the items of information needed. Classify these needed items, considering for each the best interviewer, the best respondent, and the most appropriate method.

There is a tendency in planning a study to assume that a particular method (interview, questionnaire, or observation) will be used to collect all of the data needed. If the interview method is chosen, there is a tendency to assume that the same type of interviewer and respondent will be used for all of the interviews. Often this assumption of uniformity of strategy is unfounded because there is not a corresponding uniformity of information needed. Before accepting this assumption, we must examine specific questions carefully and regroup them according to who would be most willing and able to validly answer each question.

The temptation to be apparently efficient by having all of the needed questions on the same interview schedule so that they can all be collected at the same time by the same interviewer is often the source of invalid data. This spurious efficiency in collecting data is often reinforced by the additional desire for more efficient data analysis which is possible when all of the information is on the one interview schedule. Any "efficiencies" gained at the expense of validity is gross inefficiency; nevertheless these temptations exist!

Maximize flow of specific types of information. Once the needed information is divided into different types, you should plan the strategies, techniques, and tactics to maximize the flow of each particular type of information and then see where a common method may be used and where different methods must be used.

Sometimes information that is potentially ego-threatening, such as getting a person to report any delinquencies he or she has committed, can be obtained simply by using an appropriately structured questionnaire with safeguards of anonymity that are trusted by the respondent. This has been demonstrated by Clark and Tifft, who used the questionnaire approach to elicit reports of delinquent acts and were able to show by means of a later interview and polygraph analysis that the results were valid.[2]

Sometimes the conditions of the community are such that no promise of anonymity will be trusted by the respondent. For example, a study on industrial conflict collapsed early in the data-collection phase because valid responses from respondents were conspicuously unobtainable. The study took place in a community where a Textile Workers Union of America (TWUA) strike was in progress. The textile workers were questioned as to their sentiments regarding the TWUA and were asked to weigh the importance of various sources for such sentiments.

---

[2]John P. Clark and Larry L. Tifft, "Polygraph and Interview Validation of Self-Reported Deviant Behavior," *American Sociological Review* 31 (1966), pp. 516–23.

According to Roy there were several reasons for the failure: the respondents did not trust the interviewers to keep the information anonymous; the potential consequences of information leakage to the management of the mill were perceived as very serious; and conflict in the organizing campaign was intensive.[3] This points to the possibility that a strategy for collecting certain information might be perfectly valid at one point in time and useless later if a conflict situation develops, making a leak of the particular information dangerous to the respondent.

In a study of the phenomenon of rape in a large city, a team of information gatherers is used in which each member obtains a different type of information. Later, all of the information is assembled to obtain a holistic picture. The strictly medical information is determined by a physician; a description of the rapist and certain facts such as the time, place, and circumstances of the attack are obtained by a policewoman. A female psychiatric social worker elicits details about the precise nature of the attack, how the victim responded, and how she feels about the experience and about reporting the attack. Other information is obtained to cross-check the story given to the police department. Gradually, this multi-interviewer strategy is being developed to improve the relevance, validity, and completeness of the data. All this is necessary because of a tendency for policemen to be unsympathetic to rape victims and for the victim to be reluctant to report being attacked for fear of damaging her reputation. The project is also developing other strategies to persuade victims to report attacks that previously would have been unreported.

Even the most potentially threatening information will be given to a skillful interviewer under the right circumstances. This is clearly demonstrated in a study by Ball, who interviewed in Puerto Rico fifty-nine narcotic drug addicts who had been formerly incarcerated at the U.S. Public Health Service Hospital at Lexington, Kentucky.[4] The respondent's report of the time and place of his first arrest was validated against FBI arrest records; his report of whether or not he was currently using the drug was validated by a urine analysis. According to Ball the information collected in the interview was highly valid because of the skill of the interviewer, the absence of the police function, and the use of a carefully structured interview.

Do not overgeneralize from experiments. Studies and experiments on different strategies, techniques, and tactics of interviewing may appear totally contradictory if we do not take the social context of the interview into consideration.

---

[3]Donald F. Roy, "The Role of the Researchers in the Study of a Social Conflict," *Human Organization* 24 (1965), pp. 262–71.

[4]John C. Ball, "The Reliability and Validity of Interview Data Obtained from Fifty-Nine Narcotic Drug Addicts," *American Journal of Sociology* 72 (1967), pp. 650–54.

The contextual model is not only useful as a sensitizing framework in planning interviewing methods for a particular study; it is also useful for determining the applicability of studies and experiments of interviewing methods to a particular situation. Frequently, the apparently contradictory results among experiments testing the validity of the same strategy, technique, or tactic can be accounted for by differences in the triadic relationship within the interview, or by differences in the relationship of the interview situation to the local community and larger society.

All too frequently, researchers may select a method proven successful in a different setting, only to be disappointed by its failure in the situation where it is currently applied. There is a danger also that a particular approach, potentially effective in the current situation, is rejected because of studies showing its inadequacy in quite different circumstances. Both of these unfortunate errors can be reduced by applying the contextual framework when making comparisons of results of different studies of interviewing methods.

Now that we have given an overview of the interview in its social context, let us turn to the basic tasks of the interviewer in any interview situation and look at some of the problems that may arise in trying to carry out these tasks. Here we do not pretend to furnish any of the tools for dealing with these problems; that will be the subject matter of Chapters 7 through 17. Here we simply want to show some of the general problematic dimensions of the interaction between interviewer and respondent.

OBJECTIVES, TASKS, AND PROBLEMS OF COMMUNICATION

There are basic *objectives* common to all interviews. These objectives, in turn, present the interviewer with very general *tasks* common to all interviews. These basic tasks generate certain general *problems* found in all interviewing situations. Now let us consider these objectives, tasks, and problems in a general way.

Objectives of the Interviewer

The general objectives of the interviewer in any interview are three: *relevance, validity,* and *reliability.* Assuming that we already have clear informational objectives for a study and that we have already designed questions relevant to these objectives, then the interviewer is responsible for obtaining relevant, valid, and reliable responses to those questions. Once the respondent understands the question, he or she has at least four logical alternatives as a response. In rare cases the respondent might say nothing, as may happen when a psychotherapist interviews a schizophrenic patient. However, a normal person who wishes to avoid answering the question can do so gracefully by saying something irrelevant or ambiguous. If the interviewer does not accept irrelevancies or ambiguities, the respondent may then do one of two things: simply fabricate an answer that is relevant to the question but untrue, or give an answer which is both relevant and true. If all respondents said nothing, responded with the truth, or said "I won't tell you!" the tasks of the interviewer would be much simpler! Unfortunately the respondent can avoid appearing uncooperative by responding voluminously with irrelevancies or misinformation, and this presents a challenge to the interviewer.

Tasks of the Interviewer

In harmony with the distinction between relevance, validity, and reliability, we divide the interviewer's basic tasks into essentially two groups. The first deals with obtaining relevant information, and the second with increasing the validity and reliability of the information given by the respondent.

The relevance-related tasks include (a) having a clear understanding of the purpose of the interview, (b) clearly communicating specific questions in accordance with the purpose, (c) detecting and correcting misunderstandings of the question by the respondent, (d) distinguishing between the irrelevant, the potentially relevant, and the clearly relevant, and (e) guiding the respondent to avoid the irrelevant and probing the potentially relevant to convert it into actually relevant information.

The validity-reliability related tasks depend upon maintaining generally good interpersonal relations with the respondent and include (a) being aware of the potential inhibitors which make the respondent unwilling or unable to give valid information, (b) using both verbal and nonverbal means to help the respondent become more willing and able to give valid information, (c) detecting symptoms of resistance in the respondent, and (d) refraining from pressuring the respondent for information before the respondent is willing or able to give it.

The interviewer must be constantly alert and ready to modify his or her own behavior in a way that will maximize the flow of relevant and valid information. To do this the interviewer must clearly understand the objectives of the interview, observe the behavior of the respondent, and be aware of his or her own behavior as it influences the respondent.

Problems of Communication

Both of the interviewer's tasks depend upon verbal and nonverbal modes of communication. Nonverbal communication includes the tone of voice, facial expression, gestures, posture, and pacing which accompany the words.

Verbal communication problems. Rarely is there lack of communication because either the interviewer or the respondent does not understand the dictionary definition of a word. More frequently the interviewer's problem is becoming acquainted with special jargons currently used by subcultures associated with an occupational group, social class, age level, ethnic group, political party, religious group, or geographic region.

The successful interviewer must be willing to learn special universes of discourse. Without the interest and sincerity to master the knowledge needed to make the question meaningful to the respondent and to understand the answer, the interviewer has no right to the respondent's time. Interviewing auto mechanics about the problems of their business without a familiarity with their special, extensive vocabulary is insulting and fruitless. The interviewer who does not understand what he or she is being told cannot show a vital interest in what the respondent is saying.

This need of an appropriate vocabulary is more obvious when interviewing someone with more education or higher social status or when the interview deals with a specialized problem. Nevertheless, the need is often just as urgent in interviewing a respondent of lower social status about a nonspecialized problem. For example, in preparing to interview scientists about recent cancer studies, it is apparent that the interviewer would have to learn a special vocabulary to be effective. It is not so obvious, but just as important, to learn a special vocabulary to interview an Arkansas farmer about his experiences in a tornado.

It is sometimes *more* important to know the correct vocabulary when interviewing a person of lower social status. The lower-status respondent feels less free to educate the interviewer, and the interviewer is less likely to perceive his or her misunderstandings. Even though the interviewer assumes the role of the "ignorant but willing student," the respondent still is less inclined to assume the role of teacher than would be the case if the respondent had higher social status.

As an example of the necessity of special vocabularies, an interviewer planning to interview the personnel of a mental hospital about morale problems should not approach the first respondent without knowing the meaning of common abbreviations such as EST, BM, IV, GP, GI, or GU. Respectively, these usually stand for electroshock treatment, bowel movement, intravenous injection, general paresis, gastrointestinal, and genitourinary. In addition to the medical vocabulary, the interviewer would encounter the vocabulary of abnormal psychology and the highly specialized vocabulary dealing with the local physical and social structure of the hospital.

Similarly, if a study of employee morale is to be done in a large telephone company, the interviewer must understand terms such as CO, ACO, PBX, rate structure, traffic department, plant department, ICC, AT&T, employees' concession, and key-pulse dialing. The same symbol can have entirely different meanings in different universes of discourse; for example, the first abbreviation, CO, means carbon monoxide to the chemist, chief operator to the telephone employees, commanding officer in the army, and conscientious objector in a Mennonite community.

The examples above have perhaps been misleadingly obvious, since abbreviations are frequently used to express the most unique vocabulary in any occupational group. It is also quite easy to detect special meanings when they are conveyed by words or phrases which are *not common* to the universe of discourse of both the interviewer and the respondent. If a college student from New York heard a farmer say, "We just built a new water closet"; or a carpenter say, "This ladder needs new dogs"; or a mechanic say, "Your worm-gear is growling"; or a farmer in a semitropical area say, "We use triple-deck farming here"; or one plumber say to another, "Give me the snake, Joe"; or a man on skid row say, "Pete is a snowbird," he or she would probably be aware of not understanding some of these phrases.

However, the same student might hear an Arkansas farmer explaining his experiences in a tornado with, "I wasn't excited during the big blow, but I studied all night the first four nights afterward." He or she would probably *not* be aware of not understanding him since only common words are used and the context does not give a clue to the special regional meaning of two of the words: *excited* and *studied.* In this case saying that he was not *excited* does not mean that he was not terrified or that his pulse was not up to 140 beats per minute but that he was not demonstratively screaming, running in panic, or hysterical. Also, the word *studied* has no academic implications but means that he worried all night and couldn't sleep.

Another type of universe of discourse is illustrated in the following example. It is more difficult to detect because it is associated with a particular person's life history.

A local women's political organization was studying academic freedom at three colleges in the area by interviewing all members of their social science faculties. One of the interviewers arrived for her appointment with a faculty member and felt that she should first build *rapport* with a friendly conversation before launching into the formal interview.

I: Good morning! I am Mrs. Kirk from the Politics Club.

R: Oh yes, how do you do! I have been expecting you.

I: It's nice of you to give me an appointment. You are helping us with such an important project. We feel that it is important to have academic freedom in our colleges.

R: I can certainly agree with you there. Won't you sit down?

I: Thank you. I am so glad to have a chance to interview someone in the sociology department. When I was young I used to enjoy reading about Eugene Debs and that sort of thing. I think everyone should know how the other half lives. . . . (Pause) Could you tell me how many social workers your department graduates each year?

In this dialogue, the interviewer has unintentionally damaged rapport with the professor. Let us consider the last line which, although not part of the formal interview, is the only question. In its denotative aspect, it is simply *asking* for a concrete number of social workers who are graduated in a year. The answer is "zero." However, the context of the question allowed the professor to induce several assumptions on the interviewer's part that he felt needed correcting.

First, he was amazed by the question but recovered in time to explain the relationship between socialism, social reform, social work, and sociology. Since the interviewer knew she was talking to a member of a sociology department of an undergraduate school, yet expected them to be graduating social workers, the professor knew she did not understand the difference between sociology and social work. Furthermore, her remark about Eugene Debs implied that she saw a connection between socialism and sociology.

The professor's immediate response was to the *connotative statement*, rather than to the simple *denotative question*. He hastened to explain that sociology had no more in common with socialism than it did with capitalism, vegetarianism, or fascism, except for the first four letters.

The general effect upon the respondent was to make him distrust the interviewer because he doubted that anyone so grossly ignorant of his field could sympathize with the problems of academic freedom or be able to accurately record his opinions on the matter.

These confusions of universes of discourse can be prevented in most cases. Sometimes it is practical to recruit interviewers from the same cultural background as the respondents, interviewers already familiar with the particular universe of discourse. If a large number of interviewers are needed and it is not possible to recruit and train them, exploratory interviewing can be done by a few experienced interviewers. When special words and meanings are detected, they can be taken into account in modifying the wording of the questions and a special glossary can be included in the instructions to warn the interviewers of the special meanings which might appear.

Experimental studies of interviewing show that different respondents sometimes read different meanings into the same questions and, therefore, they are actually answering different questions.[5] These different interpretations are due to differences in the basic assumptions

[5]R. S. Crutchfield and D. A. Gordon, "Variations in Respondents' Interpretations of an Opinion-Poll Question," *International Journal of Opinion and Attitude Research* 1 (September 1947), pp. 1–12.

held. C. Wright Mills points out that different sets of basic assumptions are expressed in different "vocabularies of motive" used from one historical period to another.[6] Thus, an act that would have been explained in terms of the "battle between God and the devil" in the Middle Ages would be explained in Freudian terms of "the battle between the *id* and the *superego* in the arena of the *ego*" in a later era.

For example, a tornado took a diagonal path (from southwest to northeast) across White County, Arkansas, destroying four towns along the highway running in that direction. The disaster team which followed in its wake asked the following question (among many others): "Why do you think the tornado struck the way it did?" This question brought into play the "vocabulary of motives" of this local subculture. Most of the responses were based upon the assumption that God controlled the fate of men and that the tornado was an instrument of God's justice. Based upon this premise, then, the respondents were asked to explain how the inhabitants of one village had been more sinful than those of another and why certain people in their own stricken village were killed and others spared. Some typical responses were, "God does not have to explain his ways to man!" "The youngsters in this town have been going straight to the devil!" "Who am I to judge the ways of God?" In contrast, the members of the disaster study team thought the explanation was to be found in the statistical regularity with which tornadoes traveled from southwest to northeast through "tornado alley" and could be explained in terms of the rotation of the earth, prevailing winds in the northern hemisphere, local atmospheric conditions, and rapid changes in temperature.

The field team members were initially prepared for this question to elicit some pseudoscientific manifestations of anxiety such as: "They shouldn't seed those hurricanes in Florida because it just broke up one big hurricane which might have stayed out to sea into a lot of tornadoes which pop up all over the South!" Indeed, such explanations did come from some of the respondents.

With this wide gap between the interviewer's and respondent's silent assumptions, there was a danger of a breakdown in communication if the interviewer was not aware of the respondent's assumptions. The unaware interviewer might think that the respondent did not hear the question correctly, that the respondent was joking with him, or that the remark about the supernatural was merely a manner of speaking rather than a serious intellectual attempt by the respondent. Rapport would have been shattered if the interviewer had laughed, or even smiled, and said, "Really now, why do you think it struck the way it did?"

---

[6]C. Wright Mills, "Situated Action and the Vocabulary of Motives," *American Sociological Review* 6 (December 1940), pp. 904–13.

Garfinkel's study shows how this "cognitive substructure" of silent assumptions is not only associated with the more stable values, beliefs, knowledge, and expectations of a subculture; but it is also being constantly reformed and shared in the interaction between members of a group such as the family.[7] Thus, the understanding of the real meaning of today's conversation in the family depends upon having shared yesterday's experiences which provide the unspoken context.

Nonverbal communication problems. We now turn our attention to the interviewer's tasks which relate to nonverbal communication from respondent to interviewer. The interviewer must listen to *how* the respondent says what he does. Auditory clues include changes in pace, pitch, intensity, and volume level. In addition, there are visual clues such as facial expression, gestures, bodily position, and movements of hands, feet, and head.

Many respondents have learned to hide certain nonverbal clues to their feelings and attitudes. This control is usually exercised either by maintaining a neutral or noncommittal expression or by pretending an opposite feeling. In exercising such control most respondents manifest this inner conflict by inconsistencies. They are unable to control all of the symptoms of their attitude. For example, the respondent might display a calm facial expression and a casual tone of voice, yet betray anxiety by twisting his hands.

The interviewer can observe these inconsistencies by developing the habit of watching the *total* bodily response rather than concentrating only on the tone of voice and facial expression. In ordinary conversation, most people look to facial expression more than to other bodily changes for clues to feelings and attitudes. Perhaps it is precisely for this reason that we learn to control the facial expressions more readily.

There is also a problem of accurately judging the meaning of various visual and auditory nonverbal clues. One reason is that respondents vary greatly in their normal range of expressive behavior; unusual tension for one person would be normal for another. The interviewer can deal with this by focusing attention on *changes* in the level of these expressive symptoms.

Also, if the interviewer has more than one contact with the respondent or can observe the respondent in another setting, it is easier for the interviewer to make more accurate judgments of the respondent's emotional state.

The nonverbal clues noted by the interviewer have little meaning if isolated from the verbal communication and the situational context of

---

[7]Harold Garfinkel, "Studies of the Routine Grounds of Everyday Activities," *Social Problems* 11 (Winter 1964), pp. 225–50.

the interview. Only when the nonverbal clues and the denotative and connotative verbal messages make a consistent picture, can the interviewer feel sure that his or her interpretation of the respondent's message is correct. If there is some inconsistency, the interviewer should probe further until the matter is clarified for the objectives of the interview.

Thus, for maximal utilization of nonverbal respondent-to-interviewer communication, the interviewer's tasks are:

1. To observe a broad range of nonverbal activity and be alert for inconsistencies.

2. To be alert for *changes* in the respondent's nonverbal activity rather than being aware of only the general level which distinguishes one respondent from another.

3. To interpret the meaning of any inconsistencies and changes in nonverbal behavior in the broader context of the verbal communication and the situation in which the interview is taking place.

Now let us examine the interviewer's tasks related to nonverbal communication in the other direction, from interviewer to respondent. This aspect of communication will be studied extensively later under "Nonverbal Techniques." Here we will merely point out the nature of the task.

In general, the interviewer must strive to communicate certain positive attitudes toward the value of the interview itself, toward the respondent as a person, and toward the respondent's cooperation. This does not imply that an interviewer can change attitudes as the chameleon changes its colors. However, several precautions can be taken to minimize negative attitudes which might damage interpersonal relations sufficiently to invalidate the information obtained.

First, the interviewer can be selected to fit the task. From the viewpoint of a field supervisor, this is a matter of selecting the right interviewer for a particular topic and respondent. From the point of view of the single independent investigator, it is a matter of being aware of personal limitations and avoiding interview situations where the interviewer cannot control negative attitudes.

Second, the interviewer may deliberately seek the kinds of topics or respondents toward which he or she has a negative attitude in order to broaden personal views, gain tolerance, and learn to control the expression of these negative attitudes. However, the same interview which is used for this educational purpose will be of little value as a source of valid and complete information.

Third, the interviewer must learn certain techniques to counteract his or her negative attitudes. Even with ordinary precautions to match the interviewer with the topic and respondent, or to retrain the interviewer's attitudes, there will be some degree of self-control necessary, since it is hardly possible to find any one person who agrees with everything another person believes or has done. Just as it is difficult for the respondent to hide attitudes with a neutral expression, it is also difficult for the interviewer to hide attitudes from the respondent.

The interviewer's task is to displace real negative attitudes with equally real positive attitudes. This way, the interviewer avoids the problems inherent in attempting to remain neutral or refusing to admit to having such an attitude. Thus, if the interviewer strongly disagrees with the attitudes and beliefs being expressed by the respondent, he or she must be vitally concerned with the information-gathering task enough to show sincere appreciation for the respondent's frankness. Or the interviewer can manifest a strong interest in how the respondent arrived at these views, if this is an objective of the interview. In both of these cases, scientific objectivity rather than cold neutrality allows the interviewer to demonstrate positive attitudes of appreciation and interest rather than negative attitudes of disagreement and rejection.

In summary, the interviewer achieves the main goals—obtaining maximum relevant information and maintaining optimum interpersonal relations—by being sensitive to both verbal and nonverbal communication. The interviewer's tasks occur in the following cycle:

First phase. The interviewer must accurately receive information through both verbal and nonverbal modes of communication.

Second phase. The interviewer must then make valid inferences regarding the adequacy of the information and the condition of the interpersonal relations.

Third phase. The interviewer must then translate what is learned to modify his or her own behavior at the verbal and nonverbal levels to maximize the flow of relevant information and to maintain optimal interpersonal relations.

It will be noted that although the aim in the third phase is twofold, we have guarded against interviewer ambivalence or vacillation by not giving the two aims equal weight. The aim is *maximal* information with *optimal*, rather than maximal, interpersonal relations. Optimal interpersonal relations is whatever form and degree of relationship that will maximize the flow of information, or at least not interfere with the flow. Thus, the satisfaction of spontaneous interpersonal relations is viewed as a means to an end.

The precaution of using the word *optimal* is necessary, since there are situations where the best way to *maximize* the feeling of warm interpersonal relations is for the interviewer to "stop asking all those questions!" Often the neophyte thinks he or she has conducted an excellent interview because "rapport was perfect" and the respondent was "completely at ease, talked spontaneously, and commented that she had enjoyed the interview." Yet when the interview is analyzed for the amount and clarity of relevant data, it is found to be incomplete, superficial, and ambiguous.

Often there may be a conscious or unconscious desire on the part of the interviewer, respondent, or both to avoid any psychological strain in the interview. The interviewer may retreat into rapport-building chitchat or the ritualistic asking of required questions, while uncritically accepting irrelevant, evasive, incomplete, or ambiguous answers, instead of probing. The respondent may cooperate with the conspiracy by appearing cooperative while contributing a verbal smoke screen, obscuring the relevant material.

At times, a respondent may take the initiative in this disguised resistance, inundating the interviewer with meaningless verbiage, which the interviewer is unable to appraise systematically for its relevance in time to fulfill the objectives of the interview. The loquacious respondent who decides to sidestep the interviewer in this manner often presents a much more difficult problem than the taciturn respondent whose reluctance is more obvious.

Just as it is possible to overemphasize the importance of interpersonal relations, it is also possible that the interviewer becomes so concerned with gathering the appropriate information and neglects to lay even a minimal foundation of interpersonal relations. In this case, the interviewer gives the impression that the respondent is merely a means to an end. The respondent begins to feel like the patient whose medical specialist obviously loses interest upon discovering that the patient does not have a rare disease but merely a common but painful malady.

Thus the interviewer's task is to be approached as the acrobat approaches a balancing stunt. The interviewer must balance the information-gathering task with the rapport-building task and should develop a sensitive awareness of moments when more attention should be devoted to one or the other.

This chapter has tried to show in a general way how the flow of relevant, valid, and reliable information depends not only upon the interaction within the interview situation but also upon the relationship between that situation and the local community and larger society. Against the background of this contextual model the chapter tried to show general objectives, tasks, and problems to be dealt with by the interviewer in all interviews.

Care was taken in the chapter not to overcomplicate the exposition with any details on specific forces that tend to inhibit or facilitate the free flow of relevant information. To gain a more analytical and practical understanding of how to maximize the flow of relevant information, it is helpful to see the interview situation as a social-psychological field in which forces act as either facilitators or inhibitors of the information flow.

DISCUSSION QUESTIONS

1. What important factors help determine the respondent's ability or willingness to give the information he or she has other than the actions of the interviewer?

2. In planning an interview or series of interviews, which must be done first: selecting the respondent, choosing the interviewer, picking a time and place, or clearly defining what information is needed? Why?

3. Why do experiments on the use of certain interviewing techniques sometimes arrive at contradictory results even when the methodology is valid and reliable?

4. What are the central tasks of the interviewer?

5. What is a universe of discourse? How does it affect the interview? Give an example of some part of your own universe of discourse that would be unintelligible to outsiders.

Selected Readings

The references below were selected because they are studies of social conduct where much of the information was collected by interviewing and where the type of information needed makes the importance of the *social context* of the interview evident. Most of the studies involve deviant or at least private behavior.

Bryan, James H. "Apprenticeship in Prostitution," *Social Problems* 12 (1965), pp. 287–97.

Douglas, Jack D. *Investigative Social Research: Individual and Team Field Research.* Beverly Hills, Calif.: Sage Publications, 1976.
Most of the empirical examples are from a study of the massage parlor and the nude beach.

Gaylin, Willard. *In the Service of Their Country: War Resisters in Prison.* New York: Viking Press, 1970.

Hess, Robert D., and Gerald Handel. *Family Worlds.* Chicago: University of Chicago Press, 1974.
This deals with the attitudes and emotions involved in family interaction.

Humphreys, Laud. *Tearoom Trade.* Rev. ed. Chicago: Aldine Publishing 1975.
    This is a study of the relationships of homosexuals to each other and to the
    straight world.
Irwin, John. *The Felon.* Englewood Cliffs, N.J.: Prentice-Hall, 1970.
    An in-depth study of the felon.
Wiseman, Jacqueline P. *Stations of the Lost.* Englewood Cliffs, N.J.: Prentice-
    Hall, 1979.
    A sensitive study of the life of alcoholics.

Chapter Four

Ethics of Interviewing

The discussion of ethics in interviewing will attempt to touch on some of the most vital ethical issues of data collection, with emphasis on the interviewer's rights, obligations, and ethical choices.

This author is acutely aware of the fact that, when any of us takes sides on a particular case, we are expressing our own ethical choices. Rather than pretending that these choices are obvious deductions from universally accepted principles, the author sees them as an effort to find a resolution of the conflict between competing values.

WHAT IS ETHICS?

For the sake of brevity let us define ethics as the application of social values to concrete behavior. It is the practical application that distinguishes ethical problems from the problems of building a system of values or a set of ideals. In the abstract world of thought we can imagine a set of harmonious and mutually reinforcing values which never compete with one another. However, in the empirical world of deeds and actions, the most attractive set of ideals can be thrown into conflict.

Ethical choices are problematical at two levels. First, we must decide what value to assign to a particular action on the basis of its assumed or known result. This is necessary because most acts are not good or bad in themselves but are judged so according to their known or assumed probable effects. Only those who have no moral scruples, or who have never engaged in any intentional action to change society, can easily assume that there is no problem in doing the right thing as an actor in society. Second, once the results of each alternative act are evaluated in terms of different standards of competency, then the actor must choose among the possible actions by deciding how to weigh each of the competing standards.

To the uninitiated there can be no conflict among values if each one alone is considered good. It seems logical to say only good and evil conflict, not one good with another, but this is not true! For example, here are three statements which all sound "good" to many people but frequently are in direct conflict with each other:

1. Social science should help bring equality of human rights!

2. Social scientists should never use deceit in any form!

3. Social scientists should never be backed by physical force to obtain what they need to carry out a scientific project!

Merely to declare these three values is not an ethical act. But we are forced into ethical decision-making as social scientists if we start to act toward objective 1. Under certain conditions the attempt to achieve the first value will conflict with the maintenance of the second two values.

To give a concrete instance, Pierre van den Berghe, a Belgian, wanted to pursue objective 1 by doing an empirical study of *apartheid* in the Republic of South Africa.[1] It was clear that he would not be admitted to the country for this purpose. Yet it was important to gain a detailed understanding of *apartheid*, which is perhaps the most extreme application of racial segregation and discrimination in the world today. In order to obtain a visa admitting him to the country he stated that he wanted to study the economic growth in that booming economy. Thus, to attain value 1 he violated value 2, which was to "never use deceit." Some might argue that he then should have stayed out or worked for the liberation of the blacks through insurrection and revolution. If he did this of course he would be violating value 3, which is that social scientists should never be backed by physical force.

To give another illustration of values in conflict, assume that you agree with the following three value statements:

1. Social scientists should use their skills to improve the system of justice!

2. No one should intrude on the privacy of jury deliberations!

3. Social scientists should not use deception in their pursuit of knowledge.

The first value is not the pure scientific value of the "right to know" or that "knowledge of any subject is always better than ignorance" but is an amalgam of the pure scientific value and the general societal value of improving justice. The University of Chicago fielded a research team funded by the Ford Foundation in 1953 to study the jury system, to understand better its strengths and weaknesses in bringing about justice.

---

[1] Pierre L. van den Berghe, "Research in South Africa: The Story of My Experiences with Tyranny," chap. 8 in *Ethics, Politics and Social Research*, ed. Gideon Sjoberg (Cambridge, Mass.: Schenkman Publishing Co., 1971).

As the study evolved, consultants in the legal profession suggested that the use of simulated trials, mock juries, and interviews with real judges and jurors after a trial would leave certain crucial aspects of the process in obscurity. It was suggested that the actual deliberations of real juries in noncriminal trials be tape-recorded so that their understanding of the facts of the trial, the judges' instructions on points of law, and the jurors' patterns of influence upon one another could be analyzed.

This was done with elaborate safeguards to protect the jurors and the judicial system.[2] The judges whose permission was needed initially suggested that the jurors would have to be informed in advance that their deliberations were being recorded. However, the judges were persuaded that this attempt to avoid the deception of the jurors, value 3, would make jurors conscious of the recording and result in the interference with the free deliberations of the jurors, thus violating value 2. The only way to resolve the conflict between 2 and 3 would be to give up the recording of the jury deliberations, thus relinquishing the original purpose: basing reform of the jury system upon solid knowledge of what actually happens in jury deliberations.

The fact that this attempt exploded into public controversy clearly illustrates the first principle that acts are usually judged as good or bad on the basis of the *assumed* probable outcomes under certain conditions. In this case the outcomes, as pointed out by Vaughan, were very different from those anticipated.[3] First, the attempt to keep recordings secret failed. Second, the lawyers and judges cooperating with the social scientists did not represent the same point of view on the value of a scientific investigation as that held by the members of the Internal Security Subcommittee of the Senate Committee on the Judiciary, who carried on widely publicized hearings in which those on the research team

---

[2]For example, the recording device was locked so that the tape could not be removed except by the judge, who had the only key. No recordings would be made of criminal cases. After the trial the recording would be sealed and remain in the custody of the trial judge until final judgment had been entered and all appeals had been terminated. Then the research committee would produce a single transcription and destroy the original. The committee would then edit out all identifying information, such as the name of the court, the geographical locations, the dates, the names of all participants. This edited manuscript, along with the verbatim transcription, would be submitted to the court for any further editing and approval. The entire project of the recordings was to not receive any publicity until after the project was completed. All additional expenses incurred by the court in aiding in the process would be paid by the research project funds.

[3]Ted R. Vaughan, "Governmental Intervention in Social Research: Political and Ethical Dimensions in the Wichita Jury Recordings," chap. 3 in *Ethics, Politics and Social Research*, ed. Gideon Sjoberg (Cambridge, Mass.: Schenkman Publishing Co., 1971), pp. 50-75.

were called as witnesses, ostensibly to "determine how and why the recordings were made." Actually, the subcommittee chairman, in asking
the questions, showed that he was not really interested in the *how,* the
why, or the *ethical* issues involved. Instead, this subcommittee, which
in those years had been accustomed to looking for communists' subver-
sive activities, saw this as an opportunity to discredit the University of
Chicago and the Ford Foundation.

The inconsistency between the stated objectives and the hidden
agenda of the subcommittee was indicated in the fact that when witnesses tried to explain *how* they had done the recording, in terms of the
safeguards taken, or *why* they had done it, in terms of the need to know
and the need for secrecy to avoid affecting the deliberation process,
they were cut short by the chairman of the subcommittee. Never was
there any free discussion of the ethical problems of resolving the conflict
between the different values involved. Another possible inconsistency
on the part of the government was that the same people who strongly
supported legislation to prevent recording jury deliberations for any
reason were supporting a bill to permit wiretapping under certain conditions for nonscientific reasons. Attorney General Herbert Brownell
scored the research project particularly, and the University of Chicago
generally, for "spying on panels' deliberations in sociological study," yet
his office sponsored the wiretapping bill.

One of the most lamented outcomes of this conflict from the point
of view of the social scientists was that a law was passed in 1956 to prevent recording jury deliberations for any purpose and under any condition. This became another barrier to the free discussion of the ethical
merits of any particular case and the possible values to be derived by social justice from such a study. The law, in effect, says that either we must
never modify the jury system in the United States or we must do so
without any adequate knowledge of how juries currently function.

These two studies, *apartheid* in the Republic of South Africa and
the Wichita Jury Study, are mentioned merely to establish the fact that
making ethical decisions in social science is not a facile exercise in the
self-righteous recitation of ideals. Such decision-making is a series of
knotty problems which force us not only to make choices among different values but also to make predictions regarding the probable results of
any decisions we make. It becomes clear that values and ideals often rest
on certain assumptions and knowledge regarding cause and effect in the
real world. Perhaps as we can more accurately predict or control the results of our actions we will be able to become more ethically responsible.

INTERVIEWER ETHICS AS CONFLICTING LOYALTIES

The ethical problems of social science research could be viewed from
the perspective of the larger society, the client organization for whom

the study is done, the larger scientific community, the research organization doing the work for the client organization, the interviewer, or the respondent. For the purposes of a book on interviewing we will view the ethical problems from the point of view of the individual interviewer, for whom ethical problems often present themselves as conflicting demands from these different segments of society, or as a set of sometimes conflicting obligations to these different segments. Fortunately, in the majority of instances all of these possible conflicts of loyalty or obligations do not actually develop; many can be avoided by an appropriate delineation of the problem and by seeking an optimum field strategy.

In examining ethical conflicts from the point of view of the interviewer, we assume that the interviewer is a responsible ethical agent, and cannot escape the ethical implications of his or her acts by claiming merely to be "following orders." Interviewers are never forced to carry out their tasks; they can make decisions ranging from whether they will work on a particular project to how they shall carry out their specific responsibilities.

RESPONSIBILITIES TO THE LARGER SOCIETY

Analyses of the ethics of interviewing are relatively rare. In the few examples that do exist, there is a tendency to regard the ethical behavior of the interviewer only in relationship to the sponsoring organization, to scientific objectivity, and to the respondent, thus leaving out the larger society. The implication seems to be that there could be no conflict between the aims of the sponsor of the study and the values of the larger community. Actually there is often a direct conflict of interest, particularly in those cases where the sponsor of the study is interested in influencing or manipulating people as consumers, as workers, as taxpayers, or as clients.

Suppression of Findings

To give examples of the sponsor of surveys using information which helps exploit the public while withholding information which might be helpful to the public, the author needs only to think back to his experiences with commercial motivation-research interviewing projects he was acquainted with while he was a graduate student. For example, in a survey for a whiskey company it was found that a majority of the men over fifty years of age had been advised by their doctors to quit drinking alcohol, but this information was suppressed and not reported in the findings. Another unpublished survey involved interviewing men who had at different times in their life used a straight razor, a safety razor, and an electric razor. At that time it was clear that those who had tried all three preferred the safety razor because it was quicker and easier on the face, yet they bought electric razors as gifts for others because "you can't buy a man a $1.59 safety razor for a gift and not look like a cheapskate." The electric razor company was not anxious to be seen as the most frequently unused man's product.

Not only commercial concerns but also public and private social agencies may try to hide the results of studies which they have commissioned. For example, when the author was on a team of three researchers representing a joint effort of a college, a private welfare council, and a city plan commission, he did a detailed study of the social problem rates in a metropolitan area. Several attempts were made to suppress his findings, which were relevant to all of the organizations and citizens in the area. The data indicated that Boy Scout troops were not located in lower-class areas and that there was a city-wide dropout rate from Boy Scouts which started at twelve years of age and rapidly accelerated until most had dropped out by the age of fourteen, the age at which the delinquency rate began to climb. This irritated the local Scout officials who were accustomed to making appeals during the United Fund drive that implied that the Scouts were a strong character-building force to prevent delinquency. In desperation they even tried to claim that the information they had given was false or inaccurate. The Council of Churches (Protestant) in the same city insisted that the County Juvenile Court routinely record the religious affiliation or nonaffiliation of each delinquent so that they could show the positive effect of the church in the community, but when the resulting figures indicated that those who went to Protestant churches were *most* likely to be delinquent, Catholic next, then nonaffiliated, while the lowest rate was among Jewish youth, the Church Council tried to suppress publication of the results.

The City Plan Commission and the Community Welfare Council, with some urging from the prominent citizens who were angling to win a City Beautiful Award, tried to suppress the publication of the whole package of data relating social organizations to the rates of social problems such as schizophrenia, school dropouts, adult crime, illegitimacy, juvenile delinquency, divorce, and separation. The report was organized so that all of the information on each of ninety-five census tracts appeared in a two-page format. Instead of publishing and widely using the whole report, the Plan Commission and the Welfare Council each wanted half of the information on each tract in its office and the other half in the other office with only one copy in existence. This, of course, would give these two organizations a monopoly on the information which should have been in the hands of every school, church and social agency in the city. As the third partner on the team, the college insisted on full dissemination of the report in printed form, and a local publishing house did the printing free of charge.

In each of these cases it was one of the front-line field workers, viewed as "hired hands" by the sponsoring agencies, who had to press for full dissemination of the findings to the public at large. In the cases of the commercial firms the demand was ignored, but in the case of the public and private social agencies the attempt to prevent repression was successful. Even though much of the applied research by business, industry, and government is considered "in-house" evaluation and not for publication, there are still ways that the lasting results can be disseminated. One way is to lump together statistical data on several institutions or organizations of the same type so that not only are individuals not identified but also the organizations and the geographical locations are obscured. In some cases the researcher may have to agree to wait one to ten years before the results can be published. Whether or not such a prior agreement is ethical depends upon the nature of the study, which of the competing organizations or special interest groups might be harmed or benefited by the findings, and the significance for basic social science.

In some instances an individual researcher has initially accepted certain restrictions on dissemination of information, but upon discovering the nature of the information decides that his or her loyalty is to the larger society rather than to the special interest group. For example, Daniel Ellsberg, an economist on the staff of the Rand Corporation, went to Vietnam convinced that the defeat of the communist-led forces was essential and that social science could lend a strong helping hand.[4] At that time he saw no conflict of interest between the Pentagon and the American people. However, upon becoming acquainted with the contents of a massive forty-seven-volume Pentagon-sponsored history of American involvement in Vietnam, classified as top secret, he felt his duty was to let the American people know; and in June 1971, he turned documents over to the *New York Times.* Whether or not one agrees that this was an ethical decision, it is clear that it was a painful decision of conscience from which no personal gain was expected. It is clear that this exposé of the "Pentagon Papers" gave impetus to the anti–Vietnam War movement in the United States.

The moral conflict between the interests of any special interest group or organization and the larger society manifests itself in the use of secrecy. Any time the researcher is working for an interest group or must get the permission of an interest group which acts as the gatekeeper controlling access to respondents, there is a chance that the researcher will soon become involved in an ethical conflict. For example Gaylin, a psychoanalyst, hoped to understand the young men who had refused induction into the U.S. Army in protest against the Vietnam War.[5] To

---

[4]Myron Glazer, *The Research Adventure: Promise and Problems of Field Work* (New York: Random House, 1972), pp. 173–78.

[5]Williard Gaylin, *In the Service of Their Country: War Resisters in Prison* (New York: Viking Press, 1970).

do this he needed regular access to the inmates of a federal prison. His approach was to use a nondirective (nonscheduled) interview with the draft resisters who were desperate for someone, particularly an intellectual, to talk to. He was able to collect insightful information on their reasons for refusing induction, their relations with their parents, with fellow resisters in prison, with other prisoners, their fears of homosexual attack, their sense of isolation, and the lack of any rehabilitating influences in the prison.

Gaylin's preliminary manuscript of his book also included a general critique of prison life and the unpredictable nature of the parole system. The reaction of the prison officials was to exclude him from further contact with the men before his study was finished. His argument that this was government censorship was to no avail. Although he was never again given access to the prisoners, the government officials made no effort to suppress the book which was published in 1970.

To this point the examples of conflict between the interviewer's loyalty to a particular interest and to the larger society have been those in which a relatively powerful and conservative organization was pitted against the interests of a relatively weak segment of society. This is not always the case. Sometimes the social scientist is opposed and hampered by those who may be of a radical ideology and claiming to speak for the suppressed minority. This claim is sometimes true, in that they actually know how to and are in fact helping a minority. In some cases they would like to do so but either do not have the necessary knowledge and skills or they are too constrained by a straitjacket of simplistic ideology to be of any help to anyone. In other cases they may be using idealistic rhetoric to hide the fact that they are engaged in a form of political manipulation of the downtrodden who have value as potential recruits to swell the ranks of the cause. In some of these circumstances some radicals interfere with studies which could be useful to the oppressed and to anyone seriously interested in helping them.

For example, Lansberger, a sociologist with long experience in studying peasant movements in Latin America, decided to study the cooperative movement among black farmers in southern United States. He wanted to bring his experience to bear on the struggle of southern blacks. When the Ford Foundation financially supported the development of farm cooperatives among blacks in the South, Lansberger acted as a consultant to evaluate the effectiveness of the program. As a Ford Foundation consultant, he was cordially welcomed by the indigenous farm leaders who made up the board of directors of the Federation of Southern Cooperatives as well as by members of the individual black farmers' co-ops and their officers; but the organizers from outside the community were hostile.[6] According to Glazer, "Lansberger never

---

[6]Henry A. Lansberger, "Southern Rural Cooperatives: A Provocative Preliminary Assessment of Their Past and Their Prospects," Unpublished paper.

received the cooperation of his youthful, often urban-born, more highly educated, and certainly more radical, critics."[7] These men wanted Ford Foundation support, but they did not want an independent evaluation of their efforts to help the rural blacks. According to Lansberger, the facts were perceived as a threat by middle-class radical leaders who were proposing to help the poor.

> To query the feasibility of a project for the poor or the black on any basis except that it is really "an establishment plot to avoid tackling the underlying problem," is to lay oneself open to charges of racism, insensitivity, and the like. But to query a project on such specific bases as the possible lack within the poor or black communities of technical or managerial skills; or to conclude that membership apathy is a fact of life among poor blacks (as it is among poor and rich whites) is to make certain that such accusations will be made. . . . [but] . . . I think well enough of my fellow man—both the humble in the co-ops, and the powerful in the foundations and in the government—to believe that they frequently, and increasingly, welcome the truth.[8]

Lansberger's position in this situation is a most difficult one for the educated person so often reluctant to be labeled a reactionary or a racist. Yet he held to the hard-nosed position that any successful attempt must be based upon objective, relevant information on the local situation rather than upon reactionary ritual or radical rhetoric.

Evaluative investigations have been opposed by both conservatives and radicals. The conservatives fear that such studies will show the establishment's foibles and methods of maintaining power. The radicals fear that the information will be used by the establishment to repress them, that it will show a gap between their ideology and their practice, or that their attempts at social change are ineffective. Both the conservative and the radical objector will try to clothe his objections in terms of freedom and ethics, when the real issue is often power.

All these examples are intended to illustrate the fact that there is a tendency to prevent studies of human behavior and to suppress the findings of such studies if they are not to the liking of a particular individual or group. This tendency is found in all groups to some extent, whether they are weak or powerful, uneducated or educated. None makes an absolute value of truth for truth's sake. Not only do those agencies who pay for studies sometimes try to control them, but the research organization or individual hired by the sponsoring organization may also try to suppress the truth to some extent for fear that any findings unpopular with either the sponsor or the public in general may weaken future ability to attract research funds. This fear throws into gear all of the mechanisms of self-preservation in any organization.

---

[7]Glazer, *Research Adventure*, pp. 157–58.
[8]Ibid., p. 158.

Intentional Bias in Data Collection

The conflict between the researcher's loyalties to the humanistic values of the larger society, the survival values of a particular organization, and the scientific values of pure truth may pose some agonizing dilemmas, resulting in disagreement on what is ethical. It is often easier to obtain consensus on the ethics in a situation where the researcher intentionally uses his or her skills to distort the truth to deceive the larger community. Although it may be difficult to establish that the deception was intentional, it makes little difference if the distortion was in fact the result of incompetence on the part of a person claiming to be a social scientist.

An infamous example of the biasing of the data-collection process or the misrepresentation of the representativeness of the data is given by Cain.[9] He points out that a study billed as a national sample of the aged and their attitudes regarding health, medical care, medical insurance and related topics was in fact a systematically biased sample. Even though respondents in many states were interviewed to get a geographical spread, the sample was powerfully biased in that it excluded all blacks, all persons receiving old-age assistance, and anyone in hospitals, homes for the aged, nursing homes, or other institutions; a large portion of those remaining were also excluded if they were in the lower economic class. Furthermore, 20 percent of those falling in this "sample" did not respond. It is possible that over 55 percent of the aged were excluded, and all of these were the less affluent.

This study became the center of a national controversy when the American Medical Association used the report to support their opposition to the Medicare Bill then before Congress. Press releases were issued and congressmen quoted the study as showing that 90 percent of the aged had no unfulfilled medical needs and that the remainder listed lack of money as one of the least important reasons for failure to relieve their needs. Several of the research associates complained about this interpretation and said that they had been uninformed about the overall nature of the national sample when they were doing their geographical portion of the interviewing. The study was discredited at the National Gerontological Congress and was later generally discredited, but the whole controversy indicated the lack of clearly ethical conduct on the part of some individuals within the social science profession as well as a lack of any developed means of enforcing ethical conduct within the profession.

---

[9]Leonard D. Cain, Jr., "The AMA and the Gerontologists: Uses and Abuses of a Profile of the Aging: USA," chap. 4 in *Ethics, Politics and Social Research*, ed. Gideon Sjoberg (Cambridge, Mass.: Schenkman Publishing Co., 1967), pp. 78–114.

Probably if those who worked on the study had known in advance how the findings were to be used, they would have raised serious objections to participating in the study.

Intentional Bias in Interpretation

It is not necessary to introduce bias into the data-gathering process to have a detrimental effect on the community at large. In some cases the valid results of a study can be used to the disadvantage of those studied. Even though those doing the study may be motivated by the desire either to improve the performance of the existing program or to design a better one, it is possible for any results showing shortcomings of the program to be used politically as an excuse to simply cut it out rather than build something better. This is a particular danger in program evaluation studies done to measure the effectiveness of any action program in the areas of health, education, and welfare. An example of this problem is provided by Pilisuk from a case in which investigators working with a grant from the Office of Economic Opportunity produced findings which questioned the effectiveness of the Headstart Program, particularly in its ability to improve the preschool child's reading-readiness scores.[10] These findings were successfully used by those arguing for a cutback in funds. Instead of benefiting more children and families with a higher quality program—the real need shown by the investigation—there was a lower quality or smaller program because of the resulting cut in funds. The researcher does not have to be willingly seeking to prostitute his or her craft in order to be taken advantage of, and therefore the researcher must be constantly alert to the uses and misuses of the research findings.

It may seem to some readers that this discussion of obligations to the larger society, which are sometimes in conflict with obligations to the sponsoring organization, is not a legitimate responsibility of all interviewers on a project. These ethical decisions may apparently belong to only those who are charged with the responsibility of choosing the problem, finding a funding organization, designing the field strategy, analyzing and interpreting the data. To some extent this is true, but there is a better chance of achieving a high level of ethical behavior if everyone recognizes that he or she has certain choices of action.

Every interviewer has the opportunity to decide whether to work with a particular project. Everyone should know who the sponsor of the study is and to what purpose the findings are to be used. As some of the illustrations have shown, it is also wise to be alert for how the findings

---

[10]Marc Pilisuk, "People's Park, Power and the Calling of the Social Sciences," in *Toward Social Change: A Handbook for Those Who Would*, ed. Robert Buckhaut et al. (New York: Harper & Row, 1971).

are used and to see that they are not misused. Once the interviewer is assured that the aims of the study are harmonious with the common welfare of the larger society and that the sponsoring organization will use it accordingly, the interviewer may find it is easier to handle those ethical conflicts arising from his or her loyalty to the research organization, the research team, and the respondent.

RESPONSIBILITIES TO THE RESEARCH ORGANIZATION

There are some ideals regarding the interviewer's relationship to the research organization that are easily stated but under some conditions may be difficult to follow.

Always Follow the Sampling Instructions

In studies where it is necessary to obtain responses from an accurate representative sample, it is extremely important either to make no substitutions or to have a predetermined system for making random substitutions. The temptation to make an unauthorized substitution of a more available and willing respondent may become strong near the end of a study when it is necessary to clean up the remainder of the random sample, but this can result in considerable bias in the results that cannot be compensated for by simply increasing the total number of interviews.

Do Not Fictionalize Responses

Fictionalizing may occur in the most mild form when the interviewer is instructed to take *verbatim* notes but abbreviates words and phrases and then fills in the missing portions immediately after the interview is over. There is a temptation at this point for the interviewer to slightly pad the response with some concrete imagery to make up for a failure to probe more deeply during the interview. An intermediate form of fictionalizing sometimes occurs when the interviewer discovers after leaving the respondent that certain questions were omitted. Here the temptation may become strong to fill in the occasionally missing answer by guess. It is better to leave a blank so that later random answers may be substituted, a phone call may be made to the respondent, or the space simply left blank in the tabulation.

It makes research directors shudder to think of the most extreme form of fictionalizing in which the interviewer fills out the whole interview schedule or questionnaire for an imaginary respondent. This sometimes occurs when a study has been going for some time, the work load has been heavy, and the obstacles to contacting the respondents are many. The obstacles may be physical things like an above-ninety or below-zero temperature, or social-psychological things like fear of being refused. It is more ethical for the interviewer to protest the work load, the working conditions, or the lack of a high morale-producing atmosphere rather than to avoid conflict by fictionalizing an interview now and then. Such fictionalizing subverts the whole purpose of the enterprise.

Descriptions of the conditions under which cheating arises and some telling case studies are given by Roth under what he aptly calls "hired-hand research."[11] He shows how interviewers who were supposed to probe for five reasons why parents had put their child in an institution could rarely extract that many reasons from the same person. They would often fill in the blank with an imaginary reason, particularly after the director of the study had criticized some for not getting five reasons as others had done.

If pressures exist to encourage the falsification of information, it is more ethical to bring these to the attention of the study director *early* in the project rather than devoting more time to the collection of useless data. If one interviewer finds that others are cheating, it would be better to try to discuss with that person the pressures which cause the behavior and get the interviewers to agree jointly to bring the problems to the attention of the project director. If this is done early it is more likely to be appreciated.

Probe Fully Where Needed

There is a tendency for interviewers to become less thorough in probing for complete, adequate, and valid responses as they become fatigued, bored, or simply lose their initially fresh curiosity. For example, the writer discovered that a team interviewing disaster victims over a ten-day period averaged about two and one-half depth interviews per day.[12] The interviews were long and there was considerable difficulty in finding the sample of respondents who had moved after their houses had been destroyed by a tornado. Over the ten-day period, the average length of each interviewer's first interview of the day dropped from about thirty-five to twenty-eight pages of transcription. Analysis of the interview transcriptions revealed that the shortening of the interview was due somewhat to increased efficiency in obtaining relevant information. However, the main cause of the drop in interview length was

---

[11]Julius Roth, "Hired Hand Research," *American Sociologist* 1 (August 1966), pp. 190–96.

[12]Raymond L. Gorden, "An Interaction Analysis of the Depth Interview" (Ph.D. dissertation, University of Chicago, Department of Sociology, 1954).

the flagging curiosity of the interviewer who had heard so many respondents' accounts that he felt he knew what the respondent would say without having to probe to really find out.

The thoroughness of the probing becomes an ethical problem in those settings in which boredom, fatigue, and a lack of interest in the purposes of the study tempt the interviewer to take a shortcut. Any director of any project involving many repeated interviews, particularly when they are done on a full-time basis, must realize this danger of settling for the stereotyped response. In some cases this can be remedied by rotating functions such as locating respondents, monitoring tapes, editing interview schedules, transcribing tapes, public relations chores, and preliminary data analysis.

This principle of relieving boredom and increasing responsibility for completeness of the information was applied by the writer in developing a system for outreach workers in a local poverty program to collect data on each client. Instead of having an interviewer collect the information, another person punch the cards, and a third person do the statistical analysis, a McBee keysort card was developed on which the interviewer could record the information on the spot; then the same person would punch his or her own cards, and later do a statistical analysis of the accumulated cases every three months. In this way the interviewer became acutely aware of missing information, of faulty punching, of his or her own accumulated accomplishments, and of the meaning of the data in the aggregate. Training these interviewers, many of whom had not finished high school, to carry out a wider range of functions required considerable effort. This was a continuing operation to be carried out by the same people over several years, so it was well worth the trouble.

Do Not Bias Responses

Interviewers can bias the responses by the tone of voice used in asking the question, by gestures, and by facial expression as well as by deviating from the required wording of the question or structuring of the answers. Sometimes consciously or unconsciously an interviewer will try to bias the responses, particularly if he or she has a strong emotional attachment to the issues involved and the use of the results. In some cases an interviewer may frankly feel that because of strong emotional bias and problems of self-control, that for the good of the scientific objectivity of the study he or she should not interview on the subject. Sometimes this is not discovered by the interviewer until after a few interviews have been done. In this case the problem should be discussed with the project director. A later chapter deals with this problem of manifesting nonbiasing attitudes.

Report Possible Invalidities in the Interview Schedule

Ethical problems may develop if the interviewer discovers that while he or she has no difficulty in exhibiting unbiasing behavior, the wording of a single question, a particular sequence of questions, or the structured answer choices of a particular question may be highly biasing in its effect. Under these circumstances it is the interviewer's ethical duty to report this opinion to the project director and give as clear evidence as possible for the opinion. In this case the interviewer should be prepared to discover that the bias is intentional because the results are intended to be used as propaganda or advertising to deceive "enemies, clients, constituents, or customers" to the benefit of the sponsoring organization. Here the interviewer must decide whether his or her loyalty is to the larger society or to the sponsoring organization. Also involved are the interviewer's loyalty to the respondent whose opinion should not be distorted for someone's gain, and loyalty to one's own conscience. This ethical dilemma most frequently arises in studies involving conflicts over public issues or in commercial motivation research where product competition is strong.

It requires moral courage for an interviewer to approach the project director with the proposition that the interview schedule is biased. If the bias is intentional and the interviewer persistent, the interviewer may be fired. On the other hand the project director may be grateful for the help, particularly if the problem is dealt with early in the field work. Again, the joint opinions and experiences of all the interviewers would be more useful than those of just one. From the project director's point of view, assuming that the project director does not want to bias the responses, it is helpful to have the same interviewers do one or two field tests and revisions to make the questions more relevant or valid.

The interviewer has an ethical obligation not only to report possible bias in the wording of questions but also any possibility that certain very crucial questions are omitted. The interviewer might discover that some of the questions are in a form which misses the most relevant dimensions of the issue or that different kinds of respondents need different kinds or wordings of questions. These are all things which should be worked out in the development and field testing of the interview schedule, but there is always the possibility that some serious errors remain.

Even if such problems are discovered and reported very late in the data-collection process, the report is still useful and will be welcomed by the truly scientific project director since it will be helpful in making interpretations of the responses. Obviously, for practical purposes, at least in a survey where the data are to be statistically summarized, it is impractical to keep changing the form of questions or adding and subtracting questions throughout the duration of the study, but it is never too late to weigh the relevance, validity, and reliability of the information.

The probability of an interviewer's reporting these problems grows with any increase in the interviewer's understanding of the purpose and importance of the study, faith in the project director's integrity, and general allegiance to scientific standards.

The number and kind of ethical problems which arise seem to depend on the extent to which the purposes of the research organization and the problem under study are consonant with the values of the larger society and the values of the scientific community. In those happy situations where there is consonance, the interviewer's obligations to society in general, to the research organization, and to his or her own conscience are one and the same. However, this happily harmonious state is rare in situations where the purpose of the research is to evaluate existing organizations or to develop better patterns of human behavior. We can expect that, with the growing interest in applying social science to social change, ethical issues will be generated at an increasing rate.

RESPONSIBILITIES TO THE RESPONDENT

Again, the discussion of ethical responsibilities to the respondent will represent each value that should ideally be pursued in this relationship. Yet it must be pointed out that often these values conflict with others, and therefore the interviewer has to make an ethical choice, whether or not this is a conscious decision.

Gaining Access to the Respondent

There are several possible ethical problems involved in gaining access to the respondents needed for a particular study. One problem might be called "getting past the gatekeepers." This is an obvious problem in the case where the potential respondents are in some closed institution as was true in the case cited earlier in which Dr. Gaylin needed to interview war resisters in prison. In that case the conflict arose between the scientific value of completing the study and the institutional value of the prison's protecting itself from criticism. Another type of gatekeeper problem arises when it might be physically possible to sidestep the gatekeeper but the gatekeepers could facilitate access to the respondent. The gatekeeper could orient the interviewer and point out where certain people, things, or information could be found. In this case the gatekeeper is not in a position of absolute power but may attempt to drive a bargain for favors in exchange for information. Under these conditions the researcher may be lured to promise more than he or she can produce as in the case of Berreman's study of an Hindu village.[13]

Berreman was tempted to exaggerate the possible values of his study of the village in "putting the village on the map." This appeal would fit into the villagers' feeling of having underdog status because they were on a mountain rather than on the plain. Berreman's experience also points out a danger in entering a community through the usual channels of the high status gatekeepers. This may make it difficult for the interviewer to assure respondents that no harm may come to them, or it may prevent the respondents from providing complete relevant and reliable information. For example, the gatekeepers of the Himalaya village were high-caste merchants who were viewed by the villagers as dishonest, cheating exploiters of the common people. This was a negative force in the early portion of the study.

Another example of the danger in going through instead of around a gatekeeper is given by Babbie who tells of a study of church women, in which the ministers of the churches were the gatekeepers:

> The ministers in a sample of churches were asked to distribute questionnaires to a specified sample of members, collect them, and return them to the research office. One of these ministers read through the questionnaires from his sample before returning them, and then proceeded to deliver a hell-fire and brimstone sermon to his congregation, saying that many of them were atheists and going to hell. Even though he could not know or identify the respondents who gave particular responses, it seems certain that many were personally harmed by the action.[14]

It becomes a field strategy problem to decide whether to use one gatekeeper or another or none at all. For example, in a study of employees of a large corporation, it would be convenient to interview them at work. A list of the employees and an opportunity to interview them at work might be sought by approaching either the union or the management. Either could play a maximum role by furnishing a list of names and a time and place at the plant to interview and by expressing approval of the study. Either could play a minimum role by providing a list of employees' names and addresses; the researcher could then interview each employee at home. The former procedure would require less time and be more convenient; the latter procedure would reduce the interviewer's obligations to management or the union.

[13]Gerald D. Berreman, *Hindus of the Himalayas* (Berkeley, Calif.: University of California Press, 1972).

[14]Earl R. Babbie, *Survey Research Methods* (Belmont, Calif.: Wadsworth Publishing, 1973), p. 350.

It becomes apparent that the ethical problem and the methodological one become intertwined. In some cases it is particularly difficult if the gatekeeper has absolute power to deny access to the respondent. In other cases the gatekeeper has relative power as a nuisance or a convenience for the researcher. In either case the interviewer must be careful not to sell his scientific soul, his obligations to the larger society, or the rights of the respondents in exchange for the gatekeeper's cooperation.

Voluntary Participation

Voluntary participation is desirable but often impossible because of its conflict with other values. One of the most obvious conflicts is with the democratic ideal that everyone's opinion is important. Since all adult citizens can vote, any attempt to poll all voters cannot strictly adhere to the principle of voluntary participation. If we define a volunteer as anyone who would come to the interviewer to be interviewed, representative studies could not be done. If we mean that anyone who is "busy" or "doesn't know anything about that" on the first contact should not be interviewed, then accurately representative polls would be impossible.

Fortunately, our ethical dilemma dissolves to some extent when we make a distinction between the pure volunteer, the "persuaded," and the "coerced." Most "volunteers" are actually "persuaded" cooperators or at least nonresisters to gentle coercion. There are many legitimate claims which can be made to persuade the respondent to be interviewed. These have been described earlier as *facilitators* of communication. From an ethical point of view, to appeal to the respondent's altruism, and even to the respondent's need for recognition, is an appeal to the values and ideals of the larger society.

Often the respondent can be activated by evidence of selflessness on the part of the interviewer. For example, Babbie points out that certain interviewers are more persuasive than others in obtaining cooperation of respondents; he says, "experience has shown an eight-month-pregnant interviewer is more successful than the average in this regard."[15] The author has also found that the interviewers who understand most clearly the purposes of the interview and have the most respect for the respondents are most successful in obtaining cooperation.

The fact that social pressure and altruism can persuade volunteers to undergo extreme privation has been demonstrated by the experiments at the University of Minnesota during World War II, in which volunteer conscientious objectors were subjected to slow starvation of 500 calories per day for months at a time, reducing them to walking

---

[15]Ibid., p. 348.

skeletons.[16] Undergoing this privation can probably be accounted for to a great extent by the conscientious objectors' feelings that they did owe something to their country and would like to make a sacrifice equal to that of many of the men and women in the armed forces without having to kill a fellow human being. Were these conscientious objectors, then, volunteers or were they coerced by the draft law and the fact that their country was at war? Regardless of the answer to this question, it is clear that they chose this more sacrificial route when others were legally available to them.

Once we discover the extent to which respondents can be persuaded to cooperate, we have solved a practical problem but are in danger of running aground on the ethical question of *how* we persuade them. There is a temptation to promise anything feasible to obtain cooperation: promising respondents a copy of the results of the study, promising to help them in some way, or promising to pass their name along to some other agency which can help them. Of course, these strategies and many more are ethical as long as we are prepared to actually follow through on the promise and as long as it does not injure anyone else.

The respondent's cooperation can be gained not only by giving some positive incentives but also by reducing the costs to the respondent. This cost-reduction approach includes choosing a time when there will be the fewest competing demands on the respondent's time, avoiding the use of unnecessary time in the interviewing, or offering to come a second time to finish. The problem of offering the respondent incentives is particularly important in gaining the initial contact. Once the interview begins we can usually rely on the *facilitators* to keep the motivation.

Do Not Harm the Respondent

Rarely does anyone argue with the idea of avoiding harm to the respondent, yet the naïve interviewer can injure the respondent in many ways. In some situations it may be harmful to the respondent to even be seen with the interviewer. This was the case when the writer was interviewing college professors about violations of academic freedom at colleges where the president had refused to allow the interviewers from Louis Harris Associates on the campus. To avoid possible retribution from the presidents of such colleges, the author interviewed the professors at their homes. This problem arises in many conflict situations in which "anyone who is not a known friend must be treated like an enemy." Even

---

[16]Ancel Keys, *Human Starvation* (Minneapolis: University of Minnesota Press, 1950).

though someone might feel like a captive of an in-group and might want to contact a neutral outsider, he or she may be viewed as a traitor.

Harm can be done to the respondent by leaking information which could be used against him or her either by legitimate authorities such as the police, by company management, or by the dean of students—these might have power either to withhold rewards or to mete out punishment to the person on the basis of the information given. Protecting the respondent from any harm resulting from the interview becomes an ethical problem when the respondent has engaged in deviant behavior punishable according to the values of the larger society. This problem can arise when an interviewer discovers that a manager has falsified company records, that a worker has made personal long-distance phone calls on the employer's charge account, that a person has committed a felony for which he or she was never apprehended, or that a person shoplifts regularly to pay for a heroin habit.

To give a concrete case, a field study was done in a Mexican-American neighborhood to evaluate the effectiveness of gangworkers and to formulate certain generalizations about the development of delinquency within the context of a lower-class urban ethnic group:

> In another instance a social worker was contacted late at night by one of his boys, who was a drug addict. The boy was scheduled to go on a voluntary commitment to the federal narcotics hospital, but his bus did not leave until the next morning. His supply of drugs had been raided and he had no money. If he was to get through the remaining twelve hours, he needed a "fix." In San Antonio at present, there is no way for an addict legally to get a fix. On the other hand, if he didn't get it the withdrawal symptoms would become "unendurable," at which point he might try to steal some money in order to get more drugs. This would place the boy in jeopardy, and if he were caught, it would lead to imprisonment, a criminal record, and possibly involuntary commitment to a hospital.
>
> The social worker was in an extremely delicate ethical position. . . . The worker's solution was to place the boy in a situation where he could get a fix, although the worker was not present when the boy bought and used the drug. The worker stayed with the boy part of the night and met him in the morning to get him on the bus and on the way to voluntary withdrawal from drugs. The boy stayed in the hospital until his release and has been off drugs ever since. Had these events led to some unfortunate consequences for the worker or for the boy, we might have had to view the ethical issues in a somewhat different light.[17]

---

[17]Richard A. Brymer and Buford Farris, "Ethical and Political Dilemmas in the Investigation of Deviance: A Study of Juvenile Delinquency," chap. 13 in *Ethics, Politics and Social Research*, ed. Gideon Sjoberg (Cambridge, Mass.: Schenkman Publishing Co., 1971), pp. 311–12.

Clearly this field worker was protecting his respondent from any harm resulting from the knowledge he had gained; yet this made the social worker an accessory to the crime of buying and using illegal drugs. At the same time the social worker was fulfilling the values of both the respondent and the larger society by making available a voluntary treatment to cure his addiction. As the author implies, the whole ethical decision-making process depended upon the social worker's correct prediction of the outcome which he helped to bring about. Thus, values in their application cannot be separated from knowledge about cause and effect, prediction and control. What would be ethical under one set of circumstances becomes unethical under another.

Precisely where to draw the line in protecting a respondent would depend upon the value to be served in the larger society, the potential value of the research project to society, and the effect on the scientific community, on the respondent and on the interviewer. Obviously, we are not going to propose a formula for doing this; but it is realistic to note that people must make ethical decisions involving both human values and assumptions or predictions about the probable effects of their decisions. Even inaction is a decision by default.

Anonymity and Confidentiality

The major way of protecting the respondent from harm resulting from information he or she gives is to keep that information confidential or anonymous. Confidential means that no one except the interviewer knows from whom the information came. Anonymous means that not even the interviewer knows from whom the information came.

The discussion of methods of preserving anonymity or confidentiality will be left to the next chapter, but the discussion in the remainder of this section emphasizes the differences in the potential ethical issues in each. First, the social research interviewer (whether a professional sociologist, psychologist, anthropologist, social worker, manager, or a paraprofessional interviewer of any type) has no legal guarantee of privileged communication as does the lawyer, physician, or clergyman. If a court wants to subpoena a tape recording, interview transcription, or interview schedule, or if it calls the interviewer to the witness stand to report what he or she was told, there is no clear legal recourse. Therefore, if we promise confidentiality to our respondent, there may be certain circumstances in which the promise is hard to keep.

If the information is collected by an anonymous questionnaire and if there are enough cases so that no individual can be pinpointed by some combination of characteristics, then there is no possibility of the information being used against the respondent or interviewer. Often, the kind of information needed and the field methods required make the anonymous questionnaire impractical. In this case, if the interviewer has an ethical obligation to protect the respondent against the effects of the information, the interviewer may have to destroy the original form of the data and refuse to depend upon his or her faulty memory for testimony.

This precise issue arose when Humphreys reported on his study of the behavior of male homosexuals in public toilets.[18] The study was a Ph.D. dissertation financed by the National Institute of Mental Health. The university administration tried to have NIMH withhold a second grant pending an investigation of the methods used to obtain the information.

In order to be an observer, Humphreys had played the role of a lookout in the public toilets to warn the homosexuals of any possible intrusion by police or other unfriendly strangers during their brief intimate encounters. Then in order to see how their homosexuality fit into the rest of their lives, he traced automobile license numbers to locate the men's home addresses; allowed a year to lapse, changed his hair style, manner of dress, and car to avoid recognition and introduced himself as a researcher studying community health patterns. Most homosexuals were heads of families and this gave him an opportunity to see them prepare barbecues, have their evening drinks, and talk with their families. In addition he did an intensive study of a dozen of these men who were willing to talk freely with him about their homosexuality after knowing the purposes of his study. He did not secretly observe or interview anyone.

The study flared into public controversy when Nicholas von Hoffman, writing in the *Washington Post*, accused Humphreys of the same invasion of privacy as police are often charged with.[19] Others charged that no human being should be trusted with such incriminating evidence about another and that more clear ethical codes should be drafted to govern the conduct of social science investigators.

Humphreys himself says that he took each step in the study only after agonizing appraisal of the ethical pros and cons, the practical dangers to himself and his respondents, and the ultimate value to society of such a candid descriptive study. He totally rejects the analogy to the police violations of privacy. He made a large distinction between the violation of his own privacy by the police who arrested him and his intrusion into the private domain of his respondents:

---

[18]Laud Humphreys, *Tearoom Trade*, rev. ed. (Chicago: Aldine Publishing, 1975).

[19]Nicholas von Hoffman, Irving L. Horowitz, and Lee Rainwater, "Sociological Snoopers and Journalistic Moralizers: An Exchange," *Transaction*, May 1970, pp. 4–8.

The real concern of the founders of our liberties was with protecting the citizen against the awful force of military and social control agencies, who have the power to arrest, prosecute, imprison, and destroy those whose privacy they violate. As I wrote Nicholas von Hoffman shortly after my arrest: "You see, the real point is that the former (John Mitchell et al.) can and do arrest the latter." (Laud Humphreys et al.)[20]

There is general agreement among psychologists, sociologists, penologists, and administrators of social agencies often dealing with homosexuals that we need more unbiased description of the development of homosexuality itself and how it affects the lives of the homosexual, his family, and the community before we can reform current irrational practices. For example, those who would like to send boys to the army "to make a man out of them" must face the fact that homosexuality is more prevalent in the army, in prisons, and in other sexually segregated institutions than it is in the community at large. Perhaps it is the reluctance to face some of these apparent dilemmas that generates some hostility to the study of homosexuals.

Even though it is true that in this case the private information given to Humphreys was never used to blackmail or to legally prosecute any of his respondents, it must be admitted that in the hands of less careful and courageous researchers there could have been some backlash affecting the respondents. Even those social scientists who feel that Humphreys did the ethical thing recognize that this modus operandi is not possible for everyone:

> My conversations with Humphreys convince me of his extraordinary courage and ability to withstand condemnation and abuse. Yet these very characteristics make him a poor model for others to emulate without the most painful self-scrutiny. . . . While admiring Humphreys, I know that I could not pursue such research myself and would attempt to dissuade others from such a path.[21]

Fortunately, such painful dilemmas rarely arise in the attempts to keep private information anonymous or confidential, but the basic ethical point here is that any researcher who wants to study deviant behavior of any kind should take very seriously the responsibility to prepare for possible attempts to get the original data for use illegally in blackmail or legally in prosecution of either the respondents or the interviewer. Part of this preparation is a careful soul-searching of one's own motives, of the study's probable value to society, and of the dangers to the social science professions, and to individuals involved in the study.

Why do social scientists engage in the study of deviant behavior if the data cannot be used to reform the individual deviants? One answer

---

[20]Glazer, *Research Adventure*, p. 164.
[21]Ibid., p. 116.

is that any rational decision making about the value of eliminating any form of deviant behavior requires seeing that behavior in a broader context of alternatives, and evaluating the possible effects of various methods available to reduce deviance. Second, evidence shows that most of society's attempts to reform or to cure individual deviants, whether we are thinking of drug addicts, criminals, schizophrenics, or alcoholics, are not successful. The major hope for success in reducing antisocial forms of deviant behavior lies in *prevention*, and any successful prevention program must be based upon a realistic knowledge of the process by which the individual becomes a deviant member of society. A third answer is that by studying deviant behavior we can further basic social science knowledge regarding the nature of generic processes such as socialization, personality development, social control, conformity and nonconformity to norms, and changes in social values and norms. Obviously, Humphreys probably believed more strongly in the value of his research to society in the long run than those who advised him that it was not worth the risks to all concerned. The relatively happy ending to the affair was due mainly to his foresight in destroying the evidence, including the list of respondents, *before* he was asked for it by authorities.

Help the Respondent, If Possible

Helping the respondent is both a means of attracting or maintaining his or her cooperation and of ethically reciprocating or showing appreciation for what the respondent has contributed. Often the non-social-scientist interviewer conducts an interview in order to obtain information which can be used to help a person. In some cases the information may also be used to the person's detriment, particularly from the point of view of the respondent. In either case the non-social-scientist is obtaining the information in order to directly influence the respondent one way or another. Often this effect depends upon the nature of the information elicited.

This is the typical situation with the employment interviewer, the social work interviewer, the poverty outreach worker, and the college admissions interviewer. When the interview results in a person's obtaining some needed social service, obtaining a job or a promotion, or in getting into the college he or she chooses, then we have certainly helped the respondent. However, when the result of the interview is not what the respondent wants, there is often little thought of how some secondary help might be given to the person on the basis of the same diagnostic information. Such help could be built into the interview as a fallback position to show the respondent that the interviewer is still interested in his or her welfare as a fellow human being. For example, a person who is found to lack the qualifications needed for a job could be informed of the probable nature of the future job market, what additional knowledge or skills should be developed, where the appropriate schooling or on-the-job-training could be obtained to make the respondent more marketable. As a minimum the interviewer could refer the respondent to other agencies which could provide these types of information.

The situation of the social scientist interviewer is quite different with regard to his or her opportunities to help the respondent. Rarely does the study itself call for attempting to bring about some change in the respondent as a result of the information obtained. For this reason the rewards used, either to elicit the respondent's cooperation or to maintain the respondent's goodwill, must be less connected to the nature of the information sought.

In community studies social scientists have often undertaken some practical social service project which will keep them in contact with the respondents or will generally make them more welcome in the community. When the writer was field supervisor of a disaster study team, he noted that the interviewers began increasingly to develop guilt feelings for taking up the time of the disaster victims with interviews which could help future disaster victims but not those being interviewed. Since the project was short term (about one month in the field), the interviewers could not donate time or services, but they decided to make a cash contribution for a disaster relief fund to be administered by the local village council.

Berreman in his longer-term study of the Hindu village developed some ad hoc forms of helping the village by letting villagers listen to his radio and by supplying simple medical remedies.[22] Liebow obtained cooperation by offering Tally a ride to the courthouse where he had been subpoenaed as a witness in the trial of his friend Lonny, accused of murdering his own wife.[23] From this time on, Liebow was looked to for advice on a wide range of things. Lewis, in his study of a Mexican village, Tepoztlan, found that the Mexican government was interested enough in the value of his study to attach to his project the services of two agronomists, two doctors, and two social workers to give direct practical help to the villagers.[24]

All of these aids to the respondent might be classified as extrinsic rewards in our framework of facilitators and inhibitors. However, the rewards given in community studies may go to many people in addition to the respondents and may have little quantitative relationship to the amount of time or effort expended by a particular respondent.

[22]Berreman, *Hindus.*

[23]Reported in Glazer, *Research Adventure*, pp. 18–19.

[24]Oscar Lewis, *Life in a Mexican Village: Tepoztlan Restudied* (Urbana, Ill.: University of Illinois Press, 1970).

There are several ethical problems which can arise in the attempt to follow the rule of helping the respondent when possible. First there is the temptation to promise more than can be produced as a result of the study. This typically occurs when the respondents have strong hopes that the study will help them in a particular way.

Another ethical problem arises when the interviewer, in order to get the respondent's cooperation, promises to give him or her the results of the study. Unless this has been included in the budget for the study, there is very little chance that it will be done. Also the respondent population may be so transient that with the lapse of time needed to complete the analysis, the problems of getting the results to individual respondents is overwhelming. Preparations must be made in advance to share results with the respondents. This can be done even in cases where the respondents are anonymous. For example, in a study of the racial attitudes of students, parents, and teachers in a public school system, one copy of the study was put in each school library, in the local neighborhood branches of the county library, and also was given to all social agencies in the city.

A third problem arises when the field phase of the study is long and the needs of the respondents are great. In studying ethnic ghettos, rural villages, or any low status groups, there is the danger that the research staff in empathizing with the respondents or acceding to their expectations will gradually shift their activities from science to service to such an extent that science is lost.

The writer experienced this problem when he attempted to train field workers in an antipoverty program whose purpose was to discover the obstacles to getting families out of poverty. Even though it was clear that the program had at least a 90 percent failure rate despite its multi-million-dollar budget, and the workers were interested in discovering and removing the causes of this failure, they became diverted from the purpose of discovering and describing obstacles by such activities as finding a pair of shoes for a child or raising emergency funds to pay delinquent utility bills. In their more rational moments the workers would admit that these activities would not get families out of poverty and they interfered with that objective. However, after long exposure to the poor, their urge to do something concrete predominated over the more frustrating task of objectively determining how the mass of conflicting regulations of many different human service agencies could be untangled to allow the effective coordination of services essential in getting families out of poverty. In this case, the short-run urge for concrete, but ineffective, action conflicted with the long-run goals.

Do Not Deceive the Respondent

Even though ideally it may be good to tell the truth, the whole truth, and nothing but the truth to the respondents, all this is not necessary to conform to the rule not to deceive the respondent. There are many circumstances in which telling the respondent too much can cause considerable problems. For example, Whyte, in his study of street corner society in an Italian slum, found that it was not possible to explain the purpose of his study to the slum dwellers. He had no reason or desire to deceive them but simply could not explain the theoretical purpose of his study in terms that people of a different background could grasp. Often what is done in such cases is to give a very general explanation that will include all of the researchers' activities. In community studies such an explanation as "doing a history of X community" is acceptable and broad enough to include the kinds of data collected.

It has already been shown that in many cases giving a respondent a complete explanation may stop the study before it gets off the ground if that respondent is one of the gatekeepers of the organization or community to be studied. Having a legal or moral right to do the study may have no persuasive effect upon the gatekeeper if he or she feels threatened by the sponsorship of the study or its purpose. A precise explanation of the purpose or sponsorship not only has the possibility of preventing the study but also of biasing the responses if the respondents tend to want either to please or deceive the sponsoring organization. The researcher to be honest must be prepared for the possibility that if he or she is to stay within the bounds of ethics certain types of studies simply cannot be done at certain times and places. It is not always possible for the researcher to become convinced that the potential value of the study to the larger society or to the scientific community is great enough to justify the means to that end.

Often the question of deceiving the respondent is more personal than either the purposes or the sponsorship of the study. Since the interviewer is the instrument by which relevant information is elicited from respondents, it is often desirable or necessary to change the nature of the instrument to fit the social environment in which it must be used. This change may involve how the interviewer presents himself or herself to the respondent. In some cases interviewers have merely chosen from among their various real roles the one that may have the most appeal to the particular respondent. That fact that an interviewer lives in California, that her grandfather was a Baptist minister, that she graduated from Berkeley, that she belongs to a women's liberation group, that she wants to be a child psychologist, or that her mother speaks Spanish more fluently than English may all be true, but it is obvious that under certain circumstances one of these roles might have a different effect upon the respondent's willingness to trust and cooperate than would another one. Is this deceiving the respondent if the interviewer put his or her best role forward?

This is a common tactic in everyday interactions between people, and the author personally does not feel it is unethical as long as the study is beneficial to society and will do no harm to the respondent.

In other cases interviewers must decide whether to assume behavior that is not their own in order to conform to the demands and expectations of the people being studied. This was the problem Daniels found in a study of the U.S. Army practices in the training of recruits.[25] Her self-concept was of a competent professional, director of a research project with a mandate from Washington, and equal to the officers with whom she dealt. Her use of humor, her strong handshake, her steady gaze, and her brisk competent manner were seen as inappropriate for a woman. The initial response to her was either to resist any spontaneous cooperation or to try to seduce her. She did not realize that in many situations according to the army subculture she appeared to invite seduction. In order to gain access to the needed interviews and observation situations, she had to change her manner to more "feminine" helplessness: less aggressive, less self-assured, waiting to be helped by the officers.

In this case the researcher was engaging in a type of deception as to the kind of person she was in order to conform to the expectations of the group she wanted to study. This was the price of her admission to the group. Is this an unethical form of deception or is this merely adjusting to the field situation and showing respect for another subculture? In this case the fact that the researcher was emotionally involved with the basic issue of women's rights in her own society made it more difficult to separate the value of fighting for a new status for women from the value of gathering valid, reliable, and complete information on the army training process. Clearly the pressure to assume a specific role came from the respondent.

In contrast, in Humphrey's study of homosexuals the pressure to assume the role of lookout did not come from the respondents but from the interviewer's desire for access under circumstances where an opportunity to observe and interview would not be assured without it.

It is interesting that researchers often have more conflict and feelings of hypocrisy when they adjust temporarily to subgroups in their own culture than they have when they go through the ritual of crossing an ocean to a foreign land or an exotic culture.

A more thorough deception of respondents is reported by Festinger, who was a member of the team doing a study of an apocalyptic group led by a woman who believed that through "automatic writing" she had received messages from beings living in outer space forecasting the destruction of the earth by flood on a certain date in the near future.[26]

---

[25]Arlene Kaplan Daniels, "The Low-Caste Stranger in Social Research," chap. 12 in *Ethics, Politics and Social Research*, ed. Gideon Sjoberg (Cambridge, Mass.: Schenkman, 1967), pp. 267–96.

[26]Leon Festinger, H. W. Riecken, and Stanley Schacter, *When Prophecy Fails* (New York: Harper & Row, 1964).

Since the predicted date was close, it made possible a study of how the group behaved during the time before that date and how they would adjust to the failure of the prophecy. To gain access to the group the research team posed as a group of traveling businessmen; this provided an excuse in advance for the team to leave after the date of the prophesied destruction. They posed as being interested citizens who merely happened to hear about the prophecy. The case of "misrepresentation of self" is different from the previous two in that it combines the masquerade of personalities with the misstatement of purpose of the study.

Another type of masquerade is that of showing sympathy for a cause in a way that may either contradict the neutral objectivity stance or exceed the amount of uncritical acceptance actually felt for the cause. This was the situation when Bonilla and Glazer did a study of the professional and political attitudes of Chilean university students.[27] Since it was a participant-observation study, they engaged in informal political discussions with students in which they were expected to share their own political views. In some situations they allowed their respondents to feel that they agreed more with the discussion than they actually did by either emphasizing points of agreement or refraining from expressing their disagreements. This raised the ethical question for the researcher: What right do I have to expect the respondents to give me their candid political views if I do not give an equally candid account of my own political position?

The above examples do not pretend to cover all possible forms of masquerade in the process of presentation of self to obtain information from others, but they should serve to illustrate the reality of the problem. If we were blindly to follow the formula of telling nothing but the whole truth to our potential respondents and their gatekeepers, it would be impossible to study many important controversial issues or to get an inside view of any group we do not already belong to.

Share the Results with the Respondents

The scientific value of sharing information with fellow human beings is obviously served by showing the results of any study to the respondents who furnished the information. It also serves the general humanistic value of reciprocity to the respondent, and it is frequently necessary to disseminate the results of a study if they are to be applied to any action toward larger societal goals. Superficially, it may seem rather difficult to generate an ethical problem through the sharing of the results of a study.

---

[27]Frank Bonilla and Myron Glazer, "Note on Methodology. Field Work in a Hostile Environment: A Chapter in the Sociology of Social Research in Chile," app. A: in *Student Politics in Chile* (New York: Basic Books, 1970), pp. 313–33.

Yet problems do arise. For example, one of this author's former respondents in a study of miscommunication between North Americans and Latin Americans on reading the rough draft of the report said, "Yes, that is true, but I don't think you should say that; it makes Americans look like fools, and they were actually a much better than average bunch in their sensitivity to the host culture." True, they were better than average. Also, it should be noted that nothing in the text of the paper suggested that their behavior could be explained by their lack of concern for the Colombians; yet objectively reporting the results was perceived as a threat, even though the specific individuals were not identified.

A more dramatic example of this tendency to reject certain reflections of reality was encountered in this same study.[28] A group of Peace Corps trainees, not yet accepted as volunteers, had lived in a Colombian home for several weeks. They were then asked to "Describe how the Colombian home you now live in differs from North American homes as you know them," and they gave written responses. The remarks in these short essays were classified into general categories and quoted back to the trainees as a group. A hot discussion ensued with some hostility toward the researcher because the trainees recognized the statements as a series of complaints about the lack of physical comforts and conveniences in even the middle-class homes of Colombia. This image did not jibe with the official image of the volunteer or with the trainees' stated desires to get out into the villages with the volunteers where the discomforts would be even greater. When the trainees learned that this information was used in a course orienting other North Americans in Bogotá, they went on strike against attending classes in the training program.

They protested that they had been promised that the information would be confidential. This charge lost steam when it was pointed out that the preface to the questionnaire, which all respondents were required to read, stated that no individuals would be identified, but that the results would be used in training programs for other Peace Corps groups and for North American undergraduate students coming to Colombia. In resentment of the nonidealized image of themselves, they had forgotten their initial enthusiasm for providing information useful for orienting other arriving North Americans.

If such results are shared before a field study is completed, there is the danger that the backlash can prevent the study from going any further. On several occasions such sharing of information has put researchers in

---

[28]Raymond L. Gorden, *Living in Latin America: A Case Study in Cross-Cultural Communication* (Skokie, Ill., National Textbook Co. in conjunction with the American Council on the Teaching of Foreign Languages, 1984).

the position of having to compromise their scientific value of giving a full, uncensored report because some of the facts shown were threatening to one of the gatekeepers. For example, in studying the effects of a tornado on a small company town built of scrap lumber around a lumber mill in Arkansas, suddenly the complete 100 percent cooperation of the respondents reversed to a 100 percent refusal rate. After consulting with the owner of the company town and the lumber mill, it became clear that the researchers would not be allowed to continue the study unless they agreed to stop collecting information on the income of the mill workers which was less than 30 percent of the rate for similar work in other places in the same state. In this situation just the realization of how such information would look in print was highly threatening to the gatekeeper.

In general the ethical problem about sharing results arises when the potential findings will be perceived as a threat by individual respondents, by the organization or community studied, or by some other interest group. This immediately raises the question of the ethics of suppressing the facts or the interpretation of those facts by the people who collected them. In some cases the suppression is indirect; the research organization may exercise "prudence" in reporting to their client, for fear of angering them and risking the loss of future research grants. For this reason an individual researcher may resist censorship of findings more easily than can a research organization with a large investment in staff and equipment which they must protect.

In sharing results of a study there are ethical rules of thumb: (*a*) promise to share results unless there is some very unusual reason why this would be harmful; (*b*) when the promise is given, prepare and follow through on the promise; (*c*) give respondents a chance to comment on what they feel are errors of fact or interpretation before the final draft is completed; (*d*) do not back down from the facts and your best interpretation merely because it would put someone in an unflattering light; (*e*) do not distort the findings to avoid embarrassing yourself or the research organization doing the study. Usually, all or most of these norms can be followed without great agonizing over conflicting values, but any researcher must be prepared to meet possible conflict courageously.

ETHICS AND HYPOCRISY

The information gatherer cannot hope to be ethical by being innocent or naïve about how society works. The timid information gatherer may try to avoid ethical questions by studying only topics that are safe at the moment, but there is no necessary relationship between the ethics of one's action and the likelihood that it will stir up controversy. Often very noncontroversial information-collection activities—for example, gathering data in the area of motivation research—may be used to victimize the consumers, add to pollution problems, and channel human and other resources into nonproductive areas. The fact that this may be accepted as operating procedure does not mean that it is an ethical use of social science.

Earlier an example was given of the senators who supported a bill in Congress to permit wiretapping but desperately fought the idea of studying the effectiveness of the jury system by tape-recording the deliberations. It is not unusual for interest groups to deplore methods used by social scientists as unethical when they are commonly used by the same interest group making the complaint.

Often a controversy arises in which the social scientist's actions are likened to the police state's invasion of privacy. This completely obscures the importance of the fact that in one case the invasion of privacy may be backed by force, used to terrorize the weak and to punish the person whose privacy is violated, and used to maintain a form of illegitimate power; while in the other case every effort is made to avoid harm to the respondent and to resolve the types of conflicts in the larger society that lead to the use of terror, suppression, and force. Thus, in situations where there is the least congruence between the welfare of individuals and the aims of power elites, we can expect the most difficulty for the social scientist and the most hypocrisy in the double standard of ethics as applied to social scientists versus the practices of the power elite.

The banner of ethics is raised not only by powerful groups in an offensive battle to monopolize information but also "ethics" can be a phony slogan sounded by the less powerful to defend themselves. For example, as a consultant, the writer designed an information system for a five-county antipoverty program. There followed a long period of resistance by many in the organization to the recording of certain basic information about the clients they were supposed to help. Among those bits of information that workers resisted collecting and recording on a McBee data card were the following: full name, address, telephone number, age, race, sex, source of income, social security number, marital status, and draft status. Despite the fact that each of these items was needed to help the respondent obtain social services and income maintenance, some staff argued that "we have no right to that information," "it might be used to throw my client off welfare," "it takes too much time to get all that stuff," "to record the person's sex, race, or ethnic background engages in discrimination," "I don't think we should be interested in people in categories," or "it is not humanistic to try to reduce people to numbers and statistics."

Some arguments were conscientious, but others were inspired by fear of exposure. This was true when field workers had been making up fictitious clients to make their work load appear greater. In other cases they did not want the central office to discover that they were serving more nonpoor than poor, that they were not serving as many blacks as they should, that they were dealing only with acquaintances in their local neighborhoods, or that they were reporting more mileage than actually traveled in the line of duty. Thus each item of information could be perceived as a threat to different field workers, depending on which of their own activities or nonactivities they were trying to hide. Yet the rhetoric was in terms defending the privacy of their clients.

These are all examples of interest groups trying to stop someone else from seeing or collecting certain information. There is another form of hypocrisy in which the interviewers raised the issue of the "ethics" of their activities only after they had gotten themselves into an embarrassing, boring, or dangerous situation. For example, a group of graduate students in sociology had begun a study of the city government in a steel-industry city. They discovered by accident that the city attorney was in collusion with a local group connected with a large underworld syndicate. They discussed the ethical and practical problems of bugging the city attorney's office to record possible conversations with those with whom he plotted, and they decided to do this.

In their enthusiasm for the intellectual super sleuthing, they forgot to consider seriously the probabilities of getting caught in their amateur effort or the possible repercussions if the "bug" were discovered. One of the students who worked in the mayor's office arranged to have a microphone placed in the light fixture above the city attorney's desk. They were amazed at the content of the conversations which intimated bribery and plans to fleece the taxpayers and deceive the voters. Just about the time they began to discover the awesome power group involved and the full extent of the corruption of the city attorney, a most untimely accident occurred. The fluorescent bulb in the fixture above the city attorney's desk burned out. The janitor came to replace it and found the planted microphone. By following the wire, he discovered that it led to the office of one of the graduate students. As soon as the student heard it had been discovered, he left for an early lunch, called the other members of the team, and they all left town without returning to work that afternoon.

After what they had already learned from monitoring the tapes, they realized that the organization might resort to violence against them. Perhaps one thing that saved them was the fact that the recorded tapes had been numbered and dated and left in the student's office only because he was afraid to return for them. But this made it possible for those who traced the wire to find the tapes and destroy them all. The point to note here is that *before* the bug had been discovered, the students seemed to have no pangs of conscience and no doubts regarding their own ethics because they had no intention of giving the information to the mayor or to the police department; they were trying to discover some of the basic conditions under which such violations of trust by people in public office developed. All this could be used to design better city governments without necessarily exposing the individuals involved in this particular case.

It was not until *after* they had been seriously frightened by the discovery of the bug that some members of the team began to feel genuine remorse for having violated the city attorney's privacy. These members argued that the ends do not justify the means, that they should have gotten the mayor's permission, or that what they did was illegal. Those who still felt the bugging was not unethical argued that they should have not been so amateurish, they should have used a wireless bug, that it had proven impractical but not immoral, or that it certainly could not be called immoral to listen in on crooks out to victimize the citizenry.

Regardless of what the team would decide if they had an opportunity to study the same kind of situation in another city, it is clear that their ethical discussion would be more serious and would take into consideration a wider range of factors than before. Their amateurish enthusiasm would be more tempered by realism.

The important point in this episode is that we must have some way of sifting out the difference between right and might, between ethics and politics, between fear and reason, lest we become frightened into elevating pure expediency to a high moral principle. If we are unwilling to admit fear, we are in danger of taking the side of the corrupt in any situation where they are powerful enough to punish those who would disturb peace with the truth. We cannot realistically demand that all seekers of truth be beyond the reach of fear, but fear will have a less insidious effect if we recognize it for what it is.

It does not always require such a threat of violence to make the information gatherer doubt his or her own ethical position. More typically, any direct contact over a long period of time with members of any group under observation can become uncomfortable and lead the observer to look for escape under the banner of ethics. This occurred when four undergraduate students undertook, as their senior project, a participant-observation study of faith healing. They observed evening meetings at the Church of the Open Door which were held for the purpose of "revival of our faith in the Lord and to cure the sick with our faith."

After three weeks of observing three times each week, one of the students on the team wanted to drop out because he felt that it was "unethical" to attend the meetings as an observer. He felt he was "deceiving the people there into thinking that he was one of them." Yet he admitted that others came who were not yet "saved" and in fact the minister made it abundantly clear that all were welcome, "sinners and saved alike." In our discussion about his feeling, it developed that he was from a Protestant background and had been to Latin America where he had repeatedly attended a Catholic church without feeling hypocritical. We explored the differences between his experiences in this American lower-class Protestant church and the lower-class Catholic church and discovered some important facts: He could feel detached in the Catholic church because he did not have to interact with others in the congregation during mass, while in the Church of the Open Door he was immediately surprised and embarrassed by how warmly and personally the members of the Protestant sect had received him. He was immediately accepted as a unique individual, and there was obvious concern for the fate of his soul. Genuine affection was displayed among the members; there was considerable body contact among the men and among the women; even though the students were considerably younger than the average male member of the church this did not stand as a barrier as far as the members were concerned. Much of his complaint of embarrassment over the demonstration of affection resulted from the fact that he was obviously expected to participate, not simply to observe. Pure observation was easier at the Catholic Mass.

He seemed to feel a bit like this author's carpenter friend who accepted a job doing repair work on buildings in a nudist camp. His initial enthusiasm turned to retreat when it was explained upon his arrival that he would have to take off all his clothes while he worked to avoid embarrassing the members who were nude. He had gone to observe and not to participate and be observed.

Other sources of the student's discomfort at the healing meeting seem to be related to his vague fear that he might actually be converted to the church after seeing paralyzed people walk away from their wheelchairs. There was also an attractive feeling of security in the warmth and simplicity of the people's faith which he felt he should not yield to. He would have felt less uncomfortable if he were not required to make any systematic observations, yet he felt that it was precisely this requirement of disciplined observation which kept him from succumbing to the lure of the group. All of these cross-pressures exerted upon him could be escaped by finding a legitimate excuse for dropping out of the research team. Since he began to feel subjective strain, he interpreted this as guilt feeling resulting from his "unethical" behavior. This very understandable reaction should not be confused with ethics.

These examples illustrate the principle that under certain conditions the banner of ethics can be used to hide unethical practices in a struggle for profit or power or to disguise a retreat from battle as an ethical advance.

SUMMARY

This chapter has tried to deal only with some of the most vital issues which directly affect the interviewer's ethical choices. Contrary to the naïve view that only good and evil conflict, any social action contains conflict or competition between propositions, each of which may be considered good in its own right. The process of making ethical choices involves two dimensions: the *valuation* of particular acts in terms of assumptions or knowledge regarding their probable effects and the *weighing* of the relative importance of different values. Thus, ethics does not merely involve some fixed hierarchy of abstract ideals isolated from knowledge of cause and effect in the empirical world; ethics involves decision making guided by both values and knowledge. Knowledge of the concrete situation and of the general principles of cause and effect in that situation is needed.

The ethics of interviewing is seen as the interviewer's choice of actions in which his or her moral obligations to the larger society, to science, to the research organization, and to the respondent must all be taken into consideration to find the best short-run and long-run effects. There is no way the interviewer can avoid making ethical choices, whether or not the interviewer is aware of them.

There is no escape through the claim that "I was only following orders," because any interviewer decides whether to work on a particular project, whether to work for a particular organization, and how to carry out a particular assignment. We cannot rest assured that we have made the best ethical choice merely because no one is complaining or no obvious conflict results. Nor can we escape responsibility for the information collected and the use to which it is put by saying that we just collect the facts which speak for themselves. This is unrealistic; facts are collected for some purpose and should be relevant to that purpose. To interpret them we must show how they are relevant. We cannot escape ethical decisions by avoiding the study of controversial areas or of social change; such avoidance is a decision. Once we accept the idea that we cannot escape making ethical judgments, we become more conscious of *how* we make them.

Heightened awareness of ethical decisions allows us to resolve some of the ethical dilemmas by creative data collection. The point in the data collection process at which the most ethical problems can be resolved or avoided is at the strategy phase when decisions are made on who should get what information from whom, where, when, and how. The next section of this book will deal with such strategy decisions.

DISCUSSION QUESTIONS

1. What is the difference between ethics and ideals?

2. In what way do knowledge and values interact in ethics?

3. Why is it often difficult to determine whether a person is acting ethically?

4. Give an example of social research that you feel is clearly unethical. Why is it unethical?

5. Give an example of social research which you feel offers the toughest ethical dilemma. What makes it so difficult?

6. Do you feel that the ethical obligations of the interviewer are clearest in relationship to the larger society, to the research organization, to the scientific community, or to the respondent? Why?

7. What conflict may be encountered when the interviewer tries to fulfill his or her obligations to the respondent?

8. What are some of the ways that the accusation of being unethical can be used by the unethical? What are usual motivations in these cases?

Selected Readings

Glazer, Myron. *The Research Adventure: Promise and Problems of Field Work.* New York: Random House, 1972.
The book deals mainly with the field strategy problems encountered by social scientists in Chile, India, South Africa, and Vietnam, as well as in American subcultures such as the Indians in Alaska, the Italian American slum, the black ghetto, the military, the judicial, the homosexual, and the small town. Woven throughout the whole presentation are implicit and explicit ethical problems.

Klockars, Carl B., and F. W. O'Connor, eds. *Deviance and Decency: The Ethics of Research with Human Subjects.* Beverly Hills, Calif.: Sage Publications, 1979.
Twelve authors discuss the central issue of whether ethical behavior of any professional group, particularly social scientists, can be formally regulated for the good of society either by the professional group itself or by the government with such regulations as those proposed by the National Commission for the Protection of Human Subjects to apply to all federally funded research.

Orlans, Harold. *Contracting for Knowledge.* San Francisco: Jossey-Bass Publishers, 1973.
Orlans's purpose is to make an assessment of the value and limitations of government-sponsored research. He summarizes and evaluates evidence and expert opinion on such sensitive subjects as the politics and biases of social scientists, the politicization of social science associations, the evaluation of government social programs, the scholar's ethical responsibilities to government, and the kinds of research for which universities, nonprofit institutes, and other organizations are best suited.

Sjoberg, Gideon, ed. *Ethics, Politics and Social Research.* Cambridge, Mass.: Schenkman Publishing Co., 1971.

This is an excellent collection of writings by fourteen different authors all squarely focused on ethical issues in social research. Each case illustrates the pressures and counter pressures exerted by sponsors, by government, by professional associations, by political pressure groups, by the respondents, by colleagues. The conflicts among the values of science and politics are clearly shown.

Wax, Murray L., and Joan Cassell, *Federal Regulations: Ethical Issues and Social Research.* Boulder, Colo.: Westview Press, 1979.

Eleven authors defend responsible social research as essential for intelligent social policy and discuss the differential effects of federal regulations on qualitative versus quantitative studies, the formation and nature of the federal regulatory system, and conflicts among professional associations with regard to regulation.

Chapter Five

Inhibitors of Communication

This chapter will deal with the *inhibitors* of communication in the interview and Chapter 6 will deal with the *facilitators*. Each inhibitor is seen as a barrier or obstacle to communication that should be avoided, circumvented, or removed from the respondent's mind. Each facilitator, on the other hand, is not merely the absence of an inhibiting barrier but is a positive force motivating the respondent to communicate. Within this framework the interviewer's task of maximizing the flow of relevant information is transformed into the more specific objectives of *minimizing the inhibitors and maximizing the facilitators of communication.*

LINKING THEORY AND PRACTICE

The inhibitor and facilitator frame of reference (IF) does not claim to be a theory, nor does the author feel that a single theory of interviewing is currently possible. Interviewing is a microcosm of many forces operating within the human personality, within the interaction situation we call the interview, and within the whole community, society, or culture. Separate theories would be needed to explain each different system. The lack of a single theory of interviewing does not mean that theory is not applicable. Interviewing is a practical art to which many types of theory apply. Concepts drawn from anthropology, sociology, social psychology, and psychology all are involved in interviewing. For example, the concepts of culture and subculture, role and status, social structure, role theory, group dynamics, perception, memory, ego-psychology, trauma, competition, and definition-of-the-situation all are borrowed without apology from the social sciences and without pausing to develop the total theoretical schemes from which they come. If we tried to do this, we would be in danger of losing sight of the practical objective of learning to interview. Furthermore, we would become paralyzed by the realization that there are gaps and ambiguities in some of the theory.

The IF frame of reference has been developed as a sensitizing frame-work to connect the specific theories which often lay behind the experi-mental studies of interviewing and the practical problem of planning and performing an interview. To some, the eight inhibitors and the eight facilitators may appear to be an eclectic hodgepodge, lacking in symme-try and elegance. Yet analysis of hundreds of verbatim interviews shows that these *are* the types of things which from the point of view of the practitioner hinder and help the flow of relevant information.

The reader will note that all of the inhibitors and facilitators be-come more meaningful when viewed within the general framework of the *social context of communication* presented in Chapter 3. We are not concerned, for example, with generally inhibited personalities but in how a person is either unable or unwilling to give some particular type of information, to a certain type of interviewer, at a particular time and location for the interview which is defined by the respondent in a cer-tain way. Thus, we see that the triadic relationship (involving the type of information sought, the type of respondent having the information, and the type of interviewer asking for the information) is brought into play within the interview situation which has certain characteristics be-cause of its relationship to the larger society, community, or culture.

Even though the *science* of interviewing draws upon experimental studies and theoretical concepts, the practice of interviewing involves more. The additional element might be called the *art* of interviewing. In both the planning and execution of the interview, the art of interviewing consists of making judgments as to whether a particular inhibitor might be present and of making judgments as to which strategy, technique, or tactic might be most effective under the conditions at hand. In short, the application of theory in interviewing, as in any field, becomes an art.

In interviewing, the practical art accounting for success depends not only upon the interviewer's clear knowledge of the theoretical concepts and the informational objectives of the particular interview at hand, but also upon the interviewer's *skill* in anticipating potential inhibitors and facilitators so that he or she can plan to minimize one and maximize the other. This anticipatory skill is based on experience, empathy, and commitment to the purposes of the interview. Another set of skills comes into play once the interviewer-respondent interaction begins. These skills include the ability to listen empathically while evaluating the relevance and completeness of the response, proficiency in quickly adopting tactics appropriate to the stage of the interview, and expert-ness in controlling one's own behavior to conform to the objectives of the interview.

There is no doubt that both the knowledge and skills, the science and the art, of interviewing can be learned. This has been proven by demonstrations of improvement in performance of interviewers after a period of training. That "interviewers are born not made" and its opposite, that "anyone can learn to be a successful interviewer," both have some truth. It is clear that the cognitive concepts of theory can be learned rather quickly, but the basic human skills come more slowly. For this reason studies of improvement of interviewing through training show that even though the training improved everyone's interviewing performance, those who had the most effective performance before the training period tended to have the most effective performance at the end of the training period. The importance of the training is demonstrated by the fact that often the performance of the best interviewer on the pretest was not so good as the performance of the worst interviewer on the posttest.

All the evidence seems to show that such personal qualities of the interviewer as intelligence, empathic ability, listening habits, and observation skills take a long time to develop, but new concepts, strategies, techniques, and tactics can be learned relatively quickly and will pay increasing dividends as we gain skill in their application. In short, interviewers *can* be made.

RECOGNIZING EFFECTS OF INHIBITORS

Often the neophyte interviewer is deceived into thinking that the interview has been productive because the respondent has "talked on and on." The interviewer may accept this as evidence that no inhibitors were at work in the situation. Unfortunately, this is not necessarily true. If inhibitors always had the effect of making the respondent quiet, their presence would be easy to recognize. Often a respondent will talk animatedly without saying anything relevant to the question at hand. In this case the response is a smokescreen of words designed to hide his or her noncooperation.

Of course the respondent's flow of irrelevancies is not always a verbal smokescreen consciously intended to hide the withholding of relevant information. Frequently the respondent simply does not have any relevant information; not wanting to appear uninformed, the respondent protects the ego by saying something even though it is not relevant. In other instances respondents may simply want to be polite to the interviewer, show good intentions, and avoid appearing uncooperative. Other respondents may simply seize the opportunity to emote on their favorite topic with little concern for its relevance to the question at hand.

In the author's experience people in positions of power and responsibility, who are caught in a crisis where things for which they feel responsible are going wrong, are much more prone than the average person to use the intentional smokescreen when an interviewer questions the handling of that crisis. In contrast to the average person, this leader is more likely to have relevant information, has more reason to hide the information for fear of being blamed, and has more political pressure to *appear* cooperative.

This smokescreening was very apparent in interviews with police chiefs and mayors of small towns struck by tornadoes. Even in these situations when it was not humanly possible to "handle the situation," the officials would hide certain facts that would make it apparent they were unable to cope with the crisis. They felt they would be blamed for not handling the crisis but that it would be political death to appear uncooperative with the investigation. The officials' solution to the dilemma was often effusively to praise such things as the spontaneous grass-roots rescue operations or the solidarity of the community across racial, ethnic, religious, and political lines.

Thus, the effect of inhibitors such as *ego threat* and *etiquette* may not be to stop the respondents from talking; under many circumstances they may have the effect of producing a lot of irrelevant information. Just as it is wrong to conclude that high verbal productivity indicates the absence of any inhibitors, it is also incorrect to conclude that the respondent's failure to talk freely is an infallible indicator of the presence of inhibitors. If a particular respondent fails to give certain relevant information or shows a reluctance to elaborate on the essential facts, this may indicate simply that there is very little relevant information to give. In some cases the respondent's personality is basically taciturn, or he or she may be concerned with being precise, efficient, and to the point.

For these reasons we must keep in mind that for the purposes of interviewing we must define an *inhibitor* as any social-psychological barrier which impedes the flow of *relevant* information by making the respondent *unable* or *unwilling* to give it to the interviewer at the moment.

INHIBITORS

The eight categories listed under this heading operate more frequently to inhibit rather than to facilitate communication. The first four categories tend to make the respondent *unwilling* to give information, while the last four categories tend to make the respondent *unable* to give the information even though willing.

Competing Demands for Time

The respondent hesitates to begin an interview because of other ways he or she should or would like to be spending the time. The respondent does not necessarily place a negative value on being interviewed but must weigh the amount of time he or she is asked to devote to the interview against other activities competing for this segment of time. The interviewer must sell the idea of being interviewed to obtain the respondent's initial cooperation.

This inhibitor functions only in situations where the respondent is free to decide whether to participate in the interview. Sometimes the respondent is obligated to participate, even though the respondent would rather not do so; here, competing time demand is not a factor. This would be the case if the personnel department of a company decided to interview all employees or if a social worker decided to interview a mother to determine whether she were still eligible to receive certain welfare services or if a clinical psychologist wished to interview a patient in a mental hospital. In these situations, the problem is not obtaining the respondent's time for the interview, but the sophisticated interviewer knows not to assume that the captive respondent is *willing* or *able* to give the information needed.

In the free-choice situation, the initial problem is to obtain the respondent's cooperation. Once this is accomplished there may be few obstacles to obtaining the information if the amount of time needed is small and if the nature of the interview was clear to the respondent before he or she gave consent to participate.

It is possible, however, for an interview to begin without interference from competing demands but to continue into a block of time where other current or anticipated activities compete for the respondent's attention. In this case, the respondent's interest diminishes. For example, the housewife may begin a market research interview gladly but may begin to lose interest and feel apprehensive as it grows closer to the time for her husband to return for dinner.

Ego Threat

The respondent tends to withhold information which may threaten his or her self-esteem. The effect of an ego threat can range from mild hesitancy in giving information to complete repression. The importance of ego threat as a barrier to communication in the interview is emphasized by Polansky, who devotes most of his book to the various ego-defense mechanisms used by different respondents in social work and therapeutic interviews.[1] Unfortunately, he does not follow through with suggestions for any methods the interviewer can use to overcome these ego-defense mechanisms.

---

[1]Norman A. Polansky, *Ego Psychology and Communication: A Theory for the Interview* (New York: Atherton Press, 1973).

Three broad categories may be defined according to the strength of the effect of ego threat. The strongest effect is repression. The respondent not only refuses to admit the information to the interviewer but also hides it from self to preserve self-esteem and avoid a guilty conscience. The respondent is being honest in answering that he or she does not know or has forgotten. This level of ego threat primarily occupies the psychiatrist, psychoanalyst, and clinical psychologist but is sometimes a factor in the information-gathering interview.

Scott found that in 1955 people were very worried about the possibility of an atomic attack upon the United States, yet it was threatening to admit fear.[2] In many cases people had repressed their anxiety to the point where they would not admit their anxiety to an interviewer or even to themselves. When the respondents in a survey were asked "Are you worried about an atomic war?" there were many fewer admissions than when a projective picture test was used. The picture showed a woman standing in what might be a doorway scanning the sky in which some distant objects are seen only as formless specks. If the question about the picture was "What do *you* see?" there were many fewer admissions of anxiety than when the question was "What do you think *others* might see?" This tendency to project one's own feelings onto others and to deny them in ourselves is a common mechanism for avoiding ego threat.

A less intense, but more common, effect of ego threat is found when the respondent, although consciously possessing the information, hesitates to admit it because he or she anticipates that the interviewer may disapprove. Often the respondent is torn between withholding the information and a yearning for catharsis. Since the respondent has not successfully repressed the memory which is threatening self-esteem, he or she may have guilt feelings. If made to feel confident that the interviewer will not be condemning, the respondent may welcome the opportunity to divulge the information.

Sometimes the shrewd respondent indirectly interviews the interviewer to discover the latter's attitudes. For example, the respondent who would like to confess socially disapproved forms of sex behavior may first try to discover the interviewer's probable reaction. The respondent may mention a case similar to his or her own and may even try to provoke the interviewer into condemning it. If the interviewer condemns the hypothetical case, the respondent will not confess. Confession is usually easier if the interviewer is a stranger whom the respondent never expects to see again. In any case, a generally accepting and sympathetic attitude toward the respondent as a person goes far toward eliciting candid responses.

---

[2]William A. Scott, "The Avoidance of Threatening Material in Imaginative Behavior," *Journal of Abnormal and Social Psychology* 52 (1956), pp. 338–46.

A lesser threat to the respondent's self-esteem exists if the respondent is willing to give information to the interviewer but fears losing status if the information becomes public. This respondent must be assured that anonymity will be respected. This is not always easy to do. The respondent may fear that the interviewer, even with the best of intentions, will be unable to conceal the source of the information. The higher the respondent's status, the more difficult it is to describe his or her actions in the community without revealing the respondent's identity.

This greater fear in higher status people of losing anonymity was demonstrated in the contrast between the attitudes of the officials in disaster-stricken towns and those of average citizens toward tape-recorded interviews. It was rare to find an ordinary citizen who, as an anonymous number of a random sample, objected to the tape recorder. However, objections from officials were quite common. Even though the official was willing to talk candidly to the interviewer, who was a stranger in the community, he felt that his anonymity would be sacrificed if the tape recording were heard by some member of the local community. He was aware that any of the small-town populace could identify the speaker's voice.

The interviewer not only must assure the respondent of anonymity at the beginning of the interview but must also be sensitive to any need for further assurance as the interview progresses. Often the respondent is too shy at the beginning of the interview to show open concern about anonymity; but as he or she gathers confidence during the interview, the respondent becomes more willing to show hesitancy. This delayed reaction may be more common when the respondent's cooperation is not voluntary. Bain, in his analysis of interaction between a research team and workers in a laundry plant, found that the workers' initial cooperation changed to hostility.[3] The researchers did not need the workers' permission to gain access to the plant. Therefore, a thorough, systematic, and convincing explanation of the study had not been given to the workers. Latent doubt flowered into open suspicion when a temporary recession caused the layoff of a few workers. Rumors spread that the researchers were company spies hired to inform management of who should be laid off next. Several weeks were required to rectify this misperception so that the study could continue.

The numerous symptoms of ego threat can be seen as different effects upon the information flow. These effects may range from simply refusing to volunteer any information to fabricating information as a cover-up. A respondent might defend his or her ego in an interview in various ways. Assume that an interviewer is talking to a person whose home town was destroyed by a tornado. The interviewer asks, "How

[3]Robert K. Bain, "The Researcher's Role: A Case Study," *Human Organization*, Spring 1950, pp. 23–28.

did you *feel* when your house took off over the pecan orchard?" Here are examples of answers by several respondents.

Evasion. "I looked out the window and could see the tops of the pecan trees below. The roof had blown clean off the house, but it was still holding together. I don't even remember a jolt when we landed in the trees!"

Simple, emphatic denial. "Well, to tell the truth I wasn't scared at all. There's no sense in getting excited 'cause there is nothing you can do. Of course, the women and children screamed, but there is no sense in a man getting scared at a thing like that."

Elaborate, subtle denial. "Ordinarily, anybody with good sense would be scared stiff but I think that it all happened so fast I had no time to think about it. I couldn't really believe it. Could you believe it if you looked out the window and saw that you were sailing over the trees? I was just trying to hold the door shut and the next thing I knew was when we landed about 300 feet away from where the house left the foundation."

Depersonalization. "I imagine most people would be plain scared at a time like that. People were all scared and excited. Who wouldn't be at a time like that?"

Minimization. "I was nervous, of course, but not really scared like a lot of people were. I'd been through worse than this in the war, so it didn't seem so bad. I'm sort of the calm type, myself, so it didn't have too much effect on me."

Although, in general, the respondent's ego threat leads to omission, distortion, and fabrication of information, there are exceptional circumstances where it is even more ego threatening to withhold the information than to reveal it. For example, when a respondent who has certain information realizes that the interviewer knows he or she has it and will insist on having the truth, the respondent may give the information even though it damages the self-image. This use of pressure to obtain information becomes more successful as the power and prestige of the interviewer increase and as the respondent has more assurance that giving the information will not result in any reprisals from the interviewer or others. We are all familiar with children confessing to an adult rather than risking the disfavor of such a powerful figure.

When the interviewer is of a lower social status than the respondent, as would be a newspaper reporter who was interviewing a senator, it is usually impossible to pressure the respondent into giving ego-threatening information. There are even institutionalized responses for handling such a situation. The person of higher status and power merely says, "I don't care to comment on that at this time," or simply, "no comment," or "I'm sorry, but I am not free to give such information."

In general, ego threat is an inhibitor of the free flow of information from respondent to interviewer. Even in cases where pressure seems to succeed, it is unlikely that the response will be as detailed and candid as under conditions where no pressure is applied.

In some cases the purpose of a study is not to penetrate the ego-threat barrier, but to directly study the specific nature of the ego-defense system. We may want to know how people in a particular culture or subculture go about verbally defending their actions which have not measured up to the group or community's expectations. Often, the respondent feels that the interviewer will hold him or her morally accountable for some untoward behavior which the respondent has admitted or about which the interviewer has previous knowledge. In this case, the respondent tries to bridge the discrepancy between his or her actual behavior and the ideal by giving an account designed to neutralize any negative feeling from the interviewer. Whether or not this account is honored depends upon the underlying assumptions held by the respondent's community regarding the nature of human beings and society. Scott and Lyman give many examples and a refined conceptualization of this process of giving "accounts" in the form of excuses and justifications.[4]

Etiquette

The etiquette barrier operates when the answer to the interviewer's question contains information perceived by the respondent as inappropriate to give to the type of person doing the interview or inappropriate to the situation in which the interviewing is done. Answering candidly would be considered in poor taste or as evidence of a lack of proper consciousness of one's status relationship to the other. The etiquette barrier inhibits the flow of certain types of information both up and down the status hierarchy.

To understand this phenomenon, society must be viewed as not only a web of communication between people in different roles and statuses but also a pattern of conscious and unconscious barriers to the indiscriminate flow of information. All types of information do not flow equally well among all persons in society. There cannot be a pattern of communication unless there is also a complementary pattern of noncommunication.

---

[4]Marvin B. Scott and Stanford M. Lyman, "Accounts," *American Sociological Review* 33, no. 1 (February 1968), pp. 46–62.

Etiquette is one of the inhibitors of communication which acts as a qualitatively selective filter, encouraging the passage of certain messages and obstructing the flow of others between two people with a certain relationship to each other. This selectivity may be governed by the nature of the situation as well as the relationship between the sender and receiver.

To a great extent, we learn these subtle patterns of noncommunication unconsciously, but we are painfully aware of them when they are violated. The five-year-old who repeats some bit of intimate family life to his kindergarten teacher learns from her reaction that he has done something wrong. The teenager who uses obscene language in front of the high school teacher knows that the topic is inappropriate for the teacher. However, the teenager often has not yet learned that the teacher does understand this vocabulary, even though the teacher never uses these words in front of students. The teacher who is afraid to let the student know that he or she understand such words may be handicapped in meeting the situation.

It is known that there are things which men do not discuss in front of women and vice versa, things that married couples do not discuss in front of unmarried people, things students do not tell teachers, things doctors do not tell patients, things parishioners do not tell the clergy, and so on. These inhibiting effects of etiquette are often taken for granted as acceptable barriers as long as their inhibiting effect applies to someone else. The problem is that each person's ego, particularly in a democratically oriented society, tends to blind that person to his or her own limitations as a receiver of communication due to the etiquette barrier.

This can be seen in the case of the American returning from a trip around the world who says, "I found nothing but love for Americans everywhere I went." Similarly, a manager of a large corporation may assure the consultant that it is perfectly all right for the middle management people to interview the employees regarding their attitudes toward management because, "We have spent years building up good relations between management and workers; we are just one big happy family." And then there is the parent whose child has been charged with a delinquency who tells the social worker, with all sincerity, "But I asked him if he did it and he said he is innocent. I believe him because he always tells me everything he does." Usually, under these circumstances the person involved can admit that the etiquette barrier would *ordinarily* be operant but wrongly assumes that because of his or her charm and desire to hear the truth there will be an exception.

This desire to avoid embarrassing, shocking, or threatening the other person is quite distinct from the fear of exposing oneself, as in the case of an ego threat. The distinction becomes useful when it is demonstrated that the treatment of one barrier is quite different from the treatment of the other. The ego-threat barrier can be reduced by the interviewer's demonstrating a nonjudgmental attitude toward the respondent's information and by guaranteeing the respondent's anonymity. This would not facilitate communication if the respondent's information was harmless to his or her self-image but was felt to be inappropriate for the interviewer.

The effect of the etiquette barrier may go beyond simply withholding information to spare the interviewer's feelings and may extend to the point where the respondent, through selective reporting or fabrication, tries to please the interviewer by telling the interviewer what he or she wants to hear. This desire to please may be particularly detrimental to the validity of the information when the interviewer consciously or unconsciously suggests the "appropriate" answer.

Often the negative effects of the etiquette barrier can be forestalled by selecting the appropriate interviewer and situational setting for the interview. Also, if there is a choice of respondents having the desired information, the respondent having the most appropriate relationship to the interviewer should be selected. Sometimes these precautions are not enough in themselves and special techniques and tactics described later can be used.

Trauma

Trauma is used to denote an acutely unpleasant feeling associated with crisis experiences. The unpleasant feeling is often brought to the conscious level when the respondent is reporting the experience. This is distinctly different from the fear of losing self-esteem, as in the case of an ego threat, or the fear of shocking the interviewer, as in the case of etiquette. Here, the unpleasantness of the topic results from forcing the respondent to relive the original emotions associated with the experience. In these circumstances, there is no tendency for the respondent to vacillate between evading a topic and talking about it in order to obtain a cathartic release from guilt feelings. The respondent does not feel remiss for his or her acts, but has an unpleasant feeling regarding something which happened.

The marriage counselor talking to a recently divorced person, the physician obtaining a detailed case history of a person whose close relatives have had untimely deaths, the detective interviewing the widow of a recent murder victim, the social worker interviewing a mother regarding legal charges brought by neighbors against the father for beating his wife and children, the policeman or insurance investigator interviewing the survivor of an auto accident, the personnel counselor interviewing an applicant regarding the circumstances under which he was fired from his last position, the teacher talking to a student suddenly rejected by his peer group because of a rumor regarding the student's family—these and other interview situations are likely to involve some probing of traumatic experiences.

The four inhibitors above (competing time demands, ego threat, etiquette, and trauma) are similar in that they reduce the respondent's *willingness* to talk about a certain topic. There are exceptional cases in which both ego threat and trauma in the extreme may render the respondent unable, as opposed to unwilling, to respond. When the ego threat or trauma is so severe that it leads to repression, then for all practical purposes the experience is forgotten and the respondent is unable to give the relevant information without special interviewer techniques or even hypnosis. In most circumstances, however, these four inhibitors make the respondent unwilling to give certain information even though the respondent has it.

There are another four inhibitors which reduce the respondent's *ability*, rather than his or her willingness, to provide valid information. This inability has two general results. First, and least problematical, the respondent may simply admit that he or she cannot supply the information at the moment for some reason. Second, the respondent, in trying to cooperate, may supply "information" which is no more than a well-meant mixture of imagination, guesswork, and confusion. The second type of respondent poses a much greater problem for the interviewer. The interviewer must learn to anticipate, detect, and counteract this tendency in the respondent. In practice, the solution of the problem is not so difficult as it might seem because much of the respondent's feeling that he or she has to "say something" is due to a general atmosphere created by the interviewer.

Of the factors which make the respondent *unable* to report relevant information, the first is forgetting.

Forgetting

A frequent inhibitor is the respondent's inability to recall certain types of information. This is not a problem if the objectives of the interview deal only with *current* attitudes, beliefs, or expectations. However, the moment we move into the area of facts we are dealing largely with the past.

This natural fading of the memory (which may be hastened by selective psychological repression) makes it easier for the ego-defense system to reconstruct one's image of the past by simple omission, addition, or distortion. This idea of the "reconstruction of biography" is a continual theme in the insightful writings of Alfred Schutz.[5]

The memory problem is a much more frequent obstacle than is generally expected by interviewers. Even some of the most seemingly simple and obvious facts cannot be obtained by superficial interviewing methods.

---

[5]Alfred Schutz, *Collected Papers*, vol. 1, ed. Maurice Natanson (The Hague, Netherlands: Martinus Nijhoff, 1962).

For example, a simple fact such as the date of starting work at a factory cannot be accurately determined in a superficial interview. This was demonstrated in an experiment by Moore in which the respondents' replies to an interviewer were checked against the company records.[6]

Historians have been aware of the "treachery of recollection" in trying to reconstruct even recent historical events.[7] More recent experiments have been done to determine the extent to which forgetting is a function of elapsed time versus the nature of the facts to be remembered. For example, Dakin and Tennant found in a survey at different time intervals after the fact that, although the greater the time lapse the less accurate the memory, there were also great differences in accuracy of remembering one fact versus another at the same time interval.[8] In one example, only 24 percent could remember their income while 98 percent could remember their former address.

Fortunately, the respondent's experience of a particular event is not simply either remembered or forgotten. The respondent's ability to remember depends, in general, upon three types of factors. First, the vividness of recall of the experience is related to various dimensions such as its original emotional impact, its meaningfulness to the person at the time, and the degree to which the person's ego was involved. Second is the simple problem of the amount of time elapsing between the event itself and the interview pertaining to it. Third is the nature of the interview situation, including the interviewer's techniques and tactics.

Knowledge of these factors as they are related to a particular respondent will help the interviewer to *predict* probable trouble in certain areas of subject matter. The second factor, time lapse, is sometimes controllable by the interviewer if he or she is free to select respondents whose experience is fresh. If the interviewer has no control over the amount of time lapse between event and interview, knowledge of the length of this time span will at least warn the interviewer when special techniques and tactics are in order to refresh a respondent's memory. That a once-forgotten event can subsequently be recalled is frequently demonstrated in interviews when the respondent has given a spontaneous and sincere reply early in the interview, only to contradict himself later when his memory has been more adequately stimulated. There are many strategies, techniques, and tactics available to help the alert interviewer overcome the memory barrier.

---

[6]B. V. Moore, "The Interview in Industrial Research," *Social Forces* 7 (1929), pp. 445–52.

[7]Daniel Aaron, "The Treachery of Recollection: The Inner and Outer History," in R. H. Bremner, *Essays on History and Literature* (Columbus: Ohio State University Press, 1966).

[8]Ralph E. Dakin and Donald Tennant, "Consistency of Response by Event-Recall Intervals and Characteristics of Respondents," *Sociological Quarterly* 9 (1968), pp. 73–84.

Chronological Confusion

This term refers to the respondent's tendency to confuse the chronological order of his or her experiences. This may occur in two ways: *(a)* Two or more events may be correctly recalled, but the respondent is unsure of the sequence of their occurrence, or *(b)* only one condition or event is recalled and is incorrectly assumed to have also been true at an earlier point in time.

The second type of confusion is more complicated and merits further explanation. It usually occurs when the interviewer is inquiring into a *developmental* sequence such as relations between people or the respondent's past attitudes, beliefs and expectations, and in his or her interpretation of past events. Often the original conditions are forgotten and subsequent conditions which are recalled more readily are assumed to have also been true in the prior situation. There is a strong tendency for the respondent to utilize hindsight in interpreting events of the past. Therefore, if we are interested in discovering what the respondent's original interpretation was at the time of the event, special techniques and tactics must be used.

For example, in a suburb of Rochester, New York, leaky gas lines exploded damaging the reducing valves which prevent natural gas from entering homes at an extremely high pressure. When the gas pressure suddenly increased 100 times, houses filled with gas and began to explode one at a time over a period of three hours until forty-five houses had been completely demolished.

When respondents were asked why they ran from their homes when they first heard an explosion, some said that they wanted to get out of the house before it exploded. Actually, there was no way for people to suspect that the initial explosion was to be the first in a series; the causal connection between the first and succeeding blasts could not have been known immediately. But once the facts were known, running out of the house appeared the rational thing to have done. These respondents, because of chronological confusion, did not realize that they were explaining their behavior at one point in time as being motivated by an idea not gained until *after* they had acted.

This type of problem is commonly encountered in interviews seeking case history information. This would include studies of how people's attitudes and values change, how interpersonal relations in the family or any other group develop, how conflicts arise and are resolved, how people's interpretation of events change, or studies of any problem involving a chronological dimension.

Inferential Confusion

This term designates confusion and inaccuracies resulting from errors of inference on the part of the respondent. These errors fall into two general categories: *(a)* those errors due to faulty *induction*, when the respondent is asked to convert concrete experiences into a higher level of generalization and *(b)* those due to faulty *deduction*, when the respondent is asked to give concrete examples of certain categories of experience supplied by the interviewer.

It is common for the respondent to make a misstep in either ascending or descending the ladder of abstraction. Even though the respondent's memory of an experience might be correct, the moment the respondent begins to interpret, explain, or generalize from these experiences he or she can make an inferential error. There are two main sources of inferential error, regardless of whether it is the inductive or deductive type. The first is simple; the error may result from the respondent's failure to comprehend the interviewer's abstract concepts. The second is a distortion of thinking which may be produced by strong attitudes and preconceptions.

Errors of the first type are often caused by the interviewer's providing categories of experience which are not clearly defined for the respondent. In this case, the respondent's attempt to provide concrete examples fitting the categories may fail. For example, the interviewer who is studying family conflicts, and who needs to categorize the specific examples of conflict into role conflict, value conflict, and lack of communication, would not be wise to ask, "What are some examples of role conflict in your family?" The probability of the respondent's giving an example which was totally or mainly a case of role conflict is very low, even if an attempt is made to define the term "role conflict" for the respondent. A request for such an example places too much of the burden of analysis upon the respondent.

In order to help the respondent up and down the ladder of abstraction, the interviewer must break the general question into steps which will accumulate relevant details, allowing an accurate analysis to determine which category is appropriate for a specific conflict episode. Often, the respondent is quite adept at giving examples which correctly fit into categories that are his or her *own*. However, the problem arises when these categories are irrelevant to the purpose of the interview and the respondent is forced to think in unfamiliar terms. The interviewer should use techniques and tactics that either avoid the necessity of the respondent's making inferences or that help the respondent to make them accurately.

Errors of the second type, those involving distortions of inference due to strong attitudes and preconceptions, are common in many types of interviews. These errors usually occur when the objectives of the interview call for some generalized forms of information such as, "How do the black and the white people get along in this school?" "How were the rescue operations handled in the disaster?" "What philosophy of child rearing do you use with your child?" An accurate response to these questions would involve a thoughtful process of inductively reaching a generalization on the basis of a representative sample of observed, concrete events. All of these questions also involve value judgments which are liable to act as premises for a deductive process resulting in the unconscious line of reasoning which says, "This is the way things *should* happen and, in the absence of glaring evidence to the contrary, let's assume that is the way it *did* happen." Thus, the teacher reports that race relations are "tranquil" in her school, the disaster victim reports that the rescue operations were carried out in a "heroic fashion," and the parent reports that she handles the child in a very "permissive and democratic way." In each instance, the respondent may be simply expressing a desire, intent, or assumption. This must be checked by bringing the generalization down the ladder of abstraction to specific concrete events. Often the interviewer will discover that there is no concrete experience to back up the generality.

Unconscious Behavior

Often the interview objectives call for information about a person's unconscious behavior. Behavior that is not consciously directed may be classified into three types. The most common is simply custom or habit. The degree to which this is unconscious is indicated by Sapir.[9] Into this category would fall those questions about repetitive behavior such as, "What is the difference between the way you speak to a male and a female on the phone?" "When do you use the prepositions 'of' and 'at' after a verb in the English language?" "Which sock do you usually put on first in the morning?"

Next, there is a type of unconscious behavior which Blumer calls "circular reaction," or the immediate, unwitting response of one person to the subliminal, nonverbal cues furnished by another.[10] This is not usually a repetitious form of behavior, but one which arises only under special circumstances. The following questions would be asking about this type of behavior: "What made you dislike him when you first saw him?" "How did you decide to join the lynch mob?" "How did you know that she loved you?"

The third type of unconscious behavior is found under conditions of acute emotional stress in crises where the behavior does not follow a habitual pattern and where it does not result from circular reaction with others. For example, in a disaster interview a respondent was unable to report how he traveled from his house to a cousin's house in the neighborhood. The evidence indicated that the behavior forgotten by

---

[9]Edward Sapir, "The Unconscious Patterning of Behavior in Society," in *The Unconscious: A Symposium*, ed. E. S. Dummer (New York: A. A. Knopf, 1927), pp. 114–42.

[10]Herbert Blumer, "Collective Behavior," in *An Outline of the Principles of Sociology*, ed. Robert S. Park (New York: Barnes & Noble, 1946), p. 224.

the respondent covered a five-minute interval. The interviewer thought the respondent could have been knocked unconscious and then either blown through the air to that point or carried by a rescue worker. Later, the interviewer discovered that both possibilities were incorrect because other witnesses had seen the respondent climbing frantically over the rubble on the way to his cousin's house and heard him shouting to his wife who had been at the cousin's house before the storm struck.

In general, this type of information is difficult to obtain by interviewing, but it is not uncommon for respondents to say that they had never been aware of certain aspects of their behavior until after the interview had been in progress for some time. When interviewing methods fail, the information must be obtained through direct or indirect observation.

SUMMARY

Of the eight inhibitors we have named, four of them (competing time demands, ego threat, etiquette, and trauma) tend to make the respondent *unwilling* to give relevant information. The other four (forgetting, chronological confusion, inferential confusion, and unconscious behavior) tend to make the respondent *unable* to give relevant and valid information to the interviewer.

The effects of these inhibitors are not always obvious to the interviewer because the unwilling respondent may fill the air with irrelevancies, ambiguities, or pure fabrications to make a smokescreen concealing his or her lack of cooperation. The respondent who is willing but unable to give relevant and valid information may use these same tactics if the interviewer exerts too much pressure to cooperate without critically evaluating the relevance and validity of the information given.

Fortunately, the effect of inhibitors is not absolute. Inhibitors should be viewed as potentials to be avoided or counteracted. They can be avoided to some extent by methods aimed at minimizing their intrusion into the interview situation. Their effects can be counteracted by maximizing the facilitators which act as counter forces in the interview situation.

The next chapter will describe and illustrate eight facilitators which can be used as positive forces to counteract or displace inhibitors.

DISCUSSION QUESTIONS

1. What is an inhibitor of communication?

2. How is the inhibitor-facilitator model helpful to interviewers?

3. To what extent is interviewing seen as an art or a science?

4. What is the author's response to the idea that "interviewers are born not made"?

5. How many inhibitors are there? Under what two more general categories can they be grouped?

6. To predict whether a certain inhibitor will come into play in a particular interview, what do we have to know about that interview? Give an example of an interview situation in which you would expect a certain inhibitor to be present.

LABORATORY PROBLEM 2

Detecting Potential Inhibitors

Below are examples from a variety of interview situations. Select the inhibitor most likely to intrude in each. Note that after some items there are letters in parentheses corresponding to one or more of the inhibitors to be omitted from your selection. This rules out the most obvious possibilities in those cases with multiple inhibitors. There is no absolutely correct answer since it depends on the assumptions you happen to make regarding any unspecified but relevant aspects of the interview. Write the answers on a sheet of paper after the problem numbers 1 through 10, using the following answer key:

a. Competing time demands   *e.* Forgetting

b. Ego threat   *f.* Chronological confusion

c. Etiquette   *g.* Inferential confusion

d. Traumatic experience   *h.* Unconscious behavior

1. The prosecuting lawyer in a murder trial asks a witness for the defense, "Has your lawyer coached you on what to say and what not to say?"

2. A mother in the Parent-Teacher Association who has a spoiled child asks a teacher during a conversation at tea, "How is my son doing in your class?" (Not *b*)

3. One Vietnam veteran asks another, who is a close friend, "How did you feel when you came back from Vietnam last week and found Jane had broken your engagement and married an old high school friend?" (Not *b*)

4. A psychology student, in obtaining a case history from a neurotic teenager, asks, "Did you ever have any big fights with any of your brothers?" (Not *d*, *e*, or *g*)

5. A student asks his roommate, who has some difficulty keeping up with the reading assignments, "When you read, do you read words or groups of words; and do you 'back track' over a word or phrase very often as you read?" (Not *b*)

6. At 5:30 P.M. a public opinion interviewer knocks on the door of a dwelling unit falling in the random sample. He does not know the family's name, but he does know that the husband is a junior executive in a local firm, that there are three children in the family (ages one, three, and five), and that he must interview the wife. The wife answers the door and the interviewer explains that he is studying an important problem of improving the nursery school and kindergarten facilities in the area, and would appreciate cooperation in an interview which takes about an hour.

7. A public opinion interviewer who is studying the preelection political situation says to the respondent near the middle of the interview, "You mentioned that you don't like the Democrats because they say so many foolish things . . . could you give me some examples of what you mean?" Not *b*, *c*, or *e*)

8. One young businessman (about 25 years old) says to another of about the same age, "That's interesting—you know I am a Princeton man too . . . we must have been there at the same time. Which eating club did you belong to?" (Not *c*)

9. Two politicians who have been personal friends since childhood are discussing their political careers when one asks the other, "I remember how you correctly predicted the election of Senator Young even though his opponent, Bricker, was the forecasters' choice. How did you know that Bricker wasn't going to make it?" (Not *e* or *h*)

10. A detective is trying to discover how the victim (who is still alive) was poisoned. He asks the victim, "What did you eat for lunch five days ago?" (Not *f* or *h*)

Chapter Six

Facilitators of Communication

This chapter will emphasize the potential *facilitators* of communication in contrast to the inhibitors emphasized in the previous chapter. The two chapters together present the inhibitor-facilitator model of communication that views the interview situation as a field of social-psychological forces. These forces arise from the relationships between the information sought, the respondent, the interviewer, the interview situation, and the larger social context as described in Chapter 3.

THE FACILITATORS

The facilitators will be approached from the point of view of the respondent as were the inhibitors. And like the inhibitors, these facilitators are also treated as social-psychological resultants of the relationship between the information and the situation in which it is communicated. Some of the situational stimuli for communication apply to any type of information and others only to more narrow categories of information. Although these facilitators occur in other forms of conversation and can be illustrated with examples from a wide variety of settings, the main concern here is with their value in the interview for both maximizing the flow of relevant information and for maintaining optimal interpersonal relations.

Fulfilling Expectations

One of the important forces in social interaction is the tendency for one person to communicate his or her expectations verbally and nonverbally to another person. The second person then tends to respond, consciously or unconsciously, to those expectations. This may be viewed as one manifestation of the more general human tendency to conform to the group of peers and to the suggestion of higher status persons in the society. It is in this conformity to the group norms that security is sought and usually found. The theoretical and empirical treatments of this basic human tendency are so abundant that we will not attempt to review them here.

More specifically relevant to interviewing is the question of *how* the interviewer communicates *which* expectations to the respondent. In answer to the latter part of this question, we must be aware that the interviewer should communicate both a general expectation of cooperation as well as the more specific expectation of an answer to specific questions. Although the respondent reacts to his or her own perception of these expectations, we cannot assume that the response will always mechanically (in a stimulus-response fashion) fulfill the expectation. Instead, by the steady and consistent communication of general and specific expectations to the respondent, the interviewer will exert a steady, and often cumulative, force affecting the respondent's cooperation. This expectation may be communicated between persons of equal or unequal status, but cooperation requires a type of creative reciprocity that has been described as *dyadic creativity* by Murray.[1]

When we turn to *how* the interviewer communicates expectations, we must clearly distinguish between *asking* for cooperation and *expecting* it. The former is mainly a verbal communication while the latter is mainly nonverbal. As pointed out by Rogers there must be harmony between what one says and what one feels if the interviewer is to be "dependably real" to the respondent.[2] The inexperienced interviewer who lacks confidence, or who fails to see the importance of the task, will often ask only verbally for the information. The interviewer dutifully poses the question, while the interviewer's whole nonverbal manner communicates doubt that he or she has any right to expect an answer. It is this neutralizing effect of the verbal and the nonverbal communication which often causes the novice to lose faith in the "power of positive expectations." The novice may say, "I told him it was all right to tell me anything that was on his mind, but I'm sure he was withholding important information." This problem persists where the interviewer is not aware of also communicating nonverbally with the respondent.

In some cases, the interviewer's negative expectations also interfere with his or her ability to observe the respondent accurately. The interviewer's attitude so colors the interpretation of the respondent's behavior that the interviewer imagines resistance. This makes the interviewer more doubtful and the reinforced attitude is then communicated unwittingly to the respondent. Thus, a form of circular reaction is set up with

---

[1]Henry A. Murray, "Dyadic Creations" in *Interpersonal Dynamics*, ed. Warren G. Bennis et al. (Homewood, Ill.: Dorsey Press, 1964), pp. 638–46. © 1964 The Dorsey Press.

[2]Carl R. Rogers, "The Characteristics of a Helping Relationship," *On Becoming a Person* (Boston: Houghton Mifflin, 1961), pp. 39–58.

one aspect reinforcing the other until the interviewer feels it almost unbearable to contact another respondent.

The strong expectation, based on experience, that the respondent will answer the question is illustrated in the following dialogue in which a television news interviewer (a former officer on the vice squad in another city) did an on-camera interview with a prostitute on the street. Most inexperienced interviewers would shrink from the assignment but not this experienced news reporter.

I: What do you think of the mayor's new policy of getting tough on prostitutes?

R: It's a laugh. It's re-election time!

I: He says you should get an honest job like teaching school. What do you say to that?

R: I couldn't get a job teaching kindergarten. I'm doing my own form of social work and do well at it.

I: How many tricks do you do in a good week?

R: About thirty, sometimes more.

I: How much a trick?

R: Forty dollars.

I: That's $1,200 a week!

R: That's right . . . couldn't make that much teaching. Sorry, I've got to go now to meet a John.

I: Thank you. (To the audience) You see it isn't hard to find prostitutes in this city if you just know where to look!

Most reporters who had not been former vice-squad members would have grave doubts about the willingness of a prostitute to give such information on camera. But this reporter knew from previous experience that a matter-of-fact approach could get results, and he *expected* to get results.

Usually interviewers gain confidence with experience. However, the experience must be mostly successful. The wise novice accepts his or her limitations and begins with easier assignments and, with increasing confidence and skill, progresses to more difficult ones. Confidence is not all that is needed, but it is one of the positive forces in the interview situation. When the interviewer gains a better understanding of the numerous factors which make an interview successful or unsuccessful, he or she is less likely to lose confidence through failures caused by forces beyond the interviewer's control. Just as the physician, lawyer, and minister, in their roles, can expect and receive privileged communications, the interviewer learns a role and is able to communicate it in a subtle way to the respondent.

Recognition

All human beings need the recognition and the esteem (as distinct from affection) of others. Much literature of social anthropology, social psychology, and sociology is concerned with concepts which involve this element of recognition. Studies of such factors as competition, social status, prestige, or approval all involve this element. W. I. Thomas was one of the early sociologists who consciously conceptualized the idea as one of the "four wishes" basic to human motivation.[3] The desire for recognition is fitted into a carefully developed theoretical framework of *social exchange* by Homans, who shows that social interaction often depends upon an exchange of social goods such as esteem and admiration for certain activities.[4] In short, people will "perform" in exchange for recognition and other social rewards. Parsons and Bales use the words *approval* and *esteem* to cover what we refer to as recognition.[5] In their scheme, approval refers to that positive attitude in response to *specific* performances by the other person, while esteem is reserved for the positive *overall* evaluation of that person. Sutherland has demonstrated that even criminals find ways to gain esteem, approval, or recognition (and hence self-respect) by conforming to the norms of the underworld.[6]

The need for recognition is fulfilled by attention from people outside the individual's intimate circle. Being appreciated and loved by one's wife is gratifying, but does not fulfill the need for recognition as we use the term. People may enjoy recognition even though it is based upon notoriety or upon a good reputation which is not deserved.

The skillful and insightful interviewer takes advantage of every opportunity to give the respondent *sincere* recognition. Experimental studies of interviewing have shown that praising the respondent's cooperation has a definite positive effect on the interview.[7]

---

[3]Edmund H. Volkart, ed., *Social Behavior and Personality* (New York: Social Science Research Council, 1951, reprinted by Greenwood Press, 1981), pp. 125–29. Thomas's "four wishes" are the desire for new experience, security, response, and recognition.

[4]George C. Homans, *Social Behavior: Its Elementary Forms* (New York: Harcourt Brace Jovanovich, 1961), pp. 51–82.

[5]Talcott Parsons and Robert F. Bales, *Family, Socialization and Interaction Process* (New York: Free Press, 1955), pp. 86–87.

[6]E. H. Sutherland, *The Professional Thief* (Chicago: University of Chicago Press, 1956).

[7]Joan B. Field, "The Effect of Praise in a Public Opinion Poll," *Public Opinion Quarterly* 19 (1955), pp. 85–90.

In addition to direct, sincere praise, there are many sources of ego gratification for the respondent. For example, the respondent may be flattered that he or she was *selected* because of having some information that is *needed*. The same feeling may result because the respondent's town, place of employment, school, or any other group with which the respondent identifies is being studied. It is no accident that there have been several magazine articles on the theme, "I was interviewed by Mr. Kinsey." People who have had such an experience are unique in the eyes of those around them.

Altruistic Appeals

There seems to be a human need to identify with some high value or cause that is beyond immediate self-interest. This may be a form of identification with the objectives of some larger group. The group may be real or imaginary, contemporary or not. Altruistic deeds usually increase self-esteem whether or not the person's deeds have been public. This distinguishes altruism from recognition.

In every case, the individual is responding to some group value which has been internalized. In some cases, value may be *latent* in that the holder seldom acts upon it because more immediate practical values take precedence. Often the interviewer who understands the respondent's value system can use strategy, techniques, and tactics to reactivate the latent value.

Altruism is of major importance in motivating many respondents in sociological, psychological, and anthropological studies. For example, the Martin brothers gave detailed case history material on their crimes, feeling that this might help other youths stay out of the underworld.[8] In some cases, respondents have volunteered information that was obviously painful to give because they felt it would be of value to others. In a study of marital adjustment, it was obvious that some of the husbands and wives volunteered information beyond what was asked and accepted the blame for an unsuccessful marriage because "it might help someone avoid the mistake I made." Also members of a disaster-stricken community willingly gave information with the hope that it might help future disaster victims.

Sympathetic Understanding

Human beings need the sympathetic response of others. They like to share their joys, fears, successes, and failures. This need of understanding differs from the need for recognition which requires success and increased status in the eyes of people with whom one does not share an intimate relationship; in fact, a person can feel "famous" without knowing

---

[8]Clifford R. Shaw, *Brothers in Crime* (Philadelphia: Albert Saifer, 1952).

any of the "fans" personally. In contrast, sympathetic understanding may be obtained in connection with failures and shortcomings as well as successes, and it is usually extended by a member of the primary group, but it may also be extended by the therapist or interviewer.

This need for sympathetic understanding has been incorporated into many schemes of human needs and it has been given several names. Some of the concepts most closely synonymous with sympathetic understanding are: the "desire for *response*," as used by W. I. Thomas,[9] and a combination of the desire for *acceptance* and for *approval*, as used by Parsons and Bales.[10]

This desire to be understood and to have someone offer a sympathetic ear is seen not only in the therapeutic interview but also in many information-gathering interviews. Teenagers often need someone who "really understands" them and who knows what they mean by "problem parents." Old people are often easy to interview, not only because they are retired and have more time, but also because they have problems which no one takes time to hear. Also, until recently their problems have received much less attention than the problems of youth in the American culture. Shut-ins, socially deviant persons, and other types of isolates often cause the public opinion pollster great difficulty because they want to chat about everything but the subject of the interview. In this case, the need for sympathetic understanding interferes with the efficiency of the interview, and the interviewer must decide to what extent to allow the respondent to talk about his or her own problems in view of the effect upon interpersonal relations and the adequacy of the information.

People do not have to be obviously isolated to have a pent up need for a sympathetic ear. In their routine pattern of living, many people have few opportunities to meet a good listener. Ordinarily, when they begin to talk about their problems, the listener retaliates with a long list of his or her own grievances which tend to pale the first person's difficulties. Often, people refrain from expressing their feelings because "my husband hears that from me all the time," or "he hears people's gripes all day long at the office and doesn't want to hear more of the same thing when he comes home."

Interviewers who reflect a sympathetic attitude and who know how to direct it toward the objectives of the interview will find their percentage of successes much higher than those who do not.

New Experience

All human beings welcome some form of new experience.[11] Even though variety may not be the only spice of life, escape from the dreary

---

[9]Volkart, *Social Behavior*, p. 129.

[10]Ibid., p. 86.

[11]Ibid., p. 121.

routine is sought by everyone. In interviewing personnel in hospitals, industry, and schools, there have been many cases where the interview appeals to the respondent's need for new experience. For example, educators who were cosmopolitan by training and who found themselves temporary captives of a small, local community, found it stimulating to be interviewed on such subjects as academic freedom, foreign trade, or trends in the development and application of social science.

When interviewing industrial employees, it was often obvious that they welcomed a coffee break during which they could discuss anything. After the formal interviews were completed respondents commented, "Do I have to go back to work now?" "That was very interesting. I had never thought about a lot of these things before." "I hope I didn't bore you with all this talk, but I found it very exciting." "I'm not much of a talker, but if we can talk on company time that's fine with me." "This is a lot more fun than what I do all day at the plant."

Similarly, as market research people know, the homemaker has a certain pattern of activities, and although these may vary in detail from tenement house areas to suburbia, a break in this routine is often a welcome relief. Many homemakers have little contact with other adults during the day, much less have the opportunity to be interviewed by one.

Sometimes the respondent is motivated by curiosity regarding the interviewer, and the interviewer should consider this in deciding what to say about himself.

We must not assume, simply because an interview is a new experience for a particular respondent, that it will satisfy his need for new experience. There are some negative effects when certain aspects of the respondent's perception of the new situation are ego threatening. The respondent may be anxious about whether he or she will make a good impression on the interviewer or whether there may be some hidden purpose in the interview. This apprehensiveness can often be detected by the interviewer at the beginning of the contact. Once these fears are dispelled, the respondent frequently finds the interview a new and interesting experience.

Catharsis

By *catharsis* we mean the process by which a person obtains a release from unpleasant emotional tensions by talking about the source of these tensions and expressing his or her feelings. The psychotherapist is most often concerned with catharsis as a release from guilt feelings which may be repressed in the subconscious. Similarly, the religious confession usually involves an expression of guilt in an attempt to relieve the pangs of conscience. Although catharsis is often associated with deep personality disturbances, in its broadest concept it is found in the everyday experience of most people. We have mild guilt feelings over the way we have treated someone during the day, or we have pent-up feelings of frustration and inhibited aggression against our associates. This tension may be released by kicking the cat or by pouring out our difficulties to another person.

Although we are all familiar with the frequent need for catharsis in ourselves, we do not always perceive the same need in others. Most people dealing in human relations know that this need to "air our gripes," to verbalize our feelings of hostility, guilt, and frustration, is omnipresent. The sensitive field worker frequently recognizes his role as the itinerant "father confessor." For example, a college professor, whose colleague was fired during loyalty hearings, feels guilty for not having come to the defense of his friend. Although he knew his colleague had no communist connections, he was afraid he, too, might lose his job. A mother of a delinquent son might blame herself for his behavior. More commonly, a mother might feel frustrated because her three children keep her so exhausted that she cannot be a good companion for her husband or use her college training creatively. In any of these cases, the need for catharsis increases the spontaneity of the interview once an atmosphere of sympathetic understanding has been established.

The need for sympathetic understanding and the need for catharsis are related, but they are not the same thing. A person may satisfy a need for sympathetic understanding by sharing with the interviewer personal joys, plans, and achievements that do not involve any past frustration, aggression, guilt, or repression. Since no moral connotations are involved, it is not so necessary for this respondent to feel assured that the interviewer will respect his or her confidence. The respondent is mainly concerned with finding someone to talk to and does not consider whether the interviewer will divulge the information or not.

Frequently, motivation behind the conversation may move by imperceptible degrees from the simple need for a sympathetic listener to the need for catharsis. Although at some points in this process it is difficult to distinguish which motive is dominant, this does not make the distinction between the two motivations meaningless.

There can be a situation in which the need of sympathetic understanding is being fulfilled without catharsis. However, it is impossible to fulfill the need for catharsis without first establishing an atmosphere of sympathetic understanding. For this reason sympathetic understanding usually *precedes* catharsis. The interviewer who does not have time to listen to what might be considered inconsequential egocentric talk will not find the respondent ready to share important confidences.

The need for catharsis is usually a positive factor, but once the proper atmosphere has been established, there is sometimes a detrimental delayed reaction, and the respondent begins to feel embarrassed or resentful toward the interviewer for "making" him or her talk about ego-threatening topics. Once the respondent's need for catharsis has been fulfilled, the respondent may become concerned about the possible results of having given the information. The respondent's doubts grow when the interviewer is no longer present to provide the constant reassurance of anonymity and to display a nonjudgmental attitude toward the respondent. As a result, any second contact with the respondent may begin with coolness or hostility. In cases where no second contact is needed, the respondent may still damage the study by negatively influencing other potential respondents. Ways of minimizing this possibility will be shown later.

The Need for Meaning

Another general human trait is the need for meaning. The desire for an answer to such questions as "Who am I?" "Where did I come from?" "Where am I going?" or "Why do events happen as they do?" often tempts a person in higher status to give a person in lower status an answer that he or she does not believe personally but which he or she thinks will satisfy the questioner. For example, a child may ask his mother, "What holds up the moon?" and in desperation she may reply, "It hangs on a string," or "It is full of gas like a balloon." Most primitive tribes have a myth which explains the origin of their tribe, if not of the whole universe, which fills the void between desired knowledge and available knowledge.

Every society has a set of assumptions, values, explanations, and myths lending order to the confusion of reality in which the members of that society live. Cantril has spelled out in some detail the interrelationships between different parts of the system as they are internalized in one personality.[12] Particularly relevant to the problem of interviewing is his general observation that under changing social conditions, the individual's system of meaning becomes inadequate to explain real events from which he cannot escape. When the social matrix is disturbed, the individual embarks upon a search for meaning which often makes him highly susceptible to suggestion and a likely candidate for some social movement.

This concept of the *need for meaning* has been dealt with experimentally by Festinger and others as the need to resolve *cognitive dissonance.*[13] They point out that there is a psychological tension set up

---

[12]Hadley Cantril, *The Psychology of Social Movements* (New York: John Wiley & Sons, 1967, reprinted 1971 by R. E. Krieger Pub., Huntington, N.Y.).

[13]Leon Festinger, *A Theory of Cognitive Dissonance* (Stanford, Calif.: Stanford University Press, reissue 1965).

when the individual becomes aware of any incongruence of facts, assumptions, or interpretations. This tension is painful and its reduction is rewarding to the individual.

As the interviewer with wide experience knows, these disturbances of an individual's belief system result from wars, depressions, catastrophes, and other large-scale crises. Disaster interviews often show that the crisis left the members of the disaster-stricken town groping for the meaning of what has happened. They would wonder, "Why did some people get killed while others were spared? Why was I spared? How could a just God allow this to happen to innocent children who are too young to be sinners? What would have happened if Robert had been late to the high school dance as he usually was . . . would he have been killed on his way?"

This need for meaning and the tendency to search for answers was noted in these people's increased attendance at several different local churches for some weeks after the disaster. Usually, each minister responded to his congregation's expectation of an explanation by showing how these events could be reconciled to the concept of a "just and loving God." The need for meaning was also shown in the respondents' reflections during the interview.

More common sources of insecurity accompanying loss of meaning are seen in the life cycle of individuals. In a dynamically changing society, the adolescent is beset by confusion as he or she tries to adjust to the process of becoming an adult. The examples set by the adolescent's own parents may no longer seem to apply to conditions of life in the computer age. At the other end of the life cycle people in later maturity pressed by questions of sickness, loneliness, and death may find that their philosophy of life needs to be reevaluated.

In those cases where the interview topic deals directly with the sources disturbing a person's system of meaning, there is a strong motivation for the respondent to talk it through, once the respondent is convinced of the interviewer's interest in this search for meaning. It is sometimes possible for the interviewer to elicit the respondent's interest by pointing out contradictions, inconsistencies, dilemmas, or facts that might stimulate the respondent's need for meaning. In other words, the interviewer may try to disturb the respondent's equilibrium by involving the respondent in a problem. This is usually more difficult than dealing with a problem in which the respondent is already involved. Valid public-opinion polls on "controversial issues" are often difficult to do, because problems defined as public issues by the information collectors may not concern those who are answering the questions.

Once the interviewer has been sensitized to this omnipresent need for meaning, he or she can use skills, techniques, and tactics to maximize the stimulation and fulfillment of the need, thus utilizing another basic motivation to communicate.

Extrinsic Rewards

This term refers to those rewards motivating the respondent other than those gained directly from interaction within the interview itself. These extrinsic rewards are helpful insofar as the respondent sees the interview as a means to an end. Even though the objectives of the interview may not coincide with the respondent's objectives beyond the interview, the interviewer may skillfully utilize various extrinsic rewards in order to obtain the respondent's cooperation.

Many forms of extrinsic rewards have been used. Money may be given in exchange for the respondent's time, or the interviewer's study may help solve some problem in which the respondent is interested. A respondent may submit to an interview, or even seek it, as a means of obtaining a job. A recently divorced mother may agree to an interview with a social worker, hoping that she will be able to obtain financial aid and psychotherapy for her daughter. A businessman may cooperate in an interview because he is interested in reducing juvenile delinquency, particularly shoplifting from his own store. A college professor may have an interest in being interviewed on the topic of academic freedom, hoping that the study might stir up public sentiment for the protection of this freedom.

Extrinsic rewards are usually not needed to obtain cooperation in studies involving human interest, but they become more necessary as intrinsic rewards decrease and as the amount of time and thought demanded from the respondent increase. For example, it is more necessary to pay people to submit to a psychological study of sensory perception or reaction time than it is to pay respondents to cooperate with an opinion poll on a current issue. Sometimes an extrinsic reward is desirable even though the respondents are members of a captive group who do not give their permission as individuals. This is true particularly if the reward is given by the agency sponsoring the interviewer rather than by the agency that allowed the interviewer access to the respondents. The extrinsic reward sometimes helps overcome initial resentment or allows a series of contacts without causing the respondent's increasing resentment of time spent.

There are circumstances in which any extrinsic reward, particularly money, is detrimental. If the offer of a reward has the effect of attracting one type of respondent and repelling others, this selectivity may bias the study. Offering money may damage the prestige of participating in the study or may encourage bargaining by people who are interested only in the money. The effective use of extrinsic rewards will be explored in the next chapter on field strategy.

Extrinsic rewards are rarely needed and then mainly for obtaining the initial contact. Once the interview begins, the interviewer must bring as many of the intrinsic rewards into play as possible.

SUMMARY

From the interviewer's point of view, there are two basic tasks to be accomplished. The main one is to *maximize* the flow of relevant and valid information. As a means to this end, the interviewer must maintain *optimal* interpersonal relations with the respondent. Unlike a social conversation, the task of maintaining optimal interpersonal relations is subordinated as a means to the end of maximizing the flow of useful information.

It is helpful to view the interaction in the interview-respondent dyad in the broader theoretical framework of *social exchange* to which we have referred from time to time.[14] This framework helps us focus upon the essential fact that the interviewer must take stock of the social-psychological rewards that can be offered in exchange for the information he or she seeks from the respondent. From the point of view of the respondent, we can see that the exchange in the interview involves both *costs* and *rewards*.

The *cost* to the respondent is represented by the respondent's effort to overcome the inhibitors classified as (1) competing time demands, (2) ego threat, (3) etiquette, (4) trauma, (5) forgetting, (6) chronological confusion, (7) inferential confusion, and (8) unconscious experience. The *rewards* to be offered by the interviewer to offset the costs consist of the facilitators classified as (1) fulfilling expectations, (2) giving recognition, (3) providing altruistic appeal, (4) supplying sympathetic understanding, (5) providing new experience, (6) facilitating catharsis, (7) fulfilling the need for meaning, and (8) supplying extrinsic rewards when the preceding seven intrinsic rewards are not sufficient.

Figure 6–1 summarizes the interviewer's tasks in terms of the social-psychological forces over which he or she has some control in the interview situation. The interviewer's task consists of *reducing the costs* to the respondent by minimizing the eight inhibitors and of *enhancing the rewards* by maximizing the eight facilitators of communication.

The remainder of this book provides a variety of strategies, techniques, and tactics to be used by the interviewer in performing the two basic functions in the dyadic social exchange we call the interview.

DISCUSSION QUESTIONS

1. What are the eight potential facilitators of communication in the interview?

---

[14]Peter M. Blau, *Exchange and Power in Social Life* (New York: John Wiley & Sons, Inc., 1964). Contains one of the best formulations of social exchange theory.

FIGURE 6–1   **Facilitators and inhibitors of communication**

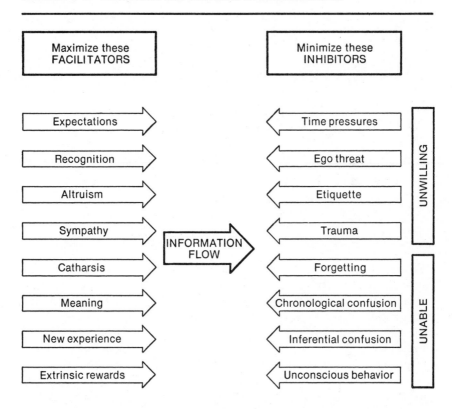

2. What is the difference between asking for the respondent's cooperation and expecting it?

3. Would a woman be more able to give her husband recognition or sympathetic understanding? Why?

4. What is the difference between altruism and recognition as facilitators of communication in the interview?

5. Which two of the following three are most closely related and how: catharsis, recognition, or sympathetic understanding?

6. To predict whether a certain facilitator might come into play in a particular interview, what do we have to know about that interview? Give an example of an interview situation in which you would expect a certain facilitator to be present.

LABORATORY PROBLEM 3

Detecting Potential Facilitators

Below are examples from a variety of interview situations. Select the facilitators most likely to be present in each. Note that after some of the examples there are letters in parentheses corresponding to one or more of the facilitators to be omitted from your selection. This rules out some of the most obvious possibilities in those cases with multiple facilitators. There is no absolutely correct answer since it depends on the assumptions you happen to make regarding any unspecified but relevant aspects of the interview. Write the answers on a sheet of paper after the problem numbers 1 through 10, using the following answer key:

a. Fulfilling expectations   e. New experience

b. Necessary recognition   f. Catharsis

c. Altruistic appeal   g. Need for meaning

d. Sympathetic understanding   h. Extrinsic rewards

1. A physician asks a patient who is having his semiannual physical exam, "How frequently do you usually have bowel movements lately?"

2. A newspaper reporter asks a miner to explain how he rescued five of his fellow miners after an explosion a week earlier. (Not *a* or *e*)

3. A sociologist, studying the effects of the arrival of the first child upon the adjustment between the husband and wife, is interviewing a mother with a two-month-old girl and begins the interview in the respondent's home by saying, "I know from my wife's experience that the first few weeks after you return from

the hospital can be very trying, so I have waited until Janet was two months old to do this third interview we had arranged. How do you feel now?" (Not *a* or *f*)

4. A juvenile-court social worker, in obtaining a case history of a twelve-year-old delinquent child, asks in a matter-of-fact tone, "When did you first skip classes at school?" (Not *b*, *e*, or *f*)

5. Mr. Farnsworth, interviewing for the National Opinion Research Center, is studying a sample of students in a secluded women's college to obtain their views on U.S. foreign policy. (Not *a* or *c*)

6. A minister is talking to a mother about her child who has recently been sent to a juvenile detention home. "You mentioned a while ago that it is hard to know whether you have done the right thing with your children and that you had made some mistakes in raising yours. Would you like to tell me a little more about that?" (Not *a* or *c*)

7. A public opinion interviewer says to a farmer, "I understand that you have lived and farmed here in Boyd County for twenty-seven years. With that much experience, what is your opinion of the present federal farm policy?" (Not *a* or *e*)

8. Two partners in a small business have been independently studying a new income tax law, reducing the amount of state tax on small business incomes, which just arrived in the mail. One partner asks the other, "Is there anything you don't understand about the new tax law?" (Not *a*, *f*, or *h*)

9. A market research interviewer promises a ticket for a free chance on a color television set to all those who give an interview on their movie attendance.

10. An interviewer, studying the social-psychological problems in disaster-struck communities, approaches a respondent in a random sample of the inhabitants of a town three miles from one which had been devastated by a tornado just two days before. He says, "I'm Mr. Gower. I am working on a study for the government of the problems arising in the rescue and relief activities in major disasters. We need to interview not only those people who were directly involved but also some of the lucky ones in nearby areas which the tornado missed." (Not *a*, *e*, or *g*)

Part III

STRATEGY OF INTERVIEWING

The preceding chapters focused mainly on problems rather than solutions. We considered interviewing as a *communication problem* in which the aim was to minimize the inhibitors and to maximize the facilitators of the flow of relevant information from respondent to interviewer.

The next three parts of this book present three general types of *tools* available to the sophisticated interviewer to enhance the flow of relevant information by minimizing the inhibitors and maximizing the facilitators of information flow in the interview. The six chapters in Part 3 describe the many *strategy* options available and some of the criteria for selecting the most appropriate. The two chapters in Part 4 present verbal and nonverbal *techniques* and some criteria for selecting one over the other. The three chapters in Part 5 explain different *tactics* and the conditions under which each should be used.

Figure 7-1, near the end of this chapter, provides a summary of the seven strategy areas and a preview of eight technique areas and seven tactic areas. Although the items listed in Figure 7-1 imply a definition of strategy, techniques, and tactics, it would be useful at this point to attempt a more formal definition of each type of interviewing tool so that their differences as well as their complementary aspects can be seen more clearly.

All three categories of interviewing tools refer to certain methodological decisions that must be made by someone in the process of gathering information relevant to some clear purpose. If these decisions are not consciously made according to some basic social psychological principles, then the method is left to chance.

Strategy

Strategy deals with those more general decisions affecting the basic relationships between information sought, interviewer, respondent, interview situation, and larger society as previously depicted in Figure 3–1. These relationships are affected by answers to such questions as: Who should be interviewed? Who should do the interviewing? When should the interview be done? Where should the interview be done? Should the interview be done in person or on the telephone? How is the interview situation to be explained to the respondent? Should the interview be standardized or unstandardized, scheduled or nonscheduled, tape-recorded or not?

Most of these facets of strategy are put into effect in the approach to each respondent *before* the first question is asked. Strategy does *not* include decisions on details regarding the wording of the questions, the structuring of the answers, the nonverbal behavior of the interviewer in either asking the questions or responding to the answers. Nor does strategy include considerations of the most appropriate sequence of topics and questions, or how to adjust to particular behaviors of the respondent. All of these methods are to be classified as techniques or tactics.

A detailed overview of the types of strategy questions that can be raised is presented in the checklist, Figure 7–2, at the end of this chapter.

Technique

Technique refers to the verbal and nonverbal behavior of the interviewer in isolated statements, questions, or probes. As shown in Figure 7–1 the verbal techniques consist of supplying contextual statements to clarify the meaning of a question, structuring the answer, and selecting a loaded or unloaded question.

The nonverbal techniques include the use of silence, the pacing and inflection of the voice, and any other show of attitude in connection with a specific statement, question, or probe.

Techniques, then, are the verbal and nonverbal ways of communicating a *single* utterance of the interviewer.

Tactic

Tactic refers to a *sequential pattern* of either content or techniques. For example, moving from impersonal to personal topics is a content sequence, while moving from broad- to narrow-scope questions is a technique sequence. These sequential patterns are important because they provide a context which affects both the meaning of a specific question and the respondent's willingness or ability to answer it.

The interviewer must be aware of the differences in strategy, technique, and tactics to understand the full range of interviewing methods. Sometimes the flow of relevant and valid information is best enhanced by careful planning at the strategy level, while at other times the solution may be at the level of techniques or tactics.

Parts 3, 4, and 5 discuss the creative process of selecting various combinations of strategies, techniques, or tactics to fit the interview situation and purpose. This creative process is the essence of the art of interviewing.

Chapter Seven

General Strategy

The central task of the interviewer is to minimize the eight inhibitors and to maximize the eight facilitators of communication to increase the flow of valid, relevant information. The tools for this task are of three general types: strategies, techniques, and tactics.

The first of these three, *strategy*, involves making those decisions which determine the general social-psychological setting of the interview. In dramatic terms, we would say that strategy determines the *plot* (purpose or objectives), the *scene* (time, place, and definition of the situation), and the *cast* (who is to interview whom). However, it does *not* include writing the *script* (the interview guide or schedule). The script, or who says what to whom, includes both techniques and tactics as will be defined here. Unlike the cast of a stage drama, the interview is usually limited to two persons, and only one has a script.

In making strategy decisions we must specify the purpose of the interview as clearly as possible since the selection of the cast and scenes depends upon the plot. The research director may seem free to determine the purpose of a study but is never completely so because he or she may be limited by the availability of funds, by theoretical problems, and by methodological shortcomings in view of the particular field conditions in which the research must take place.

One of the most general of these field conditions is the subculture in which the study is to be carried out. Often we take for granted that the cross-cultural communication problem must be dealt with in the strategy of the anthropologist who travels afar to exotic cultures, but we are not prepared for some of the same problems in our own land. A subculture may be associated with an occupation (policeman, teacher, circus performer, etc.), an institution (college, prison, hospital, etc.), a geographical location (southern U.S, Greenwich Village, inner city, etc.), an ethnic group (Jewish, Chicano, WASP, or French Canadian), or a race (Nisei, Afro-American, etc.).

Each subculture has its own characteristics, its way of distinguishing insiders from outsiders, its way of deciding whom to trust, and its sensitive issues vis à vis other subcultures and the larger power structure. The potential strategy problems depend on how the topic of the interview, the sponsorship of the study, and the identification of the interviewer relate to that subculture's *current* sensitivities in relationship to the larger society.

For example, Gaylin's experience interviewing prisoners indicated that only cooperation came from the inmates themselves who were resisters to the draft during the very unpopular Vietnam War.[1] The only serious backlash came from the "gatekeeper" administrators. In contrast, Giallombardo, who deals with the problems of interviewing more typical prisoners, shows that we can anticipate considerable resistance from the prisoner-respondents themselves, since the problem of establishing mutual trust is very different from that of winning the trust of war resisters who did not identify with the criminal underworld.[2]

During the 1960s there was a growing hostility to surveys and community studies in the black ghettos of the United States. For example, Josephson discusses the resistance to community surveys in Harlem in the late 1960s and concludes that it was extremely important to screen prospective interviewers in terms of race, accent, and attitudes.[3] Also, he admits that there are times and places where it is difficult if not impossible to collect data on deviant behavior because of the suspicion toward outsiders, regardless of the personal characteristics of the interviewer.

There are two dimensions to the ghetto culture that affect communication between interviewer and respondent: the social characteristics associated with race and those associated with socioeconomic class. There are barriers to communication between lower and middle classes regardless of race. As pointed out by Fein, experience in inner city interviewing shows a number of general barriers to cross-cultural communication.[4] One of these is that the forms of verbal expression and the thought processes in the lower-class respondent are different. Furthermore the idea of research as an established institution, a way of examining social phenomena, and the possible benefits seem unreal to the respondents. This is a type of general apathy underlying the hostility

---

[1]Willard Gaylin, *In the Service of Their Country: War Resisters in Prison* (New York: Viking Press, 1970).

[2]Rose Giallombardo, "Interviewing in the Prison Community," *Journal of Criminal Law, Criminology and Police Science* 57 (1966), pp. 318–24.

[3]Eric Josephson, "Resistance to Community Surveys," *Social Problems* 18 (1970), pp. 117–29.

[4]Edith Fein, "Inner-City Interviewing: Some Perspectives," *Public Opinion Quarterly* 34 (1970–71), pp. 625–29.

which may flame up on certain sensitive issues. She suggests that one way to convince the less-educated respondent that we are serious in saying that their participation is meaningful and valuable is to pay them for the interview time. Here we are in effect substituting a cash extrinsic reward for an appeal to the respondent's altruism. Others oppose the cash payment, saying that respondents might expect cash even when the U.S. census taker comes around, or that it might only be interpreted by the respondent as an indication that the interviewer himself does not believe in the value of the study to the larger community. More research needs to be done on the conditions under which certain amounts of cash payment may be both effective and ethical.

Once we have a tentative formulation of the plot we can then choose the actors. In selecting potential respondents we must think about who has the needed information, who is most likely to give the information, and who is most accessible in terms of the efficiency of the project. In selecting the interviewer we must think of the types of persons who will have the best understanding of the purposes of the study and the best relationship to the people who have the needed information.

We cannot mechanically proceed from the consideration of the plot, to the selection of the cast, and then to the specification of the scene. Instead, realistic choices of scene, in view of the actual field conditions, must be taken into consideration in selecting interviewers or respondents and in revising or specifying the purpose of the research. The researcher, unlike the playwright, is not completely free to create the scene from imagination but must consider the actual field conditions in which he or she must operate. Nor can the researcher proceed effectively without creative imagination to conceive of ways to exercise some control of the scene by the selection from among real possibilities of time and place, and by devising effective ways of influencing the interviewer's and respondent's definition of the situation in a way that will minimize the inhibitors and maximize the facilitators of communication.

The researcher does not have a choice of either making or not making strategy decisions. The researcher uses a strategy whether he or she is aware of it or not, whether he or she consciously selects from among alternatives or not, whether it is guided by any theoretical rationale or not. The fact that a particular interviewer is not aware of these problems does not mean that the decisions have not been made by someone. In large-scale research projects these strategy decisions are rarely made by the corps of hired specialized interviewers. Instead, they may be made by a research director, a supervisor for the specific study, or a special consultant-interviewer. Regardless, the person making the strategy decisions should be someone intimately familiar with the purposes of study, with the types of potential respondents, and with various possible settings in which the interviewing might be done. Frequently it is necessary for the strategist to do some pilot interviewing and, usually, some of the early pretesting of the first drafts of the interview schedule, if it is to be used by a team of specialized interviewers. The larger the research organization and the greater the amount of data to be collected on a particular study, the smaller the proportion of the total personnel involved in the strategy decisions.

Whether it is a small-team effort or a large-scale survey, it is advisable to clearly specify all of the strategy decisions as part of the instructions to the interviewers. It is not uncommon for the instructions for a ten-page interview schedule to be as long as forty to fifty pages. The neophyte is often unaware of the importance of this manual of instructions for a particular interview study. It is important to their performance and morale for the interviewers to understand what decisions have been made regarding strategy, techniques, and tactics, and why these are necessary.

ASSUMPTIONS UNDERLYING THE TREATMENT OF STRATEGY

It may be assumed that other sources of information such as personal documents, official records, census data, questionnaires, participation, and observation have been considered and that there has been a decision that some or all the information must be collected by interviewing.

A myriad of practical specific questions must be resolved to meet minimum requirements of any field operation. Specific problems such as how to select a random sample of respondents (if such a sample is needed), how to obtain a list of special respondents, how to locate respondents once they have been selected—will not be taken up here. This is not because they are considered unimportant, but because the concrete answers to these questions vary infinitely, owing to the variety of specific settings, and the questions themselves do not deal with the central problem of minimizing inhibitors and maximizing facilitators of relevant information.

It is useful to discuss *general* types of problems, and an array of problem-solving tools, without giving rules to cover the multitudinous specific situations which might arise. These general problems must be considered by the designer, field supervisor, or sophisticated interviewer so he or she can effectively select from among several possible strategies. The principles which we might illustrate in only one or two cases are often applicable to many different specific settings.

CONTRASTING TYPES OF FIELD SITUATIONS

It has already been pointed out that the researcher, unlike the playwright, cannot create the scene completely from imagination but must operate within the limitations of the realities of the field situation in which the study must be done.

The following classification of field situations sensitizes us to three vital dimensions of the broader context in which studies operate. Each dimension has important consequences in that it places different types of limitations and poses different types of problems calling for different types of strategies. These three dimensions are: friendly versus hostile, open versus closed, and single versus multiple contacts.

Friendly versus Hostile Territory

Logically, there might be three points on a continuum which indicate community attitude toward the interviewing. At one extreme would be the completely hostile situation with a minimum of cooperation expected. This would be approximated in the military interrogation of a prisoner of war or in the policeman's questioning of a suspect. Less extreme would be the case of the sociologist interviewing the president of a college to discover flagrant violations of academic freedom. Similarly, a social scientist studying the effects of the "sit in" against restaurant segregation would encounter hostility in interviews with leaders of a restaurant association formed to combat the "sit ins."

At the other extreme of the continuum would be a group inviting a social scientist to help them achieve some goal they have spontaneously agreed upon. This type of field situation, as long as it remained one of pure cooperation, would not pose any particular problems for the strategist. However, even though the interviewer had been invited to do the study, initial cooperation might change as the interviewing progressed and disturbed the social equilibrium. The good strategist is prepared for this possibility.

Between the two extremes of hostility and complete cooperation is a middle ground encountered more frequently. Three classes of intermediate types can be delineated. The first is simply a form of *limited cooperation* where the cooperation has certain implicit or explicit limits. These limits may consist of certain quantitative of qualitative conditions which are imposed. For example, the middle-management people in a large corporation might be happy to be interviewed by a consultant regarding problems of management training programs if a "reasonable limit" was placed upon the amount of time or the number of interviews involved. If this limit was exceeded, the initial cooperation might turn to mild hostility.

The implied limitation may be qualitative. A civic organization that invited a consultant to interview a sample of suburban residents later withdrew its support because he asked "personal questions" such as the source of the respondent's income, and his religion.

Another type of intermediate point might be called *ambivalence.* This is a more volatile circumstance in which individual respondents have the potential for both excellent cooperation and explosive hostility. The respondent's ambivalence may be due to either conflicting values and desires within himself or potentially opposite perceptions of the interview situation. This type of ambivalence was sometimes found in respondents recounting their marital difficulties; they would feel torn between confessing certain actions to obtain catharsis and cutting the interview short to avoid confessing such ego-threatening information.

A third type of middle ground might be called the *polarized* situation. Here, as in ambivalence, both ends of the hostility-cooperation continuum are actually or potentially present in the group. However, each individual is consistently cooperative or hostile depending upon his or her attitude toward some issue related to the interview topic. The split in the community or organization might occur between strata of power or prestige, between subcultural groups, or between occupational categories. The polarized situation would be probable in a study of labor-management conflicts. In this case, the interviewer who was perceived as partial to the union would also be perceived as unsympathetic or hostile to management, and vice versa.

Open versus Closed Communities

Here, closed refers to the degree to which persons of power or prestige can prevent the interviewer from contacting or gaining the cooperation of subordinates in the group. If a group is open, each individual respondent is free from any legal or other direct social pressure determining the decision to cooperate with the interviewer. The degree of closedness of a group, organization, or community depends upon the degree to which the power figure has absolute control over members, the degree to which the membership of the group overlaps with other groups, and the degree to which the members feel committed to the wishes of the power figure, even though they can be contacted through other groups or in the open residential community.

To illustrate these dimensions, assume that we wish to interview prison inmates. The prison warden has absolute control over the inmates in his institution; during their stay in prison inmates are not members of any group through which the interviewer might gain access to them as respondents. However, if the criminal were interviewed after his release from prison, he would not feel any obligation to the warden.

On the other hand, in doing a social-psychological study of certain monastic orders, we would find a different pattern of closedness. In some orders, the person in charge of the monastery may grant or deny permission to anyone who wishes to enter or leave, and each monk's total life pattern may take place within the monastery walls. In these characteristics, the organization is as closed as the prison, but if a brother were to leave the order and return to the outside world, he may have internalized the point of view of the church hierarchy and still be strongly under its influence. A different pattern of closedness prevails in a delinquent gang not in custody. No one's permission is needed to make contact with any members of the gang, since they all have homes and may even go to school regularly. Nevertheless, obtaining information about their illegal operations is very difficult unless the informal leader gives an affirmative nod.

The closed community is not always easy to recognize or to antici- pate because of various possible complications. The community may be polarized between two nearly equal power groups, one favoring and the other opposing the interviewing. The opposition may be hidden from view, while the favoring group may be reluctant to acknowledge the op- posing group's existence. The control over the respondents may be either legal or extralegal, while the sanctions for violation may be either punishment or withdrawal of certain privileges or status. The followers may perceive their leader's desires as external pressure or as "the right thing to do."

Strategy problems are not necessarily greater in the closed commu- nity than in the open, but the problems are different. Regardless of the quality or amount of closedness in a group, certain common strategy must be planned to obtain the goodwill of the power group which can allow contact with respondents and give some assurance of their coop- eration. If this sanction is given by the leaders, plans must be made for maintaining their support throughout the study. If the community is not only closed but also polarized between power strata, an interesting di- lemma arises. The support of the superordinate group, which must be obtained to gain access to the subordinate group, is double-edged; the interviewer may be suspected by the respondents *because* the interviewer has the approval of their superiors. Finally, if the power group does not give its support, plans must be made, if no other community can be sub- stituted, to gain access to respondents without the leader's sanction. The extent to which this can be accomplished depends upon to what degree the respondents are completely controlled by the one closed group or community.

Single versus Multiple Contacts

Whether or not each respondent must be contacted more than once de- pends upon several conditions. For example, if the interview calls for a wide variety of special respondents, the first contact may be devoted to checking the respondent's qualifications in terms of his or her experi- ences and the ability and willingness to report them. Or, if the type of information needed requires a more intimate relationship than can be established quickly, the first contact may be devoted mainly to building a suitable relationship. In other cases, multiple contacts are required simply because the amount of information to be obtained is too great to obtain in a single interview without encountering fatigue or competing time demands.

Another common type of information requiring multiple contacts is the panel study or any study where the objective is to trace changes in individuals over a period of time. Also, the study may be in the initial stages of exploration so that the interviewer does not know during the first interview all the questions which must be asked. There are times when the interviewer needs to return to the respondent to clarify or to verify some of the information obtained in the first contact. Finally, there is the strategy based on the interview followed by a questionnaire. Although it is often possible to do both the interview and the question- naire in the same session, it may be valuable to use the multiple-contact strategy either because the combination would be too long for one ses- sion, or because it is desirable to allow more time for the respondent to mull over the issues stimulated in the interview before filling out the questionnaire.

In either case it has been shown by Alderfer that, even though highly structured questions and answers are wanted, more relevant informa- tion can often be obtained from the questionnaire method when it has been preceded by an interview.[5] In some cases the interview provides an equally important portion of substantive data; in other situations it may simply furnish qualitative verbatim quotations to give meaning to the statistical results of the questionnaire. The interview may furnish no data in itself but may be used to stimulate the respondent's thinking in certain areas, to provide a context for interpreting the meaning of the questionnaire, or to build a more personal relationship between the re- spondent and the agency sponsoring the study.

Regardless of whether the multiple-contact strategy is used for one of the foregoing reasons or whether the job can be done with a single contact, there are problems associated with either of the strategies. If only one contact is to be made, there may be a problem of building good rapport in the short time available. However, there are advantages to the single contact in that the interviewer is usually perceived as a stranger who will leave the local scene immediately and therefore will not be- come involved in local matters.

In some circumstances the single contact seems to be advisable re- gardless of the large amount of information to be collected from each re- spondent. A very long interview makes it more difficult to find a suffi- cient block of time uninterrupted by competing demands. However, the

---

[5]Clayton Alderfer, "Comparison of Questionnaire Responses with and without Preceding Interviews," *Journal of Applied Psychology* 52 (1968), pp. 335–40.

efficiency of the interview might be improved by using auxiliary questionnaires or check lists, by pruning out all unnecessary questions, and by carefully selecting a time and place for the interview which will minimize competing time demands. Of course, the latter solution will often spread the same number of interviews over a longer period of elapsed time.

A danger to guard against in the long interview is simple fatigue or loss of interest by both the interviewer and respondent. Fatigue is not necessarily a result of the length of the interview; there is considerable evidence that fatigue is often more the result of the presence of the communication inhibitors and the absence of the facilitators. It has been demonstrated that it is possible to interview one person for eight hours at a time without fatigue seriously interfering with the flow of information.[6]

In making strategy plans involving the possible use of extremely long interviews, pilot interviews should be done to explore any negative effects of fatigue. It might be found necessary to abandon plans for a single contact and split the interview into two sessions.

When single contacts are to be made with a large number and variety of special respondents, a much larger proportion of the interviewer's time will be spent locating and contacting than would be the case where a series of contacts is made with the same person. This is an unavoidable consequence which must be recognized in planning the rate of progress of the field study.

Let us now examine some of the potential problems present when the interviewer makes multiple contacts and stays longer in the community. First, we must guard against the contamination effects of one respondent directly or indirectly influencing another. This influence may be negative. For example, a respondent might feel uneasy about confidences given even though the interview had a pleasant cathartic effect at the time. His delayed reaction may cause him to warn others in the community about "that interviewer who makes you say things you don't mean." Often, this possibility can be reduced by ending each interview with a short informal conversational period aimed at building the respondent's ego. In some cases, the respondent will use this ego-building period to rationalize or "explain" things he said but "didn't really mean." If the interviewer simply accepts these rationalizations without question and praises the respondent where it is possible to do so conscientiously, there is less tendency for the respondent to try to retaliate after the interviewer leaves.

---

[6]N. Gross and W. Mason, "Some Methodological Problems of Eight-Hour Interviews," *American Journal of Sociology* 59, no. 3 (November 1953), pp. 197–204.

Another contamination effect is found where one respondent tries to explain to a potential respondent the purpose of the interview, the sponsorship, and so on. Although intentions are good, his or her account may distort the facts so that the interview is seen as simply worthless or even ego-threatening. This difficulty can sometimes be forestalled by preparing a written explanation, combined with a note of appreciation, to be left with each respondent after completing the interview. This pamphlet or letter should contain clear information on the purpose, sponsorship, and anonymity of the interview. Perhaps more important, it should include the name, address, and phone number of some locally trusted person who endorses the project and who can quell any doubts. Another safeguard is to give news releases to local papers explaining the study, reporting its progress, and praising the community for its cooperation. Also, the possibility of contamination can be reduced by maintaining contact with key informants regarding any developments of rumors or opposition.

Another problem arising when the interviewer stays longer to make multiple contacts might be called *role confusion.* On the first contact, the interviewer may be given confidential information because of being perceived as a stranger who will not remain long enough to carry confidential information to others in the community. When the same interviewer is in the community weeks later talking to neighbors, a respondent might temper remarks in the next interview or show suspicion of the interviewer's purpose.

Much of this role confusion can be prevented by stating clearly at the start how long the interviewer intends to stay in the community, by reassuring respondents regarding the interviewer's integrity, and by showing the necessity of interviewing all types of people. Also, the topics to be covered in a series of interviews may be planned to leave the most ego-threatening information to the last in the series.

Another strategy is to use different interviewers to contact respondents who fear the possibility of information being passed among them by the interviewer. This problem is greatest when the community is polarized or fractionalized over issues conceivably related to the topic of the interview. The interviewer's association with members of one group is perceived by members of another as "fraternizing with the enemy." When this polarization is extreme, multiple contacts with each respondent become almost impossible. In this case, one interviewer could specialize in respondents on one side of an issue and another interviewer could deal with the opposite camp.

In contrast to this situation, where the problem is to avoid contamination from one respondent to another or to keep contending parties apart, there is the *group interview* which aims to get the interacting parties together and to stimulate both verbal and nonverbal interaction among them. Here the interviewer is a participant-observer. Although the group interview strategy has been developed mainly for therapeutic purposes, it can also be used for pure information-gathering or diagnostic functions. Friedman provides an example of the group interview with the families of schoolchildren.[7] The study gives data on fifty-three families and detailed summaries of four cases showing the dynamics of the relationships among family members as expressed in the interview situation. In this study the aim was to diagnose the possible causes of the student's learning disorders.

Hill shows how the group interview, again with the family, is used in a hospital setting for the diagnosis of health problems.[8] He demonstrates that there are both values and pitfalls to be avoided in the conjoint family interview. Much research remains to be done to explore the conditions under which the group interview may be fruitful for predicting a person's performance in small group situations, for overcoming the memory barrier by using the collective memory of the group, and for other information-gathering functions.

GENERAL TYPES OF RESPONDENTS

In addition to the contrasting types of field situations, another important dimension of strategy is the type of respondent needed for the purposes of the study. Broadly, the types of respondents can be said to correspond, in general, to the kinds of information sought in a study. Here, we are not concerned with personal characteristics of the respondent, but with the general type of information the respondent can offer.

Key Informants

The key informant is any person who gives information relevant to any of the strategy problems of a study. In this role, the person does not give information directly related to the objectives of the interview. Instead, the key informant helps by supplying information on the local field situation, by assisting in obtaining cooperation, by locating or contacting respondents, and by relaying information during the progress of the study to help meet its objectives. Key informants are particularly necessary in hostile and closed communities.

---

[7]Robert Friedman, "A Structured Family Interview in the Assessment of School Learning Disorders," *Psychology in the Schools* 6 (1969), pp. 162–67.

[8]William G. Hill, "The Family as a Treatment Unit: Differential Techniques and Procedures," *Social Work* 11 (1966), pp. 62–68.

Special Respondents

The special respondent is any person who gives information directly relevant to the objectives of the study and who is selected because he or she occupies a unique position in the community, group, or institution being studied.

Special respondents are needed because their unique position qualifies them to give special information, either on their own thoughts and actions as they function in that particular position, or on their observation of others' feelings, thoughts, and actions from a special vantage point.

Special respondents also provide information on the *structural* aspects of the group, institution, or community. Such special respondents would be useful in discovering the difference between the formal and informal organization of an industrial plant, mapping out the channels of political influence in a community, or analyzing the structure of a boys' gang.

A different type of information may be obtained from each special respondent since his or her unique perspective is a chief contribution to the study.

Representative Respondents

The representative respondent, like the special respondent, gives information directly relevant to the objectives of the interview. The representative respondent is chosen because he or she is *like* other respondents, in that he belongs to a certain category, universe, or population. The representative respondent, as one of a sample of representatives from the same class, contrasts with the special respondent who might be the only member of the special class to be interviewed.

Several important characteristics distinguish the use of special respondents from the use of representative respondents.

1. Representative respondents are worthwhile only when there are enough of them to represent certain variations in the universe or population from which they have been selected.

2. The same questions must be asked all members of the sample.

3. The sample is considered as an *aggregate* of individuals having a range of characteristics similar in variation to the universe. Likewise, the universe is also conceived as an aggregate rather than a *structure* of relationships between individuals.

4. Since the sample is an aggregate, the measurements obtained from individuals are subject to mathematical and statistical

operations such as addition and multiplication or to finding a mean, standard deviation, and measures of association.

None of the above characteristics applies to the use of special respondents.

Uses of Kinds of Respondents

It is important to realize that a single study might require the use of key informants, special, and representative respondents. Furthermore, the same person may be a key informant at one time in the study; later he or she may be a representative respondent, and even later a special respondent.

To illustrate the use of key informants, special respondents, and representative respondents, let us examine a field study in which all three types are needed. In studying teenagers' conflicts with parents and the relationship of these conflicts to juvenile delinquency, we might begin by contacting key informants, such as the staff of the state juvenile authority, to help select a location for studying the problem. These informants might help find locations with extremely high and low delinquency rates; they might also estimate the extent to which the differences in the official rates reflect actual differences in delinquency rather than in booking systems.

In addition, these key informants could furnish the names of special respondents in the local areas, such as the superintendents of schools, juvenile parole officers, truant officers, and family case workers, who deal directly with known delinquent children. Additional special respondents such as high school counselors, teachers, playground directors, and local police would be able to provide information on many unrecorded delinquencies. Another class of special respondents would be each delinquent's closest friend or the whole gang to which he belongs.

The representative respondents could include a sample of teenagers and their parents from each of the two communities. These teenagers and their parents could supply information on the number and types of conflicts they have experienced. If the two communities were large, with a population of more than 100,000, a 1 percent sample of teenagers and their parents might easily include some of the special respondents.

It is possible to have a study requiring only special respondents, such as a study of a small community's division-of-labor pattern. At the other extreme, a public opinion poll for predicting election results usually involves only representative respondents. Thus we see that the types of respondent depend upon the purposes of the study and the types of information to be collected.

STEPS IN FIELD STRATEGY

After the problem of the study is clearly formulated and the types of information needed are specified as precisely as possible, the next step is to determine the types of respondents required. With the ideal types of respondents decided upon, it is then necessary to determine the means of locating and contacting them.

Locating and Contacting Representative and Special Respondents

If the study calls for a sample of anonymous representative respondents, locating and contacting them may involve merely knocking on the doors of a random sample of an area's dwelling units. If special respondents are needed, there are usually several channels through which they may be identified, located, and contacted. In this case the advantages and disadvantages of one channel must be weighed against those of other channels.

For example, in studying the process of professionalization of occupational therapists, there are several possible channels of contact. The interviewer might obtain the names and addresses of OTs from the national or local association and interview them at their homes. This would avoid seeking the permission of the administration of the hospital where they work. If the study also requires interviewing physical therapists, physicians, nurses, and orderlies working in the same hospital, it would be desirable to obtain the hospital administration's approval so that the names of all of these employees in the local hospital could be acquired. It might also increase the efficiency of the project if some or all of the special respondents could be interviewed at the hospital. This would require additional cooperation from the administration.

After discovering which channels of contact exist and how cooperative each will be, further consideration must be given to the possible effects of each channel of contact upon the respondent's motivation to cooperate.

Securing the Cooperation of Key Informants

If a key informant's permission must be obtained to gain access to several respondents in a closed community or organization, we should try to learn as much as possible about the informant. The following questions should be answered: Would the study threaten the key informant in any way? What competing time demands might make the key informant reluctant to give access to the respondents? Would this person take an ambivalent position because of conflicting desires or because of an ambivalent picture of the study's purpose or effect? If this person gives his or her wholehearted permission for the study, what might be the effect of this knowledge upon the respondents?

Some information relevant to these questions might be obtained from written sources if the key informant is a leader or professional person in the community or organization. Company newspapers, college catalogs, local newspaper files, local newspaper reporters, and directories of professional, administrative, business, and occupational groups are all useful sources of information about a person's status and function in a given social setting. Available public documents may yield such facts as the person's full name, address, correct title and position, phone number, age, race, organizational affiliations, educational background, job history, public activities, and possibly a photograph. Further information might be obtained from other key informants who have contact with the person and can give impressions of his or her probable attitudes toward the proposed study.

Prepared with this background information, and guarding against prejudices, preconceptions, and stereotypes, the interviewer can approach the person whose approval is desired. The interview with this key informant may accomplish several objectives. It may explain the purpose and sponsorship of the study, and show how the information is to be used. It may demonstrate how the study can help the key informant, or the interviewer may appeal to an altruistic motive and show precisely how the key informant can help the project. It might also be desirable to show the extent of anonymity involved in the collection and the publication of the information.

The interviewer may also want to ask for advice on such things as the best time and place for interviews. The interviewer should also take advantage of every opportunity to show sympathy for any of the problems confronting the key respondent in the decision to cooperate and should probe to clarify the precise nature of the problems instead of trying to discount them as imaginary or inconsequential. This information allows the interviewer to deal more intelligently with the obstacles, and the interviewer's interest in the key informant gives a sympathetic and responsible impression.

This interview should create an atmosphere encouraging the informant to ask questions and clarify any doubts. It is always good strategy to leave written materials covering the same points as the oral explanation, along with details of where the interviewer and the sponsor might be contacted. In this way, channels of communication remain open.

If there is reason to believe that serious resistance will be offered by the target community, it is often practical to do a small pilot study in a similar community or organization at a distance to obtain perspective and forewarning of some of the potential strategy problems. For example, if a university sociology department wishes to study the problems of public school superintendents in five counties surrounding the university, it would be useful to do a small pilot study in a remote county of the state where a serious strategy error would not damage the final study.

If there is reason to suspect opposition from leaders of a closed community, plans should be made to meet it with constructive counterstrategies. One of the most problematic situations occurs in the study of a closed community in which the power figures are not in sympathy with the study, but do not feel free to publicly refuse cooperation. In this case, covert measures such as keeping the interviewer busy with irrelevant activities, stalling, red tape, and subtle threats to respondents may be used to sabotage the interviewer without directly refusing cooperation. It is well to anticipate, if possible, some of these potential evasions and have countermeasures ready. For example, it is useful to prepare face-saving explanations for the person of influence in case his initial resistance weakens and he wants to avoid the appearance of having acquiesced to pressure. In some cases, it is even necessary to prepare for a hasty retreat if a final rejection seems imminent. If possible, a final "no" should be avoided even at the cost of a temporary retreat.

If permission is refused. If the leaders' formal permission or informal approval is not obtained, there are still several paths toward the next step. At this point it is necessary to deal with several interrelated questions: Is it crucial to study this particular community or organization or can the study be carried on equally well in more friendly territory? Is the leader's power so complete that all channels of contact to the respondents are closed, or is it still possible to contact the respondents as individuals rather than through the group? If the respondents can be contacted as individuals, will the influence of the power figure still prevent their cooperation? These judgments must be made on the basis of information obtained in the local setting.

We must never forget that refusals to cooperate with the formal interviewing of a study may, nevertheless, provide much relevant information. In the discussion of the person's public reasons for noncooperation, real fears and suspicions or some of the powerfully competing time demands will frequently be manifested. In spite of the respondent's adroit mixing of public information and official explanation, the interviewer can find clues to some of the underlying causes of resistance.

In addition, it is possible to obtain relevant factual information while the person is refusing to cooperate. For instance, if an interviewer wished to study conflicts in a small town during desegregation of the public schools, the local mayor would be a good key informant regardless of his attitude toward the study. Even though he would not give confidential information about the performance of the local police force, for example, he would probably be willing to review specific incidents, name parties to the dispute, and give his official interpretation of the events. Regardless of the accuracy of his interpretations, the verifiable facts of time, place, and names would provide leads to other special informants on both sides of the issue.

On rare occasions, it is necessary and effective to challenge the power figure by pointing out that his or her resistance appears defensive in view of the guaranteed anonymity. In equally rare cases, it can be pointed out (where it is true) as a last resort that the study will have to be carried out with or without sanction of the power figure. Of course, in a completely closed community such a statement could not be made.

If permission is given. Plans should be made to maintain cooperation, once it has been obtained, because initial approval, either in an open or closed community, may turn to resistance. For example, people who originally assumed the study to be a survey of public opinion may subsequently feel that "confidential" information is being collected. They may simply be unable to see the relationship between the stated purpose of the study and the specific information gathered, and feeling threatened, they may accuse the interviewer of misrepresenting the nature of the study. This problem must be guarded against early by providing a written explanation which can be referred to later. This explanation may cover the range of information to be collected, or it may allow for more detail to be added from time to time with each interview with the same respondent.

Often, while not objecting to a particular question, the respondent objects to what he or she believes are certain implications in the relationships between the questions. An example is provided in a study of the social-psychological factors determining the success of rescue operations after a community-wide disaster. The officials of the city were not reluctant to give figures on the number of men and the amount of police, fire, and medical equipment sent to the scene. However, these facts were often viewed differently by the respondents after they had been asked the extent of the disaster, the time when the rescue workers and equipment were needed, and the precise time of their arrival on the scene. Initially, the rescue work was often carried out informally before any of the official organizations (such as the National Guard, Red Cross, Civil Defense, or local police) could mobilize; thus, manpower and equipment in excess of the need were sent, draining the surrounding area of its normal fire, police, and medical personnel. Even though the information was not to be used in judging, praising, or penalizing officials for their performance or for assuming responsibilities outside their jurisdiction, the interview questions were ego-threatening to people who liked to think of themselves as always having things under control.

In this type of situation the ego threat can be reduced by separating the facts so that the ego-threatening relationships are not perceived by the respondent. This may be done by having a series of interviews with the same person. In this way the relevant facts are collected in widely dispersed time, or parts of the picture are collected from different respondents and later assembled into a meaningful whole.

In some cases the initial cooperation of the power figures of a closed community precludes the enthusiastic cooperation of the respondents. This happens if the community is polarized between the superordinates and subordinates. Since the interviewer must have the permission of the leaders to gain access to the community members, the respondents may view the interviewer as a representative of the superordinate group. This difficulty can be ameliorated by the interviewer's frankness in explaining to the respondent that he or she is not sponsored by the power group but had to gain their permission to do the interviewing. This explanation in itself, truthful and logical as it is, will not necessarily gain the immediate trust of the respondent. The interviewer will have to show by an interest in the respondent's point of view that he or she is not a spy for the dominant group.

This discussion of possible steps in field strategy has presented a necessarily pessimistic picture, since its aim was to warn of certain problems which might arise and to suggest possible solutions. At each step the worst was assumed by supposing (*a*) that the respondents could not be contacted directly, but were in a closed and potentially hostile community; (*b*) that the situation within a community was complicated and sometimes polarized; (*c*) that it was necessary to persist in the study even though cooperation was refused; and finally (*d*) that even if permission were given, it might turn into resistance unless certain precautions were taken. Fortunately, it is rare to find all of these complications arising in any one field study.

All the possible strategy problems are never encountered in any one study. However, it can never be assumed that any information-gathering project will lack resistance merely for being a good cause in pure or applied human relations. Nor can we assume that all potential respondents will be disarmed and freed from ego threat by the fact that the social scientist is not going to use information for personal gain or for penalizing any individual or institution.

Instead of the naively optimistic or the hopelessly pessimistic approach to the strategy problems, a constructively cautious approach will be more useful—preparing for the worst and expecting the best.

Successful strategy involves doing the right things in the correct order and avoiding assumptions about the nature of the field situation without first checking available facts. The researcher must obtain reliable information about the field situation in order to prevent the rise of misperceptions, rumors, and suspicions before having an opportunity to explain the study to persons whose cooperation is needed. Unless there is a degree of success at the strategy stage, the interviewer will not have an opportunity to use his or her skills in interviewing.

FIGURE 7-1 Tools for interviewing

Strategy areas	Technique areas	Tactic areas
1. Selecting respondents.	1. Supplying context for question.	1. Regulating sequence of topics.
2. Selecting interviewers.	2. Selecting appropriate wording.	2. Providing transitions.
3. Selecting the time and place.	3. Regulating scope of question.	3. Varying sequence of questions.
4. Structuring the interview site.	4. Structuring the answer.	4. Varying topic control.
5. Selecting recording method.	5. Loading questions appropriately.	5. Meeting resistance.
6. Selecting mode of contact.	6. Using silence.	6. Preventing falsification.
7. Deciding number of contacts.	7. Using pacing and inflection.	7. Using informal post-interview.
	8. Showing appropriate attitudes.	

So far, the discussion has dealt broadly with strategy by defining strategy in contrast to techniques and tactics, discussing some of the general types of field situations, delineating three types of respondents, and discussing some of the possible steps in field strategy as a decision-making process. This serves as a background for a more detailed treatment of four basic tools of strategy: selecting appropriate respondents, selecting appropriate interviewers, selecting the optimum time and place for the interview, and structuring the interview situation.

Figure 7-1 presents an overview of all of the *tools* for interviewing dealt with in this book. There the strategy portion of the tools is divided into seven areas. In Figure 7-2 these seven areas are expanded into a checklist of thirty-three detailed strategy decisions that can serve as both a preview and a summary of the major points covered in Chapters Seven through Twelve. When you plan any interviewing project these strategy decisions must be made early. Not all of the thirty-three decisions must be made in every project because the practical circumstances often limit or predetermine the answer to a question. However, the checklist can be very helpful in guarding against the failure to consider certain strategy options due to the automatic acceptance of strategies developed in previous projects or laid down by tradition in a certain organizational setting.

In some cases incorrect strategy decisions may make it difficult, if not impossible, for the most skillful interviewer to succeed; yet, strangely enough, most treatments of interviewing deal only with the techniques and tactics while omitting the strategy considerations in the broader social context.

FIGURE 7-2   Checklist—Strategy decisions

1. What specific items of information must be obtained for this project?
2. Which of these can be most effectively obtained by interviewing?
3. Is the information to be collected in an open or closed community?
4. Is the setting friendly, neutral, or hostile?
5. Is it necessary to prevent one respondent from reporting an interview to a potential respondent?
6. Are key informants needed to give advice on the situation or on contacting respondents?
7. Are special respondents, representative respondents, or both needed?
8. If representative respondents are needed, how is the sample to be selected?
9. If representative respondents are needed, how will follow-up contacts be made with those who are not home or refuse to cooperate on the first contact?
10. If special respondents are needed, how are they to be located and contacted?
11. Does the study call for standardized, unstandardized, or both types of interviews?
12. Is advance publicity of the project needed to reduce resistance and increase cooperation?
13. Which respondents are most likely to have the relevant information?
14. Which of those who are able are also willing to give relevant information?
15. Of those respondents who are able and willing, which are the most accessible?
16. Should an appointment be made in advance with the respondent?
17. In view of the type of information to be collected, the type of respondent, and the type of setting of the interview, who would make the best interviewer?
18. Is more than one type of interviewer needed?
19. Should respondents be interviewed more than once by more than one interviewer?
20. What auxiliary roles can and should the interviewer assume in the interview?
21. What special knowledge is needed by the interviewers regarding the topic, the respondent, or the situation?
22. Where should the respondent be interviewed?
23. When should the respondent be interviewed?
24. Should the interview be done on the telephone or face-to-face?
25. How should the interview be recorded?
26. How is the mode of recording to be explained to the respondent?
27. How should the interviewer be introduced to the respondent?
28. How is the purpose of the interview, the selection of the respondent, and the sponsorship of the study to be explained to the respondent?
29. Should an information sheet be left with each respondent after the interview?
30. Should any extrinsic rewards be given?
31. How is the respondent to be assured of anonymity?
32. Is the respondent to be offered the results of the study?
33. Should rapport-building, lead-in questions be used?

DISCUSSION QUESTIONS

1. What is interviewing strategy?

2. Is it possible to not use a strategy in interviewing? Explain.

3. What are some of the most important things we need to know about any subculture to plan a strategy for studying its members?

4. What are three important dimensions which characterize contrasting field conditions? Give an example of how one or more of these dimensions affect the strategy.

5. What are the three general types of respondents and in what way is each valuable?

6. What are some of the problems which may arise at the strategy phase of any study?

7. What general attitude of approach does the writer suggest in planning a field strategy?

Chapter Eight

Selecting Appropriate Respondents

The type of respondent needed depends mainly upon the type of information sought. The interviewers available and the setting for the interview will also have a bearing; but in discussing the selection of respondents, we will assume that the optimum interviewer and interview situation obtains.

If a special respondent occupies a unique position, then that respondent is irreplaceable. If representative respondents comprise a sample which cannot be altered without damaging its representativeness, then each individual in the sample is irreplaceable. If both types of respondents are irreplaceable, there is no choice in selecting respondents. Then the query becomes, why deal with the *selection* of respondents?

Special respondents are *chosen* in two senses. First, it is necessary to determine which of the many unique positions (role, status, or function) are relevant to the purposes of the study. Second, similar positions are frequently occupied by more than one person. Thus, the special respondent is not a unique individual, but any person occupying a special position in society giving him access to certain observations, actions, and knowledge.

Representative respondents, on the other hand, offer fewer opportunities for purposive selection other than determining whether each is a member of the universe as defined for the study. However, there is an opportunity to maximize the flow of relevant information by "selecting" cases even after the complete sample has been chosen. This is done by deciding which respondents are to be interviewed by which of the interviewers (who are also already selected).

Logically, there are at least four basic criterion questions which must be answered in selecting respondents. Who *has* the relevant information? Of those having the information, which are physically and socially *accessible*? Which persons having the information are most *willing* to give it? Which persons having the information are most *able* to give an accurate accounting?

The first two of these questions depend so heavily upon the specific information needed and the specific nature of the field situation that we will deal with them only superficially and then devote the remainder of this section to the last two criterion questions.

WHO HAS THE RELEVANT INFORMATION?

If we are seeking to measure subjective orientations of individuals—such as the attitudes, beliefs, expectations, desires, preferences, or loyalties of a certain population—then obviously everyone in that population has the relevant information. If we want to generalize to that population, we must either interview all or a representative random sample so there is no opportunity to select or reject respondents on any criterion other than being randomly selected from that population.

In contrast to this situation are the many studies which are not interested in the subjective orientations of an aggregate of individuals but in objective facts external to the individual, obtainable from a single person, verifiable through more than one person. Such facts would include objective information about a community, institution, organization, group, or event. For example, all of the following questions seek information of the objective type about Greenville, Ohio:

1. Who is the mayor of Greenville?

2. When will Greenville celebrate its centennial?

3. Who is the superintendant of schools in Darke County?

4. What is the property tax rate for public schools?

5. How long must children remain in public school according to Ohio law?

6. Who hires Mexican-American migrant farm labor in Darke County?

7. What are migrant workers paid per day?

8. Is there a Headstart Program for children of migrant workers?

9. Are there literacy classes in the evening for migrant workers?

10. How many attend literacy classes?

11. How is eligibility for food stamps determined?

All of these questions deal with Greenville, and any one of them could be validly answered by one person in Greenville if we found the right respondent. The number of people in Greenville having the information would vary tremendously from one question to another. Thousands of people could answer either question 1 or 2, but perhaps only two or three would know the answer to question 11. Despite the fact that hundreds of families in Greenville may receive food stamps through the local county welfare office, it is doubtful whether any of the recipients could be relied upon to know precisely how eligibility is established. The person to ask would be the person in the welfare office who processes the applications and makes the decisions on eligibility.

Ideally we should have a systematic scheme for relating general characteristics of respondents to the types of information they are most likely to have. Many descriptive studies relate to this problem, and some attempts at generalization have been made; but the fact that much remains to be done is evident in the apparent conflict between generalizing statements. Most of the literature simply demonstrates that one type of respondent is a better source of certain information than another, without inducing any general statement with appropriate qualifications regarding the type of information in relation to the type of situation. The following will attempt some tentative generalizations.

High-Low Status

Often the high-status respondents in any organization or community are much better than the lower-status person in providing an overall view of the organization or its relationship to other organizations. They are also more likely to be familiar with the legal and financial structure of the organization. They often are more able to report on the past history and future plans of the organization.

Usually lower status persons can be relied upon for the details of daily operation, but they often show reluctance to answer questions of policy. Even among lawyers within a large law firm this tendency was found by Smigel, who noted that those lower down in the power structure, and usually younger, were reluctant to discuss policy matters or to make generalizations.[1] They preferred to discuss the technical details, procedures, and routines involved in carrying out the policies. Often the only time the lower-status person is articulate about policy is when he or she feels its pinch and disagrees with it.

If we want an estimate of the subjective state of mind of the rank and file in an organization, it is often more valid to ask even a few of the lower status people than to try to get an overall estimate from the top manager. This has been found in many different organizational settings. For example, Campbell did an experimental study which showed that

---

[1]E. O. Smigel, "Interviewing a Legal Elite: The Wall Street Lawyer," *American Journal of Sociology* 64 (1958), pp. 159–64.

Navy enlisted men made a more accurate rating of morale among the submarine crews than did the officers.[2]

There are several possible reasons for this lack of awareness by high-status people in any organization. First, the etiquette barrier might stop the men from disillusioning the boss who is proud of keeping high morale. Also, ego-threat to the employee might be strong if the boss does not like to hear any "complaining about low morale." Finally, the boss may tend not to notice any evidence of low morale because it would be seen as a personal failure. This same pride in keeping high morale was demonstrated when a manager in a company with over 25,000 employees rejected evidence of low morale provided by a consultant, because management had launched a program five years earlier to develop the atmosphere of "one happy family" among all employees.

Active-Passive Types

In studies of community structure and process there seems to be considerable evidence that those who are active in community affairs regardless of their position in the social status system are more knowledgeable than the nonparticipants. Of course there are occasional astute observers who rarely directly participate, either because they are outsiders or because they wield indirect power requiring that they remain anonymous. Yet, information regarding the interplay of groups within the community, particularly around public issues, can be obtained better from the community activists. For example, Merton found in his study of community housing that the particularly cooperative respondents were local leaders, who were active participants in organized and informal group life, and who identified strongly with the community.[3]

Just as there are gatekeepers who can provide or deny the interviewer access to certain types of respondents, there are gatekeepers who because they provide certain types of information to the community make particularly good special respondents. Lewin's conception of the gatekeeper was a person who linked the interpersonal communications network within a particular group to the outside world.[4] This may include a link between a very small group like an office staff and the larger organization, or the link between the mayor's commission and the federal

[2]Donald T. Campbell, "The Informant in Quantitative Research," *American Journal of Sociology* 60 (1955), pp. 339–53.

[3]Robert K. Merton, "Selected Problems of Field Work in a Planned Community," *American Sociological Review* 12 (1947), pp. 304–312.

[4]Kurt Lewin, "Group Decisions and Social Change," in *Readings in Social Psychology,* ed. Swanson, Newcomb, and Hartley (New York: Henry Holt, 1952), pp. 459–62.

government, or between the home office of a U.S. company and its Latin American branches. These gatekeepers have the outside information first and decide what is relevant, when to release the information, and may even have suggestions about what should be done about it. These gatekeepers may be either one-way or two-way communicators who also interpret the group to outsiders.

This gatekeeper is the same person that Katz and Lazarsfeld found particularly influential in linking the mass communication media and informal groups.[5] In a sense these gatekeepers act as the on-off switch, even for information in the mass media, by calling the attention of their group to certain content of the newspaper, radio, or television, by interpreting the meaning of the content, or by setting an example of what should be done about the information.

Insider-Outsider Types

A person may be an outsider in different ways. He or she may simply be an outsider who never intends to get inside and is therefore useful, not for any insider information, but for the perspective as an outsider. This may mean that the outsider is more objective, or it may mean that the outsider has stereotypes of the in-group or hostility toward them. The latter case is more likely if the outsider belongs to a competing or conflicting group. If the outsider is from another culture, he or she may be particularly useful in having a different frame of reference for raising useful questions and suggesting alternatives which would never occur to the insiders. On the other hand danger lies in the outsider's tendency to misinterpret observations of the other culture. This is clearly shown by Gorden, whose study shows that American Peace Corps trainees living with Colombian families in Bogotá made consistent errors in conclusions drawn from their observations and conversations in their Colombian homes.[6] For example, the majority of Americans, after living in the Colombian home for several months, mistakenly believed that their host did not expect them to take a bath every day or wrongly concluded that they were not expected to make their own beds. Thus, the outsider from a different culture may give information based upon false conclusions drawn from misinterpretations of his or her observations.

Just as the outsider has strengths and weaknesses as a potential informant so does the insider. The insider may be better acquainted with the details, but the insider's perspective may be too narrow.

---

[5]Elihu Katz and Paul F. Lazarsfeld, *Personal Influence: The Part Played by People in the Flow of Mass Communications* (Glencoe, Ill.: Free Press, 1955).

[6]Raymond L. Gorden, *Living in Latin America: A Case Study in Cross-Cultural Communication* (Skokie, Ill.: National Textbook Co., 1984).

A person is not always simply an outsider or an insider. In some cases a person is both, or is a "marginal man." The marginal person may be a *novitiate* coming from outside but being assimilated as a permanent member of the group. The novitiate is more useful in seeing the processes of initiation, socialization, assimilation, and social control in any group or organization than are the long-time members who have forgotten the pain.

Another type of marginality is the *sojourner* who comes into a group with the intention of staying only a short time and therefore does not try to gain complete acceptance in the group nor submit completely to its control. The sojourner, as we have already noted, can sometimes raise significant questions about what he or she observes, but often the sojourner's own answers to these questions may be fallacious. This is particularly true of sojourners in foreign countries. For example, when the author was studying the miscommunication between North Americans and Colombians in Bogotá, he found that most Americans, even after living as a guest in a Colombian home for months, had gained many incorrect ideas about the daily routine in a Colombian home. When asked, for example, "What does your Colombian family expect you to do with your towel after taking a shower?" not a single American said that it should be hung in the patio to dry in the sun.[7] Yet this was the answer given by a large majority of the Colombian housewives in these same homes. Significantly, none of the Americans said "I don't know." This demonstrates how the sojourner can remain isolated from many aspects of the foreign culture in which he or she is a guest. These same sojourners, when they returned to the United States, often felt like and were treated like authorities on how to be a guest in a Colombian home when they were questioned by other Americans, including Peace Corps volunteers bound for Colombia.

Another general type of marginal person is the *ex-member*. This is someone who used to be inside and is now outside. The type of information the ex-member has depends upon what was his or her role as an insider, how long the ex-member has been outside (since he or she may forget or may have out-of-date information), and the relationship between the ex-member and the group. To clarify this relationship we must know whether the ex-member was rejected by the group (becoming a rejectee, exile, or outcast)—or whether the ex-member took the initiative (becoming a fugitive, escapee, expatriate, or defector). Although both the expelled and the escaped may have feelings of fear or hostility toward the in-group, there is usually a difference in the type of

---

[7]Raymond L. Gorden, *American Guests in Colombian Homes: A Study in Cross-Cultural Communication*, a report to the U.S. Office of Education, 1970, p. 43.

information they have. If the in-group sees the larger world as threatening its interests, then the escapee may have information considered more dangerous than has the rejectee. Both the rejectee and the escapee are the result of tension and conflict. This is not so with all ex-members.

There is another type of ex-member who does not result from any conflict with the group but simply moves out as a part of the normally expected social process. This includes such persons as the graduate, retired, promoted, pensioned, emeritus, ex-officio, exogamic, ex-patient, vacationer, postdoctoral, postjuvenile, etc. All of these may have an advantage in having been a member at one time and now having a larger perspective. They may not be so biased against the organization and so willing to provide negative information; they may, however, bias the information positively either because of a romantic nostalgia or a feeling of obligation to protect the group's interest.

A very special type of marginal person is the one who is still in the group but in conflict or disagreement with it to some extent. This is the *disaffected* person. This type of person has special knowledge of the social control system and how it feels to be subjected to it. Also, since the marginal person is still a member, he or she can continue to be an informant regarding the processes of control, at least until being considered incorrigible and becoming an outcast.

Mobile-Stable Types

Some people by virtue of their mobility have a better-than-average overview of the connections between groups or organizations. Such people as taxi drivers, police, interoffice errand boys, delivery people, and textbook salesmen often have a unique understanding of activity between groups.

A special perspective on a community can often be gained from transients or new residents. In field strategy we often have to locate mobile individuals through agencies which specialize in dealing with them. The most challenging problem often arises in mapping a strategy for locating respondents who have left the organization or community we want to study. This is often difficult, but not impossible.

No systematic treatment has been done of the assets and liabilities of the different types and degrees of mobility in the context of information-gathering problems. We can only suggest that mobile people often have a kind of information rarely attained by stay-at-homes, yet they are often left out of community studies where their knowledge would be of special benefit.

The above classification of respondents into high-low status, active-passive, insider-outsider, and mobile-stable types is a sensitizing frame of reference to use in answering the question: Who *has* the relevant information? These four dimensions help to see where the person fits into the social matrix and make some crude preliminary estimations of the person's opportunity to acquire the information we seek. There is no guarantee that a person will be *willing* to give information merely because he or she has it or is *able* to give it at the time of the interview. Let us now turn to the question of which type of respondent is the most willing and able to give relevant information in a valid way.

WHO IS ACCESSIBLE?

The problem of *accessibility* of respondents is often great. Although a respondent must be accessible in order to be interviewed, there is a danger that the most easily accessible respondent might not have the other qualifications. In public opinion polls and market research, for example, there is frequent danger of a systematic bias in the selection of respondents when quota sampling is used. For example, the interviewer who must obtain a quota of ten males between thirty and fifty years of age from a certain neighborhood might choose those who are conveniently near the subway station or other artery of transportation. Or the interviewer might select those who are most psychologically accessible in that they seem to be middle-class educated people who can "express themselves more clearly." Numerous studies indicate that the opinions of members of the articulate middle class often differ markedly on many subjects from those of people from other socioeconomic classes that will always appear in a strictly random sample of the population.

Respondents in the upper socioeconomic class are often difficult to reach. They are highly organized and feel no obligation to respond to the desires of a lower-status person. They may fear that information given might be used to their disadvantage; furthermore, they are suspicious of con men and burglars who might be disguised as interviewers. In this stratum of society sponsorship, recommendations, and introductions are extremely important. There are notable exceptions to this reluctance to be interviewed—for example, in cases when the mass media interview a person as an expert or as a philanthropist. This provides the respondent with an opportunity to both propagate a point of view and to strengthen a public image.

It is also difficult to obtain access to lower socioeconomic class respondents under certain conditions. For example, in ethnic-group neighborhoods of urban areas, the interviewer might be suspected of being a bill collector, a salesman, a detective, or truant officer. To complicate matters, some families live in tenement houses or apartments, and the interviewer has no opportunity to speak to the respondent face-to-face before being refused. When someone shouts down the stair well or speaking tube, "Who is it?" the interviewer can only hope that the door does not slam as he shouts back the shortest and most enticing version of his purpose.

WHO IS WILLING TO GIVE RELEVANT INFORMATION?

In dealing with this question we will assume that it is known who has the relevant information, and that those who have it are physically and socially accessible. It will also be assumed that the study requires special respondents, but that more than one of each type of special respondent are available.

The question then becomes that of how to select from among the *available* special respondents those that are most *willing* to give relevant information? A more refined version of this question is how to best circumvent the four inhibitors (competing obligations, ego-threat, etiquette, and trauma) which tend to make respondents less willing to give information?

Competing time demands. Often it is possible to reduce the pressure of competing obligations in the interview situation by choosing a lower-status person who may be able to provide the same information as a higher-status person. The lower-status person will feel more obligated to spend time in the interview.[8] In addition, certain facilitators of communication are more likely to be brought into play in an interview with a lower-status respondent. For example, it is more likely to be a release from boring routine, thus appealing to the need for new experience. Also, the lower-status person is more likely to feel he or she is gaining recognition in the experience.

It is possible in some circumstances to reduce the competing time demands by selecting a respondent who has large blocks of unoccupied time. If the same information regarding a teenage gang fight could be obtained either from firemen or drugstore employees who witnessed the event, it would be better to go to the firehouse than to the drugstore for an interview. Again, if equal information is possessed by a mother of five children or a retired senior citizen, the latter would feel fewer time pressures.

Interviews with senior citizens have shown that they are often very willing to be interviewed at length if their health permits. Zelan reports on a survey on the use of medical resources by 678 surviving veterans of the Spanish-American War.[9] When the interviewing was done, the youngest were in their late seventies; yet a response rate of 92 percent

---

[8]Lewis A. Dexter, "Goodwill of Important People: More on the Jeopardy of the Interview," *Public Opinion Quarterly* 28, no. 4 (Winter 1964), pp. 556–63. Some of the dangers of intruding upon the time and privacy of high-status persons are cited here.

[9]Joseph Zelan, "Interviewing the Aged," *Public Opinion Quarterly* 33 (1969), pp. 420–24.

was achieved. He suggests that anyone needing to study the aged population will find them very willing to talk, providing that they are in reasonably good health and the topic touches them personally.

When interviewing the aged, however, there are some possible disadvantages in using reports of their observations of events and people. For example, Bahs points out, in his study of homeless men, that those who consent to be interviewed are no more likely to be consciously untruthful in replying to questions than are members of any other disadvantaged population.[10] However, because they are aged and some drink excessively, they are somewhat disoriented and tend to be unable to answer questions which have any complexity. Thus, they are very willing, mainly because of a lack of competing time demands and a desire for sympathetic understanding, yet they are unable to answer complex questions or those which might involve chronological confusion or inferential confusion.

Ego threat. The ego-threat barrier can sometimes be reduced by the proper selection of respondents. The general principle is to find some person whose ego is not involved in the information sought. There are many kinds of information given much more freely by one person than by another who feels threatened by admitting the truth. The most obvious example is the choice between a respondent who actually perpetrated an act of which he is ashamed and a respondent who saw another commit the act, but is neither identified with the perpetrator nor afraid of any reprisals if he gives the information. This is a situation familiar to the legal profession, where the witness for the prosecution has less ego threat than the defendant.

Perhaps more familiar to the social scientist is the situation where one person reports information withheld by another because he or she does not realize the stigma attached. The person is not consciously "tattling," nor acting as a witness against the other, but merely giving a straightforward answer to a question. This is seen in cases where a child or youth tells the straight truth, while the adult, who realizes the implications, tries to alter or completely deny the facts. For example, in a study of teenagers' adjustment problems in school, the child is likely to admit having been suspended from school for three days. In contrast, the middle-class *mother*, who feels that the child's bad behavior is actually due to her own failure, is less likely to be truthful. Also, children are often more free in admitting sibling rivalry than are the parents.

This difference between the frankness of children and adults seems to be just one example of a general principle. The greater the responsibility a person assumes for some deviation from the public norms, the

---

[10]K. C. Bahs and K. C. Houts, "Can You Trust a Homeless Man?" *Public Opinion Quarterly* 35 (1971), pp. 374–82.

greater is the pressure to pretend that the actual behavior conforms with the norms.

Concrete examples will illustrate this principle. The public relations office of a college is more reluctant to admit any conflict between the administration and the faculty over academic freedom than is the student body president. Also, public school superintendents are less likely to admit their schools' basic problems in achieving high-quality education than are the young teachers. Similarly, the superintendent of a state mental hospital testified before a state legislature that there was adequate staff to give good care to the patients, an opinion which shocked the nonadministrative staff.

Unfortunately, there is sometimes a dilemma when the person who has the most accurate information will be the least likely to give it because of being most directly connected with the events being studied. This leads to the danger of depending upon more indirect sources of information. In these cases, strategies, tactics, and techniques other than selecting the nonthreatened respondent must be used.

There are circumstances where people in top power positions have valuable inside information that they are unwilling to give until they are ousted from the organization as renegades. Once they are out they no longer are subject to ego threat from the organization and many become very willing to talk. Sjoberg points out that these renegades from top power positions are often both very able and willing to give social scientists information, particularly regarding the decision-making processes ordinarily considered secret.[11]

Etiquette. In some cases, it is possible to avoid the etiquette barrier by selecting the appropriate respondent. The problem arises in situations where the interviewer is perceived by the respondent as a person who would be surprised, shocked, or chagrined by candid answers.

The etiquette barrier commonly appears when a person in a responsible position sincerely attempts to evaluate the human relations aspects of an organization by interviewing his or her own subordinates. If a junior executive in a large firm wants to evaluate a new employee-information program, he would wisely select respondents who do not know him as the designer of the program, since there would be a tendency for the respondents to avoid hurting his feelings by giving any negative impressions. If the information needed calls for representative respondents, this method of eliminating the etiquette barrier is not available. Instead, the *interviewer* must be carefully chosen to avoid selecting anyone who might be perceived by any of the respondents in the sample as having a vested interest in the program to be evaluated. In

---

[11]Gideon Sjoberg, "The Interviewee as a Marginal Man," *Southwest Social Science Quarterly* 38 (1967), pp. 124–32.

rare cases, the employees in the sample might fall into two or more distinct types requiring different types of interviewers to minimize the problem.

Often, the etiquette barrier is more effectively minimized if we are free to select the appropriate interviewer, rather than the respondent; but an administrator, or any authority, is often placed in a position where some knowledge is better than none and must proceed to gather it personally. In such situations, we cannot warn too strongly against the effects of the etiquette barrier. If it is necessary to minimize the etiquette barrier by selecting the best respondent, the interviewer must be intimately acquainted with the norms governing what can be politely communicated from whom to whom. Lack of this knowledge results in serious miscalculations.

Often such knowledge is not possessed at the outset, in which case it becomes part of the strategy phase to discover the relative validity of information coming through certain channels. This can frequently be done in a small pilot study where two or more categories of respondents are asked for the same factual information. The frequency with which the two groups mention events tending to discredit or embarrass the interviewer can be compared. It is also possible to compare written comments from a group of anonymous individuals with oral statements made by the same group to the interviewer. This difference for one category of respondents could be compared with that of another category of respondents.

In general, if a respondent is not inhibited by the etiquette barrier which would usually apply, it is because of one of the following reasons:

1. The respondent does not realize that the information he or she gives has a negative value in the eyes of the interviewer. Children are often immune to this type of inhibitor for this reason.

2. The respondent might be so in accord with the interviewer's effort to obtain accurate information that he or she will be candid although being truthful may be painful.

3. The respondent may have a desire to embarrass, belittle, or hurt the interviewer's ego and therefore welcomes the opportunity to elaborate upon all of the details which tend to threaten the interviewer. Although this might be a strain on the interviewer, it often has a cathartic effect, reducing the respondent's hostility toward the interviewer.

4. The respondent may have a relationship with the interviewer which permits such information to flow freely on the particular topic as long as the interviewer's questions are considered genuine, rather than rhetorical, and sincere, rather than designed to obtain a compliment.

Trauma. The trauma barrier is not so rare in interviewing as we might think. Of course it is rarely found in the opinion poll on current public issues or in the practical surveys made in most communities. However, certain interviewers, because of the problems with which they deal, frequently encounter the trauma barrier: these would include the police investigator of homicides and suicides, the coroner who holds inquests, the insurance investigator, the case worker attached to the family relations court, the industrial safety investigator, the minister, the Red Cross disaster worker, and the social scientist investigating such problems as causes of auto accidents, causes of suicide, or adjustments to mental illness in the family.

Often, the problem cannot be circumvented by selecting respondents because the person with the most direct knowledge of the crisis also had the most traumatic experience. But there are occasions when the interviewer can select a respondent with no traumatic experience to supply the relevant information. A police investigator of auto accidents needs facts such as the time of the accident or the number of passengers in the car which hit a child crossing the street while her mother watched from the curb. In this case, the investigator can choose between interviewing the mother or the two shopkeepers who were eyewitnesses.

It should not be assumed that merely because a respondent has had a traumatic experience he or she will refuse to report it or will stint on detail. This has been shown untrue in interviews with families who have just lost children in a disaster. In these cases it seemed that the respondent's altruism and needs for meaning, sympathetic understanding, and catharsis were stronger than the urge to repress the memory.

WHO IS MOST ABLE TO GIVE THE INFORMATION ACCURATELY?

Even though two people have the same experiences and are equally willing to report them, there may be a wide variation in the precision or efficiency of their reports. Having had the appropriate experiences does not guarantee the person's ability to report these experiences.

Forgetting. If the interview seeks information on events repeatedly experienced by many people, respondents who have experienced the event most recently can be selected in order to minimize the problem of stimulating the memory. Of course, if the event experienced is a rare one, we may need to wait for it to happen and be ready to interview people immediately while their feelings and images are fresh.

Assume we are studying the changes in family relationships resulting from the arrival of the first child. In an interview one year after the child's birth, it would be difficult to obtain an accurate and detailed picture of these subtle changes. It would be better to obtain from local hospitals a list of patients who have been discharged from the maternity ward long enough to have recovered physically, but who were still establishing their new family routine.

In addition to selecting respondents who have been most recently exposed to the experience, we can select those for whom the event was the most meaningful, problematical, ego-involved, or direct. For example, in studying childhood diseases of primary school children in the Puerto Rican district of New York, the information would be more accurately obtained from the mother than from the father, who feels strongly that raising babies is the mother's complete responsibility.

Chronological confusion. Since chronological confusion is partially a function of a fading memory, any method of selecting respondents which reduces the memory-fading process will also reduce the amount of chronological confusion. There are other safeguards in selecting respondents which can minimize chronological confusion.

First, we might cross-check chronological accuracy by selecting more than one person to give the same information. The two or more respondents selected should have participated in, or observed, the same situation. For some purposes, it may be more revealing to interview those whose observation or participation was completely independent of each other, and for other purposes, it is necessary to select people who interacted in the situation. In either case, the cross-checking of the respondents' stories will alert the interviewer to problems of chronological confusion. It is sometimes effective to have the two or more respondents discuss the event in a group interview. Whether the group interview should precede, follow, or replace individual interviews is decided in the specific setting.

Second, it may be possible to select a person whose role in the situation provides a special perspective for remembering details in chronological order. In an investigation of crowd reactions at an air show where a stunting airplane had crashed into the full grandstand, it was desirable to discover the precise chronology of events immediately preceding the crash. The one person capable of doing this was the master of ceremonies for the show. He was aware of the order in which events had originally been scheduled and the deviations from this order. Also, he could relate the informal, nonscheduled events to the scheduled events, thus establishing a complete chronology.

Inferential confusion. Any selection of respondents which reduces the fading of memory or chronological confusion is helpful in reducing distortion of the facts upon which inferences are to be based. This does not necessarily mean that the inferences made by the respondent will be logically correct.

Most of the solutions to inferential confusion lie in the areas of tactics and techniques; however, we may still reduce the interviewing problems by selecting the respondent who has the best understanding of the types of generalizations to be made, and has no strong prejudices on the topic to bias his or her logical processes.

Unconscious behavior. The reader will recall that we use *unconscious behavior* to refer only to actions that were automatic at the time they were performed rather than to memories of actions which, although accompanied by a high level of awareness when they were being performed, have been *repressed* into the unconscious because they would constitute a severe ego threat. This aspect of the unconscious has been subsumed under the inhibitor category of ego threat.

If the objective of the interview is to study some segment of human behavior which is experienced at a low level of consciousness, it is often impossible to obtain a valid account in retrospect, even though the behavior was very recent. For example, if we need to know which shoe a person put on first this morning, it is rare to find a person who is sure that his or her guess is correct later in the day.

It may be impossible to stimulate recall of certain behavior. A different approach is often more valid and practical. Instead of dealing with respondents' past behavior, we can select respondents who are about to undergo certain relevant experiences and will report them, or who can observe others carrying out the behavior in question.

The participant-respondent is asked to participate in the event or situation, observe his or her own behavior of which the participant-respondent is ordinarily unconscious, and then report it to the interviewer. This approach would be useful for describing such unconscious patterns of behavior as tying one's tie, doing a complicated dance routine, playing a musical instrument, or shaving with a safety razor.

When an observer-respondent is used, he or she is first given the problem and then sent to observe others' unconscious behavior. The best observer-respondent is one who makes interested, unbiased, acute observations, and who has access to the situation in which people indulge in the type of unconscious behavior being studied. The observer-respondent is needed only if the interviewer himself does not have access to the situation.

This approach is particularly useful in cases where the act of self-observation might change the pattern of behavior being observed or where self-consciousness might completely invalidate the information.

It would be invalid to ask a mother to observe her own behavior toward her two-year-old son to note how frequently she attempts to avert undesirable behavior of the child by physically removing some object of his attention rather than by first using a verbal command, request, or distraction. The mother, consciously posing this question to herself and observing her own behavior toward the child, might recognize her reliance on the physical method which became a habit before the child learned to speak. In this situation using an older sister as observer-respondent would probably yield more accurate information.

Thus far the problem has been in choosing the respondent to minimize the inhibitors which make him or her less willing or able to supply relevant information. The respondent was selected with regard to his or her relationship to both the relevant experiences and to the interviewer. Here, it was assumed that the interviewer-respondent relationship could be manipulated only by the selection of the respondent. In the next section, the assumption will be that the respondent is predetermined. In this situation, the relationship can be manipulated only by selecting from among possible interviewers or by the interviewer selecting the most appropriate role from his repertory.

DISCUSSION QUESTIONS

1. Would the most thought have to be given to the selection of representative respondents for a public opinion poll or to the selection of special respondents for a large-scale community study? Why?

2. What are some of the most important social-psychological forces that tend to make a person *unwilling* to give relevant information but that might be reduced by careful selection of respondents?

3. What are some of the most important social-psychological forces that tend to make a person *unable* to give relevant information but that might be reduced by careful selection of respondents?

4. Give one example of information which one person would be *able* to give but another would not.

5. Give one example of information which one person would be *willing* to give but another would not, despite the fact that both are able to do so.

LABORATORY PROBLEM 4

Selecting the Appropriate Respondent

This problem requires creative imagination (empathy) in applying principles of communication to this important phase of field strategy. You should imagine interview situations in which one main inhibitor can be either maximized or minimized by the selection of a good type or bad type of respondent, assuming the same interviewer in both cases. You should concentrate on the relationship between the type of information needed, the type of interviewer used, and the type of respondent most likely and least likely to give the needed information.

Give *three* examples of interviews, using the following format for describing each of the three situations. Assume that both respondents have the needed information but one is more willing or able to give it.

    a. The specific *question* to be asked.

    b. The type of *interviewer* used.

    c. The type of respondent *most* likely to give the information.

    d. The type of respondent *least* likely to give the information.

    e. The main *inhibitor* of communication operating between the respondent mentioned under (*d*) and the interviewer.

Here is one example. Note that there is no need to elaborate with detail.

    a. (Question) "What methods are used by building contractors to defraud the client?"

    b. (Interviewer) A newspaper reporter.

    c. (Best respondent) Clients who are suing contractors for failure to fulfill the specifications of the contract.

d. (Worst respondent) Building contractors who have never been involved in any complaints from clients.

e. (Inhibitor) Ego threat.

Be prepared to defend your examples in a class discussion by explaining why you would expect the particular inhibitor to be most important and why you would expect a different respondent to minimize it.

Chapter Nine

Selecting Appropriate Interviewers

It is fruitful to think of two phases of interviewer selection. First, we look for the most appropriate person for some portion or all of the information-gathering in a particular project. Second, we select a particular person who, from among the possible roles, can play the ones most suitable for specific phases of the project. Let us first examine the process of selecting the person.

SELECTING THE PERSON

The field supervisor, the self-directed research team, and the individual researcher must all be concerned with selecting the most suitable person as interviewer. The field supervisor may find some of the suggestions useful for hiring interviewers for a special project, for selecting from among the continuing staff of interviewers the one best suited for a particular project, or for deciding which ones might be most easily trained for certain types of studies.

When a new interviewing team is being organized, it is important that the members be selected for their information-gathering potential. When a study calls for contacting a wide variety of special respondents, it is often more effective to allow each member of the team to specialize in one or two types of special respondents with whom he or she has the most effective relationship.

The criteria suggested below are useful to sensitize the interviewer to some of his or her immutable characteristics such as sex, race, and physique, which limit the possible role relationships in the interviewer's repertory. This in turn restricts types of studies the interviewer personally should undertake and suggests the need for collaborators on certain aspects of information gathering.

Some of the suggested criteria will point to areas in which the interviewer must prepare himself before contacting the respondent. Specific knowledge of the interview topic or of the type of respondent and situation in which the respondent is to be contacted fall into this category. In addition, criteria such as the role repertory, attitudes, and situational skills will suggest a long-range program of personal development for the serious student of human behavior.

For this discussion, it will be assumed that skill in interviewing is possessed by all interviewers. Not all possible personal characteristics are considered relevant to selecting interviewers. The criteria will be limited to those having a *direct* bearing upon the problem of maximizing the flow of relevant information between respondent and interviewer. These criteria will be grouped under four headings: overt characteristics, basic personality traits, attitudes, and knowledge. These areas are all interrelated and are significant in that they affect the role repertory as it relates to the interviewing task.

It should be noted that the selection of an appropriate interviewer does not affect as many of the inhibitors as does the selection of an appropriate respondent. This is true because selection of the appropriate interviewer does not affect the respondent's *ability* to give the information, but only the respondent's *willingness* to do so. Although there are four inhibitors (competing obligations, ego threat, etiquette, and trauma) which generally reduce the willingness to give information, only two of these, ego threat and etiquette, are clearly influenced by the choice of an interviewer. In addition, it is possible to maximize three of the facilitators of communication (recognition, sympathetic understanding, and new experience) by choice of interviewer, quite independent of skill in interviewing techniques and tactics.

It is not enough to accurately assess the qualities of an interviewer; it is also necessary to know how these characteristics will be perceived and evaluated by the potential respondent. During the strategy phase, and within each subsequent interview, we should be alert for clues to the respondent's perceptions of the interviewer. It is often possible for the interviewer to make tactical corrections within an interview which will clarify his or her role or will correct misperceptions. If not, it is frequently possible to change the strategy of the approach toward future respondents or more effectively match interviewers with respondents.

It should be noted that the relative importance of the interviewer's overt physical characteristics is greater in single-contact than in multiple-contact field situations. These overt characteristics are also more significant in the scheduled than in the nonscheduled interview. The less structured the schedule, the more freedom the interviewer has in expressing basic personality traits.

In discussing the effects of certain characteristics of the interviewer on the flow of relevant information, we are using a shorthand expression for "probable effects in general" or "effects possible under certain conditions," or "tendencies which may or may not be counteracted by certain tactical and technical skills." We must assume intelligent and empathic use of these suggestions which, in specific situations, are to be treated as hypotheses checked by feedback from key informants, by observation of the respondent, and by analysis of the interview results.

Overt Characteristics of the Interviewer

Such characteristics as sex, age,[1] race,[2] ethnicity, social class,[3] manner of dress, and speech are important. Not only do they create an immediate impression and help determine whether or not the respondent will consent to be interviewed, but they also place certain limits upon the roles which the interviewer may successfully occupy. Many studies on interviewer bias have shown differences in the results when the interviewers vary in these overt characteristics. One of the most systematic studies has been done by Hyman and his associates at the National Opinion Research Center.[4]

In reading and evaluating the many studies done on interviewer bias, we often find apparently contradictory results. Often this is because there is no guiding theory to relate type of interviewer and type of respondent with the type of information to be obtained. Often, studies try to determine the effect, for example, of a "white collar" interviewer versus a "blue collar" interviewer in a random sample survey. The results are likely to be ambiguous since the random sample is composed of both white collar and blue collar respondents. Even if the effects were separated according to type of respondent, the effect would be different depending upon whether the topic of the interview were attitudes toward labor unions or preferences for types of shaving cream.

Here, we will try to show how the overt characteristics are meaningful only insofar as they affect the relationship between the interviewer and respondent, which in turn affects the potential barriers to communication.

---

[1]Mark Benney, David Riesman, and Shirley Star, "Age and Sex in the Interview," *American Journal of Sociology* 62 (September 1956), pp. 143–52.

[2]Aaron Bindman, "Interviewing in the Search for Truth," *Social Quarterly* 6, no. 3 (Summer 1965), pp. 281–88. This deals with the effects of using black versus white interviewers.

[3]Daniel Katz, "Do Interviewers Bias Poll Results?" *Public Opinion Quarterly* 6 (Summer 1942), pp. 248–68. This classic study compares the results of using white collar and working-class interviewers to obtain opinions on war and labor issues.

[4]Herbert Hyman et al., *Interviewing in Social Research* (Chicago: University of Chicago Press, 1975).

Sex. Selecting an interviewer of the proper sex can sometimes reduce the etiquette barrier. For example, male market research interviewers can obtain more spontaneous information about men's shaving habits than female interviewers. Likewise, female interviewers are more successful in obtaining information on feminine hygiene from women. The use of a female interviewer for a market research survey on shaving methods and materials would not be as serious a strategy error as using male interviewers on the feminine hygiene study.

The sex of the interviewer may also operate to increase the facilitators of communication. It would appeal much more to the need for *new experience* to use a male interviewer with respondents in a women's prison or to have a Wac interview soldiers in an isolated garrison post or to send a male interviewer to an electronics plant where 90 percent of the workers and supervisors are women.

Also, the sex of the interviewer may determine the extent to which the respondent will perceive the interviewer as a person capable of giving *sympathetic understanding* to certain problems covered by the interview. A female interviewer would probably be more welcome in interviewing mothers regarding the problems of the homemaker. A male interviewer would probably be perceived as more sympathetic in an interview with crane operators about their grievances.

In some cases, the sex of the interviewer is important not so much because of the effect it will have upon communication in the interview as upon the probability of even starting the interview. In single-contact interview studies in metropolitan areas, one of the large problems is gaining entrance to the home. For example, it is not rare for the male interviewer in an urban poverty area to notice someone peeking out the window as he comes up the sidewalk; then the radio is silenced and no one answers his knock. This may be because the occupants of the house think he is a bill collector, a truant officer, parole officer, or a salesman. Sometimes in areas which have had recent violent disturbances, whether man-made riots or natural disasters of some type, a male interviewer is mistaken for a newspaper reporter. All of these mistaken identities of the male interviewer usually present problems.

Age. The main social significance of a person's age is that it limits both the roles which the person can assume and the status the person has vis-à-vis another person. In general, an older person has higher status than a younger person when other visible signs are equal and when neither knows the other's function in society. The effects of status difference on communication will be discussed when we focus on the status dimension of the relationship.

Since age offers both possibilities and limits to the role repertory, the individual investigator may examine a typical life cycle of a person of the same sex in his or her culture and realize that at one time in life he or she will be a better interviewer on one set of topics; at another time he or she will excel on another. A high school student doing a study of family relations might find the etiquette barrier arising in the interview with parents regarding child-rearing problems. Yet the same high school student, with minimal skills in interviewing, could do an excellent job of interviewing students about "problem parents."

Often, it may be necessary to interview people in a very different age bracket because there are few interviewers among the age group being studied and the interest in the specific problem is not widely shared. The interviewer, by skillful tactics and techniques, can often overcome this initial disadvantage. For example, Krause found that as a graduate student, when she interviewed people over sixty years of age on problems of personal adjustment in old age, she had to exercise care to avoid conveying the feeling of superiority because of her higher education.[5] She learned to show by every word and gesture that she appreciated the wisdom they had gained with experience. They were quick to appreciate her sincere respect which they felt was rare in the younger generation. In effect, she had to escape the stereotype of university student and become a personal disciple of the respondent.

Race or ethnicity. Whether or not an interviewer who appears to be of a certain race or ethnic group is an appropriate interviewer depends upon the respondent's perception and evaluation of that group and the role the respondent feels appropriate for the interviewer to assume. Since this affects the status relationship between the interviewer and respondent, there is the possibility of the barriers of ego threat and etiquette inhibiting the flow of certain types of information.

For example, it might be a distinct advantage to be a black in studying nationalistic attitudes of Africans or attitudes of Indian students toward racial discrimination in the United States. On the other hand, in an industrial relations study, a white field worker might find it very difficult to obtain spontaneous information from black workers even after spending months in the plant.[6]

Racial differences between interviewer and respondent not only affect the respondent's attitude toward the interview but also the interviewer's attitudes and stereotypes of the respondent. The respondent who is a member of the minority race is quick to sense the stereotyping

---

[5]Luise Krause, "Problems of Interviewing Older People," in M.A. thesis, "Personal Adjustment in Old Age," (Department of Sociology, University of Chicago, 1950).

[6]Robert K. Bain, "The Researcher's Role: A Case Study," *Human Organization* 9 (Spring 1950), pp. 23–28.

by the interviewer. The respondent may resent it, conform to it, or both; but in any case, it will affect the flow of information.

There is the additional communication problem caused by differences in the universe of discourse. Racial or ethnic group cultures are quite distinct in some ways from the middle-class white cultures, and this difference impedes communication.

The effect of race of the interviewer and respondent depends, of course, upon the meaning of those particular racial differences within the culture in which the interview is taking place. The problem would be quite different in Hawaii, Brazil, and Arkansas. Only insofar as race is a symbol of role and status will it affect the flow of information in the interview. Whether this effect is positive or negative depends upon the meaning of race, in general, and its significance to the topic of the interview.

An example of clear experimental effects of the race of the interviewer is shown in two studies by Athey in which the white respondents scaled down their expressions regarding nonwhites for both the black and Asian interviewers in comparison with their remarks to white interviewers.[7]

One of the symptoms of the effect of the interviewer's race is in the respondent's reluctance to elaborate on responses with spontaneous detail. For example, Ledvinka did an experiment in which seventy-five black job-seekers were each interviewed by a white and a black interviewer in the natural course of their contact with the employment service.[8] On each of six different measures of language elaboration, the respondents elaborated more on their answers to the black interviewers. In a different cultural setting, Alers found that Indian respondents had a poor reaction to the *mestizo* interviewers who came to their village.[9] The basic attitude of the Indian was one of distrust.

We have already warned that no general statements can be made about what characteristics of the interviewer act as inhibitors of communication without also taking into consideration the *triadic* relationship between the interviewer, the respondent, and the topic of the interview in the context of the larger society. To illustrate, Schuman showed

---

[7]K. R. Athey, J. E. Coleman, A. P. Reitman, and J. Tang, "Two Experiments Showing the Effect of the Interviewer's Racial Background on Responses to Questionnaires Concerning Racial Issues," *Journal of Applied Psychology*, Spring 1960, pp. 244–46.

[8]James Ledvinka, "Race of Employment Interviewer and the Language Elaboration of Black Job-Seekers" (Ph.D. dissertation, University of Michigan, 1969).

[9]J. Oscar Alers, "Interviewer Effects on Survey Responses in an Andean Estate," *International Journal of Comparative Sociology* 11 (1970), pp. 208–19.

that the effect of the race of the interviewer depended upon the particular questions being asked.[10] His study using data from the Detroit Area Project showed that, when northern urban blacks were interviewed, questions dealing with militant protest and hostility to whites showed considerable sensitivity to interviewer effect; but the respondents' reports of racial discrimination, poor living conditions, and personal background showed little distortion due to the race of the interviewer. Similarly, an experiment done by Weller used three white and three black interviewers to interview twenty-eight black and twenty-seven white respondents who were applicants for job training.[11] All six interviewers were middle-class, college graduates, with the same rating on interviewing skills and with almost identical personality profiles as measured by the Minnesota Multiphasic Personality Inventory test. On the questions about family relations white interviewers obtained more high-quality responses from black respondents than did the black interviewers. However, the race of the interviewer made no difference in the quality of information obtained from the white respondents. Weller feels that this was because the black respondents felt more sure that the white interviewers would not use the information for gossip within the black community, while the white respondents could see no difference in the amount of anonymity afforded by a black versus a white interviewer.

Whether or not communication barriers can be overcome only by training interviewers better or by the selection of interviewers depends on the kind of information sought, and the kind of relationship which must be established between interviewer and respondent to obtain this information. In a review of the literature on the helping interview, Banks concludes that more attention needs to be turned to training black interviewers to help blacks rather than doing more studies of the black respondent, hoping to learn how to overcome his or her distrust and resistance.[12]

The problem of the effects of the race of the interviewer is much more complicated than often assumed by those doing oversimplified or underconceptualized studies of interviewer effects. For example, it should be clear at the outset that the effect of race depends upon the *meaning* which race has to the topic of the interview in the context of

[10]Howard Schuman and Jean Converse, "Effects of Black and White Interviewers on Black Responses in 1968," *Public Opinion Quarterly* 35 (1971), pp. 44–68.

[11]L. Weller and E. Luchterhand, "Interviewer-Respondent Interaction in Negro and White Family Life Research," *Human Organization* 27 (1968), pp. 50–55.

[12]G. P. Banks, "Effects of Race on One to One Helping Interviews," *Social Service Review* 45 (1971), pp. 137–46.

the larger society at a given moment in history. First, physical racial differences between interviewer and respondent must be translated into social-psychological relationships such as social distance, status differences, power differences, in-group–out-group relations, or anonymity. Then these relationships must be translated into potential inhibitors or facilitators of communication of a particular kind of information.

For example, a black respondent may feel free to air personal complaints about discrimination to the white interviewer who is sponsored by a white mayor clearly interested in eliminating discrimination. The interview becomes a means to recognition or the extrinsic reward of removing discrimination. At a later time the black respondent may not elaborate on discrimination to the white interviewer who is not sponsored by a new black mayor.

The respondent's *definition of the situation* determines whether the respondent would feel more free if the interviewer is like or different from him or her, whether the respondent prefers anonymity to avoid ego threat, or whether the respondent wants publicity to obtain recognition. As a reflection of these complications Dohrenwend found that under some circumstances there could be an inhibiting effect by either having too much or too little social distance between interviewer and respondent.[13]

At the present state of knowledge of the effect of race on the inhibitors and facilitators of communication in the interview situation, we can only say that—for certain topics under certain conditions—racial difference between interviewer and respondent sometimes has a negative effect on information flow, sometimes it makes no difference, and perhaps more rarely, sometimes it has a positive effect on the information flow. In the practical situation the decision must be made tentatively on the basis of translating what is known about the nature of the questions, the meaning of race in society at that time, and the respondent's probable definition of the situation. Often this tentative decision can be pretested in the field, using interviewers of different races, before going on with the larger study.

Speech. Our vocabulary, accent and diction can provide glaring signs of ethnicity, status and role. As such, they affect the flow of information in the interview. In some cases, an accent is sufficient to nullify the effect of obvious racial characteristics. Identical black twins born in England and speaking with a crisp British accent would encounter different reactions in a southern railroad station if one freely demonstrated his accent and wore a turban while the other said nothing to betray his accent.

[13]Barbara S. Dohrenwend et al., "Social Distance and Interviewer Effects," *Public Opinion Quarterly* 32 (1968), pp. 410–22.

This is further demonstrated by the experience of a white graduate student studying at the University of Chicago who was doing his master's thesis on a black Muslim cult hostile to white Americans. Upon first contact with the group, the researcher was trying to locate their meeting place in the basement of a vacant building. There he was caught by surprise, frisked, and taken to their leader who explained that the "snooper" was fortunate to have a foreign accent or they would have dealt with him more harshly. Upon discovering that the student was from Baghdad and was a wrestler, they invited him to teach in their "college," which he did for a few months while writing his thesis on the development of the movement.[14]

Dress and grooming. These factors of appearance are symbolic of social status and role as well as of the subculture to which a person belongs. The more superficial the contact with the respondent and the stronger the solidarity of the respondent's "in-group," the more important the effect of dress and grooming. Part of the strategy phase of a field study must sometimes include getting information on the most appropriate way to dress. However, it is usually not possible, practical, or ethical to try to pass oneself off as a full-fledged member of the group being studied. Nor is this usually necessary, although it is often advisable to prevent the interviewer's being falsely perceived as an outsider in a threatening role.

For example, a person studying the activities of teenage gangs in a city's high delinquency area might give the impression that he is a detective by wearing black shoes. Or, if he carries a briefcase, he might be suspected of being a bill collector. Without trying to impersonate the members of the respondent's group, the interviewer must discover how to dress to prevent mistaken identity. In addition, it is possible to reduce the social distance between the interviewer and respondent by dressing more nearly like the respondent without trying to imitate him. A person studying the problems of controlling migrant children from farm areas in an urban neighborhood might do well to dress like the local graduates of the junior college rather than like an Ivy Leaguer.

Physical deviance. There are many settings requiring interviews with persons physically handicapped or otherwise deviant from the normal. Very little research has been done on the effects of using normal versus physically deviant interviewers. An experiment was done by Comer and Piliavin in which handicapped men in wheelchairs and leg braces were interviewed by the same interviewer posing as handicapped

---

[14]This account was given by Hatim Sahib, now returned to Baghdad, in a personal conversation with the author.

(in wheelchair and leg brace) for half of the respondents and as his normal self in the other half of the interviews.[15] The topic of the interview in this case was one which allowed for much elaboration and free-association by the respondent. The questions ranged from "Tell me about yourself," to "What do you think about the importance of sports, religion, money, women, etc., in a person's life?" In those cases where he appeared as his normal self, the interviews were terminated sooner, the respondent showed greater motor inhibitions, smiled less, had less eye contact with the interviewer, and admitted feeling less comfortable during the interview. Since the same interviewer was used none of the differences in response to him could be attributed to any of his personality traits.

To what extent can we generalize to other types of deviants? Should those who interview criminals be criminals? Should only homosexuals interview homosexuals? The general approach to the answer to these questions is the same as to those regarding the effect of race of the interviewer. We must judge each case on its own merits, but the specific facts of the situation must be ultimately translated into the same set of social-psychological variables we have mentioned earlier.

Basic Personality Traits of the Interviewer

An excellent interviewer need not conform to the popular image of a pleasing personality. The sparkling personality is sometimes a valuable asset in making the initial contact or getting in the door, but the same qualities might interfere with communication by stealing attention from the respondent.

Basic personality traits are relevant only insofar as they help or hinder the performance of the interview. Three important assets would include flexibility, intelligence, and emotional security. Flexibility allows the interviewer to assume a very active role when it is called for and to assume a more overtly passive role when this will facilitate communication. Intelligence permits the interviewer to clearly appreciate the objectives of the interview, to learn to evaluate critically the information that is received, to remember what information has been given, and to probe for greater clarity and completeness. Emotional security frees the interviewer from personal anxiety and allows the interviewer to direct full attention toward the tasks of maximizing the flow of information and maintaining optimal interpersonal relations.

---

[15]Ronald J. Comer and Jane A. Piliavin, "The Effects of Physical Deviance upon Face-to-Face Interaction," *Journal of Personality and Social Psychology* 23 (1972), pp. 33–39.

The absence of flexibility severely limits the interviewer. Some personalities find it impossible to slow down the pace of an interview, allow relatively long silences, and permit the respondent to say what he or she wishes when he or she wishes. For this type of person, silence is intolerable; it is a vacuum which must be filled at any cost. This type of interviewer panics when the respondent does not immediately respond in an appropriate manner. This type of interviewer tends to dominate the situation in a way which threatens the respondent's ego. He or she does not build a permissive and thoughtful mood, and frequently distorts the information unknowingly by suggesting answers.

Some interviewers tend to be rigidly passive. This type of person does well as long as the task calls for letting the respondent take the lead, but he or she can be easily lured into irrelevant bypaths or sociable conversation when this is neither necessary nor desirable. The passive interviewer is reluctant to assume an active role by holding the respondent to the topic, to evaluate critically the information received and to probe for completeness and clarification.

The importance of sufficient intelligence to the tasks of eliciting the information, evaluating it in terms of interview objectives, and probing for clarity and completeness is obvious. This does not imply that any intelligent person will carry out these tasks efficiently at the first attempt. Rather, any person must have the basic ability to learn once the task is clear and must have the opportunity to practice.

The interviewer's emotional insecurity could have several detrimental manifestations in the interview. The interviewer may display a compulsive urge to dominate and may challenge remarks unnecessarily. In some cases, the challenging response is compulsive and unconscious. The insecure person is often so anxious that he or she (a) fails to observe the respondent's emotional needs, (b) communicates insecurity to the respondent rather than a positive expectation of cooperation, (c) may be unable to empathize with the respondent at crucial points in the interview, (d) cannot communicate warmth which leads the respondent to reach for sympathetic understanding and perhaps cathartic communication which might bring relevant information; and (e) is incapable of giving sincere praise to the respondent for his or her efforts or performance.

This is not to suggest that anyone having personal insecurities will always manifest them in these detrimental ways, nor does it necessarily indicate that any person who commits any of these errors is a hopeless victim of personal insecurity. As a neophyte interviewer, any conscientious person is likely to be doubtful, self-conscious, and anxious. An experienced interviewer may feel the same way about the first few interviews of a new study. Before the interviewer can devote full attention to the respondent's needs, he or she must take care of personal anxieties which arise in a new situation or with a new study.

Some people show these symptoms of insecurity only in certain types of interviews. Often, the distinguishing factor is the status relationship between the interviewer and the respondent. Some find it very easy to interview people of lower status, but if a respondent tends to assume an equalitarian relationship, the interviewer finds it intolerable. Some find that they cannot interview anyone who is not a peer, while others function most adequately in a subordinate role such as student or seeker of advice.

Ideally, the interviewer should have a flexible personality, free of defense mechanisms which limit the interviewer's sensitivity to the respondent or ability to shift roles as the situation requires. If the well-rounded interviewer cannot be found, we should as least recognize the limitations and avoid assignments which demand behavior of which a particular person is not capable.

Much personal insecurity can be controlled to suppress detrimental manifestations. The best prescription is to master some of the basic interviewing techniques, tactics, and skills and to prepare thoroughly for a particular interview by being completely familiar with its purpose, by planning some tentative alternative tactics, and practicing whatever recording techniques are to be used.

Attitudes of the Interviewer

Since the positive attitudes intentionally displayed by the interviewer will be discussed later, this section will focus on only those uncontrollable negative attitudes which can be eliminated only by selecting the appropriate interviewer. These attitudes may be negative toward the type of respondent from whom the information must be obtained, toward the topic of the interview, or toward some particular information given by the respondent.

To speak of selecting an interviewer devoid of such negative attitudes does not imply that one must be completely free of such attitudes to be effective. Nor should it be said that training of the interviewer does not help overcome these attitudes, or at least teach how to avoid displaying them so that they affect the interview. Whether we depend upon selection or training depends upon the availability of interviewers, the time available for training, the strength of the negative attitudes, the delicacy of the interview topic, and the degree to which the interview is scheduled.

Here the intent is not to quantify these factors but to give some examples of their symptoms and the direction of their effects. Often a strong attitude toward a certain type of respondent is accompanied by strong stereotypes. The attitude may be toward certain religious, racial, occupational, ethnic, educational, or political groups. Leighton found that some research workers in the Japanese relocation centers were unable to lose their stereotypes of Japanese even after living in the center for months.[16] This stereotype acts as a barrier to communication, since it represents a form of insensitivity to individual differences which prevents the interviewer from adjusting his or her behavior to that of the respondent.

In training social scientists for field work in mental hospitals, high delinquency areas, and foreign cultures, the author has often found fear, suspicion, or a feeling of superiority toward the respondent. Even though these feelings may be controlled to the point of not being manifested to the respondent, nevertheless they may have an effect upon the interview.

The interviewer's attitude may be so strong that it is perceived by the respondent and brings ego threat or etiquette into play, inhibiting the response. The attitude toward the respondent may cause the interviewer to use loaded questions in a way which biases responses.

Even if the interviewer suppresses all visible manifestations of his or her attitude so that it is not perceived by the respondent, there are three important ways in which the interviewer's attitude still may minimize the flow of relevant information. (1) The interviewer's effort to control his or her negative attitude may succeed at the price of failing to manifest the positive attitudes of recognition, appreciation, sympathetic understanding, and the expectation of cooperation. Thus, some of the most important facilitators of communication are neglected. (2) The interviewer may attempt to exude a warmth which deceives the respondent, but still fails to empathize with the respondent enough to probe points important to both the respondent and the objectives of the interview. (3) When the completely structured interview prevents the interviewer from using loaded questions, when the interviewer is experienced enough to avoid letting personal attitudes show in the interview, and when the respondent actually gives ample relevant information, there is still the possibility that the interviewer will bias the result in taking notes on the respondent's replies.

An excellent experimentally controlled study done by Fisher shows that the interviewers with strong political attitudes did not accurately record the responses and that the direction of the error was consistent with the direction of the interviewer's political attitudes.[17] This bias in the recording phase of the interview is most likely to occur when the interviewer is attempting to take verbatim notes on responses to broad questions and the respondent is speaking too rapidly to allow the interviewer to actually write everything.

---

[16]Alexander Leighton, *The Governing of Men* (Princeton, N.J.: Princeton University Press, 1968).

[17]Herbert Fisher, "Interviewer Bias in the Recording Operation," *International Journal of Opinion and Attitude Research* 4 (Spring 1950), p. 393.

The negative attitude toward the topic of the interview need not be in the form of taking sides in a controversial issue. Just as common is the apologetic attitude which seems to say, "I'm sorry to ask such questions. I'm not sure I have the right to expect you to answer them." This communicates the expectation of failure and may stimulate precisely the anticipated reaction. Such an apologetic attitude would have scuttled studies such as the Kinsey report[18] or Becker's study of marijuana users.[19]

Certain types of negative attitudes can be overcome even if they have not been eliminated by the careful selection of interviewers. It has been shown that often interviewers have certain negative expectations about the prospective respondents which are simply not true. It is possible during a short training and orientation period to reduce or eliminate these attitudes. This was shown experimentally by Kumar, who told interviewers in advance whether the respondent was a friendly or a hostile type of person.[20] The interviewers gave an account of each respondent after the interview. These accounts showed that respondents who had been described as hostile appeared to be more hostile than they were, and those described as friendly appeared more friendly than they actually were. This difference can be partly because the interviewer's expectations actually affect the respondent's behavior or affect the interviewer's selective recording or memory of the responses.

Some effective ways to overcome an interviewer's false expectations of resistance are to have the interviewer hear tape-recorded interviews of the type that is going to be done, talk with interviewers who have had a lot of experience in the type of interview, or have the trainee go with an experienced interviewer to listen and take notes. Depending on the topic, the last of these three ways may have some inhibiting effects.

Special Knowledge Possessed by the Interviewer

Special knowledge refers to specialized information or skills needed by the interviewer in order to gain access to the situation where the respondent can be interviewed, to gain the respect of the respondent, or to understand the topic of the interview. This special knowledge often goes beyond any superficial knowledge or skills which can be gained by the interviewer for the occasion. For example, Howard Becker's study of the jazz musician would not be as thorough and insightful if Becker had

[18]Alfred C. Kinsey et al., *Sexual Behavior in the Human Male* (Philadelphia: W. B. Saunders Co., 1948).

[19]Howard S. Becker, "Becoming a Marijuana User," *American Journal of Sociology* 59 (July 1953 and May 1954).

[20]Usha Kumar, "Client and Counselor Responses to Prior Counseling Expectancies" (Ph.D. dissertation, Ohio State University, 1965).

not played in dance bands at the time.[21] Again, Hatim Sahib's study of the black Muslim sect was greatly facilitated by his knowledge of the Koran and of Arabic as well as by his skill in wrestling and his ability to teach Iraqi cooking.

Not only does special knowledge act as a key to gathering information through sustained contact with the respondents, but it also is needed for certain types of single-contact interviews. For example, in a study of the performance of state police in a local crisis, the interviewer should have considerable knowledge of the usual function, organization, and jurisdiction of the police. To understand their accounts of their activities during the crisis, the interviewer should also be familiar with the local geography and relevant locations such as police headquarters, the radio transmitter, and the highway system.

Regardless of whether he or she has one or many contacts with the interviewer, the respondent often judges the interviewer not on the basis of his or her skill in interviewing, but on the basis of his or her knowledge and interest in those subjects in which the respondent is an expert. Where continued contact is needed in a participant-observer field study, the interviewer who can show competence in an area which is understood and respected by the community has an advantage.

Sometimes it is practical for the interviewer to acquire the special knowledge needed for a specific assignment. At other times, the topic is so technical and complex that it would be more practical to select a person who is already a specialist in the area. For example, to discover some of the problems of coordinating a team of researchers, it would seem advisable to use a social scientist who has had previous experience in team research. To discover some of the problems of the adjustment of American students in Latin America, the interviewer would need to be familiar with the Latin American culture and the Spanish language.

When doing a study of international organizations, Miles wrote a research note intended for graduate students and others without previous field experience in studying international organizations.[22] In giving suggestions about how to interview, he points out that one important factor is the interviewer's knowledge of the *organizational subculture*. International organizations develop a subculture that is not the same as that of any one of the nations represented. The knowledge of the organizational structure, the power hierarchy, the universe of discourse, all act as a cultural context needed to determine the meaning of what the researcher sees and hears.

---

[21]Howard P. Becker, *The Professional Dance Musician in Chicago* (M.A. thesis, Department of Sociology, University of Chicago, 1949).

[22]E. Miles, "The Logistics of Interviewing in International Organizations," *International Organization* 24 (1970), pp. 361–70.

Special knowledge, then, helps the interviewer gain access to the respondent *in situ*, helps the interviewer understand the respondent who refers to local detailed information, provides him or her with the universe of discourse needed, and gives the respondent respect for and confidence in the interviewer. If the interviewer shows that he has not bothered to familiarize himself with needed special knowledge, it may be difficult to persuade the respondent to devote serious time and effort to the project.

SELECTING THE APPROPRIATE INTERVIEWER ROLE

Role is probably the most important characteristic of the interviewer. All other characteristics (such as sex, age, race, speech pattern, basic personality traits, knowledge, and attitudes) gain some portion of their significance from the fact that they all create opportunities or limitations for the role behavior of the interviewer.

The Nature of Role-Taking

Selecting the proper role for the interviewer to assume might involve selecting the appropriate interviewer, or the interviewer might need to select from among his or her role repertory the one or ones most appropriate for the task at hand. Role-taking is distinct from role-playing. The former refers to selecting from among a person's actual roles those which are most appropriate to display under the circumstances; the latter refers to taking a role which the person has never assumed in real life or which he or she is assuming in an artificial situation. Role-playing is done in psychodramas, sociodramas, and ordinary dramatic productions and games. Role-taking is done in everyday life, usually quite unconsciously. The minister in the pulpit does not usually choose to behave in the role of a father or a husband. Within his minister role he may choose to display certain aspects or to withhold them; he may act as a Christian, as a Protestant, as a mentor, or as a chastiser.

Role-taking should not be confused with an unethical form of deceptive playacting, a childish game of cops and robbers, or a romantic cloak-and-dagger operation. In interviewing, role-taking is a conscious selection, from among one's actual role repertory, of the role thought most appropriate to display to a particular respondent at the moment.[23] Most of us have no occasion to take an inventory of the roles we play, but when we do the number is usually much larger than expected. For example, a woman who is a lawyer may have only one professional role

---

[23]It should be noted that in discussing the role repertory of the interviewer we are concerned with auxiliary roles peripheral to the *central* interviewer role.

but many auxiliary roles that might be helpful to display on different occasions. Some of these auxiliary roles might be sibling, daughter, wife, mother, neighbor, taxpayer, consumer, voter, student, client, patient, card player, employee, tourist, foreigner, adviser, writer, musician, swimmer, subscriber, contributor, driver, bicyclist, or pedestrian. She would probably have many others.

Functions of the Auxiliary Role

All of these roles constitute the role repertory from which one or more may be selected as auxiliaries to the principal role of interviewer. For example, the Fund for the Republic sponsored a study of the state of academic freedom on the campuses of American colleges. Of the sample of 180 colleges, 20 had refused to allow interviewers on campus to interview the social science faculty. One interviewer was assigned to visit some of the 20 reluctant colleges to try to convince the president to change his mind and to interview faculty members and students to discover what, if anything, the college was hiding. Which of his many roles should the interviewer display to which respondents on the college campus? He could, in honesty, present himself as "a representative of the Fund for the Republic," "a consultant hired by Elmo Roper Associates," "a college professor interested in theoretical problems of social conflict," "a sociologist," "a grandson of a Presbyterian minister," "a specialist in interviewing methods"—these roles and many others would be equally true.

Actually, many of these selections from the role repertory proved valuable at certain times with certain respondents. In contacting a sociology professor, it was helpful for the interviewer to mention that he, too, was a sociology professor working as a consultant for the Fund for the Republic. In dealing with the President at one college, it proved an asset for the interviewer to be the grandson of a Presbyterian minister, since the President was a Presbyterian minister himself. In no case did it seem advisable to be presented as "a specialist in interviewing methods," since this would probably cause some ego threat. Even the role of bicyclist was useful in breaking the ice with one professor when the interviewer commented that he, too, rode a bicycle to work if the weather permitted.

The respondent often wants to know "What kind of person is this who is asking the questions?" In a study of family relations, the respondent is relieved to know that the interviewer is not a bachelor but married and the father of two children. Even though this does not necessarily qualify the interviewer to understand the particular respondent's problems, that respondent is less inhibited by the etiquette barrier than if he or she perceived the interviewer as a bachelor.

A field situation may require the interviewer to actually *function* in an auxiliary role for the duration of the study, rather than merely presenting himself as a person who has a role other than interviewer. The interviewer may choose to function in an auxiliary role in order to gain access to respondents in a certain situation. For example, a researcher studying the professionalization process in a group of occupational therapists might work with several occupational therapists in the hospital in order to discuss their work *in situ*. Or instead of interviewing the occupational therapist as he or she works in the hospital, the interviewer might have formal interview sessions after working hours in the respondent's home. In the latter case, the interviewer's work in the hospital one or two days per week would have several useful functions. It would acquaint the interviewer with the universe of discourse of the hospital setting, clarifying communication in the interview. Furthermore, the interviewer would be more capable of sympathetic understanding. The etiquette barrier would be reduced, since the interviewer now would be considered more of an equal, and this greater equality would usually reduce the ego threat. Also, if the interviewer carefully arranged his or her working hours in order to actually reduce someone's work load, this might be an effective extrinsic reward to the respondents or their supervisors and make the interviewer's continued presence more welcome.

In general, when taking an auxiliary role, it is advisable to make it clear from the beginning that the main purpose is to study the situation and that the auxiliary role is a way of gaining a more intimate and sympathetic view. Often the key informants in a closed community and prospective respondents are favorably impressed by the interviewer who will take the assignment seriously enough to get his or her hands dirty in the situation. This is something perceived as a form of recognition and often reduces the respondent's defenses against an "ivory-tower" approach to problems.

Approaches to Role Selection

There are three basic ways in which an auxiliary role may be selected and brought into play. First, the interviewer may choose from among his or her own repertory of real roles the one most appropriate to use in view of the purpose of the study and the type of respondent. One uses a role or brings it into play by what one tells the respondent about himself, by mentioning other people, places or events connected with this role, by displaying knowledge or skills connected with the role, by vocabulary and manner of speech, as well as by dress, grooming, and manner. In this whole approach there is no contrived acting. It is a matter of displaying only part of oneself as is usually done automatically and unconsciously in everyday social life. The difference is that the role displayed is an auxiliary role in addition to the central role of interviewer, and the role selected must be in harmony with the objectives of the interview.

Second, the interviewer can actually take on a new role that is not included in the background repertory. Again, this role, although new, is not a matter of contrived acting but a real functional role. For example, a sociologist wanting to understand the union member's attitude toward management may take a real job on the production line in an automobile factory. In this case he or she may never have been a factory worker before but for the duration of the study must assume all of the responsibilities, rights, and duties of the other factory workers. This might restrict the interviewing to coffee breaks, lunchtime and after work; but the role offers opportunities for direct observation of individual behavior and for understanding the scene making up the background of the workers' daily life, thereby making the interviews more understandable and the probing more effective.

Third, the interviewer may intentionally create an impression that he or she has a role when it is not true. For example, a researcher might want to understand the effects of the everyday interaction in a mental hospital on the state of the patients. To do this he or she could arrange to be admitted to the hospital as a patient in such a way that none of the staff would know that the new "patient" was actually doing research and was not mentally ill. This strategy would provide the interviewer with access to the other patients on the ward as well as to the staff members coming into daily contact with those patients. Also, it would provide a rare opportunity to record systematically how the staff members treat the interviewer they believe to be a patient. With similar purposes white researchers have dyed their skin black to obtain firsthand experience with the differences between the way whites treat whites versus the way they treat blacks in a given situation. Similarly, researchers have been admitted to prison to study prison life; they have joined social movements, religious sects, gone to massage parlors, or frequented places of homosexual encounters.

Some researchers take the position that it is always unethical to *pose* as something you are not regardless of the purpose. Others feel that if it adds to scientific knowledge without doing harm to the people being studied it is justifiable. The author, along with many other social scientists, takes the position that "posing" or creating impressions or letting people jump to the wrong conclusions is not always ethically wrong, nor is it always ethically defensible, but that we must carefully examine every case, taking into consideration all of the factors mentioned in Chapter 4, The Ethics of Interviewing. If social science is to make progress in finding solutions to contemporary and future social problems, such ethical questions will continue to arise. In resolving these ethical issues we must be careful not to assume that a research strategy is unethical anytime it proves to be physically dangerous, personally uncomfortable, or socially unpopular. Such an egocentric interpretation of ethics appears to the author to be quite unethical since it takes into consideration neither the short-run benefits to those being studied nor the long-run benefits to society in general.

Of the three approaches to role selection, it is clear that this third way, posing or creating false impressions, is the most controversial. However, it can often be avoided by more creative effort in locating, selecting and training for special projects interviewers who have the appropriate natural roles. Another alternative is to gain the cooperation of people who are already members of the groups, organizations, or communities being studied and to obtain the information needed indirectly through them.

Dimensions of Role Relationships

Rather than attempting to show the relative values of an almost endless list of specific roles to be taken by interviewers, it is more useful to deal with two salient dimensions of role relationships. The significance of the interviewer's central role as interviewer and his or her auxiliary roles lies in the *relationship* generated with the respondent. Two of the most important dimensions of the relationship may be conceived of as the horizontal, or in-group–out-group, relationship and the vertical, or subordinate-superordinate, dimension.

The effect of the interviewer's presenting himself as a physician cannot be predicted unless we know whether the respondent is, for example, another physician or a nurse. The difference is these two pairs can be expressed in terms of relative status. The physician-physician relationship is one of equality. The physician-nurse relationship is one in which the physician is superordinate. To view these same relationships in the in-group–out-group dimension would require additional information. For example, the physician-physician pair would be furthest toward the in-group end of the continuum if both were members of the American Medical Association, lived in the same town, and constituted a clinical team. They would tend to view each other as outsiders, however, if one were a physician from the Soviet Union wanting to practice in the United States, or if one had lost his license through malpractice.

In many instances, it may appear that two people have an in-group relationship *because* they are of equal status. Upper-class people may welcome other upper-class people into their homes, but will erect barriers to keep lower-status people at a distance. On the other hand, there are instances where two people have an out-group relationship because they are of equal status. This is often true in competitive situations where there is conflict between equals. If the chief body designer for X Motor Company were sent to interview the chief body designer of Y

Motor Company, the interviewer would be treated politely perhaps, but would be suspected of spying.

These two basic dimensions of role relationships can either inhibit or facilitate the flow of various types of information.

In-group–out-group relationships. There are advantages and disadvantages to either type of relationship. Which is more desirable depends upon the type of information needed. In some cases, we need information from both vantage points and must use two interviewers to obtain complete results. Since the outsider role is often the easiest for the interviewer to attain, it is valuable to begin by indicating some of its advantages.

Advantages of the outsider role. The outsider has the advantage when seeking information on violations of the in-group code. Here, the outsider, not bound by these codes and with no power or desire to enforce them upon the respondent, has an advantage over the insider. The interviewer is not an ego threat to the respondent. Thus, a criminal would more willingly admit to a sociologist than to a member of the underworld that he once squealed on a partner to reduce his own sentence. In another situation, members of a teenage gang admitted to an interviewer that they had never been to a prostitute, but this fact was never admitted to the other members of the gang who would have considered it a sign of inferiority.

This tendency to make one's verbal behavior conform to the perception of the group norms has been experimentally demonstrated in several settings. For example, the author demonstrated that when the interviewer asked members of a group for their opinions on the Soviet Union, they tended to compromise their private attitudes to conform with what they perceived to be the group norms with respect to the Soviet Union.[24]

Another general circumstance in which the outsider has the advantage is in obtaining information on methods of manipulative control used by those in power to keep subordinates in line. Anthropologists have found that adults of one tribe will give totemic secrets to neighboring tribes, but not to their own children.[25] Similarly, it was found that ministers gave information on how they manipulated their congregations by interpreting and reinterpreting scripture, yet they vehemently denied any such purposive manipulation in a men's club discussion of

[24]Raymond L. Gorden, "Interaction Between Attitude and the Definition of the Situation in the Expression of Opinion," *American Sociological Review* 17, no. 1 (Spring 1952), pp. 50–58.

[25]Marcel Griaule, "L'enquette Orale en Ethnologie," *Revue Philosophique de la France* 142 (October 1952), pp. 537–53.

the minister's role in the church. To give such information to the in-group in which he has status would constitute an ego threat to the minister.

The outsider again has the advantage over an insider when the group is looking outward for some type of assistance. This is often experienced by social workers. The outsider in this case has some potential extrinsic reward to offer.

Often, the outsider does not have the disadvantage of facing the etiquette barrier which exists between certain in-group members. For example, a sociologist whom the respondents have never seen before can obtain detailed information of the premarital sex lives of a husband and wife which they have never discussed with one another because it was considered in bad taste.

Another valuable function of the outsider role is to evaluate the effectiveness of social-psychological experiments requiring the manipulation or control of the subjects' definition of the situation. The experimenter often tries to set up the experiment to control the participants' perception of the purpose of the experiment, but he does not always know when he has succeeded. Altemeyer tested the relative value of having the experimenter or an outsider interview to find out.[26] He set up the experiment making it obvious that the respondents were not supposed to know the purpose of the experiment. One of the researchers then "leaked" information about the "real purpose." The experimenter and an outsider both did postexperiment interviews. None of the subjects interviewed by the experimenter admitted that they had been given information about the purpose of the experiment, while 50 percent of those interviewed by an outsider admitted that they had been given information. This illustrates the general principle that giving certain types of information to an insider may constitute more of an ego threat or etiquette barrier than giving it to someone from outside.

The outsider may also have a certain advantage in that the respondent's need for new experience can be fulfilled by talking to an outsider. Anthropologists, sociologists, public opinion pollers, and social workers all have moments when they feel that the respondent is more curious about them than they are about the respondent. The respondent may waver between excited curiosity and apprehension. When a later maturity study was done in a deteriorating apartment-house area of Chicago, a charming old lady of eighty years shyly admitted to the interviewer, "I saw you talking to Mrs. Podolsky and I was curious about what you were talking about, but I don't think I would have let you in if you weren't talking to a friend of mine."

---

[26]Robert Altemeyer, "Pool Pollutions and the Post Experimental Interview," *Journal of Experimental Research in Personality* 5 (1971), pp. 79–84.

Often a respondent will perceive the interview as means of getting recognition. He or she may not be appreciated at home, at the office, or in the community. Or it may be that the respondent has already told all his or her friends, neighbors, and coworkers about certain highlights of his or her life. In this case, if the interviewer is interested in obtaining a life history the respondent will welcome the chance to have the complete attention of another human being. Such an opportunity to talk about oneself is rare indeed. An insider who already knows certain public facts and perhaps more intimate aspects of the respondent's life has little reason to ask the respondent to "begin at the beginning and tell me everything you feel is significant in your life."

In some circumstances, a strong in-group feeling is developed in a group of people who have suffered together some catastrophe, hardship, or persecution. This common experience is the badge of membership for the in-group. In this case, there is no possibility of an outsider's becoming a full-fledged member of the group unless he or she too has shared the same experience. If the interviewer has not had the experience, it is sometimes harmful to rapport for the interviewer to pretend to appreciate the respondent's experience. In this case, the interviewer's approach should be as a sympathetic outsider.

For example, in interviews with respondents who had experienced a community-wide disaster, resentment could be detected in the respondent's manner if the interviewer pretended to fully appreciate the horrors of the experience. It proved a better tactic if the interviewer admitted to being an outsider striving to catch a glimpse of what it was like to live through a devastating tornado. When a respondent told her listener, "You have no idea how horrible it was. The only way to know is to go through it yourself," the interviewer's best response was that of a sincere and concerned outsider, shown in his reply, "Yes, I've never been through anything like that in my life. I'm sure I can't begin to really grasp what it was like. I can only hope to learn through someone who has lived through such an experience. What would you say kept you going through all this?"

In this kind of situation the interviewer who takes the humble approach has a distinct advantage over the insider, because those who have shared the experience feel little reason to talk about their misfortunes to someone who has been equally unfortunate. The respondent seems to feel that he or she has more of a right to demand sympathy from the outsider.

In some instances, respondents of an in-group welcome the outsider, hoping to fulfill their need for meaning by raising meaningful questions, by clarifying confusion, by settling a controversy, or by sharpening the issue. The outsider is more trusted than the insider, who is suspected of taking sides if the group has been polarized, or who is considered too close to the problem to have the required perspective. It is often difficult for the outsider to maintain this advantage for a long period of time because the insider may expect the outsider to understand, to see the light, and to take the "right" side in the issue. For this reason it may be necessary to replace an outsider with a new outsider after a period of time if additional information is required. Even in situations where the respondents belong to a closely knit in-group, suspicious toward all outsiders, there are still certain kinds of information which can be obtained by the outsider. He or she may discover the official line given to the outsider, the extent to which the group is interested in recruiting or proselytizing others, and the in-group's fears and stereotypes of the outside world.

Advantages of the insider role. With all the advantages of the outsider role, there are still many situations when the insider has a distinct advantage. Most of these advantages revolve around situations where the outsider is perceived as an ego threat, where communication with an outsider is restricted by etiquette, or where the outsider is perceived as a person incapable of sympathetic understanding. In some instances, even though the respondent is able and willing to give the relevant information, an outsider is unable to use the jargon fluently enough or is ignorant of the local facts needed to understand what he or she is told. This last possibility has already been discussed, so let us examine more closely those situations in which communication with the insider involves less ego threat, fewer etiquette restrictions, and a greater satisfaction of the need for sympathetic understanding.

An outsider may constitute an ego threat to the respondent guilty of violations of public norms (laws and mores), who is afraid that such information might be used to damage his or her reputation. Thus, a person studying social organization in a slum would not have access to much information on underworld activities until the person had achieved the status of insider. This might be called a form of in-group defensive secrecy. Thus, Whyte spent months becoming accepted as a friend by the "corner boys" in an Italian-American slum section of a large city before he began to obtain information on certain organized crime activities in the area.[27]

Similarly, studies of Japanese-Americans interned in relocation centers during World War II recorded the difficulties interviewers had becoming accepted as "friends."[28] Some Caucasian researchers never achieved this status. Others succeeded within four or five months. Even

---

[27]William F. Whyte, *Street Corner Society: The Social Structure of an Italian Slum* (Chicago: University of Chicago Press, Third edition, 1981).

[28]Dorothy S. Thomas and R. S. Nishimoto, *The Spoilage* (Berkeley: University of California Press, 1946).

the Nisei members of the research team had difficulty avoiding being perceived as "informers" by the camp members although none of the information they received was ever given to the government. Much of the relevant information could not be elicited until the insider role was established.

Another type of information withheld from outsiders might be called trade secrets. These are not withheld for being distasteful, immoral, or illegal, but because they give the possessor advantages in the competitive struggle. This information must not fall into the hands of a competitor. If the interviewer were perceived as a person who could not conceivably pass on the information to a competitor, the respondent would be less reluctant.

Another disadvantage to the outsider role lies in the etiquette barrier. Even though no ego threat is involved in the outsider's presence, there may be a tendency to treat the outsider as a guest or a "visiting fireman," and the respondent tends to put on company manners.

Finally, the interviewer from the outside is perceived as a person unlikely to sympathize with the in-group's problems and who has no real interest in the respondents except for what they offer the study. There is a feeling that there is nothing in common upon which to build rapport. Students studying some of the social-psychological aspects of the church meetings in store-front churches report this "feeling of emptiness" between themselves and their respondents. In this case, the respondent correctly senses the lack of any sympathetic understanding on the part of the middle-class college student. Although an interview can be conducted under such conditions, little information on the more subtle feelings, aspirations, and beliefs of the respondent can be obtained, because the answers are not motivated by a desire to share experiences with a sympathetic person. Therefore, responses tend to be short, unspontaneous, and not always relevant.

Establishing the insider role. In spite of the advantages of the outsider role, there are purposes for which the interviewer must have an insider role. How is this role established? There is no simple formula for attaining it with respect to an individual or group, but there are general ways to approach the problem.

The first general way to be accepted as an insider is to participate in the group, institution, or community being studied. The intimacy of the interaction demanded depends upon the nature of the information sought. If the group is very closely knit, the intimacy of participation needed before one is considered "in" is very great. For example, to become an insider in a religious sect actively opposed to existing religious institutions requires more intimate association and active participation than being an insider in a conventional denomination. Joseph Zygmunt found in studying the Jehovah's Witnesses that faithful attendance and participation in the weekly meetings was not enough.[29] He had to spend additional time "witnessing" on street corners and distributing the literature where there was opposition before he was considered really sympathetic.

Religious groups differ not only in their degree of hostility toward the "outside" world but also in the degree to which they are interested in recruiting new members. For example, the Jehovah's Witnesses are both hostile toward conventional religion and actively proselyting for new members. The black Muslim sect mentioned previously is hostile to the white Christian world, but is not interested in trying to convert the enemy. Not hostile to the outside world, the Bruderhoff communities in the United States and England want to explore a new communal way of life and welcome the outsider as long as he participates in their work. The Hutterite communities in the United States and Canada are not at war with the larger world, do not seek recruits, but are withdrawn and generally want to be left alone.

When groups practicing protective secrecy are suspicious of outsiders trying to gain entrance, it is often necessary for the field worker to enter in a subordinate role or not at all. One convenient subordinate role is that of student. By showing a sincere desire to learn from the members of the group something in which they excel and something which distinguishes them, the interviewer can reduce hostility and suspicion by reducing ego threat.

The language of the group can often be learned to gain rapport. This was found true by Whyte in his study of "Cornerville," where he found that learning Italian helped to gain the group's trust. Thomas and Nishimoto also reported that in their study in Japanese relocation centers, the Caucasian interviewers found it useful to learn Japanese, even though they did not become fluent enough to use it in interviews.

This role of student can be adapted to a variety of situations. Bain found that in interviewing workers in industry, the role of student could take the form of asking the respondent to explain his job and the equipment. In interviewing senior citizens, Krause, as a person sensitive to problems of interpersonal relations, found it quite natural to assume the role of a youth seeking insights and perspectives possessed only by her elders.

In addition to the approach of becoming an insider through direct participation, it is often possible to be perceived as an insider through an indirect method of being sponsored or recommended by some trusted person. The degree to which this entrance by sponsorship is successful depends upon how hostile, how closed, and how locally autonomous

[29]Joseph F. Zygmunt, "The Role and Interrelationship of Symbolic and Structural Processes in the Development of a Sectarian Movement" (Ph.D. dissertation, University of Chicago, 1960).

the group is, and the nature of the information sought. These problems of sponsorship will be dealt with later in this chapter.

Subordinate-superordinate relations. Any two persons having functionally related roles, directly interacting with each other, can be located on a continuum showing that one is superordinate, equal, or subordinate to the other.

In the following pairs having a reciprocal relationship, it can be seen that in each pair there are superordinate-subordinate roles: captor-captive, master-slave, captain-lieutenant, manager-worker, physician-patient, teacher-student. Note that the first three might be called power relations, since they are based upon the use or the threat of force. Even though the subordinate in each case might like to escape the role, he or she would be forcefully restrained from doing so. The second three might be called dependency relationships. Although the subordinate in each case may break off the relationship he or she usually endures the subordinate role because it is more beneficial than breaking it off. This attribute alone is not enough to determine the existence of the super-ordinate-subordinate relationship; it would be possible to have a mutually beneficial relationship where both would suffer equal injury if it were broken. Therefore, to be an unequal relationship, termination must clearly be more injurious to the subordinate.

For the purposes of interviewing, we are interested in this dimension of the interviewer-respondent relationship only insofar as it inhibits or facilitates the flow of relevant information. It is not always clear when the interviewer is in a superordinate, equal, or subordinate role. The reality of the relationship depends not only upon the respondent's perception of the interviewer and upon the interviewer's perception of the respondent, but also upon the degree to which these two perceptions agree.

Upon initial contact between interviewer and respondent, there may be mutually agreeable or clashing perceptions of each other. This relationship develops and fluctuates as they size each other up. For this reason status relations may develop clarity or even reverse directions in the progress of a single interview. This is particularly true when the situation is not clearly defined at the outset and when the interviewer has wide latitude in techniques and tactics.

It is possible to initiate an interview in a superordinate position to gain initial cooperation and then shift to a more equalitarian role to obtain information which would be withheld from superordinates. The initial social distance can be reduced by a skilled interviewer who finds among his or her role repertory status attributes comparable to those of the respondent or which at least help in conveying to the respondent a nonthreatening image. It is probably easier for the interviewer to move from a superordinate position to an equal or subordinate one than vice versa.

Advantages of the superordinate position. In general, it is easier to make contact, to obtain an appointment, or to begin the interview, if the interviewer is perceived as occupying high status. The obligation to the higher-status person tends to reduce the effect of competing time demands. This does not necessarily mean that the interview, once begun, will be successful.

In some cases, the higher status of the interviewer will not only make the initial contact easier but will also facilitate the flow of information, because the interviewer's position symbolizes a moral obligation so strong that refusing to give accurate information would threaten the respondent's self-esteem. The reality of this ego threat depends upon the extent to which the respondent has actually internalized the moral obligation. For example, a child will sometimes lie to a peer, but when confronted with its mother's sternness, will admit the truth.

Sometimes the high status of the interviewer does not have this happy effect because the respondent has not internalized the norm. Or, the ego threat involved in giving a truthful answer would be more painful than the conscience pangs generated by lying. In this type of conflict, the respondent can show great creativity in developing rationalizations for not giving the information. If the ego threat involved is due to the authority position of the interviewer, then the superordinate role is double-edged. This is often the situation where the witness in a trial has taken an oath to tell the truth, but feels threatened if he or she does.

In some circumstances, the superordinate interviewer has the advantage of appealing to the respondent's need for recognition. The respondent may even hope for some publicity as a result. Of course, this, too, can be double-edged in rare cases where the respondent believes a more sensational tale has a better chance of being published. This was occasionally encountered in interviewing "heroes" in disaster situations. More often, however, the respondent who had been featured as a hero in the local newspaper showed embarrassment over the exaggerations or fiction furnished by an enthusiastic and creative reporter who had found a human interest story for the day.

If the interviewer's higher status is based upon higher education, specialized knowledge, or experiences in a certain area related to the interview topic, the respondent may be motivated by a need for meaning. The father of a delinquent child being interviewed by the social worker, the teenager feeling the first emotional attraction to a member of the opposite sex being interviewed by the high school counselor, or the supervisor who did not receive an expected promotion being interviewed by the personnel department—all might be motivated to talk by a need to orient themselves to the realities and to make sense of the events.

Finally, the interviewer in the superordinate position has the advantage of being able to offer extrinsic rewards while the lower-status interviewer cannot. The interviewer or sponsor may pay respondents a flat rate per interview "as a symbol of our appreciation of the time and effort you have given us." Other inducements—paying transportation and lodging for the respondents to come to a central point to be interviewed, offering to obtain appointments with influential people, or taking the respondent to lunch—have been beneficial in some instances. Gross and Mason's study of the role of the public school superintendent illustrates this.[30]

Service in some form may also be rendered by the field worker in exchange for information. For example, Oscar Lewis found that to establish good rapport with the people he was studying in the Mexican village, Tepoztlan, it was necessary to help them.[31] Similarly, Albert De Graer found that his role as medical doctor gave him an acceptable reason for intimate contact with both the patients and "doctors" of the Azande tribe in the Belgian Congo.[32] This technique is not only useful when working in exotic cultures but also in our own culture, whether in a factory, hospital, school, or community.

In general, the fact that the researcher is rendering a service to the group or individual being studied gives a reason for his or her presence that is much more understandable to many people than the abstract idea of research on human behavior. The service function gives the researcher an opportunity to do more than formal interviewing. It also allows the researcher to be a participant-observer with access to certain situations which might be considered taboo even if he or she were accepted as a researcher.

In some cases, it is possible for the service to take the form of giving useful information; however, there are some important safeguards which must be observed. First, the information must not have been confidentially obtained from a previous respondent, even if that respondent is anonymous. There is always the danger that the current respondent will be afraid that his or her information will also be passed along. Second, there are many situations in which it is harmful to even give the respondent a statistical summary of the type of data which has been found up to that point in the study. For example, some disaster interviewers tried to reassure a respondent, who felt guilty because he had become so frightened that he could not eat or sleep for two days, by pointing out that "more than 60 percent of the people in other communities studied have shown these same symptoms." This is dangerous for several reasons. In some cases, the respondent may not have been aware that he had been communicating his guilt feelings. Also, he may resent being "just another statistic" and want the interviewer to view his

---

[30]N. Gross and W. Mason, "Some Methodological Problems of Eight-Hour Interviews," *American Journal of Sociology* 59, no. 3 (November 1953), pp. 197–204.

[31]Oscar Lewis, *Life in a Mexican Village: Tepoztlan Restudied* (Urbana: University of Illinois Press 1970).

[32]Albert De Graer, "L'art de Guerir Chez les Asande," *Congo* 10, pp. 220–21.

case as unique. And from a psychotherapeutic standpoint, the respondent finds it difficult to obtain catharsis if the very basis for his or her guilt is denied by the interviewer. Finally, there is the danger that giving certain kinds of information will confuse the respondent about the interviewer's role.

Many harmless forms of information can be supplied. For example, an interviewer in a factory may become quite popular during the World Series games by giving the latest report on the scores. Or, an interviewer in an academic institution may pass along some interesting information on new publications and current research projects in the respondent's field.

The effect of extrinsic rewards may often depend upon whether they are of the discriminating or nondiscriminating type. Those discussed previously are nondiscriminating, in that all respondents receive the benefits regardless of their performance in the interview. This type of extrinsic reward is more common in the social science interview in which the interviewer is not in a power position even though he or she may have high status. The discriminating extrinsic reward is one which is given only to those respondents who have completed the interview successfully according to certain criteria set up by the interviewer. This is often the situation when the social worker is interviewing a respondent; the information obtained may be used to determine eligibility for welfare measures. The personnel interviewer speaking to the job applicant holds out the hope of a job if the respondent is successful according to some criteria which may or may not be known to the respondent. The prison parole officer; the administrator of loans, grants, or fellowships; the manager in charge of promotions; or the physician examining a person to determine eligibility for medical insurance—all these and others interview people to determine whether they are deserving of some reward.

It can readily be seen that the nondiscriminatory extrinsic reward is more clearly an asset to the interviewer than the discriminatory reward. In the latter case, the respondent is highly motivated to pay attention, to comply with requests, and to devote extended periods of time, but there is always the ego threat of possible failure in reaching an admitted objective. To avoid failure, the respondent is tempted to withhold information he or she feels might be damaging to the case or to exaggerate certain points while distorting others. Whenever it is feasible, information should be collected in situations where no discriminatory rewards are used.

Advantages of equality. The advantages inherent in an equality relationship assume the absence of a competitive or conflicting relationship between equals. Thus, the advantages of equality are gained when there is an in-group relationship between the two. The principal advantage under these conditions is the absence of ego threat.

There is an advantage also in the absence of certain etiquette restrictions. There may never be any relationship completely devoid of etiquette restrictions, but for the purposes of interviewing we are interested in eliminating only those which inhibit the flow of relevant information. Abstractly, we can say that in the equal relationship the quality of the etiquette restrictions is different from that in unequal relationships.

The absence of any power or prestige leverage by the interviewer may make it difficult to obtain the cooperation of an equal unless some bond of friendship, sentiment, or symbiosis is present. The interviewer must depend upon some intrinsic reward to obtain the cooperation. In the equality relationship at its best, it is possible for the respondent to be a true collaborator in a common problem, and once his or her interest is captured, it can be sustained.

Advantages of subordinate role. The principal advantage in the subordinate role for the interviewer is the absence of any threat to the respondent's ego. The interviewer who demonstrates a high level of competence can be respected although in a subordinate role. The respondent who is not pleased by the purpose of the interview, the sponsorship, or some aspect of the strategy is often more apt to express displeasure to an interviewer "who is just doing a job assigned to him" than to someone in higher status where etiquette might interfere.

Sometimes the respondent gives the information because he or she feels sorry for the interviewer who has such a "distasteful" job. Or, the respondent may feel no obligation to furnish more than a modicum of information and dismiss the interviewer. Since there is no possibility of applying direct pressure to the respondent, indirect pressure in the form of an appeal to the respondent's altruism may be used. To do this successfully, the interviewer must know which values, reference groups, or membership groups might be legitimately identified with the purpose of the interview in the respondent's mind.

The low-status interviewer is not in a position to offer any of the discriminatory extrinsic rewards as is the high-status interviewer, but the low-status interviewer is not completely without resources in offering nondiscriminatory extrinsic rewards. If he or she is familiar with the type of respondent and the general setting and is sensitive to opportunities to offer small favors in a nondiscriminating way, the low-status interviewer may smooth the path of the interview for the single contact or be more sure of appointments for a series of contacts with the same person or organization.

As mentioned previously, the interviewer's auxiliary role might involve a form of participation which is beneficial to the organization or the individual respondent. There are also many types of small services which can be rendered upon a single contact. Helping the respondent bring in the groceries, watching the baby while the respondent puts the groceries away, bringing an armload of wood from the barn into the house, explaining the latest treatment recommended by the Department of Agriculture for a parasitic corn fungus, bringing the newspaper from the foyer to the respondent's third-floor apartment—these types of services, depending upon the setting for the interview, can have a positive effect where the interviewer does not have to worry about losing a superordinate position.

Just as it is possible for the interviewer initiating the interview in the superordinate role to move toward a position of equality as the interview progresses, the subordinate interviewer can also move upward to a position of equality during the interview. The downward shift of the superordinate interviewer is most likely to be accomplished by emphasizing auxiliary roles the interviewer has in common with the respondent. The upward shift of the subordinate interviewer is more often accomplished not by emphasizing auxiliary roles but by performing well in the central role of interviewer.

The Central Role of the Interviewer

Thus far, the discussion has focused upon the *selection* of the appropriate role for the interviewer, which involves both the selection of the right person to do the interview and the selection of the most appropriate roles from the interviewer's natural role repertory. Since the *selection* process required us to focus upon the background characteristics of the interviewer, the emphasis was upon his or her auxiliary roles. With the attempt to sensitize the reader to these factors we have perhaps overemphasized the importance of the auxiliary roles and neglected the central foreground factor of the person *qua* interviewer.

In the final analysis, the auxiliary roles are important only as they impinge upon the central role of interviewer. More directly relevant to the problem of maximizing the flow of relevant information is the way in which the interviewer plays the role of interviewer vis-à-vis a particular respondent. It is often apparent that the respondent has only a very hazy notion of the interviewer's role. This is unavoidable since respondents rarely have extensive practice in their role as a respondent. One exception is the respondent who has undergone treatment by a psychiatrist or clinical psychologist; these respondents are often more secure in a nonscheduled, low topic-control interview, aimed at collecting information on subjective experiences.

The general vagueness of the average respondent's concept of the interviewer's role has advantages and disadvantages. If the concept is vague, the interviewer at least has a clean slate upon which to communicate his or her expectations of the respondent. If the respondent does have a strong conception of the interviewer's role, often it is a stereotype not appropriate to the particular situation in which he or she is being interviewed. These incorrect expectations must be detected and corrected by the interviewer.

METHODS OF SELECTING INTERVIEWERS

The manager of a field research team can use a combination of approaches to assess interviewer candidates. Such objective information as sex, age, educational level, and experiential background can be obtained in the application questionnaire. Other characteristics such as race, dialect, accent, speed and intonation of speech, posture, dress, grooming, or body movement can be observed in a personal interview with the candidate. In research where the interviewer's attitude either toward the topic of the interview or toward a certain type of respondent is likely to bias the results of the interview, an appropriate attitude scale can be constructed and administered as part of the application process. In research where the interviewer needs special knowledge to do a valid interview, the manager can either construct a test of that knowledge or devise a way of quickly conveying that knowledge as part of the interviewer training sessions.

In order to test a prospective interviewer's basic sensitivity to interviewing problems, a pencil-and-paper test such as Laboratory Problem 1 along with the scoring system given in the *Instructor's Manual* can be used while keeping in mind that the ability to do well on this pencil-and-paper test is generally a necessary but *not sufficient* condition for doing good interviewing.

One of the most valid methods of assessment is to have the interviewer candidates do, as part of the application process, a tape-recorded interview relevant to the particular field research project for which they are being hired. The project director should not only listen to the tape but should also interview the interviewer candidate about the tape to obtain general reactions and answers to specific questions about problematic points in the interview. In some cases listening to only the first five minutes of the interview will show clearly that this person would not make a good interviewer on this particular topic and no follow-up interview with the candidate is necessary. In other instances where the respondent seems particularly difficult it is advisable for the project director to interview the interviewer candidate to determine the extent to which he or she is aware of such things as irrelevant answers, evasive answers, incomplete information, or possible lies. Also, it could be determined whether or not the interviewer candidate was aware of mistakes made or of alternative approaches which could be used in another interview on the same topic.

SUMMARY

We have viewed the process of interviewer selection as having two phases. The first phase is the selection of the person; the second is selecting the most suitable roles a particular person can take vis à vis the respondent. These two phases are functionally related in that the selection of a person determines certain opportunities and limitations for the role-selection phase.

In selecting the person we need to consider his or her overt physical characteristics (sex, age, race, ethnicity, speech pattern, dress and grooming, and physical handicaps), basic personality traits, attitudes (toward the subject of the interview, toward the respondent, and toward his or her own role as interviewer) and, finally, the interviewer's background of knowledge and experience relevant to the subject matter of the interview, the type of respondent to be interviewed, or the social context in which the interview is to take place.

In selecting the most suitable role for the interviewer, we must not assign new roles for him or her to play but select from among his or her actual role repertory (such as mother, parent, daughter, taxpayer, church member, voter, consumer, musician, etc.) those which should be emphasized as *auxiliary* to the central role of interviewer. This distinction between role *playing* and role *taking* is essential both in terms of the ethics of avoiding deceit and of the effectiveness of the interviewer.

These auxiliary roles are selected in a way calculated to minimize the inhibitors and maximize the facilitators of communication. Therefore we must consider their effect on the respondent's perception of the interviewer-respondent relationship and the respondent's definition of the interview situation. In thinking of the probable effects of certain characteristics of the interviewer on the interviewer-respondent relationship, there are two major dimensions to keep in mind: the in-group–out-group relationship and the superordinate-subordinate relationship. Each of the combinations of this two-dimensional relationship has its advantages and disadvantages, depending upon the type of information sought in the context of the interview situation and the larger society.

All of the characteristics of the interviewer and his or her auxiliary roles are relevant only insofar as they affect the performance of the central role as interviewer. All of the effects of the interviewer's characteristics depend upon the meaning they have for the particular respondent in the concrete situation.

Some general methods of collecting relevant information for choosing the best interviewer candidates include the candidate's application questionnaire, a personal interview with the candidate, assigning a trial tape-recorded interview to be done by the candidate and assessed by the project director, and discussing the tape-recorded interview with the candidate.

The credibility of the interviewer and the predictability of the respondent's definition of the situation can be augmented and supported by selecting the most appropriate scene for the interaction. So within our dramatic frame of reference, we can say that the interviewer, to emerge convincingly as a real character, must be backed by appropriate

props and scenery. Setting the scene is the topic of the next two chapters, which begin with the assumption that the respondents, the interviewers, and their appropriate roles have already been determined.

DISCUSSION QUESTIONS

1. What is the one most important thing to do before selecting inter-
    viewers for a particular project?

2. In general why are visible characteristics of the interviewer impor-
    tant?

3. What are some of the most important visible characteristics of in-
    terviewers? Explain how they can affect the results?

4. What are some of the most important nonphysical or "invisible"
    characteristics of the interviewer? How can they affect results?

5. What are the two most important dimensions of the interviewer-
    respondent relationship? Give an example of how one of these di-
    mensions might affect the results positively? Negatively?

LABORATORY PROBLEM 5

Selecting the Appropriate Interviewer

This problem requires creative imagination (empathy) in applying principles of communication to this important phase of field strategy. You should imagine interview situations in which one main inhibitor can be either maximized or minimized by the selection of a good type or bad type of interviewer, assuming the same respondent in both cases. You should concentrate on the relationship between the type of information needed, the type of respondent at hand, and the type of interviewer most likely and least likely to give the needed information.

Give three examples of situations, using the following format for describing each of the three situations. Assume that the respondent has the needed information but is more willing or able to give it to one interviewer than to the other.

a. The specific *question* to be asked.

b. The type of *respondent.*

c. The type of interviewer *most* likely to obtain the information.

d. The type of interviewer *least* likely to obtain the information.

e. The main inhibitor of communication operating between the respondent and the interviewer described in (*d*) above.

Below is one example. Note that there is no need to elaborate with much detail.

a. (Question) "What do you think of the new open-space middle school pioneered here in Yellow Springs by your superintendent of schools?"

b. (Respondent) Teacher in that school.

   c.   (Good interviewer) Teacher from nearby school district.

   d.   (Bad interviewer) Member of the Yellow Springs school board.

   e.   (Inhibitor) Etiquette.

Be prepared to defend your examples in a class discussion by explaining why you would expect the particular inhibitor to be most important and why you would expect a different interviewer to minimize it.

Chapter Ten

Time and Place of the Interview

Too frequently the time and place of an interview is not consciously chosen with care because the scene is not considered an important force in determining the quality of the interview. Instead, too often the scene is determined by custom, by the physical or psychological convenience of the interviewer, or by the invalid criterion of dollar cost per interview rather than per item of valid information. The rigid rituals of time and place are seen in such examples as the school principal who always interviews students in his office, in the teacher who always interviews students in front of other students in the classroom, the psychiatrist who has never seen a patient at home, the lawyer who has never interviewed the client at the scene of the issue, or the manager who has never gone to a subordinate's office to talk with him. Perhaps these customary scenes are generally correct, but there are many instances in which consideration of the potential inhibiting effects would call for abrupt departure from the routine.

In discussing the problems of selecting an appropriate time and place for the interview, we will concentrate upon the circumstances that often link the spatial and temporal dimensions of the situation with social-psychological facilitators and inhibitors of communication. No attempt will be made to deal with the relative cost of the different time-space strategies. Most of the experimental studies of the effects of time and space upon both the costs and the validity of the interview have been done in connection with polls and surveys and will be referred to in a separate chapter.

Before dealing with our main concern for the social-psychological meaning of time and place, we will first list the most salient physiological aspects of the situation that can affect the quality of the interview. It is common sense to recognize that the time and place should maximize the respondent's physical comfort as well as the interviewer's, with the temperature, humidity, light, and odors conducive to comfort. Also there should be no visual or auditory distractions that make concentration difficult for the interviewer and respondent. In addition to these physiological aspects, occasionally we must consider physical characteristics such as the spatial relationship between the interviewer and respondent; and if a recording machine is to be used, we should check the location of a functioning electrical outlet, whether there is alternating or direct current, and where the machine and microphone can best be placed. Once these details are known, the more important problem is the social-psychological *meaning* for the respondent of the prospective situation.

There are several interesting and relevant connections between the time-space aspects of a situation and the communication problems which result. These general relationships are pertinent to many interviewing problems.

SOME EFFECTS OF PLACE

Minimizing Inhibitors

The selection of an appropriate place for the interview can minimize the competing time demands. This statement may appear to be a contradiction of terms in that it proposes to deal with the *time* dimension by manipulation of the *space* dimension. This is possible only because places contain people, things, and interests that might compete with interview time. Although the aphorism "out of sight, out of mind" is not completely true, there is a tendency in this direction.

To illustrate this, an interviewer studying morale problems of the public school teacher could arrange to interview the teacher in the classroom during a free period, in the faculty lounge if there is one, or at home in the evening. In the first setting the desk may be stacked with unread English themes, or the bulletin board may contain a display two weeks behind schedule; the blackboard may contain an assignment for which the teacher must prepare. Although the faculty lounge may be free from these distractions, it may have less privacy than either the classroom or the home. In any case, the types of competing time demands activated by each situation are qualitatively and quantitatively different.

The appropriate selection of place can also minimize ego threat. Place is connected with ego threat insofar as it influences the respondent's conception of the role and status of the interviewer and the purposes of the interview, or reminds the respondent of certain values that must be upheld or roles that must be performed. In addition, the place may suggest various probabilities of information leaking out to some ego-threatening audience. This suggests that the *place*, like a stage set in a play, provides the context in which the interaction takes place and therefore gives support to each actor's role. The interview setting should be chosen to reinforce the respondent's perception of the interviewer's most appropriate auxiliary role. If inappropriately chosen, the impression of the setting can overpower any attempt of the interviewer to communicate a nonthreatening image of himself.

For example, in studying the reasons why high school students choose nursing as a career, the interviewer should not arrange appointments with new recruits in the office of the director of the school of nursing if he or she wants to avoid identification with the authority of the nursing school. In one study, the interviewer did accept the invitation to use the director's office for the interviewing. He tried to overcome the handicap by explaining that he was not working for the hospital, but was doing research on his own initiative. Later, it was discovered that several of the students still did not understand that the interviewer was not on the hospital staff. Some remembered and believed his explanation, but assumed that the interviewer was interested in administration of hospitals or schools of nursing. While some very real reasons for going into nursing were given to the school counselor over a cup of coffee in the cafeteria, they were not mentioned in the more formal interview. For example:

R: Letha and I were talking the other night about her home background and were surprised to find the same things. We are both from strict farm families. In our home town, the Lutheran church does not allow boys and girls to mix in the teenage Sunday School classes. Things are pretty dead in the country and the boys get to run around while the girls just sit at home. The only way you can get away from home is to get married, go away to college, or go into nursing.

I: Why not get a job as a stenographer, waitress, or store clerk?

R: You don't know my dad. He doesn't think waitresses are respectable. And you can't get a job in an office unless you can type well. I went to a school where they don't teach typing, bookkeeping, and that sort of thing. All the girls working in the offices in this town are graduates of the city high schools.

In contrast, in the formal interview situation there was a strong emphasis on such factors as the social usefulness of the nursing profession, the desire to "work with people," and the practical combination of the nursing profession with marriage. Here, the place of the interview considerably affected the information obtained.

Similarly, an interviewer should consider carefully invitations to use the principal's office to interview teenagers on their adjustment problems, the dean's office for interviewing college students, or a management conference room for interviewing employees on their morale problems and perceptions of management. More neutral ground should be used for the interview, if possible.

Of course, if ego threat is to be minimized, it is usually necessary to find a place where privacy is assured. Sometimes the person's home, if there is privacy, provides the greatest security. In other cases, lower-status respondents may feel defensive about their economic condition as reflected by the home. This is particularly true of minority groups who are forced to live in slum housing, even though they dress well and drive a late-model car. Also, crowded living conditions may make privacy rare in this kind of home except at certain times.

Sometimes there is the problem of achieving the proper balance between privacy and complete isolation. For example, when males are interviewing female respondents, either the respondent or others in the community or organization may become fearful or suspicious of the intimacy that might result.

Considerable ingenuity is often required to find privacy needed for the purposes of the interview. It is very difficult and sometimes impossible to obtain valid information from a subordinate when his or her superordinates can listen. This obstacle is familiar to the public opinion poller who finds that wives more frequently have "no opinion" on controversial issues when their husbands are present. If it is essential to the results, the need for privacy should be tactfully and firmly explained to the respondent.

Just as the situational setting tends to influence the respondent's perception of the interviewer's role, it also makes the respondent more conscious of one of his or her own roles than of another. Therefore the ideals, obligations, expectations, and other subjective orientations connected with that role are brought into the foreground of the respondent's consciousness. A respondent who is a father, a businessman, and a deacon of the local church might give different answers to questions from the same interviewer on controversial issues such as local option liquor sales, taxes for schools, or federal aid to religious education, depending on whether the respondent was interviewed at home, in his or her business office, or in the office of the church. In each setting it is possible that different moral frames of reference gain ascendency in weighing issues. What is considered threatening to the ego depends upon the person's self-concept, which he or she strives to maintain. It is highly probable that individuals vary considerably in the degree to which their self-concepts remain stable and consistent as they move from one role to another. Therefore, whatever flexibility exists will be associated with those changes in setting that highlight different roles.

Many of the same points regarding the connection between the place, role emphasis of inter iewer and respondent, and ego threat can be said of the relationship between place, role, and the etiquette barrier which acts as a filter of communication allowing some items to pass and prohibiting others, depending upon the role relationship between the two communicators. Any change in the role of either the interviewer or the respondent will have some effect upon limiting communications. To apply this principle, the interviewer must know how the selection of the place for the interview will affect the respondent's perception of his or her own and the interviewer's role. In addition, the interviewer needs to be familiar enough with the situation to know which etiquette restrictions are attached to which role combinations.

Although this seems complex, which it is in theory, in actual practice all mature adults are able to govern their behavior according to many of the subtle requirements of etiquette. The problem becomes acute, however, when an individual in the role of interviewer is required to operate in situations where he or she is not familiar with the nature of the etiquette restrictions. A vital part of the strategy phase of any study is to become familiar with the restrictions in the new settings.

Simple forgetting and chronological confusion may both be reduced, in some cases, by the selection of an appropriate place. It is important that the place be quiet and private so that the interviewer can establish the appropriate pace and mood for careful recall of events. Without this quiet privacy it is impossible to use some of the techniques and tactics useful for stimulating recall.

Another way of utilizing place to stimulate recall is to effect a return to the scene with certain physical objects prodding the memory. It is sometimes possible to interview the respondent while walking through the actions in their original setting. Where this is impractical, it may be possible to use photographs, maps, tape recordings, and other physical traces of settings and events that relate to the interview.

Often an accurate presentation of the spatial arrangements of the original scene (regardless of whether these are seen in the real setting or in a photograph) will facilitate the untangling of the chronological order and perception of events. This was observed in interviews with building contractors to discover the types of conflicts they had with clients. By either visiting the house he or she built or by looking at photographs and floor plans, the respondent was stimulated to remember in considerable detail misunderstandings and issues of conflict with the client.

Finally, in choosing the place of an interview we must find a location that is quiet because the interviewer must be able to use subtle vocal expressions and intonation patterns to convey the complete meaning to the respondent. It is equally important that the interviewer can hear the most subtle nonverbal expressions of the respondent. With considerable background noise or competing conversations, this level of communication is lost. Second, if the interview is to be tape-recorded, the competing noises can make the playback relatively unintelligible, greatly increasing the amount of time needed to transcribe reliably or to code the material, and causing the loss of both verbal and nonverbal meaning.

Maximizing Facilitators

If the type of information to be obtained requires the establishment of a sympathetic and understanding mood, the place must be quiet and private. In some cases, the location may represent a new and interesting experience for the respondent. Or, the trip to the place of the interview might be an extrinsic reward that attracts respondents. The main value in the location of the interview, however, is the absence of distractions.

SOME EFFECTS OF TIME

Many of the effects of *place* also apply to the selection of a *time* for the interview, in that the relevant characteristics of a particular place change from time to time. Therefore, this aspect of time in relationship to place was assumed as a consideration in selecting the place for the interview.

There is another important aspect of selecting a time for the interview. This is the relationship between the point in time when the interview takes place and the events or experiences about which the interviewer is seeking information. In assessing current opinions and attitudes, this time dimension is not involved. However, in many interviews the time of the interview in relationship to events and experiences determines both the respondent's *ability* and *willingness* to give relevant information.

The most significant effect of timing is upon the respondent's ability to remember, accurately and completely, avoiding chronological and inferential confusion. To avoid simple forgetting, the interview should take place as soon after the relevant events and experiences as possible. Much psychological research indicates the distorting effects of fading memories. Specific facts, if remembered, may be quantitatively or qualitatively distorted. Complex events may be retained in an essentially correct pattern with nonessential detail omitted; or the whole gestalt of the event may be distorted, thus reversing its significance.

What is forgotten depends not only upon the recency of the experience but also upon how ego-involved it was, whether it was a completed task, whether it was considered a success or a failure, and whether it was routine, dramatic, or traumatic. Regardless of the cause of the forgetting, in general, time is an important factor.

Events are not simply forgotten or clearly remembered. Often the faded memory can be revived by special interviewing techniques and tactics. At the strategy level, information on events more than a month in the past is more efficiently obtained by giving the respondent some advance notice of the interview topic. If the topic of the interview is explained when making an appointment (with or without the suggestion that the respondent might like to think it over), and if this is one or two days in advance, it is often easier to obtain more complete detail in the interview. The advance notice may be given to all respondents at once in the form of individual letters, a public announcement in a newspaper or on a bulletin board, or by radio or any other available public channel. Whether or not the advance notice should be individualized or simply made public depends on the topic of the interview and the nature of the group, community, or institutional setting.

Generally, immediate interviewing will not only reduce the loss of accurate detail, but will also help to avoid chronological confusion, which becomes a major problem in studies of changes in attitudes and beliefs over a elatively long period of time. There is a tendency to forget or représs previou attitudes, beliefs, and expectations. The author has had occasion to interview the same persons on international relations at six-month intervals. People who at one time vehemently expressed a conviction that war with the Soviet Union was inevitable would deny with equal vigor six months later that they had ever taken such a "defeatist position."

In this case, two interviews six months apart discovered shifts in the respondent's attitude that would not have been revealed by simply asking the respondent, "What is your opinion on the probability of war with the Soviet Union?" and "What was your opinion on this issue six months ago?" The respondent tends to feel that his present position is rational and right and, therefore, the same as it has always been.

Similarly, attempts to discover why a person "chose" to work for his or her current employer, why the person "selected" the college he or she now attends, or why the person "elected" to enter a particular vocation, are all fraught with the danger of chronological confusion. Each ingroup, whether it is an industry, college, profession, or community, supplies its members with certain ready-made rationalizations for how and why they came into the group. The virtues of the in-group may be systematically extolled in rhapsodic indoctrination by its myths and ideals, or the individual may develop a self-congratulatory version of why he or she made such a wise decision. In either case, it is extremely difficult in retrospect to uncover the original forces accounting for the final decision.

Even though the respondent has selectively forgotten certain things because he or she desires to forget, we nevertheless classify this in a later interview as an *inability* to give the information. Although originally the memory was repressed, the respondent is being perfectly honest when saying he or she has simply forgotten since the respondent is not consciously withholding or distorting information. If at the strategy level we can eliminate the need for extensive retrospection, the technical and tactical problems in the interview will be greatly simplified.

The strategy planner must always keep in mind that sometimes it is either impossible or impractical to depend upon interviewing to obtain information that has been forgotten and that other sources, such as diaries, public records, personal letters, or other documents should be used, either as a principal source or to supply cues to stimulate the respondent's memory and to guide the interviewer's probing.

There are many other situations in which not only the respondent's ability to remember but also the respondent's willingness, depend upon *when* he or she is interviewed. Information which could be given freely at one time becomes an ego threat to the respondent at another. When the author was interviewing college presidents and faculty to discover why the college had refused permission for interviews about academic freedom, he was given an important observation by one of the professors:

> It's a peculiar thing—perhaps if I weren't a social scientist I wouldn't have noticed it—when there was the big dispute on campus about firing Professor X, several faculty members besides myself defended his right to academic freedom. Some of them continued to criticize the administration after the professor's services had been terminated. All of these people except myself have since left, more or less voluntarily. The others who defended Professor X up to the time of his dismissal, but then dropped their objections, are still here. My point is, that of those who are still here, most of them will not admit *now* that the action of the administration was a violation of academic freedom. Yet no new evidence has been admitted to change their original point of view. To me it is quite simple. These people do not want to admit that they would continue to teach in a place which does not have academic freedom because this would be an admission that they are willing to knuckle under; so to save face, they deny that there has been any restriction of academic freedom. Perhaps I am just projecting, but that is the only way I can make sense out of their change in behavior.

If this respondent's assessment of the situation is correct, interviews with the faculty would have been much more fruitful *before* the administration had made the decision to dismiss Professor X. It is now an ego threat to the respondent to admit that X's dismissal was a breach of academic freedom.

Selecting an optimum time for the interview can also increase the respondent's conscious willingness to give the relevant information. One of the simplest ways is to select a time when the respondent has the fewest competing time demands. To do this, the interviewer must be familiar with the daily, weekly, monthly, and seasonal patterns of the respondent.

These patterns vary with the culture, the person's roles in that culture, and personal preferences. The interviewer who sets out to interview students the last week before the semester ends, farmers during harvest season, fishermen leaving in two days for a six-week's voyage, lifeguards on duty, factory "graveyard shift" workers at 11 A.M., housewives at 5:30 P.M., or a fireman immediately after a fire, shows either ignorance or a lack of sympathy with the respondent.

The interviewer should not assume that he or she can guess what the competing time demands will be in a strange situation. Often, the most obvious commonsense assumptions are completely wrong. For example, it was assumed that respondents who had experienced a disaster of major proportion (such as the burning of their house, the injury or death of members of the family, the crashing of an airplane into their home) would be reluctant to spend one or two hours in an interview the next day. The assumption seemed sensible, in view of the fact that under these circumstances such respondents would have many new tasks to complete as a result of the disaster.

This assumption is essentially correct *if* the disaster involves only one person, one family, or only a few families in a community. The assumption is completely fallacious, however, in large-scale disasters where the total community is devastated; the community is not yet functioning as an organization, each individual is unable to play normal roles, and therefore, has few competing time demands. The man whose house has blown away, whose horse and cow have been killed, whose barn and tractor are damaged beyond repair, and whose strawberry patch is covered with heavy debris cannot begin to do anything about his condition. His every move depends upon someone else's making a move. He would like to go to the next town to make arrangements with the insurance adjustor for a new tractor. Ordinarily he would phone, but the telephone lines were destroyed by the tornado; he would drive his car, but it is damaged; although a bus line ordinarily passes the house, the highway is obstructed by fallen utility poles, trees, and high-power lines; he would use his power chain saw to remove some of the trees from the road, but he has no gasoline for the motor and since the electricity is off, there are no pumps working at the local gas station, so he cannot refuel. Thus, he is caught in the paralyzing web of a nonfunctioning community. In his frustration, he is perfectly willing to talk about his troubles and has ample time to do so. Under these conditions, there is no difficulty in obtaining a two- or three-hour interview from the average respondent.

Sometimes an etiquette barrier arises in cases where the interviewer is asking information before it has become public. Etiquette often requires that a hierarchy of people be notified of an event or decision before it becomes public. If the interviewer attempts to obtain the information too soon, the request may be denied. This problem often arises when the interviewer is studying some ongoing community action program *in situ*. If the interviewer must continue work in the same community or organization over a long period, repeated requests for advance information could become a serious source of irritation.

In rare cases, the time for the interview may be selected to minimize the inhibiting effects of trauma by providing sympathetic understanding which will lead to catharsis. Immediately after a traumatic experience, the respondent is often more willing to talk about it than he or she will be later. Perhaps this is because the event is vivid in the respondent's mind and it cannot be repressed. Since the respondent's mind is full of images and internalized conversation about the event, it is no more painful to externalize these thoughts in conversation with the interviewer. Later, when the experience is less fresh and the respondent can cast the thoughts from mind, he or she is reluctant to renew the pain by discussing the topic. For example, after a community-wide disaster, interviewers noted a sudden decrease in respondents' willingness to discuss their experiences once the funerals were over. The funeral ceremonies seemed to symbolize the community's return to normal routine.

An interview may be timed to maximize the appeal to the respondent's need for meaning by catching the respondent while he or she is still undecided, confused, and trying to pin down a future that is in a state of flux. If the purpose of the interview is to study value systems, decision-making processes, role conflicts, or processes of defining situations, then although it might be possible to wait until after the decision has been made before interviewing the respondent, this delay would allow greater memory distortions and deprive the respondent of the opportunity to use the interviewer as a sounding board for ideas, dilemmas, and ambivalences during this struggle for meaning.

This immediate timing would be fruitful in studying such problems as decisions to marry or divorce, occupational choices, selection of a college, labor turnover, migration, and other major decisions that change a person's life pattern.

Thus far, we have discussed some of the implications of the time of the interview in relation to the individual's pattern of time demands and his or her experiences to be reported in the interview. Another aspect of the time dimension is selecting the most appropriate *sequence* of interviews with the different respondents.

If a random sample selects representative respondents who are so widely dispersed socially and geographically that they do not communicate with one another, the chronological order for contacting them is usually a matter of convenience and efficient use of the interviewer. But, if there is a possibility of contact between the respondents, so that they might discuss the interview either in prospect or retrospect, the effect of this communication upon the flow of relevant information should be carefully considered in the strategy planning.

Several types of questions should be answered in terms of the specific field situation in which the interviewing is to be done. Should the respondent of higher or lower status be interviewed first? Should the most willing or the most reluctant be interviewed first? Should certain respondents be interviewed first because they will not be available later? Should those special respondents who can give the broadest picture of the situation be interviewed first?

Ordinarily, it is best to interview the people of higher status first. Those of lower status may wish to wait to see if those higher up are going to cooperate by being interviewed. Also, those of higher status may be insulted if they are the last to be asked for their opinions on some community issue. This resentment, in extreme cases, might make it impossible for the interviewer to continue if the offended person has the power or prestige to blacklist the study.

Where the status of the prospective respondents is equal or irrelevant, it might be desirable to select the most willing respondents first in order to build a background of experience with the interview topic and the type of respondent. This experience might be useful in dealing with reluctant or resistant respondents. Also, the fact that all the others have cooperated and found it painless and even interesting might exert some pressure or arouse the curiosity of the reluctant.

In some situations, the interviewer knows in advance that some segments of the community or the institution will be moving or going on vacation and should be approached first. Also, certain special respondents might have the type of information which gives a broad view of the situation helpful in understanding the more specialized experiences of the respondents to follow. Such respondents may also give information on the relationships between the other respondents or information about them as individuals.

If there is a possibility of collusion between two or more respondents, this can sometimes be prevented by interviewing them separately and simultaneously. This method was used by Burgess and Wallin in gaining information on sexual adjustment in marriage.[1] A husband and wife were given questionnaires and were interviewed at the same time in different rooms. Each knew that the other was asked the same questions. This technique was able to elicit private information with great accuracy, and it provided validity checks.

SUMMARY

We have suggested that all too frequently the time and place of the interview are determined by rigid ritual, but better results can be obtained if the time and place are viewed as strategy tools consciously used to maximize the flow of relevant and valid information. The time and place can either inhibit or facilitate information flow. There are certain physiological inhibitors that must be avoided such as a room that is too hot, too cold, too noisy, or unpleasant smelling, but the more frequently

---

[1]E. W. Burgess and Paul Wallin, *Engagement and Marriage* (Philadelphia: Lippincott, 1953).

encountered barriers associated with time and place are the social-psychological ones and can be understood only in terms of their *meaning* to the respondent.

The *place* of the interview should be chosen to minimize the inhibitors of communication. For example, competing time demands can be reduced by getting the respondent away from distractions which remind the respondent of his or her other roles and obligations in life. Ego threat can be reduced by providing privacy as a defense against being overheard or of being seen cooperating with the interviewer; privacy can protect the respondent against being quizzed later by others about the interview. The scene can be chosen to reinforce the credibility of the interviewer's most appropriate auxiliary role, thus reducing ego threat and dissolving the etiquette barrier. Forgetting and chronological confusion can be reduced by interviewing the respondent at the scene of the event being discussed.

The *time* of the interview is important in three different perspectives. The first is in the relationship between the time of the interview and the regular cycles of events in the respondent's life. This perspective is important in choosing a time to minimize competing time demands and in knowing when to catch the respondent in the most opportune place. The second perspective is in the relationship between the time of the interview and the point in time when the event under discussion took place. Often by interviewing people as soon as possible after an event, we can minimize the effects of forgetting and chronological confusion. Also, if the events to be discussed had a strong psychological impact on the respondent, his or her need for catharsis, for meaning, and for sympathetic understanding will be highest immediately after the event. The third time perspective is in the sequence in which the respondents are to be interviewed. Often it is best to interview high-status persons first if their cooperation will insure the cooperation of lower-status persons. If status is not as important as a general willingness to be interviewed, then the most willing respondents can be interviewed first so that they will recommend the interview to others. At other times we need to choose the sequence of respondents to give the interviewer an overview of the situation as early as possible, so that the interviewer will have the context to understand the more detailed information to come later from other respondents.

Once we have gotten the right interviewer together with the right respondent at the most opportune time and place, we have solved most of the strategy problems. Before the opening question marking the beginning of the technique phase of the interview, there remains the final strategy step of defining the interview situation by the arrangement of physical props and by the interviewer's verbal explanation of the interview. This final bit of strategy is the subject of the next chapter.

DISCUSSION QUESTIONS

1. Is the selection of an appropriate time and place for the interview considered a strategy, technique, or tactic?

2. Explain how the *meaning* of a particular time or place of an interview might affect the respondent's ability or willingness to give relevant information.

3. What else about time or place, besides its meaning, might affect the flow of information from the respondent?

4. Give an example, not furnished by the author, of how the time or place of the interview might inhibit the respondent.

LABORATORY PROBLEM 6

Strategy Problems of Time and Place

In each problem below specify the most appropriate *time* and *place* for the interview. Consider how the relationships between the interviewer, the respondent, and the information sought might generate inhibitors which could be minimized by the selection of the appropriate time and place for the interview. After you have done this independently, compare your solution with others in the class and discuss why you chose the time and place you did. There may be legitimate differences in solutions depending on the assumptions you make regarding certain unspecified aspects of the situation. The discussion will be valuable in bringing out the different assumptions and showing what additional information might be needed to make the decision.

1. A graduate student from the School of Business Administration wants to interview middle-management people in large industries regarding their problems in bridging the gap between the top policy-making managers and the supervisory personnel. The interview will take from two to three hours.

2. A counselor with the County Employment Training Program is to interview an unwed mother, with a two-year-old child and now on welfare, regarding her possible interest in getting the child into a day-care program and attending a six-month vocational training program during which she would receive a small amount of money for transportation and lunch per day from the Job Training Partnership Act.

3. A police officer from the Traffic Division is studying a certain type of accident in order to design a better prevention program. He needs to interview a woman who witnessed an accident a

248

couple of blocks from her home as she was walking home from the drugstore.

4. A medical interviewer for the U.S. Public Health Service needs to interview General Motors workers who have been treated for venereal disease within the past year. He needs to ask about symptoms to discover whether the treatment was successful and whether there has been any new contact with the disease. All fifty of the follow-up cases work at GMC and live in a nearby community.

Chapter Eleven

Structuring the Interview Situation

DEFINING THE INTERVIEW SITUATION

Here "defining the interview situation" refers to only the final phase of strategy, from the moment the interviewer first contacts the respondent through the opening question of the interview. What the interviewer says and does during this time provides the immediate context of the interview and can greatly affect communication. Decisions must be made in advance relating to eight questions: (*a*) How should I introduce myself? (*b*) How should I explain the purpose of the interview? (*c*) How should I explain the sponsorship of the study? (*d*) Should I explain how and why the respondent was selected? (*e*) Should the respondent be anonymous? If so, how should this be explained? (*f*) Should any extrinsic reward be mentioned? (*g*) How should the interview be recorded, and how should the recording technique be explained? (*h*) What are some appropriate alternative wordings for the opening question?

Interviewer's Introduction

In presenting oneself to the respondent, what is said is significant mainly in helping the respondent crystallize his or her perception of the interviewer's role. Therefore, all that has been said regarding selection of the most appropriate role from one's repertory applies to the introduction. In addition, the manner of the introduction will preview the interviewer's degree of aggressiveness, responsiveness, competence, self-assurance, warmth, or objectivity.

Giving one's name to the respondent helps reduce suspicion that might arise if the interviewer remained anonymous. This is true even though the respondent may remain anonymous. This common courtesy personalizes the relationship to some extent. If the respondent is not to remain anonymous to the interviewer, and if the respondent's name is known, then the interviewer should use the respondent's name when presenting himself. Generally, the following two phrases would leave considerably different impressions:

"I'm interviewing residents of this community on. . . ."
"Hello, Mrs. Bishop, I'm Mr. Rolph. I'm helping X Organization with a survey of this community on. . . ."

It is often necessary to remind the neophyte interviewer, with his or her enthusiasm or anxiety to obtain the information, of the desirability of observing such common amenities.

If it is essential that the respondent remain anonymous to the interviewer, the interviewer may nevertheless give his or her own name and proceed in a way that makes clear that the respondent's name is not needed.

Sponsorship

Often the next phrase of the introduction includes the sponsorship of the study, if it has one. The value of having an organization as a sponsor generally increases in more urban settings and when the interviewer is a stranger to the respondent. In a small village, folk society, or primitive groups, organizational sponsorship is often meaningless. The only meaningful sponsor in this case would be a *person* known to the respondent.

The central strategy problem here is to obtain information on the field situation. Which type of sponsorship and which organization or person will be helpful? Which might be fatal? Again, the significance of sponsorship is its effect upon the respondent's conception of the interviewer's central and auxiliary roles and the effect of this upon the inhibitors and facilitators of communication.

It may be helpful to have both a formal organization and a local person as sponsors. For example:

Mrs. Jones, how do you do! I'm Mrs. Beals from the Association for the Aid of Crippled Children. Reverend Rolf said that you would be a good person to talk to about some of the problems in Yellow Springs.

If the respondent is to remain strictly anonymous, it is still possible to use a personal sponsor in the following manner.

How do you do! I'm Mrs. Beals from the Association for the Aid of Crippled Children. Perhaps you have read in the paper that Reverend Rolf is the Yellow Springs representative for the study now under way here. I would like to talk to you about some of the problems of crippled children in your neighborhood.

In some cases, it is advisable for the interviewer to carry some written credentials which include his or her name and the name, address, and phone number of the sponsoring organization. Respondents will rarely ask but will be reassured when identification is routinely shown. Even in cases where the sponsoring organization is unknown to the respondent, he or she may be favorably impressed by the interviewer's willingness to give information. The credentials may be a lapel button with either an official or informal look, depending on the nature of the study; or the interviewer may have a letter of introduction; or a photo identification card may be very persuasive that the interviewer is not bogus.

If the interviewer expects to spend several days in the community or organization under conditions where the respondents and potential respondents do not see him or her every day, it may be advisable to have the credentials reproduced in a form to be left with each respondent, along with a thank you note, so that questions from potential respondents can be answered accurately. This prevents the rise of rumors regarding the identity, sponsorship, or purpose of the interviewer.

Although the optimum sponsorship may be very helpful for getting in the door, it will have to be followed by good interviewing performance to maintain the initial advantages. Since the same sponsorship may not impress all respondents equally, some additional explanations will have to be given.

One of the most difficult situations in which to select sponsorship occurs when studying a group which has polarized for and against an issue related to the topic of the interview. Special care must be taken to find a sponsor perceived as neutral or disinterested. If a disinterested organizational sponsor can be found, it sometimes also helps to find a personal sponsor in each of the opposing camps of the controversy.

Explaining the Purpose of the Interview

The purpose of the interview should be explained in terms the respondent can understand and in a manner which will account for *all* the types of questions which are going to be asked. If the initial explanation is too narrow or vague, the respondent may not be able to connect certain questions with the stated purpose. The respondent's suspicions may be aroused because he or she feels the interviewer is hiding the "real" purposes. This is particularly likely to happen in a hostile or polarized community.

This does not mean that all of the possible uses of the data must be pointed out but that the most widely acceptable and most easily understood purposes should be stated so that none of the questions that follow seem to be off the subject. In some situations a complete explanation of the purposes would tend to bias the responses of those who would like to influence the results for their personal benefit. In these situations a minimal explanation omitting such temptations would be best.

In order to keep the initial explanation as simple and clear as possible, it may be necessary to plan additional explanations as the interview proceeds, pointing out the relevance of each new line of questioning to the originally stated purpose. In the interests of clarity, the language used should be appropriate to the background of the respondents and free of any technical jargon.

The next problem is to include as many points as possible which will maximize the facilitators and minimize the inhibitors of communication. In the explanation, it is often possible to avoid ego threat while appealing to the need for recognition, sympathetic understanding, new experience, the need for meaning, or some combination of these. For example, if the problem is to discover why one area of a city has much higher delinquency rates than another, and the hypothesis is that social control functions of the family break down when these are not supported by an organized community, we could use the following type of explanation to open an interview with a parent in a high delinquency area:

> You have probably read in the newspaper that Metropolitan Community Studies is interested in the problems of youth in our city. We are talking to parents all over the city to discover if it is more difficult nowadays for parents to bring up children than it used to be when your parents were raising you. What do you think are some of the problems in bringing up children nowadays?

This explanation of purpose is designed to help the interviewer get inside the door. It is short and directly connected to the opening question. It indicates that the study is publicly supported, is a good cause, and is interested in the respondent's practical problems. It appeals, therefore, to the respondent's altruistic impulse, promising sympathetic understanding and possible recognition. Further explanation may be needed and given at transitional points in the interview where the questions in a new topical area are not obviously related to the initial explanation. For example:

> Some people feel that there are different problems for parents living in different parts of the city. Do you feel that there are any problems which you have

with children in this neighborhood that parents in other neighborhoods might not have?

The type of explanation needed, the sequence, and the timing of the various vital points depends upon the situation.

Explaining the Selection of the Respondent

It is not always necessary to explain why and how a particular respondent is selected. Often, the respondent does not question the point, particularly in the more traditional census or opinion poll. But it is especially important to give a clear explanation when interviewing in potentially hostile or polarized territory. In this case, if the *representative* respondent can be persuaded that he or she has been chosen in an objective and impartial manner and that he or she will remain anonymous, ego threat and hostility will be minimized. If the person is a *special* respondent, and thus not anonymous to the interviewer, it would be helpful to mention that the respondent had been recommended by some person who is known and trusted.

Even in the most friendly territory, the respondent may suggest that the interviewer contact "somebody else who knows more about the problem," or "who has more time." In this case, it is particularly important to explain to the *representative* respondent that he or she was selected by an impartial sampling procedure and that it is necessary to obtain the point of view of everyone in the original sample, including people who are very busy and do not happen to be experts on the topic at hand. If the person is a *special* respondent, it is usually easier to appeal to his or her ego by recognizing the respondent's unique value to the study. Often, an appeal can be made by pointing out that the respondent was selected because he or she has, by implication, certain altruistic tendencies. For example, "You have been recommended as a person who has done a lot of volunteer work with youth of the community," or "You have shown an interest in the problems of the senior citizens of Akron," or "You have taken an active interest in the PTA."

There are also ways of explaining the selection of the *representative* respondent that will give him or her recognition as a member of a particularly interesting or meritorious local group, community, or institution. In a study of the causes of delinquency, the interviewer was collecting information to compare a high delinquency area of a large city with an equal population in a village. Although a random sample of villagers was interviewed, each one was made to feel somewhat unique by the following explanation:

We are analyzing some of the causes of juvenile delinquency by comparing places with very high delinquency rates with those having a very low delinquency. You can be very helpful to us, since you live in a town with the least delinquency in this part of the state.

The explanation can communicate positive expectations of cooperation by assuming that everyone will cooperate since, thus far, everyone else has. For example:

We have been able to interview the families in every ninth house in this area and it looks like we will be able to finish today.

This strategy must be used with caution to avoid being interpreted by the respondent as pressure tactics. Careful wording and the appropriate context must be employed. The expectation should be mentioned casually as an interesting sidelight.

Thus we see that even though the respondent is willing to cooperate without an explanation of how and why he or she was selected, it is often desirable to provide an explanation appealing to altruistic tendencies, giving recognition, and communicating positive expectations of cooperation. All of these precautions, although not always 100 percent successful, should help to assure optimum interpersonal relations at the outset.

Providing Anonymity and Confidentiality

Often in order to minimize the respondent's ego threat, it is necessary to use a strategy that will provide some degree of anonymity or confidentiality to the respondent. The relationship is *anonymous* if the respondent's identity is not known to a member of the research or helping team. The relationship is *confidential* if a member of the team knows the identity of a respondent and can link the information given to that respondent but does not reveal the respondent's identity to anyone else. Thus some members of a team may have an anonymous relationship and others a confidential relationship with the respondent.

There are degrees of anonymity. For example, the most complete anonymity would be achieved if no member of the team and no one using the information knew the respondent's name or address or how he or she could be contacted again. Often this extreme degree of anonymity would defeat the objectives of the study because respondents (whether representative or special) usually have to be selected according to some criteria relevant to the purposes of the study. Also there needs to be some way of spot-checking to determine whether interviewers have in fact interviewed the right respondents or to check the reliability of the information collected by allowing for some reinterviews of the same person. In many of the applied social science fields, such as counseling, social work, journalism, or crime investigation, there must be a continued relationship between the interviewer and the respondent, so anonymity is out of the question.

A less extreme degree of anonymity holds in situations where the respondent's name is not known but a prior arrangement is made regarding a time and place for a subsequent contact. Even less anonymous is the situation where the name of the *individual* is not known but either the address or phone number of the *household* is known.

In cases where the anonymity is complete, there is no question that the individual's identity will of necessity be confidential; but when the anonymity is not perfect, the question of the amount of confidentiality to be provided arises. For example, if only the director of a research project knew the names, addresses, or titles of a sample of employees of a company, there could be several different degrees of confidentiality promised to the respondent. The respondent's identity could be withheld from everyone else, given to the interviewer only, given to all members of the research team but not to anyone in the company management, or attached to the published study for all to see. Once the respondent's identity is known by anyone, it becomes a question of how far along the lines of communication this information should be shared.

In the helping professions not only the interviewer must know the respondent's identity but so must other members of the helping team and their supervisors. This is necessary in order to coordinate and supervise the services to be given. Here the respondent's identity and the information given remain confidential in the sense that the information is not passed along to any individual or agency outside those represented by the helping team.

It should not be assumed that the respondent, whether special or representative, desires or should be given anonymity. Often, the respondent does not care to be anonymous because this might detract from his or her recognition. At times, it might be necessary to make clear that the results will be anonymous even though the respondent prefers to tell the world what's on his or her mind. This is the case where the respondent sees the interview as a means to some personal gain and colors his or her report hoping for approval of superordinates or for the discreditation of peers. Under these conditions, the respondent's motivation is not to give an objective report but to select, censor, exaggerate, and rationalize, as it best fits the respondent's purpose.

There are circumstances where the respondent would prefer to remain anonymous but should not be granted this wish by the interviewer. This would be the case in studying a controversial issue in a community and attempting to predict who will take what public stand. If the respondent does not feel strongly enough or is not courageous enough to give his or her point of view to the interviewer, he or she is less likely to take a public stand later than is the person who gives his or her views in a forthright manner. This principle may be carried further by having the interviewer bring up arguments of the opposition and ask for permission to quote the respondent in a report to some public body or the press.

Thus, we see that the granting or withholding of anonymity is not decided upon the basis of tradition or the respondent's desires, but upon the purpose of the interview. One ethical point must be observed in any case. If the respondent is promised anonymity, that promise should be scrupulously kept; if the respondent is not to be given anonymity, this should be clear to him or her before the interview begins.

Another important dimension of anonymity is the degree of identification of groups versus individuals. In some cases, respondents are almost as reluctant to have information published about their particular group, organization, or community as they are about having information published about themselves. This may be because each respondent's role in the group is so conspicuous that he or she too would be identifiable, even though the respondent was not named, or the respondent may simply be so ego-involved in the organization that he or she feels any threat to its reputation as a personal threat. Here, it is difficult to assure anonymity for the organization if only one such organization is studied. Organizations are easily kept anonymous when many of the same type are studied, and the results reported as either a statistical summary or as case studies which are frankly camouflaged by changing nonessential details and omitting unnecessary identifying materials.

Even though one of the above methods of preserving the respondent's anonymity may be used, there are occasions when a particular respondent is not convinced of the interviewer's sincerity. Sometimes the interviewer's promise is put to a severe test. One respondent may quiz the interviewer for information obtained from another respondent. A management person may ask for some "off the record" information about one of the workers who has been interviewed. In rare cases, the interviewer will be threatened with jail or prosecution for not giving the information. This situation arose in a study of a disaster-stricken community where the chief of police ordered an interviewer to surrender her tape recordings for him to hear. After refusing and explaining that the information was confidential and that the respondents had been promised anonymity, she was threatened with prosecution for "withholding evidence." Of course, such a charge was groundless, since no crime had been committed for which evidence was needed. Probably, the chief was anxious about the possibility of people reporting the shortcomings of the police department during the crisis. Knowing that he was not on firm legal ground, the chief did not attempt to use physical force to obtain the tapes. When the field supervisor explained the situation to the chief, he reluctantly relinquished his claim.

Let's look at a few methods of preserving anonymity or confidentiality. For example, if we are studying a group whose members are willing to answer the questions but demand complete anonymity and do not trust any outsiders (including the information-gathering team) to keep their identities confidential, there is a way to handle this situation. First, the group is asked to elect a qualified person to select individuals to be interviewed according to criteria provided by the information-gathering team. This elected go-between selects the respondents and works out an interview appointment schedule. If it might be necessary to reinterview or send a questionnaire to some of these same people and to match the original interview information with the second set of information, the following added procedure will make the matching possible while keeping the respondent anonymous. The elected go-between assigns a number to each person before the first interview and makes a record of the names and corresponding identification numbers. Each respondent is then given an identification card with nothing but this number on it. The respondent presents this card at the interview appointment so that the interviewer can record this as the "case number" on that person's interview form. If later the interviewer wants to reinterview any individual, he or she gives this number to the elected go-between who contacts that person and makes another appointment. The same system can work for telephone interviews.

A less complete anonymity can be achieved in the case of the random sample survey of a community. In this case the interviewer would know where the respondent lived but would not know the respondent's name or telephone number. The procedure would be as follows. A random sample of households would be selected according to the procedure described in Chapter 12, *Sample Surveys.* Once the sample house or apartment is located, the individual to be interviewed can be selected at random or according to certain characteristics such as the male head of household, teenaged son, registered voter, or certain sex and age, and so forth. To do this properly the interviewer must explain that he or she does not want to know the names of members of the household, but the person answering the door is expected only to say whether the person in the wanted category resides in the house, whether that person is home, and if so, to bring that person to the interviewer. To allow follow-up information-gathering or supervisory checkups, the interviewer will indicate on the face sheet of the interview schedule the case number, address, age, sex, and other characteristics of the respondent.

In many surveys the name, address, and telephone number of the respondent appear on the face sheet of the interview schedule before it is given to the interviewer. In this case a degree of confidentiality can be preserved by the following procedure. Each interview schedule is given a case number. This number is repeated on every page including the face sheet which has the identifying information. When the interview is completed, the interviewer removes the face sheet and gives it to the project supervisor for safekeeping. In this way no one but the supervisor can match the names with the information given, in case a particular respondent has to be recontacted. In the meantime other members of the team can start editing, coding, and entering data in the computer using the identification numbers. None of these members of the team would have any need to know the identity of any person giving the information. It is important to keep the face sheets locked in a secure place so that curious personnel will not be tempted to try to discover who gave the responses in a particularly interesting interview.

Even in cases where the name of the respondent is never obtained, there is still the possibility of anonymity being violated by *inferred identity*. In cases where some members of the information-gathering team are familiar with the local community, it is possible that the answer to one or more questions in the interview will clearly identify a specific person as the respondent. For example, if the questions asked for the respondent's age, sex, and occupation, there might be only one twenty-three-year-old female auto mechanic in the town. Even in a big city inferred identity is a possibility, as in the case of a thirty-five-year-old bank teller whose father's occupation is "mayor." The only solution to this is to train those who handle the data to respect the ethical standards when confidentiality is promised. Once the data from all the interviews are aggregated for statistical purposes, any individual's identity is usually obscured. However, if there are cross-tabulations in the analysis and report, we would have to be careful to avoid any categories that contained only one or two people. For example, if the mayor was in the survey, we could lump the occupation of mayor into some larger category like city employee or politician.

One controversial technique for preserving anonymity or confidentiality is to mark each interview schedule with a secret or invisible mark of some kind so that case numbers do not appear and it does not occur to anyone that there would be any possible way to match the questionnaire with any particular respondent. Some field researchers feel that as long as this technique is not used in any way to harm or take advantage of the respondent it is ethical. Others make the added stipulation that the respondent should not be lied to and told that the responses are anonymous. Others make a third stipulation that the respondents be told about the deception and why it was considered necessary to obtain valid information only *after* all of the information has been collected. Still others take the position that to mark the forms secretly and allow the respondents to assume that they are not identifiable is unethical under all conditions.

The researcher has the ethical responsibility to actually provide whatever degree of anonymity or confidentiality he or she has promised. This means that the researcher should carefully and honestly assess the possibility of demands by the court for interviews to be used in civil or criminal proceedings. This is essential to consider in view of the fact that social scientists do not have the client-professional legal immunity that protects physicians, lawyers, and the clergy. If the researcher is not willing to endure the consequences of refusing to surrender identified interview material (such as contempt charges, legal suits, or jail), then anonymity and confidentiality should not be promised.

The foregoing discussion on maintaining various degrees of anonymity indicates the need for some serious strategy planning to avoid problems in this area. Closely related to the problems of anonymity in general are the problems that arise regarding tape-recording of interviews, which bring up the question of how the interview should be recorded and what explanation of the recording technique should be made to the respondent.

RECORDING THE INTERVIEW

The best method for recording the interview must be decided on the basis of various criteria. For example, the method chosen may be one that obtains the most complete and accurate detail, that affords optimal interpersonal relations, or that makes the analysis of the data most efficient. We assume the most valid criterion is that of obtaining complete and accurate information, regardless of the effects upon the problems of analysis. Information collected efficiently is of questionable value if it is not also valid. Of course, there are degrees of reliability and validity which must be considered in relation to the purpose of the project and weighed against the merits of efficiency.

"Taking notes" may consist of either recording the respondent's statements in his or her own words, noting important relevant central ideas, classifying the responses by checking some predefined answer categories, or taking "probe notes." Probe notes are specific points jotted down to be elaborated or clarified later, rather than notes taken to record detailed relevant information.

Note-Taking on Informal Interviews

Recording the interview covers many kinds of activities. In the case of informal interviewing (as in anthropological studies), where the respondent does not see the researcher in the formal role of interviewer, the researcher should not take notes of any kind during the interview. It is typical in participant-observation to make notes on one's observations of others and of one's own reactions after leaving the scene.

Note-Taking on Structured Interviews

In a more formal interview, the problem of noting the relevant information varies according to the scope of the questions to be asked and the degree to which the answers are structured. Where the scope is broad and the answers left open-ended, there is greater difficulty in recording the answers, unless the breadth and openness are used mainly to facilitate the spontaneous flow of communication and the proportion of relevant information is low and falls into anticipated, clearly recognizable categories. In this case, recording the relevant data can be efficient and does not tend to interfere with the interviewer's tasks of critically listening and evaluating the information. The interviewer may be simply required to check a box or to circle a number.

Sometimes the response is not clearly codable into the response categories given. In this case, the interviewer should give the response as completely as possible, and in some cases, check the category which seems nearest to fitting the response. This then becomes a coding problem.

In cases where it is advisable to let the respondent know the answer choices, they may be included as part of the question or the choices can be printed on a card to be handed to the respondent, as illustrated in the chapter on interviewing techniques.

Verbatim notes. For some purposes, it is necessary for the interviewer to record the responses verbatim. In many situations, it is not humanly possible for the interviewer to record the total interview verbatim. When the respondent is highly emotional, ungrammatical, or erratic in verbal pacing, and yet a complete report is needed, the only solution is to use a tape recorder. The verbatim recording of responses in longhand that is a common practice of many survey-type studies is valid only in the following situations:

1. We need the exact words and phrases used by the respondent.

2. The responses cannot practically be categorized in advance.

3. The scope of the question is narrow enough that the relevant response is short and uncomplicated.

4. The essence of the relevant response can be written without damaging rapport in the interview.

5. The interviewer can complete any missing words immediately after the interview before going on to the next.

6. The interviewer's handwriting is corrected or clarified before going on to the next interview so that the people who code the responses may reliably read them.

Under these conditions, when verbatim notes are needed, the interviewer must carefully discipline himself to avoid paraphrasing or summarizing the respondent's ideas.

One method of obtaining verbatim or other fairly detailed notes without either being distracted from listening to the respondent or using a tape recorder is to use a two-person interviewing team, with one person asking the questions while the other takes notes. In some cases it is useful for the two to exchange roles from time to time. A few of the pros and cons of these "tandem interviews" are discussed by Kincaid and Bright.[1] Although this system has advantages, in that it leaves the interviewer free of note-taking to give full attention to what the respondent is saying and yet avoids the possible objections to a tape recorder, we must carefully evaluate the probable inhibiting effects of the third person in the context of a particular interview situation.

Probe notes. Another type of note-taking is the use of probe notes. In contrast to verbatim notes (which are aimed at storing the information received), the probe notes are taken to remind the interviewer of specific points which should be elaborated or clarified later in the interview. They are similar to verbatim notes in that they include the exact word or phrase used by the respondent rather than a paraphrase or summary. The less the interview is structured by a detailed interview schedule and the more important it is to not interrupt the respondent's association pattern by immediately probing any unclear or incomplete response, the more necessary it is to take probe notes so that the relevant points may be elaborated and clarified later.

Effects of note-taking on rapport. Taking notes in an interview may have several effects. Intense note-taking may distract the interviewer from the task of observing and listening to the respondent. Also, the respondent may feel the interviewer should not neglect him or her and should show more spontaneous appreciation. When few notes are taken, the respondent may feel that when the interviewer is writing, something important has been said. In hostile territory, it is usually better to leave note-taking until after the interview if the session is short and the details are few. The interviewer can often detect the respondent's positive or negative reaction to the note-taking by the latter's tendency to elaborate at those points where the interviewer is taking notes, to go back and qualify or "correct" those points, or to quickly pass on to a new topic.

In some situations, the poised pencil seems to act as a nonverbal probe to "tell me more about that." Where note-taking seems to have a

---

[1]H. V. Kincaid and M. Bright, "The Tandem Interview: A Trial of the Two-Interviewer Team," *Public Opinion Quarterly* 21 (Summer 1957), pp. 304–12.

negative effect, the interviewer can ameliorate some of the effect by devoting his full attention to the respondent and taking as little notice of the note-taking as possible. The interviewer should never attempt to take notes secretly. If the effect of taking notes is detrimental, then the danger of being caught or even suspected would be much more detrimental. The best approach is to assure the respondent of anonymity and to explain that notes must be taken to ensure completeness and accuracy. When the respondent does not accept this idea, it is better to refrain from taking notes.

Tape-Recording the Interview

The tape recorder is not used in most interviewing. In some cases this is simply because the information is so simple that it can be readily represented by merely checking an answer category on the interview form. In other cases it is clear that much relevant data might be lost without the tape recorder, yet it is not used because of cost considerations. Even though the cost of tape recorders and tape has been greatly reduced over the last two decades, the cost of transcribing and coding tape recorded material has risen considerably. If every word of the interview is to be transcribed, it may require two to six hours of typing for each hour of tape. This ratio varies with the speed of the speech, clarity, pacing, complexity of vocabulary, accents of the interviewer and respondent, clarity of the recording, and the amount of background noise, as well as with the technical skill and background knowledge of the typist.

Despite these disadvantages of economy, particularly for large-scale projects, the tape recorder is an invaluable tool for certain phases of interviewing. Even on those projects which depend mainly on highly structured interview schedules, the tape recorder is an excellent tool in the initial exploratory interviewing and subsequent pretesting of the interview schedule.

The tape recorder is almost indispensable for the teaching and supervising of interviewing. It would seem ludicrous to try to teach painting without seeing the student paint a picture, or to teach swimming without seeing the person in the water, but people are often taught to interview without the advantage of having any experienced person actually hear them interview. Instead, an attempt is often made to learn by reading detailed instructions or basic theoretical ideas, perhaps doing some role-playing, and then going out to learn by doing. Also, the supervisor of the interviewers on a large project may determine the interviewer's skill by noting such objective indexes as whether all the questions have been answered, whether verbatim notes are clearly legible, and whether the quota of interviews is completed on schedule. All of these indexes do not tell us whether the interviewer unwittingly loads the questions with a particular tone of voice, interrupts the respondent, probes for more information at appropriate points, and correctly codes or records what the respondent has said.

Also, for the person who wants to improve his or her interviewing independently, the tape recorder is a boon. Without it, the person cannot be fully aware of where inadequate information was accepted without probing, where specific opportunities to probe were missed, and where chances to note important nonverbal cues from the respondent were overlooked. All of these can be recorded on tape and heard more accurately by the interviewer later when he or she is free from the strain of listening, recording, and deciding what to say next. Another unique advantage is that precisely the same behavior can be analyzed several times by the same or different people.

In addition to being used as a tool for teaching, supervision, and self-instruction, the tape recorder is sometimes needed for all of the interviews in some types of data-gathering projects. In deciding whether the tape recorder should be used in this way, there are many variables to consider. Objective evidence has been accumulated showing that much of the apprehension about the inhibiting effects of using the tape recorder are valid only under certain limited circumstances. One of the most comprehensive and thoughtful treatments of the pros and cons of using the tape recorder is given by Bucher, Fritz, and Quarantelli.[2] Another article by Engle[3] deals with the advantages of using the tape recorder in consumer research, and Womer and Boyd[4] show the value of the tape recorder in the simultaneous training and selection of an interviewer for a particular field study. These and other more atomistic experimental studies can be subsumed under some general principles to guide our decision as to whether or not we should plan on using a tape recorder on a specific project.

The more complex the information, the less the method should depend upon the interviewer's memory. The more rapid the flow of relevant information, the less we should depend upon taking longhand notes. The more we wish to explore for unanticipated types of responses and the less sure we are of what categories of information are relevant to the problem, the more we should use a tape recorder, which omits nothing and allows the relevance of the responses to be decided later.

---

[2]Rue Bucher, Charles E. Fritz, and Enrico L. Quarantelli, "Tape Recorded Interviews in Social Research," *American Sociological Review* 21, no. 3 (June 1956), pp. 359–64.

[3]J. F. Engle, "Tape Recorders in Consumer Research," *Journal of Marketing* 26 (April 1962), pp. 73–74.

[4]S. Womer and H. W. Boyd, Jr., "The Use of a Voice Recorder in the Selection and Training of Field Workers," *Public Opinion Quarterly* 15 (Summer 1951), pp. 358–63.

The greater the significance of the precise words used and the order in which ideas are expressed, the more necessary it is to use a tape recorder. The less topic control is used, and the less the sequence of topics is controlled, the more important it is for the interviewer to be relieved of verbatim reporting in longhand and allowed to devote more attention to probe notes. The more important it is for the interviewer to devote full attention to the respondent to obtain optimal interpersonal relations, the more important it is to use the tape recorder.[5] However, because of the time consumed in transcribing or coding, the tape recorder should never be used if all relevant data can be validly recorded on the spot by the interviewer. One exception would be the situation where the interviewer tape records in order to improve his or her technical and tactical skills.

One sometimes crucial advantage of tape-recording an interview is that it makes it possible to measure and improve the reliability of the coding operation. This may be done by either having the same person code the same interview twice or by having two different people code the same interview independently and then compare the results. By discussing any disagreements, the coders can determine whether the disagreement is due to a lack of clarity in the definitions of the coding categories, due to the failure of the coders to apply the definitions logically, or due to the failure of the interviewer to probe to obtain relevant, clear and complete answers. By using the interviewer as one of the coders of a few pretest interviews, it is possible to sharpen the code definitions, to make the interviewer more acutely aware of the need to probe for clarity and completeness, and to make the coders more reliable in their application of the coding categories. The tape-recorded interview is to the research team as the instant replay video tape is to the football or dance coach. It is an indispensable tool in the process of perfecting our act. In some social science circles the historic significance of this bit of technological revolution has not yet been fully realized or exploited.

Even though the vast majority of interviews done by both specialized and auxiliary interviewers are not done with a tape recorder, the writer feels that it has a unique function in the exploratory interviewing phase of many large-scale projects, for teaching, supervision, and self-instruction in interviewing, as well as for collecting all of the data on certain types of projects. Thus, it is worthwhile to deal with some of the basic ideas involved in using the tape recorder for any one of these purposes.

---

[5]Charlotte H. Wilkie, "A Study of Distortions in Recording Interviews," *Social Work* 8, no. 3 (July 1963), pp. 31–36. This study shows how distortions in recording seriously limited the worker's understanding of the client's problems.

When a tape recorder is to be used, here are several precautions that should be taken to facilitate optimal interpersonal relations:

1. The interviewer should become thoroughly familiar with the machine so that he or she does not feel insecure in its use or devote too much attention to it.

2. The physical setting should be arranged, if possible, so that the tape recorder is out of the respondent's sight.

3. The microphone should be inconspicuous and out of the direct line of sight as the interviewer and respondent face each other.

4. The use of the recording machine should be explained in forthright and matter-of-fact way.

5. Once the interview begins, the interviewer should show no awareness of the tape recorder's presence.

In explaining the use of the tape recorder to the respondent, the interviewer realizes, with experience, that it is rare to find a respondent who will object to its use. It is possible for the interviewer to raise doubts in the respondent's mind by *asking* for the respondent's permission to use the machine rather than *explaining* why it is used. The interviewer should show by his or her manner that it is merely routine procedure. Some explanation such as one of the following is usually sufficient:

I am interested in getting all the details of your story in precisely your own words. Since I can't take shorthand and don't want a third person present, the best way is to let this machine do all the work.

or:

We always record the interview so that the information will be accurate. I listen to it and type the relevant material so that the tape can be used over again.

Transcribing Tape-Recorded Information

The problem of transcribing the information from a tape-recorded interview depends on how much of the total flow must be transcribed, either because it is clearly relevant, near-relevant, or provides a context in which to interpret the relevant. The proportion to be transcribed from the tape could vary from none to 90 percent. It would be none only if coders were to listen to the tape for information clearly falling into relevant categories for which only a frequency count is necessary. If such information occurs rarely, the only way to do a reliability check is to have two coders listen independently to the same tape, record the location on the tape (giving the numbers on the tape meter at that moment), and then check to see if they recorded the same numbers in the same categories.

If the *form* of the statements, their *contexts*, or their *sequence* is important for the coders to know, the relevant information must be transcribed regardless of how little or how much is relevant. Ideally, the interviewer should also be able to type fairly rapidly while not being concerned about misspellings, typos, or crossed-out words. Let us look at some of the conditions under which it would be beneficial to have the interviewers transcribe their own interviews.

Interviewers transcribing their own interviews. First, if because of field conditions there is poor audibility in the tape, the person who did the interview is much less likely to make errors in transcribing. Second, if the interviewer has been careless in those details essential to obtaining a clearly audible recording, he or she will directly reap the results of this carelessness and be strongly motivated to obtain better audibility on subsequent interviews. Third, if there are peculiarities of speech, such as regional or foreign accents, the interviewer is more likely than the typist to understand them. Fourth, it is an excellent training device, since it makes the interviewer acutely aware of errors in techniques and tactics. Fifth, the interviewer becomes aware of the amount of missing information and is then motivated to probe more persistently in subsequent interviews. If it is not practical to have interviewers transcribe all of their interviews, it would still be highly desirable to have each interviewer transcribe at least the first interview in a series.

The relevant material should first be transcribed in the order it occurred on the tape with no attempt to organize it systematically. Keeping the information in sequence is not only more practical than attempting to code it as we go, but this also preserves the unique context. This practice assumes that the interviewer who is doing the transcribing has a clear grasp of the problem and therefore is capable of selecting the *relevant* information. This assumption is warranted since, as we pointed out previously, unscheduled interviewing cannot be done successfully by anyone who does not thoroughly understand the problem. This selection process sharpens the interviewer's awareness of the problem and makes the interviewer acutely aware of any shortcomings in the information he or she has obtained. As a general rule, unless material is clearly irrelevant, it should be transcribed. It can later be rejected in the coding process.

Dictating relevant material. If only a portion of the recorded material is relevant and the interviewer cannot type or is more urgently needed to interview, the following tactic can be effective. The interviewer listens to his or her recording and then *dictates* the relevant information onto another tape which is then transcribed by a good typist. When this system is used, it is critical that the interviewer does not *interpret* the "real meaning" of the respondent's words to make them more relevant, more clear, or more complete. The exact words of the respondent must be used. Of course it is permissible to edit the respondent's words to the extent of leaving out "guggle" such as the "ahs," "uhs," "well . . . erh," by omitting repetitions, or by inserting the referents where the relevant sentence uses "this," "that," "these," "those," "them," or "it" to refer to a sentence which was not transcribed. This method has all of the advantages of making the interviewer aware of his or her own techniques and tactics as well as the relevance, clarity, and completeness of the information obtained.

The transcribed material should then be coded by the interviewer and another person familiar with the problem. As a reliability check, the material should be coded by independent coders who are familiar with the problem. There is a real danger in using the test-retest measure of reliability if this is done only by the original interviewer, because in many cases the interviewer tends to read into the material more than is there. If the second coder does not code some material in the same way, it is often because the coder sees less information in the material than the interviewer does. In this case, the interviewer might become aware that he or she is judging on the basis of additional information and insights which have not been transcribed from the tape. Often, there is a certain *gestalt* in the total interview which is lost in the transcription, thus possibly making the original interviewer's judgment more accurate. At any rate, the cross-check between the interviewer and the noninterviewer provides a more balanced view and forces the interviewer to support his or her interpretations with clearer evidence. Often, the interviewer becomes aware that he or she should include in the transcription significant nonsymbolic cues which influenced the interpretation of the material. This usually increases the agreement between the interviewer and the noninterviewer coding the material.

The interviewers on the project should transcribe and code their first interview as soon as possible so that subsequent interviews will benefit from the experience. This practice is beneficial whether the main purpose of the project is to learn interviewing techniques or whether the main aim is to obtain complete, reliable, and valid information. Having the interviewing, transcribing, and coding all done by the same people improves the quality of the data in situations where nonscheduled interviewing is needed; therefore, the sooner these experiences are combined in one interview, the sooner the next interview will be improved.

Another distinct advantage of alternating interviewing and transcribing is that it provides a more balanced variety of activities throughout the life of the project and saves the interviewer from continuous long hours of tedious transcription and coding of data.

Sometimes the objection is made that having the interviewing, transcribing, and coding done by highly skilled people will make the cost of the operation prohibitive. We have no choice if we decide that tape-recorded nonscheduled interviews should be used only to get information that could not be obtained just as effectively by a questionnaire or a highly structured interview. Open-ended data cannot be reliably coded by people who do not thoroughly understand the problem. Nor can nonscheduled interviewing be done by people who are merely following mechanical rules. Since it takes a considerable investment of time to familiarize someone with the problem, it is more efficient to use the same people for both the coding and the interviewing.

There are certain conditions under which it is more efficient to have typists do the transcribing. If the audibility of the tape is extremely clear, if the typists are sufficiently impressed with the importance of accuracy, and if the proportion of relevant data is so high that it is quicker to transcribe the whole interview than to select out the relevant material, then the use of typists may be satisfactory.

We have found the proportion of directly relevant interview material to vary from 1 to 90 percent. For a number of reasons, the use of typists is probably not economical when, for example, only 40 percent of the information is relevant. They often make errors at crucial points in the interview which can be checked only by having someone familiar with the interview situation listen to the tape and check it against the typescript. Also, the length of time required to type the total interview is sometimes greater than that required for the interviewer, who may not be as good a typist, to select and type 40 percent of the interview. The coding process is cumbersome when there is a large proportion of extraneous material. Also, the amount of inaudible material will be much greater if the interviewers are not responsible for doing their own transcribing.

Poor audibility is one of the main causes of transcribing difficulty! Sometimes one hour of tape-recorded material can be transcribed in as little as three hours if the rate of speech is average and the audibility perfect. However, ten hours might be needed to transcribe one hour of tape with poor audibility.

PLANNING THE OPENING QUESTION

Even though the interview is not scheduled to the extent of providing exact questions or an order for covering subtopics, it is advisable for the interviewer to prepare several opening questions. The importance of the opening question is too great to leave to caprice, yet neither should it be rigidly predetermined.

There are several important and unique functions of the opening question. It may either be broad enough to delineate the entire topic of the interview, or it may select a single point of departure. In either case, it should be clearly connected with the explanation of the interview so that the respondent is immediately aware that the interviewer is pursuing the stated purposes. If possible it should ask for information which is relatively easy for the respondent to give so that there is no chance of ego threat at the outset. The opener may also begin with a point on which the respondent feels particularly qualified to speak, thus appealing to his or her need for recognition. A well-phrased question might also demonstrate sympathetic understanding of the respondent's problems. Finally, if the interview requires free-flowing and detailed answers rather than simple yes-no responses, it is important that the respondent realize this at the beginning.

In studying the attitudes and problems of the community's senior citizens, an excellent opening question was found to be, "Do you think there is some age at which people should stop working?" A question equally appealing to teenagers in a study of parent-child conflict was, "What are some of the things you feel parents and other adults should know to get along with teenagers?"

It is often desirable to plan opening questions for different categories of representative or special respondents, so that each can begin the interview at a point that concerns him or her.

In interviews where the main problem is to stimulate the respondent's memory of experiences during a certain period of time, it is useful to begin the interview with a question regarding a point in time prior to the events the interviewer wants reported. This "lead-in" helps establish associations and builds an appropriate mood and pace before dealing with the critical time period. The lead-in portion of the interview may last from thirty seconds to ten minutes, depending on how far in the past and how detailed the experiences to be reported. The time needed for the lead-in discussion increases when it functions to supply certain background information about the respondent or the event providing a context for the interview.

When approaching each respondent, the interviewer should make it a point to get to the opening question as quickly as possible. The introduction, the explanation of the purpose and sponsorship of the study, the explanation of how the respondent was selected and the extent to which he or she is anonymous, and any explanation of the recording should be as economical and clear as possible in order to get into the opening question. In some cases, not all of these preliminaries are needed because the respondent understands the situation. At other times, the explanation needed is so long and involved that further explanations of the objectives of the interview, the use of the data, the respondent's anonymity, or the recording method might be made as the interview progresses, at points where the context makes it more meaningful.

SUMMARY

Strategy includes the overall planning done before the actual interview is under way. This planning is done carefully on the basis of information gained regarding the field situation, but the strategy plans must be considered tentative and subject to revision on the basis of additional information gained after the interviewing begins.

Three dimensions of the general field situation (friendly-hostile, open-closed, and single-multiple contacts) affect the general strategy to be used. These general types of field situations provide a backdrop for making basic decisions.

These basic decisions include the selection of appropriate respondents, of appropriate interviewers and interviewer roles, choosing an appropriate time and place, and structuring the interview situation. All of these decisions are made on the basis of their probable effect upon the respondent's willingness or ability to give the relevant information. All of them are strategy tools which can be used to minimize the inhibitors and to maximize the facilitators of relevant information. All these decisions, and their effect, depend upon their meaning to the respondent.

In selecting appropriate respondents, a distinction must be made between *key informants*, who provide strategy information on how to obtain information, and *respondents*, who provide information directly relevant to the objectives of the interview. Respondents are either *special* respondents, who have specialized types of information which can be obtained only from people in a certain role or status, or *representative* respondents, who are chosen because they share certain characteristics defining a group or category of people.

In selecting respondents, the problem is to determine who has the needed information, who is most able to give it, and who is the most willing to give it. Whether or not the person has the relevant information depends upon his or her experiences in relation to the purposes of the interview. The respondent's ability or willingness to report experiences depends upon the degree to which the facilitators and inhibitors of communication are present.

Once we know what information is needed, the field situations where it must be sought, the kinds of respondents who possess such information and are most able and willing to report it, the next problem is to decide what type of interviewer is most likely to be able to obtain the information completely, validly, and efficiently. Certain overt characteristics such as sex, age, race, ethnicity, speech patterns, dress, and grooming place limits upon the role repertory of the interviewer by determining the respondent's perception of the interviewer. Of these overt characteristics, only dress and grooming are easily changed. The others can be controlled only by selecting the appropriate person as interviewer. The interviewer's basic personality traits are also important insofar as they determine his or her ability to perform the interviewing task. Since, by definition, these traits cannot be changed to fit the interview situation or the type of respondent, the problem must be solved by selecting the right interviewer for a particular task. Interviewers may also be selected on the basis of certain special knowledge needed and for the presence or absence of certain attitudes. To a certain extent, the relevant knowledge can be acquired for the particular interviewing task and attitudes can be controlled by training, but there are practical limits upon both.

From the point of view of a particular interviewer, the task is to determine which auxiliary role or roles in his or her own natural role repertory should be presented to the respondent or which new auxiliary role can or should be taken to facilitate interviewing. The particular role taken by the interviewer is important only insofar as it puts the interviewer in a different relationship with the respondent. Role relationships exist along at least two dimensions: the in-group–out-group dimension and the superordinate-subordinate dimension. In appraising the in-group–out-group dimension certain conditions can be specified giving advantages to both ends of the continuum. Similarly, there are advantages and disadvantages in both the superordinate and the subordinate role. The desirability of a particular role relationship depends upon how it affects the respondent's willingness to give relevant information.

The place of the interview provides the opportunity to communicate and, like a stage set, acts as a context for action which brings certain auxiliary roles to the foreground for both the interviewer and the respondent. The respondent's self-perception and the respondent's perception of the interviewer have an effect upon the degree to which certain information is inhibited because of ego threat or etiquette. In addition, the setting may minimize competing time demands, stimulate recall, and provide the conditions needed for the interviewer to use his or her techniques and tactics to full advantage.

The temporal setting of the interview is significant in its relationship to the time of the experiences which the respondent is reporting. When the interviewer asks the question determines to a great extent both the respondent's ability and willingness to give the information. The selection of an appropriate time can minimize the inhibiting effect of forgetting, ego threat, and competing time demands, as well as maximize the facilitating effect of sympathetic understanding, catharsis, and the respondent's need for meaning.

The final phase of strategy consists of structuring the interview situation before the actual questioning and probing begin. To assure best results, the interviewer must have planned how to introduce himself, how to explain the sponsorship and purpose of the interview, how to explain the selection of the particular respondent, how much anonymity should be promised, how to record the interview, and several possible opening questions. These aspects influence the respondent's views of the interviewer's role and of what information is relevant, as well as the respondent's willingness to give relevant information.

Strategy problems have many dimensions. It is impossible to provide a specific solution for each possible problem. Instead, we have pointed to some of the available strategy tools and must leave their application to multitudinous specific situations to the interviewer. The author's experience in consulting and in training interviewers shows that many of the strategy errors were avoidable in that the interviewer had at his command resources to solve the problems. Failures most frequently resulted from not raising the right questions before leaping into the situation.

Selected Readings

Douglas, Jack D. *Investigative Social Research: Individual and Team Research*. Beverly Hills, Calif.: Sage Publications, 1976.
> One of the less conventional treatments of informal interviewing in the context of participant observation, in that it deals with the *conflict model* of field research where a team is operating in situations in which the respondents have something to hide. Many of the empirical examples are from studies of the massage parlor and the nude beach in which the respondents have devised elaborate "fronts" to conceal their real purposes.

Einhorn, Lois J., et al., *Effective Employment Interviewing*. Glenview, Ill.: Scott, Foresman, 1982.
> Chapter 6 deals with opening the interview and strategies for structuring the interview.

Chapter Twelve

Sample Surveys

This chapter deals with the sample survey as one type of field strategy which may provide the context for interviewing as well as other modes of data collection. We will concentrate mainly on the sample survey from the viewpoint of the interviewer and the field supervisor. We will omit the research design phase of the survey by assuming that the purpose of the survey is clear, the specific questions have been formulated, the universe of respondents has been delineated, the statistical treatment of the information has been planned, and arrangements have been made for appropriate data processing. We will deal with sampling design only as it affects the behavior of the interviewer or supervisor and omit the mathematical theory of sampling which is available in standard statistics books.

BASIC TYPES OF SAMPLE SURVEYS

It is desirable to know the basic dimensions that distinguish one type of sample survey from another in order to decide when a sample survey rather than some other strategy should be used and to fit the survey design, when it is needed, to its purposes.

Any study that requires the analysis of only one case *cannot* use a sample survey. The word *case* is used in this context to refer to the element to be analyzed regardless of whether it is a person, a group, an organization, institution, or event. But any study which calls for making statements about an aggregate of many elements belonging to the same category (population, or universe) without studying every case in that category *can* use a sample survey.

Once it is clear that a sample survey is needed, we have the choice of several kinds. First, we must decide whether the sampling element is to be individual people, families, groups, organizations, institutions, events, or processes of change. Second, we can then decide whether the purpose can be best accomplished by a one-shot, cross-sectional survey or a longitudinal sampling at different times. Third, if the time dimension is important, we then must choose among a trend study, a cohort study, and a panel study. Fourth, after these decisions are made we are ready to choose among different sampling strategies. Now let us look at these distinctions one at a time.

Sampling Element

The sampling element is the object or events to be analyzed. Too frequently it is assumed that in a survey the sampling element must be an individual. Perhaps this restricted view springs from the assumption that if we *interview* individuals then we are trying to *analyze* individuals. For example, if we want to understand the process of school desegregation in large cities we would have to interview a large number of individuals, but the aim is to understand specific cases of an *event* called desegregation. Our element of analysis would be the desegregation event in big-city schools. If we studied only one case, we would not have a sample survey even though many individuals might be interviewed because we would deal only with the key informants who were actually involved in the one decision either to desegregate or not. If, however, we wanted to study many cases of successful and unsuccessful desegregation in order to generalize about the process we would have to take a sample of schools that was representative of all schools of a certain category and compare segregation versus desegregation decisions.

In thinking about the sampling element it is also useful to distinguish between studying static characteristics of any element and studying actions or processes in which it may engage. For example, we can either focus on relatively fixed characteristics of a person such as sex, age, political affiliation, religious background, and race, or we can focus on events or behaviors of that individual, such as how the person decides to vote for or against a particular candidate. In the first case we may engage in a spatial sampling of people as physical objects, but in the second situation we must have some way of pinpointing the event in time. Some events, such as births, deaths, marriages, bankruptcies, are already neatly recorded and listed, so that a random sample can be easily drawn. Other events, such as starting to smoke marijuana, having extramarital sexual relations, or deciding to shoplift, are not recorded in any systematic way so that sampling becomes a much more difficult problem.

Cross-Sectional versus Longitudinal Surveys

Once we have specified the sampling elements, we must choose between two general types of sample surveys: the cross-sectional and the longitudinal. The *cross-sectional* survey is used to describe certain properties of the elements at a single point in time. Even though there may be two or more samples or subsamples to allow comparison, the point of the comparison is between two different universes at the *same* point in time. A *longitudinal* survey is one that samples the same universe at two *different* points in time. There are three different varieties of longitudinal surveys: trends, cohorts, and panels.

Trend studies. In *trend* studies the universe is defined as all of those units (persons, groups, institutions, or communities) in a certain category or geographical location at the different points in time they are sampled. For example, trends in Bostonians' attitudes toward divorce could be shown by taking a random sample of the residents of Boston on April 1 of each year. In the trend study the sample will be different people each year because a different sample is taken. Also, the characteristics of the people (age, sex ratio, race, etc.) may differ from sample to sample because of change in the composition of the population of the city from year to year. In this case we do not know whether any change in attitude is due to a general change in U.S. public opinion or to a change in the composition of the city's population unless we also collect information on such demographic variables as age, sex, race, religion, and ethnicity so that we can compare trends among these subsamples.

Cohort studies. A second type of longitudinal survey is the *cohort* study. In the cohort study the universe is defined as a certain age group. The particular age group chosen for the first survey is followed through time. Thus, if we sample eighteen-year-olds in 1975, we then take a sample of nineteen-year-olds one year later. In essence the cohort study follows a certain age group through time, so that the sample is one year older each year. The cohort may be either uniform in age, as in a study beginning with first graders in the public schools, or varied in age, as in a study of people leaving the Army in 1975. The requirements of a cohort study are fulfilled as long as the successive samples of the same category of people are getting older each year. The point of the cohort study is to focus on changes that take place as a person (or any other sampling element, such as an institution) goes through the life cycle.

Both the trend study and the cohort study preclude any direct analysis of the *causes* for the changes in individuals since different people are in the different samples. For example, if it is found that 50 percent of the twenty-one-year-old college students in 1970 felt it advisable to put the Panama Canal under United Nations' jurisdiction and 90 percent of the thirty-one-year-olds felt this way in 1980, we could not study why certain individuals did change and others did not since there is no way of knowing which people had switched their views. Furthermore, it is possible that the percentage of the sample favorable to United Nations' jurisdiction would be precisely the same in the samples despite the fact that a sizable number shifted from pro to con, because an equal number may have shifted from con to pro. This deficiency is overcome in the panel study.

Panel studies. In the case of the *panel* study the same individuals are studied at successive points in time. Thus, at point B in time the panel can be divided into those who did not change and those who did. Those who did change are further divided by their direction of change. Then additional information about the members of the panel may be used to account for change or lack of change.

There are several limitations to the panel study. It is necessary to select a sample of a given population and faithfully collect all the needed information in repeated interviews of the *same* people. This rules out any secondary analysis of previous studies of other people done by different researchers—which is possible in trend studies and cohort studies. Another limitation lies in the fact that, even though the sample may accurately represent the population at the first point in time, they get a year older each year, thereby omitting any representation of the younger portion of the population. This might be called the *life-cycle* effect. Another way in which the panel becomes unrepresentative is in the *education effect* of the repeated interviewing. It has been shown in some studies that the panel members become more sophisticated on the topic of the interview than the population in general because of the thought stimulated by the repeated interviewing. Another difficulty with the panel study is the greater difficulty of analysis, since each individuals' "before" and "after" opinions must be matched and cross-classified into different categories of change or nonchange. However, this objection is invalid since it is a logical necessity in view of the unique aim of the panel study.[1] A final source of decreasing representativeness of the panel is the *attrition* of members.

The life-cycle effects and the attrition effects in the panel study are minimized when the panel is used to explore the causes of short-range changes in the attitudes, knowledge, or opinion of the group. For example, a typical use of the panel study is to discover how people make up their minds to vote for or against a political candidate. In this case the respondent might be interviewed once a month for the last six months preceding the election. However, this short-run use of the panel does not preclude the possible educational effect. The amount of educational effect would depend upon the nature of the topic, how specific the interview questions were, the frequency of the interviews, and the relative force of other factors operating to change the respondent's opinion.

---

[1]Donald C. Pelz and Frank M. Andrews, "Detecting Causal Priorities in Panel Study Data," *American Sociological Review* 29 (1964), pp. 836–48.

Approximating Longitudinal Surveys

There are several ways in which cross-sectional studies may approximate a longitudinal study without actually interviewing at more than one point in time. All have their strengths and weaknesses. First, the respondent may be simply asked how he or she feels about a certain topic at this moment and then asked to remember how he or she would have answered the same question at a previous point in time. This runs the risk of inaccuracy due to the memory barrier. However, it is possible with excellent depth interviewing, using tactics designed to help free the association process of the respondent, to minimize the effect of forgetting. Of course this would increase the cost per interview.

Another method of approximating the longitudinal study is to compare different age groups within the one cross-sectional sample. For example, if we want to know whether attitudes toward premarital sex relations are changing, we could compare the attitudes of the twenty to twenty-nine-year-olds with those of the thirty to thirty-nine and the forty to forty-nine-year-olds. The obvious danger here is that we will confuse a life-cycle change in attitude with a historical trend.

A third way to study processes of change is to analyze the data in one cross-sectional survey according to a *scaling pattern*. For example, if we find that everyone who has done act C has also done acts A and B, and that everyone who has done act B has also done A, then we can assume an ordinal chronological relationship exists: that A must be done before B and B before C. Concretely, this could be applied to discovering the order in which people begin using certain drugs. If, for example, all heroin users had used marijuana, and all marijuana users have smoked tobacco, then we could say that there is an order in which people begin using these drugs. Or in a market research survey, we might find that everyone who owns an electronic oven also owns a freezer, television set, and refrigerator; that all those who own a freezer also have a television set and refrigerator; and that everyone who owns a television set will also have a refrigerator; and some who do not have a television set do have a refrigerator. We would then know that the order in which people acquire major electrical appliances would be as follows: refrigerator, television set, freezer, and electronic oven.

Although this application of scaling to the current pattern does give us a valid description of the chronological order of events, it cannot be interpreted as showing any causal sequence. That is, we cannot say that, because people use marijuana before heroin, this is evidence that the use of marijuana is the cause of the use of heroin. Nor can we validly conclude that since only 5 percent of those who used marijuana ever used heroin the use of marijuana is not one factor in a causal pattern leading to the use of heroin. This would be logically equivalent to saying that only 5 percent of those people exposed to a cold virus actually caught cold and therefore the virus is not a cause of colds. All we can say scientifically is that if X is not always followed by Y then X alone is not the total cause of Y.

All of the one-shot, cross-sectional attempts to study change have weaknesses compared to the longitudinal study. However, for practical purposes the shortcomings are sometimes tolerated, either because the cross-sectional survey is so much less costly than repeating the survey, or because there is not enough time to do repeated surveys into the future so a trend must be established now by reconstructing the past.

BASIC SAMPLING STRATEGIES

Once we understand the differences among basic sampling strategies, we are better able to fit a particular sample design to the type of survey we need to do. Although theoretically all of the basic sample designs could be applied to any survey, regardless of whether the sample element was a person or an institution or whether we needed a cross-sectional or longitudinal study, practically, the problems of identifying sample elements and locating respondents rule out the use of certain sampling strategies in a particular instance.

Simple Random Sampling

Simple random sampling assumes that we have been able to identify every member element in the universe to be sampled and that each element is represented in some way so that it can be randomly selected. By randomly selected we mean that, each time an element is selected, all of the elements in the universe have an equal chance of being chosen. For example, if we wanted to take a simple random sample of all students at State College, we could take a list of students, number them consecutively, turn to a table of random numbers (which can be found as an appendix in standard texts on survey research methods or statistics), pick an arbitrary starting point and proceed systematically across the page in any predetermined pattern to find the numbers corresponding to those to be taken from the list as the sample. The number needed for a good sample depends upon several factors which will be discussed later.

This simple random sampling method can be applied whether the sampling elements are people, groups, institutions, or geographical areas (such as blocks within a metropolitan area or counties within the United States). However, there are some very real practical limitations. First, you must be able to obtain a complete list of all elements in the universe to be sampled. This is no problem if sampling the patients in a hospital at a given moment or all of the Presbyterian churches in California; in either case there is a list of all units in the universe to be sampled. If we need a sample of all the people in Chicago, San Francisco, New York, or New Orleans, no such ready-made list exists and the cost of making such a list would be prohibitive.

Even in cases where all of the elements in a large universe are already listed (for example, the universe of telephone subscribers in New York, or the people listed in the city directory of Dayton, Ohio), there is the time-consuming task of identifying every member of the universe with a unique serial number so that every time a sample element is selected every element in the universe has an equal chance of being selected. This chore makes simple random sampling impractical when the universe has millions of elements. There are rare situations in which the universe is large and each unit already has a serial number.

One of the principal advantages of the simple random sample is that you may stop at any point in the selection of the sample with the assurance that the sample is as representative as possible for a sample of that size. A small sample may be drawn and, if it proves to be too small to obtain the amount of accuracy needed, it may be enlarged one element at a time until the needed amount of accuracy is reached. In other types of sampling it is necessary to decide in advance the exact size of sample needed; and during the process of selection the sample does not become truly representative until all sample elements have been drawn. The implications of this will be more clear as we compare simple random sampling with systematic sampling.

Systematic Sampling

In systematic sampling we must first decide how many elements we need in the sample, calculate what proportion the sample is of the universe, and then use this proportion as the sampling interval. If the sampling proportion is 10 percent, then the sampling interval is stated as "one out of ten" or every tenth unit. To select every tenth element randomly, all elements of the universe must be arranged in some consistent or systematic order. There are two basic systematic arrangements: chronological order and spatial order. In the first case we are doing a time sample in which we could either take every tenth event in chronological order or we could sample every tenth time unit of a second, minute, hour, day, week, and so forth.

There are several versions of systematically sampling a spatial order. If we were to sample every tenth household in a city, we would simply start with one house and move through space in one systematic pattern taking every tenth house in the whole universe. We would not have to identify every dwelling unit in advance but merely identify each separate unit as we went along, skipping nine between each one we took.

Another version of systematic space sampling, not so obviously related to space, is sampling from an alphabetical list or a file of cards. For example, if we take every tenth name in the telephone directory we are sampling ordinal space on each page of the telephone book. In essence it is the spatial arrangement of all of the elements of the universe on a piece of paper which is significant. Whether the people are arranged in spatial sequence on the page according to their height, weight, or alphabetical order is irrelevant. Similarly, in sampling from a card file, then, it would not matter whether cards were arranged alphabetically, by social security number, or in random order.

The advantage of the systematic sample over the simple random sample is obvious. There is no need to identify every unit in the universe with an individual number or name, which in a practical situation is a tremendous savings in time. The basic disadvantage is that we must know in advance the size of sample needed, and we must proceed systematically through the *whole* universe before the sample is representative. For example, selecting 100 names from the telephone directory by taking every tenth name from A through M would not be as representative as taking every twentieth name from A through Z. If we did a survey on the assumption that a sample of 100 would be large enough and then found that we needed more cases, we would have to redesign a new sample by taking, for example, every fortieth name from A through Z to get an additional sample of fifty cases to increase precision.

The one condition under which the systematic sample is not representative occurs when the sampling interval happens to correspond to some periodicity in the spatial or temporal arrangement of the units in the universe. For example, if in sampling households we are using the sampling interval of ten, and there happens to be 10 houses to the block in the city we are sampling, this could introduce a bias if we began with the corner house. Every house in the sample would be a corner house which might be a second-floor residence above a corner store of some type. The result may be that we have over-represented small-store owners or renters in the sample.

A second type of systematic bias can be introduced by using an interval scale of either time or space when only the ordinal one is appropriate. For example, if in time-sampling programs broadcast by a certain television network, we tuned in every hour at ten minutes past the hour we would introduce a bias toward the longer programs; obviously any two-hour program would have four times the chance of any half-hour program of being chosen for analysis. In order to get an unbiased sample we could simply select every Nth program in ordinal chronology rather than using some interval scale of time units.

Systematic bias could also be introduced into the space sampling of five file drawers full of mental health case folders. If we pull the cases falling at five-inch intervals, the thicker folders would have a greater chance of being chosen than the thinner folders. This would possibly bias the sample by overrepresenting the cases that were more complicated or that involved clinical tests, or cases that had simply been with the agency for a longer period of time.

If each case occupies an equal amount of time or space, then the interval scale is superior to the ordinal scale sampling interval. Using an interval scale we avoid counting the number of units in the universe to determine the sample interval needed to get a certain size of sample. We also avoid counting the number of cases in each sampling interval. For example, suppose we wanted to take a sample of 500 cases from the two million automobile owners in Los Angeles. If each owner was represented by a card in the file, we would not have to count the number of cards to determine the sampling interval but only measure how many inches of cards are in the file and divide this figure by 500 to obtain the sampling interval in terms of inches. (Thus, if there were 100 cards to the inch those two million cards would occupy 20,000 inches of space in the file drawers. Dividing by 500 gives us a sampling interval of forty inches.) This represents a tremendous savings in time and tedium since you would be measuring off 20,000 inches with your measuring tape rather than counting the two million cards. Even if the total number of cards is known in advance, this would still represent a huge savings in time because a sample of 500 from a universe of two million gives a sampling interval of 4,000. Just picture yourself counting out 4,000 cards once (this is a stack over one yard high) and then repeating the process 500 times! More time could be spent in selecting the sample than in collecting the data from the sample.

Multistage Sampling

To discuss multistage sampling it is necessary to distinguish between the sampling *unit* and the sampling *element*. So far we have spoken only of sampling *elements* which are the entities to be ultimately studied and compared. The sampling *unit* is the particular entity containing the sampling element at some stage in the sampling process. In the one-stage samples we have discussed to this point, the sampling element and the sampling unit are the same entity, but in multistage sampling they are different. For example, in multistage sampling we might use three stages to arrive at a sample of 500 people from the adult population of Minneapolis. The ultimate sampling element is the adult person, but first we might use the city block as the sampling unit by selecting a random sample of blocks from the universe of city blocks. Then we could use the household as the sampling unit by selecting a random sample of households from those in the randomly selected blocks. Finally we could use the individual as the sampling unit by randomly selecting individual adults from all the adults in the randomly selected houses. Thus in this case the adult person is both the sampling element and the sampling unit in the third stage of sampling.

The multistage sample becomes more advantageous as the universe has a larger number of elements and covers a larger geographical area. If we wanted to select a sample of 5,000 voters to predict a presidential election, it would be impossible to identify each of the millions of registered voters in the thousands of precincts in the United States in order to select a simple random sample or even a systematic sample. Instead, it would be much easier to identify all of the cities and all of the rural counties and take a random sample of each. This would be the first stage of sampling. Then we could identify each city block in each of the sample cities and each enumeration district in the rural counties. These are already mapped and identified by number by the U.S. Census Bureau. We could then take a random sample of city blocks and rural Census Enumeration Districts. Up to this point the sample design is done from maps and census data without going out into the field. The last two stages must be done in the field, and are usually done by the interviewers.

Each interviewer is given a map showing the location of all the sample blocks or enumeration districts in a certain portion of the city or county. There should also be a blowup of each block or enumeration district which fills a whole page so that each street is clearly seen. Then the interviewers may begin the *block listing* process. The interviewer goes to the first sample block, starts at one corner and proceeds around the block, drawing in each residential building along the way. For those buildings which are not single-family dwelling units, the interviewer must indicate the number of dwelling units in the building.

Once all of the dwelling units in the sample blocks are located and identified by address and apartment number, the sample of dwelling units may be selected in one of three ways. *Simple random sampling* could be applied by assigning serial numbers to each dwelling unit. Then using a random numbers table, we could select the appropriate number of dwelling units from the whole pool. *Systematic sampling* could be used by taking every Nth dwelling unit from the total list of dwelling units using whatever sampling interval would obtain the size of sample needed. *Cluster sampling* could be applied by randomly or systematically selecting only one dwelling unit from each block or enumeration district and then taking an additional number immediately adjacent to make a cluster of two, three, four, or five. This saves time by not having to select the remaining units in the cluster randomly, and it reduces travel time in reaching the respondents. However, this efficiency of reduced travel time is bought at the price of decreasing the precision of the sample's representativeness. For any given size of sample, precision increases as we reduce the number in each cluster and increase the number of clusters.

If the survey is to be done in a census year or in an area where there has been little change in the number of occupied dwelling units since the last census, we can avoid actually listing all of the units in the block in order to get the sample. By consulting the U.S. Census block publications, we can identify all of the blocks and know the number of dwelling units in each block. When we know in advance the total number of dwelling units in all of the sample blocks and enumeration districts, we need to record only the addresses falling into a systematic sample. For example, if we need a sample of 400 respondents, and there are 40,000 dwellings in our sample of block and enumeration districts, we know that the sampling interval is one out of every hundred dwelling units. Each block lister would walk or drive through the area counting the dwelling units and recording the address of only each 100th unit. This is simple in areas with only single-family dwelling units, but in apart-ment-house areas we must count the apartments in each building. In this systematic area-sampling process we must have some consistent pattern to follow (around the block and within apartment buildings) in counting to the 100th unit. The details of one method of systematically selecting dwelling units is given by Backstrom and Hursh.[2]

The fourth stage would be the selection of individual respondents living in the sample of dwelling units. This is usually done by the inter-viewer at the time of the interview. The method for making this selec-tion depends upon the purpose of the survey, and the nature of the uni-verse we are trying to sample. For example, in sampling the whole adult population in a survey of political opinion, we might want the views of all registered voters, or we might be interested only in information from heads of households.

In principle, the procedure is simple. Have some adult in the house-hold give the first names of all members of the household who fall into the universe in which we are interested. If it is heads of household, we ask, "Who is the head of the household?" If it is all persons eighteen years old or over, we then ask, "Would you tell me how many persons living here are eighteen years or over?" Then if there is more than one, "Please give me the first name of each, beginning with the oldest person down to the youngest." Once all members of the universe are listed, then we must have some random way of choosing the one person to be the respondent. If there is only one adult in the household, then there is no problem of selection because this person has already been selected randomly along with the household. If there are two or more, there are several different systems which fulfill the criterion of randomness. One system is illustrated in the respondent selection chart, Figure 12–1.

This respondent selection chart would appear as the first page of ev-ery interview schedule. The Xs show which person is to be interviewed, depending on the number of adults in the household. This is accom-plished by randomly assigning the Xs to columns 2, 3, 4, and 5. It is suf-ficient to allow for a maximum of only five adults in a household since larger households are mostly children under eighteen years of age. This

---

[2]Charles H. Backstrom and Gerald D. Hursh, *Survey Research* (New York: John Wiley & Sons, 1981).

FIGURE 12-1

RESPONDENT SELECTION CHART
(version A only)

(a) Ask: "How many people 18 years or older live here at the present time?" Circle this number at the top of the appropriate column <u>and</u> circle the X in that column.

(b) If there is more than one such person, ask: "Who is the oldest person living here?; "Who is the next oldest?"; "Who is next oldest?"; etc., until all members of the universe are listed.

(c) The name appearing opposite the circled X is the person you must interview.

First names, oldest to youngest	Number in family				
	1	2	3	4	5
1	X		X		
2		X			
3				X	
4					X
5					

Note: This has the Xs filled in in one of the five different random patterns running through the set of interview schedules.

means that there will be five different versions of the respondent selection chart alternating systematically throughout the series of interviews. The questionnaires would be given serial numbers; and to be sure that respondents were selected randomly, the interviewer would have to use the interview schedules in serial order. If a respondent is not at home, that same interview schedule is assigned to that respondent and used later when calling back. When duplicating 400 copies of the interview schedule, since there are five different versions of the respondent selection page, there would be eighty copies of each version. The five versions would have to be alternated so that they would repeat the series a, b, c, d, e all the way through the 400 copies in serial order. Another technique for selecting the respondent from among the members of the household is given by Backstrom and Hursh.[3]

Stratified Sampling

In designing a sample we can increase its accuracy without increasing the size if we stratify the sample into subsamples of different portions of the universe. These portions of the universe must be identified by certain characteristics of the respondents known to be related to (correlated with) the opinions, beliefs, or attitudes we are trying to sample. For example, if we were going to sample opinions on the women's liberation movement, we would want to stratify the universe into subsamples by sex, age, region, and educational level, since, in general, people are more sympathetic to the women's liberation movement if they are female, younger, Northerners, and highly educated. The more we know about the respondents in the universe and how their characteristics correlate with the opinions we are trying to measure, the more effectively we can stratify the sample to gain precision without increasing the number of respondents in the sample. The greater the correlation between the characteristics by which we stratify and the opinions of the respondents, the greater the gain in precision by stratification of the sample.

The problems involved in designing different types of stratified samples and the implications for the field operations are so many and technical that we cannot deal with them here. Because of these complications and costs the stratified sample is usually designed for those national surveys that are done repeatedly, or for longitudinal studies where the initial cost of the sample design can be amortized over several surveys.

GAINING ACCESS TO THE RESPONDENT

There is always a possibility that the respondent will refuse an interview. One thing that may be increasing the tendency to refuse an interview is the increased use of the commercial sales pitch disguised as a survey. Typically, this fake survey begins with some questions to discover whether the respondent is in the market for the product being sold and then subtly shifts to questions designed to obligate the respondent to attend a demonstration, to receive a sample, or to buy. This practice has helped to develop a widespread public allergy to surveys, especially in large cities. Biel found in a sample survey of 240 respondents in Chicago that 60 percent had at one time been approached in a phony survey either personally or on the telephone.[4] This sometimes explains why a respondent backs off as soon as the interviewer says the word "survey."

Some supervisors of interviewers who have done little interviewing under the conditions of a particular survey may feel that it is always the

---

    [4]Alexander Biel, "Abuses of Survey Research Techniques: The Phoney Interview," *Public Opinion Quarterly* 31 (1967), pp. 298–99.

interviewer's fault if he gets a refusal. This is far from true, and if the supervisor persists in this unsympathetic view, it will increase the pressures that sometimes result in fabrication of interviews by an interviewer.

Studies have shown that refusal rates vary with the ethnic background of the respondent regardless of who the interviewer is. For example, Snell and Dohrenwend in a study of a sample of 214 respondents in New York found that Irish-Americans had a much higher refusal rate than Jewish, Negro, or Puerto Rican respondents, regardless of ethnic background of the interviewer.[5] Also older people and those who have been in the United States a shorter time refused more often.

Perhaps this lower refusal rate of the native Americans is because the survey is beginning to be recognized as a legitimate feature of the American scene. Even as early as 1966 a large minority of the U.S. population had been a respondent at some time in a survey. Hartmann did a sample survey of 1,000 household heads which showed that 35 percent of the population had responded to some type of survey.[6] There were 25 percent who responded to a face-to-face interview, 20 percent to a telephone interview, and 12 percent to a mailed questionnaire. The rate was 40 percent among married women thirty-five to forty-four years old and 65 percent if above $15,000 income. While 57 percent of the sample in the Northeast had been surveyed, only 21 percent in the South Atlantic states had the experience.

There is also evidence that the American public is becoming more sophisticated in making distinctions between the disguised sales pitch, the vested-interest commercial surveys, and the survey aimed at promoting the common welfare. For example, Brunner did a survey on pharmaceutical products in which one sample of interviews was sponsored by a private research corporation and the other by the University of Maryland.[7] The first sample had a 33 percent refusal rate and the one sponsored by the University had only a 16 percent refusal rate. There was probably a tendency of the public to assume that any survey by a commercial firm is more concerned with increasing profits than in improving the product and that a university is more closely identified with the interests of the consumer, taxpayer, and voter.

In trying to reduce the number of refusals a common mistake is made by inexperienced surveyors who first make a telephone call to set up an appointment at a convenient time for the respondent. This strategy

---

[5]Barbara Snell and Bruce P. Dohrenwend, "Sources of Refusal in Surveys," *Public Opinion Quarterly* 32 (1968), pp. 74–83.

[6]Elizabeth Hartmann, "Public Reaction to Public Opinion Surveying," *Public Opinion Quarterly* 32 (1968), pp. 295–98.

[7]G. A. Brunner and S. J. Carroll, "Effect of Prior Telephone Appointments on Completion Rates and Response Content," *Public Opinion Quarterly* 31 (1967–68), pp. 652–54.

has been repeatedly proven ineffective by experimental studies. For example, Brunner, in the same experiment referred to above, showed that the refusal rate among the respondents who were first contacted by phone was much higher than in the cases where the first contact was the personal call. Those contacted by telephone had a refusal rate of 63 percent in contrast to only 33 percent for the face-to-face contacts. In the sample sponsored by the University the rates were 55 percent and 16 percent, respectively.

Other studies have shown that matters are also not improved by first sending a letter instead of making a telephone call. For example, Cartwright and Tucker sent a letter to half of their random sample, explaining that they would like the respondent's cooperation in an anonymous survey of people's health and their use of doctors.[8] The effect of the letter was to *increase* the refusal rate from 22 percent to 34 percent for the middle class, from 15 percent to 64 percent for the working class, from 10 percent to 61 percent for all men, and from 23 percent to 30 percent for all women.

It seems easier for people to refuse when the interviewer is not face-to-face with them at the moment. The difference between the refusal rates with the different modes of initial contact varies not only with the type of respondent as shown above but also with the topic of the interview. If the topic of the interview is viewed as potentially unpleasant by the respondent, he or she will be more likely to refuse in the absence of any personal influence from the interviewer. The attempt to make an appointment in advance by mail or telephone only increases the refusal problem. Fortunately, there are ways the respondent can be prepared for the survey in advance to reduce the refusal rate.

In general we can say that any advance information received by the respondents should not offer the opportunity to refuse to be interviewed. Instead, information should blanket the total population to be sampled through the news media thus avoiding a direct approach to any individual in the sample. This advance publicity should include who is sponsoring the study, why it is being done, what potential benefits might arise from it, why it is so important to obtain responses from 100 percent of the members of the sample, how the sample will be selected, how it is anonymous, how the community is receiving recognition from the larger world for its cooperation in the project, and how the results can be obtained by all interested individuals.

In effect we want to indicate general acceptance of the survey in a tone that assumes that the individual respondent will cooperate. At the

---

[8]Ann Cartwright and Wyn Tucker, "An Attempt to Reduce the Number of Calls on an Interview Inquiry," *Public Opinion Quarterly* 31 (1967), pp. 299–302.

same time there should not be any advance warning to a particular respondent that he or she has been selected and will be interviewed on a certain date.

Of course it cannot be assumed by the interviewer that every respondent in the sample has seen the advance publicity. Even when the respondent has not seen it, the interviewers can take advantage of the advance publicity if they each carry a copy of the story showing clearly the name of the newspaper and the date of publication. Also, as Hills points out, his strategy of mailing a reproduction of a local newspaper story on the impending research, with a newspaper photograph of the interviewer, to each member of the sample was one of the major factors contributing to the 98 percent interview completion rate in his survey of participation in local voluntary associations.[9]

The news photo is particularly helpful in communities where people are reluctant to open the doors to strangers. There is no reason why this strategy could not be used when there are three or four interviewers. Of course it is most effective if there is only one interviewer who happens to be a relatively prestigious person so that the respondent feels that he or she gains recognition by being interviewed.

The refusal rate can also be reduced by carefully selecting interviewers whose visible characteristics are most likely to make the respondent want to at least open the door to give them an opportunity to speak. The sex, race, and dress of the interviewer should be matched with the respondent, considering the topic of the interview and where the interview is to take place. The props which the interviewer carries such as a notebook, a clipboard, a zipper case, briefcase, handbag, umbrella or other item should be specified in view of what is known about the local community's cues for identifying various types of people who might come to the door. The problem is to avoid being mistakenly identified as some type of person the respondent does not want to talk to such as a bill collector or salesman.

Finally, the refusal rate can be reduced if the time for the interview is chosen to minimize any competing time demands upon the respondent. The principle is simple to state but its application depends upon considerable knowledge of the particular population to be sampled and the pattern of demands upon their time. For example, if the population to be sampled is households in the sense that the information needed is facts that can be obtained from any member of the household over sixteen years of age, then the time of the day or the day of the week will not be crucial. Whoever is available or has the most time or is most willing can be interviewed. In fact one person could begin the interview and

---

[9]Stuart L. Hills, "Increasing the Response Rate for Structured Interviews in Community Research," *American Behavioral Scientist* 11 (1968), pp. 47–48.

another respondent could finish it. In some cases it might even be a group interview.

In contrast, if the population to be sampled is a specific category of persons, we can accept no substitutes because the information sought is the attitudes, beliefs, preferences, or expectations of each person in the sample. The difficulty in finding a most appropriate time for interviewing such a sample depends upon how homogeneous it is with respect to the pattern of demands upon their time. For example, if the population is unemployed housewives with school-age children, then the best time to interview most of the members of the sample is probably after lunch and before the children come home from school. But if the population includes all persons over eighteen years of age in a poll on political beliefs, then we are dealing with a more heterogeneous set of time demands.

To find appropriate interview times for such a heterogeneous population, we must abandon the attempt to decide in advance a particular time in common for all members of the sample. Instead, we must either have some relevant advanced information on each member of the sample to pick a most likely time for them, or be content with covering the same geographical territory two or three times to accommodate all of the respondents.

In sampling some populations it is conceivable that interviewers might spend the whole first day in the field without actually finishing one interview. The time is well spent, however, if interviewers finish the first day with some appointments for that week, some information on the best time for call-backs on those who were not home, and some acquaintances among neighbors, relatives, and friends of his or her respondents.

For interviewer morale it is important that the interviewers clearly understand that this field activity is an unavoidable and necessary step in getting the job done. The supervisor must be able to provide a realistic picture of the contact strategy and show the interviewers that gaining access to respondents requires as much skill and resourcefulness as the interview itself. With some survey topics making the contacts is the major aspect of the job.

Once the interviewer is face-to-face with a respondent in the sample, there comes a critical moment which depends entirely on the interviewer's power of verbal persuasion. In a small minority of cases the respondent will show some resistance or skepticism and will need to be convinced. At this point the interviewer need not panic; he or she should realize that most of the forms of resistance have been discovered in previous surveys and certain interviewer responses have been shown effective in the large majority of situations. Also, there are some respondents who would not cooperate regardless of how they were approached. Some of the most typical forms of verbal resistance in sample surveys are succinctly given in a list by Backstrom and Hursh, reproduced here in Figure 12-2. Some of the answers might vary slightly in specific surveys, but the forms of resistance are typical of a variety of survey situations. The interviewer's responses should not necessarily be worded exactly as in these examples, and should not sound like memo-

FIGURE 12-2 Stock answers to respondents

What you should say . . .

1. *If respondent asks:* Who is doing this survey?

   This survey is being conducted by the Research Division of Model State University. We are trying to get some idea about what people think about current issues in Model City.

2. *If respondent presses for a better answer on auspices:*

   Well . . . I'm a professional interviewer. The people in charge of this survey are at the Research Division at Model State University. They'd be glad to explain the survey to you. Would you like their phone number so you could call them? (If "Yes," give trouble number.)

3. *If respondent wonders why he is being interviewed, or suggests interviewing someone else:*

   You were selected completely *by chance* according to procedures worked out by my office. So *your* opinions are important and interviewing someone else wouldn't be as good.

4. *If respondent says he doesn't have time to be interviewed:*

   The questions won't take long. You can go right on with your work and I'll just run through these items. (Begin questioning immediately.)

5. *If respondent insists he is too busy:*

   What would be a better time soon for me to come back? I'll note down an appointment that would be more convenient for you.

6. *If respondent says he doesn't know enough to give good answers:*

   In this survey, it's *not* what you know that counts. Rather, it's what you happen to think about various topics that is important.

7. *If respondent is afraid to answer some question or asks:* What are you going to do with these answers? or Why do you want to know that?

   Well . . . many people are being asked these same questions, of course, and what you say is confidential. We are interested in these questions only to see what a *lot* of people in Model City generally are thinking about.

8. *If respondent resents questions that talk down to him:*

   The people in my office made up these questions, and we are instructed to read each one just as it is written.

9. *If respondent is annoyed and just plain refuses to answer a question:*

   Of course, you don't have to answer any question you'd prefer not to. I'm only trying to get your opinion because our study is more accurate that way. Then if respondent still refuses, don't comment, just go on quickly to the next question. Mark the item "Refused."

Source: Charles H. Backstrom and Gerald D. Hursh, *Survey Research* (New York: John Wiley & Sons, 1981).

rized automatic responses but should have a spontaneous ring because they are understood by the interviewer.

This section on gaining access to the respondent in a sample survey has shown some of the conditions that should be considered in gaining the respondent's cooperation. This is a critical problem when we need a high rate of return to have a fair amount of precision in representing the whole population on the basis of a sample. This section has warned against the mistaken practice of making an initial contact by telephone or letter to obtain permission, or an appointment with the respondent before the interviewer makes a personal appearance on the respondent's doorstep. This section has also given a few basic suggestions on the types of plans, preparations, and approaches designed to reduce the number of refusals, and finally, it has shown that at the last critical moment access may depend upon the interviewer's ability to respond verbally to the various forms of resistance that may be shown by some respondents.

Now we will show how the format of the interview schedule or questionnaire is an important link between the field research team (respondent, the interviewer, and the field supervisor) and the data analysis team.

FORMAT OF THE INTERVIEW SCHEDULE OR QUESTIONNAIRE

The interview schedule in a sample survey is not a simple list of questions; it is a complicated, precision instrument. This section will show the basic functions of the interview schedule and its principal parts as these relate to the sample survey. The interview schedule can be divided into two general functional parts: the face sheet and the body.

Face Sheet

Face sheet refers to the initial pages of the schedule which precede the questions dealing with the topic of the interview. There are several important kinds of information on the face sheet, some furnished in advance by the research team and some obtained from the respondent. Some of the items that may be included in the face sheet are described here.

Sample assignment. It is often convenient to identify a particular interview schedule *before* the specific respondent is selected. For example, in multistage sampling the interview schedule can be identified as a particular element in the sample by indicating that the respondent represented by that particular interview schedule is the first in a cluster of three from Block Number 522 in City A.

This sample element identification allows the field supervisor to know which elements of the sample have been assigned to an interviewer and to assign geographically adjacent respondents to the same interviewer. As the completed schedules begin to come in, the field supervisor can record which portions of the sample have been completed and which remain to be done. This identification also assures that the appropriate form of the respondent selection sheet is used in each case. If the interviewers were free to use any interview schedule with any respondent, and thus control which respondent selection chart was used in a particular case, the sample could be seriously biased.

Respondent selection chart. If the sampling method calls for randomly selecting the individual respondent from a household or other group, then the respondent selection chart, discussed earlier, should be included in the face sheet. Since different schedules have different forms of the respondent selection chart, it is important that no substitutions of face sheets be made. For example, if one interview schedule is damaged before it is used, the substituted face sheet should have the same version of respondent selection chart as the original. For this reason it is useful to identify the different selection charts as version A, B, C, etc., on the face sheet. Without this, it is difficult to quickly recognize the different face sheets.

Introductory statement. It is usually helpful to include a suggested introductory statement which the interviewer should use with each respondent. The statement may include the interviewer's name, the organization for whom he or she works, the organization for whom the survey is being done, the purpose of the survey, the degree of confidentiality or anonymity provided, and how the respondent was selected. Occasionally, some of these elements are omitted or additional ones added. In any case, the interviewer should master the content and meaning so that he or she may spontaneously give the introductory remarks in a natural manner in his or her own words.

Respondent identification. In any sample survey it is necessary to have some way of identifying a particular respondent so that the field supervisor will know whether the sampling procedure has been followed and will have some way of spot-checking whether the selected respondent has actually been interviewed. The supervisor must also be able to assign a particular respondent to a different interviewer if necessary.

How the selected respondent is to be identified depends on the amount of confidentiality or anonymity which must be provided. If call-backs have to be made by an interviewer other than the one who did the original random selection of the respondent, then it will be necessary to include the street address, apartment number, and some designation such as "husband," "wife," "eighteen-year-old daughter," and so on. In some surveys there is no reason for not using the full name, address, and phone number for identification. As long as the names of the individuals in the sample are known to no one except the interviewer and field supervisor, the information is still confidential, since the report to the sponsoring organization or to the public in general does not identify any person in the sample.

Contact record. In obtaining a perfect random sample, it is necessary to locate and interview all members of the sample without any substitutes. For this reason, it is often necessary to try several times to contact some of the hard-to-reach respondents. The contact record allows the interviewer to record all attempts to contact the respondent. He or she records attempts made when the respondent was not at home. If the respondent was home but must be interviewed later, the appointment time should be recorded. When the appointment is kept, the interviewer must record whether or not the interview was completed or whether a second appointment was made.

If the respondent was not at home on the first call, the interviewer should record when the respondent is usually home according to other members of the household or neighbors, so that he or she or another interviewer would have a better chance to contact the respondent on the second try.

If the respondent is identified but not contacted on the first try, the interviewer may obtain enough information about the respondent (such as age, sex, race, etc.) to know that it would be advisable to have a different interviewer make the second attempt to reach the respondent in order to have a better match between interviewer and respondent.

Interviewer identification. The face sheet should provide for indicating the name of the interviewer to whom the case was originally assigned and the names of all interviewers making subsequent contacts. It is essential for any interviewer to know what previous contacts the respondent has had with the study. It is also important to the field supervisor, who can obtain the cooperation of the interviewer in filling in missing information and in interpreting handwriting in "verbatim" responses. Also, the supervisor must know who was responsible for selecting, contacting, and interviewing the respondent in order to exercise the quality control essential for a valid survey.

Demographic data. The face sheet should provide for easy recording of certain demographic characteristics of the respondent. Such demographic facts may serve several purposes. If the sample is stratified by demographic characteristics of the respondent, it is necessary to record these characteristics in each case to determine whether the respondent does in fact fall into the intended stratum. Also, such demographic descriptors may be used simply to determine in which subpopulation of the sample the variables measured by the survey are the strongest. For example, if a periodic national survey is used to determine trends in racial attitudes, it may be helpful to know whether prejudice is strongest in males or females, or in older or younger people. This would provide information useful in reaching the right target audience or in designing educational materials for the reduction of prejudice. A third purpose of the demographic data might be to test hypotheses regarding the causes of a particular attitude or opinion measured in the survey. Usually the demographic variable such as age, sex, or level of education is viewed as the independent variable and the attitude, opinion, or knowledge is the dependent variable. For example, we might hypothesize that the respondent's attitude toward fundamentalistic religion on radio programs might be a function of his or her educational level.

Some of the demographic characteristics most useful because of their association with beliefs, opinions, attitudes, and knowledge, and with the channels of communication through which these subjective orientations may be formed or changed, are listed below:

1. Sex.
2. Age.
3. Race.
4. Ethnic background.
5. Marital status.
6. Income level.
7. Educational level.
8. Occupation.
9. Religion.
10. Home ownership.
11. Residential mobility.
12. Political affiliation.

All of these characteristics of individuals tell us something about their probable social environment and their point of view on that environment. Of course, this relationship between individual characteristic and social environment is not simple and absolute.

The answer categories needed for each of these demographic questions vary from the simple male-female sex dichotomy to the most complex classification of occupation. Although many surveys use only the fourteen occupational categories used by the U.S. Census Bureau, each of these general categories may include a number of more specific jobs. Using these categories permits the proportion of each occupation in the sample survey to be compared with the proportion in the census publications. The specific jobs to be included in each category are given in U.S. Census publications and in Backstrom and Hursh.[10]

Case number. The face sheet should provide for a case number, essential for easy identification and location of a particular interview schedule. Once the schedule has been edited for omissions, errors, and ambiguities, it may be desirable to delete the name and/or address of the respondent before passing the case on to the data processors if confidentiality is important. It may also be desirable to retain names and addresses of all members of the sample listed in serial order by case number in the event that some future contact may be needed. This would reduce the number of people on the research team who could link the interview schedule with a particular individual.

Often it is desirable to take the pages of the interview schedule apart so that the keypunch operator can finish with the first page of questions for all cases in the sample before going on to the next page. This is more efficient and accurate than going through one whole interview schedule before going on to the next. In this case it is absolutely essential to put the *case number on every page* before taking the questionnaire apart. Otherwise there is no way of getting all the data belonging to one case together again.

Body of the Interview Schedule

The body of the interview schedule includes the actual questions to be asked, the answer categories, the code numbers assigned to each question-and-answer category, instructions to the interviewer regarding asking questions or recording answers, coder's spaces and instructions, and possibly one or more sets of response cards which the interviewer hands to the respondent at certain points in the interview.

Question-Answer types. There are four basic types of question-answer formats, depending on the type of information sought. First is the *open-ended* question which has no prefabricated response categories but requires the interviewer to write verbatim the relevant portion of

---

[10]Ibid., pp. 99–100.

FIGURE 12-3   Examples of basic question-answer formats

Open-ended question

1. What do you feel are some of the most important qualities to look for in a candidate for mayor in the next election? _____

_____

_____

Nominal-scale question

2. Which of these qualities do you feel is the *most* important in a candidate for mayor in the next election? (*Hand card to respondent.*) Give me the number of the one most important quality. (*Circle appropriate number.*)
   1. Well educated
   2. Honest
   3. Political experience
   4. Black
   5. Republican
   6. Democrat
   7. Experience in city government
   8. Interested in this city's problems
   9. Other (*Write in.*) _____

   _____

   X No answer

Ordinal-scale question

3. President Jones of State College says the time of political upheaval on American college campuses has passed and will not return in the 1970s!
   Would you agree, disagree, or have no opinion of his statement? Would you say you agree (disagree) *strongly* or just agree (disagree)? (*Circle the appropriate number below.*)
   1. Strongly agree
   2. Agree
   3. Neutral
   4. Disagree
   5. Strongly disagree
   X No answer

Interval-scale question

4. Which of these categories includes your annual family income? (*Hand card.*) Just give me the *letter* in front of the category. (*Circle appropriate number below.*)

a.	(1)	Under $5,000	e.	(5)	$20,000–$24,999
b.	(2)	$5,000–$9,999	f.	(6)	$25,000–$29,999
c.	(3)	$10,000–$14,999	g.	(7)	$30,000–$34,999
d.	(4)	$15,000–$19,999	h.	(8)	$35,000–or over
			X		No answer
			Y		Don't know

---

the response in the space provided. Samples of this type and of the others are shown in Figure 12–3.

Second, there is the question with the *nominal scale* answer categories provided in advance. A nominal scale is a set of qualitative (nonquantitative) categories belonging to a single dimension such as sex (male and female), political affiliation (Democrat, Republican, independent), or marital status (single, married, divorced, separated, widowed).

Third is the *ordinal scale* response format in which the interviewer records quantitative information in the form of ranks rather than some absolute amount. The ordinal-scale item is most commonly used to measure attitudes or to rank preferences or feelings about something. The format of the response usually consists of a five-point scale (for example, strongly agree, agree, neutral, disagree, strongly disagree) in which the point most nearly corresponding to the respondent's feeling is circled.

Fourth, the *interval scale* item calls for information which is quantifiable in terms of absolute values.[11] In measurements of human social behavior most interval scales deal with types of information resulting from enumeration or counting of discrete units, such as years as in age, dollars as in income, or crimes as in crime rate. Interval-scale information may be recorded either by simply writing a number in a blank or by checking a particular class interval in which the number falls. For example, the response to the question, "How old are you?" could be recorded by simply writing in the number twenty-five or by checking the class interval "25–29." If it is not necessary to record the number of years, it would greatly facilitate the data analysis if the prestructured set of class intervals of age were used instead of merely writing in the number.

Response cards. When the structured response categories are numerous, or difficult to understand or to retain in one's memory, it may be advisable to use a response card. This allows the respondent to see all of the choices while making a choice. Also, if the interviewer requests the respondent to choose by simply calling off the appropriate number or letter designating the category, this can help to reduce ego threat, particularly if there is some danger that someone is overhearing the interview.

In question 4 of the examples of basic question-answer formats (Figure 12–3), the response card would have only the letters *a* through *h* designating the categories, because if the interviewer said, "Just give me the *number* of the category," the respondent might feel that he is asking for the number of dollars, but if the categories are designated by letters this ambiguity is eliminated. On the interview schedule, however, both the alphabetical and the numerical designations are used since the numbers are needed by the keypunch operator.

---

[11]Mathematically, there is an important distinction between interval-scale and ratio-scale data in that the interval scale has equal-sized units throughout the full range of the scale, while the ratio scale has the additional feature of a natural zero point. But this distinction is irrelevant to the format of the interview schedule.

When the answer structure contains more than five or six nominal-scale categories, it is well to use different forms of the response card in which the order of the categories is changed so that the aggregate of responses will not be systematically biased by the respondent's tendency to pay more attention to the first and last items in the list. In this case it is good to reproduce the different forms on different colors of cards in addition to giving them a number identifying each version. The same code letter or number should be used to correspond to a particular response category on all versions of the set of answer categories. This eliminates the need to have different versions of the interview schedule and avoids confusing the keypunch operator by either having different codes for the same response category or by having the same response category located in different positions in the list. The keypunch operator does not need to see the response cards.

Contingency question format. In many surveys the interview schedule contains more questions than are asked of any one respondent because it is often necessary to ask one question before knowing whether other questions apply to the particular respondent. These questions that determine which line of questioning to follow are called *contingency* questions, *filter* questions, or *pivotal* questions. It is important that the format clearly show the alternative routes to follow in the sequence of questions as illustrated in the contingency question format (Figure 12–4).

Note that each question or set of questions that is contingent upon the answer to the previous question is indented further than the preceding one. This makes it easier for the interviewer to see how far ahead to skip when a series of questions does not apply. For example, if the answer to question C-1 is anything but "yes," then the interviewer jumps ahead to the next question with the same amount of indentation as C-1 which is C-9. The clearer the format, the fewer omissions will be made by the interviewer. Clear formats make it easier for the supervisor to check for omissions. The keypunch operator can punch more efficiently from a clear format.

In the set of answers to those questions which are contingent upon the previous question, it is often wise to include the "not applicable" category so that every column will be punched. Otherwise there would be some confusion as to whether the failure to punch a column corresponding to a particular question was because of the keypunch operator's error or because the question did not apply to a particular respondent.

Schematic sets of questions. When there is a set of questions having identical response categories and related to the same stem question, it is often convenient and efficient to form the set into a *schematic* or tabular form so that the stem of the question does not have to be repeated and

FIGURE 12–4

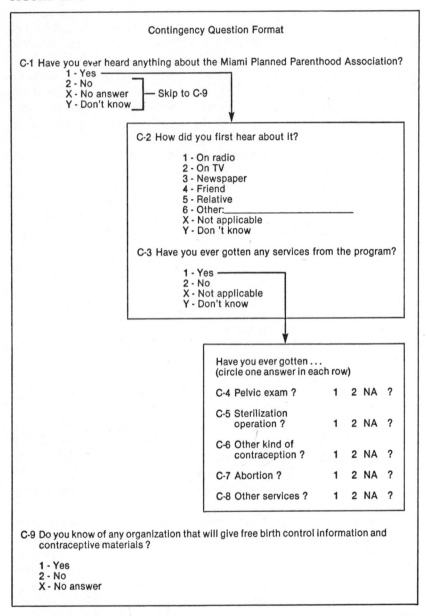

Contingency Question Format

C-1 Have you ever heard anything about the Miami Planned Parenthood Association?
1 - Yes
2 - No
X - No answer
Y - Don't know

— Skip to C-9

C-2 How did you first hear about it?

1 - On radio
2 - On TV
3 - Newspaper
4 - Friend
5 - Relative
6 - Other:_____
X - Not applicable
Y - Don 't know

C-3 Have you ever gotten any services from the program?

1 - Yes
2 - No
X - Not applicable
Y - Don't know

Have you ever gotten . . .
(circle one answer in each row)

C-4 Pelvic exam ?   1 2 NA ?

C-5 Sterilization
operation ?   1 2 NA ?

C-6 Other kind of
contraception ?   1 2 NA ?

C-7 Abortion ?   1 2 NA ?

C-8 Other services ?   1 2 NA ?

C-9 Do you know of any organization that will give free birth control information and
contraceptive materials ?

1 - Yes
2 - No
X - No answer

the amount of space used for the answer categories can be greatly reduced. This is illustrated by questions C-4 through C-8 in the contingency
question format. In the interview specifications, the interviewer should
be told that in contingent schematics the column heading NA means *not
applicable* and that ? means *don't know.*

SUMMARY

This chapter has treated the sample survey as one highly specialized form of field strategy. In a relatively short space this chapter has tried to describe some of the basic types of surveys classified according to whether the unit of analysis is the individual, group, institution, or community, and whether the aim is a cross-sectional study or a longitudinal study. The chapter has distinguished between three types of longitudinal studies (the trend study, the cohort analysis, and the panel study) and has indicated some of the differences in the purposes, problems, and prospects of each. It has also discussed three ways of approximating the longitudinal study with an interview at a single point in time.

The strengths and weaknesses of different sample designs have been pointed out, and the most salient steps in applying simple random sampling, systematic sampling, multistage sampling, and stratified sampling were described. The reader interested in the mathematical theory and calculations involved in determining the size of sample needed or in measuring the level of statistical significance should consult standard texts on sampling methodology.

To concretize all of the dimensions of the sample survey, the discussion concentrated on the interview schedule as a technical instrument for coordinating such activities as designing the sample, selecting respondents, contacting respondents, questioning respondents, recording information, supervising field activities, editing interview schedules, coding, and keypunching the data. The interview schedule is the focal record of all of these activities.

Since the sample survey was being viewed as a special type of field strategy, the assumption was made that all questions had been formulated correctly, their sequence was optimally arranged, and that the interviewer had the skills for communicating the questions, determining the adequacy of the responses, and probing for complete and valid answers. The next chapters on techniques and tactics will treat all of these steps as problematical.

DISCUSSION QUESTIONS

1. What is a *sampling element* in a survey? Give examples.

2. What is the difference between a cross-sectional and a longitudinal survey?

3. What are the basic types of longitudinal surveys and how do they differ in *method?*

4. How do the different types of longitudinal surveys differ in the *purpose* for which they can be validly used?

5. How can the purposes of a longitudinal survey be approximately accomplished by a single cross-sectional survey? What are the major limitations of this use of the cross-sectional survey?

6. What are some of the comparative advantages and disadvantages of the simple random sample versus the systematic sample?

7. Under what basic condition is the systematic sample going to be biased?

8. What is the main advantage of the multistage sample over the single stage sample?

9. Under what conditions can we gain an advantage by stratifying the sample?

10. What are some pointers to remember in gaining access to a respondent in a personal interview survey?

11. What are some of the functions of the interview schedule in a sample survey other than supplying questions and answer choices?

12. What are some of the major question-answer types?

13. What are some general suggestions for good format in designing an interview schedule for the sample survey?

Selected Readings

Babbie, Earl R. *Survey Research Methods*. Belmont, Calif.: Wadsworth Publishing, 1973.
  Part One deals with the scientific context of survey research; *Part Two* gives a good overview of all of the steps in designing a sample survey; *Part Three* details various models for analyzing survey data; and *Part Four* raises the questions of the ethics of applying the results of the survey and its scientific implications.

Backstrom, Charles H., and Gerald D. Hursh. *Survey Research*. 2nd ed. New York: John Wiley & Sons, 1981.
  Chapter 1 on Planning a Survey, and Chapter 2 on Drawing the Sample, are particularly useful in giving practical details on how to plan and carry out a sample survey. Although the most detailed treatment of sampling mechanics is given for cluster sampling, this includes all of the ingredients for other sampling models.

Bradburn, Norman M., Seymour Sudman, et al. *Improving Interviewing Method and Questionnaire Design*. San Francisco: Jossey-Bass, 1979.
A comparison of four survey techniques (face-to-face, telephone, self-administered questionnaire, and randomized responses) to determine which produce the most truthful responses to slightly, moderately, and highly ego-threatening questions. They describe the effects of length, structure, and wording of questions, and different characteristics of respondents on the validity of the responses.

Part IV

TECHNIQUES IN INTERVIEWING

Chapter Thirteen

Verbal Forms Used by the Interviewer

Earlier *techniques* were defined as specific forms of verbal and nonverbal behavior used during the interview, and *tactics* as the way in which specific techniques are varied to meet problems as they arise in the context of a particular interview. Techniques can be classified in isolation from the larger context of the interview, while tactics are the patterns or sequences of questions as they relate to the progress of the interview as a whole. Thus, each question or statement by the interviewer has a technical form in itself and is part of a larger tactical pattern.

Techniques and tactics are functionally intertwined in the dynamics of interviewing, but to simplify the exposition, the two will be separated. In an actual nonscheduled interview, the interviewer must direct his or her attention toward tactical problems as they arise unpredictably; therefore, the successful interviewer must have mastered a wide range of specific techniques so that their use is automatic before attempting the more complex task of adjusting the pattern of questioning to the ongoing context of the interview. These techniques include the verbal forms and nonverbal expressions of attitude used by the interviewer. This chapter will focus on the verbal forms and the next will focus on the nonverbal forms and their effects on the inhibitors and facilitators of communication.

Several good experiments clearly demonstrate that disciplined interviewers can consciously control both their verbal and nonverbal behavior to affect the completeness and validity of the information received. Sometimes the verbal behavior is determined by the particular wording of the question and sometimes by more general instructions to verbally show appreciation for the respondent's efforts. Of course, the nonverbal behavior of the interviewer must be consistent with his or her verbal behavior. Marquis did a survey of health problems of adults in which interviewers acted according to two different sets of instructions.[1] Each time the respondent reported an illness, the experimental interviewers used a *reinforcing* statement which showed appreciation for the information and interest in the respondent's problem. The experimental interviewers also used a longer introduction to each section of the interview schedule in order to establish a context showing the survey's interest in the respondent. The experimental interviewers also looked at the respondent when talking to him or her and smiled frequently. The control interviewers omitted all of these verbal and nonverbal techniques and simply asked the questions in a neutral way. The experiment showed that the experimental interviewers obtained 25 percent more reports of symptoms and conditions than did the control interviewers.

In spelling out specific verbal forms and attitudes making up the interviewer's kit of techniques, the discussion will also indicate their purposes and probable effects upon the respondent's ability and willingness to give relevant information. The verbal forms and their effects to be discussed here will include (*a*) providing specific *context* for the question, (*b*) selecting the appropriate *vocabulary* in wording the question, (*c*) delimiting the *scope* of the question, (*d*) supplying *answer categories*, and (*e*) *suggesting answers*. All of these verbal forms when appropriately used help the interviewer with the two major tasks of maximizing the flow of relevant information and maintaining optimum interpersonal relations.

CONTEXTS AIMED AT COMMUNICATING THE QUESTION

Every specific question occurs in a context which helps convey its meaning to the respondent. Context is furnished at the strategy level by the respondent's perception of the purpose of the study, the sponsorship, the interviewer's auxiliary roles, and the time and place of the interview. As the next chapter explains, context is also furnished at the tactical level by the sequence of questions and answers in a particular interview. At this point, the discussion will be concerned only with the context provided at the technique level by wording a particular question to include the context or by supplying a contextual statement which immediately precedes the question.

Several useful functions can be performed by the provision of an appropriate context with the question. The context may simply clarify the meaning of the question; it may increase the respondent's ability to give the relevant information by stimulating the respondent's memory, by decreasing the chronological confusion, or by bringing unconscious

---

[1]Kent H. Marquis, "Effects of Social Reinforcement on Health Reporting in the Household Interview," *Sociometry* 33 (1970), pp. 203–15.

norms and assumptions to the surface; it may also increase the respondent's willingness to give the information by decreasing ego threat, removing the etiquette barrier, appealing to the need for meaning, or stimulating altruistic motives.

Defining terms. It is often necessary to preface a question with a contextual statement defining crucial terms which might be unclear to the respondent. Ego threat is prevented by giving the definition before the respondent shows that he or she needs it and without asking whether the respondent understands the term. For example:

> There are cases where a man and woman live together as husband and wife, set up housekeeping, have children and take care of them, but do not get a marriage license or have a wedding ceremony of any kind. *Do you think children of these common-law marriages should be entitled to the legal rights of inheritance?*

This is better than either asking if the respondent knows what a common-law marriage is or assuming that the respondent understands the term.

The same question might have different meanings to different respondents who use different sets of assumptions to interpret the meaning of the question. Garfinkel shows how, in different situations in everyday social interaction, people interpret the actions of others in terms of common sense theories.[2] These theories are composed of assumptions about human behavior, as they know it, which help them to make sense out of what people say and do. He goes further to show that this *context* of unstated assumptions, particularly the cognitive assumptions, changes within a group as a result of the members' past interactions. Each person, therefore, brings to any communication situation a set of assumptions (normative and cognitive) which are derived both from his general cultural background and from the more unique experiential background of the groups of which he is a member. Usually, in the interview situation the respondent and interviewer are establishing a new relationship in which neither knows the unstated assumptions of the other that would bear upon the interpretation of the particular questions to be asked. Under these conditions, if the interviewer does not explicitly furnish a context for interpretation of a question because he or she unwittingly assumes that there is only one possible context, the interviewer is leaving the respondent free to use a set of assumptions that are unstated and unknown to the interviewer. Thus, not only is the question different in the minds of these two people but also the response has a different meaning to each.

---

[2]Harold Garfinkel, *Studies in Ethnomethodology* (Englewood Cliffs, N.J.: Prentice-Hall, 1967; Cambridge: Polity, 1984 reissue).

Of course, the context for the interview as a whole is partially established by those dimensions of the situation previously treated under the heading of strategy, but at this point we are concerned only with contexts as a verbal technique for more clearly communicating the question.

Studies involving controversial issues on a national and international scale often involve terms not clearly understood by many people. In a random sample of the population such words as *monopoly, savings, profit, free-trade, mandate,* and *right of way* carry only a vague meaning for the majority. In many cases, respondents will not ask the meaning because either they think they know or are embarrassed to ask.

Providing a time perspective. Often the answer to a question can be completely reversed by a shift in the time perspective. This is particularly true when obtaining facts or opinions on *trends* of any type. For example, in response to the question, "Do you think that the amount of academic freedom on American college campuses has increased, decreased, or stayed about the same?" a respondent's answer might be "increased" or "decreased," depending on the period of time the interviewer has in mind. To bring about a clearer time perspective, the context could be, "Try to remember some of the things happening on this campus five years ago, in 1956, and compare that with the present time. Think of the general psychological atmosphere and its effect upon academic freedom."

If the interviewer has information on some specific events in the local, national, and international scene occurring in 1956 this would be helpful in providing a more vivid time perspective.

Providing a spatial perspective. Just as an answer could be reversed by the time perspective, it could also be reversed by the spatial perspective of the respondent. A citizen's civic improvement organization interested in knowing the public's reaction to its efforts in one section of a large city questioned a random sample of respondents in and near the area where its work was going on, asking, "Do you feel that your neighborhood has got better, worse, or stayed about the same in the last years?" The problem here was that the psychological boundaries of each respondent's neighborhood varied. If the respondent's own psychological boundaries did not coincide with the area the organization had in mind, the answer could be negative since the surrounding area was rapidly deteriorating in its physical and social condition. This was easily remedied by preceding the question with this clarifying context: "Perhaps you are familiar with the area between Wentworth and State streets from 43rd to 57th. Just think of this area and forget for the moment all the areas right around it."

The responses to this question after the context was furnished would be significantly different, particularly for respondents residing near the outside edges of the designated area.

Supplying a social-psychological perspective. A myriad of examples could show that a question in its logical purity, even with clearly defined terms, could be answered differently depending on the circumstances which the respondent has in mind. For example, we could define "bureaucracy" as a pure form of social structure and then attempt to discover people's attitudes and opinions on the desirability of such a form of human organization by asking the question, "Now that we have defined the bureaucracy as we will use it in this discussion, what do you think of it as a general form of organization?"

The answer to this question would vary, depending upon whether the respondent was thinking of the probable effects of such an organization when manned by "those government bureaucrats in Washington" or by "the managers of America's great business enterprises, such as X Motors." The respondent might very well have no opinion on "bureaucracy" in the abstract, and in order to give the question some meaning the respondent would supply his or her own context if none was supplied by the interviewer.

Supplying criteria for judgment. Closely related to the previous type of context is one which clearly specifies the criteria the respondent is to apply in making a judgment. Of course, in the previous example the respondent might use different criteria in judging a business bureaucracy versus a government bureaucracy, but the interviewer has no way of knowing in advance what the criteria are. The following example is an attempt to focus the respondent's attention on one of many possible criteria for making a judgment.

As you know, there are some counties in this state which have not yet integrated their public schools. Many reasons are given for favoring and opposing the integration, but I am interested in your opinion on the economic efficiency of integration. I am not asking whether you favor or oppose integration. Just assume for the moment that the only problem is one of getting the best education for the most people for the least money from the taxpayer. Do you think integrated schools would be a more efficient or a less efficient use of public funds? (Probes: Why do you say that? Could you explain that a little more?)

It will be difficult to persuade the respondent to use the criterion of efficiency if he or she is strongly opposed to integration on other grounds. For this reason, it would be necessary to probe carefully as to *why* the respondent feels the integrated system would be more or less efficient.

Supplying needed facts. Many times, the point of an interview is to discover how a person will decide an issue if given certain relevant facts. Instead of either assuming that the person has them or asking the person if he or she is "well informed," the interviewer supplies the salient facts, and thus is sure they were taken into consideration insofar as the respondent gives them weight.

For example, in a study of public opinion formation in a small community, the following question was one of those asked of a carefully selected group of opinion leaders:

As you probably read in the *News-Sun,* the Village Council must make a decision at next month's meeting on whether to put in a new gravity-flow sewer system at the cost of $400,000, which will still serve the population twenty-five years from now, or to put in a new sewer pumping station at the cost of $100,000 but which will have to be enlarged at the cost of $50,000 in five years. With each five-year period, the cost of enlargement would be greater, so that the total cost at the end of twenty-five years would be about $600,000. Do you personally favor the gravity-flow or the pumping station? (Probes: Why do you favor that? Is there any special reason you favor that? Could you explain that a little further?)

The use which the respondent makes of the supplied facts varies, depending on the respondent's additional facts, knowledge of the general problem, and questions generated in the analysis of the information he or she has. For example, in the discussion brought out by the probing, one of the better-informed respondents said:

If you look at it from the standpoint of long-run efficiency of service, it is difficult to decide which would cost the taxpayers the most because the total cost of either system depends upon how much money must be borrowed, at what interest rate, for what period of time and, finally, how much inflation or deflation there will be in the local economy during the period for which the money was borrowed. Since I don't know these things, there is no way to make an intelligent choice.

More typical responses were in the direction of the two below, representing both those who favored and those who opposed the gravity-flow sewer.

I think it is best to do what is cheapest in the long run. If it is going to cost the taxpayers $200,000 more within a twenty-five year period to use pumping stations, I think we should put out a little more money right now by getting the gravity-flow sewer and saving in the long run.

I have heard the argument that it would save us money in the long run to get the gravity-flow sewer, but who is "us"? I may not be here in twenty-five years or even ten years. Also, this might be a ghost town by that time and not even need as big a sewer system as we have now. I don't believe in these predictions of the future.

It is clear that both respondents considered the facts but reached opposite conclusions by putting these facts in different perspectives.

Discovering the respondent's own contexts. So far, we have shown how the interviewer may need to provide some context with a particular question in order to define terms, provide a time perspective, give a spatial perspective, locate a particular social-psychological circumstance, supply criteria for judgments, or furnish specific facts to be used in making a judgment. All of these uses of context are aimed at communicating the meaning of the question more precisely to the respondent. Thus, we assume that the interviewer has a particular context in mind which he or she desired to make clear to the respondent.

There is a contrasting purpose of the interview where the main objective is to discover the respondent's own context which gives meaning to certain words, facts, slogans, or any form of abstraction. In this case, it would *not* be appropriate to furnish the context; special tactics may be needed to discover the respondent's context without appearing to be cryptic or nonsupportive. This problem will be dealt with in the next chapter.

CONTEXTS AIMED AT MOTIVATING THE RESPONDENT

The preceding types of contexts are aimed primarily at communicating to the respondent the precise meaning of the question. Once the respondent clearly grasps the question, it is sometimes also necessary to make the respondent either more *able* or more *willing* to answer fully. The respondent's willingness may be increased by a context which arouses his or her interest in the topic, acknowledges the respondent's special qualifications, or reduces any ego threat or etiquette barrier. Contexts may also increase the respondent's ability to give relevant information by stimulating his or her memory, by obviating chronological confusion, and by stimulating unconscious behavior patterns and attitudes.

Arousing the respondent's interest. Often a respondent has a low level of motivation because he or she fails to see significance in the information being given. If it can be done without "loading" the question, supplying contexts from time to time in the interview can help motivate the respondent. For example:

There has been a lot of discussion in Congress recently about free trade. Slogans such as "Trade, not aid to the underdeveloped areas" have been invented.

There are two bills before Congress at the moment dealing with the problem. *What does the term "free trade" mean to you?*

This context does more than arouse interest; it provides a perspective suggesting international free trade rather than interstate free trade in the United States. If the international perspective is correct for the purpose of the interview, then this context would not distort the information.

Recognizing the respondent's special qualifications. It is not only useful to remind the respondent of his or her qualifications at the beginning of the interview when explaining how and why he or she was selected, but it is also helpful to remind the respondent of these special qualifications at other points in the interview. One way of doing this is to preface a question with a reminder of the respondent's qualifications as is done in the following examples:

You have had much more experience with life than I and can see things in a broader perspective. What advice would you give to young people today to make the "senior citizen" period of their lives more full and happy?

Since you were at one time a member of the gang with the biggest "rep" in East Harlem, could you give me some idea why teenagers join these kinds of gangs?

Within one interview, different aspects of the respondent's qualifications can be mentioned in order to support the respondent's need for recognition.

Reducing ego threat. Questions can be worded to include a face-saving preface to reduce the ego threat. For example, "I know people nowadays do not have time to keep up on everything that is going on in the world, but would you tell me if you have read anything about the Near East crisis?" Several studies of the validity of people's statements regarding current events have demonstrated that they exaggerate the amount of reading they have done and tend to feel guilty about how little they know about current world issues. A preface of this type will reduce the urge to overestimate one's reading and reduce the ego threat involved in an admission of ignorance.

Another approach is to show that "even the gods have clay feet," and celebrities, too, have failures. This helps place a respondent's possible weaknesses in a nonthreatening perspective. For example:

As you probably know, Winston Churchill, Albert Einstein, and others of that calibre failed in some of their college courses. How many courses have you failed so far?

Depending on the purposes of the interview, the interviewer's knowledge of the respondent, and the general setting of the interview, this principle can be adapted to soften many potentially ego-threatening questions.

Preventing falsification. It often saves a tremendous amount of time and energy to prevent the respondent's committing himself falsely. Once the respondent has taken the false position, he or she will feel honor-bound to defend it even though the respondent may regret the falsification. Often, an elaborate web of lies has to be built up to preserve consistency with the original lie. It is mainly in detective stories that the culprit breaks down when inconsistencies are discovered in the story. In the interview situation the respondent is not obligated to submit to continual pressure. Neither is a suspicious attitude on the part of the interviewer considered within the bounds of etiquette. Under these conditions prevention is more efficient and less embarrassing.

For example, an employer is interviewing a prospective employee who has been fired from her former job. If the interviewer wants to know something about the respondent's relationship with her former employers, he should let the respondent know that the former employer has informed him the respondent was fired. A straightforward question, after rapport has been built up, would not only save time but would also indicate to the intelligent respondent that the interviewer has no desire to trap her. The interviewer could simply say, "I was told by your former employer that you were fired. They gave me their side of the story, but I would like to hear it from your point of view."

Reducing the etiquette barrier. In the strategy phase, the interviewer-respondent combinations should be selected to avoid role relationships which erect an etiquette barrier. However, there are still situations in which the respondent may identify the interviewer with a role which would damage the flow of information. If the interviewer takes advantage of opportunities to clarify his or her role as the interview progresses, the probability of the etiquette barrier arising can be reduced. For example, a college professor who was interviewing students regarding their experiences in a new foreign extension of the college conducted a group interview with five students recently returned from abroad. The professor was the designer of the program and this fact was known to most of the students. He assumed that students would be reluctant to criticize the weaknesses of the new program and therefore introduced the discussion as follows:

As you probably know, I was instrumental in designing the original program set up in Guanajuato in 1958. I have had no official connection with it over the past three years and I am somewhat out of touch with what is going on there. I am interested in doing what I can to improve the program at this time. I suspect that in its actual operations the program has certain weaknesses which should be brought out in the open and discussed. That is why I have invited you here today, not to obtain a pollyannaish report of the program, but to get some insight into your personal experiences so that I can see it from the point of view of the students it is supposed to benefit. What are some of the things that should be done to improve the program there in Guanajuato?

Of course, beginning the discussion with a one-paragraph statement aimed at reducing the etiquette barrier is not to be depended upon completely. The group began with some minor criticisms as well as some praise of certain aspects of the program. The interviewer's success in obtaining criticism of the program rested heavily upon his reactions to the group's initial criticisms. When they observed that he did not swell with pride when the program was praised, nor attempt to defend it against their criticisms, they were encouraged to express themselves more candidly. All etiquette barriers were not eliminated by this technique. For example, students interviewing the same groups discovered objections not raised in the discussion with the professor, but these were matters withheld because he was a member of the older generation and not because he was the originator of the program.

Several ways have been dealt with in which an appropriate context might reduce the respondent's resistance to giving relevant information. Now the discussion will examine some of the ways to increase his or her ability to report experiences.

Stimulating the memory. By reviewing some of the objective facts about a certain situation, the interviewer often can stimulate the respondent's memory of his or her experiences in that situation. In the following example the interviewer is attempting to reconstruct the pattern of interaction between members of a family when a tornado struck their rural village. He needs to obtain an accurate report of the actions of each person and the extent to which other family members were taken into consideration.

Now after the wind stopped blowing and the house had crashed into the pecan orchard, it was still dark, raining very hard, and someone outside the wreckage was shouting, "Anybody in there?" At that moment did you know where your husband was?

It is not always necessary for the interviewer to know that the respondent was conscious of all the circumstantial facts mentioned, as long as all the facts are accurate and were occurring at the time of the respondent's relevant experiences. In contrast to the example above that describes *events* occurring at the relevant time, the context might focus upon a description of the physical *scene* of the event. In any case, the interviewer should attempt to include those circumstantial facts most salient to the respondent.

Reducing chronological confusion. Often the respondent is less aware of the chronological order of his or her actions and observations than of their relationship to certain salient observations of events not directly related to the objectives of the interview. Even if the respondent does not know the correct order of the irrelevant events, the interviewer who knows their order can use this information to unscramble the respondent's sequence of experiences.

We have been able to clearly establish the order of some events that you might remember from the day of the explosions here in Brighton. First, there was the explosion in the reducing-valve vault under the sidewalk at Twelve Corners, then the gas jets in people's stoves, furnaces, and gas dryers began to make a hissing noise, then the Mellinger house exploded, the next house exploded about twelve minutes later. The first explosion was south of your house, the second was directly west. What were you doing when you heard the first explosion? Where were you when you heard the second explosion?

This technique of preventing chronological confusion is simply an extension of the general principle of using known facts to stimulate recall of additional actions and observations.

Discovering unconscious factors. Of the types of unconscious experience a respondent might have, the one most amenable to verbal techniques is that of the values or norms which govern a person's behavior. Frequently, they cannot be clearly reported because the respondent is not aware of the norm in the abstract, but expresses it in his or her behavior toward concrete situations. In this case, it is often helpful to use a hypothetical case as the focus for discussion. Several hypothetical cases may be required to delineate the particular norm or pattern of norms in question.

Suppose our problem is to discover the norms governing the relationship between nurses and doctors in a large metropolitan hospital. The interviewer might ask a nurse how the higher status of the doctors is shown in their behavior toward nurses and in their treatment by the hospital administration. The following is one hypothetical case:

Suppose a maternity patient in the hospital is about to give birth to her baby, but the physician in charge of her has not yet arrived. Her labor is in the final phase and the child will be born in a few minutes. This is the patient's fourth child, she is in good health, and her medical history is known to the nurse in charge of her case. Three hours previously, the physician called to say he would arrive at the hospital in four hours which would be in another hour. (1) What would the nurse in charge of her case do? (2) What would the supervising nurse on the maternity ward do? (3) What would the physician probably say if he could be reached by phone and it was explained that the birth was going to take place before he could arrive?

The interviewer who has some hunches of what constitutes a violation of the norms in this situation might suggest these to obtain the respondent's reaction. Very frequently, we are more aware of specific actions which would constitute a *violation* of a norm than we are of the norm itself. In some problems of this type, the interviewer can simply ask, "What would be the wrong thing for the nurse to do in this situation?" or "What could you say for sure the physician would *not* suggest for the nurse to do in this case?"

To stimulate discussion of this hypothetical case, it might be useful to suggest possible actions to obtain a response. For example, "Would the nurse go ahead and deliver the baby herself, if she knows there are no complications in the case?" "Would the supervising nurse ask one of the physicians on the ward who was not busy at the moment to perform the delivery?" "Would the nurse in charge, by previous arrangement with the physician, retard the delivery until the patient's regular physician arrived?"

This extension of the hypothetical case by suggesting possible action solutions must, of course, be constructed so that a full range of action is included, or so that each action or action alternative involves the norms in which the interviewer is interested. Otherwise, we may bias the responses by suggestion or by exclusion of certain relevant alternatives. If the interviewer is not sure of the adequacy of the alternative actions, they could be used only as possible answer choices for the interviewer to check without mentioning any of them to the respondent.

An interesting study in the use of hypothetical cases is reported by Weaver, who wanted to study the norms among Spanish-Americans governing the decision whether to call a *curandero* (folk medicine specialist) or a medical doctor.[3] Instead of asking the question, for example, "When do you usually ask the *curandero* to come?" the respondent was given hypothetical cases of illnesses and asked direct questions about the symptoms, diagnosis, and treatment. In this way the criteria for actions, which were mostly unconscious in the respondent, could be tested by a carefully selected set of hypothetical examples. The hypothetical example as a particular form of context has been shown to be useful not only for teasing out unconscious patterns, but also for avoiding ego threat in situations where, if the respondent were aware of the

---

[3]T. Weaver, "Use of Hypothetical Situations in a Study of Spanish-American Illness Referral Systems," *Human Organization* 29 (1970), pp. 140–54.

pattern of his or her behavior, he or she would refuse to verbalize it to the interviewer. Under these conditions the interviewer can assume the task of inducing the pattern from the concrete examples, while being careful not to point it out to the respondent. Another value of the hypothetical example is to avoid inferential confusion by not asking the respondent to abstract the rule logically from the specific examples, but by letting the interviewer handle the inference process.

The hypothetical case is often an excellent focus for discussion and will, if well chosen, stimulate salient responses. Good hypotheses cannot be constructed from a swivel chair but must be built upon previous knowledge. Often it is not until the later stages of a study, or at least until after several interviews have been done or some participant-observation used, that relevant hypothetical examples can be produced, since they should contain problematical situations which could really occur.

SELECTING APPROPRIATE VOCABULARY

Without becoming enmeshed in a multitude of possible examples, let us look at some of the main problems in selecting an appropriate vocabulary for the interview.

1. The words should be clearly understood by the respondent.

2. The words should aid in establishing an optimum role relationship between the interviewer and respondent.

3. In some cases, the question should be worded to include the vocabulary needed by the respondent to give an answer without violating the etiquette of the situation.

4. Emotional words which might unintentionally "load" the question should be avoided.

These apparently simple principles may be very easy or very difficult to put into practice.

The first principle can be thwarted by very subtle differences in the universe of discourse of the interviewer and the respondent. For example, the two questions below obtained quite different responses from rural victims of a tornado:

What were some of the problems which arose during the rescue operations right after the tornado struck?
What sorts of trouble did people have trying to help folks who were hurt or trapped in the wreckage?

The second question obtained a straightforward and spontaneous response relevant to the purposes of the study. The first wording of the question seemed to puzzle some respondents because the word "problems" had a connotation narrower than intended by the interviewer.

The second principle, using a vocabulary that will establish an optimum role relationship between interviewer and respondent, has many manifestations, but it can be viewed in the same two-dimensional system suggested in the previous chapter. The interviewer must recognize that the respondent can quickly classify him as an "insider-outsider" or "subordinate-equal-superordinate" on the basis of his or her choice of words. For example, in an interview to obtain voters' attitudes toward certain policies of the Department of Agriculture, the interviewer might ask, "What do you think of our policy of allowing farmers to vote on alternative types of farm programs we administer through the Department of Agriculture?" In exploratory, nonscheduled interviews, the interviewer noted that most of the respondents referred to any department of the federal government as "they," rather than "we," as did the interviewer. This prevented the interviewer from being perceived as an "insider" by the farmer. On certain controversial issues, this brought the etiquette barrier into play.

It is often helpful to word the question so that it is clear to the respondent that the interviewer understands the local universe of discourse. This allows the respondent to speak more spontaneously without having to "translate" for the interviewer. Usually, only the more educated or experienced respondent will bother to do this, while the respondent with a narrow range of experience does not realize he or she has a special jargon. The interviewer can indicate that there is no need to "translate" by using the local jargon in the wording of the question. For example, in an interview with a supervisor in a telephone company, the interviewer said, "I understand, according to one of the COs, that they expect to install key-pulse dialing when the new rate structure filed with the ICC is approved. When do they expect the ICC to give its decision?" Immediately the respondent was aware that the interviewer understood "CO," "key-pulse dialing," "rate-structure," and "ICC."

There is a danger in using the local jargon if the interviewer does not actually understand it or if it puts the interviewer in the insider role when it would be more desirable to be an outsider. Often, the outsider role can be retained without forcing the respondent to translate if the interviewer explains that he or she has learned as much of the jargon as possible for the occasion and will ask for further explanations from time to time. Only a few questions early in the interview will clearly indicate that the interviewer is an outsider.

In some cases, the vocabulary used is crucial in helping the respondent classify the interviewer as an equal or a superordinate. In cases where the interviewer is perceived as a superordinate, the respondent is sometimes reluctant to answer a question, sensing that his or her vocabulary would be considered vulgar outside the respondent's own group, yet the respondent does not know what vocabulary would be considered appropriate by the interviewer. In this case, the interviewer can be careful to supply the vocabulary by the wording of the question so that the meaning is obvious. Then the respondent can use the same vocabulary in answering. For example, in a study of child-rearing practices of mothers in the lower socioeconomic level, the question, "How did you go about toilet training your child?" was ineffective. Instead, it was necessary to use a series of questions to provide the polite vocabulary needed by the respondent. Mothers were asked, "When were you first able to depend on Johnny asking to go to the toilet to have a bowel movement?" and then, "When did he quit wetting himself and start going to the toilet instead?" Once these questions were answered, a more detailed discussion of the mother's attempts to toilet-train the child followed rather smoothly, since "bowel movement" had become a common phrase.

It is common sense to avoid using emotionally loaded vocabulary in wording the question. The actual implementation of the principle is not so simple, but depends upon the interviewer's knowing which words have a biasing effect upon the respondent. For example, in a study of communication between North Americans and Latin Americans, the use of the word *gringo* in Mexico to refer to North Americans would have a strongly negative emotional loading. *Gringo* would not have this effect in Colombia where the word *yanqui* is reserved for negative connotations.

There are times when it is appropriate to use emotionally loaded words as long as it is intentional and the direction of the effect is known. This intentional use of the "loaded" question will be discussed later.

DELIMITING THE SCOPE OF THE QUESTION

Questions and probes by the interviewer may vary tremendously in their scope. A question may be so broad that it includes within its confines more than the total objectives of the whole interview, or it may be so narrow in scope that hundreds of minutely specific questions are necessary to cover the same topic. The scope of each question used in an interview is not automatically determined by the objectives or the topic of the interview. People experienced in nonscheduled interviewing realize that it may require twice as many questions to obtain the relevant information from one respondent as from another. In one case, broad questions provide sufficient stimulus for the respondent to cover many specific points within the scope of the general question, while in another the interviewer must specify each bit of information needed.

It is important for an interviewer to become aware of this dimension, called "scope," since most people have an unconscious habit, developed in social conversation, of being unnecessarily restrictive in the scope of their questions. Perhaps it is a way of saving time or of restricting the other person's remarks so that we may express our point of view sooner. Or perhaps the efficient businessman, the incisive lawyer, or the police detective who "get to the point" in mass media portrayals influence our conversational patterns. Regardless of the source, in training interviewers the author has found that it is usually more difficult for them to ask broad questions than to ask each specific point separately. Frequently, the neophyte interviewer behaves as if his or her motto were "never use a general question if several specific questions can be used instead." By developing a sensitivity to how apparently small differences in the wording of a question make vast differences in its scope, the interviewer may guide his or her own behavior in accordance with the objectives of the interview, rather than be guided by unconscious habit.

To illustrate this difference in scope, let us compare three opening questions used by different interviewers in an interview with teenagers to discover some of the educational values of the county fair for city children.

1. Tell me what happened at the Greene County Fair when you were there last Saturday.

2. Tell me what you did at the Greene County Fair when you were there last Saturday.

3. Did you like the horse show at the county fair?

Regardless of which question is the best opener for this type of interview, the vast difference in scope is clear. The first question, by using the term "what happened," leaves the topic open for the respondent to report what he or she did, what others did, what he or she saw, what others saw, what he or she felt or thought about what was done or seen and what he or she felt and thought about what others did and saw.

The second question logically restricts the area of discussion as much as 90 percent by asking only what the *respondent did.* This unnecessary restriction of the topic might constitute an ego threat in this case, because the respondent probably was mainly a spectator and could more spontaneously report what he or she saw than what he or she did. Also, the impersonality of "what happened" versus "what did you see, do, or think" often makes the respondent less self-conscious.

The third question restricts the conversation to some fraction of one percent of the respondent's impressions of the fair. It also inhibits the spontaneous flow of information, because it prevents the respondent from talking about what, for him or her, were the most memorable aspects of the fair. It also implies that a simple "yes" or "no" answer is required.

Dimensions of Scope

Rather than examining scores of illustrations of differences in scope and discussing their possible effects on the flow of relevant information, we have devised a scheme to show some of the important dimensions of scope. This allows the reader to generate his or her own examples. Figure 13–1 (next page) delineates five dimensions of scope, represented by the column headings, which apply to all questions. The columns are arranged in the order in which each dimension usually appears in the sentence structure of a question. Within each column the scope becomes broader as we progress from top to bottom. With some imagination, the reader can construct questions for a hypothetical interview topic, using different breadths of the five dimensions.

To illustrate some questions constructed from different breadths of each of the five dimensions (see table below), we will assume that the interview topic is a robbery that occurred the week before. Each of the six questions becomes successively broader in scope.

Although many more sentences could be constructed from different combinations of breadths of the five dimensions, it is not possible to construct a meaningful sentence corresponding to every logical combination of breadth. Which combinations are meaningful depends to some extent upon the topic of the interview. In spite of the lack of refinement, this scheme can help sensitize the interviewer to the fact that the scope of a question can be expanded or contracted by gradual degrees, and that the answer to several of the narrower questions could be logically included in the answer to one of the broadest questions on the same topic.

| | *Dimension* | | | | | |
Breadth	A	B	C	D	E	*Questions*
1	1	1	1	1	1	"Did you give the gun to Jim in the car before the robbery?"
2	1	1	1	2	1	"Did you give a gun to anyone before the robbery?"
3	2	2	1	2	2	"Who could have provided the gun for the robbery?"
4	3	4	4	4	2	"How did the robbery happen last Thursday night?"
5	4	1	3	4	3	"What were you doing last Thursday night at eight?"
6	4	4	4	4	4	"What happened last Thursday night?"

FIGURE 13-1 Scope of the question

| | Dimensions of question | | | | |
Breadth	Interrogative A	Actor (subject) B	Action (verb) C	Relationships (objects) D	Scene E
1	(Request for information) Did....? Was....? Will....? Has....?	(A specific person or thing) "You," "Tom," "your boss," "car," "wind."	(Specific action verb supplied) "Run," "sing," "say," "lift," "drill," "give," "take."	(Both the direct and indirect objects are specified)	(Specific point in time and space specified or implied)
2	(The facts) Who....? When....? Where....? How much....? How many....?	(Unspecified persons or things other than "you") "People," "others," "everyone," "things."		(Only one object is specified)	(A certain event within the scene specified)
3	(Interpretation-explanation) Why....? How....?	(Does not specify "you" or "others") "Anyone?" "Anything?"	(General class of action specified as to overt or covert) "Do," "think."	(Only one object is specified)	(A certain limited time period or spatial location)
4	(Request for unspecified information) What....? Tell me about.....	(No actor category specified)	(No specific action or class of action is specified) "Happened?"	(Neither the direct or indirect object specified)	(No time or place limitation; includes the whole scene or topic of the interview)

Consciously or unconsciously the interviewer makes a choice in the nonscheduled interview between (*a*) using broad questions and encouraging the respondent to elaborate to obtain specific details or (*b*) using many narrow questions to cover the same topic. The tactical problem of shifting from broader to narrower questions or vice versa will be discussed in the next chapter. At this point the discussion will examine some of the most probable values of broader and narrower questions and indicate some of the limiting circumstances for the use of each.

Values of Broad Questions

Broad questions have two general values: First, they must be used to obtain certain types of information which would be distorted by the effect of many specific questions; second, they have certain motivational effects upon the respondent under certain conditions.

Interviews with any or all of the following objectives often require the use of broad questions: (*a*) discovering the respondent's paths of association regarding a certain topic, situation, or event; (*b*) discovering the relative importance of various aspects of a topic, situation, or event experienced by the respondent; (*c*) discovering the frame of reference used by the respondent in observing, analyzing, or acting in a situation; (*d*) discovering the chronological order of the respondent's experiences in a given situation; (*e*) discovering the vocabulary used by the respondent in discussing certain aspects of a topic, situation, or event.

In each of these objectives the interviewer must be careful not to impose his or her own organization upon the topic, but must encourage the respondent to discuss the topic in the respondent's own terms. It is practically impossible for the interviewer to divide the topic into many specific questions without imposing his or her own frames of reference, without using a vocabulary he or she is not yet sure is appropriate, without interrupting the respondent's natural paths of association, and without imposing different perspectives or hierarchies of importance upon the specifics reported.

Broad questions not only help the interviewer to avoid giving rather than receiving information, but also help to increase the respondent's ability and willingness to give relevant information in several ways.

Reducing ego threat. Often certain facts regarding a topic, situation, or event might constitute an ego threat to the respondent if the interviewer calls the respondent's attention to the significance of the relationship between these facts. If the interviewer asks for each fact, the respondent may become concerned with how the interviewer is going to evaluate the information. However, if the interviewer does not ask for but is given the facts, the respondent does not know the interviewer attaches any particular significance to them. In rare cases it might be necessary to pose a broad question that focuses on an area only indirectly related to the specific facts needed so that the respondent will not feel threatened by direct questioning on sensitive areas.

Stimulating memory. The objective of the interview may not be to discover the respondent's individual paths of association. Still it is often advisable to allow the respondent to follow his or her own inclinations in order to assure that the respondent is not forced to give information before having had an opportunity to recall it. When specifics are asked for before the respondent volunteers them, there is a danger that the respondent will fill the gaps in his or her memory with imagination. The respondent may be reporting what he or she assumes must have been done in view of the logical or moral requirements of the situation; the respondent need not be consciously fabricating.

Giving the respondent recognition. By merely introducing a broad topic of discussion and allowing the respondent to tell his or her own story, the interviewer implies a respect for the respondent's ability to report relevant material. This lack of restriction also allows the respondent to mention information to his or her credit even though it may not be directly relevant to the objectives of the study.

Giving sympathetic understanding. Giving the respondent more freedom to tell the story in his or her own way usually implies to the respondent that the interviewer is more interested in him or her as a unique person than as a source of information. The respondent perceives that the interviewer is "interested in what is important to me" and is encouraged to take advantage of the opportunity. The more that specific, narrow questions are asked, the more likely that the emphasis of the interview will shift away from each respondent's unique concerns.

Encouraging catharsis. Once an atmosphere of sympathetic understanding is established, the respondent will be encouraged to "get certain problems off his chest" if they are important to him at the moment and are related to the topic of the interview. Of course, whether or not the interviewer should encourage this catharsis depends upon whether the information is relevant, whether the catharsis is helpful or harmful to the optimum relationship between interviewer and respondent, and how efficient the interviewer must be.

Need for meaning. In some cases, the freedom from the restrictions of specific questions and a generally permissive atmosphere will encourage the respondent to soliloquize. He or she begins to think out loud and expresses doubts, fears, and even the decision-making process used in forming answers to questions. This usually occurs when the interview topic itself or the life situation of the respondent touches upon confusion or crisis. If the interviewer needs to stimulate the respondent's need for meaning by pointing out problems and dilemmas, the broad question does not always allow the interviewer to do this.

Values of Narrow Questions

As in the case of the broad question, the value of the narrow question depends to a great extent upon the type of information sought and the type of motivation which must be stimulated. In general, if specific facts and opinions are needed rather than more complex structural relationships, a more specific question will be more efficient. For example, if we wish to know a person's age, religion, and marital status and if such information is not ego threatening under the circumstances, then it would be ridiculous to attempt to obtain the information by asking, "Would you please tell me about yourself?" On the other hand, if we wanted to know which were the most salient aspects of a person's self-concept, we would need to know not only the person's age, religion, and marital status but also many other characteristics, as well as their relative importance and interrelationships in the mind of the respondent. In this case, the broader question would be more appropriate. However, under certain circumstances the narrower question has advantages in motivating the respondent.

Reducing ego threat. There are circumstances where the topic and the respondent are such that broad questions have little meaning to the respondent. He or she may feel at a loss to begin the report or to organize it into some meaningful whole. This is particularly true when the topic itself is not vital to the respondent or is put in terms that are too abstract. Under these conditions the ego threat is not in the information itself but in the fact that the respondent is embarrassed because of feeling that he or she has nothing to say. The respondent is given encouragement and support by the interviewer who dissects the topic into more manageable specifics.

Reducing the etiquette barrier. In some interviews, the respondent is willing to give any information as long as he or she is sure that it is considered useful or necessary by the interviewer. If the interviewer has a relationship with the respondent that makes the respondent reluctant to report certain information, he or she will tend to omit it unless the interviewer specifically asks for it.

Stimulating the need for meaning. Often a person's interest in the topic of the interview can be increased by stimulating his or her need for meaning. This can be done by asking specific questions posing dilemmas, inconsistencies, or problematical relationships. The respondent can often be enticed by the realization that things are not as simple as they might appear at first glance.

Structuring the Answer

Questions may include varying degrees of answer structure. The categories of acceptable answers may be explicit or implicit. The respondent may be instructed to choose one or more than one. Answer categories may be mutually exclusive or overlapping. The respondent may be given the choice of either using the answer categories supplied or giving a more detailed answer in his or her own words. The categories may be qualitative or quantitative.

In general, questions which do not supply the answer categories are called open-ended and those that limit the answer choices are called closed. An example of an open-ended question would be, "What did you see at the County Fair?" An example of a closed question would be, "Which of the following did you see at the county fair: sulky racing, the hog show, the milking machine display, the fruit exhibit?"

The answers to a question need not be either completely open or closed, but may fall in between. Rather than supplying categories, the wording of the question may imply choices, as in these two examples: "How many times a month, on the average, do you go to church?" and "Do you go to church every week?" The first example implies that the answer should be in terms of times per month. The second implies that either a "yes" or "no" answer is needed. A more completely structured form would be as follows: "How many times, on the average, do you go to church: more than once a week, once a week, two or three times per month, once a month, or less than once a month?"

Of course, none of the above three forms should be used unless preceded by a filter question to determine whether or not the particular respondent did in fact attend some religious body that would be appropriately called a church.

In deciding upon the amount of structuring to use, it is necessary to consider the type of information sought and the effects of the structuring on the respondent's ability and willingness to give the relevant information.

Some of the same information objectives requiring questions with a broader scope also require open-ended questions discovering the respondent's paths of association, frames of reference, and universe of discourse.

If the information can be obtained equally well by either open-ended or closed questions, then the closed question should be used because it increases the efficiency and reliability of the coding and analysis of the data.

In a semischeduled interview in which specific items of information are to be obtained but no wording of the questions or sequence is specified, it is still possible for the interviewer to structure the answers and to record the responses on a multiple-choice code sheet. This eliminates having to convert verbatim notes into code categories. Also, if the correct category for the answer is unclear to the interviewer, he or she can probe for further clarification.

Structuring answers can have several possible effects upon the facilitators and inhibitors of communication.

Competing time demands. The use of structured answers not only saves time for the interviewers, coders, and analyzers but also for the respondent. If the information is of the type where it is appropriate to structure the answers, the respondent is often happy to see that the interviewer knows exactly what he or she wants and is businesslike and efficient.

Ego threat. Under some conditions respondents feel threatened by open-ended questions which sound "as if they would require a dissertation to answer." The respondent's insecurity can often be reduced by placing the choices before him or her.

Etiquette. Often the etiquette barrier can be reduced by supplying specific answer categories which show that the interviewer expects such information. Answer categories can supply the respondent with a vocabulary compatible with the etiquette requirements of the situation. For example: "With which of the following did you have your first complete heterosexual intercourse? (1) With a prostitute? (2) With an intimate acquaintance before marriage? (3) With a girl 'picked up' for the occasion? (4) With your wife before you were engaged? (5) With your wife after engagement and before marriage? (6) With your wife after marriage?" Such a question put in a matter-of-fact tone by a mature interviewer would be more likely to elicit a valid response with less strain on the respondent than would the open-ended form of the same question. If there is no reason why the information must be collected by interviewing, a questionnaire would probably be still more effective in reducing both the ego threat and the etiquette barrier. A compromise between an interview and a questionnaire can be arranged by stating the question orally and then handing the respondent a card with the answers on it and asking the respondent to give the *number* of the correct answer.

Forgetting. Under certain circumstances it is more efficient, valid, and reliable to obtain facts which have faded in the respondent's memory by asking him or her to choose from among several specific alternatives. It is usually easier to *recognize* the correct answer when it is presented by the interviewer than it is to *recall* it without a suggestion of the possibilities. This is a valid procedure only if the interviewer knows in advance that the suggested choices include the correct answer and that only one answer could be correct. It is also helpful to eliminate as many incorrect answers from the list as possible and to offer possible answers clearly different in their meaning or their sound. For example, students returning for a summer session in Guanajuato, Mexico, were interviewed to determine some of the effects of the cross-cultural experiences. The interviewer wanted to establish where the person stayed during his six weeks there. After learning that it was "some hotel with a Spanish name, but I can't think of it at the moment," he asked:

I: Was it at El Orozco, La Posada de Santa Fe, or El Castillo?

R: Oh, yes, La Posada de Santa Fe, we called it the Posie, or the hotel, because it had such a long name.

In this case the interviewer knew the names of the only three hotels in town so there was no danger of omitting a possibility or of suggesting something that was not possible.

Once a memory has faded completely, it is not always possible for the respondent to recognize the correct answer even though it is included in the choices. A good interviewer can often detect when the respondent is unsure or simply guessing. The danger of not detecting this is that the respondent may "invent" the answer. In such a case the respondent is not lying but is merely giving what at the moment is believed to be the correct answer.

When there is no single answer about an objective situation but multiple subjective possibilities, the checklist of answers may coercively suggest invalid answers. For example, when we asked physicians to list as many positive and negative aspects of being a doctor as possible, this open-ended approach elicited no mention of "having to make emergency calls in the middle of the night" as one of the negative aspects. Yet when a checklist was supplied later in the same interview, a significant proportion of them checked this reason.

One way of avoiding the biasing effect of suggestion is to use a list of bi-polar dimensions which suggest both the positive and the negative extremes of each dimension. For example, if we want to discover a person's self-concept, we could provide a list of bi-polar pairs of traits such as secure-insecure, friendly-unfriendly, or we could give a set of hypothetical situations and ask the person to respond in quantitative terms. This direct self-rating has the advantage of stimulating memory by suggesting possible dimensions without loading the answer positively or negatively, but it does not eliminate the ego threat involved in giving oneself a negative rating. The second method of using responses to hypothetical situations does not directly ask the respondent to rate himself nor does it necessarily call to the respondent's attention the fact that dimensions of his personality are being measured. Of course the more educated the respondent, the more he or she is able to understand that responses to hypothetical situations may be an indirect way of measuring dimensions of personality. In this case ego threat may not be so easily circumvented.

An interesting example of a creative structured approach to obtain the respondent's self-concept is reported by Tudor and Holmes who instructed their respondents to introspect about themselves in terms of analogies and opposites.[4] This technique elicited significantly more information about each person in the experimental group than was obtained from the control group whose members were simply asked in an open-ended way to give a description of their self-concept.

Chronological confusion. The interviewer can often help the respondent avoid chronological confusion by supplying a set of events known to be arranged in chronological order and then asking the respondent whether the event in question occurred before or after each event in the list. For example: "Let's see if we can get a little more exact age at which Johnny had the skin allergy. Was it before he could walk, after he could walk but before going to nursery school, or after he was in first grade at Mills School?"

If the events arranged chronologically are also meaningful to the respondent and have some connection with the event to be recalled, this technique may be very helpful to the respondent and save considerable interviewing time.

Thus far, we have indicated some of the conditions under which closed questions are particularly useful. The conditions for using open-ended questions are the same as those calling for the use of broad questions and these have already been discussed.

USING LEADING QUESTIONS

The term *leading questions* refers to any question, including its context and answer structure, which is phrased so that it appears to the respondent that the interviewer desires or expects a certain answer; yet the interviewer's expectation could not have been derived solely from what the respondent has already said in the interview.

---

[4]Thomas G. Tudor and David S. Holmes, "Use of Analogies and Opposites in Helping Interviewees Verbalize Their Self-Concepts," *Journal of Consulting and Clinical Psychology* 38 (1972), pp. 445–48.

Forms of Leading

A question may be leading because of the *context* in which it appears; this leading context may be of a personal or impersonal type. The following is an example of the personal context.

> The President has made several public statements advocating freer trade between nations. Do you think we should eliminate some of the tariff barriers that have been erected against free trade?

The direction of the effect of this loaded context cannot be predicted unless the respondent's attitude toward the president is known. Nevertheless, it is highly probable that changing the context, as in the example below, would obtain a different response from many respondents.

> Socialists have historically advocated free trade among nations. Do you think we should eliminate some of the tariff barriers that have been erected against free trade?

In contrast, the impersonal context does not mention the point of view of any individual or group, but brings into play certain facts and logical relationships which tend to influence the answer in one direction. The next question is put into two different contexts tending to bias the response in opposite directions.

> In view of the fact that the United States is the richest country in the world do you think that the defense budget should be cut as much as 25 percent? In view of the fact that about 80 percent of the total federal taxes are spent on past, present, and future war expenditures, do you think that the defense budget should be cut as much as 25 percent?

There is little doubt that a random sample poll of the United States, using the two forms of the question, would show significantly different results.

Even when no leading context is provided, the question may be loaded by simply using *emotionally charged* words. For example, compare these two questions:

> How do you feel about blacks moving into this area?
> How do you feel about blacks invading your neighborhood?

Even though in sociology *invading* is not an emotionally charged term, to the respondent *moving into* would appear more neutral.

A third way of loading a question is to structure the answer in a way that restricts the respondent by *omitting a category* most appropriate for him or her. Compare these two questions:

What is your religion? Protestant, Catholic, or Jewish?

What is your religion? Protestant, Catholic, Jewish, agnostic, atheist, or free-thinker?

It is highly probable that the second form would elicit a smaller number of Protestant, Catholic, and Jewish responses.

A fourth way of leading is to make *challenging statements*. The respondent will often change his or her general point of view expressed in the interview if the interviewer consistently challenges one type of statement and allows the opposite type to go unchallenged. Any of the following would be considered a challenge to some degree: "How do you know that?" "Do you think you could back up that statement with evidence?" "Give me a specific example of that." "That sounds very unusual, I have never heard of such a thing happening. How do you account for that?" "Are you sure that your observations are correct?" "That seems to contradict what you said before."

The effects of such challenges depend upon how sure the respondent is of his or her rapport, the extent to which the respondent is inclined to show deference to the interviewer, and the tone of voice in which the challenge is made.

Effects of Leading Questions

In the literature on interviewing there seems to be a preponderance of opinion, usually based upon direct experience in interviewing, that the leading question should be avoided. For example, Cannell and Kahn suggest that "Questions should be phrased so that they contain no suggestion as to the most appropriate response."[5]

Kinsey takes an opposite position at one point in his discussion of interviewing methods used to obtain information on the respondent's sex behavior. He advocates putting the burden of denial on the respondent:

> The interviewer should not make it easy for a subject to deny his participation in any form of sexual activity. It is too easy to say "no" if he is simply asked whether he has engaged in a particular activity. Consequently we always begin by asking when they first engaged in such activity . . . and since it becomes apparent from the form of the question that we would not be surprised if he had had such experience, there seems to be less reason for denying it. It might be thought this approach would bias the answer, but

---

[5]Charles F. Cannel and Robert L. Kahn, "The Collection of Data by Interviewing," in Leon Festinger and Daniel Katz, *Research Methods in the Social Sciences* (New York: Dryden Press, 1953), p. 346.

there is no indication that we get false admissions in forms of sexual behavior in which the subject was not actually involved.[6]

Becker, who takes the position that challenging the respondent in an aggressive manner does not necessarily bias the response, points out some of the conditions under which he could obtain more valid information from public school teachers regarding race relations problems in the school. He says that a basic condition for success was

> the professional bond of courtesy which the teacher feels obligated to extend to the interviewer. She felt she must avoid being unpleasant. Such tactics will not prove effective in all situations nor would one want to use them . . . where, for example, your research places you in continuous contact with those being studied, as in a long-term community study, it might be wisest to avoid the possibility of antagonizing informants which lies in this stratagem. . . . Finally. . . the informant must not be of a higher social status than the interviewer because the unspoken etiquette of such a relationship leaves the informant free to be rude through evasiveness and implausibility, free to ignore the demands of the questioner who is stepping out of the confines of his deference role.[7]

None of the authors cited base their conclusions on experimental studies aimed at testing the relative effectiveness of using leading versus nonleading questions. Richardson[8] and Dohrenwend[9] have done experiments which show that the question, "Should leading questions be used?" is not well put, since the answer can be neither "yes" nor "no." Instead, we should try to account for the conditions under which they are successful or unsuccessful. After reviewing much of the literature and his own experiences, the author suggests that the following factors account for the different effects of leading questions.

It is helpful to distinguish between three types of situations, one in which the leading question helps to obtain more valid information, another in which valid information is obtained in spite of the leading question, and a third situation where the leading question actually distorts the answer. Here are some of the most important characteristics of the type of situation in which the leading question would obtain more valid information than the neutral question.

----

[6]Alfred C. Kinsey et al. "Interviewing," *Sexual Behavior in the Human Male* (Philadelphia: W. B. Saunders, 1948).

[7]Howard S. Becker, "A Note on Interviewing Tactics," *Human Organization*, Winter 1954, pp. 31–32.

[8]Stephan A. Richardson, "The Use of Leading Questions in Non-Schedule Interviews," *Human Organization* 19, no. 2 (1960), pp. 86–89.

[9]Barbara Dohrenwend and Stephan A. Richardson, "A Use for Leading Questions in Research Interviewing," *Human Organization* 23 (1964), pp. 76–77.

1. The respondent has the relevant information clearly in mind. This is in contrast to a faded memory, a confused image or feeling which would leave the respondent open to the power of suggestion in the leading question.

2. The respondent has a tendency to withhold the information either for fear of violating the etiquette requirements of the interview situation, or because the correct answer is potentially ego threatening since it admits a violation of public ideals of some type.

3. The respondent either accepts these ideals as valid or assumes that the interviewer does so.

4. The interviewer loads the question in a direction contrary to the public ideals.[10]

Regardless of whether the bias of the question is toward or away from the correct answer in the case of a particular respondent, such a leading question will be helpful. If the respondent's correct answer happens to be in violation of the public ideals, then the question is biased *toward* the correct answer and the respondent is more likely to admit his or her deviant experience. This is particularly true when the interviewer's manner shows that he or she expects the respondent to have had such an experience and that he or she does not condemn the respondent for it. The respondent who has not had the deviant experience is less likely to pretend that he or she has committed a violation of public ideals. Thus the use of the leading question under these circumstances is based upon the assumption that in general people are less likely to falsely plead guilty than they are to falsely plead not guilty; therefore the bias should be toward guilty.

An interesting experimental example of the creative use of the leading question is given by Dohrenwend reporting on a study of abortion.[11] When the loaded question was used, 58 percent of the respondents admitted knowing how an abortion was performed, while only 37 percent admitted such knowledge when the unloaded form of the same question was used. Similarly, 51 percent admitted having at least one friend who had an abortion when the loaded form of the question was used, in contrast to only 25 percent when the unloaded form was used.

---

[10]Lois R. Dean in "Interaction, Reported and Observed," *Human Organization* no. 3 (Fall 1958), p. 36, demonstrates the tendency of the respondent to falsify his report in the direction of the acceptable norms.

[11]Barbara S. Dohrenwend, "Experimental Study of Directive Interviewing," *Public Opinion Quarterly* 34 (1970), pp. 117–25.

There are circumstances in which valid information is obtained in spite of the use of leading questions. Here the following conditions are important:

1. The information is clear in the respondent's mind, free from fading memory, chronological or inferential confusion.

2. Neither the information to be reported nor the relationship between the interviewer and respondent constitute an ego threat.

3. There is no etiquette barrier between respondent and interviewer.

To illustrate these circumstances, let us assume that an interviewer is attempting to discover what happened at a meeting attended by the respondent and how the respondent felt about what transpired. Further assume that the meeting lasted one hour, that fifteen people attended, and that it consisted of a short speech and a discussion of the pros and cons of an increase in the public school tax levy. The meeting occurred the night before the interview. Note that all the questions are leading in that they either suggest possible answers or exclude other possible answers, yet none of them cause distortion in the respondent's information.

I: How many people were at the meeting, about 100?

R: Oh no, there were fifteen including the speaker; I know them all. There are very few people interested in the public schools, particularly in the summertime.

I: What time did the meeting start, 8 or 8:30?

R: We always start at 7, as we did last night.

I: Did you just have an informal discussion?

R: No, we also had a speaker from Columbus.

I: Was his talk about the usual sort of things which education people have to say about child psychology?

R: The topic was "What can the taxpayer buy for his school tax dollar."

I: Oh, I see. Did you feel that the speaker had little of value to say as is so often true of people speaking on this topic?

R: No, he had quite a bit to say; we selected him because of his analytical objectivity.

I: Do you feel that an excellent speaker of this type will exert a strong influence on improving the public schools?

R: He won't have any strong *direct* influence on the community since he was speaking to only fifteen people, but there is a possibility that this will spark some activity among the vitally interested people.

To avoid being led astray by the "harmless" leading question, the interviewer should be reminded that often he or she will not know in advance that all the necessary conditions are present for rendering the leading question harmless. In some situations the interviewer may know in advance that a certain condition is present but often cannot know in advance that other conditions are also present. In any case, it is a good plan to avoid the use of leading questions rather than hope they are of the harmless variety unless the situation calls for their intentional use.

There are types of situations in which leading questions are definitely harmful because they bias the response away from the truth. The following conditions are significant:

1. The respondent does not have the information clearly in mind because of fading memory, chronological or inferential confusion; he or she is therefore susceptible to suggestions from the interviewer.

2. The information requested is not important to the respondent, and there is little motivation to strive to remember the accurate information.

3. The respondent does not feel free to say "I don't know," because he or she has an ego-threatening relationship with the interviewer or because the etiquette of the situation requires that the respondent show deference to the interviewer.

4. The question leads in the direction of a false answer.

These conditions typically prevail in settings where the respondents are subordinates in the same community or organization as the interviewer.

For example, Company X, a large corporation, has been carrying on an intensive "educational" program pointing out the virtues of working for Company X—such as its pension plan, job rotation plan, retraining for automation, and family health insurance. In the excerpt below the interviewer is working for the personnel department and is studying the problem of recruiting workers to reduce labor turnover. Four years ago when the respondent came to work for the company, the same interviewer had talked with him. The objective of the present interview is to obtain a complete picture of the factors accounting for why the respondent came to work for Company X. In the course of the interview the following loaded questions obtained these responses:

I-1:   We are doing a study of why people come to work for Johnson Electric and why they stay so long. How long have you been working for us?

R-1:   About four years, I guess.

I-2:   Why did you pick this company to work for?

R-2:   Gosh, that was a long time ago. Let me see . . .

I-3:   Yes, it was quite a while ago. Who were you working for before you came here?

R-3:   For Central Electric.

I-4:   Why did you leave there? Didn't you like it?

R-4:   No, it wasn't a very pleasant place to work.

I-5:   Did they have a pension plan like ours or a job rotation plan, training for automation, family health plan, or that sort of thing?

R-5:   No, they didn't have any of those benefits like we do here.

I-6:   What did your wife think about your choosing Johnson Electric?

R-6:   She was glad I could get the job . . . she likes the family health plan very much, and I like the system of rotating jobs every three months after you have been here a couple of years. It makes things interesting. I learn a lot that way about the company as a whole. I can't understand people who like to hold down one job all the time.

I-7:   Did you hear about this company through ads in the paper?

R-7:   I spent a lot of time looking at the ads to find a good job.

I-8:   Why did you choose to work for Johnson Electric?

R-8:   It is a very progressive company. It has a lot of good personnel policies like I mentioned before. For example, I hope I can benefit from the in-service training program so I can be upgraded when we get more automated.

With question 1 the interviewer begins to furnish a biasing context in the phrase "why they stay so long" rather than "why people come and go." Question 2 is loaded with the assumption that the respondent "picked" the present company to work for when actually he might have preferred another but was not accepted. Question 4 suggests an easy way for the respondent to avoid the ego threat of saying that he was fired. Question 5 supplies the answer for questions 6 and 8. In questions 5 and 6 the interviewer does not probe to distinguish between what the respondent and his wife like about Johnson Electric now that he is here and what they knew about it before he applied for the job. Only the latter could have been a reason for coming to Johnson Electric.

Question 7 supplies an answer to what would have been a less biased question: "How did you first hear about Johnson Electric?" After four years the respondent's memory might be vague on how he heard about Johnson Electric and any suggested answer would be tempting. In question 8 the interviewer again assumes that the respondent chose to work at Johnson Electric. Response 8 gives the "company line" answer suggested by the interviewer in question 5 even though response 2 indicates a possible fading of memory.

The overall effect of the leading questions in this situation is to suggest invalid answers which are readily given by the respondent due to the type of communication barriers operating.

The following conditions describe another type of situation in which the leading question has a distorting effect upon the response.

1. The information is clear in the respondent's mind and he or she is, therefore, *able* to give it accurately.

2. The correct report would constitute an ego threat since it is in violation of public ideals or the apparent wishes of the interviewer.

3. Or, the correct report would violate certain etiquette requirements of the situation.

4. The question is slanted toward the public ideals and, for the respondent, toward a false answer.

These conditions frequently prevail in situations where the interviewer is perceived by the respondent as a superior. The main difference between this situation and the preceding one is that here the ego threat, the etiquette barrier, or the leading must be stronger to distort the response since the respondent has the correct information clearly in mind. The respondent must consciously distort his or her report to compromise in the situation. In this case, the respondent often produces rationalizations for his or her falsification such as, "He doesn't really want to know the truth anyway, so why should I give him the benefit of it." "He wouldn't do anything constructive with the information so why give it to him?" "He just wants to find out how to get me to work harder; why should I whip myself?" "I don't want to be a stool pigeon!"

By specifying and illustrating some of the relevant conditions determining the positive, neutral, and negative effects of the leading question, this section hopefully can encourage the creative use of leading questions under appropriate conditions.

It is important to note that in some situations the interviewer cannot be sure that the conditions prevail to make the loaded question more effective than the neutral question. Therefore, in order to guard against false "confessions" the interviewer should refuse to accept the respondent's statement at face value without cross-checking. The interviewer should press the respondent with probes on how the act was done and on precise details of the setting in which the act took place. In doing so it may become apparent that the respondent has confessed to something he or she did not do.

SUMMARY

This chapter has presented a variety of *verbal* techniques that can be used by the interviewer to minimize the inhibitors and to maximize the facilitators of communication under certain conditions.

Among the verbal forms used as techniques are providing context with the questions, selecting an appropriate wording, defining the scope of the question, structuring the answer, and using leading or nonleading questions. Providing the verbal context with a question is one technique for communicating the question more accurately to the respondent by providing definitions of terms, time perspectives, spatial perspectives, social-psychological contexts, criteria and facts to be used by the respondent in making judgments. In questions where the objective is to discover the respondent's own frames of reference, definitions, criteria, and perception of the facts, the interviewer must scrupulously refrain from providing the context.

Verbal context provided with the question may also motivate the respondent by arousing interest in the topic, by giving recognition to the respondent's special qualifications, reducing ego threat, preventing falsification, stimulating memory, reducing chronological confusion, and discovering unconscious subjective orientations of the respondent.

In wording the question itself, the interviewer should try to use a vocabulary which is clearly understood by the respondent, which aids in establishing an optimal relationship, and which does not unintentionally load the question in favor of a particular response.

The scope of a question may vary from the broad type which includes the whole topic of the interview to one which delimits some particular aspect of a particular person's behavior in relation to a particular object at a specific time and place. Broad questions are useful in discovering the respondent's paths of association, hierarchy of values, perspectives, universe of discourse, definitions of terms, perceptions of facts, and chronology of personal experiences. Under some conditions, the broad question can reduce the respondent's ego threat, stimulate memory, give recognition, provide sympathetic understanding, encourage catharsis, and stimulate the need for meaning. Under other conditions, the narrow question can help reduce ego threat, circumvent the etiquette barrier, and stimulate the respondent's need for meaning.

In structuring the responses, the interviewer should consider the type of information sought as well as the effects upon the respondent's motivation to give such information. The open-ended question is sometimes more useful in discovering unanticipated responses, the respondent's paths of association, universes of discourse, perspectives, definitions of terms, hierarchy of values, and perceptions of facts. Closed questions are preferred over open ones when equally valid information can be obtained because of the greater efficiency in coding and analyzing the results.

Under certain conditions, the closed question has great motivational value. By speeding up the interviewing process and shortening the interview, the probability of encountering competing time demands is reduced. Providing answer choices reduces the size of the task for the respondent and the ego threat which might be involved when the boundaries of the response are unknown. The structured answer is useful in stimulating the respondent's memory if the correct answer is among the choices. Similarly, choices provided in chronological order may be helpful in reducing the respondent's chronological confusion.

Leading questions are those which tend to indicate that one answer is expected or preferred over another when such expectations or preferences are not based on previous information given by the respondent. The question may be loaded by associating it with a personal or impersonal context having emotional meaning to the respondent. Questions can also be loaded by providing answer categories which stack the cards in favor of a particular response. In extreme cases, the question may be loaded by an accompanying direct challenge.

In some circumstances the leading question seems to obtain more valid answers than a nonleading one. This is true when the respondent has the information clearly in mind, but tends to withhold it because it violates certain public ideals which the respondent either accepts or assumes that the interviewer accepts. Under these conditions, if the question leads in the direction contrary to the public ideals, it can often obtain more valid results than the nonleading question. Under other conditions, the leading question seems to have no effect; valid information is obtained in spite of its use. More common, however, are situations in which leading questions distort the response.

This chapter has focused on only the *verbal forms* of interviewer behavior and discussed the possible effects of the verbal techniques both in communicating to the respondent what information is needed and in affecting either the inhibitors or facilitators of communication that govern the respondent's ability and willingness to provide complete and relevant information. A checklist of these verbal techniques is given in Figure 13–2 in the form of questions you should ask yourself when preparing an interview.

This verbal facet of techniques is only half the story. The other half is the use of nonverbal techniques to be discussed in the next chapter.

FIGURE 13-2   Checklist—Verbal techniques

Questions to ask yourself about verbal techniques when preparing an interview

---

Should a *context* be supplied to *communicate* the question more clearly by providing:

1. Definitions of terms to be used?
2. A time perspective?
3. A spatial perspective?
4. A social-psychological perspective?
5. Criteria for judgment needed to answer?
6. Facts to consider in giving the answer?

Should a *context* be supplied to *motivate* the respondent by:

7. Rousing the respondent's interest?
8. Recognizing the respondent's special qualifications?
9. Reducing ego threat?
10. Preventing falsification?
11. Reducing the etiquette barrier?
12. Stimulating the respondent's memory?
13. Reducing the respondent's chronological confusion?
14. Using concrete hypothetical cases?

Is the *vocabulary* that has been used the type that:

15. Is clearly understood by the respondent?
16. Establishes the best role relationship between respondent and interviewer?
17. Supplies the vocabulary needed for the respondent's answers?

Should the *scope* of the questions be:

18. As broad as possible?
19. As narrow as possible?
20. In the middle range?

Should the *answer structure* be:

21. Left completely open?
22. Completely structured?
23. Completely structured except for an "other" category?
24. A combination or sequence of open and structured questions?

Should *leading* questions be used? If so, should they be loaded by:

25. Loading the context or sequence of questions?
26. Loading the question with emotional words?
27. Loading the answer choices?
28. Using a challenging statement?

DISCUSSION QUESTIONS

1. In what ways can preceding a question with a contextual statement help in communicating the question?

2. How can contextual statements preceding the question help to motivate the respondent?

3. What are some of the most important problems to be solved or avoided in selecting the appropriate vocabulary for wording the question?

4. What are some of the dimensions of question scope?

5. What are broad-scope questions best for? What are narrow-scope questions good for?

6. What are some of the ways of structuring the answers to questions?

7. How can answer structures inhibit or facilitate communication?

8. Under what conditions are leading questions good or bad?

Selected Readings

The three references below are examples of demonstrations of the use of highly structured verbal forms (leading questions, analogies, and hypothetical cases) to elicit generally hard-to-verbalize information.

Richardson, Stephan A., et al. *Interviewing: Its Forms and Functions.* New York: Basic Books, 1965. Chapter 7, "Expectations and Premises: The So-Called 'Leading Question'," pp. 171–97.
  One of the best treatments of the use of the *leading question.* Reviews some of the experiments done on the problem and suggests basic principles.

Tudor, Thomas G., and David S. Holmes. "Use of Analogies and Opposites in Helping Interviewees Verbalize Their Self-Concept," *Journal of Consulting and Clinical Psychology* 38 (1972), pp. 445–48.
  An excellent study demonstrating one application of the general principle of using highly structured stimuli to tease out subtle subjective orientations, in this case the respondent's self-concept.

Weaver, T. "Use of Hypothetical Situations in a Study of Spanish-American Illness Referral Systems," *Human Organization* 29 (1970), pp. 140–53.
  An excellent example of the use of indirect techniques to discover norms, values, expectations, attitudes, or other difficult-to-verbalize subjective orientations. The hypothetical situation gives the respondent the chance to *demonstrate* his norms rather than being asked directly what his norms are.

LABORATORY PROBLEM 7

Verbal Techniques in Studying
Parent-Child Conflicts

PURPOSE

The purpose of this laboratory problem is to provide a challenge to creatively link the general purpose, the specific information objectives, and the verbal techniques of an interview. Throughout the whole process you must strive to word the questions so that (a) they are *relevant* to the general objectives of the study, (b) they clearly *communicate* to the respondent the specific information needed, and (c) they *motivate* the respondent to give relevant information as completely and accurately as possible.

STEPS IN PLANNING

The steps below are not intended to imply a simple, rigid one-way progression since in the actual creative process you may have to move backward and forward several times. However, each of the steps must be taken at least once to complete the process.

1. *Specify the objectives.* The general purposes of any study must first be converted into specific questions without losing track of the general purpose. Any problem stated in common sense terms is open to a variety of interpretations. The particular interpretation of the problem should be accurately reflected in the wording of the specific questions.

2. *Word questions tentatively.* Before finally specifying the particular interpretation of the objectives, brainstorm a lot of tentatively

worded questions to get an idea of how the general objective can be broken down into specific questions aimed at various items of information.

3. Anticipate inhibitors and facilitators. Once you see the form and content of the specific questions to be asked, you are in a better position to try to empathize with the respondent to anticipate some potential inhibitors and facilitators.

4. Review the verbal forms. The verbal techniques should be reviewed and selectively applied in wording questions in the light of the potential inhibitors and facilitators.

5. Word the question. In view of the probable effects of the various verbal forms, select the best for the purpose at hand.

Obviously, the five-step process is not infallible and is only as good as the planner's ability to empathize with the potential respondent and to apply the different verbal forms available. In a real study this five-step process produces the tentative rough draft of the interview schedule which must then be field-tested and revised at least once. Also, any weaknesses in the instrument due to its inapplicability to a particular respondent are compensated for by the tactical behavior of the interviewer in adjusting to a particular respondent. However, serious creative work in developing the rough draft saves much floundering in the early stages of the field work.

THE STUDY (PARENT-CHILD CONFLICTS)

Assume that you are to plan an interview to discover the sources of intergenerational conflict in the American culture by interviewing a random sample of high school students regarding the kinds of conflicts they have with their parents. You are interested in all types of conflicts from the most mild to the most violent and want to discover the range of issues involved. You are to explore all conflicts in the year preceding the interview. A comparison of the nature and frequency of the conflicts in different types of communities may render important clues to some of the causes of mental illness and delinquency in teenagers. Assume that the respondent is a sixteen-year-old high school girl being interviewed by a twenty-two-year-old college student.

The interviewer says, "My name is Linda Johnson. I am helping with a study of family relations sponsored by the U.S. Public Health Department. We want to get the teenager's point of view on family relations and that is why we are talking to hundreds of high school students. Your name was selected randomly for an interview."

Problem 1. What question will open up a free discussion of the types of conflicts the respondent has had with her parents in the past year? This is to be the opening question following the introductory explanation above.

Problem 2. Design two or three questions to discover which kinds of behavior the teenager hides from her parents to avoid open conflict.

Problem 3. Design three to five questions which will also be asked of the parents and will allow you to compare the teenager's point of view with theirs in the area of economic responsibilities and privileges. How you would word the main question? What subsidiary questions are needed? To limit this problem deal with only one type of economic responsibility or privilege, some economic issue over which parents and teenagers are likely to have conflict.

Problem 4. Design three to five questions to discover the respondent's criteria for judging the relative seriousness of conflicts she has had with her parents in the past year.

Chapter Fourteen

Nonverbal Techniques

Although both verbal and nonverbal techniques have the dual function of communicating the question and of motivating the respondent to answer, the author feels that the verbal communication dealt with in the previous chapter has the predominant function of communicating the question, and the nonverbal techniques to be dealt with in this chapter have the main function of motivating the respondent to answer candidly and completely. In any case the overall effect on the respondent depends upon the combined effect of the verbal and the nonverbal communication.

Even though nonverbal communication tends to be less subject to conscious scrutiny, it has been demonstrated by numerous experiments that people can learn to be aware of nonverbal communication, can analyze it, and can experiment with it as a conscious tool in interviewing. Nonverbal cues are essential ingredients in both interviewer-to-respondent and respondent-to-interviewer communication. From the standpoint of the development of skills, the interviewer must learn to be sensitive to both the nonverbal cues received from the respondent and those sent to the respondent.

THEORY OF NONVERBAL COMMUNICATION

The following presents a short overview of the general nature of nonverbal communication without concentrating on its application to the interviewing task. First, general ideas are provided on the importance of the nonverbal portion of a conversation; second, some of the general principles are described that govern nonverbal communication; and third, the major types or channels of nonverbal communication are described.

Importance of Nonverbal Communication

Studies, for example the one by Rosenthal, show that some people are more sensitive than others to nonverbal cues and that these people

generally function better both socially and intellectually.[1] This same research also found that younger people are less sensitive to nonverbal
cues than are older people, which suggests that the ability to read these
cues comes with life experience and can be learned. This empathic ability
to read nonverbal cues and to control one's own nonverbal behavior
can also be improved by systematic study and practice.

Everyone seems to realize that in a conversation the words themselves do not carry all of the meaning; even so the impact of the nonverbal cues is probably greatly underestimated. For example, studies which
raise the question of the relative importance of the verbal versus the
nonverbal portion of the message estimate that as high as 65 percent of
the meaning is carried by the nonverbal cues such as tone of voice, facial expression, gestures, posture and dress.[2]

Another study showed that, if the listener is allowed to hear the
tone of voice of the speaker but is deprived of seeing the head and hand
gestures, there is a 20–30 percent loss in comprehension.[3]

There are possible objections to assigning precise percentages of
meaning to the verbal versus the nonverbal since the effect of each is not
completely independent, and their relative importance would depend
upon the social context of the conversation, the style of speech, and the
content of the message. Despite these caveats it is clear that in everyday
speech much of the comprehension depends upon the nonverbal cues.

Nonverbal communication is important not only because it affects
the comprehension of the message but also because it establishes some
kind of *relationship* between the communicators which transcends any
specific message. As we will show later, the nonverbal signals sent out
by the interviewer determine to a great extent whether the respondent
sees the interviewer as "good," "likable," "sympathetic," "trustworthy,"
or the opposite. The nonverbal cues and the verbal communications
must be consistent, particularly if the interviewer expects the respondent to share private information.

Finally, the nonverbal component is extremely important in that
it communicates general *emotional states*. People communicate their
current feeling state by unconscious physiological reactions. The close

---

[1]Robert Rosenthal et al., "Body Talk and Tone of Voice—the Language
Without Words," *Psychology Today*, September 1974, pp. 64–68.

[2]Randal Harrison, "Nonverbal Communication: Exploration into Time,
Space, Action and Object," in *Dimensions in Communication*, ed. James
H. Campbell and Hal W. Hepler (Belmont, Calif.: Wadsworth Publishing,
p. 101. See also Timothy G. Hegstrom, "Message Impact: What Percent Is
Nonverbal?" *The Western Journal of Speech Communication* 43, no. 2 (Spring
1979), pp. 134–42.

[3]William Rogers, *Communication in Action: Building Speech Competen-
cies*, (New York: Holt, Rinehart & Winston, 1984), p. 80.

connection between emotional feeling and physiological state is evident in the verbal expressions developed in common daily speech such as "lost your head," "chin up," "hair-raising," "butterflies in the stomach."[4] These emotional states can be communicated verbally or nonverbally, but the communicator usually has less conscious control over the nonverbal expression of feelings. Often we are tempted to think of the nonverbal cues as something the interviewer observes in the respondent and forget that the interviewer's nonverbal behavior is also being observed by the respondent. In many interview situations the information conveyed nonverbally about the respondent's feelings is very relevant if not the major point of the interview.

In short, any analysis of human communication which sees it as only a rational exchange of verbal symbols will leave most of the process unexamined and will fail to explain much of what happens in human interaction. The nonverbal communication is at least as important as the verbal. Let us look at some of the general principles governing nonverbal communication before looking at the specific types or channels of nonverbal expression.

Some Principles of Nonverbal Communication

The nonverbal message is often not intentional or conscious on the part of the sender; it has a strong influence on the receiver, and it tends to be believed; it is not isolated from the verbal message; its meaning depends upon the situational and verbal context, and the specific cues vary somewhat from culture to culture; and it has several different relationships with the verbal message. These five principles of nonverbal communication will be presented on at a time in the discussion that follows.

Unconscious behavior. To a great extent nonverbal behavior is at a less conscious level than is verbal behavior. Nonverbal behavior tends to be nonrational in that the communicator often is not aware of his or her own nonverbal cues being sent out; and the response in the receiver is direct and immediate, circumventing the conscious deliberative process. Nonverbal messages tend to follow a stimulus-response pattern without any intervening conscious decision-making process we commonly call thinking. For these reasons nonverbal communication is less conscious than verbal communication, but it may be the more powerful force in face-to-face interaction, particularly as a determinant of motivation.

The classic demonstration of people being unaware of the nonverbal signals they are emitting is found in the case of Clever Hans, the

---

[4]W. Schutz, *Joy: Expanding Human Awareness* (New York: Grove Press, 1967).

horse that could give the time, the date, and answers to arithmetic problems by tapping his foot. A group of skeptical horse experts tested Clever Hans and found that he did for them the same feats he had done on stage for his owner. As it was discovered later, the people testing the horse had watched the horse carefully as it tapped out the answer; once it had reached the correct number, the observers would relax and make a slight movement of the head which was Hans' clue to stop tapping. This is an excellent illustration of the principle that the observer, concentrating on the other party to the communication, is unaware that he or she is sending out signals which are also being observed. It never occurred to the testers that Hans was clever enough to watch them and to interpret correctly their unconsciously emitted signals. Later it was shown that if the testers were out of the horse's line of sight when they posed the question and awaited the answer, Hans could not give the correct answers.[5]

In human communication these nonverbal cues can result in circular reactions in which not only the original signal is unconscious but the observer's response to it is also nonverbal and unconscious, which in turn triggers off another unconscious response in the original sender. This process can build strong emotional states leading to riots, brawls, and lynchings. In the interview such circular reaction can lead either to greater spontaneity of exchange or to an almost total blocking of communication depending on the nature of the emotion being reflected back and forth between interviewer and respondent.

Nonverbal communication is believed. The degree to which the receiver is aware of the nonverbal message depends on the context of the nonverbal cue. For example, if the person's verbal message is not congruent with his or her nonverbal cues, the receiver is more likely to be aware of the nonverbal because it is in conflict with the verbal and poses the question of which message is to be believed. For example, Gazda suggests that in a counseling interview, if there is contradiction between the interviewer's verbal and nonverbal cues, the nonverbal ones are usually believed by the client.[6]

This principle that the nonverbal communication is most convincing may be fortunate or unfortunate depending on the situation. Not only is the principle useful in social science and the helping professions, but it also can be put to use by con artists to bilk people of their life's

---

[5]Mark L. Knapp, *Nonverbal Communication in Human Interaction*, 2nd ed. (New York: Holt, Rinehart & Winston, 1978), p. 2.

[6]G. M. Gazda et al., *Human Relations Development*, 3rd ed. (Boston: Allyn & Bacon, 1984), Chap. 6, "Awareness of Nonverbal Behaviors in Helping."

savings or the used-car salesman who has mastered the candid look. Often if people are using nonverbal cues to deceive others, only the most skilled will succeed against those taught to detect the lack of congruence between the verbal and the nonverbal, or between one nonverbal cue and another given out at the same time. This brings us to the third principle of nonverbal communication.

Nonverbal cues are seldom isolated. The same emotional state such as fear, for example, can be manifested in several simultaneous nonverbal physical reactions rather than in a single isolated expression. The voice pitch rises, the eyes open wider, the pulse rate increases, the skin becomes damper, the respiration rate quickens, the limbs become more rigid, and the mouth becomes dry. A person trying to deceive the police in an interrogation may be able to keep the eyes from widening and keep the pitch of the voice down, but the polygraph will show an uncontrollable reaction in the pulse rate, respiration rate, or dampness of skin. A person telling a verbal lie, even of the most mild type, such as "I feel fine," may still express the truth in the tone of voice, posture, or facial expression which say "I feel terrible." This unconscious verbal message is called "leakage" and can occur even if the speaker is successful in controlling some of the nonverbal cues.

Leakage is the unintentional sending of a valid (truthful) message. It is the failure to suppress the truth completely. Just as the verbal communication is under more direct conscious control than is the nonverbal, so are some forms of nonverbal behavior more controllable than others. Typically, people learn to control tone of voice and facial expression better than they can control movements and positions of the hand and feet. For example, a video camera operator produced a special show by merely comparing two views each of several television talk shows and quiz shows where the participants were all seated at a table facing the audience. When the usual above-the-table angle was compared with the simultaneous under-the-table shot, a dramatic contrast became evident. Above the table people had confident smiles while below the table some had slipped off their shoes, some were scratching their leg with their big toe, some hands and feet were writhing, handkerchiefs were being twisted into knots, and the general impression was one of stress and tension.

Studies of counseling and therapeutic interviews show that much of the client's nonverbal behavior may be obvious to the interviewer but hidden from the client who is much more aware of the verbal behavior.[7]

---

[7]W. R. Passons, *Gestalt Approaches to Counseling* (New York: Holt, Rinehart & Winston, 1975).

Much depends upon the interviewer's skill in detecting both verbal slips and nonverbal leakage and interpreting them accurately.[8] Success in any form of interpersonal relations is enhanced when we apply the principle that nonverbal cues are not isolated from either other nonverbal cues or from the verbal message. Skill in observing and noting the congruence or lack of congruence is the critical factor in applying this principle.

Meaning of a nonverbal cue depends on the context. Context is being used in a broader sense than the relationship between a particular cue and the other verbal and nonverbal signals which accompany it. Instead, *context* is used to refer to social settings and cultural differences that can determine the meaning of a particular cue. For example, weeping can indicate happiness, sadness, disappointment, frustration, and even a mixture of happiness and sadness. Weeping at a wedding does not indicate the same emotion as weeping at a funeral. Just as the meaning of weeping varies with different situations in the same culture, we also find that the same situation may allow a different display of emotion in different cultures. For example, in some African cultures there is a free and audible display of sadness and mourning at funerals, but in other cultures funerals call for a "stiff upper lip" or even smiles.

Cultures also vary in what is considered the proper volume level in face-to-face conversations. For example, some Americans have louder voice levels than do people in other cultures,[9] and what is considered an appropriate nose-to-nose distance in the Latin American or Arabic culture is usually considered too close for comfort by Americans.[10] Similarly, what is considered the optimal amount of eye contact varies from culture to culture, and from one social class to another, as well as from one situation to another in the same culture. Contrary to popular opinion, lack of eye contact does not always indicate deception or lack of truthfulness.[11] In some cultures one shows respect to others by *not* looking them in the eye.

---

[8]P. Ekman and W. V. Friesen, *Unmasking the Face* (Englewood Cliffs, N.J.: Prentice-Hall, 1975).

[9]D. W. Sue and D. Sue, "Barriers to Effective Cross-Cultural Counseling," *Journal of Counseling Psychology,* 24 (1977), pp. 420–29.

[10]Edward T. Hall, *The Silent Language* (New York: Doubleday, 1973). See Chapter entitled "Space Speaks."

[11]S. C. Sitton and S. T. Griffin, "Detection of Deception from Clients' Eye Contact Patterns," *Journal of Counseling Psychology,* 21 (1981), pp. 269–71.

Verbal-nonverbal relationships vary meaningfully. There are three basically different relationships that can exist between the verbal message and the nonverbal message. First, the two messages may be *congruent* or consistent. This congruence may take different forms: The nonverbal cues may simply *repeat* the verbal message, may *substitute* for part of the verbal message, may *complement* (modify or elaborate) the verbal message, or may *accent* or emphasize certain points in the verbal message.[12]

Second, the two messages may be *incongruent* in that the nonverbal cues express one feeling while the verbal messages denote another feeling. We are all familiar with this incongruence in situations where one person asks "How are you?" and the other person responds in a bored, depressed, or tired voice, "I'm fine." This phenomenon has already been noted in connection with the concept of leakage discussed earlier and will be elaborated later as it applies to interviewing.

Third, the nonverbal cues are used to *regulate* the flow of the conversation as opposed to affecting the meaning of the content of the conversation. The nonverbal cues are used in several ways as regulators. A gesture may say, "Speak up, I can't hear you," or "Slow down, you're talking too fast." Similarly, the speaker may increase the volume level to indicate to the conversation partner "Don't interrupt yet." As we will show later the regulation of turn-talking is one of the most important functions of nonverbal cues in the interview situation.

To summarize the principles of nonverbal communication, we have pointed out that (*a*) much nonverbal communication is unconscious either on the part of the sender or the receiver of the message or both, (*b*) nonverbal behavior tends to be uncritically believed, (*c*) nonverbal cues are not isolated either from the verbal message or from the other nonverbal cues, (*d*) the meaning of nonverbal cues depends upon both situational and cultural contexts, and (*e*) there are three basically different functional relationships between the verbal and the nonverbal content of a conversation.

TYPES OF NONVERBAL COMMUNICATION

Most nonverbal cues fall under the headings of *proxemics, chronemics, paralinguistics, kinesics, haptics,* or *aromatics.* Proxemic communication is the use of interpersonal space to convey meaning. Chronemic communication uses time in interpersonal relationships to convey meaning. Paralinguistic communication is the use of voice qualities

---

[12]Mark L. Knapp, *Nonverbal Communication in Human Interaction*, 2nd ed. (New York: Holt, Rinehart & Winston, 1978).

such as volume, pitch, and timbre to convey meaning. In kinesic communication the use of body movements including facial expression, eye movements, hand gestures, and body posture conveys meaning. Haptics is the use of the sense of touch as a channel of communication. Aromatic communication occurs through the sense of smell. Let us now examine each type of nonverbal communication in turn.

Proxemics

It is clear that the relationship between interviewer and respondent is both a cause and an effect of proxemic behavior. For example, when an interviewer knocks on a door and someone opens the door, the interviewer may take a short step backward to avoid appearing aggressive and pushy, which might arouse resistance in the respondent. Or the interviewer and respondent, if both are standing, may stand slightly closer together if both are females than if one is male and one is female. When the interviewer and respondent are of the same age, they might stand closer than if there is a large age difference.

It has been shown that if the distance between interviewer and respondent is greater, there is more of a tendency for them to watch each other's eyes for cues to meaning. Goldberg carefully recorded the eye behavior of the respondents when they sat 2½ feet versus 6 feet from the interviewer.[13] At the greater distance the respondents spent much more time looking at the interviewer's eyes.

As shown by Hall, the correct conversational distance varies from one culture to another.[14] In the Middle East you are bathed in your conversation partner's breath; in Latin America equals of the same sex carry on conversation at a much closer distance than do North Americans. When we invade the respondent's boundary line between private space and intimate space, the respondent will feel threatened. If we stay too far away in an interview the respondent will feel that we do not like him, that we do not want to associate with him.

In arranging the interview situation, it is important to position the respondent's chair, the interviewer's chair, and the microphone (if used) so that there can be some variation in distance (from two to four feet) to accommodate to different respondents, different sex combinations, and age variations from one interview to the next.

Relatively little experimentation has been done with proxemic communication in the context of the interview, but experienced interviewers

---

[13]G. Goldberg et al., "Visual Behavior and Face-to-Face Distance During Interaction," *Sociometry* 32 (1969), pp. 43–53.

[14]Edward T. Hall, *The Silent Language* (New York: Doubleday 1973, reprinted 1980).

agree that sensitivity to the proxemic factor is important. Often, as the subject matter of the interview changes, the interviewer can note changes in the proxemic behavior of the respondent. The respondent who is free to back away might do so when the topic is one which is unpleasant or threatens to invade his or her privacy.

Chronemics

The use of time in interpersonal relationships can convey feelings, attitudes, and desires. For example, if the interviewer or respondent is late in keeping an appointment, this may convey a lack of vital interest in the interview. The order in which members of a given organization are interviewed may carry considerable meaning. However, both of these factors would be classified as a strategy rather than a technique. The most important chronemic *techniques* which the interviewer can control are the length of pauses and rate of speech in his or her own conversation and the length of time allowed to lapse after the respondent has finished a sentence and before the interviewer asks another question. The first technique is called *pacing* and the second is the *silent probe*.

Pacing is one of the principal nonverbal methods of communicating the appropriate mood. The tense interviewer often communicates anxiety by using a rapid-fire rate of speech which in turn increases anxiety in the respondent. To establish the more thoughtful, deliberative mood needed to stimulate free association and recall or to avoid chronological confusion, the interviewer must take the initiative in establishing a more relaxed, deliberate pace, at the technique level, in a setting free from competing time-demands, chosen at the strategy level. It is up to the interviewer to break the vicious circle of mutual reinforcement of anxiety. There is a tendency for one person to unwittingly respond to the other's anxiety with additional signals of anxiety.

The silent probe is such an important technique that it will be discussed in a special section later in this chapter.

Kinesics

Much more research has been done on kinesic communication in the interview than on either proxemic or chronemic communication. Body posture, feet movements, hand movements, facial expressions, and eye movements have all been studied in the kinesics of interviewing. Carmichael experimented with hand movements by having an actor seated behind a curtain so that only his hands were visible.[15] When the viewers

---

[15]L. S. Carmichael et al., "A Study of the Judgment of Manual Expression as Presented in Still and Motion Pictures," *Journal of Social Psychology* **8** (1937), pp. 115-42.

were asked to classify the emotions the actor was trying to portray there was substantial agreement between the emotion intended by the actor and that perceived by the viewers.

Even though posture, hands, and feet all communicate, numerous experiments have shown that the communicators tend to focus more attention on the face and are more accurate in their judgments of the others' feelings if they can see the face. For example, Exline demonstrated that a group of viewers responding to head cues only were more accurate in matching photographs to verbal behavior than were respondents to body cues only.[16]

When the viewer is observing the others' head and facial movements, there is evidence that the central focus is usually on the eyes. One of the earliest sociological essays on the human eye as a communication channel was given by Simmel:

> By the glance which reveals the other, one discloses himself. By the same act in which the observer seeks to know the observed, he surrenders himself to be understood . . . the eye cannot take unless at the same time it gives.[17]

This early intuitive observation on human communication has been followed by many experiments on eye-to-eye communication. One of the general findings in many different contexts is that eye behavior communicates the desire to make or to avoid communicative contact. When people feel shame, they will drop their eyes to avoid the glance of the other not only to avoid seeing the disapproval in the other's eye but to conceal from the other the extent of their own shame and confusion. One specific manifestation of this general principle is the fact that the listener or questioner tends to watch the other's eyes more closely than the respondent or speaker tends to watch the listener. This was demonstrated in an experiment by Exline which showed that individuals in a laboratory situation looked more at the investigator when listening than when speaking to him or her.[18] This experiment also showed that people looked less often at the person with whom they were speaking when personal, rather than more general, matters were being discussed. This seems to suggest that we actively seek nonverbal cues from the other

[16]Ralph Exline, "Body Position, Facial Expression, and Verbal Behavior During Interviews," *Journal of Abnormal and Social Psychology* 68 (1964), pp. 295–301.

[17]Georg Simmel, "Sociology of the Senses: Visual Interaction," in Robert E. Park and Ernest W. Burgess, *Introduction to the Science of Sociology* (Chicago, Ill.: University of Chicago Press, 1924), p. 358.

[18]R. Exline et al., "Visual Behavior in a Dyad as Affected by Interview Content and Sex of Respondent," *Journal of Personality and Social Psychology* 1 (1965), pp. 201–9.

people to understand what they mean more than we actively observe to determine whether they understand what we mean.

The fact that the use of chronemic and proxemic communication can be effectively used as a conscious technique by the interviewer has been repeatedly demonstrated experimentally. For example, Matarazzo and Wiens have shown that the respondent can be motivated to give longer, fuller, and more detailed responses resulting in more relevant information when the interviewer makes no change in the verbal forms of the questions but nods in approval, makes interested noises like "hmm," "ah," "ah hah," "oh," "wow," and slows down the pace and uses more silent probes.[19] In essence these nonverbal activities reinforce such facilitators of communication as recognition, sympathetic understanding, the need for meaning, and catharsis by establishing and reinforcing a communicative mood.

Paralinguistics

We use the term *paralinguistic* to refer to those aspects of speech that are not verbal or linguistic, yet are much more intimately intertwined with the verbal than are the other nonverbal modes of communication. The paralinguistic factors in speech include volume of voice (loud or soft), quality of voice (tense, growly, breathy), accent (nuances of pronunciation), and inflectional patterns (intonation or pitch patterns).

One of the basic differences between written and oral communication is that the oral speech gives full range to a nonverbal accompaniment. Written communication tries to indicate some of the paralinguistic variables by italicizing words to be stressed, which takes the place of an increase in volume or pitch. Foreign language texts sometimes indicate the intonation pattern of a phrase or sentence in those cases where it is very different from English. A script for a drama might contain parenthetical instructions on how to say a line, but this is usually in terms of the emotion to be communicated rather than specific instructions on tone quality, pitch, or volume. Only the skilled actor can convert the intent of the playwright into the optimum nonverbal rendition. In many cases the nonverbal accompaniment to the dramatic lines is highly stylized and not necessarily like the real thing. The same sentence can be delivered with several different stress and intonation patterns in a way to change the meaning considerably.[20] Using the correct stress pattern can

---

[19]Joseph Matarazzo and L. Wiens, "Interviewer Influence on Duration of Interviewee Silence," *Journal of Experimental Research in Personality* 2 (1967), pp. 56–69.

[20]For example, see Leo Rosten, *The Joys of Yiddish* (New York: Pocket Books, 1970). Rosten shows several different intonation patterns used with the same simple sentence and their implications for the meaning of a dialogue.

help the interviewer give the intended meaning to a question and give clues to the meaning of the responses. Also, the interviewer can learn to listen for subtle paralinguistic communication which gives clues to the meaning or to the respondent's motivations at the moment. The verbal "yes" can carry the meaning of "maybe" or even "no," depending on the tone of voice and other nonverbal cues. The interviewer must learn to listen for changes in the nonverbal accompaniment and for whether the verbal and nonverbal are harmoniously reinforcing or tend to give conflicting signals, as happens when the respondent is trying to deceive the interviewer.

The fact that the paralinguistic factor alone without any words does carry meaning of its own has been clearly demonstrated in experiments. For example, Davitz had people recite parts of the alphabet to convey feelings of anger, fear, happiness, jealousy, love, nervousness, pride, sadness, satisfaction, and sympathy.[21] Tape recordings of these recitations were heard and the listeners were asked to identify which emotion the speaker was demonstrating. For all ten emotions there was a substantial correspondence between the emotion intended and the one identified by the listener. Some emotions, like anger and nervousness, were more reliably identified than others, like pride and jealousy.

The interviewer's bias can be communicated paralinguistically, resulting in biased information from the respondent. This was shown in an experiment by Duncan et al. in which the interviewer changed voice quality in a way to vary the amount of apprehension felt by the respondent.[22] The amount of bias in the responses was positively correlated with the amount of apprehension produced in the respondent.

Haptics

Haptics is the study of touch or tactile communication. There are laws which specify illegal ways of touching others, and there are unwritten social codes regulating who can touch whom, where, and how, but there has been little scientific study of how the code works. There have been experiments showing that people have a better feeling toward someone who touched them during a conversation than toward a person who did not touch under identical circumstances.[23] Of course, the

[21]J. R. Davitz and L. Davitz, "The Communication of Feeling by Content-Free Speech," *Journal of Communication* 9 (1959), pp. 110–17.

[22]Starkey Duncan, Jr., et al., "The Paralanguage of Experimentor Bias," *Sociometry* 32 (1969), pp. 207–19.

[23]H. Borenzweig, "Touching in Clinical Social Work," *Social Casework* 64 (April 1983) pp. 238–42.

unbridled use of touch without regard to who is touching whom, what part of the body is being touched, how often the touching occurs, and other situational factors can lead to negative reactions from the person being touched or even to a lawsuit. There are cultural differences in the type and amount of touching that occurs between members of the opposite sex and between members of the same sex.[24] Some cultures engage in more touching than others as shown by Jourard who observed heterosexual couples in cafes.[25] He found the following average number of touches per hour in different cultures: San Juan, Puerto Rico, 180; Paris, France, 110; Gainesville, Florida, 2; and London, England, none.

Social workers, counselors, and others in the helping professions in the United States seem to agree that there are times when a woman touching another woman's arm, for example, in the interview setting has a positive effect when the client is in need of sympathetic understanding and after some degree of rapport has been developed. However, much more needs to be known about the conditions upon which the positive reaction depends.

Aromatics

Aromatics is the study of communication via the olfactory sense (smell). There is not a large body of studies on this subject as it applies to humans; nevertheless it is known that perspiration and other odors relate to emotional states. The polygraph (lie detector) is based on this principle and measures, among other reactions, the changes in the rate of productivity by the sweat glands.

In the American culture natural body odors are socially taboo, so it is possible to have a multimillion dollar market for deodorants, gum, perfumes, and after-shave lotions all appealing to people's desire to attract, or at least not repel, others. The writer has heard kindergarten and elementary school teachers report that they noticed children have a friendlier reaction to them after they started using perfume. It is highly probable that the odors present in the interview setting would have some effect on the respondent's mood and definition of the situation. However, the author is not aware at this time of any studies of this question. Probably the wise interviewer would be sure to avoid body odors and bad breath since the respondent needs to be within three to five feet of the interviewer for good communication.

---

[24]Dean C. Barnlund, "The Public Self and the Private Self in Japan and the United States," chap. 2 in *Intercultural Encounters with Japan*, ed. John C. Condon and Mitsuko Saito (Tokyo: The Simul Press, 1974).

[25]Sidney M. Jourard, "An Exploratory Study of Body-Accessibility," *British Journal of Social and Clinical Psychology* 5 (1966), pp. 221–31.

Dress and Grooming

In a highly complex society we tend to use *stereotyping* to put people in some manageable number of categories in order to deal psychologically with numerous fleeting contacts with a wide variety of people. The judgments we make of others and their judgments of us depend to some extent on how we cover our bodies and the objects with which we surround ourselves.

The tendency to stereotype people on the basis of external characteristics is admirably demonstrated by Waters.[26] A group of employers who were asked to rate a prospective employee on the basis of a written resume and photo gave one woman a zero rating when her photo showed her with an unattractive hairdo and no makeup. The same employers said they would hire the same woman with the same resume when the photo showed her with a new hairdo and makeup. She was not recognizable as the same person.

Clothing, accessories, and hairstyles tend to be used to classify people according to culture and geographic region, gender, lifestyle, personality, occupation, and social status. Thus we tend to judge people as Middle Eastern if they have a certain type of turban or classify a fellow American as being conservative, flamboyant, meticulous, or experimenting in their lifestyle depending on their dress. The urbanite judges someone as a "hayseed," "rube," or "redneck" on the basis of dress. The used-car salesman on television wears a white five-gallon hat rather than a black one or a top hat to show that he is a "good guy." Similarly, college students develop a certain style of dress which distinguishes them from the townees in the town-gown encounter.

There are several books, for example Malloy's, which stress the importance of dress in creating a proper image for success in the business world.[27] They generally recommend that men dress conservatively and that women in the business world shun the "sexy" look on the one hand while avoiding imitating male styles of dress on the other if they seek the image of the successful executive.

A good interviewer must be aware of the symbolic meaning of various forms of dress in the setting in which the interview is to be done. The dress would vary depending on the type of respondent, the purpose of the interview, and the time and place of the interview. For this reason we cannot provide a set of general rules for personal appearance. However, a warning is in order. It is as important to have consonance

---

[26]Judith Waters, "The Cinderella Syndrome: A Study of the Relationship between Physical Appearance, Level of Skill, and Salary," *Fairleigh Dickinson University Magazine*, February 1980, pp. 11–15.

[27]J. T. Malloy, *Dress for Success* (New York: P. H. Wyden, 1975).

between the personal appearance and the purpose or behavior of the interviewer as it is to have consonance between one's verbal and nonverbal behavior in general. A middle-class college graduate, for example, cannot build rapport with a coal miner simply by dressing in dirty coveralls. This would probably impress the respondent as silly. A similar lack of consonance was clearly demonstrated to the author when he was studying cross-cultural communication problems between Americans and Colombians in Bogotá. The Colombians were confused, puzzled, or entertained by American Peace Corps volunteers wearing the *ruana* and sandals of the rural *campesino* when they were obviously educated and rich in the eyes of the Colombians.

Seven types of nonverbal communication that affect the outcome of any human interaction including the interview have just been discussed: proxemics, chronemics, kinesics, paralinguistics, haptics, aromatics, and personal appearance. Although they were discussed one at a time, in reality they occur simultaneously in patterns. These patterns may show consistency or inconsistency among the different nonverbal elements, and the nonverbal pattern may be consistent or inconsistent with the verbal message depending upon whether the speaker is sincere, truthful, ambivalent, confused, or deceitful.

To make the research findings on the different types of nonverbal communication useful to the interviewer, it will be helpful to look first at some of the ways the interviewer can use all types of nonverbal cues as part of the kit of techniques. In approaching the issue from this functional point of view, the question of how each of the seven channels of nonverbal communication enter into this process will be ignored since most of the channels contribute simultaneously to these basic functions most of the time. In using most nonverbal techniques the interviewer does not think about what channel should be used or whether, for example, the eyebrows should be lifted. Instead, the interviewer may decide to "show surprise" and not be concerned with how the various physical parts of the body contribute to this expression. The interviewer can put the nonverbal communication to use by concentrating on the *function* (effect to be achieved) of the nonverbal cues. The next section of this chapter describes the functions in any interview situation that are achieved mainly via the nonverbal channels.

FUNCTIONS OF NONVERBAL CUES IN THE INTERVIEW

Some of the most important general functions of nonverbal cues in the interview are self-presentation, expressing the meaning of the question, motivating the respondent by maximizing the facilitators (by showing appreciation, giving sympathetic understanding, giving recognition, and expecting cooperation), establishing a general mood and pace, and managing the turn-taking. Let us elaborate each of these general functions.

Self-Presentation

The critical aspect of the interviewer's self-presentation to the respondent depends upon the situation. For example, if the interviewer is doing a study of the effects of multinational corporations on the development of a world community and international peace, then it is important that the respondent who is a multinational corporation executive perceive the interviewer as competent and knowledgeable on the topic. On the other hand, if a welfare client is being interviewed by a social worker or counselor, it is more important that the interviewer be perceived as genuinely sympathetic and wanting to help. This self-presentation is affected by personal appearance, gestures and posture, tone of voice, rate of speech, amount and type of touching.

The effect of touching behavior in the counseling interview has been demonstrated in a study by Alagna showing that when the touch consisting of handshakes and touching the respondent's arm and back was in the context of caring, as opposed to an intimate gesture, it had a significant positive effect on the client's evaluation of the counseling.[28] Another study showed that similar tactile behavior caused the clients to perceive the counselor as having more expertise.[29]

Examples have already been given of how one's personal appearance and odor affect the self-presentation. Later, how each type of nonverbal behavior affects the image one projects to the respondent will be shown; but at this point the discussion will point out that those nonverbal cues involved in the self-presentation process have a high priority of importance because once the respondent has formed an impression of the interviewer as sympathetic or unsympathetic, competent or incompetent, this initial impression tends to override and provide a context for all the other messages (verbal or nonverbal) in the conversation. For example, if the respondent is convinced that the interviewer is competent and sympathetic, then small detailed behaviors such as drumming the fingers on the arm of the chair will not constitute a threat to the respondent; but if the interviewer had been perceived as unsympathetic or hostile the same finger drumming might be feared as an indication of impatience or even a prelude to a verbal explosion.

---

[28]F. J. Alagna et al., "Evaluative Reaction to Interpersonal Touch in a Counseling Interview," *Journal of Counseling Psychology* 26 (1979), pp. 265–72.

[29]M. A. Hubble, F. C. Nobel, and S. E. Robinson, "The Effect of Counselor Touch in an Initial Counseling Session," *Journal of Counseling Psychology* 28 (1981), pp. 233–35.

Expressing the Meaning of the Question

One of the advantages an interview has over a mailed questionnaire is that the interviewer can strengthen the meaning of a question with reinforcing nonverbal cues. By the use of paralinguistic cues such as tone of voice or stressing certain words, the meaning of a question can be altered. Also certain kinesic cues such as hand gestures can clarify the meaning of the question. By slowing down the pace of delivery the interviewer can make it easier for the respondent to grasp the full meaning of the question and at the same time avoid conveying the impression of impatience. The vocal inflections become increasingly important as the questions become longer and more complex. In learning to use the nonverbal accompaniment of the question to fullest advantage, it is helpful for the interviewer to listen to a tape recording of his or her own voice asking the questions to be used in an interview. It is an art to optimize the nonverbal meaning and at the same time avoid sounding stiff, stilted, unnatural, impersonal, or insensitive. This would reduce the respondent's motivation to answer the question even though it was clearly understood.

Motivating the Respondent to Answer

Within the framework of this book "motivating the respondent to answer" means to minimize the inhibitors of communication and to maximize the facilitators. To minimize the inhibitors the interviewer's tone of voice, posture, and facial expression must not be ego threatening and must not contribute to the etiquette barrier. Instead, all these cues should show sympathetic understanding, express interest, give recognition, and indicate that an answer is expected and appreciated.

Too often an interviewer's nonverbal cues show that he or she is tired, bored, disgusted, amused, or too detached, while the words pretend interest and sympathy. This discrepancy is usually sensed and dampens the respondent's motivation to answer fully.

Establishing Pace and Mood

It definitely helps the respondent to overcome such inhibitors as forgetting and chronological confusion if the interviewer establishes a leisurely pace and a thoughtful, reminiscent mood. This is done mainly by the interviewer's nonverbal behaviors such as allowing silence, maintaining eye contact, supplying supporting facial expressions, and by assuming postures in harmony with the respondent's. The author has found that if the interviewer delivers a question in a natural and thoughtful manner, rather than in an efficient and automatic way, the respondent is more likely to answer in a more thoughtful way, taking time to search his or

her memory. This thoughtful mood cannot always be established immediately but can usually be achieved if the interviewer moves in this direction from the beginning. The mood is caught by the respondent from
the interviewer.

Managing Turn-Taking

Perhaps the regulation of turn-taking through nonverbal behavior may
be considered as a special case of establishing the pace of an interview.
Research by Duncan explored several types of *turn signals* that serve to
regulate turn-taking between two people in conversation.[30]

Turn yielding occurs when the speaker wants to exchange roles with
the listener. To induce the listener to become the speaker, the speaker
can use several kinds of nonverbal cues in addition to the obvious verbal act of asking another question. For example, the speaker may simply use such paralinguistic cues as slowing down the rate of speech,
drawing out the last syllable, or using silence. In addition the speaker
may use such body language as gazing at the other person, raising the
eyebrows, or touching the person.

Turn maintaining occurs when the speaker wants to keep talking
even though the listener wants to speak. The turn maintaining signals
include such nonverbal behavior as speaking louder while continuing,
or generally increasing the use of gestures or other body movements
that emphasize what is being said or show a desire to finish without interruption.

Turn requesting occurs when the listener wants to talk. This is signi-
fied by such cues as an audible inhaling, an upraised index finger,
straightening or tightening one's posture, or rapid head nods.

The interviewer must be sensitive to his or her own turn-yielding
and turn-requesting signals to achieve the balance appropriate to the
objectives of the interview. Some interviewers as well as some respondents tend to want to monopolize the conversation beyond the point of
productivity.

Turn denying occurs if the listener gets a turn-yielding cue from the
speaker but does not want to talk. This is accomplished by such cues as
simple silence, a relaxed body posture, and eye-gaze. If the respondent
refuses to take a turn at speaking, the interviewer has to decide whether
to continue talking or to send out more turn-yielding cues. In some
cases it may be a signal from the respondent that the pace is too fast and
he or she is not ready to talk but would like to think a bit more. Of

---

[30]S. P. Duncan, Jr., "Some Signals and Roles for Taking Speaking Turns in
Conversations," *Journal of Personality and Social Psychology* 23 (1972), pp.
283–292. See also S. P. Duncan, Jr., "On the Structure of Speaker-Auditor Interaction During Speaking Turns," *Language in Society* 2 (1974), pp. 161–180.

course it also can mean that the respondent no longer wants to talk on the particular topic or would prefer that the interview were over. In some situations the interviewer can fruitfully turn the conversation to a discussion of the respondent's reluctance to talk. This needs to be done in a very nonjudgmental manner to avoid making the situation worse.

SPECIFIC NONVERBAL TECHNIQUES

The discussion to this point has shown the vital importance of the non-verbal aspect of communication, given some of the basic principles of how it works, described eight types of channels of nonverbal communication, and presented five general ways in which nonverbal techniques are applied by an interviewer. With this background established, focus will be placed on a core of specific nonverbal techniques that apply to a wide variety of interview settings. All of these core techniques usually apply to most *office* settings of the helping professions such as social work, counseling, or psychotherapy. Most of the core techniques are also applicable in modified form, to social science *field* settings more common to anthropologists, sociologists, or commercial pollsters.

This core of nonverbal techniques is small in number but very important and useful and can be quickly incorporated into an interviewer's set of professional tools to supplement the verbal techniques.

The Physical Setting

When the interviewer has control over the physical setting, it is possible to arrange the space in a way to maximize the flow of communication by making the client feel at home, providing privacy, reducing distractions to a minimum, and emanating interest in and sympathy for the respondent.

Furniture arrangements. To communicate interest and attentiveness the chairs for the interviewer and respondent should be facing each other from three to five feet apart. There should be no desk, tables, potted plants or other barriers between these chairs. It is also important that the two chairs be the same or very similar. One should not be the "throne of power" looking down on the "dunce stool." These two chairs should be oriented in the room so that neither the interviewer nor the respondent has the glare of the sun or artificial light in the eyes. Each should be able to see the other's face clearly and close enough to reach out and touch if appropriate. Noise should be reduced to a minimum by avoiding rooms with loud air conditioners, nearby radios, or live conversations. Also, visual distractions via the window or door should be minimized taking care not to give a "trapped" feeling to the room. Needless to say, the room temperature should be comfortable, and the air free of odors. Sometimes the temperature of the room cannot be ideal for both the interviewer and respondent as in the case of a young person interviewing elderly clients or a nurse interviewing cardiac patients who prefer a warmer room. In this case the interviewer can turn up the thermostat and wear lighter weight clothes indoors.

Props in the room. Decorations, charts, graphs, mottos, and so forth, on the walls should be in harmony with the needs of the client, the purpose of the interview, and the type of self-presentation desired by the interviewer. Props which help in attending to the client's immediate physical needs are also helpful. This might include an ashtray, matches, a hot-water pot for making instant coffee, herb tea, or even soup, tissues for the weeping client, and a restroom nearby. All of the visual cues and the other props should be selected for their most likely effect upon the client's feeling of trust, comfort, and sympathetic understanding. In the case of the helping professions this setting often serves as a psychological sanctuary for the client.

Sit Close

It is safe to say that the interviewer should sit close enough to give the respondent the feeling the interviewer is interested. Also, the interviewer should be close enough to clearly see subtle facial expressions and not have to speak louder than in a confidential tone. The interviewer should be close enough to reach out and touch the client when it is appropriate to show sympathetic understanding and give emotional support in the helping interview. The exact distance in feet for this closeness would vary with national cultures, social class, and the occasion. However, research has been done on the appropriate distance between counselor and client for adult middle-class Americans.[31] This research indicates that the most appropriate distance is three to four feet. Other research indicates that for Americans closer distances tend to inhibit the free flow of verbal information. There is also some evidence that the optimum distance is closer between females than males and that the very young and the very elderly require a closer distance to facilitate the flow of conversation.

In general it behooves the interviewer to know the respondent's background and to be sensitive for clues of discomfort in the respondent that might result from being too close or too remote.

---

[31]C. Lecomte et al., "Counseling Interactions as a Function of Spatial-Environmental Conditions," *Journal of Counseling Psychology* 28 (1981), pp. 536–39.

Face the Respondent Directly

The interviewer shows maximum interest by facing the respondent directly, less at a 45 or 90 degree angle. To turn one's back is to signal the termination of the conversation. Some of the author's students conducted experiments with video-taped interviews on the street in which the interviewer intentionally violated the respondent's private space by stepping up to about eighteen inches. There were two types of reactions to this invasion of their private space. Some respondents simply stepped back and others held their ground but turned at right angles to the interviewer as a defense. Other ways of creating a defense barrier are to look away, cross one's arms, or if seated, cross one's legs away from the other person.[32]

If the interviewer sits close, faces the respondent squarely, and notices the respondent engaging in creating defense barriers, then it is time to move back slightly while still facing the respondent directly.

Lean Forward

To lean forward is to show interest, involvement, and the expectation of interaction. To lean back signals the desire to escape, to disengage, or to reduce the intimacy or pace of the situation.[33] If the interviewer notices the respondent leaning back, it may mean that the interviewer is too close or that the respondent wants to reduce the intensity or pace of the conversation. In response the interviewer might adjust by moving back slightly or by sitting up straight rather than leaning forward. Some practitioners suggest that the interviewer lean forward far enough to rest the forearms on the thighs.[34]

The general idea is that leaning back, like looking away, crossing one's arms, or turning away, tends to decrease the intimacy or intensity of the communication and makes it more difficult to show interest and sympathetic understanding.

Make Regular Eye Contact

One reason for the interviewer being close and facing the respondent squarely is to facilitate regular eye contact. All facial expressions (re-

---

[32]M. L. Knapp, *Nonverbal Communication in Human Interaction*, 2nd ed. (New York: Holt, Rinehart & Winston, 1978).

[33]J. R. Graves and J. D. Robinson, "Proxemic Behavior as a Function of Inconsistent Verbal and Nonverbal Messages," *Journal of Counseling Psychology* 23 (1976), pp. 333–38.

[34]Robert R. Carkhuff and Richard M. Pierce et al., *The Art of Helping* (Amherst, Mass.: Human Resource Development Press, 1977), chap. 2.

gardless of whether the mouth, nose, cheeks, forehead, or eyes are involved) are very important in nonverbal communication; however, the eyes are where we most frequently look for clues to the other person's feeling and attitudes. The lack of eye contact suggests a lack of interest or sympathetic understanding. Too much eye contact, on the other hand, may suggest too much intimacy for the purpose and occasion of the interview.

It has been suggested by practitioners in counseling that more mutual gazing or eye contact occurs when the distance between counselor and client is greater, when comfortable topics are discussed, when interpersonal involvement between counselor and client is greater, when listening rather than talking, and when the parties involved are female.[35]

If a single eye contact lasts more than two or three seconds, particularly between members of the opposite sex, it might suggest that the initiator is seeking intimacy depending upon the accompanying general facial expression and/or tone of voice. If the facial expression is not friendly but the eye contact is prolonged, it may suggest the attempt to overpower and "stare down" the other person. The aim of the interviewer is to use enough eye contact to indicate sustained interest and sympathetic understanding without suggesting a too intimate or repressive relationship.

Adjust Vocal Quality

The interviewer's vocal quality (loudness, pitch, pacing, intonation pattern, and timbre) must be adjusted in two ways. First, it must be adjusted to the mood and pacing of the respondent. For example, if the respondent is sad and subdued and speaks softly and slowly, the interviewer should not respond in a happy, bubbly tone and pace. This would indicate a lack of empathy for the respondent. Also, the interviewer should avoid a loud voice which suggests a formal public speaking relationship or an attempt to show power over the respondent. In any case the tone of voice should be spontaneously conversational and should avoid any suggestion of a formal, routine, bureaucratized reading of a script.

The second way in which the vocal quality should be adjusted may sound in some ways contradictory to the aim of adjusting to the respondent's mood: Sometimes the vocal quality should be used to change or direct the respondent's behavior. It may be used to regulate turn-taking as discussed earlier in this chapter, and it may also be used to change the respondent's mood. For example, if the respondent is agitated, excited,

---

[35]William H. Cormier and L. Sherilyn Cormier, *Interviewing Strategies for Helpers*, 2nd ed. (Monterey, Calif.: Brooks/Cole Publishing, 1985), p. 73.

and speaking rapidly in an interview where a thoughtful reminiscent mood is needed to recall relevant material, the interviewer should *not* adjust his or her pace to the respondent but should slow down and try to have a soothing effect on the respondent. In other situations the respondent needs to be roused from a lethargic mood and stimulated to think, to verbalize, and to act. In these cases the interviewer should not adjust to the respondent's mood.

Preserve as Much Synchrony as Possible

Cormier defines *synchrony* as harmony between the interviewer's and the respondent's nonverbal behavior.[36] We have just discussed one aspect of synchrony under the heading of adjusting vocal quality. To maintain synchrony the interviewer must also be aware of the respondent's facial expression, body posture, hand gestures, and other nonverbal clues to the respondent's emotional state. As Cormier warns, the interviewer should not mimic the respondent's every move and facial expression but should be aware of them and respond appropriately to them. For example, if the respondent has a sad expression, the interviewer should not proceed in a tone of voice and cheerful countenance more appropriate to a party. Or if the respondent smilingly reports some minor victory in the daily battle of life, the interviewer should show happiness for the respondent.

In general synchrony demonstrates rapport, empathy, interest, or sympathetic understanding while dissynchrony generally communicates the opposite and acts as a powerful inhibitor of communication in the interview.

All of these specific nonverbal techniques mentioned, such as arranging the furniture appropriately, using props, sitting close, facing the respondent directly, leaning forward, making regular appropriate eye contact, adjusting the voice quality, and optimizing synchrony can be readily applied to interview situations common to the helping professions where the respondents usually come into the interviewer's office. Some cannot be applied in field interviewing situations more commonly encountered by anthropologists and sociologists. For example, in doing a house-to-house survey, or in interviewing executives in corporations, the interviewer cannot arrange the furniture, or supply props. Nevertheless, an awareness of the problem might help the interviewer select the best seating arrangement among alternatives when there is a choice. All of the other techniques beyond the physical arrangements may be applied in any interview setting.

The interviewer should be warned that the above section on specific nonverbal techniques was intended only to indicate some very specific,

---

[36]Ibid., p. 83.

easily described, and easily learned techniques that can be used to maximize the flow of candid information in the interview. *However, these can be used successfully only if they are consistent with appropriate basic attitudes of the interviewer.* Let us now look at how attitudes relate to nonverbal techniques.

NONVERBAL TECHNIQUES AND ATTITUDES

It would be wishful self-deception to believe that interviewers can detect conflict, ambivalence, and deceit by noting inconsistencies or leakage in the respondent's behavior, but that the interviewer's own nonverbal behavior can be neatly controlled to hide inconsistencies and avoid leakage of inappropriate attitudes toward the respondent. This is not true. In both the interviewer and the respondent much of the nonverbal behavior is unconscious and beyond the speaker's control. If the interviewer has strong negative attitudes toward the interview situation, toward the topic of discussion, toward the respondent as a person, or toward some particular information reported by the respondent, these attitudes cannot be easily hidden by some nifty technique that can be mechanically reproduced on demand. Instead, the conflict between how one feels and how one wants to be perceived will result in inconsistencies and leakage.

What is the solution to this problem? First, it is worthwhile to note that one's own attitudes are more open to conscious self-scrutiny than are the complex patterns of physical cues that go into the nonverbal communication of these attitudes. Therefore, the interviewer, instead of asking "Am I sending out the right signals?" should ask "Do I have the appropriate attitudes?" If the attitudes are inappropriate but the interviewer tries to cover them over with a veneer of the easily managed gross techniques such as facing squarely, leaning forward, and making eye contact, then the more subtle nonverbal cues such as facial expression or tone of voice will betray the real feelings. In short the interviewer can be conscious of strong negative attitudes but cannot completely control the manifestation of these attitudes.

Then what is achieved by knowing that a particular interviewer has inappropriate negative attitudes toward a particular interview situation? Instead of simply denying that these negative attitudes are a problem or pretending that they are easily hidden, there are three possible solutions. First, interviewers may be selected (or self-selected) who have attitudes and values appropriate to the particular interviewing task. For example, a woman who has been raped should not be selected to interview a rapist; a Palestinian should not be selected to interview an Israeli; a social worker who believes all poor people are lazy should not be interviewing the poor; or a fundamentalist preacher who believes that the role-playing game *Dungeons and Dragons* is a product of the devil should not interview a D&D player on what he or she likes about the game.

Second, interviewers can develop a strong set of professional attitudes toward the interviewing task in general and then concentrate on manifesting these attitudes rather than upon trying to hide any disagreement with the respondent. These professional interviewers' attitudes include such things as belief in the purpose of the interview, a desire not to bias the responses, a nonjudgmental attitude toward the information reported, critical analysis of the relevance, validity, and completeness of the response, respect for the respondent as a person, and appreciation of the respondent's effort.

Although many of the problems of negative attitudes may be solved at the strategy level by selecting the appropriate interviewer-respondent combination, there will always be at least mild disagreement of point of view between interviewer and respondent. Any possible negative effects of these conflicting attitudes are best neutralized not by concentrating one's attention on hiding the disagreements, but by concentrating on manifesting the set of basic professional attitudes listed above.

Next, the three major attitudinal foci of nonverbal techniques used by the interviewer will be discussed. These are the interviewers attitudes toward (*a*) the general task of interviewing, (*b*) specific items of information given by the respondent, and (*c*) the respondent as a person.

Attitudes toward the Interviewing Task

Attitudes toward the interviewing task tend to prevail throughout a series of interviews on the same topic; in some cases, an interviewer has certain attitudes toward the interviewing task in general, regardless of the particular topic at hand. In extreme cases, the attitudes may be a function of the interviewer's basic personality pattern.

Regardless of the pervasiveness of the source of the attitudes, we will first look at some of the negative attitudes commonly manifested toward the interviewing task. Negative attitudes often held by interviewers toward the task can be grouped into two types: those that indicate a general lack of *desire* to obtain the relevant information and those that indicate a basic anxiety over one's *ability* to obtain it.

The interviewer's lack of desire may be based upon initial lack, or subsequent loss, of interest in the topic of the interview. For example, an interviewer discovering housewives' motivations in buying soap might feel that the problem is inconsequential to the future of mankind and be bored with the procedure. Even in studies of people's behavior in disaster situations, the author noted a tendency for the interviewers' interest in the problem to decrease once they had done enough interviews to obtain a fairly clear picture of the chronology of events and the variety of reactions to the crisis.

Sometimes the lack of interest in the topic springs from the interviewer's naïve assumption that he or she knows what the respondent's answer is in advance. This dangerous attitude has been noted in cases where the interviewer is interviewing a friend or acquaintance. The interviewer's lack of interest may lie in the intrinsic nature of the topic or in the formulation of the problem. If the problem was formulated by someone else, the interviewer may have no vital interest in the topic or may not agree with or understand the formulation of the problem.

Regardless of the cause of the lack of interest in the interview, there are two results: The interviewer often fails to probe beneath the surface, and accepts incomplete information; also, the respondent often receives the impression that the interviewer is not serious or is incompetent or that the topic is not important. As a result the interviewer is not motivated to give complete, thoughtful, and accurate information and may even resent having to devote time to such unimportant pursuits. The interviewer's boredom can be conveyed to the respondent by tone of voice, posture, facial expression, and other gestures.

Attitudes reflecting the interviewer's basic anxiety over the ability to obtain the information are found in several common forms. He or she may feel apologetic for asking the types of questions required by the objectives of the interview. This apologetic attitude is seen in statements selected from two interviews: "You might not want to answer this question but. . . ." "You probably don't see much sense to this question but. . . ." "I am supposed to ask you if. . . ." "Would you mind if I asked you. . . ." "This next question is a dilly. . . ." "You probably don't remember this but. . . ."

This attitude of apology and embarrassment often negatively affects the flow of information. The respondent may feel a lack of the support and recognition desired. Or sensing the interviewer's embarrassment in asking the question, the respondent may think the answer will shock the interviewer. The etiquette barrier then arises. Another possible effect is for the respondent to perceive the interviewer's reluctance as an indication of guilt over some possible hidden purposes of the interview. Thus the respondent may feel some potential ego threat in the situation, which puts him or her on guard and inhibits the flow of information. Another frequent effect is that the respondent simply tends to fulfill the interviewer's expectations by finding the information very difficult to give. The interviewer's anxiety also manifests itself in a rapid-fire pace which invites superficiality and destroys any chance of building the thoughtful mood needed to recall memories.

The remedy for boredom is often gained with experience. For example, it is the neophyte interviewer who assumes to know in advance what the respondent is going to say. With experience the interviewer becomes sensitized to clues which should be probed further to bring out the individual respondent's unique point of view. Once this is accomplished, the interviewer can see for himself the difference between the initial, superficial responses and the more complex and fundamental underpinnings which emerge with further exploration.

It is also helpful if the interviewer has a vital stake in the study being done. He or she should understand any practical or theoretical significance of the study and have an appreciation of some of the more subtle methodological problems involved in obtaining complete and valid information. The interviewer should have the purpose and specifications of the study so clearly in mind that he or she is highly sensitive to what is relevant, potentially relevant, and irrelevant to the objectives.

To avoid an attitude of embarrassment or apology, the interviewer should ask himself the following question: "Would I be willing to answer all of these questions if I were approached by an interviewer under the same conditions?"

By "under the same conditions" we do not mean that the interviewer should necessarily be willing to answer the questions if the respondent were to reverse their roles during the interview. Instead, this means that the interviewer should be willing to answer the questions in a study planned to render useful knowledge, in which the sponsorship and purpose of the study were clearly given, and in which the anonymity of the respondent were guaranteed.

The interviewer who would not be willing will not be successful in hiding this attitude from respondents. Many field workers, including the author, feel that such an interviewer has no moral right to ask questions he or she is not willing to answer. Regardless of the moral issue, it has been demonstrated that interviewers' attitudes have an effect upon the degree of candidness of the respondent.

The interviewer must realize in advance that there is likely to be some inconvenience and psychic strain at times for both the interviewer and respondent but that this is necessary to advance applied or theoretical social science. The author has noted on several occasions that the neophyte interviewer's questions regarding the ethical rights to "ask those questions" typically arise when he or she is beginning to feel some of the tension involved in overcoming the inhibitors of communication. This tendency to feel that if it is difficult it might be unethical is understandable in terms of psychological mechanisms of guilt, punishment, and rationalization. Nevertheless, it should be avoided by the social scientist.

Now let us examine some of the manifestations and possible effects of the interviewer's *positive* attitudes toward the interview task. Instead of being bored, apologetic, or embarrassed, the successful interviewer shows an expectation of being successful. He or she is strongly interested in the topic and assumes responsibility personally for the questions asked rather than attempting to hide behind the sponsor. The interviewer is so "sold" on what is being done that there is a higher probability of appealing to the respondent's altruism. The interviewer's competence is a compliment to the respondent who realizes that he or she is not in the presence of a casual inquirer but an incisive prober with a purpose and a method. Most of these positive attitudes, just as the elimination of the negative ones, grow from the interviewer's instruction and experience.

Attitudes toward the Information Received

Here, the problem is the interviewer's attitudes toward specific statements made by the respondent rather than toward the interview topic as a whole or toward the questions which must be asked. In general, the interviewer should have a nonjudgmental attitude rather than being shocked by the information received, should show a lively interest in what the respondent is saying rather than being bored, and should usually maintain an analytical attitude toward the information and the degree to which it fulfills the specifications of the study. The interviewer should give praise and recognition to responses which are of a high quality in terms of their detail, completeness, depth, and candidness, regardless of the moral implications of the report.

It is sometimes difficult for the interviewer to avoid showing personal values when the respondent makes some completely unpredicted statements which catch the interviewer off guard, as illustrated below. In this example a group worker from a settlement house in the slums of a large city is talking to the person indicated in the records as the mother of a boy who has recently committed another delinquency.

I: Hello Mrs. Johnson. I am Mr. Brown from Roger Booth House. I would like to talk with you about John.

R: Come in, Mr. Brown.

I: John spends quite a bit of time at Roger Booth House. We are sorry to hear that he is in trouble and I was wondering if there is anything we can do.

R: That's right nice of you, but I don't think anything can be done now. I have had trouble with him for years. He seems to be just a born renegade. I have done my best but he just can't stay on the beam.

I: How's that?

R: Ever since he was two days old he has been trying to kick over the traces.

I: What does his father think of this?

R: I really can't say. You see, I never met his father.

I: (Making a quick recovery) I see, how old was he when you adopted him?

R: I didn't have to adopt him because I took care of his mother—she was my aunt's sister-in-law. I took care of her since she was nine years old, and I made her promise that when she got married she would give me her first son. Well, she wasn't married, but John was her first son. In fact, she had him right in this house. This was a much nicer neighborhood then.

The social worker with extensive experience with lower socioeconomic status people of various ethnic backgrounds would not be shocked by the respondent's last statement. However, in this case the interviewer had little experience with people in metropolitan slums and was unable to conceal being taken aback by the casual attitude displayed toward middle-class ideals of parenthood and the red tape of adoption procedures. From this point on, the respondent ceased to express herself so candidly and any constructive working relationship was made more difficult.

We could supply many examples in which the interviewer is caught off guard and shows surprise, shock, morbid curiosity, inappropriate amusement, or disapproval of something the respondent has said. The probability of such material entering the conversation depends upon the topic of discussion and the difference in experience, cultural background, and auxiliary roles of the interviewer and respondent. The interviewer must be sensitive to the problem and have wide experience before being able to take all the respondent's statements in stride.

It is easier for the interviewer to learn to inhibit the expression of embarrassment, boredom, shock, disapproval, and gullibility in reaction to a respondent's statement than it is to pretend the opposite attitudes when they are not actually felt. However, pretense is not necessary. The most constructive approach is for the interviewer to *learn to express* the following generally productive attitudes.

The nonjudgmental attitude. Generally, the interviewer should not express agreement or disagreement, approval or disapproval of anything the respondent says. The interviewer should remember that the goal is to obtain accurate and complete information and that any show of disagreement with the respondent constitutes an ego threat.

The interviewer must learn the fine but important distinction between disapproving of a certain value held by the respondent and rejecting the respondent as a person. At the same time, the interviewer should not assume that the respondent makes this distinction; therefore, it should be expected that any disagreement with the respondent's point of view will be interpreted as a disapproval of him or her as a person.

It is not suggested that a good interviewer is a chameleonlike character lacking values and merely reflecting those of the person being interviewed. On the contrary, the interviewer, in order to discipline himself not to indulge in unplanned demonstrations of approval or disapproval, must feel secure in his or her own value position, at least to the point of not needing to defend it or seek support for his or her position.

The very values which the interviewer holds and may be working for in the interview can be foiled by the expression of these values during the interview. For example, a person interested in reducing the juvenile delinquency rate thwarts his or her chance of gaining insight into the social-psychological process by which a child becomes a delinquent by expressing a disapproving attitude toward the delinquent that is being interviewed.

The main value of the nonjudgmental attitude is that it frees the respondent from ego threat, taking him or her off the defensive and allowing the respondent to candidly review his or her own behavior. There are *rare* occasions when it is appropriate to the objectives of the interview for the interviewer to express approval and disapproval. In learning to interview, however, the nonjudgmental approach is the basic discipline which must be mastered first so that any deviations from it are consciously calculated to meet interview objectives rather than emotional reflexive actions.

Showing an interest in the information. The interviewer's demonstrating or withholding a display of interest in certain aspects of the information is a technique of guiding the focus of the discussion. Also, the general level of interest shown in the information influences the amount of spontaneity shown by the respondent. Here "interest" covers a syndrome of more specific attitudes: a desire to understand how the world looks to the respondent; an appreciation of the things experienced by the respondent; sharing in the respondent's struggle to recall, organize, and express his experiences; appreciating the difficulties involved; and a desire to accurately reflect the respondent's opinions, feelings, and beliefs.

Various aspects of the interviewer's interest in the information can be demonstrated verbally as well as nonverbally. A few examples will illustrate this:

R: At that time I had three babies still in diapers and that made it a bit difficult to adjust to the divorce.

I: Three babies all in diapers! How did you manage?

The interviewer who is less sensitive or less appreciative could have merely said, "I see," or "What were some of the problems?" or "How is that?"

The following exchange is taken from an interview with a disaster victim where the objective was to obtain a complete account of the respondent's experiences during the period of crisis.

R: Jim and I were going down Highway 67; we didn't see the tornado, but just as we came to one of those banked turns we couldn't make it because the car was off the ground. We were jerked up in the air and I remember seeing a flash as our car hit the high-tension lines. Then we landed bottom side up in a swamp about four feet deep. One more gust of wind came and just flipped the car right side up again.

I: Were you going north or south on Highway 67?

After a large number of interviews this interviewer had become insensitive to the experiences of disaster victims and shows no appreciation for what the respondent is saying. True, this respondent's experiences, although dramatic, are not unusual for people in an area hit by a tornado. But from the point of view of the individual respondent there is little encouragement to elaborate and clarify the details of his or her experiences. An appropriate responsiveness on the part of the interviewer would have shown that he or she *expected* more detail at this point, *sympathized* with the respondent's traumatic experience, and *recognized* the respondent's unique qualifications to report how it feels to fly through the air in a car. All of these facilitators of communication could have been triggered by a natural expression of candid amazement on the part of the interviewer.

Fortunately, the interviewer's temporary lapses into insensitivity were not fatal to the flow of information on this particular topic because of the tremendous need for catharsis which leads most respondents to concentrate their attention on the most devastating portion of their experience. However, the better interviewers seemed to build up "credit" by showing interest in the respondent's account of the impact period of disaster. This credit carried over to the later portion of the interview dealing with information not nearly as important to the respondent himself.

The verbal techniques of showing interest responsiveness, empathy, sensitivity, appreciation, and recognition are often very simple as long as the nonverbal accompaniment rings true. For example: "That's very interesting to me." "That's exactly what I want to know; could you spell out more of the details?" "That's amazing—how did you do it?" "That's a very unusual experience, to say the least. Now let's see if I have the correct idea." "You must have been really angry by that time!"

All of these expressions of interest in the appropriate context are perfectly natural. For this reason interviewers are sometimes either suspicious of their use or do not think of them as "techniques." We must be careful to avoid the conception of techniques as tricks or insincere play acting.

There are occasions in some interviews when an undisciplined expression of interest, sympathy, or curiosity by the interviewer, even though sincere, will derail the interview so that the interview is very interesting but the information received is not relevant to the objectives of the interview. Here the over-concern with building rapport reduces the interview to a social conversation.

Critical analysis of the information. The nonjudgmental ethical neutrality and the disciplined interest in the respondent's story must be balanced by a third attitudinal stance referred to as critical analysis of the information. By *critical* we denote the process of evaluating the adequacy of the information for fulfilling the objectives of the interview.

It is not enough for the interviewer to be vitally concerned with evaluating the adequacy of the information; the interviewer must communicate this attitude to the respondent. When this attitude is perceived by the respondent, it helps prevent the temptation to give vague, superficial, incomplete replies which would require an inordinate amount of time to unscramble. The interviewer must prevent the respondent's perceiving him or her as a simple-minded, superficial, disorganized, or easily misled person.

The interviewer's attitude of critical evaluation is shown in an interest in precise facts, concern for correct inferences, and painstaking care in establishing accurate sequences of events when they are relevant. The interviewer also demonstrates it in the desire to get beneath clichés or instantaneous conclusions, in willingness to help the respondent remember, and in a conscientious attempt to correctly reflect the respondent's attitudes. These persistent efforts of the interviewer establish an appropriate mood. In order to help the respondent give the quality of response expected, the interviewer may have to slow down the pace of the interview and establish a thoughtful mood to facilitate memory. The interviewer may have to tactfully call the respondent's attention to apparent inconsistencies, contradictions, or omissions in the report.

This critical attitude has two general functions. First, it can be thought of as a balance wheel governing the two previous attitudes of nonjudgment and interest. The interviewer must discipline himself by restricting interest to those experiences which are relevant to the problem. Similarly, he or she must restrict the nonjudgmental approach to expressions of approval and disapproval of the respondent or the information given rather than to the completeness, accuracy, or general relevance of the information as measured by the objectives of the interview. The critical attitude reserves expressions of sympathetic understanding for only candid information; it prevents the misplaced expression of appreciation for efforts not up to the capabilities of the respondent.

The second function of the attitude is in its motivation of the respondent, who sees that a high-level performance is expected by the interviewer. The respondent sees more potential ego threat in being caught in an attempt to falsify than in a candid report, and this forestalls fabrication. The memory barrier is minimized by impressing the respondent with the importance of an accurate report. Indirectly, the respondent is given recognition because the respondent who perceives the interviewer as being competent will be apt to feel that he or she was respected enough to merit a good interviewer. The appeal to an intelligent respondent's altruism is enhanced because the respondent is more likely to be willing to give time for a good cause if he or she feels the cause is in the hands of competent people who will see it through to a successful conclusion. For some respondents a careful interview which insists upon achieving somewhat difficult objectives constitutes a challenging new experience. The interviewer's attempts to get beneath a superficial level often stimulate the respondent's need for meaning by pointing out certain inconsistencies of thinking of which the respondent had not previously been aware.

Now that some of the manifestations and functions of three general attitudes toward the information received by the interviewer have been examined, let us turn to some important aspects of the interviewer's attitude toward the respondent as a person.

Attitudes toward the Respondent as a Person

It is not possible to make a perfectly clear distinction between the interviewer's attitudes toward the information received and toward the person giving the information because, as has already been pointed out, the interviewer may tend to dislike the respondent if he or she dislikes many things the respondent says, and the respondent may tend to feel ego threat if the interviewer disagrees with some of the respondent's ideas.

For the purposes of this discussion the phrase "attitudes toward the respondent" will be used to refer only to those attitudes toward the respondent that are independent of anything the respondent has said in the interview and that are based upon the interviewer's image of an attitude toward a particular type of respondent. The type of respondent may be distinguished by such characteristics as sex, race, age, personality type, role, social class, and educational background.

There are several specific manifestations of the interviewer's attitudes which hinder communication with one class of respondent. An attitude may range in feeling from a strong dislike, through indifference, to a strong affinity. A negative feeling makes it difficult for the interviewer to empathize with the respondent. The author has found in the analysis of tape-recorded interviews that interviewers with some experience rarely express a negative attitude toward the respondent in a *direct* manner. Even though they learn to control such direct expressions, there are several indirect ways which betray a lack of interest. An awareness of these indirect manifestations will help an interviewer control negative attitudes toward a particular category of respondent.

Forgetting previous responses. This is a typical indirect manifestation of a lack of interest in the respondent. In the nonscheduled interview there is always the danger of asking the same or a similar question twice. However, the author has found that some interviewers, when interviewing certain types of respondents, were more prone to forget what the respondent had already told them even though it was something extremely important to the respondent. For example:

R: I called out "Victor, Victor, Victor" . . . as loud as I could yell. The next door neighbor was trying to calm me down, but I just couldn't control myself.

I: What was your husband doing meanwhile? . . . Oh yes, that's right you said he was unconscious all this time.

In this case the interviewer caught his own mistake and softened the blow. Such lapses of memory on the part of the interviewer are readily detected by the respondent when the information he has given is vitally important to him. This is ego threatening to some respondents, and if it happens more than once, it is often interpreted as an indication of the interviewer's lack of sympathetic understanding.

The interviewer can give this unsympathetic impression even when he or she has not forgotten that the question was asked and is asking a slightly different question for clarification. There is a danger that the respondent will feel or say, "I told you that once." To prevent this, the interviewer may positively give the respondent recognition by acknowledging the information previously given before probing further. The interviewer might say, for example, "You told me that your husband was unconscious after being hit by a board off the barn. What was he doing before that time?"

Neglecting to probe in crucial spots. This neglect communicates a lack of empathy for the respondent. If often pays to probe for elaboration and clarification of ego-involved or emotionalized responses even though the information does not seem to be directly related to the objectives of the interview. Showing an interest in what is important to the respondent is a good rapport-building technique. For example, in an interview to discover some of the factors contributing to the low morale of workers in a steel plant, the conversation was as follows:

I: Are there some supervisors the men find hard to get along with?

R: You have to take a lot of guff off the foreman here. I don't know who he thinks he is—and he has been here only two months.

I: What do you mean by that?

R: Well (with great hostility), the bastard actually violated some of the agreements the union has with the company!

I: Are there any other things that you dislike in the management or supervising system?

The interviewer's last question veers away from one of the respondent's favorite gripes. When the respondent is just beginning to gather momentum and before the interviewer has discovered the actual nature of his complaint, the interviewer rushes on as if he had only a limited amount of time. From the respondent's point of view, this behavior might indicate that the interviewer is not actually interested in his morale problems, and this could discourage the respondent from elaborating on other incidents.

Using condescending tone. There is a certain saccharine tone heard in tape recordings of interviews where the interviewer is trying to patronize the respondent who is considered in lower status. This tone is often used in an attempt to conceal outright disapproval or complete lack of interest in the respondent as a person. It is rarely successful in convincing the respondent that the interviewer is interested or impressed.

Being rigidly cautious. Although male interviewers rarely use what is called the "saccharine tone," they often become rigidly cautious in the same type of situation. In this case, these interviewers show little spontaneity, perhaps because they fear betraying their own feelings in an off-guard moment. In some instances this rigidity can be traced to the interviewer's feeling that he or she might lose status in the respondent's eyes by being too informal and spontaneous. This behavior was found in corporation managers while interviewing employees, in sociology students interviewing members of low-status ethnic groups, and in social work students interviewing mental patients.

Having shown some common manifestations of the negative attitudes toward the respondent, let us now examine some of the ways of manifesting positive attitudes toward the respondent.

Interest in the respondent as a person. Often it is impossible to motivate the respondent by treating him or her strictly as a means to an end. This is particularly true where the objectives of the interview make heavy demands upon the respondent. Here, the task of the interviewer is to reconcile the apparently conflicting goals of the interviewer who wants to obtain information and the respondent who wants to be understood and considered as a unique individual rather than as a statistic or case. The solution is to show a vital interest in both the respondent and the story at those points most relevant to the objectives of the interview. This interest, to be appropriate, must not be an idle curiosity, nor a chummy intimacy, but should be mainly confined to a keen interest in the relevant, unique experiences of the respondent. Such interest is characterized by the desire of the interviewer to see the relevant experiences through the respondent's eyes.

The respondent can be reminded of this attitude not only by its nonverbal manifestations such as the interviewer's paying close attention, responding with facial expressions and tone of voice, but also by such verbal expressions as, "I want *your* side of this story!" "How do you, *personally,* feel about this?" "Tell me what happened to *you* in the tornado." "What is *your* reaction to the rising cost of living?" "Which of these things seem most important to *you?*" "I want to be sure I understand *your* point of view on this issue!"

All of these questions and statements could be worded in an impersonal manner, but with less appeal to the respondent's ego. Personalizing the request for relevant information is one way of showing interest in the respondent as a person without encouraging irrelevant responses.

Interest in the respondent as a person can also be indicated by making statements at appropriate points showing appreciation of the respondent's role, status, or values. This does not mean that the interviewer must agree with the respondent's values. In the following exerpt an interviewer with a Protestant background is interviewing a Catholic woman who has felt the pressures of prejudice from fellow college students.

R: I recall one incident where two girls were talking about how only unintelligent people could be Catholics because they had to accept dogmatic pronouncements no matter how illogical they may be. Then one of them turned to me to see if I didn't agree. I just said, "You can't expect me to agree because I'm a Catholic myself." Were they ever embarrassed! They sputtered out something about they didn't realize I was a Catholic.

I: That reminds me of the time I heard a conversation on the bus where one woman said, "How was I to know! She didn't look like a Catholic at all!"

R: That's it exactly! They think that Catholics have two heads or something. That's why, in this community, I make a point of being known as an individual *before* I mention what church I belong to. People are less likely to be prejudiced then.

Note that the interviewer did not mention any of his experiences where the same thing had happened in relation to Jews, pacifists, socialists, or any other minority group. It is often a mistake to assume that one minority member sees any similarity between his situation and that of other minorities. And there is always the danger that the comparison will be resented.

Showing appreciation of the respondent's effort. The interviewer should be sensitive to the respondent's need for appreciation and recognition at two points in the interviewing process. First, the interviewer should show that he or she realizes a particular question places great demands upon the respondent. In doing this, the interviewer should not imply that he or she expects the respondent to fail to meet the demands. If the objectives of the question demand careful searching of one's memory, untangling chronological and inferential confusion, or reporting semiconscious experiences, the interviewer should give some indication of appreciating the difficulty of the problem. For example, the interviewer might say, "This is a difficult question, but I'm quite sure you can give me some good ideas if I just let you think it over for awhile. Let's go back to the time you mentioned when you joined the Black Hawk gang . . . that was about six years ago. Why would you say you joined the gang?"

The second phase of showing appreciation is in praising the respondent for the *effort* the respondent has made and is making. Interviews with respondents regarding their experiences in a nonscheduled interview showed that frequently the respondent did not understand the reasons for having difficulty in reporting some of the relevant information. Furthermore, the respondent was often insecure not knowing whether he or she was considered successful by the interviewer. In these cases, it is important that the interviewer show appreciation of the respondent's efforts to give the information.

The interviewer must be sensitive to opportunities to praise the respondent sincerely throughout the interview. The praise need not be lavish nor even direct, but should be given at those points where the respondent has exerted special effort. For example: "That was difficult and you did it very well!" "You seem to understand exactly what I want!" "You have given me an unusual amount of detail on your experiences. This is very valuable information!" "I know it was hard for you to talk about these painful experiences and I appreciate it." "I am grateful for your candid accounts of the conflicts and disagreements you have had with your parents!" "You have done an excellent job in giving me some insight into this problem. Is there anything else you would like to add before we go on to the last topic?" "You have given me a wealth of relevant information!" "You make interviewing very easy!"

It is easy for the interviewer to be so concerned with what information is lacking that he or she forgets to appreciate what has already been given and the amount of the respondent's effort expended. It encourages the respondent to go beyond the superficial level if he or she feels that it is expected and appreciated.

SUMMARY

Nonverbal communication is a means for communicating both certain information and attitudes to the respondent and for receiving information about the respondent's attitudes.

Technically there are four basic modes of nonverbal communication: *proxemic* communication is the use of the interpersonal space to communicate attitudes, *chronemics* communication is the use of pacing of speech and length of silence in conversation, *kinesic* communication includes any body movements or postures, and *paralinguistic* communication includes all the variations in volume, pitch, and quality of voice.

Although the four modes of nonverbal communication are useful for analytical and experimental purposes, the interviewer must in practice use any natural combinations of these modes in expressing attitudes which facilitate the flow of relevant information. Usually, the interviewer focuses attention on receiving and sending attitudes rather than upon analyzing the modes by which such attitudes are conveyed. The only specific physical nonverbal activity the interviewer needs to be conscious of is the use of silence. The silent probe must be used consciously as a specific nonverbal technique.

In the transmission of attitudes the interviewer must learn to detect subtle manifestations of attitude in the respondent. The interviewer must suppress the expression of any detrimental attitudes by displacing them with positive attitudes toward the task at hand.

The interviewer must learn to avoid expressing surprise, shock, embarrassment, or disgust in response to any information received. He or she must strive to maintain a generally nonjudgmental attitude toward information given by the respondent, to maintain a strong interest in the information, and to critically analyze the information in relation to the objectives of the interview. The attitude of critical analysis should be communicated to the respondent in order to prevent carelessness or fabrication in giving responses.

Negative attitudes toward the respondent as a person are frequently shown in the interviewer's errors of omission (such as forgetting a previous response and neglecting to probe in areas important to the respondent) or in a condescending tone of voice or cautious rigidity. These negative manifestations should be displayed by a strong verbal and nonverbal expression of interest in the respondent as a person rather than exclusively as a "case," a "statistic," or "source of information," and by showing appreciation of the respondent's efforts to give relevant information.

Even though the interviewer may unconsciously use some of these essential techniques, their conscious mastery and application will significantly increase interviewing success.

Figure 14–1 gives a checklist of questions to ask yourself about nonverbal techniques whenever you are planning, doing, or evaluating an interview. It provides a concise review of this chapter on the nonverbal technique tools of interviewing.

FIGURE 14–1   Checklist—Nonverbal techniques

Questions to ask yourself about nonverbal techniques

Proxemics

1. Is the seating arrangement conducive to conversation? Have physical barriers been removed?
2. If the interview is to be in the respondent's home or workplace, how can I select the most advantageous seating arrangement?
3. Am I within three to five feet of the respondent?
4. Am I facing the respondent directly?

Chronemics

5. Does my rate of speech suggest the appropriate pace and atmosphere for the purpose of the interview?
6. Is my rate of speech compatible with that the of the respondent?
7. Does the respondent have a speech-rhythm pattern that makes it difficult to understand? If so, the respondent may also be having some difficulty allowing for my rhythmic pattern.
8. Do I unnecessarily interrupt the respondent?
9. Is the respondent using or at least tolerating my silent probes?
10. Am I using silent probes first before trying verbal probes?

Kinesics

11. Do I lean forward toward the respondent much of the time?
12. Do I make frequent eye contact with the respondent?
13. Do I avoid such body-barriers as crossed legs, arms folded on my chest, turning away, or looking away from the respondent?
14. Do I avoid such distractions as drumming my fingers, chewing gum, or tapping my foot?

Paralinguistics

15. Am I aware of the respondent's intonation and stress patterns? Do they provide any clues to the respondent's emotional state?
16. Am I aware of hesitation and the general pacing of the respondent's speech? Any changes in these patterns?
17. Am I aware of the respondent's general volume level and any changes in volume?
18. Is my intonation, pacing and general volume level compatible with the respondent's?

Haptics

19. Is it appropriate under the circumstances to establish rapport or give emotional support by touching the respondent? If so, where, when, and how should I touch the respondent?

FIGURE 14–1 *concluded*

Aromatics

20. Am I free of bad breath or other body odors?
21. Do I use perfume, aftershave lotion, or other cosmetics that might project an inappropriate image to the respondent?
22. Is the interview environment free of distracting odors or odors which might have a negative association for the respondent?

Dress and grooming

23. Am I dressed and groomed appropriately in view of the setting, purposes of the interview and type of respondent?
24. What can I learn about the respondent's economic condition, social status, lifestyle, and emotional state from the person's dress and grooming?

Interviewer's attitudes

25. Do I show genuine interest in the topic of the interview?
26. Do I show confidence in my ability to obtain the relevant information?
27. Do I maintain a nonjudgmental attitude toward the answers given by the respondent?
28. Do I show interest in the responses and show appreciation for the respondent's efforts?
29. Am I vitally concerned for the relevance, completeness, and validity of the responses?
30. Do my probes show that previous responses have been remembered?
31. Do I probe highly ego-involved responses to show interest?
32. Do I use a condescending tone of voice toward respondent?
33. Do I sound rigidly cautious rather than spontaneous?
34. Do I show interest in respondent as a person?

DISCUSSION QUESTIONS

1. What are some of the main reasons why nonverbal communication is important?

2. What are some of the important *relationships* between a nonverbal cue and other factors in the situation such as other nonverbal cues, verbal cues, and the social-cultural context?

3. What are the major *types* of nonverbal cues or channels of nonverbal communication?

4. What are some of the major *functions* of nonverbal communication as a tool in the hands of the interviewer?

5. What are some of the very specific and easy-to-learn nonverbal techniques that the interviewer can use in many types of interviews?

6. What specific kinesic stimuli are most frequently the focus of attention of the listener in the interview situation?

7. Does the speaker or the listener tend to pay the most attention to the other person's kinesic communication?

8. Give an example of experimental proof that the nonverbal "silent language" really communicates.

9. What is the function of the silent probe in interviewing?

10. What are the principal foci of attitudes affecting the inhibitors and facilitators of communication?

11. What can the interviewer do as a technique to counteract any possible negative attitudes he or she may have toward the point of view divulged by the respondent?

12. What are some of the specific attitudes that must be developed to become a good interviewer?

13. What are some of the specific negative attitudes that must be avoided or counteracted by the successful interviewer?

Selected Readings

Below are useful collections of readings for students who want to go more deeply into the subject of nonverbal communication. Unlike most of the articles cited in the chapter, these books are not restricted to nonverbal communication in the interview setting.

Harper, Robert G., et al., *Nonverbal Communication: The State of the Art.* New York: John Wiley & Sons, 1978.
This is not an introductory test but a summarization of hundreds of research and experimental studies of nonverbal communication classified under the following headings: paralinguistics, facial expressions, kinesics, eye and visual behavior, and proxemics. It also discusses methodological problems. It is highly concentrated and slow reading, but very valuable for anyone interested in either doing research or in applying research findings to practical situations.

Rosenthal, Robert, ed. *Skills in Nonverbal Communication: Individual Differences.* Cambridge, Mass.: Oelgeschlager, Gunn and Hain, 1979.
This summarizes dozens of research studies attempting to discover and describe individual differences in people's nonverbal communication skills. Skills in both sending and receiving nonverbal cues are investigated.

Kendon, Adam, ed. *Nonverbal Communication, Interaction, and Gesture.* New York: Mouton Publishers, 1981.
A collection of nineteen articles first published in *Semiotica* prior to 1980. Part I is mainly theoretical and methodological. In Part II instances of specific types of nonverbal interaction are examined. Part III is devoted to articles on gestures. An excellent fifty page introduction provides a theoretical context for all the articles in the collection.

LABORATORY PROBLEM 8

Recognizing Techniques (Vocational Choice Interview)

PURPOSE

This laboratory problem provides an opportunity to recognize a variety of techniques as they occur in the context of the free-flowing initial exploratory interview. More different verbal techniques will be used than you were asked to produce in Laboratory Problem 7.

Also, although there is no way to convey such nonverbal techniques as tone of voice or facial movements on the printed page, you are to detect any interviewer's attitudes that are verbally manifested in what he or she says or neglects to say. This interview was selected because the particular interviewer does show some of his attitudes verbally.

PROCEDURE

This laboratory problem will require from one to two hours to complete. Below you are given the purpose and setting of the study and the verbatim transcript of the initial exploratory interview. You are to take the following steps:

1. Read the description of the objectives and setting of the interview carefully before reading the verbatim transcript. Try to imagine yourself as the interviewer.

2. As you read the script, classify all of the *interviewer's* verbal behavior that falls into any of the eleven categories in the Analysis Table provided by the instructor. Not all of his behavior falls into these eleven categories, and some of the statements or questions will fall into more than one category.

a. Each classifiable verbal behavior should be identified by the number on the transcript.

b. Within any category, the identification numbers should be in *rank order* with commas between, so that your results may be quickly compared with another person's. Example: 2, 5, 6, 9, 19, 33.

c. Do this in *pencil* so that it can be changed.

d. Do this independently, without consulting others on your decisions.

3. Now discuss your classifications with a fellow student who has already done it independently and make any changes needed in your classifications as a result of your discussion.

4. Submit your revised Analysis Table to the instructor.

OBJECTIVES

The interview aims to explore factors influencing the respondent's choice of a vocation or profession. The following three specific objectives were included in the preliminary definition of informational objectives.

1. To obtain the respondent's perception of his or her own education, training, abilities, achievements, interests, values, etc., as they relate to choice of vocation.

2. To discover the respondent's perceptions of the demands and rewards of various fields.

3. To identify the sources of any social pressure, whether through personal contact or the mass media, that influence his vocational choice.

SITUATIONAL SETTING

The interviewer, a male graduate student, is interviewing a male undergraduate student. The interview takes place in the graduate student's apartment off campus. The interviewer explained why he wanted to tape-record the interview and met no resistance to the idea. There was some conversation about the interviewer's dog and then the interview begins.

INTERVIEW TRANSCRIPT

In the verbatim transcript of the interview the durations of silences are shown in seconds by the numbers in parentheses. You are to classify only the *interviewer's* words identified by I-0, I-2, I-3, etc.

I:0   As you know, we are interested in finding how people select the vocation they go into.

R:0   That should be a fascinating study!

I:1   What I thought we would start out with is some of your earlier thoughts in choosing a field. You can go back as early as you can remember.

R:1   Hmm, that is something! I can't remember a thing before my high-school days!

I:2   Can't you remember earlier than that—just think a moment. When I try, I can remember back to six and seven years old.

R:2   Well, when I was very young, I was interested in the theater. (3)

I:3   I see, how did that happen?

R:3   It has always been more or less the field that I wanted to go into. I started out wanting to be a dancer, and I continued that for two or three years (2) while I was taking lessons, and then I decided to go into the theater.

I:4   How old were you when you first wanted to be a dancer?

R:4   Twelve! (3)

I:5   Can you remember back to the time—way back—when you were interested in other things, anything from wanting to be an Indian to a cowboy? I used to want to be a motorcycle driver.

R:5   I can't remember anything like that (2) of course I suppose I wanted to be a fireman, policeman, cowboy, or something like that when I was younger, but as far as I can remember, I have always been interested in something connected with the theater. I took dancing lessons until I was fourteen.

I:6   So you took dancing lessons until you were fourteen.

R:6   Yeh, well, I moved to Arizona when I was fourteen. They didn't have a good school of the dance, so I started acting. I sort of associated with a children's theater group and became interested in that. But I wasn't there long (3) my parents were getting a divorce, and I moved out with my mother for the proceedings. We lived there over a year. Then I went back to Massachusetts to live with my mother. (3)

I:7   Do you feel that this children's theater group was the main influence leading you toward the theater?

R:7   I don't know about that.

I:8   Why don't you know? Didn't you say that your main interest was really dancing until you were fourteen?

R:8 Yeh, thirteen or fourteen. (4)

I:9 Did you have any experience with the theater before or during your dancing?

R:9 Yea, we had a tiny group at home, you know, little kids ten or eleven years old. We'd do little fairy tales, that sort of things. We'd just sort of act them out. But nothing big. (2)

I:10 That was more or less a natural occurrence of growing up, wasn't it?

R:10 I'd say that, yeh. We had a girl though that was a junior or senior in high school, and we'd do one or two shows a year, and she'd ask us to do one and be in the show herself, and it'd be the real thing (2) but as far as being really organized, I suppose you could call it a process of growing up.

I:11 Speaking of growing up—where were you from originally?

R:11 I was born in Boston, Massachusetts, but I lived in Williamstown up in the other end of the state. Well, actually my mother still lives there. Both of my parents married again, and my stepfather still lives there. (3)

I:12 You were in Arizona only about a year?

R:12 Only about fifteen months, yes. Then we moved back. It was only a temporary move. We were only going to be there three months, but stayed longer.

I:13 Ah . . . can you think of any other fields? So you just maintained this interest until you came to college? (2)

R:13 I never really wanted to be anything else. Teaching, but teaching in the theater level. Nothing . . . (3) . . . it is always something connected with the theater.

I:14 How are you at dancing?

R:14 Well, I haven't done much lately, but I was pretty good, or at least that is what I have been told. I've done some. I've taken the modern dance course here, and I suppose with a lot of work I might go somewhere, but I'm not willing to put in the work right now with all my academic work. I wouldn't want to do it for a living.

I:15 Then you don't want to make a career of it?

R:15 Well (2) I did some dancing when I was thirteen and fourteen in public—it was a lot of fun. This was in Williamstown. All my friends came to see me, and I got quite a charge out of it. I did a little of everything then, tap, modern, ballet, and even folk dancing of a rather complicated kind.

I:16   I see. What do you think is the best for you, dancing or theater?

R:16   Well, that depends on what aspect of the theater you want to talk about. In fact, dancing is part of the theater, and there are many facets even to the acting area of theater. For example, directing, stage management, business management, choreography, singing, teaching and . . . well all kinds of things. I don't know which is the most practical. (5) Do you think it might be a good thing for someone who isn't terrifically talented as an actor to go into teaching dramatics? (4)

I:17   Well—you know the old saying, "If you can't do it yourself, teach someone else to do it, and if you can't teach it, then teach others to teach."

R:17   Well, I love acting, and I'll admit that I'm not any Olivier, but nowadays you have to be either a genius or have a lot of what Hollywood is looking for. . . sex appeal. (2)

I:18   The main reason that you don't feel acting is for you is that you sort of feel that you're—well not by my standards, but by the standards of the theater—you are mediocre.

R:18   Well . . . I. . . .

I:19   Well, I hate to use that word. . . .

R:19   I think probably with training I could . . . I mean I, I've had plenty of experience. I've had any number of stock company work and things, but it would take a lot of training, but I don't have quite the right bark to be (2) you know—a *great* actor, and I'm not a he-man so I could never become another Burt Lancaster.

I:20   Or a Marlon Brando.

R:20   Yeah, you either have to be really good in your art or you have to be really bad Hollywood. There are very few really good actors in Hollywood except for people who go out to do *one* film . . . (2) . . . but people like Burt Lancaster and that sort of thing all build on their sex appeal . . . Marlon Brando too.

I:21   Well, he does pretty good things no matter how he's cast.

R:21   Yeh, he's sort of a natural.

I:22   He's got talent as well as sex appeal.

R:22   Well, talking along these lines, I saw an old movie when I was up in Akron a while back. Ray Milland, now I thought Ray Milland could do a decent job in . . . oh, I saw him in "Time Out for Murder" with Hitchcock, now he was entertaining in that film. I mean not a great dynamic or great stirring emotional actor, but pleasant as an Englishman, dignified, refined. I just hate to see somebody cast like that (2) and it tears your heart out to see somebody who really loves the theater, it makes me ill . . . don't you think so?

I:23   Yeh, that's very true. I think they should keep Broadway actors out of movies. They can't be expected to do well at both media.

R:23   To see somebody of ability. . . Well, I'm off the subject. (2)

I:24   Do you feel that your parents influenced your decision?

R:24   No, that's one nice thing about my mother and father both. They never tried to tell me "You ought to be an actor or a dancer when you grow up." Children should have a mind of their own!

I:25   What does your father do?

R:25   He teaches business administration at Harvard Business School.

I:26   And what about your mother. Did she ever have any aspirations to the stage which were interrupted by getting married? I know that sort of thing is not at all unusual.

R:26   Well, before she got married she was a bank teller at a bank.

I:27   Did she go to college?

R:27   She went three years to a college in Boston—Erskine. It's no longer in session. She never finished school.

I:28   And what was her interest there?

R:28   I really don't know. She doesn't talk about it very much, and I never asked her. I don't know.

I:29   Do you think your parents' backgrounds might have influenced your choice of field?

R:29   Well, both my parents are very (2) or have, have a lot of background in, a creative arts background. Art was a minimum, but music especially. They both liked music very much, and I do know that I do like music because I heard it ever since I was yea-high. You know, listening to it all the time whenever they had it on, good music . . . so I like good music.

I:30   Did your parents enjoy theater too?

R:30   Oh yes—doesn't everyone in Boston? Or I should say every *educated* person.

I:31   I guess that's right. Do you have any brothers or sisters?

R:31   Yes, one younger brother and some stepbrothers and sisters.

I:32   What does your younger brother intend to do?

R:32   Well, as far as I know he wants to follow in my father's footsteps in economics, that's the last thing I heard. (2) He is sort of a "papa's boy" and is easily influenced by father.

I:33   I see—he doesn't really have a strong will of his own.

R:33   I guess that's it.

I:34   When you were living at home after your parents were divorced, where did you live, with your father or your mother?

R:34   With my mother.

Part V

TACTICS OF
INTERVIEWING

Chapter Fifteen

Advance Planning of Tactics

Tactics of interviewing are dealt with in three chapters. This chapter focuses on those tactical sequences that can be developed, planned, and frozen into the interview schedule. The next chapter on probing and the following one on dealing with resistance in the respondent focus on those tactical maneuvers that cannot be planned in advance but must be selected in response to a particular respondent's behavior. The planning of tactics is a creative art, and the parry and thrust of probing and meeting resistance after the interview begins is a performing art.

Tactics in interviewing consists of choosing the appropriate order for the interviewer's statements, questions, and probes. While the interviewer's techniques can be classified according to the form of the verbal or nonverbal behavior at a given point without any reference to what came before of after, it is not possible to view any particular behavior as a tactic without seeing it in a chronological context. We must know what came before and what we expect to come after as well as how it fits into the larger aims of the total interview. Thus, what might be a perfectly good question or probe at one point in the interview may be threatening at another point. Also, the meaning of a question at one point in the interview depends upon the questions and answers which preceded it.

Tactical patterns may be planned in advance and rigidly followed, tentatively planned and loosely followed, or left completely to the discretion of the interviewer after he or she is engaged in the ongoing give-and-take of a particular interview. At one extreme the typical opinion survey may have all of the tactical patterns built into the interview schedule and may strictly forbid any deviation in question form or sequence by the interviewer. At the other extreme as administrator may spend a large portion of time asking questions to obtain information from other members of the organization, yet the administrator may never prepare an interview schedule with a fixed order of questions. Instead, he or she would have a clear idea of the information needed and begin an informal discussion, probing important points as they emerge.

The portion of the tactical decisions that can be legitimately frozen into the interview schedule depends on the type of information sought, the setting of the interview, and the amount of information needed. If many interviews are to be done on the same topic, much of the tactical pattern can be developed in exploratory interviews. Developing sensitivity to the chronological patterning is essential for anyone who wants to do exploratory interviewing more effectively, or who wants to be able to do tactical planning and interview schedule construction for others.

Assuming that the interviewer knows precisely what bits of information are needed, there are several areas in which he or she may do advance planning of tactics. However, all of these plans must be considered as tentative in the nonscheduled interview and may be changed with field testing. The interviewer must decide how many subtopics there actually are in the broad topic. The interviewer should decide which one to begin with and perhaps work out pivot questions to determine whether subsequent subtopics are relevant to the particular respondent. He or she might devise lead-in questions which are designed to psychologically prepare the respondent for questions which will follow but which do not intend to directly obtain information relevant to the purposes of the interview. When getting chronological material from the respondent, the interviewer must decide whether to begin the discussion precisely at that point in time relevant to the objectives of the interview or to go back further and do a lead-in designed to help the respondent reconstruct the scene and the situation immediately preceding the relevant period of time. Once the order of topics and the means of getting from one subtopic to another are decided, tentative plans must be made for developing the discussion within each subtopic area. Here the interviewer must decide on all possible alternative wordings of questions, on how contexts can be provided when needed, on alternative sequences of questions; and above all, the interviewer must select some clear way of recording what has and has not been covered in the progress of the interview. The latter will be a problem particularly when the interviewer does not follow a fixed sequence of specific questions.

In addition to deciding what subtopics are needed, possible orders of these subtopics, and methods of expanding each of these subtopics to cover all of the specific information needed, the interviewer must also prepare to meet certain infrequent crises which require special treatment. For example, we might find a question which unexpectedly constitutes an ego threat to the respondent. What do we do? Or what do we do if the respondent simply says, "I'm sorry, I'm too busy now to be interviewed"? What do we do if he says, "Ask someone else who knows something about this topic; I don't know anything about it"? Or if he says he does not want to have his voice tape-recorded, or he stops in the middle of the interview to ask, "Why are you taking notes?" If he responds to a question by saying he does not remember or does not know, are we to take this literally? If, in response to a question, he uses the Yankee system of asking you the question, what tactics should be used? Or what if we merely suspect that the respondent is resisting, that he is not giving all the information he has and is withholding something? What can we do to test a hypothesis of this kind?

This chapter deals with these problems of arranging topics and subtopics, pivot questions, lead-in questions, and transitions; developing each topic to cover the specifications of the interview; meeting resistance by the respondent, and testing whether or not he is actually resisting. To a certain extent, successful use of tactics depends upon basic skills which have been developed, but perhaps to a larger extent it depends upon an awareness of what kinds of tactical problems might arise and planning some possible ways of meeting these problems. Once we know how to make these plans, all that remains is to practice planning for a wide variety of interviews so that required basic skills can be developed.

ARRANGING TOPICS AND SUBTOPICS WITHIN AN INTERVIEW

It is possible to have an interview so simple in its objectives that there are no topics or subtopics. The simplest possible interview might contain only one question:

"As you know, ____ and ____ are running for President of the United States. For whom do you intend to vote?" At the other extreme, an interview's objectives might include the opinions of the respondent on several public issues, certain of the respondent's personality traits, some of the respondent's social background characteristics, such as religion, social class, political views, the amount of influence the respondent has on others, and the respondent's position in the community. The number of topics or subtopics perceived within such a complex interview depends upon the degree of relationships between the various objectives and the level of abstraction used to hold the topics within the common frame of reference. For example, a respondent's opinion on three topics such as antivivisection, the U.S. role in the United Nations, and parent-child relations in the United States might be conceived as three separate, nonrelated topics. However, if the objectives of the interview include discovering the respondent's personality characteristics and relating them to his or her opinions on selected public issues, then these three topics become merely three selected public issues and are subtopics more related to each other than to a battery of questions regarding the respondent's personality traits. This example illustrates that what might be a whole interview in one case is a topic within an interview in another case; it could also be a subtopic within a topic of another interview. Regardless of how finely we slice the total subject matter of the interview into topics, we are faced with the problem of deciding how the specific questions must be grouped into topics or subtopics and what their chronological order will be.

Chronological Order of Topics and Subtopics

Although it is impossible to provide specific rules for determining the chronological order of subtopics within an interview, it is possible to indicate some of the most important questions that must be considered when determining the order of topics. However, these questions can be answered specifically only within the context of a particular interview problem. Too frequently, the interviewer tends to arrange the order in a purely logical fashion in order to simplify the coding and analysis of the data, or to arrange questions in a sequence that seems natural to him or her. Although both of these criteria are important, the criterion which has precedence over either of these is the effect upon the respondent's willingness and ability to give the relevant information. If the order which maximizes the flow of valid, relevant information is also the logical order which will minimize the problems of analyzing the data, this is fortunate. But it is not always the case.

Let us look at some examples in which the order of topics has an effect upon the flow of information.

Ego threat. Frequently one sequence of topics is more ego threatening than an alternate sequence of the same topics. If we wish to discover the relationship between a person's premarital sex behavior and subsequent marital adjustment, the interview obviously contains a minimum of two separate topics. In this case, we might have to do several exploratory interviews to determine which of these topics seems to threaten the respondent the least. Is the respondent more likely to withhold the details of his premarital sex behavior after discussing his marital adjustment, or vice versa?

To give another example, suppose we want to discover the relationship between the respondent's opinion on foreign aid and his or her religious participation. Foreign aid is an opinion topic, while the respondent's religious participation (such as what is the respondent's church affiliation, how many times a year the respondent attends, whether he or she participates in action projects sponsored by the church) is not. In this case, it is highly probable that the interview should first discuss the respondent's opinions on foreign aid before reminding the respondent of religious connections. If the procedure were reversed, there would probably be a greater tendency for the respondent to present his or her opinions on foreign aid as being more harmonious with his or her professed religious principles.

In other instances the respondent's ego is threatened by the fact that the sequence of topics is structured in a logical fashion that makes the respondent aware that his or her arguments are not logical, and contain some threatening inconsistencies. For example, an interview might contain five subtopics represented by the following questions:

1. Do you believe that the United States has sufficient military power to destroy the Soviet Union's industrial civilization?

2. Do you think that the Soviet Union has enough military power to destroy the United States' industrial civilization?

3. Do you think that either the Soviet Union or the United States has an efficient system of defense which would prevent the other from destroying its industrial civilization in the event of an all-out nuclear war?

4. Do you think that the Soviet Union feels that the present military power of the United States is sufficient to crush her industrial civilization in the event of an all-out nuclear war?

5. Do you feel that the United States should continue to put an increasing proportion of her national wealth into augmenting her military power?

It is highly probable that the respondent who feels that the United States should continue increasing its military power would feel threatened in stating this opinion if the question were preceded by the other four as suggested above. It is possible that such a respondent would find himself in the position of saying that the purpose of armaments and military power from the point of view of the United States is to deter the Soviet Union from attacking. The respondent may also feel that we have enough military power to destroy the Soviet Union's industrial civilization and that the Soviets believe that we have such power. Furthermore, the respondent may feel that there is no way for either the Soviet Union or the United States to defend themselves against an all-out nuclear attack of the other. In view of these premises, the respondent might find it quite difficult to justify his or her feeling that we should continue to increase the military power of the United States.

Stimulating the memory. It is often possible for the sequence of topics to have an effect upon the respondent's recall of relevant detail, and subsequently upon the possibility of chronological or inferential confusion clouding his or her reports.

There are several remedies for this. For example, the respondent might be asked to give the most easily recalled facts first. These may be more easily recalled because they happened more recently or because they were more ego-involved for the respondent. In an interview to determine the relationship between student adjustment to a field of study and the factors which influenced the student to pursue this field, it might be preferable to begin by discussing the student's adjustment to the field in which he or she is presently engaged. After this has been developed sufficiently, an abrupt transition could be made to the question of how the student decided to enter the field. (Reasons for using either abrupt or smooth transitions from one topic to another will be discussed later in the chapter.)

In this case, it is clear that discussing the person's adjustment in his or her field of endeavor is inevitably going to bring about certain associations with how the person got into the field and how things actually were in the field compared to his or her expectations. When shifting to the second topic of how the person decided to go into the field, every effort must be made by the interviewer to help the respondent overcome chronological confusion by distinguishing between the respondent's reasons for preferring the field now that he or she is in it and the respondent's initial reasons which involved preliminary perceptions and expectations.

It is also possible to minimize the problem of inferential confusion in an interview having two distinctly different kinds of topics, one which asks the person for specific factual details about certain events or a certain period of time and another topic which asks the person for his or her judgments, opinions, or overall perspectives on these events or this period of time. In this case, it is highly probable that a more accurate account of the person's overall feelings and views can be obtained if we first develop the detailed facts of the events. In this way, the respondent is allowed to review in detail with the help of the interviewer the specific factual events which have to be considered in order to make a valid overall judgment of the situation.

Maximizing facilitators. If we wish to get off to a good start in the interview and build rapport, it is often helpful to begin with a particular subtopic that maximizes the amount of recognition to be given to the respondent or which gives the respondent a chance to obtain sympathetic understanding or catharsis, or to begin with a topic that stimulates the respondent's need for meaning and raises questions that arouse his or her interest.

In some complex interviews, there may be three or four topics that would have great natural interest for the respondent and another three or four that the respondent would consider quite boring or inconsequential.

Sometimes it is helpful to alternate between one type of topic and the other.

Varying the sequence of topics with the respondent. In some cases, it is quite clear that one sequence of topics is better for maximizing the flow of information and maintaining optimum interpersonal relations than another, and that this optimum sequence would be the same for all respondents. In other cases, it may be apparent that the optimum sequence varies from respondent to respondent, depending upon the nature of each respondent's particular relationship to the topic or his or her particular experience. It may be necessary to do exploratory interviews to know whether we can use a fixed sequence of topics or whether we should allow it to vary to fit the needs of a particular respondent.

There are several ways in which the interviewer can allow the respondent to select the sequence. The first way is simply to begin the interview with a broad question covering all the topics and subtopics and then allow the respondent to begin where he or she chooses. Once the respondent finishes the initial subtopic, the same general question or another one slightly narrowed may be asked, allowing the respondent to pursue any of the remaining subtopics. For example, in interviewing disaster victims, we needed to know what the person actually *observed* during the crisis period, what the person *did* during the crisis period both to protect himself and to help others, what the person thought about what was going on, and numerous subtopics covering the later phase of relief and rehabilitation which may have lasted for days or weeks. The subtopics of the crisis period could be introduced by the general question, "Tell me what happened to you in the storm." The subtopics related to the relief and rehabilitation period could be introduced by the broad question, "Tell me about some of the relief work that went on after the storm was all over."

Another means of giving the respondent the choice of topic sequence is to simply announce at the beginning that you are going to cover three or four topics and give the respondent a choice of where to begin, as in this example:

Metropolitan Studies is interested in your opinion on three issues which are being discussed on the local scene. The first is the antivivisection issue; the second is the issue of metropolitan government; and the third is the juvenile delinquency wave. With which of these would you like to begin?

A third general tactic for allowing the respondent to discuss topics in his or her own sequence is to use a pivot question to introduce a new topic area. This method is discussed in detail in the following section.

Introducing Each Topic

Once we have decided whether or not we should predetermine the order of topics and, if so, how, we need to consider how each new topic or subtopic can best be introduced.

Using lead-in questions. A lead-in question is one that is not directly relevant to the objectives of the interview but which has the function of effectively leading the respondent to a relevant question area in a way that prepares him or her to give more accurate and valid information. In some cases, where none of the questions seems to be of any great interest to the respondent, it is helpful to ask a preliminary question that is interesting to him or her and also related to the topics which follow. This we might call the interest lead-in question.

Sometimes if the respondent is not psychologically prepared for a question the answer will be inaccurate and unreliable. For example, Haberman found that without any lead-in questions the answer to the simple question, "What was the last grade in school you completed?" disagreed about 38 percent of the time with the answers given by the same people three years later.[1] He suggested using three lead-in questions to prepare the respondent for the fourth:

1. "Did you have a chance to get as much education as you wanted?"

2. "How old were you when you were last in school?"

3. "What was the name of the last school you attended?"

4. "What was the last grade in school you completed?"

In this case the lead-in questions help to stimulate the respondent's memory, give the respondent a face-saving chance to say he or she did not have a chance to get as much education as the respondent wanted, and perhaps suggest that the interviewer could possibly check with the school that the respondent names. In any case, the lead-ins improve the reliability of the answers.

Another type of lead-in question is the chronological lead-in. This is a question regarding a point or period in time which precedes the period relevant to the objectives of the interview. This type of warm-up question gives the respondent a chance to get in a reminiscent mood which stimulates recall of a particular period of time. It also prevents chronological confusion by having the respondent looking forward in his or her mind to a bit of the past rather than looking back at it from the

---

[1] P. W. Haberman and J. Sheinberg, *Public Opinion Quarterly* 30 (1966), pp. 295–301.

perspective of the present. For example, if we are interested in an employee's view of management's handling of an educational meeting for the employees, it might be well to introduce the topic with a question such as, "When did you first know there was going to be a special meeting for the employees?" This question might be followed by other lead-in questions such as, "Where was the meeting held?" "Who did you go to the meeting with?" These questions all establish a specific, concrete feeling of the past and lead the respondent up to the point of evaluating the meeting itself.

Another function of the lead-in question is to establish an appropriate atmosphere by allowing the interviewer to display the proper attitudes toward the respondent and toward a subject matter closely related to the relevant information. For example, if the purpose of the interview is to discover problems North American students have adjusting to their Colombian host families, the interview with the Colombian *señora* could begin with a lead-in question or lead-in topic about problems *other señoras* have had with their North American guests.

All types of lead-in questions (or statements that imply a question) share one characteristic. The information sought by the lead-in question is not going to be used in the analysis of the data because it is not directly relevant to the objectives of the interview.

Using pivot questions. A pivot question acts as a turning point in the line of questioning by determining which of two or more possible new topics would apply to the particular respondent. The pivot question is sometimes called a "contingency question," particularly when used in a questionnaire. Whenever we introduce a new topic for discussion in an interview, we usually make certain assumptions regarding the appropriateness of the new line of questioning. We assume that the respondent has had the appropriate experiences *(a)* to understand the question and *(b)* to have some relevant information. The pivot question is an attempt to test these assumptions before proceeding with the next topic.

We cannot always anticipate the need for pivot questions in advance simply because we are not aware of the assumptions we are making regarding the experiences of the respondent. It is often necessary, therefore, to do some exploratory nonscheduled interviews to determine the type and location of needed pivot questions. In this phase, the interviewer, instead of using predetermined pivot questions, must be constantly alert for unanticipated pivot *responses* which indicate a need for a change in the line of questioning.

For example, in a study of academic freedom it was assumed that restrictions of academic freedom would center about controversial issues in economics and politics, particularly as they related to Communism. It was discovered that in a small minority of colleges, political issues had neither arisen nor been repressed. Instead, the main issues involved conflicts between fundamentalistic religious beliefs and the findings of the biological and social sciences. A professor might be threatened with dismissal if he insisted upon discussing Darwin's theory of evolution in a biology course. Only in interviewing a professor at such a college did it become apparent that the study of academic freedom had been based upon the assumption that such controversies between science and religion were no longer live issues on college campuses.

Similarly, in interviewing respondents living in disaster-stricken communities, the interviewer would often assume that because the respondent was a resident of the community he would be able to give information on the disaster's effects on the community. In some cases, this was proved incorrect because *(a)* the respondent was out of town the day the disaster struck, *(b)* he was immediately rendered unconscious before he was aware of any approaching crisis, or *(c)* he completely withdrew from the situation and made no attempt to discover what had happened or to help any one. The respondent was usually willing to give information regarding *(a)* or *(b)* but would sometimes attempt to prevent the interviewer from discovering *(c)*. In this situation, much confusion could be avoided if the interviewer would ask, "Where were you when the storm struck Judsonia?" If the respondent had been in Judsonia at the time, another pivot question could follow: "Were you injured in any way?" If the respondent had been in Judsonia and was not injured, then a series of questions on his participation in the immediate rescue operations became relevant. The interviewer might have these specific pivot questions in mind and obtain the answers without directly asking each question. In any case, it was helpful for the interviewer to know whether he was talking to a rescuer or to one of the rescued.

Although a small number of exploratory interviews might discover all of the pivot questions that are needed, it is often impossible or impractical to do the amount of exploratory interviews needed in order to completely eliminate any surprises regarding the assumptions made. Therefore, in any interview that is complicated by several topics and subtopics, the interviewer will need to be alert for clues indicating that some lines of questioning are not applicable to a particular respondent. The preplanning of pivot questions is even less feasible when interviewing only one or two persons from each category of special respondents.

Providing transitions. Once we have decided upon the order of topics or subtopics and have located the points where pivot questions can determine the appropriateness of a new topic or subtopic, our next problem is to determine whether it is necessary to provide specific material to act as a bridge from one topic to another. There are at least three reasons for providing a special transition.

a. It may be needed to show the respondent the relationship between the old and the new topic in order to help him maximize any advantages in the particular sequence of topics.

b. It may relate the new topic to the basic objectives of the interview so that the respondent may not become confused or suspicious that the "real purpose" of the interview was not stated in the original explanation.

c. It may be needed to emphasize a change in frame of reference, perspective, or mood so that the respondent will not carry over an inappropriate context from a previous topic.

Let us give an example of transitions fulfilling each of these three functions.

In a study of the effects of foreign travel, we included the following five topics, in the order indicated:

1. The respondent's specific experiences abroad within the past two years.

2. The effects of these experiences in *changing* the respondent's views of the foreign country.

3. The effects of these experiences in *changing* the respondent's views of his or her own country.

4. Courses taken in college that influenced the meaningfulness of the foreign experience.

5. Certain personality traits that might affect the respondent's adjustment to the foreign culture.

In the first few exploratory interviews it was discovered that the respondent usually did not make the correct connection between topics 1 and 2. The respondent's tendency was often to merely talk about interesting experiences he or she had abroad under the first topic and then forget to make any connection between these experiences and specific *changes* in the respondent's views of the foreign country. It was found helpful to provide the following transition:

You have told me about many of your experiences abroad which you found outstanding. Now that you have had a chance to think about your experiences in Germany, let us move on to a more difficult topic. I would like to know how any of these experiences you have mentioned, or any others you might recall, changed your views on Germany, the German people, or their culture. It is sometimes helpful to think of those things which surprised you because they were not what you expected or those which seemed to give you a more positive or negative feeling toward the country. Which of your experiences seemed to change your views on Germany?

Even with this transition aimed at making a connection between specific experiences and changes in beliefs or attitudes, there was still a tendency for the respondent to begin discussing his or her current views on the foreign country without stating whether these were new views gained by recent experience or whether they were old views held before going abroad. The interviewer had to be constantly alert to establish which views represented *changes* and which specific experiences were associated with these changes. Needless to say, the respondent often found it difficult to link a particular change to a particular experience. In any case, providing the transition made it easier for the respondent to see the second topic in its proper perspective and reduced the number of times the interviewer had to redirect the respondent toward the objectives of the interview.

The second function of the transition as described in *(b)* above can also be illustrated with this same interview. Most interviewers discovered in the first exploratory interview that a transition was needed between topics 4 and 5. Since the first four topics had all obviously dealt with effects of foreign travel, specific questions under the fifth topic seemed out of place to the respondent. For example, questions like the following needed some transition:

In a group discussion do you usually tend to be one of the listeners or one who does much of the talking?
Do you enjoy making introductions at a party when you discover that some of the people aren't acquainted with each other?

Without some special attention to topic transition, these questions may seem so out of context to the respondent that he or she becomes suspicious that the whole interview "is really an indirect attempt to psychoanalyze me." As one respondent put it, "I thought you said you were interested in the effects of foreign experience, but now it looks like you forgot to bring your couch along." This suspicion can be avoided by a transitional statement such as the one that follows:

It is claimed by some people interested in this problem that the same foreign experience would have very different effects upon two people with different basic personality traits. I am going to ask you ten simple, straightforward questions about the type of person you think you are.

This transitional statement proved helpful in allaying suspicion about the relevance of the final ten questions and also signaled to the respondent that the questions were not intended to be deep or devious.

The third function of the transitional statement described in *(c)* above is perhaps the most frequent. When two consecutive topics involve different but related frames of reference which might become confused in the respondent's mind, it is necessary to make a complete break between the two topics so that the old frame of reference is not unconsciously retained in the new topic. For example, in a study of factors influencing college students' choice of a vocation, college seniors were interviewed to determine: *(a)* the occupational field they had chosen and the extent to which they were sure of their choice; *(b)* their conception of the ideal way of making a living; and *(c)* the compromises with reality students made in selecting an occupation. In the exploratory interviews it was discovered that the respondents found it difficult to shift from the realistic frame of reference in the first topic *(a)* to the "ideal" frame of reference called for by the second topic *(b)*. There was a tendency for the students not to want anything obviously beyond their reach. In some cases, it might have been a bit ego threatening to be reminded of the differences between one's realistic plans and one's ideal. The following transitional statement, however, helped encourage the respondent to relinquish his realism and to more enthusiastically discuss the idealistic conceptions called for in the second topic.

You have given me a clear idea of what you want to do vocationally after you graduate, and I get the feeling that you are very realistic and clear in your plans. Now I would like you to just let yourself go, throw realism to the winds and talk about what you see as the *ideal* way of making a living. By ideal, I simply mean that you are to consider only what you would *enjoy* doing for a living. Assume that there would be no question of your having the ability or talent needed, no problems in obtaining the necessary training, the job paid well and had high status in the world. The only taint of reality which I want you to retain is in limiting yourself to choosing some type of job which really exists. So take your pick, what type of job would you enjoy most, assuming that you could obtain such a job and were capable of holding it?

This preliminary statement helped the respondent make a transition into the mood needed to encourage such unrealistic talk. Once the respondent caught the spirit and realized that the interviewer was not going to judge him for his lack of realism, it was not difficult for him to relinquish the realism of the previous topic. After the second topic was carefully explored, the respondent was brought back to reality by being asked what real limitations prevented him from aspiring to his ideal job.

The preceding examples have emphasized those situations where special care must be taken in making a transition either to maintain a connection between two topics, to show the relevance of a new topic, or to abruptly sever the connection between one topic and the next to prevent carrying over an inappropriate frame of reference. In some cases, however, the flow of the topics is such that no particular care must be taken in making the transitions, because all of the topics obviously fall within the interview objectives, the relationship of each topic is obvious to the respondent, and each topic happily provides an appropriate background or frame of reference for the subsequent one. This lack of any need for special transitional statements is sometimes referred to as the "smooth" or the "natural" transition that can be achieved by merely arranging the topics in the correct order.

Preparing an Interview Guide

To clarify the meaning of "interview guide," let us compare it with two related instruments, the interview schedule and the questionnaire. Theoretically, the *questionnaire* has built-in all of the techniques and tactics of gathering the relevant information, so that nothing is left for the interviewer to do. The questionnaire may be either mailed to the respondent or handed to the respondent in person, and it is supposed to be completely sufficient in specifying what information is relevant and in motivating the respondent to write in the information.

An *interview schedule*, as the questionnaire, specifies the questions to be asked, fixes their wording, supplies contexts where the need is anticipated, and determines the degree of answer structure to be supplied by the interviewer. Here, the interviewer is still necessary. He or she is needed from time to time *(a)* to clarify the intent of the question, *(b)* to probe for any clarification or elaboration of the responses so as to meet the objectives of the interview, and *(c)* to motivate the respondent by demonstrating appropriate attitudes toward the interviewing task, the information received, or the respondent himself.

An *interview guide* is used in the nonscheduled interview. In contrast to the interview schedule, which emphasizes the *means* of obtaining information, the interview guide emphasizes the *goals* of the interview in terms of the topics to be explored and the criteria of a relevant and adequate response. The interview guide is like the interview schedule in that it provides the framework for recording the responses or for keeping a running inventory of which objectives have been met and which ones have not. Thus the interview guide provides the interviewer with a conceptual map of the areas to be covered and a convenient way of recording the progress of the interview.

In actual practice, plans made by the interviewer may fall at some point between the interview guide, which provides only the *goals*, and the interview schedule, which provides the *complete means* to the objectives of the interview. To give a typical example, an interview guide might contain not only the list of topics to be covered but also a tentative sequence for covering them, alternative wordings of some specific questions, notes indicating where contexts and transitions should be supplied, and possible sequences of detailed questions within topics which may or may not be needed in each interview.

It is advisable, even in an apparently simple interview topic, to prepare an interview guide before approaching the first respondent. This is fruitful even though it may be necessary to change the guide or to structure it in greater detail as a result of experience. In some cases, it is possible and desirable for the interviewer to memorize the interview guide. In other cases, the guide might be memorized except for an answer sheet upon which the respondent's open-ended answers are coded during the interview.

Thus far, we have examined some of the tactical problems in determining the optimum sequence of topics within an interview and of introducing new topics with lead-ins, pivot questions, and transitional statements. Let us now examine the tactical problems of guiding and motivating the respondent toward the objectives of a particular topic. Here some of the basic question patterns which can be used to develop a topic will be spelled out.

GENERAL PATTERNS OF QUESTIONS FOR DEVELOPING A TOPIC

It is usually not sufficient for the interviewer simply to have an interview guide listing the general objectives and subtopics of an interview, and then to ask only one question per topic. The interviewer must be constantly alert to guide the respondent toward the objectives of each topic by supplying any additional statements or questions to obtain further clarification or elaboration needed to meet the objectives of the interview. These additional questions, which are not specified in advance for all respondents but which the interviewer sees are needed to obtain more exact information, are usually referred to as "probes."

This chapter will deal with some of the basic patterns of questions that can often be employed in developing a topic to minimize the necessity for probing, and the next chapter will discuss several patterns of probing, showing their strengths and weaknesses.

The two general patterns of questions to be dealt with here are the "funnel sequence" and the "inverted funnel sequence." Each is useful under certain specified conditions that may usually be determined in advance of a particular interview. Both of these sequences are patterns of question-scope described as a technique in the preceding chapter.

The Funnel Sequence

In the funnel sequence each successive question has a narrower *scope* than the previous one and is either included within or related to the previous question. This type of sequence may characterize the whole interview as a unit, but it is more likely to occur within particular topics or subtopics of the interview.

For example, if we were interested in discovering how people's views of social problems are related to the magazines they read, we might want to know what sorts of things the respondent thinks of as social problems, the relative seriousness of each, the amount of information the respondent has on the subject, the sources of the respondent's information, and whether certain magazines have influenced his or her thinking on the problem. If we were to ask the following questions, the sequence given below would be a funnel sequence.

1.   What do you think are some of the most important social problems in the world today, and why?

2.   Of all the problems you have just mentioned, which one do you think is the most important one to solve?

3.   Where have you gotten most of your information about problem X?

4.   Do you read *U.S. News and World Report?*

The above example might be more accurately described as two funnel sequences, since the scope of question 2 is clearly within that of question 1, and the scope of question 4 falls within question 3, but it is not clear that the scope of question 3 falls within that of question 2.

There are several situations in which the funnel sequence will avoid tactical problems and minimize the need for probing. We will discuss the four most important ones.

1.   When the objective of the interview is to obtain a detailed description of an event or situation and when the respondent is motivated to give a spontaneous account of his or her experiences in that situation, then introducing the topic with the broadest question will often eliminate the need for asking myriad, detailed questions.

Under the above conditions it is more efficient if we can avoid asking every detailed question; also, it is often more conducive to good interpersonal relations, since the interviewer interrupts the respondent less and is apparently interested in whatever is important to the respondent. Of course, there is always the danger of the broad question allowing the respondent to roam too far afield, but the alert interviewer can prevent this with fewer interruptions that if he or she had to ask every minute question.

For example, if we wish to know hundreds of details regarding a person's experience when his town was struck by a tornado, we could either begin by asking detailed questions such as, "Were you home when the tornado struck?" "Did you see the black funnel approaching before it struck?" "What did it do to your house?" "Are you married?" "Do you have any children?" "Were any of your immediate family injured?" "Were you injured?" "Did anyone help you after the tornado passed?" "Did you help anyone else?" "Were you able to take anyone to the hospital?" This approach would be much less efficient and much less likely to give the respondent an opportunity for recognition, sympathetic understanding, and catharsis, or to fulfill his need for meaning than if the interviewer had simply asked, "What happened to you in the storm?" This question is not only broad, it puts the spotlight on the respondent's experiences and allows him to tell his own story in his own way. It shows that the interviewer is interested in the respondent and his experiences rather than in countless details.

   2.   Under the conditions specified in (1) above, the funnel approach helps the respondent to recall details more efficiently, since he is allowed to report them by following his own paths of association.

   By giving the respondent greater freedom at the beginning, it is not necessary to interrupt his train of thought constantly to ask hundreds of specific details in an order which might be meaningless or disorganized from the respondent's point of view.

   3.   By asking the broadest questions first, the interviewer can avoid imposing a perspective or frame of reference upon the discussion before obtaining the respondent's perspective.

   Once the respondent's perspective is discovered, the specific questions can be asked within this framework. Then the detailed questions could be worded to conform to the respondent's universe of discourse. Or it could be used where the broader question would allow the respondent to show the sequence in which he had certain experiences; the more detailed questions would then deal with each experience in order.

   4.   When the objectives of the interview are both to *discover* unanticipated responses and to *measure* the frequency of responses to certain anticipated categories, then the discovery function achieved by the broader question should be pursued first.

   For example, we might wish to discover the variety of reasons people have for wanting to go abroad, regardless of where they would like to go. If we also wanted to measure the relative frequency of people's preferences for Mexico, Germany, and France as a place to go, then the questions should be dealt with in that order. In this case, the funnel would consist in the sequence of the two objectives or subtopics, rather than in a sequence of specific questions. The first objective would probably have to be pursued with many questions and probes before moving on to the second which could be achieved with one well-worded question.

The Inverted Funnel Sequence

Under the heading, "Delimiting the Scope of the Question," Chapter 13 discussed the conditions under which the narrow question is preferable to the broad question. That discussion considered only the isolated question. Here we will restrict the discussion to cases where a *pattern* of narrower questions followed by broader ones should be used. The phrase "inverted funnel" is borrowed from Kahn and Cannell.[2]

There are at least two kinds of situations in which detailed questions should be followed by broader questions:

1. When the topic of the interview is one which does not strongly motivate the respondent to speak spontaneously, either because the relevant experiences are not important to him or her or not recent enough to be vivid in the respondent's memory, it is often helpful to begin with the narrower questions and reserve the broader ones until later.

It seems that the more specific questions are easier to answer than the more general ones when the respondent does not have strong positive motivation to speak on the topic. Often a respondent's feeling of inadequacy can be dispelled if he starts successfully with the simpler tasks and receives praise.

This inverted funnel often motivates the respondent to take an interest in the topic if the initial, specific questions stimulate his or her need for meaning. This form of intellectual seduction is most successful when the specific questions can be readily answered but where the answers themselves are either contradictory, inconsistent, or unsatisfactory to the respondent for some reason. The logic of the respondent's answers may violate his or her value system. These initial disturbances of mental equilibrium may rouse the respondent from complacency and stimulate the respondent to respond more wholeheartedly to broader and more profound questions.

The second situation calling for the inverted funnel deals with the problem of avoiding inferential confusion.

2. If the objective of the interview is to obtain a generalization in the form of a judgment regarding some concrete situation, and if the facts of the situation are unknown to the interviewer but are known to the respondent, then the narrower questions aimed at establishing specific facts should precede the request for an overall judgment.

Two kinds of situations require the inverted funnel tactic to avoid inferential confusion. The first, mentioned by Kahn and Cannell, is the case where the respondent has no strong feeling regarding the topic or does not have a previously formulated judgment of the type sought in

---

[2]Robert L. Kahn and Charles F. Cannell, *The Dynamics of Interviewing* (New York: John Wiley & Sons, 1957, p. 160; Malabar, Fla.: Krieger Publishing Co., reprint 1983).

the interview. The interviewer's task is to help the respondent formulate a generalization by making inferences from specific facts.

In the second type of case, the respondent may have very definite feelings on the topic and a previously formulated judgment based upon prejudice rather than the facts of the case. Here, the interviewer aims at preventing the respondent from stating a prejudicial judgment before reviewing the facts of the case. Once the respondent has stated his or her position to the interviewer, any attempt to change it constitutes an ego threat. By first reviewing the facts in detail, the respondent is allowed an opportunity to change positions without appearing to have been influenced by the interviewer.

The latter type of problem was encountered in attempts to obtain a respondent's judgment regarding the effectiveness of the rescue operations during a disaster. There was a prejudice that became strongly fixed two or three days after a major disaster that made people say that the rescue operations were carried out with miraculous speed and effectiveness. This was particularly true in communities where no organized agency involving outsiders was participating in the rescue operation. In this case, it was better to deal with the specifics first, later asking for the generalization:

1. How many people were killed in the tornado?

2. How many do you suppose were injured so seriously that they had to go to the hospital?

3. Was there a need for blood transfusions at the hospital the next morning?

4. How do you think that most of the people died (electrocution, internal injuries, brain concussions, bleeding, asphyxia, or what other cause)?

5. How long was it before most of the injured got to the hospital?

6. Did you see anyone administer first aid by giving artificial respiration or stopping bleeding? Who was it?

7. Did you have an opportunity to give any first aid yourself? If so, what kind?

8. In general, how well do you think the first aid and rescue operations were carried out?

If this eighth question were asked first, the respondent had a tendency to base the generalization on wishful thinking. The respondent was glad to be alive, and began to feel that it was miraculous that only fifty people were killed in a town of 3,000 where 90 percent of the buildings had been demolished. With this context in mind, the respondent's reply was that the first aid and rescue operation was something close to a miracle.

However, if the general question were preceded by the seven more specific questions, the respondent's account of the rescue operation would show that people were dug out of the rubble, and the seriously injured laid in rows beside the road waiting for it to be cleared so a truck or ambulance could get through. Once a victim was lined up for the ambulance, the rescuers would go back to dig someone else out. It was rainy and cold; there was often a lapse of one or two hours before a person could be taken to the hospital, and in the meantime the respondent had neither seen nor heard of anyone stopping bleeding or giving other first aid. When this picture began to emerge, the respondent became acutely aware that many people must have bled to death or died of shock while lying in the rain.

In this case, the inverted funnel sequence had the effect of making the respondent able to give a more realistic assessment of the situation, but the ego threat involved in the awful conclusion based upon the evidence the respondent himself had given would often reduce the respondent's willingness to verbalize what was on his or her mind and subject the respondent to an unnecessary shock. In this case, since the objective was not to have the respondent himself assess the factual evidence, the evidence given by the respondent could be assessed by the interviewer and the last general question omitted. In order to further protect the respondent's ego and avoid a possible breakdown in the rapport, the first five questions in the series could be asked of the hospital officials who would not blame themselves for not having given artificial respiration or having stopped bleeding in the few minutes after the disaster struck. This example illustrates how a specific tactical pattern may be technically effective, but in certain situations have an unfortunate side effect when tested in the field.

Some of the conditions have been shown under which the use of the funnel, or the inverted funnel, pattern can solve certain tactical problems. Regardless of the way the relative scope of questions is arranged in the interview, there still remains a certain amount of probing to be done to adequately meet the objectives.

SUMMARY

This chapter has been concerned with the type of tactics that can be preplanned to some extent, depending upon the nature of the topic, the extent to which the researcher has clarified objectives, the amount of exploratory field testing that has been done, and the strategic setting of the interviewing.

In many thoroughgoing studies using depth interviews an excellent interview schedule is developed over a period of time by beginning with the most unstructured, exploratory interviewing and then gradually structuring the interview schedule as the information objectives become more precise and the potential facilitators and inhibitors are defined. In the beginning of this developmental process the tactics are not pre-planned, while in the final phase of exploration the interview guide is re-fined and structured into an interview schedule with most of the tactics planned in advance.

This advance chronological structuring of the interview schedule involves selecting the most appropriate order of topics and subtopics so that ego threat will be avoided, the memory stimulated, and facilitators maximized. Once the sequence of topics is determined, then we must determine where we need lead-in questions, pivot questions, and transi-tional statements. Within any subtopic we also should be alert to the relative value of a funnel sequence beginning with broad-scope ques-tions and becoming progressively narrower, versus the inverted funnel which begins with the most specific and then ends with the most general, or broad-scope, questions.

This chapter has concentrated on the types of tactical patterns which can be built into the interview schedule and the general process by which the pattern is determined. Yet there is another phase of tactics that cannot and should not be structured in advance. This is the inter-viewer's probing to obtain complete and valid information in response to a particular question. This is a necessary phase in the development of even the most structured interview, and it may be the *major* tactic in in-terviews that cannot be structured in advance. In these situations the in-terviewer's probing skills are tested to the utmost. This important tacti-cal probing is the focus of the next chapter.

DISCUSSION QUESTIONS

1. How does the chronological arrangement of topics, subtopics, and questions in the interview potentially affect the results? Give an ex-ample.

2. What is a *lead-in* question and what are some of its most important functions?

3. What is a *pivot* question? What other names does it have?

4. What are some of the most important functions of *transition* state-ments?

5. What is the difference between the *interview guide* and the *inter-view schedule*?

6. What is a *funnel sequence,* and what is its most important function in the interview?

7. What is an *inverted funnel* sequence, and what is its most important function in the interview?

8. Under what circumstances are *tactics* the least prestructured?

Chapter Sixteen

Probing to Meet Informational Objectives

A probe can be defined as a form of verbal or nonverbal behavior used by the interviewer when the respondent's reply to the question is not relevant, clear, and complete. The interviewer does not know in advance whether a probe will be needed or what form of probe will be most appropriate. For this reason probing requires thinking on one's feet to keep the respondent moving toward the objectives of the interview.

PROBING VERSUS OTHER TACTICS

Probing is not the only tactic for obtaining needed elaboration or clarification of relevant information. The general idea of building rapport by minimizing the inhibitors and maximizing the facilitators of communication is assumed as a general background or atmosphere for the interview. But building rapport, making the respondent feel good, or getting the respondent to talk spontaneously is not a guarantee of relevant information. Nor is the giving of relevant information a guarantee that the information will be complete and clear. Probing is a way to get the respondent motivated and steered toward giving relevant, complete, and clear responses to meet the objectives of the interview.

Some interviewers use other tactics, such as sharing with the respondent their own ideas and experiences in the area being discussed to encourage the respondent to give a full and candid report. Others use the tactic of reflecting the respondent's words and feelings at those points that need elaboration and clarification. Experiments comparing the effectiveness of *probing, revealing,* and *reflecting* show that probing is the most effective, valid, and reliable tactic for this purpose.

Vonderacek did an experiment in which interviewers used probing, reflecting, and revealing as tactics for motivating respondents to reveal personal information about themselves.[1] Probing was the most productive tactic. Although there was a tendency for some respondents to engage in more self-disclosure than others, all gave more relevant information when the probing tactic was used.

Earlier we noted that one important attitude the interviewer must develop is critical listening in the sense that he or she must listen to the response to determine whether what the respondent is saying is relevant, complete, and unambiguous. If responses are not adequate in all of these ways, the interviewer must decide what to do about it.

The neophyte interviewer will often ask relevant questions and dutifully record the respondent's reply, but the interviewer's most common

FIGURE 16-1   Objectives, wording, and probing

Objectives (specified in the instructions to the interviewer)
Since the shooting of President Reagan there have been various attempts to legislate restrictions on the sale and possession of firearms to private citizens. We want to know how people now feel on this topic six months after the assassination attempt, without being reminded by the interviewer of the use of guns to assassinate public figures. We are interested in discovering *what* the respondent thinks *should* be done in this controversial area. We are not interested in what he thinks *others* want to have done, *why* he feels something should be done, or *how* he thinks it could be done.

The question (the seventh question in the interview schedule).
7. What do you think should be done, if anything, to regulate the sale of guns and rifles and other firearms to private citizens?

Possible probing instructions (immediately following the question).
1. Probe (for what respondent thinks should be done).
2. Probe if needed. Examples:
    What do *you*, personally, think should be done?
    Should anything be done or not?
    What, for example, should be done?
    Should anything else be done?

Some inadequate responses which need to be probed.
1. I really think it is time to do something about it!
2. There has been a lot of talk about that lately.
3. I agree, something should be done quickly!
4. I hope something will be done but I doubt if it can.
5. The gun manufacturers aren't going to like any change.
6. The NRA (National Rifle Association) would object.
7. I personally feel the federal government should do something.
8. I haven't the foggiest notion what can be done.

---

[1]Fred Vonderacek, "The Manipulation of Self-Disclosure in an Experimental Interview Situation," *Journal of Psychology* 72 (1969), pp. 55–59.

weakness is in not realizing that the response is inadequate for the purposes of the interview. The interviewer may move from question to question with mechanical precision, ignorant of his or her failure; or the interviewer may realize the inadequacy of the answer but, not knowing how to probe, may either rush on in panic or attempt to elicit further information in a way that suggests responses and obtains biased information.

To avoid the meager results of the innocent, ritualistic plodding or of the panicky flight through the interview, the interviewer must not only be intimately acquainted with the specific objectives of the interview but also must be able to use skillfully a variety of probing tools when the occasion demands.

In the fixed-schedule interview, probing is usually restricted to those attempts of the interviewer to obtain a more relevant, complete, or clear answer to the immediately preceding question.

To illustrate probing within the scheduled interview the example in Figure 16–1 shows the relationship between the objective of a question, the actual wording of the question, probing instructions, and some inadequate responses that would require probing to meet the objectives.

An examination of this small sample of inadequate responses shows that it is impossible to specify the exact probes to meet every possible form of inadequate answer. Instead, the interviewer must have the objectives clearly in mind, carefully listen to evaluate the relevance and adequacy of the response, then probe to help the respondent provide more relevant information without restricting, distorting, or suggesting answers.

TOPIC CONTROL

When the objectives are more exploratory and the schedule less fixed, the interviewer has a broader responsibility in probing.[2] In this case the interviewer is free to decide whether to probe in order to clarify the response to a particular question before going on to the next or to take a probe note at the time and wait until later to probe to avoid inhibiting the respondent's momentum or interrupting the respondent's chain of associations. In the less structured interview, then, the probe may concern the immediately preceding response or any of the preceding responses. The following situation is one in which the interview is not

---

[2]Barbara S. Dohrenwend and Stephen A. Richardson, "Directiveness and Non-Directiveness in Research Interviewing: A Reformulation of the Problem," *Psychological Bulletin* 63, no. 5 (1963), pp. 475–85. This is a useful step forward in the conceptualization of the idea of directiveness in interviewing.

scheduled. It illustrates the need for a wider range of probing tools. This full range of probing we call "topic control."

A lawyer is questioning in his office a possible witness to an accident in which his client has been involved. He is trying to reconstruct the scene and assess the evidence for guilt.[3]

I: I need your help in getting a clearer picture of the accident. Could you tell me in your own words what happened?

R: Well, actually I didn't see much. (3) I just came out of Kronsky's pool hall when I heard some brakes screeching, and the cars plowed into each other at the corner.

At this point the interviewer can do a variety of things. The choices are endless, and the progress of the interview will depend upon the alternative chosen by the interviewer at this point. Among the many possible forms of probes are the following:

I: *a.*   Whose fault was it?
    b.   Where is Kronsky's exactly?
    c.   Just what did you see of the accident?
    d.   Tell me a little more about it.
    e.   Pause for three or four seconds.

Here, the range of probes varies. The most topic control is (*a*) where the focus of the discussion is shifted from "what happened" to "whose fault it was." This probe also demands a *specific* answer to what might be a highly complex question. The lowest degree of topic control is (*e*), which is a "silent probe." The success of this silence depends upon whether the respondent is actually intending to continue the story without waiting for a specific question and upon the interviewer's ability to show an interested, expectant attitude. It should be noted that the silent probe, if successful, allows the respondent to continue in the same trend of thought, to elaborate some previous response in greater detail, or to change the topic completely.

Probe (*b*) does not shift the focus outside the scope of the previous response, but narrows it to a specific detail, the location of Kronsky's pool hall. Probe (*c*) controls the topic less than (*b*) because it refers to the general area the respondent is already talking about and allows the respondent to select the particular details he or she wants to mention. Probe (*d*) exercises even less topic control than (*c*) because it does not narrow the boundaries of the discussion to what the respondent *saw;* thus, probe (*d*) would allow the respondent to continue the story, regardless of whether it dealt with what he or she had or had not seen, felt, heard, or inferred.

---

[3]The numbers in parentheses indicate the number of seconds of silence.

The examples of the opinion-poll interviewer and the lawyer illustrate how the variety of probing tactics the interviewer is allowed to use is greater as the interview is less structured by a fixed schedule. Of the seven types of topic control defined below, the first four can be used in both fixed-schedule and unscheduled interviews; the remaining three can be used only in less structured interviews.

Types of Topic Control

At this point we are not yet concerned with which of the possible probes would be the most productive, but are merely illustrating what is meant by degrees of topic control. In order to be able to discuss this aspect of interviewing technique, the following categories of topic control are listed and ranked in order of the degree of control with type 1 representing the least control. This rank order usually, but not always, holds true since it sometimes depends upon the *context* in which the probe occurs. The interviewer should learn to recognize and to manage the tendency to control either too strongly or too weakly.

1. Silent probe. The silent probe is a very useful technique which will allow the respondent to proceed in whatever direction is most interesting and meaningful. In a sense, it is the most neutral of all possible probes because it neither designates the area of the discussion nor structures the answer in any way. The interviewer must learn to distinguish between the "permissive pause," which is often very productive and the "embarrassing silence," which can be damaging to rapport.

2. Encouragement. This category includes all remarks, nonverbal noises, and gestures which indicate that the interviewer accepts what has been said and wishes the respondent to continue speaking without in any way specifying *what* the respondent should talk about. This includes such things as: "uh huh," "really," "I see," "hmmm," "is that so!" a nod of the head, or an expectant facial expression.

3. Immediate elaboration. The interviewer may go beyond encouraging the respondent to continue speaking by indicating that the respondent should elaborate upon the topic at hand, whatever that topic may be. A request for elaboration may take several forms. First, elaboration might imply a need for continuing the "story" or finishing the trend of thought. This would include such probes as, ". . . and then?" "Then what happened?" "What happened next?" Note that the interviewer is not asking for anything specific. Second, the elaboration might not imply a "moving on" with the story, but merely requests the respondent to say more about the topic at hand. For example: "Tell me more." "Tell me more about that." "Would you like to tell me a little more about that?" "What else could you say about that?" "Is there anything you would like to add?" "Could you spell that out a little more?" "Would you please elaborate on that?"

4. Immediate clarification. The clarification probe not only asks for more information on the topic under discussion, but it also specifies the kind of additional information that is needed. A request for clarification may take many specific forms of two general types. First, the interviewer might request that the respondent give a more detailed *sequence* of events, beginning at a certain point in the action described in the immediately preceding response. For example: "What happened right after you opened the door?" "Where were you just before the lights went out?" "What happened that night after you got home?" Second, the interviewer might probe for more detailed information on some specific aspect, rather than some particular period of time. This would include such probes as: "*When* did that happen?" "*How* did you find out about that?" "How did you *feel* when you saw the building collapse?" "*Why* do you suppose they did that?"

5. Retrospective elaboration. In this type of probe, the interviewer indicates a general interest in a topic that has been mentioned by the respondent some time previous to the immediately preceding response, but the interviewer does not specify *what* he or she wants to know about that topic. For example: "A while ago you said that your mother didn't want you to go out with girls when you were fifteen years old. Could you tell me more about that?" "Let's go back to the point where you had the argument with your high school chemistry teacher; tell me more about that." Note that the form of these probes is in essence the same as those under (3) above. The difference is that the topic referred to is *not* contained in the immediately preceding response but was further back in the interview.

6. Retrospective clarification. This type of probe specifies what additional information is needed as in type (4) above. The difference is that the area to be clarified was not contained in the immediately preceding response. Here, the topic is changed to one which has been mentioned by the respondent before the immediately preceding response, and the interviewer specifies what he or she wants to know about this topic. For example: "You told me how you looked out the window and saw this big black funnel and realized it was a tornado; what was the first thing you *did* when you saw the funnel?" "What did you say to your mother that first time she waited up for you and you got in late?" Note that here clarification has the same meaning as in type (4) above, but the *retrospective* clarification refers the respondent to a *previous* topic of discussion.

7. Mutation.[4] This type of probe introduces a new topic that cannot be construed to be an elaboration or clarification of any preceding response. The interviewer takes the initiative in introducing the new topic, rather than waiting for the respondent to lead into it naturally. Sometimes the interviewer softens the abruptness of the transition by bridging it with some specific topic which has already been discussed or by showing how the new topic fits into the overall purpose of the interview. For example: "So far, you have given me a very good picture of how you and the rest of your family got along during the disaster, but I need to know something about what other people in the community were doing meanwhile; could you help me with that?"

The author's analysis of many interviews done by beginners shows the two most "natural" types of topic control are types 4 and 7. The other five types are relatively rare in the neophyte's interviews but are used more frequently once the neophyte becomes aware of their value. Usually the beginning interviewer is simply not aware of the wide range of topic control which is possible and so cannot consider the value of the various possibilities.

Using Topic Control

We cannot assume that the interviewer must always exercise strong topic control to attain the objectives of the interview efficiently. In some types of interviews, strong topic control may lower the respondent's motivation; it may also degenerate the interview into a "battle of wits" or into a rigid question-answer session in which the respondent plays a passive role; or it may prevent the interviewer's obtaining the respondent's own frame of reference on the topic, or tend to bias the response by suggesting certain contexts or answer categories.

In other interviews, it may be appropriate to exercise strong topic control because a low level of respondent motivation is already present, or because the respondent's task is simply to give a few salient facts such as name, address, and occupation. Or the topic may be such that if the respondent were given great freedom he or she would tend to give much irrelevant information.

It must be remembered that even though low topic control may be useful in building rapport, it also may fail to obtain all the relevant

---

[4]This term was borrowed from Merton and is used in the same general way as in Robert K. Merton, "The Focused Interview," *American Journal of Sociology* 51 (May 1946).

information. In some cases, low topic control may make the respondent feel insecure because of not being sure what information is wanted. This insecurity can grow into hostility when the respondent feels that the interviewer has no clear objectives and is merely wasting time in chitchat. As we consider some of the values and dangers of each type of topic control, it will become apparent that most interviews call for a wide range of topic control.

Values of the silent probe. The silent probe, rarely used by the beginner, has several legitimate functions. Since it exercises absolutely no topic control, it allows the respondent to follow a path of associations. This is useful when discovering associations is a purpose of the interview, or when the respondent needs to refresh his or her memory by telling the story his or her own way. The liberal use of silence also helps to establish a slower pace and a more thoughtful mood. Then, too, the only sure way to know that we are not interrupting the respondent is to use a silent probe before trying a verbal probe. Using the silent probe also gives the interviewer time to think of the most appropriate verbal probe (which is often not needed because the silent probe itself is successful).

Of course, there is a danger in using too much silence at the wrong point in the interview. For example, if the respondent is not eager to say anything, does not know exactly what the interviewer expects, and feels a need for some support and direction from the interviewer, then the pregnant pause becomes an embarrassing silence.

Values of neutral probes. The term "neutral probe" refers to two types of topic control, the encouragement probe and the elaboration probe. Both are neutral in the sense that their wording does not tell the respondent what information is desired. They merely imply that the interviewer understands and accepts what has been said and wants to hear more.

When the respondent actually has more information to give, the neutral probe has several advantages. Like the silent probe, the neutral verbal probes give the respondent freedom in following his or her own paths of association. The neutral probes also imply a strong interest in what the respondent is saying. Unlike the silent probe, they give the interviewer more opportunity to communicate positive attitudes through the tone of voice used. The interviewer can give the respondent recognition, show sympathetic understanding, and allow the respondent to obtain catharsis when the need is there.

Perhaps the most important value of neutral probes is realized when they are used to follow up a broad question. When the broad-scope question is more appropriate than a series of narrow and specific questions, we need some way of motivating the respondent to continue

speaking on the broad topic without having to suggest specific subques-
tions. As explained earlier, the value of the broad question lies *(a)* in its
ability to obtain specific bits of information without pointing out any
ego-threatening relationships between them and *(b)* in allowing the respondent to provide his or her own context, frame of reference, or perspective on these specifics without a barrage of detailed questions interrupting the respondent's trend of thought. The interviewer needs a
tactic which motivates the respondent to elaborate further but does not
control the path the respondent takes. This is the unique value of the
neutral probe.

Another important tactical function of the neutral probe is to give
the interviewer time to formulate a more specific probe which is appropriate. Often, tactical errors are made when the interviewer is caught by
surprise and blurts out some specific question that is inappropriate. A
great deal of concentration is demanded of the interviewer; he or she
must show an interest in the respondent as a person, listen carefully to
what is being said at the moment, evaluate the relevance of the information, and constantly reformulate probes that might be needed in case
the respondent stops talking. Needless to say, there are times when the
respondent stops talking at an inopportune moment when the interviewer is not clear on what to probe. In this case, the ability to use a
spontaneous neutral probe that fits the context of the interview is a
great boon. It relieves the interviewer of the fear of being caught unprepared and inadvertently biasing the response or damaging rapport. Of
course, the interviewer's nonverbal communication must not indicate
that he or she is caught unprepared or is using a time-stalling tactic. This
tactic should not be used so frequently that topic control becomes weak
when it should be strong. In most cases, even if the neutral probe does
not succeed in eliciting the desired information, neither does it interrupt
the respondent's trend of thought. Furthermore, it allows the interviewer
time to organize his or her own thoughts. This function of the neutral
probe can only be fully appreciated by those with experience in nonscheduled interviewing.

Of the two types of neutral probes (encouragement and elaboration), it will be noted that elaboration probes exert more topic control
than encouragement probes. The former must at least indicate whether
the respondent is expected to "move on" with the story or to elaborate
the current theme, while the encouragement probe merely indicates that
the respondent should keep talking. It is possible, however, that neither
one of these neutral probes will furnish the respondent with the guidance and support he or she needs. The interviewer must be sensitive to
the respondent's reaction to low topic control and not allow the respondent to develop a feeling of insecurity or hostility toward the interviewer.

In general, making encouraging noises and facial expressions both
supports and spurs the respondent to give a more complete and detailed

account. Matarazzo did an interesting experiment in which all conditions of the interviews were the same except that during the second of three fifteen-minute periods in each interview the interviewer said "hmmm" "uh huh" all the time the respondent was talking.[5] The results showed a 31 percent increase in the average duration of the respondent's utterances.

It should be recognized that when encouragement takes the form of praising the respondent for a specific response by saying "Good!," for example, we are exerting considerable topic control regardless of whether or not the respondent feels that these comments influence his or her answers. We should distinguish between encouragement by showing an interest in the respondent's efforts and in whatever he or she may say and showing interest by praising specific comments of the respondent which may bias the results as shown in an experiment by Hildum and Brown.[6]

Elaboration versus clarification. It is obvious that the clarification probe exerts more topic control than the elaboration probe because the latter merely indicates that the respondent should continue on the current theme while the former singles out some particular aspect of the previous response for clarification.

The elaboration probe is most useful in cases where the objective of the interview is to obtain detailed descriptions of objective situations or of subjective reactions and orientations. It is also helpful where the respondent is willing and able to elaborate without undue strain or without resorting to fabrication in order to fill the vacuum. Under these conditions the elaboration probe has two distinct advantages over the clarification probe: (*a*) It allows the interviewer to obtain specific details he or she might never think to ask for and (*b*) it often elicits the answer to several detailed questions without the interviewer's having to ask them. Clarification probes, both immediate and retrospective, will be needed after the elaboration probes reach a point where they are not producing much relevant information.

There are conditions where the clarification probes should be used without first trying elaboration probes. If the objectives of the interview call for only a few isolated facts, not related in the respondent's mind to a particular topic, period of time, or event, then the tactic of using specific questions followed by clarification probes where needed is more efficient and less threatening to the respondent's ego.

---

[5]Joseph Matarazzo, "Interviewer Mm-Humm and Interviewee Speech Duration," *Psychotherapy: Therapy, Research and Practice* 1 (1964), pp. 109–14.

[6]D. C. Hildum and R. W. Brown, "Verbal Reinforcement and Interviewer Bias," *Journal of Abnormal and Social Psychology* 52 (July 1956), pp. 100–111.

Immediate versus retrospective probes. The distinction between an *immediate* and a *retrospective* elaboration or clarification might seem arbitrary in that the immediate probe is related to the immediately preceding response while the retrospective probe is related to *any* of the responses before the immediately preceding one. Even though the range of choice in formulating retrospective probes is much greater than it is with immediate probes, in actual practice the distinction between the two seems to be more important than differences within either category. From the respondent's point of view, any probe regarding the current theme exerts less topic control then reverting to some previously mentioned topic. This, in turn, exerts less topic control than a mutation—changing the subject to some new topic not yet mentioned by the respondent.

An important tactical decision must be made repeatedly. Should each elaboration or clarification be obtained immediately, before the respondent can move on to other topics? Or should it be delayed until the respondent's momentum wanes or the topic has been covered as completely as possible with the use of only silent and encouraging probes? When the interviewer decides to wait until later to return to the theme at hand, he or she is exchanging less topic control early in the interview for more topic control later.

The question then becomes, when should the interviewer postpone the probing until later in the interview and when should the interviewer probe immediately for elaboration or clarification? In making this tactical judgment the interviewer should probably postpone the probe until later, if:

1. The objectives of the interview call for a wealth of detail, including some "unanticipated" information which the interviewer would not think to ask for specifically.

2. Topics, subtopics, or questions are so interrelated that there are opportunities for the respondent to give several needed specifics in response to subsequent general questions.

3. The topic is one in which the respondent can be motivated to talk fairly spontaneously in response to broad questions.

4. There is a danger that too many interruptions for needed clarifications might inhibit the respondent's spontaneity, as is often the case early in an interview.

Conditions 1 and 2 depend mainly upon the nature of the problem and are, therefore, more constant throughout the whole interview. Conditions 3 and 4 tend to fluctuate from moment to moment and therefore require the interviewer to vary the amount of topic control he uses.

Whether using an immediate or retrospective probe, the following precautions should be observed:

1. Do not interrupt the respondent in order to probe; wait until you are sure the respondent has finished the current thought. If you intend to use an immediate elaboration probe, it might be well to first use a silent probe in case it will accomplish the same purpose.

2. Be careful that your probe doesn't give the impression that you have failed to hear something the respondent has said.

3. Use the respondent's own words whenever possible in referring to something he or she has said.

The following illustrates the difference between a good and a bad probe for immediate clarification.

Example of good clarification probe:[7]

R: In general, I got along fine with both of my parents. We lived out in the country and I went to high school on the bus, so none of the kids came to my house. Of course, we had a little skirmish now and then, but basically I liked my parents and they liked me, even when I was a wild teenager.

I: I see. (3) Tell me a little about some of the skirmishes you had now and then. What were they about?

R: Well, there weren't too many of them. (3) I remember one when I wanted to use the car to go to a basketball game and Dad wanted to go to a Grange meeting. We finally compromised and he took me to the game and I went home with someone else so he could go to the Grange meeting.

Example of bad clarification probe:

R: By the time I was a senior in high school I guess I gave my folks a rough time now and then. I don't know who I thought I was kidding, because I always came out second best and usually cut off my nose to spite my face.

I: Why do you suppose you usually lost the battle?

R: I wouldn't say I lost the battle because there wasn't really any open fight. I was just stubborn and wouldn't do things just because I thought my folks wanted me to.

---

[7]The numbers in parentheses indicate the number of seconds of silence.

Although using the right tactic does not always guarantee complete success, these two excerpts are typical of the tactics and the results obtained by two different interviewers working on the same study of parent-child conflict in families with teenage children. Note that both interviewers are trying to obtain more specific description of some concrete conflict situation. The first interviewer actually has two probes in one in that he first gives an encouraging "I see" followed by a three-second silent probe. He then makes it clear that he has been listening and is interested by using the respondent's own key word, "skirmishes," in phrasing the probe. In return, the respondent gives some detail regarding a concrete instance of conflict with his father.

The second interviewer has precisely the same problem as the first, in that the previous response was general, vague, and unclear. However, his attempt to clarify is unsuccessful for several possible reasons. First, he interrupts the respondent to ask the question (since he allowed no silence before probing); second, he does not use the respondent's own words in phrasing the probe. Instead of asking, "How did you give your folks a rough time?" he attempts to paraphrase what he thinks is the central idea of the response. This paraphrase is perceived as inaccurate by the respondent who, instead of giving any concrete information, defensively denies that there was a "battle."

The interviewer must take particular care to prevent giving the impression that he or she has not heard or remembered pertinent information when using retrospective probes. It is also probably more important to use the words of the respondent so that the respondent can immediately recognize the exact point the interviewer is probing. Sometimes it is helpful to preface the retrospective probe with a contextual statement which provides a clearer orientation to the past point being probed and which gives the respondent recognition for information already given on the particular point. For example:

I: Very good! Now let's go back to the point where you had the first disagreement with your parents over dating. You mentioned that you wanted to take this girl to the strawberry festival and your mother objected. Tell me a little more about that situation.

This is infinitely better than the following probe, which indicates a certain degree of insensitivity to the problem from the respondent's point of view:

I: Now tell me something about any disagreements you had with your parents over dating!

This probe does not show the respondent that the interviewer heard, remembered, and appreciated information already given, nor does it provide a concrete "handle" for the respondent's memory to grasp.

The recapitulation probe. The recapitulation probe is a special form of the retrospective elaboration probe which takes the respondent back to the *beginning* of the time period covered by the interview. This return to the beginning of the story is a tactic which has many advantages when used correctly under appropriate conditions.

The recapitulation probe is subject to all the same conditions and precautions as any retrospective probe, plus one additional condition. The topic must be one which the respondent tends to elaborate as a chronologically organized story. There are many types of topics in which the respondent tends to relate events in chronological order, particularly when encouraged by the interviewer to do so. A person's life history or any aspect of it such as marital relations, car-buying habits, experiences in a crisis, account of an accident he or she has witnessed, views of the changes in the social structure of the community, or political behavior—all may be elicited in story form.

The following three examples of recapitulation probes are taken respectively from interviews on human behavior in disasters, car-buying motivations, and development of delinquency behavior. After each of these interviews had been under way from twenty to forty-five minutes, these recapitulation probes proved particularly useful:

You said that the sky turned sort of yellow-green and you looked out the kitchen window and saw this black funnel coming toward you. Can you tell me more about that moment?

You mentioned that the first time you drove a car was when you learned to drive a jeep in the army in Colorado. You said it gave you a good feeling. Tell me more about how you felt about driving the jeep.

Now the first time you remember ever "lifting" anything was when you were about eleven years old and used to steal candy bars and pocket knives from Schmidt's Drugstore. Could you tell me more about the gang of kids you ran around with then?

Where there is a tendency for the respondent to relate experiences in story form, he or she will usually add new detail to the story the second time through. In order to help the respondent cover the whole time period again, it is usually necessary for the interviewer to follow the recapitulation probe with a series of silent probes and neutral probes designed to keep the respondent moving forward in the story. Thus, if the respondent has once covered the relevant period of time but omitted thirty needed details, the interviewer could either ask thirty specific questions or use one recapitulation tactic which might obtain fifteen to twenty-five of the needed details.

This natural tendency of the respondent to give further elaboration in the second telling of the story gives several important advantages to the recapitulation probe. It is often an efficient method of obtaining information since it reduces the number of interruptions of the respondent's thoughts and cuts down on the number of detailed probes needed. This also encourages spontaneity and aids the respondent's memory by giving the respondent freedom to associate events in his or her own way.

Another advantage is that this tactic provides an indirect way of obtaining material where a direct question would constitute an ego threat. For example, if the interviewer were to ask directly, "Did you remember to take the children with you when you ran from the burning building?" and if the respondent had been so panicky that he ran without them, the ego threat might cause him to falsify the report by simply answering "Yes." If the interviewer, instead, has the respondent give a detailed chronological account beginning with, "What happened when you first realized that the apartment was on fire?" and then follows with recapitulation probes, it may be obvious that the respondent did not actually think about his children until he saw a neighbor woman leading them out of the burning building.

The recapitulation probe is also an effective exploratory tactic which will maximize unanticipated responses by eliciting relevant information which the interviewer would never think to ask for.

A final and obvious advantage of the recapitulation probe is in obtaining a chronological picture of the respondent's covert or overt behavior. A series of recapitulation probes will often provide a crosscheck on the chronological order of specific events.

The reflective probe. We use the term "reflective" in a slightly broader sense than defined by Rogers, who emphasizes the reflection of the respondent's *feelings*.[8] Here, a reflective probe is any attempt by the interviewer to elicit additional information by repeating the respondent's implicit or explicit statement without including a direct question. In the following excerpt, the first, the third, and the last probes are all reflective.

R: The main reason I came to Antioch College was because of the combination of high academic standards and the work program. It appealed to me a lot.

I: It appealed to you a lot?

R: That's right.

I: Could you tell me a little more exactly why it had this appeal for you?

---

[8]Carl R. Rogers, "The Non-Directive Method as a Technique for Social Research," *American Journal of Sociology* 51 (1945), p. 143.

R: I don't know—it was just that the place sounded less stuffy and straitlaced than a lot of places, with just as good an academic program.

I: You don't like places that are stuffy and straitlaced?

R: You can say that again. A lot of places spend most of their time trying to work out a way of controlling the students, assuming that they are completely incapable of self-control. They have a housemother in every dorm, require class attendance because classes are so dull that no one would come if there wasn't a cut system, and they require chaperones at every party . . . that sort of thing.

I: Why do you suppose Antioch has less supervision by the administration?

R: Well it is part of the educational philosophy, and it would be ridiculous to send students all over the United States on jobs—New York, Los Angeles, Cabbage Key, and even Paris—where they are on their own and trusted to act like adults with no one to tell them when to go to bed, what to eat, and how to behave with the opposite sex, and then to treat them like children when they get back to campus.

I: Let me see if I have grasped the whole picture—you like a school with high academic standards, but which is not too straitlaced and operates on the assumption that college students can exercise self-control if they are not treated like children. These are the things you like about Antioch?

R: That hits it on the head. People go away to college because they want a chance to grow, to be autonomous as an adult should. I think this is a vital part of a liberal education.

Note that there is considerable variation in the form and function of the three reflective probes. Within our definition there are three subtypes of reflective probes which can be distinguished:

1. the *echo* probe, which simply repeats certain words from the previous response,

2. the *interpretive* probe, which does not literally repeat the respondent's words but attempts to reflect the meaning or feeling behind the words in the previous response, and

3. the *summary* probe, which might combine selected elements from a long previous response or from several previous responses.

It is possible to combine types (2) and (3) in the same probe as the interviewer has done in his last comments above. His first remark, "It appealed to you a lot?" is an example of the echo probe and his comment,

"You don't like places that are stuffy and straitlaced?" is an example of an interpretive probe where the interpretation is limited to explicitly stating implied feelings.

Under what conditions is each type of reflective probe likely to be useful in achieving the objectives of an interview? In his experience the author has found the simple echo probe to be relatively useless if the interviewer repeats the immediately preceding phrase which happens to have little emotional content for the respondent. The most typical response is, "That's right," "Yes," "Uh huh," "That's what I said," or something to that effect. If the interviewer repeatedly uses the echo probe with purely factual details that happen to occur at the end of a response, the respondent may feel that the interviewer is not listening closely or that the interviewer is being very mechanical. Regardless of whether the echo is in the form of a statement or whether it is given an upward inflection to imply a request for elaboration or clarification, the result is about the same. However, if the echoed phrase contains material of great emotional implications for the respondent, it is enough to start him or her elaborating the topic, probably because the respondent feels that the interviewer is aware of the importance of the particular phrase.

Similarly, when the reflective probe is one which interprets what is meant by a statement or what feeling is implied by the statement, the respondent feels that the interviewer is interested in what is being said, and responds empathically to the feelings behind what is being said. It is more important to note that the attitude expressed by the interviewer in interpreting the respondent's feelings must be nonjudgmental or sympathetic. If the tone is even slightly accusing or rejecting, it would be better if the feelings were left unreflected.

There are times when the *correct* interpretation and reflection of the respondent's feelings may damage rapport. This is true when the feeling is socially unacceptable (for example, hating one's mother) and the respondent is not yet ready to accept this feeling as his own. His repression of the feeling is complete enough to hide the feeling from himself, and he sincerely believes that the interviewer either has not been listening carefully or is projecting some of his own distorted ideas.

There is also always a danger that the interviewer may incorrectly reflect the respondent's words or implied feelings. This danger is probably greater in the interpretive-summary probe where the number of opportunities to make an error is greater. Richardson found in one experiment that only one out of forty-three times did the respondent correct the interviewer who made an incorrect summary of what had been said.[9] These uncorrected, distorted summaries lead to inaccurate

---

[9]Stephen A. Richardson, "Training in Field Relations Skills," *Journal of Social Issues* 8, no. 3 (1952).

information and, in some cases, a lowered rapport with the respondent, who feels that the interviewer does not understand what is being said.

There are other conditions under which the distorted summary would stimulate a voluminous and spontaneous response that would clarify and enrich the information obtained. On rare occasions, the author has found that a summary intentionally distorted to convey an incorrect picture which is less socially acceptable than the respondent's actual behavior may lead the respondent to elaborate upon his or her actual behavior to correct the interviewer's "misunderstanding." The conditions of success are very similar to those described in the earlier discussion of leading questions.

Mutations. Although a "mutation" is certainly a type and degree of topic control, it cannot properly be called a probe, since it is actually a general question introducing a new topic not yet discussed in the interview.

If a series of topics in an interview are interrelated in the respondent's mind, it is often possible for the interviewer to avoid using mutations to introduce the next topic or subtopic by allowing the respondent to take the lead in moving into the new topic. Whether or not such a smooth transition is desirable has already been discussed earlier in this chapter under the topic of transitions.

In general, the neophyte interviewer tends to use mutations too soon, before exhausting the relevant information on the current topic. Frequently, the beginner actually interrupts the respondent, who is still giving information relevant to the current topic, and rushes on to the next topic only to discover, when analyzing the interview data, that the first topic had been sketchily discussed.

It is helpful for the interviewer to get in the habit of asking himself whether the current topic is covered adequately before going on to a new one. Sometimes, if the current topic is complex, several precautions can be taken to avoid leaving it prematurely. First, the interviewer can obtain time to check the interview guide and the probe notes (which are described in the next section) by simply saying to the respondent, "Excuse me for a moment while I check to see if you have given me all the information I need. Meanwhile you might think of something else you would like to add on this topic before we move on." Or, if the interviewer is sure that all of the anticipated information has been obtained and wants to give the respondent one more chance to give some relevant but anticipated type of information, the interviewer can simply give a summary of what the respondent has said and ask if there is anything the respondent would like to change, revise, or add. Before going on to a mutation, the interviewer should always use a silent probe to be sure the respondent has nothing more to add.

There is one situation where it is appropriate to change the topic of discussion before exhausting the current one. This would be advisable when for some reason the respondent needs to be jolted out of some undesirable rut in the current topic by leaving it temporarily. For example, the respondent may have become defensive about the topic or may be fabricating information in an attempt to be consistent with a previous, incorrect statement or to meet what he or she thinks are the etiquette requirements or the interviewer's expectations. If the interviewer suspects this, it may be useful to act as though the topic has been covered satisfactorily and go on to some unrelated topic. Later, after the interviewer has had an opportunity to establish a more sympathetic atmosphere and to show interest in critically analyzing the information, the interviewer can then approach the old topic from a new angle so that the respondent will not revert to a defensive mood.

TAKING PROBE NOTES

Taking notes in an interview has two general functions. First, note-taking is a method of storing relevant information; and second, the notes are a tactical aid to remind the interviewer which areas have been adequately covered, what points need further elaboration or clarification, and what words the respondent used in talking about points that need further probing. We refer to notes serving the second purpose as "probe notes."

The distinction becomes clear in a nonscheduled interview in which the whole conversation is tape-recorded. Obviously, notes are not needed to store the information, since it is on the tape in complete and accurate form. Nevertheless, the experienced interviewer takes probe notes if the interview is complex enough to warrant the use of a tape recorder. The less scheduled the interview, the less topic control used, and the more complex the interview, the greater the need for probe notes.

Assuming that the nature of the interview calls for taking probe notes, there are several points of techniques to be observed if the notes are to be of maximum value:

1. The notes should not be voluminous but should include only key words or phrases to remind the interviewer of what the respondent has said.

2. These key phrases should be in the respondent's own words so that the interviewer who wishes to probe can use the respondent's own words.

3. The key phrases may either be written as a continuous story in the order given by the respondent, or may be recorded under

appropriate categories provided by the interview guide. In this case, the guide should provide ample space for notes under each category.

4. If certain ideas need further elaboration or clarification, the interviewer can underline or circle the key phrase as a reminder.

5. As these points are elaborated and clarified, with or without probing, the key phrases which had been underlined can be crossed out to indicate that a probe is no longer needed.

6. If the interview is not tape-recorded and the notes must, therefore, also act as a means of storing the information, it is helpful to take triple-spaced notes. The extra space allows the interviewer to fill in omitted words and phrases immediately after the interview.

This system of note-taking can be expanded, contracted, or modified, depending upon the complexity of the interview, the degree to which the interviewer is familiar with its objectives, and the amount of topic control called for.

Even when a tape recorder is used, the interviewer often finds it useful to make notes of all the main relevant ideas rather than trying to note only the points that need probing. There are three reasons for this. First, the interviewer is not always immediately aware that a particular idea needs probing; it may become problematical later when it apparently conflicts with subsequent information. Second, it is often easier to record all relevant key phrases than to decide which ones to omit or include. Third, in those inevitable times when the tape recorder malfunctions it may be necessary to reconstruct the interview from these notes. Such an emergency reconstruction is not valid in cases where the interview is long, the material complex and subtle, and only a very small portion of the relevant information is represented in the notes. In cases where the reconstruction is valid, it should be done immediately after completing the interview. For this reason the quality of the tape recording should always be checked immediately after each interview.

Considerable experience is needed before an interviewer can gauge the appropriate amount of note-taking in various types of interviews and before the interviewer can prevent its distracting him or her from listening carefully to the respondent. The skill lies in selecting only key phrases and words. In training interviewers, the author has found that the use of probe notes in tape-recorded interviews vastly decreases the amount of missing or ambiguous information in the nonscheduled interview.

SUMMARY

By knowing many forms of probes ranging in topic control from the silent probe through the mutation, the interviewer has a better chance of steering the respondent toward relevant, complete, and clear answers to the questions without damaging rapport or doing too much violence to the respondent's natural thought processes. The probe forms for the skilled interviewer are a set of fine tools used to deftly tease out relevant information without contaminating it by subtle suggestion or restriction. Each of the seven forms has its time and place for use.

The special strengths and weaknesses of each of the degrees of topic control were discussed, and several examples of probes falling into each level of topic control were given. The silent probe and the two types of neutral verbal probes are useful when minimal topic control is needed to avoid restricting the respondent, to allow the respondent to free-associate, and to encourage the respondent to build momentum and spontaneity. The immediate elaboration and clarification probes can be used when there is no danger of blocking the respondent's momentum, and the response to the current question can be brought up to specifications before moving on. If there is danger of damaging the spontaneity, the interviewer can refrain from probing immediately to complete the respondent's story, and wait until later, and use retrospective probes referring back to points which need to be clarified or elaborated.

Since retroactive probes may have to wait a long time, the interviewer must take probe notes as the interview progresses even if it is being tape-recorded. Then, when the respondent has covered all the high spots, the interviewer can lead the respondent back over the territory to elaborate and clarify certain points indicated in the probe notes.

All of this treatment of probing assumes that the respondent has not used any particular tactics of his or her own to resist the interviewer's probing. The next chapter will describe some tactics the interviewer can use to counter typical tactics of resistance sometimes used by the respondent.

DISCUSSION QUESTIONS

1   What is a probe? How does it differ from a question?

2. When probing, reflecting, and revealing have been compared as tactics for getting more relevant information, which usually works best?

3. In which type of interview is there the most need for probing? The least?

4.   What are some of the special values of the silent probe?

5.   What is an encouragement probe? Is there any evidence that it is effective?

6.   When is an elaboration probe more useful than a clarification probe?

7.   When is an immediate probe more useful than a retrospective probe?

8.   What is the special value of a recapitulation probe?

9.   Do you need to take probe notes if the interview is being tape-recorded? Why, or why not?

Selected Readings

The two references below have some of the most thorough treatments of probing to meet the objectives of the interview. Both overlap considerably with the concepts given in this book but use somewhat different language and give different types of examples.

Kahn, Robert L., and Charles F. Cannell. *The Dynamics of Interviewing: Theory, Tactics and Cases.* New York: John Wiley & Sons, 1957; Malabar, Fla.: Krieger Publishing Co., reprint 1983.
The most relevant portion is in Chapter 8, "Probing to Meet Objectives, that deals with clues to formulating good probe questions and tactics for handling inadequate responses. A variety of examples are given from medical, employment, and other types of interviews.

Richardson, Stephen A., et al. *Interviewing: Its Forms and Functions.* New York: Basic Books, 1965.
The most concentrated treatment of probing is in the section in Chapter 11, "Achieving Response Quality through the Question-Answer Process," in which the criteria of validity, relevance, specificity, clarity, and coverage are used to determine whether probing is needed. The problems of recognizing inadequate responses and probing are related to three types of interviews: the limited response, the free response, and the defensive response.

LABORATORY PROBLEM 9

Recognizing Forms of Probing (Vocational Choice)

PURPOSE

This problem provides an opportunity to clarify the *meaning* of the different probe forms and to *recognize* them as they occur in the context of a real interview. It will also help you to solidify the difference between *techniques* which can be classified without relevance to the larger context of the interview and *tactics* which involve the context. This is done by having you apply the tactical analysis to the same interview you analyzed for techniques earlier.

PROCEDURE

The following procedure, including the discussion, should take from one to two hours' time.

1. *Review* the meaning of the seven degrees of topic control described in this chapter.

2. *Read* the same vocational choice interview you analyzed for techniques in Laboratory Problem 8 at the end of Chapter Thirteen. This time concentrate on the forms of probing.

3. *Classify* the interviewer's probes, using the *Analysis Table* provided by your instructor. Do this independently and refer to the definitions in this chapter if necessary. Do this in *pencil* and enter the probe numbers in serial order, separated by commas (for example, 2, 7, 8, 15, 23, etc.) within each category to facilitate the comparison of Analysis Tables.

4. *Compare* your classifications with another person's, also done independently, and *discuss* any differences in classification.

5. *Revise* your classifications in those cases where you are convinced by the discussion that your original classification was incorrect.

6. *Submit* your revised *Analysis Table* to the instructor.

Note: You may not be able to arrive at perfect agreement in your classifications because of the ambiguity of some of the interviewer's behavior.

Chapter Seventeen

Dealing with Symptoms of Resistance

The phrase *symptoms of resistance* has been used advisedly (rather than *resistance*) to alert us to the fact that we cannot assume that certain overt verbal phrases always indicate actual resistance by the respondent. The phrase, "I don't remember," may simply be a statement of fact rather than an attempt to evade the interviewer's question. Or it may mean "I don't remember very much at the moment" or "Let's talk about it a bit and see if I can recall some more."

In general the tactical danger lies in the tendency of an inexperienced interviewer to respond to the symptom of possible resistance in a way which converts the possibility into reality, by activating ego threat, failing to help the respondent's recall process, and converting the interview into a battle of "I can't" versus "Yes, you can!"

In describing some of the typical symptoms of resistance by the respondent and in offering suggestions for countering them, we make no promises that the countertactic will always be effective. No experimental studies have been done of a large enough number of these countertactics to show clearly what accounts for their success or failure. The countertactics are offered as possible solutions when nothing obviously better occurs to the interviewer in the situation. Each symptom of resistance will be discussed in the order in which it is most likely to occur in the interview.

SPECIFIC COUNTERTACTICS

"I'm Too Busy Now!"

In situations where the interviewer contacts the respondent without a previous appointment, there is the possibility that the respondent will be too busy at the moment to cooperate or that the respondent will use this excuse when the real source of resistance may be lethargy, ego threat, or dislike of talking to strangers.

The tactics that are possible at this point depend, among other things, on whether (*a*) the respondent must be included in a sample or whether a substitution can be made and (*b*) whether it is possible for the interviewer to return at another time.

In some cases, the interviewer suspects the respondent is making an excuse, but it is necessary to interview this particular respondent. If it is possible for the interviewer to return, the following tactic may be effective in avoiding a return trip.

I: How do you do? I am Mr. Gregg. I'm helping with a study of the community which is being done by Metropolitan Studies, Inc. You have probably read in the Dayton Daily Times about how this study is going to help plan improvements in traffic, parking, and shopping problems.

R: I think I have heard something about it, but right now I am too busy to talk about it.

I: I see. I realize that you didn't expect me at this time. Since it is so important to talk to a wide sample of people, I will be willing to come back at any time you say—this week or next week, it doesn't matter.

R: Well, I don't know—let's see . . .

I: The interview doesn't take much time, we just want to know something about your shopping habits, where your children go to school, and that sort of thing.

R: Both of my children go to high school, and I don't even go downtown to shop any more since the new shopping center went in.

I: You have already answered two of the things I wanted to know. There are just a few more questions like that.

R: Well, if it won't take long, you might as well come in and let's get it over with and you won't have to come back.

I: Thank you very much.

When this tactic is used, the person who is really too busy but would be willing to talk will usually not hesitate to make an appointment. If the respondent actually has the time at the moment, but is hoping to turn the interviewer away, she realizes that this will not work since the interviewer will return again. Also, in this case, once the respondent knew the nature of the questions, she felt less threatened and decided to "get it over with."

In some cases, the interviewer has overcome resistance at this point by explaining how short the interview is; the importance of the project;

that the respondent need not stop working while answering the questions; that Mrs. X (a friend of the respondent's) warned that she would probably be very busy, but she would be able to give the needed information; or that it is very important to get the opinions of busy people rather than the leisure class.

Often, such a situation can be prevented if the interviewer is able to launch immediately into an initial question which rouses the respondent's interest, appeals to the respondent's ego, and shows that the interview is not difficult. This can sometimes be done even before a full explanation of the purpose of the study is given. The explanation can be given in installments where it is directly relevant to the information requested.

In rare cases in which the respondent is very fearful of the interview, he or she may make an appointment and then be out when the interviewer returns. This evasive tactic was found several times in a study of marital success, when making appointments with a few of the people who felt that their marriage had been a failure and did not want the interviewer to discover it.[1] In these cases, the interviewer learned to arrive for an appointment about fifteen minutes early. In some instances, the interviewer encountered the couple leaving their apartment house ten minutes before the appointment time.

When the respondent feels the pressure of competing time demands, persuading him or her to submit to the interview is sometimes of little value. The respondent who is neglecting his or her own work may feel tense and apprehensive throughout the interview. In these cases, the interviewer might suggest returning to finish the interview at another time.

"I Don't Know Anything about That!"

The interviewer who meets this phrase from the respondent just after finishing an explanation of the purpose of the interview or after asking the first question, may become a bit panicky. For example:

I: How do you do? I am Mrs. Karen. I am working with the Community Service in doing a study of people's opinions on antivivisection. Do you know what antivivisection means?

R: Oh yes, it has something to do with cutting animals that are alive. But I don't know a thing about it. Why don't you talk to my next-door neighbor? Her husband works at the drugstore and he knows all about that sort of thing. I just couldn't help you a bit.

---

[1] E. W. Burgess and Paul Wallin, *Engagement and Marriage* (Philadelphia: Lippincott, 1953).

I: But it's not necessary to know all about it. I just want to find out what people do know.

R: That's easy! I know nothing.

I: Oh, I'm sure you have something to say. You have probably seen it mentioned lately in the paper because there has been a big controversy over it.

R: I said I knew nothing about the subject . . . I think you should interview someone else. (slams door)

Compare the interviewer's performance above with the episode which follows:

I: How do you do? I'm Mrs. Gerhardt. I am working with the Community Service in doing a study of people's opinions on antivivisection. Do you know what antivivisection means?

R: Yes, vaguely. It deals with operating on live animals, but I don't know any more about it than that.

I: I see. Why do you suppose this is done?

R: I don't know. I suppose it is done to give medical students practice so that they won't have to practice on people.

I: Is there any other reason that anyone might operate on a live animal?

R: Well, of course, veterinarians operate on dogs when they are sick or to keep them from having puppies.

The contrast between these two episodes demonstrates a basic principle which emerged from experience with a wide variety of interviews: the interviewer should avoid challenging the respondent or even persuading the respondent to cooperate. In a sense, the first interviewer is almost demanding a declaration of surrender from the respondent before formally launching the interview. The second interviewer simply accepts the idea that the respondent knows very little about the topic, but proceeds immediately with a relevant question without formally declaring the interview started and without seemingly trying to persuade the respondent to surrender.

   If possible, the interviewer should focus the attention immediately on the respondent as in the following example:

I: How do you do? I am Mr. Black with the National Opinion Research Center. We are doing a study of how people manage in disasters in order to be of some help in planning for future disasters during either peace or war.

R: Well, I can't help you none because I wasn't even in Judsonia when the tornado struck.

I: I see. Where were you at the time?

R: I was all the way over in Searcy when I saw the big clouds over Judsonia way.

I: What did you think it was when you saw the clouds?

R: I was afraid to my bones that it was a twister. And I knowed that some of my family was here and I didn't know what was happening to them.

I: Then what did you do?

R: I got in the pickup truck and high-tailed it for home as fast as I could git. It seemed like a hundred miles because I was in a hurry and the road was full of all kinds of trees, telephone poles, and everything. I had to go off the road several times, but still couldn't get through with a car. I had to walk the last mile and a half. I just couldn't believe my eyes. With all the houses and the water tower blown away, I could hardly find the way to my house, or I should say the place where my house used to be . . .

As it was, the respondent was well on the way without having formally consented to the interview. The interviewer was able to put the spotlight on the respondent by asking, "Where were *you* at the time?" Instead of this, the interviewer could have gone into a long explanation of why he had to obtain a random sample, what a random sample was, and why the respondents who were not in the town at the moment the storm struck still had useful information. All of this would be more time-consuming and more likely to cause resistance in the respondent.

In the type of study where there is no need for a random sample and where we want to locate key respondents who can give an objective report of specific facts and events, we often should not attempt to persuade a reluctant respondent to cooperate by being interviewed. Instead the interviewer should ask him or her for advice on who might have the kind of information being sought.

"I Don't Want to Be on Tape!"

On rare occasions, respondents will consent to being interviewed but will object to having the interview tape-recorded. If after an explanation the respondent still objects, the interviewer's next move depends upon whether a tape recording is essential or merely convenient, and whether the respondent also objects to the interviewer's taking notes. If the former is not essential and the latter is permissible, then written notes are the solution.

It is sometimes helpful for the interviewer to clarify the nature of the respondent's objections so that they can be met. The interviewer can simply ask, "Would you mind telling me why you would prefer not to have the interview tape-recorded?" This question followed by some appropriate probes put in a sympathetic spirit has elicited responses such as the following:

1. I have heard some of these tape-recorded interviews with newspaper reporters on TV newscasts and they sound silly!

2. I don't want everybody hearing what I have to say. I don't mind telling you, but I don't know who else might hear it!

3. My voice sounds bad and I don't see any reason to preserve it for posterity.

4. I might say something that is not correct, or that I don't really mean, and there it is on the record forever.

The first response, if it is the genuine reason for the objection, can easily be overcome by explaining the difference between the purpose of the interviewer and of a news reporter. The second response and its variations can be dealt with by giving any of the following explanations when they are true: that no one but the interviewer will hear the tape; that the tape will be used over again after relevant information is taken off; that the transcribing will be done by people who are far away and do not know anyone interviewed in the study; that no exact quotes will be used; or that if quotes are used, the respondents will not be identified.

The third response can sometimes be overcome by reassuring the respondent that the tape does not sound like the real person since it is not high-fidelity. Or the interviewer might demonstrate how his or her own voice sounds on the recorder, then ask whether the respondent thinks it sounds like the real thing. The interviewer might record the response to this question and play it back to show the respondent that having one's voice recorded is not a painful experience. If the respondent's initial resistance seems to be giving way to curiosity, the interviewer might propose that they try recording the first two or three minutes, and then if it still seems to cause "stage-fright" it can be turned off.

The last response is closely related to the first two, but is more concerned with the apparent permanence of the responses when recorded or with the fact that the tape records precisely what the respondent says rather than what he or she really means. It could also indicate a fear that the interviewer might pressure the respondent into saying something he or she does not mean, or not give time for the respondent to carefully consider or to correct his or her own responses. In this case, several tactics have been found useful. The interviewer can suggest that the tape recorder be used and if at the end of the interview the respondent still feels the tape recording does not represent his or her views accurately the interviewer can either have the recording erased on the spot or suggest any corrections or additions after listening to it. In such a case, the respondent usually discovers in the progress of the interview that the interviewer is genuinely concerned with helping the respondent express his or her views as accurately as possible without high pressure tactics, and the respondent loses any desire to eliminate the tape recording.

In this type of situation the interviewer might need to check any possible inhibiting effects of the presence of the tape recorder by using an informal post-interview which is explained later.

"Why Are You Taking Notes?"

Even though the need for note-taking might have been explained at the outset of the interview, sometimes the respondent seems to become suddenly aware of the fact that the interviewer is taking notes. The respondent may ask directly why notes are being taken or may merely show nonverbally or indirectly that he or she is concerned. The respondent's concern may be only with the interviewer's recording a particular statement or it may be with note-taking in general. If the interview is being tape-recorded, the respondent might merely be curious about what the interviewer chooses to write down and what the interviewer chooses to omit.

The sensitive interviewer who detects the respondent's concern can discover what is bothering the respondent and give the appropriate explanation. Often, the respondent is satisfied by the interviewer's offer to show him the notes. This offer should not be made if the interviewer cannot follow through without endangering rapport. If the notes are in the respondent's own words and do not involve any interpretation or evaluation, there is little danger in showing them. Any suggestions the respondent might have should be accepted gracefully. Interviewers have discovered repeatedly that the main problem lies in being sensitive to symptoms of the need for an explanation of the note-taking. Once the explanation is given, the respondent is usually satisfied.

"I Don't Remember, I Don't Know!"

Often after the interview is well under way, the immediate response to a specific question is, "I don't know" or "I don't remember." Usually, this is not a form of resistance by the respondent but merely expression of modesty, tentativeness, or cautiousness with which many people preface an answer. Systematic analysis of tape-recorded interviews has shown that only rarely does the respondent literally mean that he or she does not know. It would be safer in many cases to translate this as "give me a moment to think." Apparently, the most successful tactic in this situation is to allow a moment's silence and show by your expression that you are assuming that the respondent is thinking. If this does not bring results, the interviewer can say something to the effect, "I realize that the question might be difficult to answer without some careful thought." Also, the interviewer can supply some cues in an attempt to aid the respondent's memory.

All of this will be unsuccessful if (*a*) the respondent never had the information, (*b*) it is deeply repressed or completely forgotten, or (*c*) the respondent has the information but does not want to give it because of ego threat, trauma, or etiquette. In the latter two situations, it is good to avoid directly pressing for the information and wait for recapitulation probes to either stimulate recall or to allow time for a more permissive relationship to be built up.

There are two general types of questions that will often obtain the "I don't know" response because the respondent feels unable to give a precise enough answer. One of these types is the question dealing with the future such as, "Is your daughter going to college next year?" or "Do you think that prices will be higher or lower six months from now?" If the objective of the interview is to obtain the respondent's best estimate, then the interviewer will have to encourage the respondent to do the best he or she can. If the respondent says "I don't know," the interviewer can say, "Well, of course, nobody knows for sure, but the way it looks now, what do you think?" Another type is the question which asks for some factual or quantitative information such as, "About how many hours per week do you watch television?" To encourage the respondent, the interviewer can say, for example, "I don't have to know exactly. What is your best guess?"

In some cases, "I don't know" represents a case of incipient resistance. Here it is better to avoid pressing for an answer and to merely accept the response at face value while continuing the discussion. For example, a Colombian interviewer is speaking to a Colombian housewife about the North American student who lived in her home for six months:

I: Was your North American guest the tidy type or not?

R: I don't know.

I: I see . . . you just didn't have an opportunity to observe!

R: Well, not exactly. . . I just don't know how to put it. Because I noticed a lot of things about her behavior in my house, but they are not consistent!

I: What do you mean by "not consistent"?

R: She was very neat in the way she dressed, but she always left the bathroom a mess in the morning. Also, she would make her bed very well, but would leave her shoes and slippers on the floor. She never put her books and papers away, but left them on the desk in her room.

In this case, the interviewer skillfully led the respondent into giving the answer without the dangers involved in not accepting the response by saying, for example, "Surely, you had some impression of her since she lived in your house for six months!"

"What Do You Think about That?"

There are several reasons why the respondent might ask the interviewer this question after the interview has been in progress for some time. The respondent might have already expressed an opinion on the matter and may feel uneasy about expressing himself so freely without knowing the interviewer's opinion. This is most likely to happen when discussing controversial issues. At other times, the question merely represents the natural desire to seek some responsiveness from the interviewer. It is also possible that the respondent is simply curious about the interviewer's position on the subject.

The basic problem is to find a way to satisfy the respondent so he or she will not feel rejected or feel that the interviewer is secretive, and yet avoid offering information which will inhibit or bias subsequent responses. If the respondent's question is in response to a straightforward fact question from the interviewer, and if it is clear that the respondent does not know the answer, the only danger in answering is that it might change the respondent's frame of reference. This is undesirable when the objectives of the interview include discovering the frame of reference used by the respondent. There is also the danger that the respondent might feel inferior or that he or she is being "tested" by someone who already knows all the answers.

In many circumstances it would be better for the interviewer to say something like, "I'm not sure about that, but even if I knew I'm not allowed to give my opinions. It is your opinion that counts." Or the interviewer could say, "I'm not allowed to try to influence you by giving my opinions. My job is to understand and respect your opinion." If the respondents in the study are not in communication with each other, if the interviewer has already used statements similar to those above more than once in the interview, and if there seems to be a danger of the rapport breaking down because of the interviewer's refusal to reciprocate, then the interviewer could say, "I'm not trying to keep any secret from you, but I'm not allowed to say anything to influence your answers. But

I will be very glad to answer any questions you have as soon as I get your opinions. I would enjoy that."

There are times when it is the best tactic for the interviewer to tell the respondent how he or she feels about the issue being discussed. However, this should be done only if (*a*) the interviewer is sure of the respondent's point of view on a particular issue, (*b*) if the interviewer agrees with some aspect of the respondent's point of view, (*c*) if the respondent exhibits a need for some support from the interviewer, and (*d*) if the interviewer agrees spontaneously and naturally. There is always the danger that the interviewer might miscalculate the respondent's point of view and thus unintentionally disagree with the respondent. This tactic should be used only when there is no danger that one respondent will communicate the interviewer's point of view to a future respondent. This condition often exists in studies of a random sample of people in a large metropolitan area.

"What Do You Mean by That?"

When the respondent asks this question in response to the interviewer's question, it may be a symptom of mild resistance in which the respondent is attempting to shift the attention back to the interviewer. It may also be a way for the respondent to stall for time while thinking of the answer or finding a way to avoid giving the answer. Perhaps the most common meaning is simply that the respondent is not sure what the interviewer's question means.

Regardless of the meaning behind the question, the interviewer must treat it as a simple request for clarification. The problem is to communicate the meaning of the question without suggesting an answer and without changing the meaning so that different representative respondents are asked different questions.

If the object of the interview is to discover the respondent's frame of reference for interpreting the question, the interviewer must avoid providing an interpretation. One tactic often used is to say that the question should be answered according to what it means to the respondent and then repeat the question in exactly the same words.

This tactic is of little value if the purpose of the question is to communicate a particular frame of reference for its interpretation, but the respondent does not understand it. In this situation it is sometimes helpful for the interviewer to ask, "Could you tell me what it is about the question that you are not sure about?" Often the respondent will then say, "I don't know whether you mean X or Y." If the clarification of these alternatives does not interfere with the purposes of the interview, the interviewer can say, "I mean X in this case." Or, the respondent may point to a specific phrase which is not clear in the context of the question. In this case, the question may be reworded or a more complete context provided so that the respondent understands how the information is to be related to other parts of the discussion. For example:

I: What attracted you to your present location in Ohio?

R: What do you mean, to the neighborhood where we live, or the plant where my husband works, or the school where the kids go?

I: That's right—you live here in Wright View and your husband works in Dayton, and the kids go to school in Fairborn. Take the whole situation; what did you hear about it while you were still in Harlan County that made you decide to leave Kentucky and come to Ohio?

R: That's easy! It was the job. My husband had some friends working in Dayton and they promised they could get him a steady job, and that's something he didn't have in Kentucky. He had worked only 5 ½ months last year and the pay was bad. We had a little patch of land for vegetables and raised chickens or we wouldn't have kept body and soul together.

It was fortunate that the respondent did not understand the first question above since it did not supply the clear context needed to be sure the respondent would answer the question in terms of what she knew about the Ohio situation *before* coming from Kentucky. It would have been easy for her to list a lot of specific things she liked about the neighborhood, the city of Dayton, her husband's work, and the children's school. Most of these would be irrelevant to the question of why the family left Kentucky and came to Ohio, since the details would have been learned *after* living in Ohio.

Sometimes the respondent does not understand a particular word in the question. In this case, the interviewer must be careful to reword the question so that it carries the original meaning. In the following excerpt, a representative of the Z Telephone Company is interviewing a subscriber regarding his attitude toward the service he is receiving and toward a possible rate increase. The interviewer rewords the question to avoid the word "subscriber":

I: How do you feel most subscribers feel about the kind of service they get from Z Telephone?

R: What's that got to do with telephones?

I: I should have said, how do you think most of the people who have telephones feel about the kind of service they get from Z Telephone?

R: As far as I know they have no kicks about it, and it is improving all the time.

The interviewer had assumed that the subscriber would be familiar with the word in connection with the telephone company since much of the literature included with the monthly bills had a salutation to the "subscriber."

It is often useful to give examples to clarify a question. Although they often save time and make the respondent feel secure, there is a danger that the illustrations might suggest an answer to the respondent or unintentionally narrow the scope of the question to the area suggested by the specific example. The following is a flagrant instance of such a biasing effect:

I: How do the officers show unnecessary superiority over the men?

R: What do you mean?

I: Well, for example, officers not introducing anyone but officers to girls at a public dance, or officers not going to a certain dance hall because too many enlisted men come.

R: Yes, that's right. They do just that!

It is sometimes safer to either give examples of what is *not* intended by the question or to supply the full range of abstract categories of behavior which would be considered relevant to the question. The following example combines both:

I: How do the officers show unnecessary superiority over the men?

R: I'm not sure what you mean!

I: I assume that for purely military reasons there must be difference in rank and authority to keep order under battle conditions. I wouldn't call that *unnecessary* display of superiority, but in other areas of peacetime military ritual, religious functions, social and recreational situations, housing arrangements for families, and that sort of thing.

R: Oh, I see. Let me think . . . in the social area there are a lot of distinctions which I feel are unnecessary.

I: Uh huh. Can you think of a specific case?

Regardless of the particular tactic used to clarify the meaning of a question, the interviewer should be alert to judge by the response whether the revised question has carried the intended meaning to the respondent. Sometimes several attempts at clarification are necessary before the respondent accurately grasps the question. This problem usually arises more frequently in the early exploratory stages of interviewing on a particular topic where many of the same questions are asked of different types of special respondents to obtain their differences in perspective. In this case a particular question may be very clear to one type of respondent and unclear to another.

The interviewer must also be alert for symptoms of the respondent's misunderstanding when the respondent is not aware of his or her confusion and, therefore, does not ask for a clarification.

Again, the author would like to caution that his suggestions for dealing with active resistance by the respondent do not specify all the conditions for their success. However, sharing these experiences will sensitize an interviewer to the problem of resistance and show some of the tactics that have been successful for the author and other interviewers in this situation.

Dealing with Falsification

Falsification by the respondent is usually a symptom of ego threat or the etiquette barrier. Much potential falsification can be *prevented* if certain precautions are taken. First, if there is a possibility that the respondent may lie to hide certain facts that the interviewer already knows, it is often good to let the respondent know immediately that the interviewer has the information and makes no judgment concerning it. This often avoids the embarrassing situation where the respondent is forced to spin out an increasingly complicated fiction in order to be consistent with certain falsifications laid down early in the interview.

A second preventative tactic is useful when the interviewer has information the respondent would be tempted to hide, but rapport would be damaged if the respondent realized this. In this case, the interviewer needs to obtain a "voluntary" admission from the respondent. If this information is the subject for the remainder of the interview, then the admission must be obtained early in the interview. This is a point where the leading question strongly loaded in the direction of the least socially acceptable answer is often useful. This was the tactic used by Kinsey, a discussed earlier.

A third general preventative tactic is to leave those questions judged in advance to be potentially ego-threatening until the latter part of the interview so that the interviewer will have more time to build up the nonjudgmental atmosphere.

In spite of precautions aimed at preventing falsification, there are instances when the respondent still fabricates his or her report. This is particularly likely when the interviewer was unable to predict the potential ego threat in a question. For example, the apparently innocuous question, "Where were you when the tornado struck your house?" did not ordinarily constitute an ego threat, but in the following excerpt the interviewer correctly suspects that it does. He wisely *retreats* from the point before the respondent makes a point of denying his actual whereabouts.

I: Where were you when the tornado struck your house? Were you home?

R: No.

I: What time do you get off work at the box factory?

R: Four-thirty. (The respondent begins to appear very uneasy for the first time in the interview.)

I: How did you find out that the tornado struck your house?

Here the interviewer's natural tendency was to ask, "Where were you between 4:30 when you got off work and 6:30 when the storm struck your house?" Instead he guessed by the respondent's reaction that he did not want to divulge where he was during that two-hour period. The interviewer tactfully skipped the topic and an hour later in the interview the respondent volunteered that he had stopped by the Oasis Tavern for a drink with some of the boys. The tavern was demolished by the same tornado that struck the respondent's home and injured his wife and child. The respondent's need for catharsis led him to admit his guilt feelings for having been flirting with "one of the girls that hangs out at the tavern" when he should have been home helping his wife and child during the storm

In rare cases, the interviewer may directly *challenge* the respondent who is suspected of lying. For example, the interviewer might say, "I'm amazed that such a thing could happen! I think you are trying to kid me" or "You don't have to give that old line because I don't expect it" or "I find that very difficult to believe; it doesn't jibe with the rest of the picture" or "This is not consistent with what you said earlier; which is correct?"

These are very strong tactics and always carry the potential of completely inhibiting the flow of information. For this reason, such tactics should be used only as a last resort and, if possible, postponed until all of the other relevant information has been gathered. Also, the attitude with which the interviewer "challenges" the respondent is important. It can be done without hostility or condescension but in a spirit of equality as if to say, "You don't have to hide things from me; we both know better." Further, the direct challenge can be followed by a qualifying phrase such as, "If what you say is literally true, then you will have to explain to me how it fits in with the fact that . . ."

If all of the usually appropriate techniques and tactics are tried and the respondent still persists in fabricating, then the interviewer usually has nothing to lose by challenging the respondent as a last resort. The one danger is that even though the challenge is successful the respondent might become hostile and retaliate by contacting potential respondents to warn them of the "third degree" tactics used by the interviewer.

In cases where the interviewer is not sure the attempt to deal with symptoms of resistance was successful, it is often fruitful to use the *informal post-interview.*

THE INFORMAL POST-INTERVIEW

The informal post-interview is a "chat" that takes place after the formal interview is terminated; it is done in such a casual way that it is not interpreted as part of the interview by the respondent. The signal of the termination of the formal interview may be turning off the tape recorder, putting the note pad away, standing up, moving to another location, and so forth.

The first function of the post-interview is to note any significant *changes* in the respondent's manner that might indicate that the respondent was inhibited or resisting during the formal interview. There are times when the interviewer feels that the respondent generally has been withholding information throughout the interview. This hunch may be correct; however it may simply reflect the respondent's personality or lack of information on the topic of the interview. For this reason the interviewer must be sensitive to *changes* in the respondent's manner as the conversation shifts into the informal post-interview period.

If the respondent has actually resisted, some of the reasons could be verified in an informal post-interview. For example, the respondent might be uneasy about the interviewer's using a tape recorder or taking notes. The respondent might feel that even though the interviewer is to be trusted, the sponsor is not worthy. Or the formality of the situation might give the respondent the impression of going "on record" even though he or she has been told that responses will be kept anonymous. However, if the respondent feels threatened by the interviewer for any reason, the informal post-interview will show no better results.

The informal post-interview can also be used as an ego-building period designed to leave the respondent in a good mood so that he or she will not spread negative attitudes to other potential respondents. In addition to giving sincere praise to the respondent at crucial points throughout the interview, it is sometimes especially important to spend a few minutes after the formal information-gathering is finished to build up the respondent's ego and give the respondent a chance to express any anxieties about his or her performance and to regain composure. This is particularly important where the nature of the subject matter and the objectives of the interview lead the respondent to give information which is difficult to recall, ego threatening, or traumatic. Even though the interview may have been very successful in the amount and quality of the information obtained, it may leave the respondent disturbed. If the nature of the study calls for many interviews in the same community where one respondent knows and communicates with another, it becomes crucially important not to leave a respondent with an unpleasant feeling about the interview. The respondent might prevent others from cooperating by referring to the "third degree" or to "psychoanalysis," and similar comments. Five minutes added to the regular formal interview for ego-building may be well invested.

Launching into the informal post-interview can usually be done with little effort. For example, the casual remark, "Are you glad that's over?" will often start the respondent talking about reactions to the interview. Sometimes the respondent will ask questions about the purpose of the interview, the nature of the study, or whether he or she can see its results. This offers a springboard for the interviewer to branch off into exploration of the respondent's feeling about the interview itself. In some cases, the interviewer may have to ask a direct question such as, "Did you enjoy it in general?" "What were some of the things that made it difficult in spots?" "Do you have some suggestions on how I could make it easier for people I will interview from now on?" "What do you think might stop some people from giving information of this type?" "Do you think everyone would be willing to give me this information?" "If some people were a little reluctant or cautious, why do you think this might be?"

Interviewers who have experimented with the informal post-interview in a variety of situations agree that there is usually nothing to be lost except a few minutes of time, and often much to be gained. Some report, for example, that what they had interpreted to be a fear of the tape recorder was actually nothing but personal peculiarity of the respondent, still apparent after the tape recorder was turned off. In other cases, the respondent would confess to fabricating certain portions of the interview because of his or her perception of the possible audience. In the words of one respondent, "I don't want to insult anybody, particularly when they had done their best and their intentions were good." Sometimes the interviewer trying this tactic was shocked to find that much of the introductory explanation of the purposes, sponsorship, and anonymity of the interview had been quickly forgotten by the respondent.

The interviewer may actually try to obtain some of the information that was not forthcoming in the formal interview or may attempt only to evaluate the respondent's attitude toward the interview in order to estimate the completeness and validity of the information given. If the interviewer discovers that the respondent has withheld vital information, he or she may attempt to relieve the respondent's suspicions or fears, leaving the door open for another interview under better conditions.

SUMMARY

In using specific countertactics to meet the respondent's symptoms of resistance, the interviewer should not automatically assume that these symptoms signal some insurmountable barrier. Instead, the interviewer should merely move ahead gently without contradicting the respondent's claims of having no time for an interview, of not knowing

FIGURE 17-1   Checklist—Tactics

Questions to ask yourself about tactics when preparing an interview

Advance planning

1. Should a sequence of topics and subtopics be fixed in advance or should the sequence be controlled by the respondent?
2. How can the questions be arranged to minimize possible ego threat, forgetting, and inferential or chronological confusion?
3. How can the sequence be arranged to maximize the facilitators as early as possible in the interview?
4. If the respondent is to control the sequence, should this be done by beginning with a broad question and following the respondent's lead, by giving the respondent a choice of topic to begin with, or by supplying pivot questions in advance?
5. Are lead-in questions needed to prepare the respondent for a topic or question?
6. Should pivot questions be built into the interview schedule?
7. Should transitional statements be given between topics or questions?
8. Should a funnel sequence be used at some point in the interview?
9. Should an inverted funnel sequence be used at some point?

Probing to meet objectives

10. Should silent probes be used extensively?
11. Is the purpose and meaning of each question clearly specified so the interviewer will recognize irrelevant, incomplete, or invalid responses?
12. Should the wording of neutral probes be suggested in the interview guide or schedule?
13. In view of the nature of the interview topic, is it best to use retrospective or immediate probes?
14. Is the recapitulation probe likely to be fruitful in this interview?
15. Should the interviewer use reflective probes? If so, what kind?
16. Should summary notes, or probe notes, or both, be taken?
17. Should the interview guide provide topical categories for probe notes or should the notes be in chronological order?

Dealing with symptoms of resistance

18. Is the interviewer prepared to deal with "I'm too busy now"?
19. Is the interviewer prepared to deal with "I don't know anything about that"?
20. Is the interviewer prepared to deal with "I don't want to be on tape"?
21. Is the interviewer prepared to deal with "Why are you taking notes"?
22. Is the interviewer prepared to deal with "I don't remember"?
23. Is the interviewer prepared to deal with "What do you mean by that"?
24. Is the interviewer prepared to deal with "What do *you* think about that"?
25. Is the interviewer prepared to deal with falsification?
26. Should there be an informal post-interview?

---

anything about the topic, or of forgetting the relevant information. The success of specific verbal countertactics of the interviewer depends to a great extent upon their nonverbal accompaniment. If the interviewer shows fear, expectation of failure, or hostility toward the respondent, he or she will probably increase the respondent's resistance.

If specific countertactics leave doubt as to the respondent's full cooperation, there remains one final tactic: the informal post-interview.

Here the skilled interviewer can often elicit clues to the respondent's attitude toward the formal interview to help judge its validity and, in some cases, can obtain missing information.

All of the tactical tools are summarized in Figure 17–1 in the form of twenty-six questions to ask yourself in planning and carrying out the tactics of an interview.

To this point the book has dealt separately with the strategies, techniques, and tactics that can be used to minimize the *inhibitors* and to maximize the *facilitators* of communication in the interview. However, in a real interview it is necessary to consider strategies, techniques, and tactics jointly as they interact with one another in different interview settings. For this reason the next eight chapters in Part 6: "Professional Settings of the Interview" will illustrate the interplay between strategies, techniques, and tactics. In many cases the strategies are mainly determined by the organizational setting of the interview, and the solutions must be mainly in the appropriate use of techniques and tactics which must be adjusted to the organizational setting. The reader will be able to apply everything learned to this point in answering the critical analysis questions accompanying each of the professional settings.

DISCUSSION QUESTIONS

1. What are some of the common verbal symptoms of possible resistance by the respondent?

2. What are some types of common reactions by inexperienced interviewers to these verbal symptoms, which tend to increase the resistance?

3. What is the best way to deal with falsification by the respondent?

4. When should the informal post-interview be used?

5. What should the interviewer try to accomplish in the informal post-interview?

Part VI

PROFESSIONAL SETTINGS OF THE INTERVIEW

Each of the following eight chapters deals with a different professional setting of the interview. This is done to help the reader identify some common interviewing problems and their solutions in situations which cross-cut a variety of professional settings. Some of the concepts discussed in the previous chapters are applicable in each of these settings.

In selecting these examples the author avoided duplicating the topics used in the laboratory problems.[1] The author also tried to find contrasting settings. Then, too, he avoided those settings for which there were neither tape-recordings nor an interviewer experienced in that setting to supply the real raw materials. Even so, the author had to omit many excellent examples of settings in which professional interviewing is done.

This does not imply that all interviews done by a particular profession are alike in their objectives, problems, or solutions. On the contrary, there may be more similarity among interviews done by a social worker, a manager, and a nurse than among three interviews done in different managerial settings. Nevertheless, it is helpful to see the same interviewing principles applied in different settings.

The heart of each chapter is a *pair* of interview dialogues taking place in the same professional setting. In each pair, one interview is much better than the other. The good one is not perfect, nor is the bad one without redeeming qualities. Each pair has been synthesized from real materials and is usually a composite of several interviews. Each

---

[1]Problem 1: Critique of the telephone company interview; Problem 7: Parent-child conflict; Problems 8 and 9: Vocational choice interview; Problem 10: Car-buyer motivation study.

dialogue is edited, condensed, and constructed to include typical problems, together with both successful and unsuccessful attempts to deal with them. They also include the lack of attempts to deal with problems either preventatively or as they arise in the give-and-take of the interview.

In each pair of interviews the first is the worse one. This gives you a chance to develop your sensitivity to the problems and to actively invent solutions, rather than having the solutions illustrated before you become aware of the problem.[2]

To involve yourself most actively in the interviewing problems presented in the next chapters, you should follow this procedure with each pair of interviews in each of the professional settings.

1. Read all of the description of the professional role and setting. Read the *objectives* and *setting* of the particular pair of interviews. Be particularly alert to the objectives and setting since they determine the tasks to be accomplished and the tools to be used by the interviewer.

2. Read the first interview dialogue with the objectives and setting in mind. *Do not look at the second interview yet.*

3. Answer the *Critical Analysis Questions* at the end of the first interview. Try to use the various frames of reference given in the book to this point—such as inhibitors, facilitators, strategies, techniques, and tactics—to help in your critique of the interview. Group discussion may be fruitful at this point after you have done your critique.

4. Read the second interview dialogue, with the objectives and setting in mind, and answer the *Critical Analysis Questions.* Group discussion may also be helpful at this point.

5. Now read your instructor's handout of author's comments and critique to see if there are additional observations, criticisms, and suggestions you had not yet thought of. Take time to reflect on how to apply what you have learned to the pair of interviews in the next professional setting.

---

[2]It will also be noted that the better interview of each pair is usually longer. This reflects reality in interviews in which the topic is somewhat complex or when considerable depth and detail are needed.

Chapter Eighteen

The Social Work Interview

It is an oversimplification to speak of *the* social work interview. The settings in which social workers interview range from talking to juvenile delinquents on the street to talking in a plush office with executives planning to retire. The objectives of the interview can include a routine check on eligibility for food stamps, counseling a client on budget management, listening to a person discuss marital problems, or trying to persuade a person to get in touch with Alcoholics Anonymous. The interviews involve different proportions of information gathering, persuasion, and information giving.

Obviously, it is not possible to represent the full range of social work interviewing in the pair of interviews presented in this chapter. The case-manager interview was chosen because it represents one of the most demanding types of social work interviewing.

THE INSTITUTIONAL SETTING

The Cooperative Comprehensive Care Center aims at coordinating the efforts of the various agencies that provide *(a)* income maintenance (such as Aid to Families of Dependent Children (AFDC), General Relief, and Emergency Assistance), *(b)* support services (such as Medicaid, day-care, Head Start, and food stamps), and *(c)* human development services (such as basic literacy, high school equivalency courses, on-the-job training, vocational education, and college).

Many of the families in poverty have no male head, and the major problem of the Center is to coordinate and synchronize the delivery of the three major types of services in order to free the mother to upgrade her earning power to the point where the family income is clearly above the poverty level.

In both interviews below, the Center has succeeded in providing income maintenance, food stamps, Medicaid, and the combination of child care needed to free the mother to go to school. The problem is that in each case for some reason the mother has dropped out of school (within a few days before this interview), and the case manager is trying to discover the reason she dropped out and what can be done about it.

OBJECTIVES OF THE INTERVIEW

The specific objectives of the interview are to diagnose the cause of the client's dropping out of school and to design a treatment plan to overcome whatever obstacles inhibit school attendance. The interviewer must do three things:

1. *Locate possible objective causes.* In this type of situation there may be a breakdown in the support system. The childcare arrangement or transportation or health support may be lacking and thus preventing the mother from going to school. There is sometimes active opposition or a failure to give support by the spouse.

2. *Locate possible subjective causes.* Sometimes the mother's morale may be shaken by the problems of meeting a new challenge. She may discover that she is ambivalent in her goals, or that she has guilt feelings about a perceived neglect of either her children or spouse. She might begin to doubt her own ability to do the school work or have a fear of failure and want to escape from a vulnerable position.

3. *Develop the treatment plan.* In some cases it is possible for the treatment to begin within the diagnostic interview. For example, the person may have needed the therapeutic effect of catharsis to reduce the guilt or fear of failure. The social worker may be able to give direct reassurance to the client on the basis of what is known about the school or about the client. In other cases the treatment is to change some of the objective conditions, to provide missing support services, or to change the behavior of others toward the client.

THE INTERVIEW SITUATION

The interview takes place in the office of the case manager at the Cooperative Comprehensive Care Center. The respondent, Mrs. Johnson, is twenty-three years old, has a two-year-old daughter, Mary Beth, and a five-year-old son, Jaycee. Her husband has deserted, but the center has been able to put together a package of welfare and social services to allow Mrs. Johnson to attend vocational school to become a medical technician.

Mrs. Johnson receives AFDC checks, has a medicaid card for free medical services, receives food stamps, and has her two children in a day-care center where she attends classes at the local community college. She drives an old car because there is no available public transportation. To have all of these services applied simultaneously to the family required great effort on the part of the case manager and case worker at the center. It has also required patience and persistent effort on the part of the client, Mrs. Johnson.

Mrs. Reimer, the case manager, has asked Mrs. Johnson to stop by the center to talk about the problem. Mrs. Johnson arrives about two minutes late for her 2:30 appointment.

Interview A

I-1:   Good morning Mrs. Johnson, have a seat. I'll be with you in a minute as soon as I get these papers filed. If I don't do it right away, I'll get all the records messed up. I have over 200 cases to troubleshoot. It's a real mess sometimes.

(Mrs. J. sits and fidgets while the case manager finishes filing.)

I-2:   What I need to find out is why you have dropped out of the medical technician classes. This is important to us because a lot of taxpayers' money is going into trying to get you onto a career ladder, so it is important that we don't let you fall off! How long has it been since you attended classes?

R-2:   Only four days!

I-3:   Four days? (2)[1]

R-3:   That's right.

I-4:   Why haven't you been going to classes—have you been sick?

R-4:   I guess I look good enough but that's not sayin' how I feel! I'm tired! (2) I have been doing this just three weeks but I'm plain tired. I hate to drive in traffic, and . . . .

I-5:   That can't be avoided. That's where the vocational center is . . . there's no way you can get there by bus. Don't you have much experience driving in traffic?

R-5:   No, in Sequatchie County there was nothing like that. The only place I saw traffic like that was when my ex-husband took me to Chattanooga. (2)

---

[1]The numbers in parentheses indicate the number of seconds of silence.

I-6:   But you'll get used to the traffic when you drive to the same place every day! Besides you should keep in mind what you are giving up. You have a chance to get into a career. That is what you said you wanted. (2) We have gotten your two kids into a good day-care center, and with ADC and food stamps you have enough to get along on, particularly with the transportation allowance and the rent subsidy. With all this are you going to let a little thing about some unpleasant driving ruin your chance for a career?

R-6:   That's not the whole problem. I have been happier the last three days because I'm with my children like a mother should be! Maybe that Storybookland place is a good day-care center as far as they go but they can't take the place of a mother. While I'm leaving them there, what am I doing? (2) That Mrs. Dexter gives us nasty exams that trick you up plenty . . . and she asks questions any time someone misses a class. She harps on how our incentive allowance will be cut off if we don't come to class regularly. She thinks we are kids. And the Westside Skills Center isn't exactly in the best part of town! No, I wouldn't give up a chance to be a medical technician just to avoid a drive in a little traffic every day, but there are a lot of better reasons not to take a chance like that. Who knows what's in the future? I know one thing right now—Mary Beth and Jaycee both need a mother now, not next year or the year after.

I-7:   But didn't you think of this at the time you wanted to get into vocational school? At that time I remember you said you were climbing the walls "penned up with two kids all day and all night." And when your husband was home you got little help from him with the kids, right?

R-7:   That's the truth, but . . .

I-8:   I'm just concerned that you look out for your own best interests in the long run. That is what you've got to think about. Mrs. Dexter is right about your incentive allowance. That continues only as long as you are attending and doing well in the courses. So your job is to think it over and realize that you are making a big decision. If you get back to class on Monday you will still be in good standing, but after that there is little we can do to help you until another year and it will be harder for you to start the longer you wait. So think it over, will you?

R-8:   Sure, I've been thinking and I'll think some more! (2)

I-9:   That's good. Have a good day!

Before reading or discussing the second interview in this pair, do the critical analysis below.

CRITICAL ANALYSIS QUESTIONS

Do not repeat the question; simply use the question numbers to indicate which one you are answering. Keep your answers short and unambiguous by supplying only the word or phrase, the interviewer's behavior number (for example, I-17), the respondent's behavior number (for example, R-19), or the numerical value (percent or mean) requested. In cases where more than one item of information is to be given, put the items in chronological order from left to right, separated by commas. (For example, I-3, I-15, I-34; or R-3, R-5, R-19; or *jargon, stupid idea, afraid.*)

Your reasons for including or omitting a particular bit of behavior can be dealt with in a discussion, either with one other person who has answered the questions independently, or with a group.

1. What *appropriate* effort, if any, does the interviewer make to initially establish a sympathetic relationship with the respondent? Give the I– number only.

2. What evidence, if any, is there that the interviewer may be too concerned with her own problems to be sensitive to the problems of the client? Give I– number only.

3. Does the interviewer use an opening question that is a general invitation to talk? If so, give the I– number only.

4. What is the mean length of silence (in parentheses) allowed by the interviewer? Divide the total amount of silence by the number of Is.

5. What percent of the interviewer's questions, statements, or probes interrupt the respondent? (An interruption is defined as a lack of silence between the end of a response and the interviewer's next question.) Identify the I– numbers which interrupt.

6. What percent of the interviewer's *questions* or *probes* are in a form that implies that a *yes* or *no* answer is sufficient? Do not include interviewer's statements. List the Is in order.

7. What percent of the interviewer's behavior (percent of Is) involves reflecting and/or accepting the respondent's feelings? List the Is in order.

8. Identify the points where the interviewer asks directly about the respondent's *feelings*.

9. At what points, if any, does the interviewer say something that might sound threatening to the respondent? Give I– numbers and the words or phrases in each of the Is that might be threatening.

10. Are there any points at which the interviewer fails to probe potentially relevant responses? If so, give the R– number and the exact words or phrases that should have been probed.

Interview B

This interview takes place at the same center. The respondent's situation is very similar to the preceding one in that she has two preschool children; she is twenty-four years old and has just dropped out of school. The father, who deserted, is being sought to enforce the continuance of child support payments, but the chances of finding him are remote. Eight years earlier the respondent dropped out of high school in the tenth grade. The center has helped her attend special classes to prepare her to pass the GED (high school equivalence examination) which would qualify her to enter secretarial school.

After three weeks of special classes Mrs. Klein stopped attending, and the school notified the director of the center that Mrs. Klein dropped out for two days although she had been doing very well up to that point.

The purpose of this interview is the same as in Interview A; the interview setting is the same, but the interviewer is different.

I–1: Hello, Mrs. Klein! Mr. Malone was worried about what has happened to you and asked me to see what we can do to help at this point. Here, have a seat here where it is comfortable. (3)[2] (Mrs. K. sits down.) Before we start I was just going to have my 10 o'clock coffee. Would you like a cup?

R–1: Yes, if it's not too much trouble.

I–2: No trouble. Cream and sugar?

R–2: Just cream, thanks.

I–3: (Returning with the coffee.) It's been a while since you and I talked, so could you just tell me a little about what's happening? (2)

R–3: Well, you can say one thing, ... I have really been busy! Busier than I wanted to be sometimes! (3)

I–4: I see, you felt really busy. . . in fact, pushed at times!

R–4: That's right.

I–5: Uh huh. (2)

---

[2]Numbers in parentheses indicate seconds of silence.

R-5: I know I had both kids in the day-care center, but it takes forty-five minutes each morning to drop Joey and Lisa off at the Kinderhaus and get to the other side of Dayton to class at 8:30 so I was getting up at 6:30 to get the kids up and dressed, get breakfast and clean up so I wouldn't have to do it when I go home. (2) Then on the way back from school I'd pick up the kids and go home, and clean house, get dinner and be with the kids a bit before I put them to bed. (2) By that time I was ready for some TV but I had to study the homework assignments. Like I say, it was a rat race.

I-6: That *does* sound like a fast pace! (3)

R-6: Yeah, and sometimes I'd get hung up at the Kinderhaus because Joey would want to show me something he was working on like a map or a picture of some clay airplane or something. And you do want to be a good mother and show interest when he's so proud of his work. (3)

I-7: But you felt sort of torn because you wanted to get home to get things done! How has your health been?

R-7: It has been fine. (2) It took a couple of weeks to get used to the whole thing with everything so new to me. I had never driven in that part of Dayton before. I'd say I'm holding up fine! (2)

I-8: Could you tell me a little bit about why you haven't been to class the last couple of days? (3)

R-8: The main problem is that I can't get a dependable babysitter. (2) Last Thursday, the babysitter called at 8:00 to say she couldn't make it. And I was already fifteen minutes late! So I had to stay home and take care of the children. (2)

I-9: That's too bad! Why didn't the babysitter show? (2)

R-9: She is an older woman who lives in the same apartment building, but her daughter came from Chicago unexpectedly on Wednesday and had to catch a plane on to Atlanta at noon Thursday. (2) You can't blame the mother for wanting to be with her because it had been a couple of years. (3)

I-10: I'm a little confused. I thought you said both Joey and Lisa were in the Kinderhaus Daycare Center. Why did you have a babysitter?

R-10: Well, that was just on Thursdays, because the Kinderhaus has staff training sessions every Thursday morning and so the kids all come after lunch but by that time I'm in Dayton and can't take them with me and they are too small to leave. So Mrs. Blanchard comes before I leave for school and then gets lunch for them and takes them to Kinderhaus.

I-11:   Oh, I see, so that is the Thursday schedule. Then why didn't you go to school on Friday? (4)

R-11:   Well, after that day at home with them I began to think about why shouldn't they be with their mother like they should instead of with Mrs. Blanchard? And the more I began to think about the day-care place . . . I thought that wasn't right. (2) After all, when they are six, that's just two years for Joey, they will *have* to go to school, so what's the hurry? They should be with their mother now! (3)

I-12:   Oh, I got the idea from you that Joey at least liked the Kinderhaus! (3)

R-12:   Well, yes he has fun with the other kids his age, I guess, but he is not learning much!

I-13:   I see, you feel they should learn more. Is that why you didn't take them back to the Kinderhaus on Friday?

R-13:   Yeah, I had Thursday to think it over! (3)

I-14:   How do you feel about dropping out of the classes? (5)

R-14:   Well, I guess I can wait until both kids are in elementary school and then take the classes and I won't have to worry about babysitters or sending them off when they are so small. (3)

I-15:   How did you feel about not going to classes on Friday? (4)

R-15:   I was glad not to go so I could be with the children and . . . .(5)

I-16:   . . . and . . . what else? (2)

R-16:   You see the first exam was on Monday and Mr. Malone promised to grade them and give them back on Friday, and besides I don't like walking from the parking lot to the classroom building. (2) I know that it would be a good idea for me to go to school now and when the kids get in school I could get a secretarial job and really make some money. But who knows how these classes or the secretarial school will turn out. (2) Anyway, I can be with the kids now and go to school when they start to school. (3)

I-17:   I see. Tell me a little bit about that first exam you took on Monday! (1)

R-17:   Well, that was something else! It was the first exam I took since the tenth grade. That was eight years ago! I just know that I goofed it! (2)

I-18:   What makes you think you goofed it? (1)

R-18:   That's simple! I even had a hard time understanding the directions. And when I finally understood what I was supposed to do, I was guessing half the time at the answers. They were multiple-choice things and just none of the answers jumped out at me. I would usually know that some of the choices were wrong but there always seemed to be a couple of right ones when there is only supposed to be one! (2) As I say I was just guessing half the time. (3)

I–19: I see! You feel sort of scared about how you did on the exam!

R–19: Sure, and if I can't even do well on the first exam in a high school makeup test . . . what chance would I have in a whole year of secretarial school?

I–20: I'm surprised, because Mr. Malone said that you were doing *very well!* And he was surprised that you dropped out. He has seen people drop out before, but not when they were doing so well!

R–20: I can't believe it!

I–21: I would be surprised if you didn't do well, because I looked up your aptitude and interest test scores, which were good. (2) Now that you have a phone at home I could have Mr. Malone call you this afternoon and tell you how you did on the exam. How about that? (1)

R–21: Sure, I guess I can take it. I am curious now!

I–22: I'll do that. There is one thing you said awhile ago that I didn't understand. You said you didn't like walking from the parking lot to the classroom building . . . why is that?

R–22: It is only a block and a half and . . . (3) have you ever been to that school?

I–23: No, will you tell me about it? (2)

R–23: Well, the school is in a slum area. A black ghetto in fact. And there are a lot of young teenage blacks hanging around that look like they should be in school. (2) In a little park across the street from the parking lot there is always one or two winos sitting on the bench or shuffling about.

I–24: So you don't feel safe in that neighborhood? (1)

R–24: I sure don't. A block and a half doesn't seem like a long distance, but when there is not a white face in sight and they are all staring at you like you were something out of the zoo, it is not a pleasant feeling. (3)

I–25: I see what you mean. (3) Would it be any help to you if we could find someone else from Fairborn who goes to school there? You could have a car pool to save gas and then you could walk together to and from the parking lot.

R-25:   That *would* help a lot! Is there someone in my neighborhood that also is taking this same course?

I-26:   I believe there is more than one. I'll check it out and give you their names, so you can get together on the transportation.

R-26:   That sounds good to me. (2)

I-27:   If I get the names and call you in the morning, will you get in touch with them and make arrangements so that next Monday you can go in a car pool?

R-27:   I'll be glad to do that.

I-28:   And what about a babysitter? Do you need to find someone more dependable?

R-28:   Not really. Mrs. Blanchard does a good job and she really likes the kids . . . and her daughter will not be coming down from Chicago that often.

I-29:   Good. I'll remember to call Mr. Malone about your exam scores so you won't be worrying between now and next Monday. (3) How do you feel about getting back into classes?

R-29:   After talking to you I feel it's a great idea. (3) I was getting discouraged and started thinking it might turn out to be a waste of time, but I was also afraid that I would live to regret it if I didn't go back. (3) I might have just been fooling myself about waiting till the kids got into elementary school. (3)

I-30:   I'm sure you will make a good secretary and can find an interesting job. Please let me know if any other problems come up; maybe I could help.

R-30:   I believe it, now. (2)

I-31:   You don't have to wait till you have a problem to give me a call or come by to tell me how you're doing. So goodbye till then.

R-31:   Goodbye, and thanks.

CRITICAL ANALYSIS QUESTIONS

Answer the same questions for Interview B as you did for Interview A, plus those below.

11. Now that you have read Interview B and answered the questions, are you more critical of the method used in Interview A? If so, what additional criticisms would you make about Interview A? (This question may be discussed with another person

who has written the answer independently, or it may be discussed by the whole group.)

12. Now read your instructor's handout where the author shares his critical comments comparing the two interviews. Does the author have some observations that you missed? Did you have some he missed?

Selected Readings

Benjamin, Alfred. *The Helping Interview.* 2d ed. Boston: Houghton Mifflin, 1974.
One of the better books on the conditions, stages, and forms of interaction in the interview. Gives down-to-earth examples. It is mainly aimed at the counseling interview.

Cormier, William H., and L. Sherilyn Cormier. *Interviewing Strategies for Helpers.* 2nd ed. Monterey, Calif.: Brooks/Cole Publishing, 1985.
Skills and strategies to be used in the four major stages of the helping process (relationship assessment, goal setting, strategy selection and implementation, and evaluation-termination) are described in detail. Many readings and role-playing exercises are provided. Not specifically for social workers but for all helping professions including counseling.

Cross, Crispin P., ed. *Interviewing and Communication in Social Work.* London: Routledge and Kegan, 1974.
This English publication has five chapters dealing with the theory and sociocultural context of both the linguistic and nonlinguistic aspects of communication in the social work interview. Three chapters deal with techniques, problems, and special situations. The final chapter provides materials and instructions for the role-playing approach to training in directive and non-directive interviewing. It is perhaps a bit pedantic for a book intended as a practical tool for social workers.

Fenlason, Anne, G. Beals, and A. Abrahamson. *Essentials of Interviewing.* Rev. ed. New York: Harper & Row, 1962.
A classic in social work interviewing, originally published in 1952. An orientation to the social casework interview and related professional interviewing. Stresses the importance of knowing the background of the client, his culture, personality, and roles, and how the dynamics of the interview may be used to help solve relevant aspects of the client's problem. Gives examples of interviews but not in the form of dialogue. Instead, the interviews are reported in an "I said, then he said" format. There is little use of communication theory. It assumes that the emphasis in the casework interview is not on obtaining information from the client but upon influencing him.

Schulman, Eveline D. *Intervention in Human Services.* 3rd ed. St. Louis: C. V. Mosby Co., 1982.

This book, written "to integrate didactic with skill training . . . of under-graduates in a mental health technical program," presents a layered approach to training in which the student progresses through a sequence of observation, recording, reporting, interviewing, and counseling. It is rich in verbatim examples, insights, and exercises. It provides a broad theoretical framework of intervention as well as the interviewing skills of paraphrasing and summarizing, reflection, confrontation, and interpretation. It has useful appendices, including a glossary, psychological tests for self-understanding, and sources of audio-visual and other aids for the human services curriculum.

Chapter Nineteen

The Employee
Appraisal Interview

The appraisal interview usually has the dual aims of evaluating and improving a current employee's performance on the job. The interview can help in deciding whether to continue a person's employment and whether to give an employee a raise or a promotion. To improve the employee's performance, the interview may be used to detect the areas where improvement is needed, to determine the state of the employee's morale, and to provide support, motivation, information, or even therapy to reduce anxiety and tensions that may stand in the way of improvement.

To a great extent the success of the employee appraisal interview is determined *before* the first word is said in the interview. Every effort should be made to make the appraisal interview a normal part of the organization's ongoing process that is viewed by both management and employees as a mutually beneficial practice. The employee's willingness to participate wholeheartedly will depend on how he or she feels the appraisal interviews have been used in the past. For this reason it takes time to establish the optimal organizational atmosphere for the fruitful appraisal interview.

The appraisal interview is usually less standardized than the selection interview done with several applicants for the same position. Since the appraisal interview is done with a current employee, it has the advantage that it can be used in conjunction with other information collected on the employee's current job performance. Also, there is no need to try to compress all of the interviewing into one session since the employee could be available again.

Although the appraisal interview may be less standardized (less structured in advance) than the selection interview, it may be more standardized than other face-to-face talks not planned in advance which management has with employees. Such things as crisis management, conflict management, and problem-solving interviews are often initiated by the respondents.

All of these management interviews have one important thing in common. The interviewer is in a superordinate position over the respondent. There is no need for the manager to assert authority. The employee is all too aware of it. Instead, the manager bears the burden of proof that he or she is approachable, human, reasonable, and interested in the employee. Otherwise information will not flow freely.

THE ORGANIZATIONAL SETTING

The John McBeam Die and Mold Company employs about 1,500 workers to make master molds for rubber products such as auto tires, bushings, grommets, and containers. The company is located in a small town. It is unionized, racially integrated, and has very little labor turnover. It pays good dividends to its stockholders.

Since the plant is not doing mass production of consumer products but is designing and making the master molds (from which other molds are made to mold the finished product), the employees have a relatively high level of skill and several design projects go on simultaneously. Each supervisor works with a small team of skilled craftsmen to develop and produce the master mold according to specifications furnished by an engineer. No objective quantitative measures of productivity of the foreman or project teams have been set up. The only quantitative measure used is a rating scale filled out anonymously by the persons (subordinates, peers, and supervisors) that come in daily or weekly contact with the person being rated.

The rating scale includes such questions as *(a)* whether the person clearly explains what is to be done, who is to do it, and the general strategy for team work; *(b)* whether the person is helpful in dealing with technical problems that arise; *(c)* whether the person coordinates the supply of materials and tools so that work stoppages on the team are avoided; and *(d)* how well the person deals with human relations problems that arise within the team and with other departments. The raters are asked not only to rate the person on a seven-point scale but also to give concrete examples of the person's most salient strengths and weaknesses.

The McBeam Company has a policy of doing appraisal interviews three times per year in September, January, and May. The employee ratings are also done three times a year, about one month in advance of the appraisal interviews.

The appraisal interviews and the rating scales furnish most of the basic information used in making personnel decisions.

OBJECTIVES OF THE INTERVIEW

There are two general objectives of this appraisal interview. First, it is to improve the performance of the foreman and the team. There is intentionally no direct connection between any particular appraisal interview and merit raises or bonuses, but the interviews do supply part of the accumulated information in the employee's file used for this purpose. Second, this year the personnel office is seeking candidates for promotion to section supervisor.

The assistant personnel manager, Mr. Bronson, has an appointment to interview Mr. Romain Starsky, one of the 118 foremen in the company. This will be the second appraisal interview since Mr. Starsky was hired. Mr. Starsky is foreman of a team that includes machinists, draftsmen, and tool and die makers. It is 10:00 A.M. on a Friday when Mr. Starsky arrives at the personnel office for the interview.

Interview A

I–1:   Hello, Romy! Good to see you! It has been a while. As you know, this is the time of the year again when personnel does the appraisal interviews. Between the four of us we have 118 foremen to interview, so we will have to clip right along!

R–1:   Sounds like you're busy!

I–2:   Well I guess that's the price you pay to be in management! I have just gone through your file and was looking over the ratings done last month and would like to mention a few of my impressions!

R–2:   I see. (2)[1]

I–3:   As you know, the company wants to keep production up, so we have to get each employee to get his shoulder to the wheel and push. (2) I see from this last rating scale that you have several areas that could stand improvement. For example, here on the scale of "helping with technical problems" your average rating is below average. You will have to do something about that. Do you think you are technically qualified for this job?

R–3:   I have been here only four months! And the whole operation is very different from Frigidaire, but I am learning fast. Even some of the jargon here is different from Frigidaire even when we are talking about the same things! Also . . .

---

[1]Numbers in parentheses indicate seconds of silence.

I-4:   Well, this is an area that is very important. The men look to the foreman to at least tell them where they can get their technical questions answered. Four months is quite a while to get used to a new job and you should speed up this learning process a bit in the technical area. Don't you think so?

R-4:   Probably right. I could use some more information on some parts of the molding process used here.

I-5:   Good! Well, here on your relations with the engineers you are doing very well. Congratulations! Keep up the good work! Now, I see that on the item about "keeping the necessary tools, instruments, and materials available" your score is not so good.

R-5:   There's a reason for that. I am not the only one involved in this. There are certain things that must be shared with other teams, and the foremen that have been here for years seem to have an in with the stockroom and get things reserved in advance.

I-6:   Well, if the other foremen can do it, you should watch and learn how to do the same thing yourself.

R-6:   I'm learning the hard way . . . but . . .

I-7:   Good, as long as you are learning! The last thing I want to talk about is probably the most important. That is the item about "dealing with human relations problems." As you probably know, a good foreman is not just someone who gives technical information, keeps the tools and materials available, and enforces the safety rules, but probably the most important job is to keep the human relations running smoothly. You are below average on this, particularly in the ratings by your subordinates.

R-7:   I'll bet the ratings by Bob Jones and Joe Johnson are very low! That week the ratings were done I had just had a little run-in with them about their overtime. (2)

I-8:   Well, with more experience you will have to learn how to handle these problems before they get to the Personnel Office or the Union Steward!

R-8:   I guess I will.

I-9:   Well, that is all for now. The other parts of your rating are at least average, but these areas we have just talked about will have to be improved between now and the next appraisal interview. My job is to see that each employee does his part and I'm going to do my job. I'm sure you can understand that, Mr. Starsky. Anything else we need to talk about?

R–9: Not as far as I am concerned. (2)

I–10: OK. Good luck. We'll be seeing each other from time to time.

R–10: Goodbye.

Before reading or discussing the second interview in this pair, do the critical analysis below.

CRITICAL ANALYSIS QUESTIONS

Keep the answers to these questions short and unambiguous. Supply only the needed word or phrase, the interviewer's behavior number (for example, I–17), the respondent's behavior number (for example, R–19), or the numerical value (percent or mean) requested. In cases where more than one item of information is to be given, put the items in chronological order from left to right, separated by commas. (For example, I–3, I–15, I–34; or R–3, R–5, R–19; or *jargon, stupid idea, afraid.*)

Your reasons for including or omitting a particular bit of behavior could be discussed with another person who has answered the questions independently, or in a group discussion.

1. What *appropriate* effort, if any, does the interviewer make to initially establish a sympathetic relationship with the respondent? Give the I– number only.

2. Does the interview use an opening question that is a general invitation to talk? If so, give one I– number only.

3. What is the mean length of silence allowed by the interviewer? (Divide the total amount of silence by the number of Is.)

4. What percent of the interviewer's questions, statements, or probes interrupt the respondent? (An interruption is defined as a lack of silence between the end of a response and the interviewer's next question.) Identify the I– numbers which interrupt.

5. What percent of the interviewer's questions or probes are in a form that implies that a *yes* or *no* answer is sufficient? Do not include statements; list the Is in order.

6. What percent of the interviewer's behavior (percent of Is) involves reflecting and/or accepting the respondent's feelings? List the Is in order.

7. At what points, if any, does the interviewer say something that might sound threatening to the respondent? Give the I– numbers and the words or phrases in each of the Is that might be threatening.

8. Are there any points at which the interviewer fails to probe potentially relevant responses? If so, give the R– number and the exact words or phrases that should have been probed.

9. Give the I– numbers, if any, where the interviewer probed the immediately preceding response or a prior response to obtain additional information.

10. Give the I– numbers, if any, where the interviewer provides support, or suggests a solution to problems brought up by the respondent.

Interview B

This next interview takes place in the same company at the same time in another assistant personnel manager's office. Again, a foreman is being interviewed and for the same purposes. This foreman, Bob Furness, has been working for the company the same length of time as has Romain Starsky.

I–1:   Hello, Bob! Come in.

R–1:   Your desk looks like you have a lot of work stacked up for the day.

I–2:   Yea. Sometimes it looks worse than it should. I was going to have a cup of coffee. Would you like one?

R–2:   No, I've been off of coffee lately, since my reducing diet.

I–3:   Then I was right, you are slimmer than when I talked to you last.

R–3:   Ten pounds!

I–4:   Great! (3) This is your second progress report, so you probably recall what we are supposed to accomplish, but let me just run over it again to get us both on the same wavelength. The main purpose is for me to discover how I can help you do a better and more satisfying job and to see whether I was able to give any useful suggestions last time to get you along this far. This helps me discover how to do my own job better. . . . You are relatively new here. How do you like it so far? (3)

R–4:   Well, I like it much better than Frigidaire but there are things I have to get used to. (2)

I–5:   For example? (2)

R–5:   Mainly, with no mass production, we are one big research and development . . . mainly development plant. There is much less repetition of duties which makes it more interesting (2) but also more complicated. Sometimes things just creep along and suddenly a breakthrough and the whole thing speeds up. There's where the problem is. (2) You have to make detailed plans ahead so these leaps over the obstacles don't end up being a block. (2)

I–6: I'm not sure how the leap becomes a block. (2)

R–6: I mean that when things slow down because of some technical problem or slow, tedious development process, it gives the impression that the pace is always going to be slow so you don't have to plan ahead as if you were moving at a rapid rate; (2) then all of a sudden the tedious part is done and unless detailed plans are ready for the next steps and the new tools and materials are ready to go, there can be a hang-up and people get very frustrated.

I–7: I see what you mean. Later I would like to get into more detail on the types of problems which come up to see if there is some way I can help. But first, if you don't mind, I would just like to get an overview of your job as it looks to you *now* compared to the last time we talked three months ago. I remember at that time you were enthusiastic after being on the job for three weeks, but you felt confused about certain details. In fact it was that talk with you that made me decide to make up this brochure we've been handing out to all new employees. Everyone needs a clearer picture of how the place operates if things are to run smoothly. Anyway, just tell me how things look to you now.

R–7: Now, it looks much clearer. I know where everything and everybody is. (2) And I have gotten to know many people as individuals, so I know their peculiarities, what they're good at and what they're not; but that doesn't mean I can predict what everyone is going to do. I have gotten rid of a lot of preconceptions brought with me from Frigidaire. Here things are less formal but more efficient. (2)

I–8: Uh huh. (2)

R–8: I like the additional responsibility and flexibility of my work here.

I–9: What are some of the added responsibilities? (2)

R–9: Well, for one thing, no one hands me a production schedule of how many units will be assembled today. Here a lot of that depends on how well I can anticipate the needs of the group and plan ahead, to be ready for the next step. (2) And I can't know everything myself; I have some very skilled and knowledgeable people on my team and my job is to coordinate skills, knowledge, materials, and tools.

I–10: Very well put. (2)

R–10:   Sometimes I need to be with the team to see exactly what is going on, but there is a lot that is not visible to the naked eye, so I've learned that I have to keep in constant communication with each person on the team to see how they are coming, how long they think it will take to get to the next step, whose help they are going to need next, what problems and obstacles they see to the smooth completion of the project, and what materials, tools, instruments, and processes they are going to have to get to next. (3)

I–11:   What about this idea of the smooth completion of the project?

R–11:   By that . . . well, in a way it is impossible to have everything run perfectly smoothly, since they do not repeat a process over and over like on an assembly line . . . but you can stop the progress from bogging down completely by keeping up on what's going on in the different parts of the project and having the next steps ready. (2)

I–12:   I am very interested in the problems of coordinating the team to run more smoothly. What else have you found out that you can do besides planning ahead for the next steps to avoid bottlenecks? (2) So far you mentioned mainly the importance of keeping up to date on who is doing what, and what they will need next and when. You're right, that is very important. Is there any other dimension to the problem of keeping the team working smoothly? (4)

R–12:   It's funny that you ask, because just when I was thinking that my time and energy have not all been taken up with just coordinating people, tools, and materials on a daily basis, but there is something else that takes up maybe 25 percent of the time and energy, and if you don't take care of it daily, it could get to the point where it takes up a lot more of my time and the whole team's time.

I–13:   What is that?

R–13:   It's keeping everyone happy and feeling that everything is fair . . . and keeping up the morale! (2)

I–14:   In what way or, I mean, under what circumstances is morale a problem? (3)

R–14:   I mentioned one situation where things bog down because one member of the team is a bottleneck. Or when the bottleneck is cleared and the next step is not ready. . . people tend to get frustrated.

I–15:   Right. You mentioned pre-planning as a way to smooth that out . . . is there anything else you can do . . . after all, it is not always possible in an operation like this to perfectly synchronize everything! (2)

R–15:   Right . . . I've found that out. I guess one thing you have to do is to let all of the members on the team realize that everything can't always run in perfect sync! (2) When they get frustrated they start looking for someone to blame. Of course they look at me, or tell me I should tell the such-and-such department to get off their asses and do their part. They don't always understand that their project team does not have the full time and attention of an engineer, since he is advising on other projects at the same time. (2)

I-16: Are you satisfied with how you have been able to handle this problem?

R-16: Can't say that I am satisfied. I can see where if I can't find a more efficient way to handle it, the frustration could flare up into a real rhubarb, at least verbally and this would make it harder for the team to work together. (3)

I-17: Have you ever just taken the team over to a conference room and sat down and talked about the synchronization problem? (2)

R-17: No, it never occurred to me. I have done a lot of talking individually to the men. But somehow it never even occurred to me to move from our usual work location for anything. (3) I guess I felt it would be viewed by the division manager as a waste of time.

I-18: I don't think you have to worry at all about that. That is one thing the rooms are for! If you can't schedule a room a week in advance, and need it to handle some group problems on a quicky basis, just check with Dorothy to schedule the room to fit your need!

R-18: Sounds like a good idea!

I-19: Also, you don't have to wait until there is strong feeling in a group about some problem. Sometimes, it is a good idea when you start a new project or get to a new phase of the project, it is good to prevent frustrations by letting people know in advance either that there are specific points in the project where coordination will probably be impossible, or that in more general terms there tends to be an oscillation between coordination and uncoordination in any development project. This is true of the creative process in general and that's what McBeam is. We are always doing prototypes, never mass production, and as you say, this has more flexibility of timing but also will lead to frustration, particularly if we expect development to run as smoothly as mass production. If we all remember there is a difference and not expect everything to be perfectly synchronized, there will be less frustration. Does that make sense to you? (1)

R-19: Yes, and I guess if people feel that the speed-up and slow-down pace is SOP for this kind of operation they won't have to look for some scapegoat to blame it on.

I–20: Exactly! Also, you will find another advantage to the group meetings. It will take some of the heat off of you. If they have a chance to freely discuss problems and frustrations among themselves, they see for themselves that others have problems too. (2) They see their problems in better perspective than if you talk to each one separately and try to get them to see the others' points of view. (3) At least this way you can be more of a referee than a punching bag. Also, sometimes you can just listen and learn more in a group meeting than you can in a lot more time spent in individual conferences. (2) Why don't you try that and then get back to me and talk about how it went? I might be able to give you some more help at that time.

R–20: Sounds worth a try! I haven't become a punching bag yet, but I was beginning to see how that could happen. (3)

I–21: There is one more thing we have to do. It'll just take a couple of minutes. You remember the rating sheet that is done on all foremen by the people they work with?

R–21: Uh huh.

I–22: This is the second one for you; the first was done three months ago a few weeks after you started. This last one generally shows improvement, since you are getting used to things and have discovered some of the things you have just been telling me about. (2) From talking to you today, I feel that you are going to continue to improve! There is just one item here that it might be worthwhile to discuss. The one about "dealing with human relations problems" . . . it is a little better than last rating time but still could be improved. I would just like your idea of what it might mean. I noticed that you were rated quite good by eight out of ten people, but the other two sounded like they are disappointed. (2)

R–22: Well, I know that just before rating time there were a couple of my team who really felt that they should be getting some overtime; but actually they were not the ones who were most overloaded, and it would do no good to let them get further ahead; that would not increase production. (2)

I–23: That's certainly true if they were already ahead.

R–23: Right; and what's more they didn't get ahead by working all that hard. It is just that on this project so far there is not a lot of detailed machine work to do. In fact I have told some of the other foremen that they could borrow my two machinists for a couple of days if they really needed them. (2)

I–24: I see. That sounds fair enough. Any other problems come up in the human relations area, even little ones? (4)

R-24:   Not that I can think of now. (3)

I-25:   How do the men on your team get along with each other? (4)

R-25:   Well, there is maybe a little feeling between some of the men on my team and a young Mexican, Efraén Lopez. I heard one refer to him as a "taco bender," but I'm not sure of the attitude that goes with that. None of us have worked with Mexican-Americans before. They are rare here in Ohio compared to Los Angeles or Houston. I never heard the term "taco bender" before. I get the feeling that Efraén would not like it. (3)

I-26:   I'm sure Efraén would *not* like it. Now that we will probably be hiring a few more Mexican-Americans that are migrating into Ohio, I think we should have some in-plant seminars in ethnic relations to prevent needless conflict in this area! (3) Well, we have been at this a while. I feel that our talk is very worthwhile. As you saw, your ratings are improving, and I'm glad I had a chance to get some idea of what the "human relations" rating meant. Remember to try that group meeting and get back to me . . . I might have some suggestions after hearing how things went. Is there anything else you wanted to bring up? (3)

R-26:   No, not that I can think of. (3)

I-27:   Remember, Bob, you can come in and talk to me any time. There is no need to wait until the next progress report time!

CRITICAL ANALYSIS QUESTIONS

Answer the same ten questions as you did for Interview A, plus those below.

11. What are two or three of the most important differences between Interview A and Interview B in the interviewing *method* used?

12. What are the most important differences in the *results?*

Selected Readings

Drake, J. D. *Interviewing for Managers,* Rev. ed. New York: American Management Association, 1982.
For the business executive with the task of evaluating job applicants. Contains short excerpts from interviews. Deals with what questions to ask, how to start the applicant talking, how to keep him talking, how to evaluate what he says, and how to set up the interview situation. Provides a format for the selection interview. Bibliography not annotated. No footnotes.

Maier, Norman R. F. *The Appraisal Interview: Three Basic Approaches.* La Jolla, Calif.: University Associates, 1976.
    Provides pairs of role-played interviews to illustrate three types of interview objectives: tell-and-sell, tell-and-listen, and problem solving. Discusses the problems associated with each style. It is written for executives who want to improve their appraisal interviewing. Long bibliography, not annotated.

Maier, Norman R. F., Allen R. Solem, and Ayesha A. Maier. *The Role-Play Technique: A Handbook for Management and Leadership Practice.* La Jolla, Calif.: University Associates, 1975.
    A role-playing approach to learning management skills for a variety of tasks including interviewing. Separate chapters deal with interviewing the union steward, the personnel interview, the promotion interview, the appraisal interview, and the progress interview. Each case presents the problem, constructs the scenario, provides the role information for each participant, including the observers in the class. One of the most careful and thorough manuals on the uses of role-playing for skill learning by participants and the observers.

O'Leary, Lawrence R. *Interviewing for the Decision Maker.* Chicago: Nelson-Hall, 1976.
    Focuses on selecting candidates for employment and choosing current employees for promotion. Although it is "written to bridge the gap between behavioral science . . . and day-to-day practical hiring decisions," it has very little on social-psychological theory of communication. Some short verbatim interview bits. The appendix provides an employment interview guide.

Chapter Twenty

The Teacher–Parent Interview

Traditionally, public school teachers do not think of themselves as interviewers. Their professional emphasis is on giving oral information and instructions to groups, rather than on receiving oral information from individuals. Yet there are several situations in which teachers do interviewing in such semantic disguises as student conferences, practice-teacher conferences, parent conferences, one-to-one teaching situations, oral examinations, student counseling, and group discussions.

School administrators are becoming aware that the professionally competent classroom teacher, as well as the school psychologist or counselor, should have basic interviewing skills.

The two interviews selected for this chapter involve teachers interviewing parents whose children have applied for entrance into kindergarten.[1] However, the school's readiness testing has indicated a low probability of success for both of these children if they enter kindergarten this year.

THE ORGANIZATIONAL SETTING

The County School District put notices in the local newspapers the first of April announcing to parents that if they have a child who will be five years old by September 30 and want the child to start kindergarten in September, they should come to their local elementary school to register their child for kindergarten. About April 15, the parent is mailed a copy of the *Parent's Guide to School Readiness* and asked to bring the child to school on May 5 for the kindergarten screening program ". . . to help us know your child better and to work with you in

---

[1]Advice on this setting of the teacher-parent interview was kindly provided by Patricia Day Malone, School Psychologist.

making the adjustment easy and the educational adventure fruitful and happy."

The kindergarten School Readiness Test consists of performance tests in the following nine areas: gross motor coordination, visual and fine motor coordination, visual discrimination and perception, visual sequential memory, auditory discrimination and perception, auditory sequential memory, receptive language, expressive language, and number concepts.

The state law expressly forbids schools to refuse to accept children in public kindergarten, yet it is clear that some children at five years of age are much more ready to benefit from the experience than are others. In fact, for some who enter too soon for their stage of maturation, the whole experience may range from unpleasant associations with the idea of school to deep psychological trauma. The readiness for kindergarten can be fairly accurately determined with the combined information furnished by the nine tests, an interview with the parent, and observation of the child at play with the group before and after they take the School Readiness Tests.

OBJECTIVES OF THE INTERVIEW

The major objective in this interview is *persuasion*. The information-gathering function in the interview is a means to the ultimate objective of persuading the parent that it is best for the child to wait a year to be admitted to kindergarten. Since the state law requires the school system to make kindergarten available to every five-year-old, the school authorities cannot unilaterally decide not to admit the child. On the other hand, teachers and educational psychologists know that in some cases the admission of a child too early to kindergarten can be damaging to the child. Therefore, the teacher provides advice which the parent is free to accept or reject.

For a persuasion interview to be successful, the interviewer (the persuader) must convince the respondent (the persuadee) that the suggested course of action is in his own best interests, that the suggested course of action is practical, and that the recommendation is highly desirable or that at least it is the best choice.

The interviewer must prepare in advance by collecting the evidence relevant to the argument, planning some alternative tactics in case certain objections are raised by the persuadee, and discovering as much as possible about the persuadee's needs, values, and beliefs as they relate to the recommended action. The chances of accomplishing the specific objectives of the interview will be increased if most of this information gathering is done in advance.

Although all of the basic principles of interviewing apply to the persuasion interview, there is a characteristic tactical sequence that has been found to be effective.[2]

1. Start the discussion by establishing some common ground of values or beliefs that will serve as a logical foundation for the persuasive argument.

2. Discover the respondent's needs, desires, values, beliefs, and plans related to the alternatives for action under discussion.

3. Encourage the respondent's active participation in the discussion.

4. Establish the interviewer's credibility.

5. Be prepared to challenge any misinformation or false beliefs the respondent has that are related to the argument.

6. Show why the recommended action is in accord with the respondent's best interests.

7. Present a workable method of carrying out the recommended action.

To accomplish these tactical objectives the interviewer must use all the techniques and skills needed to discover the respondent's needs, values, and beliefs, and to learn how these relate to the recommended action in the respondent's mind. Sensitive listening is needed to detect and probe out possible misconceptions that act as obstacles to accepting the interviewer's recommendations.

If the parent accepts the basic recommendation that the child not enter kindergarten immediately, the teacher may go further in the interview to determine the possible causes of the below-average scores and make suggestions to the parent on how to improve the situation during the year the child is waiting to be admitted.[3]

---

[2]Charles J. Stewart and William B. Cash, *Interviewing: Principles and Practices*, 4th ed. (Dubuque, Iowa: Wm. C. Brown, 1985). See Chapter 9, "Persuasive Interviewing," for a good summary of the objectives, strategies, tactics, and techniques of persuasion interviews.

[3]In this situation these additional recommendations might include such things as (a) have the child's eyesight checked and fit him with glasses, (b) have the parent or siblings play simple reading games with the child, (c) get the child involved in large-muscle activities, (d) play games aimed at improving small muscle and hand-eye coordination, (e) read stories to the child, (f) have the child tell the parent a fairy tale he or she has heard several times, or (g) play some number games involving counting and recognizing numbers.

Interview A

Of the sixty applicants for kindergarten only nine seem clearly not ready to enter this September. Mary Blumer is one of these nine. The kindergarten teacher studies the results of Mary's School Readiness Test and notes that she is below average in seven of the nine areas tested. The school psychologist has sent along the additional information that Mrs. Blumer is interested in going to work as soon as Mary is in kindergarten.

Mary is an only child, and her birthday is in August, so she would barely be five years old if she entered kindergarten in September.

The interview takes place by appointment in the teacher's room at 3:00 after most of the children have gone home, and a few are waiting for parents to retrieve them. The principal directed Mrs. Blumer to the teacher and introduced them.

I-1: As you know this conference is to give you the results of the readiness tests that Mary took last week and discuss whether or not Mary is ready for kindergarten at this time.

R-1: Yes. That is what I understood.

I-2: Good! If I remember correctly Mary is the only child.

R-2: Yes.

I-3: Well, here is the summary sheet showing how Mary did on the nine tests. You can keep that copy. If you look at the two bottom lines on the sheet you can see that Mary's vision and hearing are normal, so you can rest easy that she has no problems there. Now, the table up above shows the nine areas that were tested starting with *gross motor* and down to *number concepts*. The three columns are labeled *above average*, *average*, and *needs to develop*, right?

R-3: Uh huh.

I-4: You can see that Mary's scores in seven of the nine tests fell into the *needs to develop* column . . . and . . .

R-4: That's impossible. You mean she failed seven out of nine and is only average in the other two? That's strange because my sister-in-law, who is a child psychologist, says that Mary is a delightful child.

I-5: Being a delightful child really has nothing to do with the problem, Mrs. Blumer.

R-5: Well, I don't think that mentally retarded children are delightful myself. But these sorts of tests are notoriously invalid and biased. I know that you would like to keep the class size down to make it easier but why should my child suffer?

I-6: That's just it, we don't want the child to suffer, because . . . .

R-6: And the child is not the only one to consider. Parents have rights too. I am beginning to learn this in my self-assertiveness workshop group. Are you saying that I can't put my child in kindergarten this September?

I-7: No, Mrs. Blumer, I'm not saying that at all. I said that we were going to discuss whether or not Mary is ready for kindergarten at this time!

R-7: Well, your little tests show that she is average or below in everything, but since you aren't saying that this means she should not enter kindergarten now, then I say that there would be nothing like getting her into a group of children where she can *learn* instead of punishing her for what she hasn't learned. She's an only child and hasn't had the benefit of siblings to play with, so I refuse to make this a basis for her permanent isolation from her peers. That would be cruel discrimination, blaming the child for her problem.

I-8: (taken aback) I understand how you feel, Mrs. . . . .

R-8: No, you don't! I don't want to discuss it any more. All I ask is that when Mary arrives in your group in September that you don't take it out on her because you couldn't keep her out.

I-9: Don't worry Mrs. Blumer, she is not scheduled to be in my group, so . . .

R-9: Frankly, I'm glad to hear that, but I'm sorry that we couldn't have been more friendly. Goodbye.

I-10: Goodbye.

Answer the questions below before reading the next interview.

CRITICAL ANALYSIS QUESTIONS

This interview is an obvious failure, not only because the teacher did not persuade the parent not to enroll the child but also because she has made an enemy of the parent. Even though the failure is obvious, the reasons for the failure need some analysis. The parent first takes a defensive and then an offensive position. In effect, the parent walks out on the teacher who hasn't begun to achieve most of the objectives of the interview.

Rather than analyzing this interview in terms of specific techniques, it will be more fruitful to ask whether the interviewer is even attempting to execute the essential steps in the *tactical* sequence of the persuasive interview.

1. Does the interviewer try to establish a sympathetic relationship at the beginning of the interview? If so, give the I– numbers.

2. Does the interviewer start a discussion to establish some common ground of agreement on values or beliefs to serve as a logical foundation for a persuasive argument? If so, give the I– numbers.

3. Does the interviewer attempt to discover the respondent's needs, desires, beliefs, or expectations related to the child's entrance into kindergarten? If so, give the I– numbers.

4. Does the interviewer try to encourage the respondent's active participation in the interview? If so, give the I– numbers.

5. Does the interviewer try to establish her credibility? If so, give the I– numbers.

6. Does the interviewer note any misconceptions or misinformation the respondent has that are related to the recommendations? If so, give the I– numbers.

7. Does the interviewer try to show her recommendations are in accord with the respondent's best interests? If so, give the I– numbers.

8. Does the interviewer attempt to present a practical plan for carrying out the recommendations? If so, give the I– numbers.

Interview B

The kindergarten teacher after studying the results of the screening test for Richard Helm sees that (a) the scores are all well below average except for the receptive language score; (b) this cannot be explained by the child's age since his birthday is in November, so it leaves open the possibility that there might be some neurological learning disability, that something about the child's environment slows down his motor learning and other skills, or that there are some defects of sight, hearing, or speech that need correcting.

The school psychologists who sent the test results to the kindergarten teacher added the information that the parent is anxious to get the child into kindergarten and says that she knows "that Richie is ready" for kindergarten. Mrs. Helm has an appointment for 3:30 with Mrs. Kliene, the head kindergarten teacher. The principal directs the parent to the teacher's office.

R-0:   Hello, I'm Lucy Helm, Richie's mother.

I-1:   Yes, I'm Barbara Kliene. I'm glad to meet you! How is your time schedule? I hope we have at least thirty to forty-five minutes to talk if you have time.

R-1:   That's fine. As long as you are willing to spend that much time.

I-2:   Would you sit here where it's comfortable and I'll close the door so we won't be distracted by the noises in the hall. (Sitting down) There, that's better. We have a pot of coffee. Would you care for some?

R-2:   That sounds good.

I-3:   Cream, sugar, or both?

R-3:   Just a bit of cream, please.

I-4:   These Styrofoam cups aren't elegant, but they keep the coffee warm and don't burn your fingers to hold them. (2)[4] Did you get a chance to read the *Parents' Guide to School Readiness* we sent along?

R-4:   Not all of it.

I-5:   Well hang on to it. There's no need to read it all before our discussion today. But you will see that in the Jonesburg School District we put a lot of emphasis on the importance of getting a child off to a good start in kindergarten. That's why we feel strongly enough to spend the time and effort with the screening program. Let me take a minute to explain the background of the screening program. First, the laws of Ohio say that kindergarten and first grade must be provided at ages five and six, but they do not demand school entry before age six. Second, the parent is the one who makes the final decision whether the child should enter kindergarten, as long as the child is five before September 30. So the idea of the screening tests and parent interviews is to share information provided by these tests with the parents and have a good discussion so the parent is better prepared to make a decision that is best for the child.

The reason this readiness idea is so important to the child's welfare is that if any child is pushed into kindergarten before he is ready, he is in danger of feeling like a failure. You see, kindergarten has a very special function . . . to provide an atmosphere where no *adult* has to decide to pass or fail a child on the basis of whether some particular set of information or skills is learned. It should be a place where the child cannot

---

[4]Numbers in parentheses indicate seconds of silence.

get the feeling that he has failed. That is our philosophy. Do you agree with that?

R-5:   That is exactly my idea! (2)

I-6:   Uh huh.

R-6:   In fact, there is too much putting people down and saying "you won't be able to do this or that" . . . how do we know if we've never given them a chance?

I-7:   Right! We try hard to put this idea into practice. We find that it is not so hard to get the adults who will give the child a chance to do everything he's able and who will not blame him for not being able to accomplish more. But, as child psychologists have discovered, it is not enough just to prevent adults from labeling a child a failure, because the child gets many self-feelings from the other children, either by the way they treat him or by the way the child compares his or her own skills with those of others in the play group. It does no good for the parent or teacher to say "Susie, don't worry if you can't do what Mary can do, she has a different maturation pattern from you." It is hard enough to get parents and teachers to understand that! Have you ever happened to notice that even young kids, not just teenagers, seem to compare themselves with kids their own age and look to them for approval?

R-7:   Yes. I guess I have heard it mostly about teenagers, and mine are just five and seven, but it seems that Johnny, the seven-year-old, is much more concerned with what some of his buddies are doing and thinking than he is with what the teacher thinks . . . at least on some things that may not be so important to adults but are important to him.

I-8:   Exactly . . . a good observation! Well . . . that is what the screening program is all about. Kids grow up in different ways at different rates, and if a child is thrown into the group before he is ready, there is a danger that he will get the idea by comparing himself with others. On things that seem very small to adults, he can get a feeling of failure and a negative attitude toward school which may stick with him for a long time. Before I pull out Richard's readiness scores, I would like to find out a few things about the situation at home that might help us to decide what to do. OK?

R-8:   Uh huh.

I-9:   Are you working outside the home now?

R-9:   No, I'm not.

I-10:   Have you ever worked since you have been married?

R-10:   Yes, I worked until Johnny was born, so it's been seven years since I have worked.

I-11: Do you have any plans to go back to work sometime in the future?

R-11: Yes, definitely! I can hardly wait to go back to work. I have been out for seven years and it is a little scary to think how rusty you might be.

I-12: Could you tell me just a little about why it is a little scary?

R-12: Well, when you're home with the kids all the time you don't talk with adults much, you sort of wonder if you are talking baby talk or if you are laughing only at first-grader jokes. (3) Then when you meet other adults they are usually mothers and your friends become the mothers of kids the same age and then you hear mostly about kids' problems or occasionally complaints about husbands . . . so it's still the family scene that you have enough of already. (2)

I-13: So, you're afraid you won't know how to act in a work situation where the conversation isn't about kids?

R-13: Sure, and it's not only that. I'm afraid I have lost my typing skills and how to deal with clients. Maybe they wouldn't even want me as a receptionist any more. They sometimes want some cute young thing out front. (2)

I-14: Well, you certainly are attractive enough without looking like you are flighty or immature . . .

R-14: That's the best thing I've heard all week! (Laughing)

I-15: How does your husband feel about your going to work? (2)

R-15: He's very happy with the idea. He thinks I'm more interesting when I am working and besides he admits that we can use the money. (3) I'd go back to work when the kids got in school and two is all we plan to have (Knocking on table). (2)

I-16: Is that why you want to get Richie in kindergarten now?

R-16: Yes, that is one reason, and I think it would be good for him too.

I-17: Tell me a little about your plans to work.

R-17: Well, I know a person has a better chance of getting what they want if they can take a full-time job, but I know that is impossible now. So, I am looking around for a half-time job, but haven't found anything yet.

I-18: I see. I'm glad your husband supports you in this; that isn't always the case. Now would you just tell me a bit about what Richie's day is like at home now?

R-18:   What do you mean?

I-19:   Just the schedule of activities on a typical week day. When does he get up and what does he do through the day?

R-19:   Well, he is usually up the same time or before I am, at about 6:30. I try to get my husband off to work by 7:15 so that he won't have to speed to work. Sometimes we all three eat breakfast together . . . I should say usually. Except that Richie is usually not dressed, but Johnny is because he is older and has to catch the school bus at about 7:25. After Johnny is picked up by the bus, I see that Richie gets dressed and then he plays 'til lunchtime while I get some housework, sewing, or what-not done. I try to do my errands either in the morning and take Richie with me or wait until Johnny has been home from school for a half hour when we talk. And then at about 4:00 I can get out for an hour and a half while the next-door neighbor's daughter comes and plays with Richie and Johnny. We usually have dinner around 6:30 and finish cleaning up by 7:30, and it's almost time for Richie and Johnny to go to bed. I read bedtime stories to them. Sometimes my husband reads to one while I read to the other and we switch the next night.

I-20:   Does Richie go outside much to play?

R-20:   No, that's the thing . . . we live in the upstairs of a duplex and there is practically no yard, and there's no fence between the house and the street, where there is a lot of traffic. So it's not a very great place to let children go out and play. Recently, there have even been rumors that some teenagers were giving drugs to some of the elementary school-age kids on the block. I am afraid to let Richie, especially, go out alone or even with Johnny. Luckily, the school bus picks him up right in front of the house, and I always wait to see that the bus comes and he gets picked up.

I-21:   So about how much time each day on the average would Richie be outside?

R-21:   Well, now that you put it that way . . . it sounds strange but he is probably not out except to walk to the car, or sometimes to walk with me to the post office on the next corner. He just isn't out much!

I-22:   Uh huh. How long have you lived at your current address?

R-22:   It has been four years since my husband went to work for International Harvester. We have plans to move after we build our own house. It looks like he will stay at IH so we have already bought a good lot in a nice neighborhood, but it will be a couple of years before we can build and move in.

I-23:   That sounds wonderful. It will probably be a much better place for everyone, and Richie and Johnny will probably have a safer place and more space to play.

R-23: We can hardly wait, in fact.

I-24: Well that gives me a bit of a picture of Richie's day and now I'll show you the results of Richie's readiness tests. Remember that a kid's development rate speeds up and slows down on a month-by-month basis so to look at how Richie compares with other kids his age right now does not necessarily predict how he will compare in six months or a year from now. I know you understand that.

R-24: Yes.

I-25: Well, let's get the overview first. Notice that there were nine tests, and we just classify kids into *above average, average,* and *needs to develop.* Now, in this case, average does not mean for the nation or for the state of Ohio, it only means average for the group that applied for kindergarten this fall in the County School District, OK?

R-25: Uh huh.

I-26: This summary sheet you can keep. It shows at a glance that Richie needs to develop in five of the nine areas: *gross motor, visual and fine motor, visual discrimination and perception, expressive language,* and *number concepts.* He is average in *visual sequential memory, receptive language, auditory discrimination and memory,* and *auditory sequential memory.* This is in comparison with the group of sixty applying for this fall in the county system.

R-26: Wow! That looks bad!

I-27: No, that's not bad. It just means at *this* time he is a bit behind the average kid in *this* group in *some* things.

R-27: Then you say that it is OK for him to enter kindergarten now?

I-28: No, I'm not saying that. It is up to you to decide; but what this test shows is that he would be less likely to feel inadequate in comparison with the others if he first had a chance to develop in five of the nine areas.

R-28: What does the *gross motor* test have to do with how he is going to feel about himself, for example?

I-29: Well, the test has him hop on one foot and then the other, and skip, and walk up and down steps, and balance on each foot for five seconds and that sort of thing. He really needs more experience at this type of thing. You see other little boys are quick to notice that someone is uncoordinated and there is a tendency to pick on him or make fun of him. The teacher can try to prevent that to some extent, but then there are things that Richie would notice himself, like he would probably come out on the bottom in any game requiring large muscle, speed, and balance.

R-29:   What does this *visual and fine motor* mean?

I-30:   That is sort of hand-eye coordination. For example, the child is asked to tie his shoes, cut out circles of colored paper, make block letters, cut out a flower, button buttons, and point to colors on a chart, and that sort of thing. These are basic skills needed to succeed at many of the activities most of the children are interested in.

R-30:   While we're at it, what is the *number concept* test? Is he expected to know concepts?

I-31:   Just basic approaches to counting, like counting dots, reading numbers, holding up the correct number of fingers, and giving another person a certain number of blocks. . . this is just a general basis for playing certain games and following instructions for some of the crafts activities.

R-31:   Well, that is enough to tell me it is all very useful skills you want him to know. But I can't say that I'm not disappointed. But it looks like there would be no better way for him to catch up than to get with the other kids who *can* do these things, and they will set a good example.

I-32:   When you told me that you were wanting to go back to work, I tried to think of a way to do what is best both for you and for Richie. As you said, you fear putting off the time you go back to work because you might be getting rusty and yet Richie would feel more secure if he had a chance to catch up in some areas before getting into a group of five to five-and-a-half year olds. Wouldn't it be good if something could be worked out for both of you?

R-32:   You really think he can't go to kindergarten?

I-33:   He could, but I don't think it is best for him right now. Let me put it this way. Knowing what I see as a kindergarten teacher, if Richie were my son I'd not send him into *this group at this time.*

R-33:   Well, I appreciate your frankness, but how does that help me? I've been waiting seven years . . . that is beginning to seem like a long time.

I-34:   I can imagine that it does. It's not like you didn't have experience working before. Let me see what you think of a couple of ideas I just got. I forgot to ask you whether, ideally, you would like to work part-time or full-time?

R-34:   As long as we're talking about the ideal situation, I would like to work about a 6½ hour day so I could leave home after my kids catch the bus and get back to see them get off the bus at 3:45.

I-35:   Did you know that kindergarten is only 2½ hours?

R–35:   But I thought it started at nine and let out at 2:30 or three!

I–36:   Well actually there are two groups of 2½ hours each. The morning session runs from nine to 11:30 and the afternoon group comes from 12:30 to 3:00. So each group has just 2½ hours.

R–36:   That means I would have to find a baby sitter even to be able to work four hours a day! I had never thought of it that way.

I–37:   There is one possibility that might give both you and Richie what you need at this time . . . just an idea. See what you think of it. There is a very good chance that Richie could get into the Head Start program for a half day in either the morning or the afternoon. That has the advantage that the kids will be 3½, four, and five years old. So some of them will be a lot less coordinated than Richie, and he won't feel like the low man on the totem pole. This wouldn't free you enough to get a job, but you could get some of the rust off by taking a refresher course at County Technical College, and they even have a group of women who meet every Wednesday evening who are making the transition from housewife back to a job . . . some are heading for their first job.

R–37:   That sounds interesting. I hadn't thought of anything like that.

I–38:   But there's one more very important part to the program for Richie. What would help Richie a lot at this point would be a little extra boost from you and your husband. For example, you mentioned that living in a duplex in your neighborhood is restricting the kids' outdoor play. Well, until you move into your new house you could make a special effort to get Richie to do things like walk on the curb to get practice at balancing, or you could even bring in a new two-by-four about six feet long and put it on the living room rug and have him walk on it, first forward, then sideways, and then backward. In the *Parents' Guide to School Readiness* it gives a whole list of simple activities that you can do with your child to build the particular skills he needs. Here, let me give you a copy.

R–38:   No, I still have the one you sent in the mail.

I–39:   Oh, yes, that's right. Just one more thought. Any time you spend with Richie to help him develop his readiness during this year while he's in Head Start will make it more certain that he will be happier and have a better experience when he comes to us next year.

In the meantime you can be getting ready to go to work. However, remember that kindergarten is only 2½ hours a day, and that even when he gets to first grade he will be at school only five hours. Later the school day increases to six, then six and a half.

R–39:   Well, the whole family can work into the new pattern gradually.

I–40:   It sounds like a good idea. Remember that you have to make the final decision about Richie. It isn't necessary to have him in Head Start, but in any case, you should get him involved in some of the skill activities suggested in the *Parent's Guide.* When you do that, be sure you do these activities in the spirit of a game, not as a corrective exercise.

R–40:   Yes, I can see that.

I–41:   We have a policy of not getting a decision from you while you are here. Think it over and give me a call to tell me what you decide to do. That way we know it's your own decision.

R–41:   Fine. I'll call you soon.

I–42:   Good. It's been a pleasure to meet you. Goodbye!

R–42:   Likewise. Goodbye.

CRITICAL ANALYSIS QUESTIONS

Answer the same questions that follow Interview A, and look at the salient contrasts. Then consult your instructor's handout to see the writer's critique of the pair of interviews. Note any points that you may have missed in your critiques that throw light on the nature of the problem or possible solutions.

Selected Readings

Langdon, Grace, and I. W. Stout. *Teacher-Parent Interviews.* Englewood Cliffs, N.J.: Prentice-Hall, 1954.
    A persuasive presentation of the vital need for teachers to interview parents, and interview them well. Gives excellent practical guides for what to talk about, what situations call for an interview, what to expect, and what information to try to get, what solutions a teacher may try, and what to do with special problems during the interview. Examples of content covered in actual interviews from kindergarten to high school are given. Provides detailed considerations for planning an interview. Ends with a short list of do's and don'ts.

Chapter Twenty-One

The Mass Media Impact Interview

Interviewing to evaluate the audience-effects of mass media communication is done in many forms and settings. The most common evaluations of the print medium done by the private sector are those aimed at testing, comparing, or predicting the effects of advertisements in newspapers and magazines. Sometimes publishing houses evaluate textbooks by studying the readers' reactions. In the public sector political parties and government agencies study the effects of their propaganda campaigns and of their educational materials.

The most common evaluation of the impact of television and film media (public or private) is measuring the size of the audience. Such studies of film do not require sophisticated interviewing, nor do they reveal why some members of the potential audience choose not to attend, and they do not show what those who did attend liked or disliked, understood, or misunderstood about the film.

Increasingly, the producers of films do in-depth studies of a sample audience's reactions to a preliminary version of the film. A good impact study obtains the audience's reaction to specific features of the film. Also, it compares the reactions of viewers having different characteristics. In this way it can be determined *who* reacted *how* and *why*. This allows some features of the film to be changed before it is released for general circulation.

Unlike the nose-counting surveys of audience size, the more analytic impact studies require sophisticated interviewing methods, often combined with other impact-measurement techniques.[1]

---

[1]Robert K. Merton and Patricia L. Kendall, "The Focused Interview," *American Journal of Sociology* 51 (1946), pp. 541–57. Merton coined the term *focused interview* to refer to an interview aimed at obtaining a person's reaction to some previously analyzed stimulus or situation. In this case the important

THE ORGANIZATIONAL SETTING

Both the teaching staff and the recruits at the Naval Training Station felt that the typical training films were often boring and unimaginative. The instructional staff, all naval officers, felt that the problem of trainees sleeping during the films became so serious that they had devised various forms of punishment for those who fell asleep, but the sleeping continued. This problem was most noticeable in the GMT (general military training) films that dealt with subjects deemed relevant to the recruits' post-military or civilian roles—subjects such as history, civics, economics, or consumer education.

The Naval Instructional Technology Development Center (NITDC), staffed by civilians, was commissioned to develop a series of films on the topic of consumer education that would be interesting enough to keep the recruits awake. NITDC decided to produce one prototype film with a new format designed to hold the viewers' interest. They would then carefully evaluate its effect on trainees before producing the second in the proposed series of twelve. In reaction to the boring quality of the films they had analyzed, NITDC decided to go all out to keep the audience on the edge of their seats. To accomplish this they planned *(a)* to use an entertainment format with the facts and attitudes they wanted to promote woven into the plot of a Western with a Clint Eastwood–type hero and *(b)* to use all of the best cinematography techniques and sound effects to produce a thirty-minute film that would "wake the dead."

The scenario of the film. The film opens with our hero on horseback, seen at a distance, riding slowly down from the sage-covered hills toward the camera. In the foreground a Mexican cantina stands alone at the cross-trails in the desert. The moaning wind propels tumbleweeds past the cantina door. At one table a group of Mexicans in rag-tag military uniforms are playing cards while their leader, Sargento, picks his teeth with a dagger. As the players cautiously eye the entering gringo, there is no background music and the only sound is that of the desert wind howling mournfully and the chickens squawking as the barmaid waves them out the door. An old guitarron player in the background has stopped playing as the gringo orders a drink at the bar. He takes the whole bottle, pivots slowly, leans on the bar, and surveys the card-players with a cool eye.

He is invited by Sargento to join the game. As the game proceeds most of the players, including the gringo, are cheating. All the Mexicans speak English with a stereotyped Mexican accent and only an occasional

---

feature is that the interviewer is familiar with the stimulus situation before beginning the interview.

word is heard from the gringo. Finally, the gringo loses all of his money but wants to continue and offers his life insurance policy as collateral.

This triggers off a lively discussion among the Mexicans as to whether this is "just a piece of worthless paper" or has some real value. The most skeptical is their leader, Sargento. In persuading him of the value of the insurance policy each of the four other Mexicans explains the type of insurance he has, and why each different type is a good thing for his particular stage in life. This section of the film contains all the facts about different types of life insurance. The gringo stays out of the discussion while it is decided that he can use the policy, which he bets, hoping to regain his losses.

In the final hand of the game the Sargento calls to see the hands of the other players. The first private has three aces and two kings, the second private has two aces and three queens, the third private has two aces and three jacks, the Sargento has two aces and three kings. Obviously somebody is cheating, since there is a total of nine aces; but the Sargento decides to wait to see the gringo's hand, which turns out to be *four* aces and one king. At this point the scene explodes into a collage of pistols firing, bodies falling, and gold pieces flying—all in slow motion. When the smoke clears, the guitarron player's head rises from behind the bar. He sees that all are dead, crosses the room, picks up the insurance policy, saying, "eet ees wort hees weight een gold," takes the barmaid by the arm, and walks out of the cantina into the bright sunlight. In the dark foreground a pistol aims at the guitarron player's back, the scene dissolves, and a lone shot is heard as the theme music rises up under the credits.

Method of measuring impact on audience. The film was shown to a total of 174 navy personnel including trainers and trainees. There were five showings, each with audiences of thirty to forty people. Questionnaires were administered immediately before and after each showing, and the number of people sleeping was noted during each showing. The questionnaires were designed *(a)* to measure the amount of *gain in information* about each type of insurance policy, *(b)* to determine any *change in attitude* toward the importance of life insurance, *(c)* to find which *features* of the film were *liked and disliked*, such as the mixture of entertainment with instructions, the background music, the slow-motion techniques, the camera angles, the color, the plot, the characterizations, the accent of the Mexicans, the western setting, and the ending, *(d)* to rate this film in *comparison to "most training films,"* and *(e)* to discover whether the film had any *unintended effects*, such as producing a negative stereotype of Mexicans in the minds of the viewers.

After the pre- and posttest questionnaires were done, a random sample of the 174 viewers was selected to be depth-interviewed five days later.

OBJECTIVES OF THE INTERVIEW

The information from this interview was not used to make quantitative statements about the reactions of the viewers. This was done with the questionnaire data. Nor was it necessary to cover all the same points with each respondent. Instead, the purpose of the interview was to promote spontaneous responses that could be used in five ways:

1. To discover the respondent's attitude toward the pre- and post-test questionnaires, and toward the experiment in general, that might reduce the validity of the questionnaire responses.

2. To look for discrepancies between the oral responses and what the respondent had said on the questionnaires as another check on the validity of the questionnaires.

3. To discover additional salient reactions not included in the answer categories of the highly structured questionnaires.

4. To provide direct quotes as concrete examples of the more generalized responses given on the questionnaires.

5. To provide insights as to why the person made the responses that he did on the questionnaires.

In more general terms, the purpose of the interview was to provide a cross-check on the questionnaires' validity and to supply a more qualitative meaning to the quantified summaries of the questionnaire responses.

Since the interviewers had seen the film several times and had the respondents' questionnaires to study before the interview, it was easy to focus on certain features of the film, or on certain individual responses made on the questionnaires where some potential inconsistency was apparent.

THE INTERVIEW SITUATION

All interviews were done at the Training Center of the Naval Base. Each respondent was sent to the interviewing room by the commanding officer, who sometimes failed to explain why the respondent was being sent to room 218; so it was advisable that the interviewer explain as much as necessary about the interview. Each interview was tape-recorded so that the exact quotes could be excerpted by the interviewer later.

Interview A

Before reading this interview it might help to read the critical analysis questions at the end of this chapter to give you an idea of what to look for. In any case, you will probably have to read each interview several times in order to answer all of the questions.

A seaman recruit walks past the door of the interviewing room and looks in doubtfully. The interviewer speaks to the seaman.

I-1:   Are you looking for the interviewing room? (2)[2]

R-1:   I don't know, sir. I was just told to go to room 218 . . .

I-2:   Did you see the film on insurance called *"For a Few Pesos More"*?

R-2:   Yes, sir!

I-3:   Then you are in the right place! Come on in! Sit down here. (2)

R-3:   Then I'm not going to get garbage detail?

I-4:   No, I just want to find out what you thought of the movie.

R-4:   Sure, what do you want to know?

I-5:   Well, for example, what did you think of the color?

R-5:   I always like color better than black and white like most of the training films I've seen.

I-6:   You like color better!

R-6:   Yes sir.

I-7:   And what about the background music, was that good?

R-7:   It was the same as I heard in a Clint Eastwood movie a couple of years ago.

I-8:   Right! Did you like the camera angles?

R-8:   I didn't notice any great difference from any other Western I have seen lately; they all use different kinds of camera angles.

I-9:   Like what?

R-9:   Well, at the beginning when he was entering the cantina, you saw the people inside framed by Clint . . . I mean the gringo's legs . . .

---

[2]Numbers in parentheses indicate seconds of silence.

and the spurs on his boots were up close like you had your head on the ground.

I-10: Right! What did you think of that slow-motion scene at the end?

R-10: Well, it was good that it was in slow motion because so much happened that you couldn't have seen it if it weren't.

I-11: I see. And what did you think of the Western background or setting?

R-11: Well, I like good Westerns, but I never saw one selling insurance before.

I-12: So you *like* Westerns!

R-12: Right!

I-13: Did you like the close-ups of the faces of the poker players?

R-13: Well, if you like to see every drop of sweat on somebody's nose, that is a good way to do it.

I-14: I guess that's right. Did you like the way the film ended?

R-14: That was a big surprise, the way the Sargento and the rest all started shooting at once . . .

I-15: Uh huh.

R-15: Even with the slow motion it was confusing with so much going on at once. There were a couple of things I just didn't understand about it, but it sure would wake anyone up if they had been sleeping . . . with all that screaming and Sargento's crazy laughing.

I-16: How did this film compare with most training films you have seen?

R-16: Well, I have been in boot camp only three weeks, so I can't say what *most* training films are like yet.

I-17: Right! Did you feel that you learned anything about life insurance from this film?

R-17: Sure, I didn't know much about life insurance before.

I-18: Is there anything else you would like to say about the movie? (2)

R-18: No, that about covers it I guess.

I-19: Well, thank you very much for your help!

Also read Interview B before answering the critical analysis questions which appear after Interview B.

Interview B

The setting is exactly the same as in Interview A. Again, a seaman recruit walks past the door and looks in at the interviewer who is sitting and apparently reading a magazine. The interviewer looks up to greet the seaman.

I-1: Hello, I'm Dan Goldman, are you Kevin Condit?

R-1: Yes sir.

I-2: Good. Your name was selected at random from the list of seamen who saw the experimental film, *For a Few Pesos More*.

R-2: Oh, that's a surprise! (2)

I-3: Surprise? How? (1)

R-3: Well, I was just told to go to room 218 at 0900 and no reason was given. But since this area is where you go to get disciplined, I thought I was in for it for sure.

I-4: I didn't realize that, or I would have tried to get another room. I have never been on the base before and don't know my way around yet.

R-4: I have been here three weeks and I still don't know my way around too well, but I know this is where they send you to get assigned to garbage can cleaning detail.

I-5: I'm glad you told me this so that I can explain to the next seaman that comes to be interviewed. Here's the situation. I have been hired as a consultant on instructional film evaluation. I am from Ohio and have been asked to evaluate this film before it is released for general use in the navy. The Naval Instructional Technology Development Center here naturally thinks it's a great film because they produced it. Some of the top navy brass don't agree with the producers. Actually, more important than either the producers of the film or the top navy officers is what the seaman trainees think of the film. After all, that's who it was made for. That's where you come in! To make sure what you say is confidential and you can give your honest reactions without worrying about hurting the producers' feelings, your opinions will be collected and analyzed by me back in Ohio, and my report, of course, will not have the names of any people interviewed. Do you have any questions before we start?

R-5: Sure do Can I smoke?

I-6: That's OK with me. Here is an ashtray! If you sit here, I'll put the ashtray on this box.

R-6: Great.

I-7: One more thing I need to explain. I need to tape-record our discussion so that I won't have to have a third person to take notes, and I will be able to devote my full attention to understanding what you are telling me. I will take the cassettes back to Ohio, analyze them personally, and then erase them to use in another study. Okay?

R-7: Fair enough.

I-8: I don't have a lot of specific questions to quiz you with. I just want to have a wide-open discussion to get your reactions to the film without restricting you in any way. We have a full hour before you're expected back. But first, let me play a few seconds of the sound track from the film to help you remember how you felt about it at the time you were watching. (Plays opening music, sounds of the wind storm, chickens being chased from the cantina, and the opening dialogue between the hero and the bartender.) Does that sound familiar?

R-8: It's almost as good as seeing the film again. I could see in my mind everything that was happening! (2)

I-9: Good! First, tell me a little bit about your general reactions to the film.

R-9: I liked the song when the movie first came on, but I didn't like the quality of the sound reproduction. (I: Uh huh) I realize that the movie wasn't done by Twentieth Century-Fox. The color was really good and a lot of the shots were very good, particularly at the very beginning with the horse coming in that straight-on angle. I liked the shot where the horse is coming in through the wheat field, I think it was, maybe it was even slowed down a bit, I don't know. (I: Uh huh) (3) One thing that really impressed me was when he put the policy down in the poker game. The poker game may have been drawn out a little bit, but it made good sense to use the policy in the game because it sort of brought out the value of it. It was pretty obvious that they wanted me to get to think about life insurance. (I: Hmmm) (2) I was kind of shocked by the ending. (2)

I-10: In what way? (2)

R-10: At first I didn't like it at the time, but then, afterward, when I thought about it a little more—(3) Well, it was a pretty good ending, particularly the thought behind it.

I-11: You said at first you were *shocked* by the ending. Tell me more about how you felt at *first*.

R-11:   I was kind of shocked because it didn't come out like it was supposed to. The good guy got shot. At first I didn't like it. I think the ending was sort of satirical. (4)

I-12:   That is great! You are doing very well in recalling details of your reaction. Was there anything else that surprised or shocked you?

R-12:   The way the Mexican soldiers were portrayed also surprised me. The head man kind of fit into the old TV image of Mexican soldier . . . a real ruffian. And then there were those other two, almost mousy, guys . . . the ones that came out and talked about insurance. (3)

I-13:   What else did you notice about them?

R-13:   They seemed to be a little stupid, but they weren't ignorant, at least not about life insurance. (2) I think they looked stupid because of the way they wore their hair and they were pretty sloppy. But I didn't think it had any bad ethnic overtones, I think it was very tasteful. I liked the Sargento. The gringo was sort of exaggerated, but I like that. I was impressed with the Mexican soldier with the long straight hair. I think I've seen him on TV before. And I liked the uniforms; they looked very authentic for the time. I didn't like the canteen scene—it was too dull, there was nothing colorful in it, like you'd expect for a Mexican scene. (2)

I-14:   Uh huh, what else impressed you? (1)

R-14:   The canteen was out in the middle of nowhere, where nothing was happening. I found that kind of a disappointment that the setting was not more exciting. (3)

I-15:   I see. Anything else about it that impressed you? (1)

R-15:   I think the Indian guy [the guitarron player], who ended up shooting the Sargento should have had a line of some kind; he should have at least laughed or said something or, you know, so he'd really be in it. (4)

I-16:   That's very good! Now I'd like to shift the subject just a bit. What do you think of the general idea of mixing entertainment and instruction in the same film?

R-16:   I think it's definitely a good idea to mix them and in the school system that I went to, which is one of the best systems in the state of Texas, they tried to mix interesting things and exciting things with instruction. I don't think there is any reason why education has to be drab. Even the Greeks told stories with morals to them in order to make the principles interesting. I think the film could have been better, but I just couldn't tell you how. I assume anything can be improved, but I'm no expert on films. (3)

I-17:   OK, you don't have to solve the problems, but I'm interested in what might have bothered you, if anything, about this particular film's attempt to mix instruction and entertainment. Did anything about it bother you just a bit?

R-17:   Well, I guess I agree with what some of the other guys were saying about it. It seemed strange that right out of the blue in the middle of the Old West just after the Civil War, I guess, a guy pulls out this life insurance policy. Particularly, when they started talking about the SGLI [Serviceman's Group Life Insurance] policy. I doubt if they had life insurance then. Of course the Mexicans were in old *Reales* uniforms but no one would think of them as service men, and the gringo hero was no service man, but he said he had retired. It just didn't seem right somehow. It could have been a pinochle game between two navy men and their wives; or just two civilian couples would be even better.

I-18:   I see what you mean. What other problems did you feel about mixing insurance with the Western film?

R-18:   Oh yes, some of the people I talked to afterward didn't like the Mexican accent. All of the information on the different types of insurance was given by the Mexicans who just a few minutes earlier were being put down by the Sargento as "stupid" and they spoke in such a thick accent that sometimes I couldn't understand what they were saying.

I-19:   Ahh, that's a very important point! What else did you notice about the way the Mexicans were portrayed . . . you said they looked stupid.

R-19:   Right! I don't really think the movie was putting Mexicans down that much. Sure, they show the Mexicans cheating, but not only the Mexicans, the gringo too. (2) I think that as far as the deal about insurance is concerned, they portrayed that about even, because only the Sargento was ignorant about insurance and the other Mexicans and the gringo knew about it. I do think they stereotyped the Mexicans too much. I'm against stereotyping in general. (3)

I-20:   Could you tell me a bit more about how the Mexicans were stereotyped?

R-20:   Well, I was talking to a Mexican-American who saw the film and he liked the ending because the Mexican won. It might have pissed him off during the middle of the movie, but the ending was good. He thought during the middle, hey, they're cutting down my people, but in the end that sort of picked it up. (2)

I-21:   Uh huh. What were some of the things he said about the middle of the movie?

R-21:   Well, the close-ups of the Mexicans' faces showed sweat, beard stubble, and the pulque dripped down their beards when they drank. If I were Mexican I don't think I'd like it very much. That stupidity of the Sargento would grate on me, and the way he shot all the others, and then the guitarron player gets shot in the back. It looks like just a cruel bunch of people. After the navy tries for years to eliminate discrimination and stereotyping, this film doesn't help much. The whole gang of Mexicans seemed treacherous and threatening. For example, the Sargento used a dagger to pick his teeth and to spread out the card hand on the table. And there was the drunk, barefooted Mexican who said nothing but belched a couple of times. Not the clean All-American type.

I–22: That's very good! Now I'd like to change the subject a bit and talk about the other training films you have seen here at the base. As you know this film is just an experimental pilot film and they are trying to find ways to improve training films. You have done a good job of telling me some of the good and bad things about this new film, but how does it compare with the other training films you have seen so far?

R–22: That's a good question, because even if I seem to find fault with this one, it was much better than most I have seen. I just got out of boot camp here and I've seen several films. I don't think I've seen any of the training films here that would really stack up against this film. (2)

I–23: In what way?

R–23: None of them started off with a famous movie title like *The Good, Bad and the Ugly.* And this one was in color. This one had humor in it. This film was really refreshing to see after seeing some of those really drab training films. They covered an awful lot of facts. They covered naval history from 1775 on up just like that! (Snaps his fingers.) There were still-shots of woodcuts of navy ships and naval battles, and then there would be a voice talking for several minutes about the slide while one slide was up on the screen.

When they would say we are going to see a training film, some of the guys would say "Great, I'll get a half-hour's sleep." The worst I saw was one on the Articles of War. An admiral just stood at a podium and read the articles one by one with no explanation, no historical illustrations or reasons of any kind. That was the pits. (3) In fact, when I arrived to see this movie, I thought damn it, we're going to have another one of those movies, but then it came on and I thought, aha! it's going to be a good movie. (3)

I–24: That's very interesting! You have a lot of details on the training films! You have mentioned that this film was different because it was in color, was a take-off on a famous movie, had humor, had action instead of being just a film of a stand-up lecture . . . what were some of the other differences? (2)

R–24: I remember thinking afterward that there was one outstanding difference which had nothing to do with the film technique or the training message. That was the fact that there was not one single navy uniform in this movie! I feel like . . . well . . . we're in the navy now and we have no choice but to see these uniforms every day. From the very beginning in boot camp you see movies on warfare and they talk about navy people. They show you a movie like going downtown and getting in trouble, getting beat up, your throat slit . . . and they show navy people. They just keep shoving the navy down your throat too much. Even though I am proud of the uniform, I see so much of it in shows and on the street too, and on TV, that I think it has a better effect not to have any navy men in the movie. All you see in boot camp is movies of some navy guy telling Joe sailor to do this or do that; you're never right and all that sort of stuff. So when you go to a training film you expect it to be boring and it usually is. (2)

I–25:   Being a civilian, I didn't notice that very important point that there were no navy uniforms in this film. Good point! Is there anything else you would like to say about this film or your regular training films that might help the Instructional Technology Development Center to produce better instructional films?

R–25:   Not really! (3) Well, just a couple of details in this film. There was too much change of pace. The gringo spoke very slowly and then the Mexicans chattered too fast in a heavy accent about the details of insurance. This along with an insurance policy in the Old West was quite a jolt. The idea of action, good camera angles, background music and all that was great. They just didn't quite fit insurance into this type of story, and they didn't need to stereotype Mexicans like they did.

I–26:   Right! Well, thank you very much! You gave a lot of detail and ideas that should be useful. This interview was better than garbage detail wasn't it?

R–26:   It sure was!

I–27:   Good! Thanks again, and have a good day!

R–27:   It was a pleasure. Goodbye!

CRITICAL ANALYSIS QUESTIONS

Part 1

1. Explain why certain inhibitors might operate in this interview situation. (Do not deal with more than three of the most probable ones.)

2. Which potential inhibitors did the interviewer try to prevent or treat? (Give I– numbers and quote the relevant phrases, first for Interview A and then for Interview B.)

3. What does the interviewer do to motivate the respondent to make the effort? (Give the I– numbers in which the interviewer tries to maximize a facilitator, first for Interview A and then for Interview B.)

4. What, in addition to the things you have mentioned in (2) and (3) above, did the interviewer do to build the respondent's spontaneity or momentum? (First deal with Interview A and then Interview B.)

Part 2

Assume that *you* are doing Interview A and show what you would have said at each of the following eight points: I–4, I–5, I–7, I–8, I–12, I–13, I–14, and I–17. In each case give the I– number and the question. Then *(a)* say what was wrong with what the interviewer did and *(b)* suggest the wording of a better question or statement the interviewer could have used at that point.

Use the following format:

I–10: Right! What did you think of the slow motion scene at the end?
      a. The interviewer rushes from the topic of camera angles to slow motion scenes without giving the respondent a chance to say whether he liked the camera angles he has mentioned and whether there is something else he would like to add.
      b. "Right! How do you feel about that type of camera work?"

This procedure should be repeated for each of the eight selected points.

After you have dealt with the critical analysis questions by written answers or oral discussion, consult your instructor's handout for the writer's suggestions. Decide which of these suggestions might have improved upon your own.

Selected Readings

Although there are many studies of the effects of mass media upon individuals, there are very few that deal with the interviewing methodology involved. Those that treat the methodology tend to be either superficial or too specialized to apply to a wide variety of media impact studies. One of the best is the classic annotated below.

Merton, Robert K. *The Focused Interview: A Manual of Problems and Procedures.* New York: Free Press, 1956, reprinted 1981.
    A classic on the assessment of people's reactions to mass media or any other stimulus situation where *(a)* the exact nature of the stimulus situation is

known, *(b)* the interviewer has been able to analyze the stimulus situation and hypothesize the respondent's reaction to it, *(c)* the stimulus content of the situation provides the framework for the interview schedule, and *(d)* the interviewer focuses on the respondent's subjective experience to ascertain his definition of the situation.

Chapter Twenty-Two

The Nursing Interview

Most interviewing in the professional setting of nursing consists of *informal* interviewing done as participant-observation.[1] Often the nurse is listening and asking questions while participating in some activity such as taking a blood pressure, weighing the patient, changing a dressing, or giving a back rub. *Formal* interviewing is done less often by nurses and mainly with newly admitted patients.

The purposes of the formal interview in the nursing setting include obtaining administrative types of information (such as names of family members, hospitalization insurance coverage, and type of facilities desired) and obtaining a medical history. The informal interviewing occurs mainly during the diagnosis and treatment phases.

Informal interviewing during the diagnosis phase may be used for determining whether the patient understands the requirements of diagnosis process (such as not eating, not drinking water, or resting, exercising, or whatever is needed for the particular tests being done). It can also be used to determine whether the patient has been confused or frightened by some of the medical jargon or by some other aspect of the hospital environment. If this is the case, the interviewer turns counselor, by giving information or reassurance to reduce the confusion or fear and to increase the patient's cooperation.

Informal interviewing during the treatment phase is used for determining whether the patient is taking the required medications, for determining whether the patient is conforming to the required diet, for checking on bowel and bladder functions, for checking for symptoms, and for detecting fears, anxieties, and other emotional states that might reduce the effectiveness of the treatment.

Interviewing in the nursing setting involves a strong component of sharp observation and sensitive listening. Often the patient initiates the conversation, while the nurse is constantly observing, listening, and

---

[1]Eugenie Edde, RN, assisted with technical advice for this section.

translating (with the help of a large fund of professional knowledge) what is heard and seen into medical needs. Often the nurse is alerted to a possible medical need by observing the patient's spontaneous behavior; and then to verify the possibility, the nurse will ask some incisive questions or merely encourage the patient's free expression.

Sometimes the interview has the disadvantage of being interrupted by visits from relatives, physicians, paramedics, volunteer workers, or maids, depending on the location of the interview. Sometimes the patient is in the room with another patient, sometimes the patient is in the hall, in the receiving room, in the X-ray laboratory, or at home with the public health nurse present. Sometimes the patient may be contacted by telephone.

The interviewing relationship is also affected by the nature and seriousness of the patient's illness and prognosis. This affects the patient's response to the diagnostic procedures, the hospital staff, and the treatment as well as the patient's emotional state.

Clearly, the interview setting and strategy vary tremendously within the nursing profession.

THE ORGANIZATIONAL SETTING

The Northmont Community Hospital is an excellent institution that trains student nurses and carries on considerable medical research. Sometimes the initial medical history of the newly arrived patient is taken by a student nurse under the supervision of a teaching supervisor, but usually it is done by a supervising registered nurse.

Each of the two interviews below consists of segments taken from conversations during the three phases (admission, diagnosis, and treatment) of the patient's relationship to the hospital.

OBJECTIVES OF THE INTERVIEW

The objectives of nursing interviews change from the initial admission phase to the diagnosis and treatment phases.

Admission phase. Here the purpose is mainly to obtain some specific facts regarding the patient for administrative purposes and to record certain missing information on the patient's medical history.

Diagnosis phase. While the patient is preparing or actually undergoing laboratory tests and X-rays, the nurse should *(a)* listen and observe for clues to emotional states of the patient that might interfere with the diagnosis process or with the later treatment phase, *(b)* pick up medical information not given in the earlier formal medical history interview, and *(c)* listen for clues to the patient's misunderstanding of anything about the situation that could interfere with the diagnosis or treatment of the illness.

Treatment phase. The three objectives of the diagnostic phase should be continued into the treatment phase and one new objective should be added: *(d)* detect tendencies to deviate from the prescribed treatment procedure and persuade the patient to stay on course.

In the two illustrative interviews that follow only excerpts from each of the three phases are presented; so there is no way for the reader to determine whether the interviewer completed the task within any phase, but it is possible to note in the excerpts whether the interviewer detected the clues presented by the patient and whether the interviewer made any attempt to verify and correct potential communication problems at that point in the interview.

THE INTERVIEW SITUATION

In the first interview the patient, Mr. Jones, is being interviewed upon arrival at the hospital. His family physician decided to hospitalize him for a thorough diagnosis and possible surgery. Mr. Jones has been complaining about pains in the back and stomach area, and he has not been feeling well for weeks. He arrived in an ambulance and was taken in a wheelchair to a room with two beds. The other bed is not yet occupied.

The volunteer, who brought him in the wheelchair, helps him unpack his overnight bag and shows him the adjoining bathroom, a small locker for his clothes, and his hospital gown on the bed. The volunteer tells him that in a moment someone will come to get information and then leaves him sitting in a chair beside the bed. In a moment a nurse arrives with a file folder marked *Cyril Jones.*

Interview A

Phase I: Admission

I–1:   Hello, Mr. Jones, I need to get a medical history on you, and then you can undress and put on this gown. (2)[2]

R–1:   I hope it won't take long, I'm worn out!

I–2:   No, it won't take long because your family physician, Dr. Wasby, has sent along your medical record so we can get most of the information from that.

---

[2]The numbers in parentheses represent the seconds of silence.

R–2: That's good!

I–3: Have you ever been a patient here before?

R–3: No.

I–4: Where do you work?

R–4: City Building and Loan Company. I'm a bookkeeper. (2)

I–5: Your social security number is missing from the intake sheet. Do you know your number?

R–5: Not sure, but it's on my driver's license, let me look . . . here it is . . . 556-06-9121. (2)

I–6: Good! Now just a few questions about your health. Have you ever had any kidney problems in the past?

R–6: Well, I wouldn't say so. I never had kidney stones or anything like that.

I–7: Have you had recurring headaches? (2)

R–7: Not that I would call regular.

I–8: Uh huh. Now I want to get some information on your current illness. What seems to be the problem?

R–8: I have this nagging pain in my back much of the time and then once in a while I get a sharp stabbing pain that seems to go right through me.

I–9: I see that you have acne on your face.

R–9: Yeah. I guess so, but that's not what's bothering me at the moment.

I–10: What is bothering you at the moment?

R–10: Like I said, it's this back pain and I have it right now!

I–11: On your job do you do any heavy work that might strain your back?

R–11: The heaviest thing I lift is a ledger book. I hardly think that would do it.

I–12: And how about around the house, have you been doing any strenuous work, or did you fall, or twist your back in some way? (2)

R–12: No, nothing like that. In fact since my wife has been in Europe for six weeks I haven't even mowed the lawn, because of the way my back feels and I am just generally very weak, too.

The questioning continues ten more minutes to complete the missing items in the case history and then the nurse shows the patient where to put his wallet and other belongings and says he should get into his hospital gown and rest in bed until the doctor arrived. In an hour the physician arrives and prescribes pain relief pills to allow Cyril Jones to sleep. A series of laboratory tests is planned to begin in the morning. The nurse enters his room at 7:00 in the morning and the following conversation ensues.

Phase II: Diagnosis

I-13:   How did you sleep, Mr. Jones?

R-13:   Like a log. It was probably those pills you gave me last night. I was glad that I woke up without a scar. Last night I dreamed that I was having an operation. They got me opened up and then left me . . . what a nightmare!

I-14:   Well, it sounds like you didn't really sleep so well after all. (2)

R-14:   I guess not.

I-15:   This morning you're going up to the X-ray room. Dr. Wasby ordered a full chest and abdominal view. We'll do that right away and then bring you back for breakfast. But before you go to X ray, a technician will get a blood sample, and I'll leave this bottle for you so you can give a urine specimen.

R-15:   OK. Is it all right if I keep the pills I brought from home here in the drawer?

I-16:   Sure. Just sit up in bed and rest your arm on the bed table so I can get your blood pressure.(Takes blood pressure) There, now you can lay back down and take it easy. I'll be back in a few minutes for the urine specimen and then they'll take you in a wheelchair to the X-ray room.

R-16:   I don't have to drink any of that barium stuff or whatever it is? A friend of mine had those kinds of X rays and it turned out that he had cancer. There was nothing they could do for him; it was too late.

I-17:   No, we don't want anything in your stomach for this first X ray. I'll be back in a few minutes.

R-17:   Right.

Cyril Jones has the X rays taken, returns to his room, has breakfast and is resting. But in considerable pain again, he is sitting in the rocking chair beside his bed trying to decide whether to get back into bed or go to the bathroom. Then the nurse returns.

I–18:   How was breakfast? (2) Did you like it?

R–18:   It was all right, but I'm not used to eating a big breakfast and I'm allergic to eggs, so I just nibbled at the toast and drank the orange juice. It was fresh orange juice wasn't it?

I–19:   Yes. How could you tell?

R–19:   By the pulp and the flavor was fresh.

I–20:   Now, it's time to make your bed before you get back into it. (She goes on making the bed) . . . I'm surprised that you are a bookkeeper; I'd expect you to be white as this sheet instead of having that golden boy tan (chuckling); you must get outside a bit. (3)

R–20:   Since my wife went to Europe I haven't even been out to mow the grass. My tan is probably due to all those X rays I keep getting. (Gives a painful simulation of a smile). I hope I get out of here soon or City Building and Loan might get another bookkeeper. They'd love an excuse to get a young MBA who'll work weekends and evenings for less money. I'm what they call overqualified! They're right; they don't really need a CPA to do that work.

I–21:   How long have you worked at City Loan?

R–21:   Sixteen years!

I–22:   Then you have nothing to worry about! You are a loyal employee and have seniority. (Finishes the bed) Now you have a nice fresh bed, Mr. Jones. Dr. Wasby will be here in a few minutes to tell you the results of the tests. I'll see you right after lunch.

Dr. Wasby comes to tell Mr. Jones that the X rays clearly show that he has gallstones and that the blood tests show there is an infection. This means that he will need a gall bladder removal operation. But first they will try to get the infection under control and then operate in about a week. Mr. Jones seems relieved to know that it is only gall bladder trouble.

The operation was routine with no complications, and Mr. Jones is convalescing well and is scheduled to leave the hospital in three more days. The nurse comes in and finds Mr. Jones looking at his medical chart at the foot of his bed.

Phase III: Treatment

I–23:   Good morning, Mr. Jones. Seems like you are doing fine, but you need something to read besides your medical chart.

R-23:   That's interesting enough! But you really shouldn't put all that kind of stuff on the chart and leave it where the patient can see it. Like that SOB comment! (Glaring at the nurse)

I-24:   That doesn't mean a thing, people are often that way right after an operation.

R-24:   (Angrily) I guess there are some people who just don't have any patience with patients. If I weren't so glad to get out of here I'd complain to the supervisor. (3)

I-25:   (Confused) Well, I'm glad you are getting out soon, too, Mr. Jones! . . . and . . .

R-25:   I'm going to get out of here sooner than you think! The doctor says I can leave Friday afternoon. Well, I've got news for him . . . (Then stops abruptly and looks furtively at the nurse) I'll keep *my* secret if you won't tell the doctor. Will you promise to keep my plans confidential? After all the nurse-patient relationship is a confidential one, right? (2)

I-26:   (Confused over the patient's reaction) That's right, a nurse is not supposed to blab around town any information about patients.

R-26:   (Triumphantly) Good! I knew you would see it my way! Well, the news is that my daughter is coming back from college for Thanksgiving weekend, and she will pick me up on Wednesday afternoon instead of Friday. Now don't tell the doctor . . . you promised!

I-27:   It's your body!

R-27:   Exactly! I know when I'm feeling well enough to go, and it's not my problem that the hospital has a lot of excess rooms it has to keep full! I'm in good shape. I'll probably be able to make it back to work by Monday and surprise good ol' City Loan too!

I-28:   Will your daughter be able to look after you for a while until your wife returns from Europe?

R-28:   She has to be back for classes on Monday, but by that time I'll be back to work!

The next morning Dr. Wasby comes by to see Mr. Jones and finds that he is convalescing well, but still should stay a few more days. Something occurs during the doctor's visit that changes Mr. Jones's attitude toward the nurse and toward staying a few days more in the hospital. Just before lunch the nurse returns.

I-29:   Mr. Jones, you haven't said anything to anybody about leaving today have you? (2)

R–29:   No. I decided to be a better patient and do what I'm told. It's for my own good . . . and it would be a big burden for Jeanne to come and get me . . . then she'd try to have a regular Thanksgiving for me because she knows her mother is away. She needs a rest from college. She works hard there, and I'm sure she would like a chance to see some of her high school friends who will also be back from college for Thanksgiving. (2)

I–30:   That sounds very reasonable. She can come here to visit and you can still have a nice talk without all that fuss and muss.

R–30:   Sure. But before lunch I'd like to take a little trip to the reading room. There is a nice view from there too.

I–31:   You should be able to walk that far today without any wheelchair. A little exercise should be good for you, if you just take it slow and easy.

R–31:   But that's what I want to do, take it slow and easy, and not go running around so soon. Won't you just help me to get into the wheelchair and I can do the rest? I'll furnish the propulsion.

I–32:   OK, but you can get out of bed and into the chair yourself, if you just take it easy.

R–32:   If that's what a model patient does, that's what I'll do. As I said I've decided to be a good patient. After all, you are a good nurse . . . and I don't even know your name, your first name that is . . . or your middle name for that matter. Your name pin just says M. J. Janowitz. What's the M and J for?

I–33:   That's Mary Jo.

R–33:   That's a very nice name; the two go together. I'll call you Mary Jo, that's easier than Miss Janowitz. Are you a native of Cleveland?

I–34:   No, I'm not.

R–34:   Anyhow, I've got to make it up to you for being so nasty. (2) If you give me your telephone number I'll call you and take you out to dinner when I'm back in ship shape.

I–35:   (Curtly) Nurses do not give out their phone numbers to patients. Now I've got to see to your lunch. There is going to be a nice egg custard for dessert!

CRITICAL ANALYSIS QUESTIONS

After reviewing the objectives of the interview, point out where the interviewer has *failed* to note clues to possible misunderstandings and fears, or failed to probe to verify such clues, or failed to correct the problem.

Deal with the points in chronological order and indicate with a heading whether you are dealing with Phase I (admission), Phase II (diagnosis), or Phase III (treatment) of the interview. At each of the critical points give the I– number where the interviewer's behavior should have been different. For each of these I– numbers give a two-part response: *(a)* the diagnosis of what the interviewer did wrong or failed to do right and *(b)* the words the interviewer should have said at that point, plus any other explanation that is needed.

Interview B

This interview takes place in the same hospital as Interview A, but both the nurse and the patient are different. The patient, Mrs. Frank, was brought to the hospital by her husband when she began to have severe abdominal and back pain. In the emergency room they gave her an injection for the pain and then took her to a room where she will be examined by her family physician who is already on his way. The nurse enters the room which Mrs. Frank is sharing with another patient in an oxygen tent.

Phase I: Admission

I–1:   Hello, Mrs. Frank. I'm Mrs. Langley, and I'll be your nurse most of the time.

R–1:   Hello, I'm glad you're here!

I–2:   I know you had to have a shot for that terrible pain. How does it feel now?

R–2:   Oh, it is such a relief. It was killing me. It still hurts but nothing like the killing pain I had. It was much worse than having a baby.

I–3:   I'm glad it helped! Now let's get you settled down in bed to rest before your Dr. Penningroth arrives. Put your purse here in this drawer in the bedside table, and you can hang your clothes up here in the locker. Here is your gown, or if you brought your own nightgown you can wear that for now. Do you need some help with that?

R–3:   No, thanks, that won't be necessary. I'm just glad the pain is mostly gone.

I–4:   I'll be right back to talk with you and answer any questions you might have.

Mrs. Frank is in bed resting when the nurse returns. It is about 4:00 P.M.

I-5:   Are you all settled in, Mrs. Frank?

R-5:   Yes. Everything is handy, complete with toilet and shower.

I-6:   Do you feel up to answering a few questions so we will have your medical history completed before Dr. Penningroth arrives?

R-6:   I'm much better now, so let's go ahead.

I-7:   Dr. Penningroth will bring your medical record, but there are a few things I need to know about your present illness. Tell me how your illness first started.

R-7:   I think I had something like this before, about ten years ago, but it was not nearly so bad . . . not so much pain, that is. I had some back pain and it hurt to urinate, but this time the back pain was much worse.

I-8:   When did the pain first begin this time?

R-8:   About three nights ago . . . I had a hard time sleeping.

I-9:   Which night was that?

R-9:   That was Tuesday night.

I-10:   And it hadn't been hurting before that?

R-10:   No, not at all.

I-11:   Do you remember how you were feeling on Monday?

R-11:   No back pain.

I-12:   Anything else? Any discomfort of any kind at all?

R-12:   Well, on Sunday I didn't feel hungry and on Monday I didn't sleep well . . .

I-13:   What else?

R-13:   Well, on Tuesday I felt weak and nauseated at the smell of food.

The questioning continues for a few minutes longer to complete the medical history. Then the nurse leaves and in ten minutes Dr. Penningroth arrives, examines Mrs. Frank and orders several diagnostic tests. The nurse returns.

Phase II: Diagnosis

I-15:   Dr. Penningroth wants to find out exactly what is wrong, so she has ordered an X ray, blood test, and urinalysis. The tests won't start till tomorrow . . . and we will want to keep a careful check on your blood pressure and temperature. I'll start by taking your blood pressure and temperature now.

R–15: (Whispering) Can the woman in the oxygen tent hear us?

I–16: No, not really.

R–16: I feel so bad to have someone in that condition in the room with me!

I–17: What do you mean, "in that condition"?

R–17: (Still whispering) Dying, I mean. I know the oxygen tent is the last resort. My aunt died in an oxygen tent.

I–18: Oh, I can see why you were so concerned. You thought she was dying. No, in fact she is recovering very well from pneumonia; it's just so that she can sleep better for the first twenty-four hours after her temperature is down. She's past the crisis and will be able to go home in another forty-eight hours.

R–18: Really! I'm so glad to hear that.

I–19: Her name is Nancy Tugford, and you will be able to talk with her tomorrow when the oxygen tent is off.

R–19: Yes, I'd like to.

The nurse puts the thermometer in the patient's mouth, and takes her blood pressure, then records it on the chart.

I–20: There that's done! I'll take your temperature about every two hours.

R–20: How was my blood pressure?

I–21: It is a bit high right now.

R–21: That's why I brought my medicine with me. I know when I get uptight my blood pressure seems to go up.

I–22: You brought your medicine with you? What kind?

R–22: It's my hydroDIURIL pills—my water pills.

I–23: What other medicine did you bring?

R–23: That's the only pills.

I–24: And what other medicine or stuff to eat or drink did you bring?

R–24: Well, my husband put a bottle in my overnight bag for medicinal purposes.

I–25: A bottle of what?

R–25: A bottle of gin. He knows I like my gin, and it is not usually furnished in the hospital, I know.

I-26: Mrs. Frank, I'm sorry to tell you that for the moment I'll have to take all these things and keep them safely for you until we check with your doctor. I know you should not have the gin while we are doing diagnostic tests and the pills give us a false picture of your hypertension.

R-26: (With a look of desperation) Don't take my bottle! That's my courage. I need it when I'm so scared. I won't be able to sleep without it, and I need sleep.

I-27: Oh, you're worried and anxious . . . about what?

R-27: I'm . . . I'm afraid they'll find that I have cancer.

I-28: What makes you think you might have cancer?

R-28: I've got the symptoms and it's in the family.

I-29: What do you mean? (Sitting on stool beside the bed)

R-29: My brother died of cancer about three years ago, and he had pains in his back. It . . . it started in his spleen and spread to his kidneys . . . and (crying) he was in a lot of pain for a long time.

I-30: I can see why you're upset. So since you have this back pain you're afraid *you* might have cancer. And you think it is in the family?

R-30: Yes. I know that diabetes and asthma run in families. I have a bunch of cousins with asthma.

I-31: Well, actually cancer doesn't run in families like diabetes and asthma, but I can see how you would be worried. I know you have probably been worrying about that for a long time. Have you told your husband about this worry you have?

R-31: No, he doesn't know. (3) I was so afraid to come to the hospital that I didn't say anything until the pain got so powerful I couldn't keep my mouth shut any more. (2) It just worried me . . .

I-32: And you didn't talk to anyone about it . . .

R-32: Not until I told you . . . I just had to tell somebody right out what was eating away at me. But I feel better already talking to you. (3) I won't miss my medicinal bottle so much now.

I-33: I'm glad you told me. It's probably not cancer. Cancer of the kidney or spleen is much more rare than lung cancer or cancer of the uterus or breast in women. The tests in the morning will tell us if you have a kidney infection which is what Dr. Penningroth suspects.

R-33: I hope that is what it is so I'll know right away. (2) It's the waiting that is so hard.

The diagnosis shows clearly that Mrs. Frank has an infection of the right kidney. One temporary effect of the kidney infection is to irritate the urethra so that the patient cannot urinate.

Phase III: Treatment

I–34: The doctor tells me that you are full of water; so we are going to have to catheterize you now.

R–34: Oh, this is very bad! So it is not just a kidney infection!

I–35: What do you mean?

R–35: I have water . . . dropsy; do you know what dropsy is? People with very bad hearts have dropsy.[3]

I–36: Oh no, I'm sorry, when I said "full of water" I should have said you have bladder retention, that's all. Not dropsy.

R–36: Oh, that's different!

The nurse catheterizes her and returns in a few minutes to give the patient a bed bath.

I–37: It's time for a bath, don't you think?

R–37: I need it for sure, but I don't feel like walking around yet.

I–38: No, I mean a bed bath! You might as well enjoy the service while you can get it. Tomorrow you will probably be on your own. (Nurse proceeds with the bath while talking to the patient and then hands the patient her medication.) This ought to make it easier to sleep tonight and help with your pain. This is the same thing you took last night.

R–38: I'm sure I won't get the pain again! I didn't know what I was taking last night. I don't want any more of those!

I–39: What do you mean?

R–39: I don't believe in taking pain pills. They are narcotics and they're habit-forming. I don't want to get hooked.

I–40: That is certainly right, you wouldn't want to become an addict, but that doesn't happen when you take these kinds of pills and when you really have pain to kill. These will not hook you, and you need the sleep very badly.

---

[3]*Dropsy* is a lay term sometimes used for edema.

R-40:   Well, I'll admit I can use the sleep, and if they aren't addicting I see no harm in it.

I-41:   Then you'll take this one now?

R-41:   I trust you and you know what is good for me, so there's no problem.

CRITICAL ANALYSIS QUESTIONS

After reviewing the objectives of the interview, point out where the interviewer *succeeded* in noting clues to possible misunderstandings or fears, probed to verify such clues, or corrected the problem once it was discovered.

Analyze each phase in order and identify the phase you are dealing with by the headings Phase I, Phase II, or Phase III. Within each phase identify a particular I- number or series of I- numbers in which the interviewer is successful. In order not to take such successes for granted and possibly overlook them, remember the types of clues which Interviewer A failed to pick up. After each I- number explain how it contributed to the success of the interview, as illustrated by the following probes from another interview:

Phase III: Treatment
I-97:   "Why do you say that?" This probe, followed by I-98 and I-99, leads to the discovery that the patient is afraid she has a venereal disease because her menstrual period has been irregular.

I-100:   The nurse relieves the patient's anxiety by explaining that there are many causes for menstrual irregularity having nothing to do with venereal disease of any kind.

Selected Readings

The four paperbacks listed below all deal with interviewing in the medical setting, and illustrate in varying degrees the combination of observing, listening, and questioning skills needed by medical personnel in the diagnosis and treatment of patients.

Bermosk, Loretta S., and Mary J. Mordan. *Interviewing in Nursing.* New York: Macmillan, 1973.

Enelow, Allen J., and Scott Swisher. *Interviewing and Patient Care.* 3rd ed. Fairlawn, N.J.: Oxford University Press, 1986.

Engle, George L., and William L. Morgan. *Interviewing the Patient.* Philadelphia: W. B. Saunders, 1973.

Wicks, Robert J. *Interviewing for Nurses.* Thorofare, N.J.: Charles B. Slack, 1974.

Chapter Twenty-Three

The Initial
Counseling Interview

The word *counseling* may refer to activities as diverse as the summer-camp group leader talking to a child who is homesick, the psychologist interpreting a battery of tests to a client trying to select a vocation, the lawyer discussing the pros and cons of a divorce with a client, the college professor discussing a student's academic problem, the social worker discussing budgeting and marital problems or the personnel manager discussing various retirement options with an employee scheduled to retire soon.

This chapter will focus on the *initial* phase of the counseling interview. The first interview in any series of counseling sessions is more understandable to the reader since there is no hidden history of the relationship. Also, the initial interviews in a relationship are more alike in the wide range of counseling situations; this first interview emphasizes the common themes of establishing rapport and or identifying the general nature of the problem.

Jurisdictional disputes arise between lay people, psychologists, psychiatrists, clergy, social workers, and others as to what constitutes counseling, how it differs from therapy, and who is qualified to do it. In view of this lack of clarity and consensus, the following will define how the word is being used for the purposes of this chapter:

> Counseling is the process of helping a client identify, cope with, or resolve a problem (in which the client is personally involved) through face-to-face interaction between the client and counselor.

This definition deals mainly with the *purpose* of the process and also stipulates that the *method* must involve face-to-face communication. We are careful not to further restrict the concept by specifying whether the counselor must be directive or nondirective, whether the process does or does not involve therapy, or whether one type of setting or another is required. We strongly feel that the method must depend upon the nature of the problem, the organizational setting, and the role relationship between counselor and counselee.

Depending on the circumstances, the counselor may perform various combinations of the following functions:

1. Collect formal information from the client through standardized tests, questionnaires, projective techniques, or other pencil-paper methods.

2. Interpret the results of such formal information to the client in view of the nature of the client's problems and general emotional state.

3. Elicit cognitive information in the interview on the client's background, current situation, beliefs, assumptions, or expectations, and help the client explore and gain insight into the relationship between these cognitive factors and the problem or its solution.

4. Elicit expressions of *feeling* (attitudes and values) related to the client's problem, and reflect them in an accepting way so that the client feels free to examine possible relationships between the feelings (particularly the negative or ambivalent ones) and the problem or possible solutions.

5. Provide information that is not obtained from the client regarding any realities of the counselor's situation, the client's situation, or the larger world that may be relevant to the understanding of the problem or possible solutions.

The preceding five points suggest that the counselor's basic function may include collecting, interpreting, and giving information as well as helping the client to explore the relationship between the information and the problem or its possible solution. Here we have been careful to include both cognitive information and the respondent's feelings.

In short, the counselor engages in a give-and-take of information and facilitates the client's creative use of this to gain insight into the problem and its possible solution. Whether or not this constitutes giving advice depends upon whether the counselor's approach is directive, nondirective, or somewhere in between. In some situations the information collected, along with the counselor's knowledge and insight into the problem, makes it clear that there is a particular solution that can be successful. In this case, direct advice and persuasion may be called for but can be effective only if the client is qualified to interpret and use the information; if the client is *willing* to take the counselor's advice; and if the client is *able*, in every sense of the word, to carry out the solution. The main objection to directive advice-giving is not that it is immoral for one human being to advise another, but that it will not be effective because one of these conditions is missing.

Sometimes a problem arises when the counselor feels strongly that the client should accept a specific solution, yet feels that it is required to be nondirective at all costs. This ambivalence on the part of the counselor sometimes results in surreptitious manipulation of the client by the counselor. Sometimes an otherwise nondirective counselor tries to be directive because the situation does not provide sufficient time to use a slower, more insight-building method. This will not be successful unless the conditions for successful advice-giving are present.

THE ORGANIZATIONAL SETTING

The Northside Mental Health Center has three intake interviewers who interview approximately six new clients each day in addition to performing other duties. People come to the center with problems in such areas as money management, wife abuse, health problems, emotional disturbances, child abuse, marital problems, desertion, unwanted pregnancies, and drug addiction.

Often the client is referred to the center by a crisis intervention program, by the outreach program of a community action agency, by a minister, a friend, or schoolteacher, by the county welfare agency, police department, or public defender. Occasionally, a client enters in response to a television announcement of the center's programs and services.

OBJECTIVES OF THE INTERVIEW

Since this is the *initial* interview with the client, the counselor needs to discover the basic nature of the client's problem in order to mobilize resources for its solution. Once the nature of the problem is clarified, the counselor may refer the client to specific services within the center or to medical, legal, or educational services outside the Center.

Frequently a client will begin by presenting an immediate crisis-type problem that is sometimes the basic problem and other times only a superficial symptom of an underlying long-range problem. The counselor must always skillfully probe while creating an atmosphere of sympathetic understanding to motivate the respondent to a fuller disclosure of the problem.

Often the initial interview is too short to clarify the problem validly, so the counselor may require a second exploratory interview. If it is clear that there are deep emotional problems, the client may be immediately referred to a psychotherapist as well as to other services dealing with the environmental facets of the client's problem.

Interview A

The client, Mrs. Brown, was referred to the Center by an instructor at the local community college, where the client was studying to become a medical technician. Mrs. Brown arrives ten minutes ahead of her appointment time, and sits in the waiting room until it is time, then she walks over and looks through the open door into the counselor's office and the counselor greets her.

I-1:   Hello, Mrs. Brown, I have been expecting you.

R-1:   I'm glad I could make it. For a while I was afraid my babysitter was not going to show.

I-2:   Yes, many of us are at the mercy of our babysitters. Would you sit over here, please?

R-2:   Thank you.

I-3:   How are you today?

R-3:   I'm doing as well as could be expected under the circumstances!

I-4:   How well is that?

R-4:   Really, it's not all that good! (Looking through the open door at the people in the waiting room)

I-5:   Did you come here to talk about personal problems?

R-5:   Yes. I guess you would call it personal—if my husband and my family are personal—than it's really personal.

I-6:   Is the main problem your husband?

R-6:   To be truthful, at this point I'm so confused that I don't know exactly what the problem is or who has it. All I know is that I'm unhappy.

I-7:   I see. You're confused and unhappy!

R-7:   That's right.

I-8:   Anything else?

R-8:   Everything is wrong (2),[1] but I guess I'm out of the mood to talk about it right now. When I sat in the waiting room I got more and more scared and wondered how I got up the nerve to make the appointment.

I-9:   Well, you're here so you might as well make the best use of that time!

---

[1]The numbers in parentheses indicate seconds of silence.

R–9:   I guess so.

I–10:   We are all here to help you, but there is not much we can do unless you tell us exactly what the problem is, right?

R–10:   Well, I guess for one thing I am plain tired. I am going to Community College three nights a week with classes from seven to ten, and by the time I get home the kids have been put to bed by the babysitter and I just look in on them and head for the sack myself.

I–11:   Have you been to a doctor lately?

R–11:   Yes.

I–12:   How recently?

R–12:   About three weeks ago.

I–13:   Did you have a complete physical?

R–13:   No.

I–14:   Was it just for a cold or something like that?

R–14:   No, nothing like that.

I–15:   What was the illness? (2) Was it serious?

R–15:   Nothing serious.

I–16:   That's good. (4) You mentioned looking in on the kids when you come home. How many kids do you have?

R–16:   Just two.

I–17:   How old are they?

R–17:   One is four and the baby is fourteen months.

I–18:   One boy and one girl?

R–18:   No, both boys.

I–19:   You haven't mentioned a husband, is he living with you now?

R–19:   Yes, he is very much with us.

I–20:   Is he a good husband?

R–20:   Yes, much of the time, but sometimes he can be aggravating to the bone.

I–21:   Has he ever left you temporarily?

R–21:   No, never. Not even overnight.

I–22:   Does he work steadily?

R–22:   I don't think he has missed a day's work since we were married.

I–23:   That sounds like a good record.

R–23:   But there's a lot more to being a husband and father than working, like . . .

I–24:   Does he physically abuse you?

R–24:   No, nothing like that . . . but there is a lot of tension.

I–25:   What sort of tension?

R–25:   Well, he doesn't like the idea of me going to night school. He feels that I should be home with the kids all the time.

I–26:   Do you feel he is sort of old-fashioned?

R–26:   Yes, in *that* way he certainly is!

I–27:   Is he old-fashioned in other ways?

R–27:   Well, if you mean a man who thinks the wife's place is in the home while he goes out and plays around, then I'd say he is old-fashioned.

I–28:   Yes, that's the old double standard all right. Then, if I understand you, you feel that the problem is mainly in your husband's attitude toward your going to school, right?

R–28:   That is *one* problem . . . but . . .

I–29:   Does he have a drinking problem?

R–29:   Oh no, nothing like that.

I–30:   But he doesn't like the children?

R–30:   I wouldn't say that. When he is with the children, like on Sunday afternoon, he plays with them some, particularly the four-year-old.

I–31:   Then, do you feel that he should have some counseling on his attitude toward you and your wanting to go to school? Maybe both of you could go together to a marriage counselor to help you talk it out and to help him become aware of his own attitudes and how he restricts you.

R–31:   I didn't have anything like that in mind, but now that you mention it I'm sure he wouldn't go for the idea. He thinks I am the one with the problem, and in a way he is right; but that is no excuse for him to beat me down.

I–32:   How does he beat you down?

R–32:   Like I said, he doesn't want me to go to school, and he tells me that I can't be a medical technician, I'll never pass the math and that sort of thing.

I–33: I see. You said he would not go for the idea of seeing a marriage counselor, but you didn't say whether *you* thought that he should do that.

R–33: I don't think that is so important. I'm the one that is most upset, and that's why I am here and not him.

I–34: Well, then we should concentrate on you next time. Our time is up for today. I was running a bit behind schedule. Could you come next week at this time? That is the first open time I have, and at that time I would like to get a chance to clarify the nature of your problem and determine whether I or someone else would be best to help you deal with it.

R–34: OK, at least that gives me time to arrange for a babysitter again. And I can hold on that long if I have to.

I–35: Fine (Rising) then I'll expect to see you at the same time next Thursday. Goodbye till then.

R–35: Goodbye.

CRITICAL ANALYSIS QUESTIONS

Part 1. Individual questions and probes. To each of the interviewer's questions specified below give a two-part response, with *(a)* as the diagnosis and *(b)* as the treatment as in the example below:

I–1: *a.* The interviewer not only should have greeted the respondent by name, as she did, but also should have introduced herself. It might make the respondent uneasy that the counselor knows her name but she does not know the counselor's name.

     b. "Hello, Mrs. Brown. I'm Mrs. Farnsworth. I've been expecting you! Come in."

This should be done with only the following points in the interview: I–3, I–4, I–5, I–6, I–7, I–8, I–9, I–10, I–11 through I–15, I–21 through I–24, I–28, I–29, and I–32. Note that there are two points at which you are asked to give a more general diagnosis and treatment of a *series* of questions. These are the series I–11 through I–15 and the series I–21 through I–24. In these cases the diagnosis and the treatment should treat the series as a unit.

Part 2. Overview. Make a short one-or two-paragraph summary statement of the types of errors in strategy, techniques, and tactics made by the interviewer. Include some specifics or generalities not dealt with in Part I in addition to any general observations that might include the specifics reported in Part 1.

After you have completed the critical analysis questions above, consult your instructor's handout for the author's suggestions.

Interview B

The client, Mrs. Zeller, is a registered nurse. She has not been working because of opposition from her husband, who is an alcoholic. Mrs. Zeller has been going to night school to get her B.S. so she can qualify for a better nursing position as soon as her two preschool children get into first grade. She became so distraught and frustrated by her husband's opposition that she called a crisis center just to talk to someone on the phone so that she "would not take it out on the kids." The crisis center suggested that she call the Northside Mental Health Center for an appointment, which she did immediately. The interviewer is one of the three intake interviewers and is seeing Mrs. Zeller for the first time.

I–1:   Good morning, Mrs. Zeller. I'm Esther Ferrar. I know you called a week ago for an appointment and I'm sorry we couldn't get you in sooner. (Closes the door) Here is a comfortable chair!

R–1:   Well, I know you are busy, but I'm here now.

I–2:   Right! Do you care to smoke? I can . . .

R–2:   No thanks, I don't smoke any more. I quit it.

I–3:   Good. That is a difficult thing to do!

R–3:   It was at first, but I've made it all right.

I–4:   Uh huh! How did you get here, did you drive?

R–4:   Yes. It wasn't hard to find.

I–5:   Did you park in our parking lot behind the Center?

R–5:   No. In the municipal lot across the street.

I–6:   Then if you have your ticket, I'll stamp it so you won't have to pay.

R–6:   Fine! Here, I've got it. (Interviewer stamps the ticket)

I–7:   Next time you can park in our lot right behind and you don't even have to cross the street. (3) I know you were referred to us by the Crisis Center, but they gave me no information about you, so would you just tell me what the situation is?

R–7:   Well, everything is wrong! I'm tense and depressed and jumpy. Just about everything gets to me. (1)

I–8: Uh huh.

R–8: I don't feel like talking right now. (3)

I–9: I see. Do you sometimes?

R–9: That's the problem, I get so uptight I can't get started. When I made the appointment I was ripe to talk . . . if I could have started right then. (2)

I–10: What was on your mind then that caused you to make the appointment?

R–10: I had just had another fight with my husband. You see, I'm a nurse but my husband won't let me work. (3)

I–11: What do you mean? (1)

R–11: Well, for instance, I had a chance to do some private duty, which pays a lot, for about two weeks this month, but he makes it so miserable for me . . . saying my place is home with the children. I agree but also I need to get away from them with other people, not stuck in the house all the time. (2)

I–12: Uh huh. How many children are there?

R–12: Two—three years and five years old. (2)

I–13: Uh huh (3) (Watching client)

R–13: Oh, it isn't only that. There are a dozen things!

I–14: Tell me some of them. (1)

R–14: Well, there are some things I should have known about my husband before I married him. (2)

I–15: For example. (1)

R–15: He's a chronic alcoholic; he can't leave the stuff alone! He says he can quit any time he wants but he can't (Sigh). I feel it's going to ruin me, or the kids, or all of us. (2)

I–16: Does he hold a job?

R–16: Yeah, he's a truck driver. No more long-distance hauls, so he's home every night. The minute he sticks his head inside he starts nagging.

I–17: And does he spend most evenings at home? (1)

R–17: He just eats and sleeps in the house and spends as much time as he can with a gang of older guys at the local tavern. Sometimes I think he might be homosexual. It's an insult to me.

I-18:   Hmmm. (2)

R-18:   (Sighs) Once in a while he's decent. (3) (Sigh) I keep thinking of a divorce, but that's another emotional catastrophe . . . and I don't want to do it with the kids so young. (2)

I-19:   Divorce is an emotional catastrophe . . . what do you mean?

R-19:   (Sighs) Well . . . it's . . . I think it's worse than death. If he died I think I'd be happy. I honestly would. (Cries softly)

I-20:   I'm not sure I understand what you are trying to say. (2)

R-20:   He won't get help. That's the trouble. He won't admit that it's a problem.

I-21:   Yes, I want to hear more about his problem, but first could you tell me a little more about why divorce is an emotional catastrophe.

R-21:   I can't explain it, it's just the way I feel.

I-22:   Are you opposed to divorce generally, or . . .

R-22:   Yes, I am! (3) That's why I'm here . . . because I think a lot of marriages can be saved. (Sighs, crying softly) I think the children are the ones who suffer really. It's still a stigma to divorce in our family. It's very strong. We're not Catholic. That's not the reason. We are Presbyterian. Also, the children being taunted about it. (2)

I-23:   Uh huh! (1)

R-23:   I just feel that if I divorced him, I know it would be hard for me to adjust. It's hard for me to work and support the children. You have to pay babysitters and you're lucky to have enough to eat after the week's over. All I can think of is that if I can stand it a few years more. And then I get to the point where I don't think I could stand it a few more years . . . and that's why I came here.

I-24:   What were you going to do if you could stand it for a few years more?

R-24:   Right now I'm going to school to get my B.S. and I thought I could pack up and leave and be independent if I had a good job . . . and by that time the kids would be in school. I'd consider a divorce then, but I'm still generally opposed to it because I think that I can be straightened out.

I-25:   That *you* can be straightened out? I didn't get the idea that you thought it was *your* problem.

R-25:   Well, it's making me unstable, I never used to be like this. I used to get depressed occasionally, sure! Who isn't? But not the way I am now. Not so that I wanted to turn on gas and jump out of the window. (Tearful)

I-26:   How long have you been feeling that way?

R-26:   Ever since I've been married. And on the honeymoon (voice breaks) he drank every night. He was drinking the four or five months I knew him before we were married. But I thought it was just social. I never saw him drunk. Nobody told me his father was a chronic alcoholic. Now the only way I can get him to stay with the children at all is to have a showdown. He just comes home, eats, reads the paper and then either falls asleep or goes down to the gin mill. I guess I expected him to be like my father who had five kids and worked hard but found time for us. My husband has never saved anything. He said he wanted a home and children but never spends any time in the house. I worked part-time while I was pregnant, and I had saved money before I was married. Most everything in the house I bought. (3) It's just everything . . . it's getting so the older girl is wetting the bed again. It's gotten so I have to lie down with her at night, and lie down with her in the afternoon to get her to take a nap. She's on edge all the time and running . . . a very active child but seems tense to me.

I-27:   Didn't you have a lot of doubts about whether to have a second baby?

R-27:   Yes, I did! It was an accident.

I-28:   Oh. Was the first one planned?

R-28:   Yes, (3) and I really didn't expect it quite so soon. I mean I was using a preventative. I had wanted one but wanted to wait about a year so that there'd be a period of adjustment. But three weeks after we were married she was conceived. I knew when I married him that I didn't love him. I guess I was just bored. But I believed that if you lived with a man long enough you would learn to love him. I did love him. I still love him.

I-29:   You do? What do you mean by that? (2)

R-29:   I do. I love him, but he . . . at times I hate him. I know I love him but he makes me so miserable that I can't love him sometimes. He's always telling me that I'm no good as a nurse. He doesn't see why I want to go out and work in the first place. He fusses about me going to night school. He doesn't want to stay with the kids at night, and he yells if I get a babysitter. He doesn't mind if I get a babysitter during the day to go to school. When I had the idea of inviting my sister to come and stay with us so that she could stay with the baby while I was in school, he forbade her to come. Then he told the landlady who's a paranoid schizophrenic that I was planning to have someone else living in the house and the landlady said that wouldn't be allowed. (2)

I-30: When your husband comes home drunk does he ever physically abuse you?

R-30: No, he made a pass at me once, but I got out of the way. I grabbed a knife and I guess he knew I'd use it. I was so mad! (2)

I-31: Does he get verbally abusive?

R-31: Oh, yes. Very noisy. The whole neighborhood can hear it! (Sighs)

I-32: Why have you put up with all of this?

R-32: Well, frankly because as I said before, if I had to go out and work and hire a babysitter, I don't know how we'd live, I don't!

I-33: If you felt financially able . . . you would leave him?

R-33: Sometimes I think I would and other times I don't think I'd even be able to stay away from him. I know he'd come crawling back, and I'd probably take him back.

I-34: Why? (2)

R-34: I don't know. I guess because I love him. But I want to be treated decently. According to my family doctor, I'll probably have to pack up and leave him some day because he isn't going to change. He won't go to anyone for help . . . says there is nothing wrong with him. And in the meantime now my daughter needs help and I am losing patience with her. I thought maybe I could sort of get straightened out . . . straighten things out in my own mind. I'm confused. Sometimes I can't remember things that I have done. (2)

I-35: What is it that you want to straighten out?

R-35: I think I seem mixed up.

I-36: Yes? It seems to me that is something that we really should talk about because . . . from a certain point of view somebody might say, "Well, now, it's all very simple. She's unhappy and disturbed because her husband is behaving this way, and unless something can be done about *that* how could she expect to feel any other way." But instead you come and say that you think there is something about *you* that needs straightening out. I don't quite get it. Can you explain it to me? (2)

R-36: I sometimes wonder if I'm emotionally grown up. When you're married you should have one mate. You shouldn't go around and look at other men. I look at them, but that's all.

I-37: You mean a grown-up person should accept the marital situation, whatever it happens to be?

R-37: Yes! That's the way I was brought up. If you rebel against society you have to take the consequences. If I wouldn't be so nervous and upset I could find some way to handle it.

I-38: Hmmm. Well, tell me what would you say if you had to explain to yourself what the problem is?

R-38: You don't diagnose yourself very well, at least I don't.

I-39: Well, you can make a stab at it.

R-39: Well, for one thing, I hated to grow up. I remember when I was twelve, I was on the beach, and I had the top of my suit down, and we were playing in the sand, all five of us. And my mother said, "You must put your top up. You're a big girl now." Well, my breasts had started to grow then. And I remember how I resented it. I resented the fact that I wasn't a boy. My mother wanted a boy. I tried to compete with them. And I hated them because they always beat me and . . . you know, at their games, at their sports. I resented the fact that they were a little bit too . . . ah . . . well, they wanted to be intimate and I resented that. I didn't like to be pawed and petted and finally I was roped into it.

My sister next to me wanted to go out. So in order for her to go out, I had to go along on a double date. She begged and pleaded with me, so I said I'd go. But the boy I went with never danced. He was strictly a clod and I didn't like him. I only went out with a couple from my home town, but when I went away to Chicago to work it was different.

I took care of a mentally deficient child before I went into training for four months . . . that was nurse's training . . . and I started to go out with men. I don't even remember how I met half of them. I guess I picked the first one up, or he picked me up. And I started to drink, and I got so I drank quite a lot over a period of years. Now I don't touch it. I'm afraid of it. (2)

I-40: And what conclusion do you draw from all this about why you're not adjusting *now* the way you think you should?

R-40: I've improved since then but I still don't feel that I'm adjusted. Oh, he has problems all right but that's not the whole story. I mean it's probably remorse for the past, things that I did.

I-41: What is this thing you have so much remorse about?

R-41: Well, I was a nurse in the army and I got so depressed I wouldn't even get out of the barracks . . . It seems . . . I'm going around in circles. (3)

I-42: It's something hard to tell! (1)

R-42: While I was still in the army I met a man. He was married, but I loved him anyway. (Sighs) I became pregnant. I left *him* first and went to the islands to get away. And when I came back I saw him once again. That's when it happened. I met my husband when I was already pregnant. He offered to marry me, and I said I didn't want to, and I didn't think it was fair to marry a man under these circumstances. At the end of the fourth month I lost the baby. Two months later I married him. (Sighs) I always felt he held that little bit of information above my head, that he'd blackmail me if he didn't get his way . . . and I guess that is why I married him. (2)

I-43: Yeah, so you thought he'd hold this information over you.

R-43: I did. And I still do!

I-44: Hmmm. How come it took you so long to tell me that?

R-44: It's hard to talk about.

I-45: Sure it is. I know. I'm real glad you did tell me. Got a lot of things off your chest. I think you should be talking to somebody. I don't know if they explained to you that we have this initial interview to determine whether you could benefit from psychotherapy, and I think you can. It's just a question of how soon we can take you. And I'll try to see that you get it as soon as you can. Will you be able to manage if it takes a little time?

R-45: Yeah! I just need someone to talk to. I can't tell my friends . . . They would be shocked.

I-46: All right, you'll be hearing from me about when we can take you. (Rising)

R-46: Thank you. (Rises and is walked to door by counselor)

I-47: Goodbye, Mrs. Zeller.

R-47: Goodbye.

CRITICAL ANALYSIS QUESTIONS

1. What are some of the things done by Interviewer B to set the stage for the interview that were neglected by Interviewer A? (Here "setting the stage" includes all of the interviewer's behavior up to the opening question, at the end of I–7, ". . . would you just tell me what the situation is?" List Interviewer B's behaviors in the order they occur.

2. In Interview A the client shows some resistance to talking in R–8; the same thing happens in Interview B at R–8. What is the difference between the two interviewers' tactics in handling the situation? Say which one is best and why.

3. Despite the fact that the client's husband has many faults and is obviously to blame for much of the family problem, the wife somehow feels that basically *she* is to blame.

    a. Where is the first clue dropped by the respondent that she *possibly* feels she is to blame? (Give the R– number only.)

    b. Where is the first clue to self-blame that the interviewer responds to? (Give the I– number only.)

4. Does Interviewer A or B most often probe the respondent's feelings?

5. List the I– numbers in which Interviewer B obviously probes the respondent's feelings.

6. Does Interviewer B use questions, probes, or statements which *challenge* the respondent's actions, views, or feelings? (List the I– numbers.)

7. The interviewer uses one loaded question; which one is it?

8. Where does the respondent drop clues to possible guilt feelings that are *not* probed by the interviewer? (Give R– numbers only.)

9. Where does the respondent drop clues to possible guilt feelings that *are* probed by the interviewer? (Give R– number.)

10. How many times does Interviewer B use an immediate elaboration probe? (List the I– numbers.)

After you have completed the critical analysis questions, consult your instructor's handout for the author's critique.

Selected Readings

Barker, Larry L. *Listening Behavior.* Englewood Cliffs, N.J.: Prentice-Hall, 1971.

    The author identifies a variety of common obstacles to effective listening. These are all viewed in the context of listening to public speakers but are applicable to the interviewer's listening to the respondent.

Benjamin, Alfred. *The Helping Interview.* 3rd ed. Boston: Houghton Mifflin,1981.

    One of the better books on the conditions, stages, and forms of interaction in the interview. Gives down-to-earth examples. It is aimed mainly at the counseling interview.

Cormier, William H., and L. Sherilyn Cormier. *Interviewing Strategies for Helpers.* 2nd ed. Monterey, Calif.: Brooks/Cole Publishing, 1985.

Skills and strategies to be used in the four stages of the helping process (relationship assessment, goal setting, strategy selection and implementation, and evaluation-termination) are described in detail. Role-playing exercises and extensive bibliographies are provided. Relevant to either social workers or counselors of any type.

Ivey, Allen E., and John R. Moreland. *Microcounseling: Innovations in Interviewing Training.* Springfield, Ill.: Charles C. Thomas, 1971.
Emphasis is on attending behavior as a basic skill for successful interviewing, teaching, and learning. Reviews studies on counseling training methods, and presents its own set of recommended role-playing exercises for training counselors.

Polansky, Norman A. *Ego Psychology and Communication: Theory for the Interview.* Chicago: Aldine Publishing, 1971, reprinted 1973.
Deals with the dynamics of ego-defense as it affects communication in counseling interviews.

Stewart, Charles J., and William B. Cash. *Interviewing: Principles and Practices.* 4th ed. Dubuque, Iowa: Wm. C. Brown, 1985.
The first three chapters deal with general concepts, principles, and practices, and the last five each deal with a different setting and objective to cover informational, persuasive, employment, appraisal, and counseling interviews. The appendix includes examples of interview dialogues in each of settings dealt with earlier.

Chapter Twenty-Four

The Journalistic Interview

The topic of journalistic interviewing covers a great variety of information-gathering situations in which thousands of journalists are actually engaged.[1] To help organize and simplify this complex scene we must resort to some classification scheme.

VARIETIES OF JOURNALISTIC INTERVIEWS

The tremendous variety of journalistic interviews can be put into categories based on three dimensions: the *type of information* the journalist is seeking, the *central focus* of the story to be given to the public, and the *medium of communication* to be used in presenting the story to the public.

It is helpful to distinguish at least three *types of information:* background information gathering, news reporting, and feature story writing. Each of these activities places the journalist in a different social environment and requires different strategies, techniques and tactics.

It is useful to recognize at least three kinds of *central focus* of a story according to whether the focus is an event, a personality, or an organization. Of course, in reality events involve personalities and organizations; and personalities and organizations become more significant when they have a historic connection with events, but often it clarifies the journalist's task to decide whether the major focus of the story is to be on one specific event, on a personality who may be involved in events, or on an organization's structure and processes which may repeatedly affect events or personalities.

In classifying the *communication media* as they affect the interview setting and process, it is useful to divide the media into three main types, each with two subcategories: print (daily and periodical), radio

---

[1]Suggestions on this chapter were kindly furnished by Cheryl McHenry of the WHIO-TV newsteam, Dayton, Ohio.

(audio-taped and live), television (videotaped and live). The particular communication medium to be used in presenting the story to the public governs such characteristics as the length of the story, the rigidity of the deadline, the degree of control the interviewer must exercise in the interview, the number of people that must be involved in the interview, the amount of equipment needed, whether or not the interview can be done over the telephone, the degree to which the interview must have dramatic or entertainment value, and the type of problems in taste, style, and legality which may arise.

There is not space in this chapter to trace the complex connections between all of these different interview settings and purposes and to show how they affect the actual conduct of the interview. Instead, the discussion in this chapter will try to show that regardless of the vast variety of journalistic interviews, there still remain some very important social-psychological characteristics common to all types of journalistic interviewing.

COMMONALITIES OF JOURNALISTIC INTERVIEWS

The commonality of social-psychological characteristics springs from the fact that in all journalistic interviews the destination of the information being gathered is the general public. Since the respondent is aware that all of the information he or she gives is destined for the public ear, it is not like talking to one's doctor, lawyer, psychologist, or research sociologist where anonymity can be assured.

Even in a journalistic interview in which the name of the source is not given, the fact that the information will get to the public still may affect the respondent's behavior and the kind of information the respondent will or will not give. After all, to give or withhold information from the public may have potential benefits to the respondent even though anonymous.

The relevance of this *publicness* to the task of the interviewer may be illuminated by examining its potential effects upon the inhibitors and facilitators of communication in the interview. Of the eight potential inhibitors described earlier in Chapter 5, two are most likely to be strengthened by the publicness of the journalistic interview: *ego-threat* and *etiquette*. Of the eight potential facilitators described earlier in Chapter 6, two are most likely to be enhanced in their power by the publicness of the interview: giving *recognition* and appealing to the respondent's *altruism*. First the effect of the publicness on the two inhibitors will be illustrated.

If an individual or an organization has something to hide, they do not want this displayed in public. In this case the respondent will be wary of interviewers who might ask for information that would tarnish the public image. This may be a problem whether we are interviewing a public school teacher, a corporate executive or public servant—anyone who is potentially fearful of public censure. Even in cases where the individual has done nothing immoral or illegal there can be a fear of unsympathetic and unrealistic expectations on the part of the public.

This tendency for public figures to suffer from *ego-threat* and want to hide things from the public is so general that many journalists almost automatically assume that as representatives of the press they have no choice but to be in an adversarial relationship with the people they interview. Unless the news media function merely as a channel for propaganda handouts from government or private interests, there must be this strong element of investigative reporting which aims to expose what the respondent is trying to hide.

Not as obvious as the risk of ego-threat is the possibility of the *etiquette barrier* which operates in situations where the respondent withholds information, not to protect himself but to save the feelings of the public. For example, a person may refrain from pointing out that the voters who put an obvious quack in office are to blame; a war veteran may be reluctant to disillusion a patriotic public by divulging some of the realistic details regarding relations between the enlisted men and the officers; or a close friend of a recently deceased rock 'n roll idol may not want to disillusion the public by divulging aspects of the idol's private life.

We may well ask, why would anyone grant an interview with a journalist with even the slightest tendency toward investigative reporting? The main reason is that the respondent wants to avoid the stigma of refusing to be interviewed or wants to use the news media to get recognition and to build a more positive public image. Therefore, the respondent often accepts the challenge of outmaneuvering the investigative reporter in order to get his or her own points across without divulging any negative information.

The demand among public personalities to learn the skill of managing the interview with the press has become so great that special training seminars have been developed for that purpose. Sometimes seminars for corporate executives or government officials are designed or taught by journalists or ex-journalists. The aim is to train people in the art of coming out of the press interview victorious. This usually means that the respondent gave the public his or her own point of view on some issue, got across many points to build a positive image for the organization, and avoided giving any negative information *without appearing to be evasive.* That is victory!

In the early 1980s this issue became a cause for public debate among journalists. Many felt that it was a case of "joining the enemy" for a journalist to teach public figures how to gracefully evade the journalist's probing and how to stage news events to get media attention.

On the positive side, this same publicness can enhance the power of two of the facilitators of information flow in the interview. These two are providing *recognition* and appealing to the respondent's *altruism.* In some cases the need for recognition is so great the respondent feels that even to be involved in a scandal is better than no publicity at all. Of course, this would be more true of an entertainer than of a public official or corporate executive. It is often this lure of public recognition that entices the public figure to chance the hazards of the press interview.

Another facilitator of communication that is magnified in importance by the prospect of publicity is the power of the appeal to the respondent's *altruism*. In certain circumstances the respondent's story can be helpful to thousands of others; this is true in the case of the scam victim or the person who with great ingenuity and courage avoids or overcomes some threat of injury or disease. Such altruism's effects may range from giving inspiration to providing specific solutions. Television is full of examples of respondents who have been persuaded to tell their embarrassing, humiliating, or traumatic stories because they can help thousands of listeners.

The author is not suggesting that the journalistic interview involves only two of the eight inhibitors and only two of the eight facilitators. In fact, all of the remaining facilitators and inhibitors may be brought into play depending on who the respondent is, what kind of information the respondent has, and how it fits into the current social situation. However, the basic fact that journalistic interviews of all types carry the prospect of publicity tends to make two of the inhibitors and two of the facilitators more prominent than in other professional settings where publicity is not assumed.

In searching among various types of journalistic interviews for one to use for illustrative purposes, the author sought one as different as possible from the other professional settings dealt with in this book. Therefore, the on-camera, news interview dealing with a controversial community issue was chosen. To be more typical of television news stories a videotaped interview was selected rather than a live interview.

A VIDEOTAPED NEWS INTERVIEW

Instead of following the format of the other professional settings in which separate good and bad interviews were presented for comparison and analysis, this chapter will present only one broadcast interview and look for both the good and the bad, keeping in mind that it is not a live interview so there would be an opportunity to edit out some, but not all, of the undesirable parts before broadcast. Of course the better the interview the less editing and the better the end product.

The Issue

The reporter became acquainted with the following facts of the issue before she interviewed the councilman on-camera.

The town council of Greene Springs proposed a plan to update the town's water mains in the older section of town where they were only two inches in diameter rather than the modern standard of six inches. Replacing the old mains would not only provide greater water pressure in the homes (so that one could take a shower while the dishwasher and clothes washer were running, for example) but also would allow the town to install fire hydrants in needed locations and supply a greater flow of water in case of fire.

The town engineer estimated that the cost would be $5 million, which in a town of 12,000 people seemed astronomical. A town council meeting open to the public attracted fifty residents most of whom vigorously protested an increase in water rates or taxes to pay for the improvement. The debate became even more heated in discussing whether the cost should be collected through increased water bills to everyone in town or only to those whose water mains would be replaced. Another hot issue was whether funds should be collected in water bills or in tax assessments on property owners. The town council had proposed to collect only from the people in the area where the new water mains were to be installed, but it was not clear how the funds were to be collected.

An ex-councilman entered into the debate declaring that it was the town's moral, political, and financial obligation to replace the substandard water service at no additional cost to the citizens. Others accepted the idea that there would have to be an increase in water rates but that the cost should not be borne by those who had suffered inadequate water service for so long while paying water rates just as high as those who enjoyed adequate service. One resident calculated his prospective waterline improvement bill to be between $1,500 and $3,000, a cost which the town council didn't challenge and which all the residents found shocking.

One of the three television stations in the neighboring metropolitan center did not view this as an insignificant tempest in a village teapot but as a microcosmic drama which would be repeated in epic proportions in the larger, aging cities across the nation where the costs of replacing the decaying infrastructure of sewers, waterlines, and streets are calculated to have reached into the hundreds of billions of dollars. WHZQ reserved a five-minute segment of its News Magazine for this story and sent a reporter and camera operator to Greene Springs to interview several people including a town council member.

Purpose of the Interview

In this case we do not know precisely what the reporter's purposes were beyond showing some of the kinds of issues, arguments, divisions, and vested interests that emerge when a community is confronted with the fact of its decaying infrastructure and dramatizing the deep feelings generated by this practical issue. We do not know whether or not the reporter had hopes of finding some practical guidance for other communities with a similar problem. In any case we should try to think of some very specific objectives that should have been included in an interview guide for the occasion. Then in reading the transcription of the interview we will be able to see whether the interviewer achieved those objectives or whether other objectives are apparent.

The reporter assigned to the story is fully aware of some of the potential hazards in videotaping an interview for the News Magazine. For example, village officials might want to minimize the disagreement to preserve the image of the tranquil semirural atmosphere; partisans in the dispute might want to give their point of view as the only sensible one; some loyal residents might rather not expose their disagreements to the public; local businesses might see a television interview as a marvelous opportunity to inject some profitable propaganda on the salubrious atmosphere of Greene Springs.

Preparation for the Interview

The television News Magazine is broadcast weekly and the reporter had a week's notice to produce the five-minute segment. Nevertheless, the amount of time to be devoted to the story is limited since it is not the reporter's only assignment for the week; she has the help of only a portion of a secretary's time in doing the preparatory research.

She obtained a copy of the *Greene Springs News* and read about the issue, then called the editor of the paper to see if any more detail was available and to get suggestions for specific people to interview including a town council member and residents on different sides of the issue.

Before doing the videotaped interview with the councilman, the reporter learned the points given in "The Issue" section of this chapter, but she did not have a preinterview with the councilman.

On the Scene

The interviewer arrived, with her camera operator, at Councilman Robert Wilson's home at the appointed 11:00 A.M. She went to the door, leaving the camera operator and equipment in the car, and rang the doorbell. The councilman comes to the door:

I: Good morning! Councilman Wilson?

R: Yes.

I: I'm Karen Gregory from WHZQ.

R: Oh, yes. Come in!

I: It was good of you to grant us this interview for News Magazine. We are interested in the water main issue in Greene Springs because we feel that it is an early warning of what will be happening in a big way in the large cities across the nation with their aging sewer systems, water mains, and streets.

R: Right! Where would you like to do the interview?

I: Any place where it is quiet and enough room for us and the camera.

R: Well, we could do it here in the living room or out on the patio or in my study.

I: Could I see your study?

R: It's right here between the living room and the patio. (They go into the study.)

I: Ah, this is nice! It has an atmosphere good for a councilman. But if you don't mind I would prefer that you don't sit behind your desk for this interview. It tends to put a barrier between you and the public.

R: Good idea!

I: Ah, a small world (looking at a plaque on the wall); so that was your horse that won the steeple chase. I remember the horse's name, Meadowmouse, from when I was covering the State Fair.

R: Yes, I love horses! That's why I moved to Greene Springs ten years ago. Here I can have my horses on my little five-acre "ranch."

I: Let me call in my cameraman, so he can get set up in here. (She goes out and brings in the cameraman.) Councilman Wilson, this is Tim Jenkins who will videotape our chat.

R: How do you do.

Tim: Glad to meet you. It will take just a couple of minutes to get set up.

I: In the meantime, Councilman Wilson, I can explain how we are going to proceed.

R: Good, let's sit over here.

I: Thank you. Now we just want to have an informal talk with no concern for the camera and don't worry about making mistakes because we can edit out anything that doesn't go smoothly. We will chat maybe for ten minutes, but less than five can be used in broadcast. That gives us a chance to condense and get rid of the rough spots. If you want to stop the taping at any time that's okay. If you have any visuals like a map or a photo we can arrange to piece that in at the right point. I will start the interview by first introducing you and saying a sentence or two about the issue and then pop the first question which will be—Can you tell me what the water main issue in Greene Springs is all about? You say what you want to say and I'll probe you for more details on the town's reactions. At times I may preface my questions with some statement that puts the question in context so that both the questions and answers are easier to understand. Do you have any questions?

R: Yes, do I get a chance to look at the tape before it goes on the air?

I: That is usually not practical, but if when we finish taping here today you feel strongly that something should be edited out or off the record, just say so and we'll respect your wishes.

R: That seems fair enough!

THE INTERVIEW

After the Councilman and reporter are seated in their chairs, the cameraman asks if they are ready, starts the camera rolling and says they can start anytime.

I-1:   Councilman Wilson, can you tell me what the water main issue here in Greene Springs is all about?

R-1:   Well, it is simple in a way and complex in other ways. It is simple in that even though Greene Springs is small, it is *old*; and like many of the large cities in the United States the infrastructure like streets, water mains and sewer lines are wearing out and deteriorating. This was bound to happen, but none of the previous administrations were far-sighted enough to build up an accrual fund for the day when the water mains would need to be replaced. Now we are faced with a renovation project that would cost about $5 million, and it's tough for a town of about 12,000 people to come up with the money.

I-2:   You feel this problem could have been avoided? How?

R-2:   For the past thirty years there should have been a plan to put a bit each year into an investment fund to be ultimately used to rebuild the whole water system. It would have taken about $100,000 a year plus interest to accumulate the $5 million we need.

I-3:   Right, but since that wasn't done and you are now suddenly faced with the need for $5 million . . . has this set off some hard feelings and controversy in the community?

R-3:   I wouldn't say that. Greene Springs has a long history of town democracy, and we have had some town meetings on the problem and some preliminary discussion of alternative solutions. (Pause)

I-4: Uh huh.

R-4: We are a town with more than our share of college graduates but we have a small semirural village atmosphere which people like. For example, many college professors who teach at colleges in other towns in a twenty-mile radius choose to live here rather than in the town where their colleges are located.

I-5: That's interesting!

R-5: Yes! We are semirural in appearance and in the absence of pollution or traffic congestion, but we have a sophisticated citizenry with faith in the process of democratic discussion.

I-6: That's good! Has the town council made a proposal to the community on how to meet the problem? Has it made any formal statement on how or whether it could be done?

R-6: No! We have made no formal statement. We have only held one village meeting to present the problem and get people's suggestions and reactions. We will probably have more meetings before we can make any formal statement or take any definite action. Don't you think that is the best way to proceed?

I-7: Yes, that seems ideal. But do you and the other four members of the town council agree on what to do next?

R-7: Yes, one thing we do agree on is that we should have another open town council meeting but give it more publicity in advance so that a more representative number of citizens come. There were only about fifty people at the first meeting.

I-8: I have heard that one of the ex-councilmen made a strong statement to the effect that it is the moral obligation of the town to upgrade the water service without any additional cost to the citizens. What do you think of that statement?

R-8: No comment.

I-9: What were some of the points of controversy that arose in the last town meeting on this issue?

R-9: I wouldn't say that there was any real controversy. It was all a preliminary discussion in which anyone could throw ideas into the pot for consideration.

I-10: What were some of these ideas?

R-10:   Well, some people felt that the money should be raised by a real estate tax and some felt that the costs should be covered by an increase in the water rates.

I-11:   Did everyone there agree that new larger water mains should be installed to replace the smaller mains in the older parts of town?

R-11:   No, there was one person at least who said they had gotten along all this time without knowing that they were deprived, so why get excited about the problem now?

I-12:   Did the ex-councilman who said the town should be responsible without increasing the cost to the taxpayer—have any suggestions about where the money should come from?

R-12:   Not really! He was just pissed off because he lost the election! He tried to raise the garbage collectors' salaries 40 percent plus benefits and the voting taxpayers didn't like the idea!

I-13:   I heard that the council came to the meeting with a proposal to collect only from residents of the streets where new water mains are needed. Is that the case?

R-13:   I wouldn't call it a proposal . . . it was just an idea the council had because they had followed that principle in the case of major street improvements such as widening the street, putting in sidewalks or curbs and gutters. It was just one of many ideas floating around in that town meeting.

I-14:   If you were to pay for the project by assessments on the properties on the affected streets, how much would it cost the average property owner on these streets?

R-14:   I don't know.

I-15:   Is it just that you personally do not have that information, or hasn't it ever been calculated by the city manager or anyone on the council?

R-15:   As far as I know no one has done any precise figuring along that line.

I-16:   But hasn't some official made a preliminary estimate?

R-16:   I assume that the assessment would be in proportion to the particular tax assessed value of each person's property, so it would be a bit complicated to come up with an average.

I-17:   Wouldn't it be a simple problem of dividing the total amount needed by the number of property owners to be assessed? Did nobody in the town council or administration do that before they stated the general idea in the town meeting?

R–17:   If anyone did it they didn't give me the results.

I–18:   According to the *Greene Springs News* article, one of the citizens attending the meeting estimated that his tax assessment would be between $1,500 and $3,000!

R–18:   That's right.

I–19:   Do you think the average assessment might fall in between those two figures?

R–19:   It could, but I'm not sure.

I–20:   Doesn't it seem strange to you that a town council would in effect come to the taxpayers asking them to pay for new water mains before ever calculating how big a taxpayer's bill might be? It could sound like asking a taxpayer to sign a blank check.

R–20:   As I said before, this was just a preliminary discussion to test out the water before the council or town manager went ahead with any particular proposal for raising the money. Often people are dead set against any change, so they complain about the *cost* to avoid saying that they don't want change. For example, in my first term in office I stuck my neck out by insisting that we put up street signs all over the town. The old residents couldn't understand why street signs were needed since they had gotten along without them all these years. They just couldn't imagine outsiders trying to find something in Greene Springs when the street names were only on the map but not on the street corners. Now that we have the street signs nobody will admit being against the idea. But at the time I had put my reelection on the line over that tempest in the teapot . . . and I wasn't surprised that I lost the next time around.

I–21:   Now that begins to make sense to me . . . you were mainly trying to get a preliminary estimate of public sentiment on the idea before firming up any specific proposal?

R–21:   Yes, exactly!

I–22:   I see . . . well, uh, what I mean is . . . there must be some way out of this dilemma. Are you, personally, convinced that new water mains are needed? Is it really going to cost $5 million? If so, there must be some way of spreading the cost more broadly or spreading it out over more time. Is it possible to get federal grants or long-term loans for rebuilding the infrastructure?

R–22:   Yes, I'm convinced that the new mains are needed. It has gotten to the point that as much as a third of the water delivered to an area of the town will leak out before reaching the households. And even if the mains didn't leak they are so small in diameter that in case of a fire there is not enough pressure to put out a fire in a two-story building. Another problem with leaks is not only the waste of processed water but also the increased danger of disease. In any town the sewer pipes also are bound to leak a little here or there and the water mains and sewer pipes are near each other under the street. As long as there is pressure in the water mains, there is little chance of sewage getting into the drinking water; but in times of emergency when the water pressure is lost as in the case when our town's water storage tank froze and burst, then the leaks in the water mains reverse direction and the sewage flows into the drinking water. This is why such emergencies are often followed by an outbreak of hepatitis or worse.

I–23:   That sounds very convincing! Our Channel 2 viewers would like to know from the Greene Springs case how these problems, which are bound to beset every community in time, can be prevented or solved with a minimum of conflict and a maximum of fairness. For example, would you be in favor of raising the water rates to everyone in the town or only to those in the areas which need the new water mains; or would you favor property taxes on everyone in town or only on those on the streets where the new mains are needed. Do you think some larger tax base should be exploited like a local income tax, state tax, or some federal source?

R–23:   You have just mentioned most of the possible solutions and there may be others we haven't thought of. That's why we need these exploratory discussions on the pros and cons of the different ways of raising the money. And of course, as you suggest, we need to come up with more detailed figures on who would have to pay how much, when. At this time I'm not prepared to say which way would be best.

I–24:   I see. Early in our talk when I asked you about the ex-councilman who said the town is morally obligated to upgrade the water service without any additional cost to the citizens, you said, "No comment." Could you tell a little bit about why you didn't want to comment on that?

R–24:   If I explained why I don't want to comment, that would be the comment wouldn't it?

I–25:   I suppose so, but rumors are going around that the ex-councilman knows what he is talking about and that the town treasurer has the money but wants to spend it on statues, flower beds, and raises for the council members and town manager, so I thought you should have the opportunity to comment.

R–25:   Ah! So that's what he meant by saying we had a moral obligation! There is not a word of truth in that rumor! We have proposed no statues to be erected and no new flower beds. I don't know if the ex-councilman is spreading these rumors, if so he didn't have the courage to say these things openly at the town meeting. I didn't want to comment in the first place because that man makes me angry. He was voted out of office but still wants to run things. Only an imbecile would make a statement to the effect that "not the citizens but the town" should pay for the water mains. Who *is* the town? The town is no more than all its citizens! That type of demagoguery of promising to increase spending without increasing taxes is as old as the hills. It sounds like he may be trying to get reelected.

I–26:   Uh huh. (3)

R–26:   I've said enough on that topic!

I–27:   Is there anything else you'd like to say about this whole water main problem in conclusion?

R–27:   This problem of aging water mains is not unique to Greene Springs and the problem is popping up at an accelerating rate in the communities across the nation. We have just had the problem pointed out to us and have started looking for a solution by democratically taking the citizens into the discussion at the very beginning of the process. I think that is good even though it may bring differences of opinion into the open, and provides an opportunity for the dissatisfied to complain. We have faith in the process and in the people of Greene Springs to be willing to face the reality of the problem and to contribute to its most satisfactory solution. We're on our way and I hope we will be able to set an example for other communities when they discover their own water main problem.

I–28:   Thank you, Councilman Wilson, for your time and willingness to discuss this issue with WHZQ.

CRITICAL ANALYSIS QUESTIONS

1. What are some of the good and some of the bad (commissions or omissions) things the interviewer does in preparing for and setting up the interview situation before the video camera is rolling?

2. At what points does the R seem to be resisting, evading or possibly hiding something? (Give the R–numbers.)

3. At which of these points in question 2 does the interviewer try to probe for the information and at which points does she allow the evasion to go by? (Give R–numbers.)

4. Does the interviewer ever use a loaded question? Or should she have done so at a certain point? In either case at what point is this true? (Give the I–number.)

5. Does the interviewer ever use questions in a way that shifts the responsibility for the question to someone else? (If so, give I–number.)

6. Does the interviewer ever say anything to directly remind the respondent of the audience? (If so, give I–number.)

7. Are there any points at which the interviewer uses a clearly inappropriate form of question? (If so, give I–number.)

8. Does the interviewer ever use a "trial balloon" question to which she already knows the answer in order to determine whether the respondent will have a tendency to hide something? (I–number?)

9. Does the interviewer ever miss an opportunity to sincerely praise the respondent's actions? (If so, give the I–number.)

10. What points of information do you feel the interviewer failed to get?

Selected Readings

Brady, John. *The Craft of Interviewing.* New York: Vintage Books (Random House), 1977.
  The major focus is on the steps involved in doing interviews for, and writing up, *feature stories* as opposed to news stories. Gives practical suggestions, illustrated by amusing examples, for locating and contacting respondents, getting their cooperation, doing background research in preparation for the interview, questioning techniques and tactics, and writing up the interview for publication. The author is editor of *Writer's Digest.*

Broughton, Irv. *The Art of Interviewing for Television, Radio and Film.* Blue Ridge Summit, Pa.: TAB Books, Inc., 1981.
  Deals with how to prepare for an interview, types of questions, types of respondents, legal aspects as well as technical aspects of the interview. Distinguishes between live and video-taped interviews for broadcast. Gives specific techniques for handling the sound aspects of the interview. A special feature of this book is one hundred pages of transcripts of actual interviews.

Griffin, Merv, and Peter Barsocchini. *From Where I Sit: Merv Griffin's Book of People.* New York: Arbor House, 1982.

Mainly an interesting recital of anecdotes about Merv's experiences with interviewing guests on his various television talk shows and his relationships with other people in the entertainment business. Chapter 2 has a detailed description of the roles of all members of the production staff, the technology and the staging of his talk shows.

Hilton, Jack, and Mary Knoblauch. *On Television: A Survival Guide for Media Interviews.* New York: American Management Association, 1982.

Advice to businessmen and community affairs people on how to plan for and behave in a television interview in order to be accepted, credible and to get one's viewpoint across to the audience. Good points on how not to appear to be evasive while avoiding the question, on why you should listen, on how a talk show is put together, the interviewee's rights, and on specific traps of interviewing tactics and techniques to be avoided.

Chapter Twenty-Five

The Police Interrogation

Interrogation is a particular type of interviewing in which the interviewer seeks information that can be used against the respondent.[1] In this case the interviewer is not perceived by the respondent as friend, colleague, or helper, but as the enemy, captor, or punisher. In this sense we speak of military interrogation of prisoners of war or police interrogation of suspected or known criminals.

Interrogation describes only a small portion of the interviewing done by law enforcement officers. The officer may interview a robbery victim or a witness to an accident. The law enforcement administrator also may do a variety of interviewing ordinarily associated with the management role such as personnel selection, performance appraisal, or conflict resolution. Only when the law enforcement officer is questioning an actual or suspected criminal do we apply the term interrogation.

Perhaps the clearest example of interrogation in police work is the attempt to obtain a confession. Law enforcement officers feel that it is extremely important to be able to obtain at least some leads to convicting evidence from the criminal himself, if not a confession. It may seem that no criminal in his right mind would give self-convicting information, yet experienced law enforcement officers can clearly demonstrate that this is not the case when the right methods are used by a skilled interrogator.

THE DILEMMA OF INTERROGATION

On one hand many more criminals would be allowed to escape prosecution if it were not possible to elicit self-convicting evidence. The phrase *self-convicting evidence* is not synonymous with *confession*. In most cases the suspect unwittingly gives concrete details which can lead to

---

[1]Very helpful suggestions on this chapter were kindly provided by Charles J. Gift, Polygraph Expert of the Dayton Police Department, Dayton, Ohio.

the establishment of guilt. On the other hand, if inappropriate methods are used, it is possible to force "confessions" from the innocent. If a confession is obtained in the cross-examination of a defendant by the prosecuting attorney in the presence of the lawyer for the defense, the judge and jury, then the confession has a high probability of being admissible as evidence. However, if a confession is obtained before the court proceedings in police work, it must be shown that no coercion was used and that other evidence corroborates the confession. Since 1960 several legal safeguards have been implemented, such as the 1966 U.S. Supreme Court's *Miranda* decision, to protect citizens from improper detention and questioning methods. Can skillful interrogation be used which does not violate a suspect's Constitutional right according to the Fifth Amendment to not "be compelled in any criminal case to be a witness against himself"? The answer to this is clearly *yes*, and the test of the appropriateness of a method is whether or not it would tend to compel a person to "confess" to a crime he or she did not commit. The author feels that all of the strategies, techniques, and tactics suggested below pass this test.

INTERROGATION AS A STYLE OF INTERVIEWING

Since ego threat is such a powerful inhibitor to the truth in an interrogation, the interrogator must assume a much more active role than a public opinion interviewer. This activity may take many forms in the attempt to persuade the respondent to give information. The interrogator not only asks questions but makes statements designed to convince the respondent that to try to lie is useless, or to help the suspect rationalize illegal acts to reduce the moral stigma and ego threat.

Of all the professional settings of the interview dealt with in this book, the interrogation as an attempt to obtain a confession from a criminal generally carries with it the strongest, most persistent, and most obvious ego threat. Yet experienced law enforcement people have obtained confessions or leads to other incriminating evidence from thousands of suspects by developing special questioning methods designed to overcome the respondent's tendency to withhold the truth. One of the best distillations of these methods is given by Inbau and Reid.[2]

STRATEGY IN INTERROGATION

The term *strategy* covers many important decisions regarding the time, place, and setting of the interview before any of the verbal or nonverbal techniques and tactics of questioning begin.

---

[2]Fred Inbau and John E. Reid. *Criminal Interrogations and Confessions*, 3rd ed., (Baltimore: Williams and Wilkens, 1985).

Time of the interview. It is important not to interrogate the suspect too soon because the interrogator can be much more effective with the suspect after he or she has already interviewed the crime victim, a witness to the crime, the discoverer of the crime, or people who know the suspect. If there is an accomplice, the two suspects should be questioned separately and repeatedly to allow cross-checks on the information given.

Preparation for the interrogation. In addition to interviews with other people, other sources of information should be explored such as the suspect's record for the typical modus operandi, employment record, marital status, personal habits (drugs, smoking, alcohol, gambling, hobbies, etc.). A visit to the scene of the crime will often make the interrogator better able to question and understand the answers of the victim, witnesses, and others. Also, a visit to the scene of the suspect's alibi can be very useful in designing questions to test whether the suspect was actually at a certain place at the time he or she claims. All of this information can be used in designing questions, in determining the most effective sequence of questions and in checking the veracity of the answers.

The interrogation room. Interviews with victims, witnesses, and acquaintances of the suspect may take place in a variety of locations such as the scene of the crime, a hospital, or a private home; but the suspect, who is either being detained or has been asked to come to police headquarters to give information, should be interrogated in a special room set aside for that purpose. Some small police departments have no such specialized room, but the more of those features suggested below that can be supplied the better.

Above all the room should provide *privacy.* This is easier to provide if there is no telephone. There should be no visual distractions by activities either indoors or outdoors. The room should be quiet to avoid distractions and to produce an atmosphere of timelessness free from the hustle-bustle of the urban society. There should not be pictures or other ornamentation to act as a diversion. Also, there should be no visible bars on doors or windows in order to avoid the feeling of a jail.

To facilitate communication there should be no desk between the interviewer and the respondent. They should be directly facing each other so that the interviewer can make eye contact and see the changes in facial expression of the respondent. It is important that the interrogator is seated at a slightly higher level than the respondent. Many interrogators feel that the interviewer should be seated in a comfortable chair with arms while the respondent has a straight-backed chair with no arms.

The lighting in the room should not be glaring, but there must be enough light on the suspect's face to allow the interrogator to note subtle changes of facial expression. Another important aid is the two-way mirror which allows an observer to watch the interview without being seen by the interviewer or respondent. This arrangement has several potential functions: It helps to train new personnel to become interrogators; in cases where the suspect is female and the interrogator is male, having a female observer provides a safeguard against charges brought later that the suspect was coerced or molested by the interrogator; when a team of two or more interrogators is used, it allows all the team to see and hear the whole interview with only one physically present at a time. This allows each interviewer the opportunity to build on what has gone before without having to listen to a tape or read the transcript; and it allows two or more people to note the suspect's reactions, to think of penetrating questions, and to detect inconsistencies in the responses.

If there is no state law against it, there should be concealed microphones or video cameras to record all that is being said. This has many useful purposes. It can be used to counter any charges that coercion was used to get a confession. It can provide a permanent record of all the details of information given which at a later date may become significant as evidence or as a demonstration of changes in the suspect's story. It allows others who were not present at the time of the interview to evaluate the evidence. Finally, it provides a backup to a written version of a confession which, although signed by the suspect, may be denied later. In some cases a judge may want to know why a suspect was interrogated for three hours, yet the signed confession can be read in three minutes. The question "What was the officer doing to the suspect the rest of the time?" can be convincingly answered by the recording. Even in states where the law does not allow a suspect's testimony to be recorded without his or her knowledge, it is still important to have concealed microphones. Then the suspect can be asked for permission and, if he or she gives it, the recording can proceed without any distraction to interviewer or respondent.

The interrogator's appearance. The interrogator should *not* be in uniform but in unobtrusively conservative civilian dress. This makes it easier for the interviewer to establish a less official relationship with the respondent. The interrogator should not smoke and should not allow the suspect to smoke. The interviewer should remain calm and serious but not act tough, vindictive, or threatening. Above all the interrogator should exude the impression of having all the time in the world. The interrogator should not appear impatient by pacing around the room or getting angry, nor should he or she provide comedy relief by trying to be funny or light-hearted about the situation. As we will show later, this background impression of the setting and of the interviewer's appearance and behavior is periodically reinforced verbally by statements from the interviewer.

Defining the interview situation. First, it should be made clear to the respondent at the beginning that he or she has rights as specified by the *Miranda* decision which in effect says that the suspect must be warned that anything he or she says may be used as evidence in a court of law and that the suspect must give permission to be interviewed, since he or she has the right to remain silent.

There are some fine legal points, which will not be discussed here, that revolve around the issue of whether such rights apply only to the guilty, to persons suspected of being guilty, or also to persons assumed to be innocent. The question may be raised as to whether evidence given by a presumably innocent witness that makes the witness a suspect is inadmissible in court because the respondent had not yet been "read his rights." These fine points and many others are dealt with at length in volumes such as Kamisar[3] and Schafer.[4]

Second, the interviewer should make it clear that the purpose of the interview is not to get a "confession" but to "get at the truth" no matter who may be shown innocent or guilty. In saying this the interviewer should be careful not to promise any special concessions to the respondent or anyone else in exchange for the truth. One commonly practiced exception to this rule is the use of plea bargaining. In this case the interrogator is authorized in advance to promise a lower-status member of a criminal organization that he or she will be found guilty of a lesser crime usually in exchange for evidence that will convict a higher-status member of that organization.

Third, the interviewer should by word and deed demonstrate that the respondent not only has legal rights but also will be treated with decency and respect. Practitioners in this field report instances where prostitutes, thieves, and murderers respond favorably to being treated with the recognition that everyone is human and has more to them than the label of a criminal category suggests. For this reason the interrogator should insist that handcuffs be removed by the officer bringing in a suspect from detention.

Fourth, it has already been mentioned in connection with the topic of the interrogator's appearance and actions in the interview room that the whole scene should suggest that there is plenty of time. This general background impression can be reinforced from time to time beginning

---

[3]Yale Kamisar, *Police Interrogations and Confessions: Essays in Law and Policy* (Ann Arbor: University of Michigan Press, 1980).

[4]William J. Schafer, III, *Confessions and Statements* (Springfield, Ill.: Charles C Thomas, 1968).

with an explanation to the respondent that there is no need to rush and that the interviewer has plenty of time and will be free to interview several different times if that is necessary to get the full story of what happened.

SOME SPECIAL TECHNIQUES

Most of the special techniques which have been developed for police interrogation are ways of cracking the suspect's ego-defense with a two-pronged attack: The first is to show sympathetic understanding by minimizing the moral seriousness of the crime and by supplying acceptable rationalization for committing it; the second is to demonstrate that it is impossible to fabricate a consistent story from lies. Traps are set to detect the respondent's lies and to point them out to the respondent in an acceptable manner. Some of the kinds of questions and statements the interrogator can use will be discussed here.

Vocabulary. Whether asking a question or making a statement the interrogator should strive to use the least threatening vocabulary in order to reduce ego threat. For example, instead of "kill" the interrogator says "shoot"; instead of "steal" the interrogator says "take"; instead of "confess" the interrogator says "tell the truth."

In addition to using nonthreatening words, the interrogator should use language the respondent understands and feels comfortable with. This is usually a combination of simple, nontechnical language and some of the jargon of the suspect's own social group. If the person has a previous record of a certain type of crime, the good interrogator knows the vocabulary of the trade whether it is prostitution, drug pushing, or professional theft. If the suspect has no previous record, the interrogator should listen carefully to the vocabulary used by the respondent and follow suit.

Some special questions. Most of these special questions are specific forms of the leading question found to be fruitful under the general conditions of interrogation.

First is the question based upon *pretended knowledge.* In this type of question the interrogator pretends to know something to be a fact when he or she only suspects it to be true and then tries to get the respondent to admit the fact either directly or indirectly. The respondent may admit something if he or she assumes that it is already known. For example, if the interrogator wants to know whether the suspect had an accomplice, he or she could ask a question based on the assumption that there was an accomplice. The interrogator could say, "From one of the witnesses' description I can't tell whether or not you were the one driving the get-away car. Were you or your partner driving the car?" The suspect might reply, "That had to be me driving the car because I did the job alone." Or if the suspect did not do the job alone he or she might say, "I was driving the car, but I did not hold up the cashier. I didn't even know there was going to be a holdup; my partner said he was going to buy a pack of cigarettes." In this case the interrogator has established the probable existence of an accomplice.

Second, *a trial balloon* question can be used to detect whether the respondent will lie about already established facts. For example, if the interrogator knows that the suspect used to live only a block away from the store that was robbed but the suspect does not admit robbing the store, the interrogator might ask, "Were you ever in the neighborhood of this store before?" Then the innocent suspect might say, "Sure, I used to live near the store." But the suspect who is guilty might say, "No, I've never been in that neighborhood." Then the interrogator would have an opportunity to point out that he or she knows the suspect is not telling the truth and that he or she has many other sources of information to use in verifying the suspect's answers. After a series of traps of this kind in which the truth of the suspect's statements can be tested, the respondent loses confidence in his or her ability to deceive the interrogator.

Third, to detect whether the suspect might be guilty, the interrogator asks a question aimed at allowing the respondent to display knowledge that only a guilty person or accomplice would know. The success of the *guilty knowledge* question depends upon wording a question in such a way that it does not suggest that it is seeking guilty knowledge. It should not be apparent that the interrogator knows which information could be known only by the guilty. The form and content of the *guilty knowledge* question depends upon the circumstances. If a suspect is brought in immediately after a robbery, for example, before there has been any newspaper story or local gossip circulating and if the suspect doesn't know that he or she is a suspect, then the interrogator may begin by saying "Thank you for coming in to talk with us . . . do you have any idea why you are here?" There is a chance that the respondent may suggest that it might be in connection with the robbery that has just occurred. If this happens, then the respondent has the burden of accounting for how he or she knew there was a robbery.

If a suspect is being questioned some days after a robbery and if a newspaper story has been published, then the interrogator may ask a guilty knowledge question prefaced by a statement reminding the respondent that the story has already appeared in the newspaper. For example: "There have been several news stories about a robbery at the Jewel Thursday night. Can you tell me what you know about it?" By encouraging the respondent to tell what he or she has heard or read, it is possible that the respondent might mention some detail of the real situation that has never been reported to newspapers and could only be known by the guilty person. The discussion of the event can be continued by asking questions that encourage the respondent to *speculate* about the event on the basis of public knowledge of the event. For example: "Why do you suppose the robber would pull off a holdup for only $17?" If guilty, the respondent might suggest that "Maybe the robber didn't know the owner's wife always took away the cash to make a night deposit in the bank at 10 P.M." If this was the explanation given by the store owner to the robber who asked, "Where is the rest of the money," then the probability of guilt is raised along with the possibility of getting more incriminating information in the respondent's panicky attempt to explain why he or she speculated in such an interesting way.

This discussion in search of bits of guilty knowledge can be prolonged with questions about the victim, the scene of the crime, witnesses, possible suspects, or another aspect of the event which gives an opportunity to display knowledge known only to the guilty party.

Fourth, as a further test of possible guilt, the interrogator can use a question of *fictitious fact* to see if the respondent will try to explain away the nonexistent evidence. For example, in a murder case the interrogator might say, "Well, if you didn't do it, how do you explain the blood found on the sleeve of your coat we found at your apartment?" If the person is innocent he or she might say, "I have no idea how that could be there." But if the respondent invents a long story about going rabbit hunting in the coat, or how a small cut on his or her arm began to bleed when rubbed by the sleeve, then the interrogator has another indicator that the respondent is lying. The interrogator also has another opportunity to shake the respondent's confidence in his or her ability to lie successfully by pointing out that the respondent's long explanation was wasted because, in fact, there was no blood on the coat but that the blood was actually found somewhere else and was the same blood type as the victim's.

Fifth, under some conditions a question of *assumed guilt* can be used. The success of its use depends on the circumstances and on the interrogator's ability as an actor who can control the nonverbal aspects of the question. For example, instead of asking "Did you do it?" or instead of a direct accusatory statement like "I know you did it, so don't bother to deny it!" the interrogator might say, "One thing really puzzles me. Since you are not a blood-thirsty type why did you shoot at the old man? You already had his money and all you had to do was walk away. He was so old he couldn't have even tried to chase you, so why did you bother to shoot?" The respondent, might burst forth with "He wasn't too damned old to pull the trigger on that sawed-off shotgun he grabbed from under the counter!"

Sixth is a question which may be used with no ill effect even if it fails to obtain relevant information. This is the *hypothetical case* question. In this type of question the interrogator makes no reference to the particular crime under investigation but refers to a "hypothetical" crime of the same type. For example, in the case where the robber had shot the store owner who pulled a sawed-off shotgun from under the counter as the robber was leaving, the interrogator could say, "I just want to get your opinion on a hypothetical case. Suppose a robber walked into a liquor store, stuck up the cashier who was an old man, got the loot and was walking out the door and then turned around and shot the old man. Now this old guy was sick and scared to death and wasn't about to chase the robber, and he couldn't call the police because the robber had cut the line on the only phone. What I want is your opinion on why the robber would bother to shoot the old guy who could never identify him because he was wearing a stocking mask? That kind of robber would have to be a nut case, right?" With luck the suspect would say, "Well not necessarily a nut. The old man might have been too old to chase but not too old to pull the trigger on a gun."

The above six types of special questions, singly or in combination, cannot be guaranteed to crack the guilty suspect, but their cumulative effect may persuade the suspect that he or she cannot get away with deceiving the interrogator, or may panic the suspect into a tangle of mutually contradicting statements that demonstrate guilt.

To further reinforce the effectiveness of such questions there is a battery of *statements* aimed mainly at reducing the ego-threat and playing down the psychological costs of telling the truth.

Some special statements. In general, these special statements are all aimed at reducing the ego threat of admitting a crime by either minimizing the moral seriousness of the crime or by supplying *rationalizations* the suspect may use to show that any human being might have done the same thing under the circumstances. Below are eight types of statements that experienced interrogators have found useful under some circumstances.

First, the interrogator might make statements aimed at *minimizing the moral seriousness* of the crime under investigation. For example, in questioning a suspect arrested for soliciting sexual favors from an undercover policewoman posing as a prostitute, the interrogator could say, "Well, you are the unlucky one that got busted by a policewoman. It's a strange world. Until recently there was no law saying you could arrest a man for wanting a little fun he was willing to pay for. Now, California is getting tough on men while right across the border in Nevada prostitution is all perfectly legal and the state government takes its cut."

Similarly, statements could be made by an interrogator to make child abuse sound like justified "disciplining" of the child or to make theft from a rich person sound more like a plan to "share the wealth" or to make stealing a car sound like simply yielding to the momentary impulse to "take a joy ride" in someone else's car. Even murder can be softened by pointing out that "Everyone gets mad enough at somebody to hurt them, but unfortunately you happened to have a baseball bat in your hand when he made you mad!"

Second is the type of statement aimed at *blaming someone other than the suspect* for the criminal act. In the case of a rape the rapist is very susceptible to the suggestion that the woman was to blame for acting in a provocative manner. In the case of a robbery the interrogator might say, "So they went off and left their baggage at the curb for over an hour unattended while you were eating breakfast across the street. I guess you could say they were asking for it!" Within the context of the facts of even murder cases it is not difficult for the interrogator to point out some behavior on the part of the victim that might have provoked violence.

Third, the interrogator might make comments to the effect that either the victim or the accuser is exaggerating the nature of the offense. The assault victim who claims to have been "viciously beaten" can be reduced to an exaggerator by the interrogator who says, "So you decided to slap him around a little to teach him a lesson!" In the case of a hit-and-run accident the interrogator might say to the suspect, "I realize that the witness who said your car was speeding is being overly dramatic because the skid marks show that you were doing only thirty miles per hour! A lot of people go that fast on that block even though technically it is a twenty-mile zone but unmarked."

Fourth, some interrogators express the idea that under the same conditions they would have done the same thing. For example, "If some guy rear-ended me when I stopped at a stoplight, gave me whiplash and then tried to blame me for stopping so quick, I'm afraid I would have belted him a good one!" Short of such a bold statement the interrogator can simply say that he or she understands the pressures of the situation that would make it very difficult not to do what the accused did.

Fifth, the interrogator might supply some highly laudable reasons for withholding information in the interview. For example, "I can understand why you don't want to talk. You figure that you can protect your friend. But in this case that's not the best policy when we already have enough evidence on him to prosecute. You are being very loyal, but you'd better ask yourself how we found all the details we already have and whether you want to take the rap for all three counts or just for the part you did." In any case the point is to show that the interrogator knows the suspect is withholding information and understands some apparently laudable reason, but that the good reason no longer holds under the circumstances as they have developed.

Sixth is a statement of *agreement* with a *rationalization*. The statements to this point have allowed the interrogator to supply the rationalization to the suspect, but in many cases the suspect supplies rationalizations and the interrogator makes a comment that directly or indirectly agrees with the suspect's rationalization. While it is often fruitful for the interrogator to point out that the suspect's report of his or her *actions* are fictitious, there is little to be gained by disagreeing with a respondent's *excuses* given for a real act regardless of how distorted the rationalization may be. It is usually more fruitful to accept the motivation, thereby encouraging the suspect to get on with more detail of what he or she *did* and how he or she did it.

Seventh are statements by the interrogator that flatter or appeal to the suspect's honor. It is a mistake to think of all criminals as being without moral standards of any kind or without pride. If the interrogator understands the kinds of distinctions of values and status found in the respondent's real world, these can be used to advantage in the interrogation. For example, a prostitute may respond positively to the statement, "Bonnie, I know you are not the kind of working girl that rolls drunks." To a thief the statement might be, "I know from your past record that you operate with your brains and skill not with any of this strong-arm stuff where you leave shooting the place up." Another approach is to accuse the suspect of performing a lower-status form of crime to get the suspect to admit a higher-status crime in defense of his or her honor. For example, "I know the reason why you were selling hash out in the alley. You were going to have your hidden partner mug him for the hash after you left with his money." Sometimes, the suspect may slip out with something like, "Bull, I had no partner in that alley!"

Finally is the *correction* statement which points out to the respondent that a particular response was not true and gives the evidence of the attempted deception. The correction statement later in the interview may take a more general form after attempts at deception have been pointed out more than once. For example, "As you can see, you are wasting your time trying to avoid the truth. I have many other sources of information to use to check out your story. We are going to get the whole picture sooner or later, so why don't you save yourself a lot of time and just tell me nothing but the truth?" It is important that this be said without rancor.

In summary, the special techniques of interrogation consist of using *nonthreatening vocabulary* in formulating *special questions* aimed mainly at checking and demonstrating attempts at deception, and *special statements* aimed mainly at reducing ego threat either by minimizing the moral seriousness of the crime or by supplying rationalizations that tend to provide acceptable motivations for the crime.

It may be difficult for the inexperienced interrogator to imagine that the suspect could not simply refrain from giving incriminating evidence; but experienced interrogators have repeatedly demonstrated by their performance that the proper use of a combination of lie-detecting questions and sympathetic statements couched in nonthreatening vocabulary can frequently elicit enough facts to establish the guilt or innocence of the suspect.

SOME SPECIAL TACTICS

The reader will recall that we use the term *tactics* to refer not to the form or content of the questions or statements but to the *chronological order* of topics and questions in the interview. To some extent tactics can be planned in advance and to some extent the interrogator must follow the lead of the respondent. Not all of the suggestions made here are applicable to all interrogations, but all have a place in some situations.

It is usually helpful to open the interview proper with some small talk to help the respondent realize that the interrogator is also a human being and more than a cog in the legal bureaucracy. This is particularly needed after the formal legalities of reading the suspect's rights and getting the suspect's permission to be interviewed and before the interrogator actually begins probing for specific information. The small talk also reinforces the impression that the interrogator has all the time in the world and will not have to give up after a few minutes of successful resistance by the respondent. Also, talking about harmless topics gets the respondent in the habit of responding to the interrogator.

In circumstances where the respondent has not yet been labeled as a suspect, the questions at the beginning should be the type that could be asked of any citizen as a witness, as a hearer of rumors, as an actual or potential victim, or as a possible acquaintance of the guilty person. Then if the responses indicate innocence the respondent is thanked and the interview terminated. However, if the responses indicate possible or probable guilt then the special questions and statements can be applied more fully.

After it has become clear that the respondent is a possible suspect, it is extremely important that the line of questioning begin with the time period preceding the crime before moving on to the crime period itself. This has several purposes. It allows the interrogator to note any change in the amount of detail given or in the spontaneity of the response when shifting from the precrime period to the alibi period. Even in cases where the suspect has prepared a simple alibi in advance such as "I was at the movies" and had the foresight to see the movie at some other time in order to be able to report details of the content of the movie, such a suspect may have very little to say about how he or she got to the movie, the address of the theater, the route taken, what was seen along the way, whether the person in the box office was a man or a woman, and so forth. If the respondent proceeds very cautiously about the alibi period compared to the account of his or her movements during the preceding evening, the interrogator may have reason to feel that this is significant. Also, if the suspect can report this kind of detail regarding another movie attended earlier but "didn't notice" these things during the alibi evening this may be significant.

It is during the discussion of the alibi period that some of the special types of questions are most effective. The suspect may attempt to explain away fictitious "facts," or may lie about already known facts. As much as possible the questions about the alibi period should be aimed at getting objective information which can be subsequently checked.

Once the suspect has given some detail on the alibi period, the interrogator or an assistant who has been covertly monitoring the interrogation may have a list of points to verify by visiting the alibi scene and at the same time obtaining additional facts to be checked against the suspect's story in a subsequent interrogation. In some cases critical points in the alibi can be checked by telephone.

In cases where the suspect is clearly caught in a lie the experienced interrogator learns not to react in ways common to the novice. The interrogator's response is generally nonjudgmental. For example, the interrogator should not appear to be surprised or shocked. Also, the interrogator should not yield to the temptation to gloat over the demonstrated lie or to show disdain or vindictiveness. Instead, the impression is given that the interrogator knew all along that the respondent was lying. The interrogator may even go further by stating that he or she understands why it would be natural to be tempted to withhold the truth under the circumstances. In any case the interrogator should never neglect to point out in a matter-of-fact way the futility of not telling the truth after some fabrication has been demonstrated. Furthermore, the interrogator's words and manner should show that it is never too late to give the straight truth and that there is plenty of time to work on getting the whole story.

The *restitution* tactic can be useful when investigating crimes of a certain size where the suspect has given considerable verifiable evidence of guilt but has not yet admitted it. The interrogator can test the suspect's guilt and perhaps get a clean confession by suggesting that the police have many more important cases to work on but are pressing this one because members of the robbery victim's family are angry and hostile due to the injuries to the victim which they felt were totally unnecessary, and "even if you did not do this one would you be willing to settle out of court by offering to pay the $625 hospital bill if they would drop the charges?" If the suspect agrees to this it should not be considered evidence of guilt. The clincher follows. If the suspect agrees to the $625 then the interrogator can say, "and they want $25 for the crystal decanter which broke when you threw it at the daughter." If the suspect says: "To hell with that, I never threw any crystal decanter. The only thing I could get my hands on was the fireplace wood. They'd probably like me to buy them some new lawn furniture too. Tell them doctor bills is enough!" then the suspect is trapped. To further clinch the argument the interrogator could ask "Why do you balk at paying a measly $25 more if you're willing to pay $625 . . . then you could have the whole matter forgotten." When the suspect explains that fair is fair and refuses to pay for something he or she didn't do the interrogator says, "Then the point is that even though you did the robbery and hurt the girl no one can make a sucker out of you?" The affirmative answer to this is enough to open a more detailed and direct discussion of exactly how the suspect did it in order to lead to corroborating physical evidence to clinch the case.

Only the experienced and sensitive interrogator knows when such a tactic might work to get a confession. It seems to work best when the suspect has a previous record and intends to continue in crime and feels that the amount of restitution suggested is a reasonable price for staying out of jail and in business. Also, the interrogator has to be convincing in the explanation of the attitude of the police and of the people pressing charges.

Finally, the interrogation may reach a point where it would be a helpful tactic to test the suspect's guilt by offering the suspect the opportunity to take a polygraph examination (lie-detector test) "which is not required and can't be done without your permission but will give you a chance to prove that you are telling the truth." If the suspect asserts his or her right to refuse to take the examination, this should not in itself be considered evidence of guilt. If the suspect accepts the challenge, the test may establish his or her innocence or provide leads to corroborating evidence of guilt.

A POLICE INTERROGATION SITUATION

Both of the sample interviews that follow take place in the police department of a large city. Two members of the force specialize in interrogating witnesses, victims, and suspects. One of the interviewers has more experience and training than the other, but the situation in the two interviews is very similar. In both cases the person being interrogated is suspected of having robbed a store, and in each case someone got shot.

In both cases interrogation of the suspect is essential even if no confession is forthcoming. If the suspects are totally innocent, this may be quickly discovered leaving the staff free to search elsewhere. If they are caught in lies, they may be pressured to give some facts in order not to appear uncooperative, and these facts may give clues to physical evidence. For example, there may be no assurance that, without information from the suspect the police could find the gun in order to match it with the bullet that hit the victim. However, if in the interrogations clues leak out that lead to finding the gun then an essential piece of the incriminating evidence would be in hand.

Every possible strategy, technique, and tactic should be used that would encourage the guilty to furnish incriminating evidence, but any threats, or inducements that might pressure an innocent person to confess guilt should be avoided.

INTERROGATION A

The Crime Situation

The Kroger Supermarket, open twenty-four hours a day, was robbed at 2:00 A.M. Sunday. Only one checkout counter was operating, and no manager was in the office cubicle. The only immediately visible person was the woman at the cash register. There were also some stockhandlers replenishing the shelves and two customers out of sight down one of the aisles.

Two men entered the store, walked up to the woman at the cash register and said, "This is a stickup. Put all the money in your register in this paper bag. Do it quick and quiet and no one will get hurt." When they ordered her to get money out of the other registers, she said that the money had already been taken to the bank at midnight by the manager. They still ordered her to open up the other registers and show them. As this was going on, another customer entered, saw what was happening, quietly left to call the police on his citizens band transceiver, and then returned just as the two robbers were leaving. He tried to block the door as he shouted, "I called the police and they'll be here before you can get out of the parking lot!" One robber tried to hit the man on the head with the butt of his pistol and the other robber shot the man, and they both ran to their car in the parking lot and sped off.

The police arrived and obtained a description of the men from the checkout clerk and from the shooting victim before the paramedics arrived. They also found two witnesses who arrived in the parking lot just in time to see two men run from the store, jump into their car, and leave. One woman got the license number but wasn't sure of the last two digits. The other witness could give the make and model of the car and say which direction the robbers went.

Even though the witness was not sure of the last two digits of the license it was possible to identify the car with a high probability of accuracy by an instant computer search which combined the known digits with the make and model of the car. By 3:15 A.M. the police arrived at the address of the assumed owner of the getaway car who lived about twelve miles from the supermarket. In an apartment they found two men who had not yet gone to bed. Also, the suspect's car was parked out front, and its engine was still warm. The two men were taken to the police station, booked, and put in a cell together with the plan to question them the next day.

Before the Interrogation

The police department was notified by the hospital at 6:00 A.M. that the customer shot in the holdup had died. This escalated the case from simple robbery to robbery plus homicide. The two suspects were scheduled to be interrogated first. The arresting officer, Keller, decided first to interrogate Russel Mullins in whose name the alleged getaway car was registered. He was hoping to get Mullins' alibi and then check it out carefully before releasing him from jail. Mullins was brought from his cell into the adjoining police station. Before he left his cell, the escorting officer put handcuffs on him since he was now suspected of murder. Mullins was brought to the office of one of the detectives who would not be in that morning. The uniformed officer sat at the desk while interrogating Mullins.

The Interrogation

Officer Keller came into the room immediately after Mullins had been escorted into the office by Sergeant Daniel Weans.

I-1: Thanks, Dan! I'll buzz you when it is time to take him back to his cell. (Then motioning to the prisoner) You sit over there and I'll sit here at the desk where I can take notes. I know you were read your rights when you were picked up, so I won't do that again now. (Keller takes off his jacket but keeps his pistol and nightstick.) Now I guess you know you are in a lot of trouble!

R-1: Meaning what?

I-2: Meaning that the customer who was shot in the holdup died at 6:00 A.M. in Good Samaritan Hospital. That means the charges are now robbery plus murder.

R-2: That's too bad the guy died, but that has nothing to do with me. I didn't shoot him!

I-3: Now I suppose you are going to tell me that it was your partner who did it?

R-3: No! I'm not going to say that. We had nothing to do with the robbery.

I-4: How long had you been home when we came to your house this morning?

R-4: About two hours . . . at least.

I-5: Are you sure it couldn't have been just an hour?

R-5: No! I'm sure it was at least two hours. As I said we had nothing to do with the. . . .

I-6: (Interrupting) Don't bother to tell me you never saw Kroger's Supermarket before.

R-6: Of course not. I wouldn't say that because I have been there before, but. . . .

I-7: (Interrupting) You were not only there before but you were there last night. Don't try to deny that because a witness got your license number when you left in a hurry.

R-7: Yes. That's right. We were there and we did leave in a hurry! We had seen two men waving guns come running from Kroger's. We had pulled up in front of the K mart and when we saw them run around the corner we got in the car and followed them. They roared out like a bat out of hell, so we took off after them hoping to get the license number. They took a quick turn into a side street and we lost them. That was the end of the chase. But we cruised around a while but didn't see the car again.

I-8: So that's your alibi. That's a good story but it won't hold water.

R-8: It's got to, because it's the truth!

I-9: If that's the truth . . . why didn't you mention it this morning at 3:00 A.M. when we picked you up! No, you might as well confess . . . your alibi won't hold up. When we talk to your buddy, he won't agree on the same details and you will be in the soup. So why don't you just save my time, your time, and the taxpayers' money and confess? (At this point Keller comes out from behind the desk and begins to pace back and forth looking thoughtfully at the floor.)

I-10: Do you own a gun?

R-10: No.

I-11: Did you have a gun with you last night?

R-11: No.

I-12: Does your buddy own a gun?

R-12: Not that I know of.

I-13: Did he have a gun with him last night?

R-13: Not that I know of . . . but you can ask him!

I-14: Are you employed?

R-14: Yes.

I-15: Where?

R-15: At the J. B. Autobody Shop.

I-16: How long have you been there?

R-16: For about six months.

I-17: How much do you make?

R-17: About $900 a month take-home.

I–18: Have you ever made more than that on previous jobs?

R–18: A little more as an auto mechanic.

I–19: Why did you change jobs?

R–19: That was in Lexington, and my wife got a good job in Dayton, so I thought I would take my chances on getting a job here.

I–20: How long ago was that?

R–20: About a year.

I–21: Where did you work just before J. B.'s?

R–21: I was on unemployment insurance for about six months.

I–22: How much does your wife make?

R–22: I don't know.

I–23: You don't know! That sounds a bit far out.

R–23: We're not living together anymore.

I–24: Are you paying child support or alimony?

R–24: No, we didn't have any children and she has a better job than I do.

I–25: (At this point he stops pacing about the room and returns to his desk.) Do you have any debts of any kind?

R–25: No.

I–26: Do you go in for gambling?

R–26: I went to Las Vegas once and played the one-arm bandits.

I–27: Let's go back to your alibi. You said you saw two men come running out of Kroger's waving guns. Can you describe these two men for me?

R–27: Well, they were both about the same height . . . about five-nine or ten . . . and they were both the same build . . . sort of slim. I'd say they might weigh about 150. . . .

I–28: How old, about?

R–28: Both in their twenties, I'd say.

I–29: Hair color?

R–29: It wasn't too light, so all I can say is that they were not blond.

I–30: Were they white or black?

R–30: Definitely white.

I-31:   Do you realize that you are describing yourself?

R-31:   But there was a big difference. Both of them had beards. I can't say whether or not they also had a moustache. I was too far away.

I-32:   You said you followed their car and they turned down a side street . . . what was the name of that side street?

R-32:   I haven't the foggiest notion.

I-33:   What kind of car did they have?

R-33:   It was a Chevy Citation, about 1981.

I-34:   That sounds like your car.

R-34:   But it was a light tan color. . . mine is a light gray-silver.

I-35:   What was the license number?

R-35:   We weren't close enough to even see the color of the license plates. I wouldn't even swear that they were Ohio plates.

I-36:   You said you cruised about for some time to see if you could see anything suspicious. Where did you go after you left that first side street?

R-36:   It was all unfamiliar territory to me in this residential district and I didn't know where we were and I couldn't tell where we turned right or left. We were just taking a shot in the dark.

I-37:   Can you remember where you were when you decided to give up the chase?

R-37:   Well, we had come out of the residential district onto State Route 44.

I-38:   Where was that on Route 44?

R-38:   That was at Dayton-Yellow Springs Road.

I-39:   What time was that?

R-39:   It was about ten minutes till three.

I-40:   Are you sure about that or are you just guessing?

R-40:   I'm sure. I have a digital clock in the car with lighted numbers, and it was Joe who looked at it and said "Its getting late . . . let's give up this wild goose chase," and I looked at the clock and saw that it was 2:53 A.M.

I-41:   Then what did you do?

R-41:   Went home.

I–42:   Did you speed or go at a normal pace?

R–42:   Just a normal pace, but there was no traffic at that time of the morning to hold you back.

I–43:   Well, you know and I know that you are lying to me. Because you told me at the beginning that you knew you had been home about two hours when we arrived at your apartment this morning at 3:15. It would take at least thirty minutes for you to drive from where you gave up the chase to your apartment. So you couldn't have gotten home by 3:15 not to mention 1:15 so that you would *not* have been there two hours. So all this stuff about your following the other car is a fairy tale. What kind of a boob do you take me for!

R–43:   Well, I can't remember all these details with you firing questions at me. Maybe it was 1:53 instead of 2:53. And maybe we had been at home only forty-five minutes when you came. I don't go around with a stopwatch timing everything I do all my life!

I–44:   Maybe you were drinking last night! Maybe you are confused on the time . . . and on the whole story! Could you possibly have been so drunk or high on something that you thought you could get away with a robbery and a murder and cover it up with this flimsy alibi you just gave me? That would be the height of stupidity!

R–44:   No, I wasn't drinking last night. Not even one beer.

I–45:   Have you ever been booked on suspicion for anything before?

R–45:   No.

I–46:   Ever get a traffic ticket?

R–46:   Yes.

I–47:   What for?

R–47:   A parking ticket.

I–48:   What else?

R–48:   I ran a stop light once.

I–49:   What else?

R–49:   That's all.

I–50:   (Gets up from desk and begins pacing around the room.) Did you know that your license plate sticker is out of date? You have been driving around illegally. We need to hold you 'til we are sure you are not driving a stolen car.

R-50: That's silly. . . . you claimed you tracked me to my house by my license number and now you claim that I don't own the car.

I-51: I didn't say anything about how we tracked you to your apartment.

R-51: Anyway, I can see that you are out to pin something on me. So now I demand to see a lawyer and I've nothing more to say to you.

I-52: Okay, I'll have Sgt. Weans take you to a phone. (He buzzes for the sergeant) Dan, he wants to call a lawyer.

CRITICAL ANALYSIS QUESTIONS

1. List the *strategy* errors that were made. Keep in mind that strategy is defined as all of those decisions made by the interviewer before the actual questioning begins. This includes preparation for the interview, deciding who is to be interviewed where and when, the physical arrangement and facilities in the interviewing room, and how the interviewer defines the interview for the respondent. In looking for strategy errors look for both the errors of commission and errors of omission keeping in mind that the detection of omissions is the clearer test of your ability to apply knowledge and insight. Make two lists.

    a. *Errors of commission:* In this list give the I–numbers in chronological order and a sentence with each explaining what is wrong with it. Errors occurring before the dialogue begins will have no I–numbers but explain what was done wrong.

    b. *Errors of omission:* In this list there are no I–numbers to give but just mention some of the most important things that the interviewer should have done but did not do. No more than one sentence for each omission. *Note:* If the narrative does not mention something being said or done, assume that it was not.

2. List the errors in *technique*. Remember that techniques are defined as the type of *vocabulary*, the special forms of *questions*, and the special forms of *statements* used by the interviewer. Again look for both commisions and omissions. Use the same two-list format as in question 1 above. When looking for omissions include only those techniques which could have been applied in this particular case and give an example of the exact words the interrogator should have used.

3. List the errors in *tactics*. Remember that tactics are defined as features of the chronological order of topics, statements, questions, or other actions by the interviewer which may be planned

in advance or generated in response to what the respondent does or says. Use the same two-list format as in the previous questions.

In some cases it is difficult to determine whether a particular behavior is best classified as a strategy, technique, or tactic. Do not be too concerned about this. The main point is to detect as many errors as possible!

If the instructor has assigned these questions to be answered, be sure to complete your answers before going on to read Interrogation B below.

INTERROGATION B

The Crime Situation

A small but prosperous liquor store, on the corner of Sixth and Main, called "The Jewel" was robbed just before closing time at 10:45 P.M. on a Monday night. The robber held a gun on the owner and ordered him to put all the money from the cash register in a paper bag. As he was doing so the policeman on the beat happened to walk by and see what was happening. He walked in and ordered the robber to put down the gun. Instead, the robber whirled around and shot the officer, grabbed the bag from the terrified owner, jumped over Officer Grimes who lay moaning on the floor, and ran out the door.

According to a witness, who was on the sidewalk near the store, a man with a brown paper bag and a gun came running from the store and jumped into the front seat of a car that was already moving slowly along the curb. The witness got the license number as the car sped away, and the police picked up the car owner and his friend at their apartment at midnight. Both were read their *Miranda* rights and were asked a few questions at the apartment. They claimed that they were together since 8:00 P.M. and that they had been driving around for over two hours and had stopped at a small restaurant called the Citadel for a beer and sandwich at 10:45 P.M. and then came home.

Both suspects were detained overnight in separate cells in jail, and both agreed to be interviewed in the morning without a lawyer present because they were "innocent and wouldn't need a lawyer."

Before the Interrogation

Early in the morning the officer who was shot was interviewed at the hospital by Detective Alvarez. By noon the officer died. Alvarez also talked to the storeowner again and with the witness who was on the sidewalk in an attempt to get as much detail as possible about the robbery and shooting *before* interviewing the suspects. He also talked to the only waitress who was on duty at the Citadel the night before. She said that both suspects came to the Citadel often, and they had been there the night before and left at about 10:00 P.M. He also found a witness who knew the two men when they worked together at the Federal Cash Register Company.

The Interrogation

Detective Alvarez arranged to interview one of the suspects in a special interrogation room at the police station. The room provided privacy and freedom from any distracting sounds or sights. It was equipped with a hidden tape recorder and a two-way mirror.

At 2:00 P.M. Detective Alvarez, dressed in a conservative suit, entered the interrogation room where the suspect and a uniformed officer were waiting for him.

I-1:   Thanks. Would you please take off the handcuffs? I'll carry on from here. (The officer leaves and Alvarez walks toward two chairs facing each other at one end of the room which is well lighted but has no windows.) Come, let's sit over here where we can talk. (The suspect comes over and before they are seated Alvarez says) I'm Detective Alvarez and your name is. . . ?

R-1:   James Johnson.

I-2:   Did you have lunch?

R-2:   Yea, you could call it that.

I-3:   Not like eating in a fancy restaurant is it?

R-3:   I'm not choosy about food, but the coffee at both breakfast and lunch was pretty bad!

I-4:   I know what you mean; I've tried it! I only drink it when I can't get any brought in. Do your friends call you James or Jim?

R-4:   They call me James; there are a million Jim Johnsons in the world.

I-5:   Is it okay that I call you James? (*R:* Sure!) Okay James. I have been assigned to clear up the robbery that occurred last night, but let me say at the beginning that you have the right to (*reads him the complete* Miranda *statement of constitutional rights*).

R-5:   Yea, they told me all that last night.

I-6:   Do you understand what that means or do you have some questions?

R-6:   It is clear enough.

I-7: Knowing your rights, will you voluntarily agree to talk to me without a lawyer present?

R-7: Sure, I don't mind talking to you and why should I want a lawyer; I'm not guilty of anything!

I-8: Okay, and if at any time you change your mind and want to stop talking and get a lawyer, you may do so. Okay?

R-8: Sure!

I-9: First, I would like to know a little more about you. How old are you?

R-9: Twenty-five.

I-10: Are you married?

R-10: No.

I-11: Have you ever been married?

R-11: Yes.

I-12: Tell me about it.

R-12: Well, I got married the day after I graduated from high school and Lola was still in high school so she dropped out at the end of the tenth grade. I was too young to know what the hell I was doing!

I-13: So you feel that it was a mistake, right? Was it you or Lola that was in such a hurry to get married?

R-13: Well, it wasn't according to my plan. But Lola was pregnant and felt she had to get married under the circumstances. I didn't claim that it wasn't my kid. So we got married. (Pause)

I-14: So you felt trapped, but you were too honest to try to get out of it by claiming that the kid was someone else's?

R-14: That's right! I was just sort of talked into it and was too dumb to say "get an abortion" or "go find some other sucker for a meal ticket."

I-15: How did things go in the marriage?

R-15: Just as bad as you could expect. (Pause)

I-16: In what way?

R-16: We argued a lot and I didn't like the kid a bit. I did like Lola but not enough to listen to her complain and accuse me all the time. (Pause)

I-17: Uh huh.

R-17:   Things just got worse until I couldn't stand it any longer, then I bolted. I figured that she could get on ADC and wouldn't starve. She could even get the kid in a day care center and get some work. (Pause)

I-18:   I see . . . and is that how it worked out?

R-18:   Yeah, except for one thing I didn't figure on. They tracked me down and got a court order for me to make child support payments. I had a pretty good job at the time so they nicked me for a bundle every month.

I-19:   Where were you working at the time?

R-19:   At the Federal Cash Register Company here, but they laid off about 7,000 people when they converted from mechanical to electronic cash registers and calculators.

I-20:   That was rough! And you were too young to have enough seniority to be among those kept on the job.

R-20:   Yeah, union rules; but they should have laid off some of those old duffers who got big wages and were too set in their ways to convert to the new technology.

I-21:   Right. How long ago were you laid off?

R-21:   That was two years ago. I had already been paying child support for two years when I lost the good job.

I-22:   Where do you work now?

R-22:   At a gas station, mainly pumping gas and part-time mechanic at a Sohio station. They tell me I could be station manager some day, but that is just "pie in the sky bye and bye."

I-23:   You're probably right, and how do the wages compare with Federal Cash Register?

R-23:   Good question. Even though I made 40 percent less than some of the older employees at FCR I was still making double the amount I now make at Sohio.

I-24:   That's a real come-down! Not easy to take.

R-24:   You got it!

I-25:   Now I would like you to account for your activities beginning at noon yesterday. Where did you eat lunch?

R-25:   At the same place I always eat lunch on Mondays . . . at Linda's Diner which is just a block away from Sohio.

I-26:   What did you do after that?

R–26: Went back to work at about 1:30 so that the manager could go home early.

I–27: And what time did you get off work at Sohio?

R–27: At seven as usual.

I–28: Did you make any phone calls anytime that day before seven P.M.?

R–28: No.

I–29: How about after 7:00 P.M. up to midnight when the police came to your house? Did you make any phone calls in that period of time? Give it careful thought and keep in mind that I have already talked to your friend Derrick.

R–29: I don't have to think it over! I just didn't make any calls yesterday.

I–30: Good! Where did you go when you left work?

R–30: I went to the apartment and made myself something to eat and at about 8:00 we went out for a ride and just cruised around the town looking at the sights and then we got hungry and stopped in at the Citadel for a beer and sandwich at about 10:45 P.M. After that we went home where we were when the police came at midnight.

I–31: You say you cruised around town from 8:00 to 10:45! Now start in and tell me exactly where you went. Take it slow and easy because that is a lot of time to account for . . . about sixty miles of cruising in fact . . . so start at the beginning and let's trace your route . . . I have plenty of time, there's no hurry! (Alvarez spends the next twenty minutes getting a detailed account of the route and then traces it on a map.)

I–32: I know it's hard to remember every detail of your trip when you were talking to your friend, but are you sure that you didn't happen to go through the downtown section sometime before you went home?

R–32: No, we stayed out of the downtown area.

I–33: Are you sure you never came close to Sixth and Main Streets?

R–33: That I'm sure of. If you were only half awake you would recognize Sixth and Main.

I–34: Did you drive the car anytime between 8:00 and 11:00?

R–34: No.

I–35: Did anyone besides your friend, Derrick, drive the car that night?

R–35:   No.

I–36:   Did you leave the car at anytime between 8:00 and 11:00?

R–36:   Sure, when we went to the Citadel.

I–37:   Any other time?

R–37:   No.

I–38:   Are you sure you were in the car all the time between 8:00 and the time you went to the Citadel at about 10:45?

R–38:   Positive.

I–39:   James, I can understand why you might be afraid to tell the truth. It is only human under the circumstances, but I now know for sure that you are not telling me the truth about last night. We have a solid witness who saw your car pass Sixth and Main around 9:00 P.M. Also, some of the things you say about the time you were at the Citadel don't check out.

R–39:   So, I forgot about that; but so what? That is not when the robbery happened.

I–40:   When *did* the robbery happen, James?

R–40:   How would I know?

I–41:   That's what I was wondering?

R–41:   Well, last night the police said it happened later?

I–42:   What time did they say?

R–42:   They didn't say exactly, but it was later!

I–43:   If they didn't say what time, how do you know it was later than 9:00? Don't bother to try to explain, just let me give you a friendly warning. Don't make things worse than they are. We have lots of information from other people to check out your story. Do you suppose that the route of your travels that you just gave agree with the route that Derrick is now describing to someone else?

R–43:   I can't be responsible for what Derrick might say. Maybe he had too many beers at the Citadel and is confused!

I–44:   And are you going to deny that you have a gun?

R–44:   Lots of people have guns. In America we have the right to protect ourselves.

I–45:   Sure, but sometimes we can get into trouble by shooting someone when we don't mean to in the excitement of the moment. What kind of gun is it?

R–45: A .25 calibre Berreta!

I–46: Where was it last night between 8:00 and 12:00 P.M.?

R–46: At home in a drawer in the bedroom.

I–47: Are you sure you didn't have it with you?

R–47: Yes, I'm sure.

I–48: But how do you know it was in the drawer at home?

R–48: I saw it there after dinner.

I–49: Did you ever see it after that?

R–49: Yes, when we came home after the Citadel.

I–50: Where is the gun now?

R–50: How would I know . . . I assume it's still in the drawer unless the police took it.

I–51: The police didn't take it from the drawer because it wasn't there when they searched the place this morning! It's good it was only a .25 calibre . . . you know with a .35 or .38 you can really kill someone. Last year somebody rolled a drunk in the alley and shot him three times in the head with a .22 and it didn't kill him. He walked into the police station under his own power.

R–51: Who said I wanted to kill anybody?

I–52: I'm sure you didn't intend to do that, but in the excitement of the moment when things don't go as planned, you can just shoot at anything that moves. Incidentally, I talked to the officer who got shot and he can identify your general build even though he said you had a stocking over your head. He is not a popular officer on the force . . . because he has been suspected of being on the take and shaking down businessmen and small criminals alike. One of the officers said, "Too bad it wasn't a .45!" In fact, that may be why he arrived at the store while it was being held up. There was no police radio call yet. He might have dropped in to shake down the store owner.

R–52: Yeah?

I–53: Yeah, there are always some bad ones in any large department! But let's get back to the point. When are you going to start telling me the truth? I have been checking you out and you have flunked the test on a number of points that I have already pointed out to you. But there is a lot more that we know that I haven't told you so you are just going to have to stick to the truth. You assume that you hid the gun successfully. You probably figured that you had killed the cop so didn't want the gun around, but sometimes we make a lucky guess and look in the right place! And how do you suppose the police knew where to come last night to your apartment? It wasn't done by just picking a random number out of the telephone book! Somebody saw more than you know! You are wasting your time and mine trying to make up a story while your partner is trying to do the same thing and the stories aren't going to jibe at all. You might as well tell the truth now and get it off your chest.

Don't think I can't appreciate the position you were in. You had lost your job at FCR and were making only half as much working for Sohio and then your ex-wife hounding you for child support money, and then you and your buddy had a few beers at the Citadel and began to feel very macho, so without thinking too clearly you thought you would try a little Robin Hood strategy. This kind of thing has been done before even by the local football hero or preacher's kid.

If your buddy was sober enough to drive in the traffic, he should have been sober enough to talk you out of the idea rather than egging you on and offering to drive the getaway car. I suppose you think of him as a friend but he is not doing a very good job of protecting you, not when he thinks the finger will be pointed at him as the guy with the gun!

R-53: So what do you want me to do? Confess just to make things easier for you?

I-54: I want you to tell the truth and get this thing cleared up. One thing you can do is to volunteer to take a lie detector test and it will quickly settle whether you were at that store last night and whether you shot at the officer and made a getaway in your friend's car. How about that . . . we could give you a polygraph test right now . . . okay?

R-54: Well . . . (pause, looks down at the floor) . . . so what if I told you the whole truth, what will you do for me? Suppose I did it and decided to come clean and save you a lot of legal troubles and me too, could you see that I got off with a light sentence, since I've never been booked before?

I-55: I can't make any promises except that your lack of a previous record will be taken into consideration by the judge. After all you are not the habitual criminal type but someone who made a mistake that you regret, right?

R-55: Yeah, like you said, I was working hard but was broke as long as I got nicked for child support; and when I get disgusted I sometimes have a few too many beers. And it sounded so easy when we talked it over, but then that cop walked in. If he was coming in for a shakedown . . . maybe it taught him a lesson. He may decide to quit the racket!

I-56: Now you're doing the right thing! Let me go back and get your answers at those points where you weren't telling the truth before. First, since you haven't had time to spend any of the money will you show us where it is so that we can give it back to the store owner? That would probably change the store owner's attitude in pressing charges.

R–56: You mean the police didn't find it? It's right in the apartment in the freezer compartment of the refrigerator!
(From this point the interrogator proceeds to obtain a detailed account of the robbery and the events leading up to it as well as information needed to obtain further physical evidence such as the location of the gun.)

CRITICAL ANALYSIS QUESTIONS

Here the task is to *compare* Interrogation B with Interrogation A which you may have already analyzed and may have also discussed in class or with another student. So in comparing Interrogation B with A use your complete knowledge of Interrogation A whether or not it was in your original Critical Analysis. Also, you may in the process of analyzing Interrogation B realize in retrospect that there were additional errors in A which you had not noticed at the time. In your comparison do not repeat any of your analysis of Interrogation A but simply list all of the *good* things in B that were not in A. In other words show all the ways in which Interrogation B is better.

Note: This time it is not necessary to separate commissions from omissions.

1. List all of the ways the *strategy* in Interview B is better than in Interview A.

2. List all of the ways the *techniques* in Interview B are better than in Interview A.

3. List all of the ways the *tactics* in Interview B are better than in Interview A.

4. In what other general ways was Interview B better than A?

Selected Readings

Inbau, Fred E., and John E. Reid. *Criminal Interrogations and Confessions*, 3rd ed. Baltimore, Md.: Williams and Wilkins, 1985.
Fred Inbau, law professor at Northwestern University and former Director of the Chicago Police Scientific Crime Detection Laboratory, with the help of John Reid, who was a staff member of the same laboratory, wrote this excellent distillation of most of the major strategies, techniques and tactics which can be used legally in attempting to establish the innocence or guilt of a suspect.

Kamisar, Yale. *Police Interrogation and Confessions: Essays in Law and Policy.* Ann Arbor, Mich.: University of Michigan Press, 1980.

Deals with the legal ramifications of police interrogations citing historic court decisions dealing with such questions as: What is a voluntary confession? What are some of the strengths and weaknesses of the *Miranda* decision as an interpretation of the Fifth Amendment to the Constitution? What is interrogation and how different from the third degree in the eyes of the law?

Schafer, William J. III. *Confessions and Statements.* Springfield, Ill.: Charles C Thomas, 1968.

This practical little ninety-one-page book dedicated to "those in blue" is written by a former Assistant United States Attorney and trial lawyer. It gives specific ways of avoiding the many common pitfalls which make a confession inadmissible in court or which reduce its credibility. It cites over 100 court cases that bear upon the admissibility and credibility problems.

Van Meter, C. H. *Principles of Police Interrogation.* Springfield, Ill.: Charles C Thomas, 1973.

This is a much shorter book than Inbau and Reid so describes many fewer strategies, techniques, and tactics. It is particularly useful in describing how to prepare for an interrogation and gives details on how to obtain a written confession that will stand up in court. Also, many of the points are illustrated by an interview dialogue that continues through several of the chapters.

Part VII

DEVELOPING SKILLS IN INTERVIEWING

Chapter Twenty-Six

Focal Skills in Interviewing

Earlier we said the planning of an interview is a *creative* art and its execution is a *performing* art. This chapter will concentrate on the skills needed for the performing art. In our fascination with the give and take of the drama and our admiration for an expert performer, we must not lose sight of the fact that underlying the apparent uniqueness of each interview encounter is a general cycle of repeated activity requiring a few basic skills which can be learned by thoughtful practice.

INTERVIEWING PERFORMANCE CYCLE

As shown in Figure 26-1, the performance cycle can begin with the interviewer asking a particular question or probe, which is communicated by both verbal and nonverbal cues to designate the information needed and to motivate the respondent. Since the respondent is not an automaton, he or she will first interpret the "true meaning" of the question and the intent of the interviewer, then determine whether he or she has any relevant information or not. If the respondent has none, he or she may either simply say so, or may try to meet the interviewer's expectations by saying something irrelevant or by fabricating apparently relevant information. The respondent who feels that he or she does have information relevant to the question may give it freely, withhold parts of it, or withhold it all by giving a smoke screen of irrelevant information or by inventing seemingly relevant information. The respondent's actions depend on the facilitators and inhibitors operating in the interview situation. Even in cases when the respondent feels he or she has relevant information and proceeds to give it freely, that information may be irrelevant because the respondent misinterpreted the question or simply wandered off the track. Thus the respondent, both verbally and nonverbally, may convey relevant, irrelevant or fabricated information to the interviewer whose task is alertly to evaluate each response separating the relevant from the irrelevant and the valid from the invalid. The

FIGURE 26-1

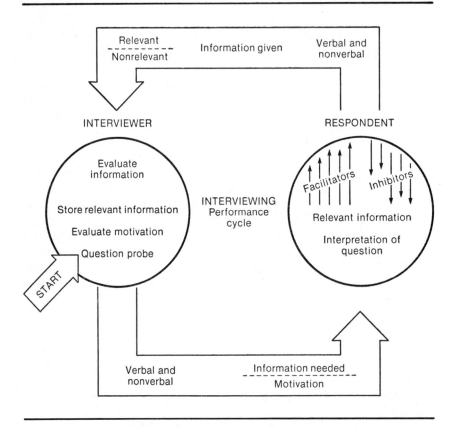

interviewer then stores (notes, records, etc.) the relevant and valid information. After estimating the respondent's ability and willingness to give relevant information, the interviewer then either formulates a probe to complete, clarify, or test the relevance and validity of the previous response or goes on to the next question.

THE FOCAL SKILLS

Assuming that the interviewer has asked a well-worded question, all of the activities which follow involve skills that can be subsumed under three main headings: (*a*) accurately receiving information, (*b*) critically evaluating the information received, and (*c*) regulating one's own behavior at the verbal and nonverbal level in selecting and delivering the next question or probe.

Accurately Receiving Information

The task of accurately receiving information can be broken down into several specific skills. It involves (a) accurately *hearing* what the respondent has said, (b) *observing* the respondent's nonsymbolic behavior, and (c) *remembering* information received. Let us examine each skill separately to see why it is important and to note some of the factors which interfere with its accurate performance.

Accurately hearing the respondent. It is important to hear accurately what the respondent has said even though every word is being recorded on tape. The interviewer must hear to be able to probe for elaboration or clarification. Also, if the interviewer shows that he or she has not accurately heard the respondent, it is likely to damage *rapport* or bias future questions and responses.

In discussing tape-recorded interviews with the interviewers themselves, the writer discovered several common conditions that interfere with an accurate perception of the respondent's words. Certain reasons were given repeatedly for situations in which the interviewer had overlooked a significant comment by the respondent that needed to be probed for further elaboration and clarification.

Often the interviewer was too absorbed in the process of *taking notes* to concentrate fully on the respondent's statements. This can be overcome by limiting the amount of writing to key phrases and not looking at the paper, by using a tape recorder to reduce the amount of note-taking needed, and simply by practicing.

Another distraction was a certain amount of *anxiety* in the interviewer, who worried over what and how to probe or over the interpersonal relations in the interview. Inexperienced interviewers would sometimes report that their minds "went blank" because of insecurity, anxiety, or tension.

A third frequently reported cause for inaccurate perception was the *loss of interest* either in the topic of the interview or in the respondent as a person. This source of inaccuracy was increasingly frequent as the interviewer had done more interviews on the same topic. The interviewer would begin with a natural curiosity which was soon satisfied and would neglect to probe relevant clues because he or she had not realized what the respondent was saying.

A fourth cause closely related to the boredom factor is simply *fatigue.* The result of fatigue has been quantitatively observed by the author while supervising the work of interviewers in the field. For example, in a field study where thirty interviewers worked for twelve days doing approximately 600 tape-recorded interviews one to two hours in length, it was discovered that the second interview of each day was always shorter than the first one by approximately five written pages. The first interview averaged almost thirty pages, and the second only twenty-five pages. The effect of the combination of fatigue and boredom could be seen in the fact that the length of the first interview of each day became shorter over the twelve day period.[1]

A fifth common cause of inaccurate perception of information lies in the interviewer's *expectations* of what the respondent is going to say and the respondent's interpretation of the meaning of the response in accord with these expectations. Instead of probing to obtain a more precise clarification, the interviewer merely assumes that the respondent means what the interviewer expected him or her to say.[2]

This difficulty arises when the interviewer has done several interviews on the same topic and begins to anticipate what all respondents or certain types of respondents are going to say. When the response is vague, the interviewer projects his or her expectations into the interpretation of the response. This difficulty often arises when the interviewer is a friend or acquaintance of the respondent or when the respondent is a stranger strongly stereotyped by the interviewer. In the first case, the interviewer assumes to know how his or her friend feels because "he feels the same way I do; that's why we are friends." In the second case, an expectation that the respondent will behave "true to type" is so strong that it blinds the interviewer to any responses that do not fit.

A sixth cause of failure to hear the respondent correctly can be distractions in the interview setting. The room temperature may be uncomfortable or the air stuffy. There may be noise or disturbing visual stimuli. Of course, the distraction is greater if it involves persons with some relationship with the interviewer or respondent. It requires diplomacy to remove a wandering visitor from the interview, particularly if that person ordinarily has access to the space being used, as in the case of the interrupting child in the home or the fellow worker in the office. All of these can distract the interviewer as well as the respondent from the central task and should be considered in the selection of a time and place for the interview.

Language barriers can also interfere with hearing the respondent. The barrier may be only a local accent, or the interviewer or the respondent may be using a second language that they understand fairly well, but which at times causes them to lose some of the subtleties of the

---

[1]Raymond L. Gorden, "An Interaction Analysis of the Depth-Interview" (Ph.D. dissertation, Department of Sociology, University of Chicago, 1954), p. 122.

[2]H. L. Smith and Herbert Hyman, "The Biasing Effects of Interviewer Expectations on Survey Results," *Public Opinion Quarterly* 14 (Fall 1950), pp. 491–506. This experiment shows that the interviewers often recorded the answer they expected rather than the answer actually given.

conversation. This problem can be dealt with at the strategy level in selecting bilingual interviewers or at the tactical level by asking the respondent to speak more slowly or to repeat. Of course, if the objectives of the interview require a spontaneous flow of associations from the respondent, the language barriers must be removed by linguistic matching of interviewer and respondent.

Accurately observing the respondent. It is important to observe the nonverbal accompaniment to the flow of verbal information both to interpret the meaning of the words and to assess the possible effect on inhibitors and facilitators of communication.

It has been demonstrated that trained observers can agree on the attitude of the respondent in an interview with a high level of reliability. Furthermore, this does not depend upon agreement between the observers on specific "operational" clues to each attitude. Oldfield shows that the observers could agree on the respondent's attitude even though they did not use the same clues.[3] Some would listen to the respondent's tone of voice, others would watch the respondent's hands, others would take special note of the respondent's posture, and so on.

Studies have shown how body motion is an indicator of a person's attitudes, and Birdwhistle has shown how observation of the eye and hand movements of the respondent can be used by the interviewer.[4]

Some of the common types of nonverbal behavior noted by interviewers are laughing or giggling nervously, using the "formal tone" as if speaking to an audience, looking about apprehensively as if someone might be listening, trailing off into a whisper or mumble, losing flexibility in pitch or pace, watching the tape recorder or the note-taking, halting abruptly in the middle of sentences, sighing, fidgeting, fingernail biting, doodling with a pencil, perspiring, grinding teeth, refusing to look at the interviewer, or playing with a handkerchief or other object.

All of the conditions which were previously mentioned as interfering with the interviewer's ability to accurately hear what the respondent is saying also interfere with the interviewer's observation of what the respondent is doing. There is an additional factor which interferes with observing the nonsymbolic behavior of the respondent which can be called *over-rapport*. In this case, the interviewer is so spontaneously responsive to the respondent's nonverbal behavior that he or she reacts to it without consciously observing it. The interviewer must retain a higher degree of detachment and objectivity than would be used when chatting with friends, otherwise the respondent will control the situation. The

---

[3]R. C. Oldfield, "The Display and Perception of Attitudes," *The Psychology of the Interview* (London: Methuen, 1947).

[4]R. Birdwhistle, "Body Motion Research and Interviewing," *Human Organization*, Spring 1952, p. 37.

problem for the interviewer is to make conscious the observation upon which his or her reaction depends.

Remembering what the respondent has said. Skill in remembering information received is particularly important in the nonscheduled interview for at least three reasons. It is necessary if the interviewer is to probe for clarification and elaboration where needed. It allows the interviewer to see inconsistencies and contradictions even though they occur at widely separated points. In studies involving repeated interviewing of the same person over a long period of time, it becomes increasingly important to recognize inconsistencies, contradictions and changes in point of view. It is important that the interviewer does not arouse resentment in the respondent by showing that he or she has forgotten information received.

Of course, the skillful use of probe notes will be a great aid in remembering what has been said. However, if the interviewer is to give the necessary attention to the respondent, the interviewer must often take very sketchy notes, giving cues to the interviewer's recall but not substituting for it. The more acute the interviewer's memory, the fewer notes the interviewer must take, the more skillfully he or she can use them, and the less the note-taking will interfere with other functions.

All of the same factors that interfere with the interviewer's ability to listen accurately to the respondent also interfere with the interviewer's ability to remember what the respondent has said. There are some additional factors which interviewers report. First, if the interviewer is unfamiliar with the topic of the interview and all its specific objectives, he or she has difficulty remembering parts of the responses that are relatively meaningless to him or her.

Another common complaint is that when two interviews are done in rapid succession, there is sometimes a tendency for the interviewer to confuse information given in the first interview with information given in the second. The same confusion also applies to questions asked. The best solution for this is skillful use of probe notes.

Another source of memory distortion not reported by interviewers but demonstrated experimentally by Fisher is the tendency for the interviewer to remember statements that agree with his or her own point of view and to forget those that disagree.[5] This principle applies to relatively inexperienced interviewers asking questions on a controversial issue.

Assuming that the interviewer has accurately received the information due to careful listening to the verbal message, thoughtful observation of its nonverbal accompaniment, clear memory of the past

[5]Herbert Fisher, "Interviewer Bias in the Recording Operation," *International Journal of Opinion and Attitude Research* 4 (1950), p. 393.

responses, and accurate recording of the key phrases, then the interviewer's next task is critically evaluating the information received.

Critically Evaluating the Information

The nonscheduled interviewer must be able to do an instantaneous evaluation of information received. He or she must be able to keep a running inventory of the relevance and adequacy of the information with respect to the objectives of the interviewer and with respect to the state of the interpersonal relations between interviewer and respondent. Without this constant vigilance there is little hope that the interviewer will be able to use his or her array of techniques and tactics successfully.

The interviewer's critical evaluation of the information depends upon two kinds of skills: (a) the ability to recognize information that is relevant or irrelevant, adequate or inadequate in terms of the objectives of the interview, and (b) the ability to evaluate empathically the presence of potential inhibitors and facilitators of communication.

The first skill, assuming that the conditions for accurate reception of information prevail, depends upon the interviewer's familiarity with the objectives of the interview. This familiarity must be intimate and precise; otherwise the interviewer may obtain large quantities of information applicable to the general topic of the interview but only vaguely related to its specific objectives.

The second skill, assuming that the conditions for accurate reception of information prevail, depends upon the interviewer's ability to empathize with the particular respondent. Many of the conditions for successful empathy are determined at the strategy level in selecting the particular combination of interviewer and respondent. Insofar as we are concerned with increasing the interviewer's skill in empathizing with the respondent, we must concentrate on creating conditions allowing the interviewer to utilize fully this empathic potential.

Appropriately Regulating the Interviewer's Behavior

After accurately receiving the information and critically evaluating it, the interviewer must then move from the diagnostic phase into the action phase. At this point the interviewer must regulate his or her own behavior in a manner appropriate to the objectives of the interview and the present state of interpersonal relations.

Before the interviewer can be successful in appropriately regulating personal behavior to fit the needs of the situation, he or she must have sufficient facility in using the full range of techniques and tactics in order to avoid feeling uneasy, stiff, or mechanical. If the interviewer does not feel natural, there is a strong possibility that he or she may sound insincere to the respondent.

In order to regulate their own behavior, interviewers must also learn to *observe themselves* much more objectively than they would in ordinary circumstances. Most interviewers find it more difficult to be constantly aware of their own nonverbal behavior than of their verbal techniques or tactics. An interviewer can be totally unaware of the fact that he or she sounds bored, unsympathetic, anxious, rushed, flippant, condescending, or unsure. The pacing, tone of voice, posture and other nonverbal cues can sometimes neutralize the positive effects of good verbal techniques and tactics. It is quite common for a neophyte interviewer who is anxious about the situation to report sincerely that all of the respondents seem to be uneasy and unspontaneous. This may be either because the interviewer unwittingly communicates anxiety to the respondent, or because the interviewer's feelings are so strong that he or she projects them into the observation and interpretation of the respondent's behavior.

Interviewers must have the *self-discipline* actually to *do* what the situation calls for without wandering from the course. The lack of this self-discipline shows very quickly when interviewers are fatigued. They will find themselves rationalizing that they need not probe any further; they may escape into a sociable chat on the pretext of building rapport; they may be distracted by the temptation to pursue therapeutic by-paths; or they may succumb to morbid curiosity or their desire to be a detective. Methods for increasing skill in the use of techniques and tactics, for improving self-observation and self-discipline are suggested in the following section.

A PROCEDURE FOR IMPROVING INTERVIEWING SKILLS

Improving one's performance skills depends upon more than simply putting in time interviewing. The effect of the practice depends upon the degree of self-consciousness with which it is done. This, in turn, depends as much upon what the interviewer does *before* and *after* the interview as during it. Therefore, this description of the learning procedure begins with preparation for the interview and ends with the analysis of the results. In a study by Parker twenty-six enrollees in a nine-month counseling and guidance institute constructed a list of the problems in learning to interview and indicated what they thought had been most helpful in overcoming these problems.[6] It was clear that actual practice interviewing and the analysis of this practice were reported as making the greatest contribution to the solution of the problems.

---

[6]Aileen Parker and Clinton Meeks, "Problems in Learning to Interview," *Counselor Education and Supervision* 7 (1967), pp. 54–59.

Experiments have also shown that although practice and analysis can quickly improve performance skills, the same skills deteriorate with disuse or with the lack of critical self-analysis. For example, a study by Wolleat showed that although interviewing performance was improved by one course in counseling interviewing, eight months later with no intervening practice all of the gains had been lost.[7] This suggests that one must keep in shape for interviewing in the same way a violinist must practice or chess player must keep playing. This does not mean that the person who had a skill and lost it will require the same amount of time to revitalize it as was necessary to develop the skill the first time.

Preparing for the Interview

Becoming familiar with the objectives. There is no possibility of success in a nonscheduled interview unless the interviewer is intimately familiar with the objectives of the study. Only if the objectives are thoroughly understood can the interviewer reduce them to specific questions to be asked, anticipate and plan for potential inhibitors and facilitators of communication, have criteria for critically evaluating information, and know what points need further probing to meet specifications.

This preparatory step of becoming familiar with the objectives contributes in several ways to skillful performance in the interview.

1. Interviewers can receive information more accurately because they can concentrate attention on making distinctions relevant to the objectives of the interview.

2. Familiarity with its complexities often increases the interviewers' interest in the problem. This increased interest contributes to a more skillful performance of all the tasks in the interview.

3. A thorough understanding of the interview objectives supplies the criteria for critical evaluation of the information and guides interviewers in probing.

4. This increased intellectual appreciation of the interview goals reduces the danger of *over-rapport* that interferes with objective observation of the respondent and oneself in the interview.

5. This understanding facilitates note-taking by allowing a faster and more accurate selection of relevant material.

---

[7]Patricia L. Wolleat, "An Investigation of Changes in Interviewing Effectiveness of Student Counselors Associated with Enrollment in a Combined Didactic-Experimental-Practical Core Course" (Ph.D dissertation, Department of Education, University of Minnesota, 1971).

Regardless of whether the objectives of the interview have been determined by the interviewer or have been assigned to the interviewer by someone else, the interviewer must become so sensitized to the specifications that the interview becomes "his problem." This is perhaps more difficult when the problem is assigned to the interviewer.

In studying and analyzing the objectives of the interview, there are several questions that the interviewer should ask himself. First, the interviewer should ask: What is the central purpose of the interview? The purpose can be viewed in terms of the central focus of the *information* and in terms of the actual *purpose* for which the information is to be used. If the purpose of the information is to test theory, then the interviewer must be intimately familiar with the theory being tested. If the purpose is to gather information as a basis for social action, the interviewer should know to what extent the alternative actions are predetermined and to what extent the purpose of the interview is to discover categories of possible action perceived by the respondents. If the alternatives are predetermined, then the interviewer should be familiar with what the alternatives are and their relationship to the specific objectives of the interview.

Second, the interviewer should ask: What categories and subcategories of information are needed to fulfill the central purpose of the interview? How are the categories defined? Do these definitions articulate with the central purpose of the interview? Can the categories be broken down into subcategories for increased clarity or to assist the respondent in more completely covering the topic? What specific questions are needed to obtain information relevant to each category? How are the categories and subcategories of information related? What level of abstractness or concreteness is required by the objectives?

Third, the interviewer should try to anticipate the potential range of relevant responses and even some of the apparently related but irrelevant responses. How abstract or concrete must the answer be to fulfill the purposes of the interview?

Interviewers often fail to appreciate the meaning of the need for *concrete examples.* To be truly concrete, an example of an object, event, or situation must be located in a *unique time and place,* and therefore involve a unique scene, objects, actors, and plots.

Anticipating potential inhibitors and facilitators. In attempting to anticipate potential inhibitors and facilitators of communication, the interviewer should keep in mind that the inhibitor or facilitator is *potentially* present, depending on the type of information the prospective respondent has to give. Whether or not the potentiality becomes actuality depends upon the nature of the interviewer-respondent relationship as seen by the respondent in the larger context of the interview situation.

Unfortunately, the interviewer does not know in advance the type of information the prospective respondent has to give; therefore in anticipating potential inhibitors the interviewer must consider the possible range of answers to the specific questions he or she intends to ask. If some of the possible answers to the question would tend to be inhibited by the respondent, then the question should be treated as a potential communication inhibitor, and appropriate strategy, techniques, and tactics should be used to minimize the inhibiting effect.

Each topic, subtopic, and question that is planned in advance of the first interview should be earmarked to show which main inhibitor or facilitator might be involved. Subsequent experiences might prove these anticipations incorrect in some instances. Nevertheless, the attempt to anticipate will be generally useful and contribute to a more skillful performance.

Planning the strategy of the approach. Now that the interviewer is clear on the precise objectives of the interview and has considered some of the potential inhibitors and facilitators of communication, he or she is ready to consider the means of obtaining the information. Usually, it is well to consider the strategy problems first. If we assume that the problem is within the interviewer's ability and role repertory, the next strategy decisions are selecting the appropriate role for the interviewer, choosing a respondent most willing and able to give the required information, setting an appropriate time and place for the interview and, finally, deciding how to structure the interview situation.

Structuring the interview situation includes introducing oneself to the respondent, explaining the sponsorship of the study, explaining the purpose of the interview, explaining how the respondent has been selected, providing anonymity, and planning the method of recording the interview. All of these facets of the situation are relevant only insofar as they relate to the respondent's ability or willingness to give relevant information. Usually, it is a good rule to say that if a problem can be anticipated and solved at the strategy level this should be done, rather than depending upon techniques and tactics. Usually enough problems will remain which can be solved only on the spot, in the interview situation.

Preparing an interview guide. The interview guide has two basic functions. It not only helps guide the interviewer through the interview but also furnishes a method of recording what has been covered. To provide a method of recording, the guide may include a list of specific topics, subtopics, specific questions or categories of answers that may be checked off after they have been covered adequately. Or, the guide might provide space under each topic or subtopic for probe notes to remind the interviewer of what should be clarified or elaborated to meet the specifications of that topic. In some cases when a tape recorder is not used, enough space is provided under each topic to take notes on all the relevant information received. Various combinations of these three formats can be used.

The interview guide, particularly before the first interview has been done, should be viewed as a flexible aid rather than a fixed outline that prevents the interviewer from using any technique or tactic that might prove to be appropriate on the spur of the moment. The degree to which specific techniques and tactics can be planned in advance depends upon the nature of the subject matter and the number of interviews that have gone into the reformulation of the interview guide.

In preparing the interview guide, the interviewer must translate the objectives of the interview into (*a*) subtopics, (*b*) questions which need to be answered that may or may not have to be asked directly, (*c*) possible probes to use, and (*d*) in some cases, categories of relevant answers that might be expected. Wording of questions should be planned carefully considering the vocabulary, context, scope, answer structure, and the possibility of using intentionally leading questions. The usual two criteria should be used in selecting among various possible techniques: (*a*) their relevance to the information objectives of the interview and (*b*) their probable effect upon minimizing potential inhibitors and maximizing potential facilitators of relevant information.

In addition to planning the verbal techniques that to some extent can be built into the interview guide, the interviewer should also do an introspective analysis of his or her own attitude toward the topic of the interview, toward the interviewing task, and toward the type of respondent to be interviewed. In this way the interviewer may be able to anticipate certain points at which special effort must be exerted to withhold expression of negative attitudes and to express positive attitudes.

Once the objectives of the interview have been reduced to specific subtopics and questions, tentative plans can be made for the sequence in which subtopics will be discussed; how they will be introduced; what transitions or pivot questions might be needed; where funnel, or inverted funnel, sequences might be needed to develop a topic; how much topic control to use in probing each topic; and how any symptoms of resistance in the respondent might be treated.

The preplanned strategy, techniques, and tactics suggested above may not be followed in every detail during the interview; nevertheless, careful preplanning will help the interviewer to improve his or her interviewing skill. In the first place, it makes the interviewer aware of the differences between what he or she expects and what actually happens in the interview and lays the foundation for the post-interview analysis where he attempts to account for these discrepancies. And second, since much of the preplanning is successful, it reduces the amount of confusion in the interview, allowing the interviewer to concentrate on the types of tactical problems which cannot be anticipated.

Of course, the process of becoming familiar with the objectives and anticipating potential inhibitors and facilitators is necessary before any of the preplanning can be done. Both are also necessary for skillful probing in the interview.

Doing the Interview for Self-Improvement

Pretesting the situation. Regardless of how much experience an interviewer might have, he or she should always pretest the specific interview situation associated with a series of interviews on a new topic. This is particularly vital for the person aiming to improve skills. By "pretesting the situation" we mean that the interviewer should become accustomed to the concrete details of the setting and the instruments to be used in the interview before doing the first interview. This would include such things as becoming familiar with the place where the interview is to be done, insofar as possible making the physical arrangements conducive to communication, becoming familiar with the use of the tape recorder in the specific setting, practicing taking probe notes and using the interview guide in the particular physical setting, and perhaps role-playing some practice introductions by which the situation is structured for the respondent.

Without these precautions it is improbable that even the best plans and sophisticated theory could be skillfully implemented because of some unanticipated, ridiculously obvious practical problem. The following are typical examples of such practical problems found by interviewers: There may be too much noise in the area, the room may be so small that it soon becomes stuffy, there may not be the right type of electrical outlet for the tape recorder, the interviewer may not know how to operate the particular tape-recording machine that is available, the machine may be out of order, there may be no available surface for writing probe notes. Most of these problems can be avoided by pretesting the situation and arriving in advance of the interview to check the setting and equipment. There is nothing more embarrassing for the interviewer than to find that neither he nor the respondent has a pencil or that some simple mechanical error in the use of the tape recorder has resulted in a blank tape. Familiarity with the interview setting eases the interviewer's mind and makes it easier for the interviewer to concentrate on the task of helping the respondent relax.

Using a tape recorder. In order to make the most of each interview for the purpose of improving basic skills, the interview should be electronically recorded. This is particularly important in learning non-scheduled interviewing because it frees the interviewer from the burden of trying to record all of the relevant details and allows the interviewer to devote more attention to the respondent and to regulating techniques and tactics. Since the interviewer is able to use tactics and techniques more self-consciously he or she is more likely to learn from the experience. In addition, the tape recording allows the interviewer to relive the experience by listening to it later when the interviewer is freer to observe his or her own and the respondent's behavior.

Using the interview guide. An interview guide is usually a necessity when the interview is even slightly complex, when the interviewer has not had experience with many interviews on the same topic, and particularly when the interviewer is attempting to improve his or her interviewing skills. Since the guide is a reminder of the specific interview objectives, it should alert the interviewer to any inadequacies of information *during* the interview in time to test various techniques and tactics for obtaining the information vis-a-vis the respondent.

Taking probe notes. The taking of probe notes in conjunction with the use of an interview guide helps the interviewer keep a running account of what has been covered. Probe notes also provide vital clues to what needs to be probed further and supplies some of the vocabulary to be used in probing. This, in turn, makes the interviewer more secure and less likely to panic, which frees his or her energies for tactical problems. This increased attention to the important problems during the interview maximizes the learning value of the experience. Taking probe notes during the interview also lays the basis for a more meaningful post-interview analysis.

Focusing on the basic tasks. Once all the preplanning is done, the situation has been pretested, and the objective procedures of using a tape recorder, taking probe notes, and using an interview guide are previewed, the problem during the interview is to *concentrate* on a few major tasks.

The interviewer should constantly be asking: What is the respondent saying? What portion of it is relevant? Is it adequate or does it need clarification or elaboration? What question or probe should be used next to meet the objectives of the interview? What are the verbal and nonverbal clues to the state of the interpersonal relations between the respondent and myself? How might these affect the informational objectives of the interview?

In becoming sensitized to the respondent's nonverbal behavior, it is often helpful for the interviewer to concentrate attention on *changes* in the nonverbal communication, whether these be changes in tempo, tone of voice, posture, hand movements, facial expression, eye movements, or forcefulness of speech. It is important to focus upon changes in the respondent's behavior rather than attempting a direct comparison of one respondent's manner with another's because of general personality and cultural differences between respondents. For example, we cannot always assume that a deliberate, measured pacing with frequent pauses indicates that the respondent is being cautious about the information being divulged. If the person's normal speech pattern is rapid and fluent and at some point becomes halting and monotonous, the interviewer should note this change and in the context of the total situation judge whether anything can or should be done about the tension which is indicated.

Analysis of the Interview for Self-Improvement

The interviewer can improve skills more rapidly in a series of interviews if he or she carefully analyzes each one *before* attempting another in the series. The interviewer must not be so disappointed with the results of the first attempt in an interview series that he or she is sure it can be improved without bothering to analyze the experience. It is tempting to assume that it was mainly the respondent's peculiarities which were to blame for the inadequacies in the information and believe that the next interview is destined to be better. Or, the interviewer may be extremely lucky in one interview and not realize how much of the relevant information was obtained *despite* rather than because of the methods used. If this is the case the interviewer may be shocked by the difficulties encountered in later interviews.

In order to make solid progress in interviewing skills the interviewer must resist any tendency to abandon impatiently a calm analysis of each interview in favor of rushing into feverish activity of "learning by doing."

The analysis of the results of each interview should be translated into improved plans for the next interview. In doing this it is important for the interviewer to avoid assuming that any technique or tactic which did not succeed in one interview should be abandoned in future interviews. It might simply be that the particular respondent did not actually have the information or that certain inhibitors of communication were operating because of the role relationship between interviewer and respondent. In either case, the specific techniques or tactic should not be blamed.

Let us now examine some of the specific steps in analyzing the results of an interview as a means to improving skills.

Analysis of strategy. In view of his or her experience in the first interview of a series, the interviewer is often aware of some improvements which can be made in selecting and approaching the respondent. The interviewer should make a checklist of all the strategy problems that might be involved and then indicate which ones were dealt with in the strategy plans, which of these were apparently adequate in actual practice, and which problems had not been anticipated. It is also probable that some of the strategy plans were not actually needed. Any suggested improvements in strategy can be incorporated in the plans for approaching the next respondent.

Analysis of nonverbal responses. Before becoming involved in the detailed analysis of the information obtained or the methods used to obtain the information, it is often helpful for the interviewer to listen to the tape-recorded interview to note the nonverbal responses. At this time the interviewer is freer to concentrate fully on the respondent since he does not have to take probe notes or plan the next question. Of course, the tape does not preserve the visual nonverbal responses but it is helpful in showing changes in tone of voice, pacing, pitch, hesitations, nervous giggling, self-interruptions, and interruptions by the respondent. As was previously suggested, it is best to concentrate upon *changes* in the quality of the nonverbal communication.

When such changes are noted, the interviewer can raise the question of whether any of the inhibitors or facilitators of communication which he or she had anticipated might underlie the fluctuations in the nonverbal communication. If any difficulty is diagnosed, the interviewer can plan to meet it better in future interviews on the same topic. The interviewer should try to recall whether all of the nonverbal messages had been noticed while the actual interview was being done. If some were not noted, perhaps the interviewer can discover why. If the respondent's nonverbal behavior shows symptoms of either inability or unwillingness to give information, then the interviewer should note what he or she either did or neglected to do about it.

Analysis of adequacy of information. By listening to the tape a second time the interviewer can analyze the information obtained. This should be done by using either the interview guide or a special coding system to categorize all of the information that is relevant to the objectives of the interview.[8]

This content analysis can be more meaningful if done by both the interviewer and another person. If two people independently analyze the results and then discuss any disagreements they have, both will increase their sensitivity to inadequate responses and the need for probing to obtain clear and complete information. Disagreements between the interviewer and the other coder about the relevance of a particular item of information are often due to the tendency of the interviewer to assume hopefully that the respondent meant more than he or she said.

---

[8]Lester Guest, "A New Training Method for Opinion Interviewers," *Public Opinion Quarterly* 18 (Fall 1954), pp. 287–99. The author shows that the interviewer's error was reduced more when coding (interview analysis) was included in the training program that when practice interviews were included.

Another possibility is that one of the coders or both do not understand the precise specifications of the information sought.

Any time there is a disagreement between coders as to the meaning, relevance, or completeness of the information, they should discuss what type of probe would have helped to clarify any ambiguity or to supply any incomplete information. It might also be necessary to discuss the criteria of relevance by clarifying the definitions of the categories of information. Either type of discussion will clarify the objectives and sensitize the interviewer to means of reaching these objectives.

Of course there will be many occasions when both coders agree that certain information which was accepted as relevant and adequate during the interview breaks down under cold analysis into a meaningless confusion. In this case, it becomes clear that the interviewer either neglected to pursue the objectives or was unsuccessful in the attempt. It has been found that in the early stages of learning nonscheduled interviewing, most interviewers do not obtain all the relevant information. Either they lack a precise understanding of the objectives of the interview or they fail to recognize the inadequacy of the information until they begin to analyze the results. A novice rarely tries to probe persistently for clarification and elaboration to discover whether the respondent is unable or unwilling to give the information.

Once the interviewer has become acutely aware of the adequacies and inadequacies of the information, he or she is in a better position to analyze the techniques and tactics he used.

Analysis of techniques and tactics. By listening to the tape-recording a third time, the interviewer can hear the techniques and tactics that were used. The interviewer should become aware of how much of the specific information was obtained by careful questioning, how much was obtained without any special effort, how much was missed because of failure to probe, and how much was missed in spite of attempts to probe.

The interviewer should critically examine every probe and question and decide whether there might have been a more appropriate one at that point. In doing this, the interviewer must consider the type of information sought and the potential inhibitors and facilitators to be dealt with. The interviewer should be sensitive to any failure to communicate the question clearly and the need to reword it, provide contexts, or change its scope. He or she might also discover misused leading questions or neglected opportunities for using leading questions advantageously.

In listening to the tape the interviewer should try to evaluate his or her own attitudes as demonstrated in the interview. Does the interviewer manifest positive attitudes toward the interviewing task? Does the interviewer show a nonjudgmental attitude toward the information received? Does the interviewer evince a vital interest in the information and indicate that he or she does not accept everything uncritically? Does the interviewer show positive attitudes toward the respondent as a person? Are there opportunities where the respondent could be praised for effort or performance? Does the interviewer give such praise? Does the interviewer sound afraid, unsure, or confused? All of these questions can be answered by listening carefully to both the verbal and nonverbal behavior of the interviewer.

There are some symptoms of confusion and tension which the interviewer should learn to detect in himself. Three of these symptoms found most frequently are (*a*) the tendency to reword questions for no defensible reason, (*b*) the tendency to use multiple questions, and (*c*) the tendency to mechanically use the echo probe. Let us examine some typical examples.

Rewording the question. The frequent recurrence of this form of verbal behavior often indicates that the interviewer is tense and fears that the respondent will not understand the question. Sometimes it indicates that the interviewer has a low opinion of the respondent's ability. Even though this is not true, there is the danger of the respondent's so interpreting the behavior. The general compulsion to reword questions must not be confused with the occasional self-correction or clarification. The following are typical examples of compulsive rewording.

I: When was the first time you ever owned or drove a car? When did you become an owner or learn to drive any type of automobile?

I: Have you had any disagreements with your parents in the last year? Have you had any squabbles, arguments, or verbal battles with them recently? Either one of them?

Regardless of the interviewer's reason for rewording the question, a failure to pause between each successive rewording tends to give the impression that the interviewer is impatient and wants to accelerate the pace of the interview.

Multiple questions. A related habit shared by many neophyte nonscheduled interviewers is the tendency to add one question to another before the respondent has an opportunity to answer the first. For example:

I: What is your general philosophy of raising children? Do you feel that modern psychology is of any value or not? Would you be more in agreement with psychoanalytic approaches or not?

This example is typical in that multiple questions are often in the form of a funnel sequence becoming increasingly specific without allowing the respondent to answer them in turn. This defeats the purpose of a funnel sequence and gives the respondent the impression that the interviewer is impatient or confused.

Sometimes such behavior is prompted by the fear that the respondent will not be able or willing to answer the broader question. Usually such a fear is groundless and is actually a projection of the interviewer's general insecurity in the situation.

Echo probes. The reader will recall that the echo probe is generally the least fruitful of the three types of reflective probes. It is usually effective only if the words which are echoed happen to be emotionally charged for the respondent. When this is not true, as in the example below, the echo probe is useless.

R: When I heard the first explosion, I thought it was the city blasting for the new water main. But then when I heard a bigger explosion next door I knew something had gone wrong. I think that was about 12:30 when I heard the second blast!

I: About 12:30?

Generally, such a probe merely elicits a "that's right" from the respondent. If the same type of echo probe is used too frequently, it may give the respondent the impression that the interviewer does not hear well or is not paying attention. For some interviewers the echo probe is unconsciously developed as a stopgap measure in cases where they do not know what else to do.

It is often worthwhile to pay special attention to the use of silence as it affects the general pace and mood of the interview. The interviewer should note the extent to which he or she adjusts to the respondent's pace or vice versa. The interviewer should check whether the pacing is monotonous and mechanical or flexible and meaningful in the context of the interview, and the interviewer should look for interruptions of the respondent, whether intentional or not.

In critically listening to these tactics, the interviewer should first be aware of any deviations from the tactical preplanning and ask whether the deviation was intentional and whether it was an improvement over the original plans. Was the original arrangement of topics and subtopics followed? Were there some questions which should have been introduced by lead-in questions, pivot questions, or transitional statements? If so, what should they have been? When was the funnel, or inverted funnel, sequence of questions used? When should it have been used?

The interviewer should listen carefully to his on-the-spot probing to detect tendencies to undercontrol or overcontrol. Awareness of one's natural tendency in probing can help the interviewer become more flexible and use a wider range of topic control when it is appropriate.

Although the basic skills in which we are interested are associated with the phases of the interviewer's activity *during* an interview, the general procedure for learning these skills emphasizes the learner's activity *before* and *after* the interview. The ultimate goals are to receive information from the respondent more accurately, evaluate this information more critically, and to exert more control over one's own behavior during the interview. However, these goals can be reached more rapidly by thoughtful preparation and by careful analysis after each interview before rushing on to the next.

SUMMARY

Despite the many purposes and settings of the interview, there are common basic interviewer tasks in the *interviewing performance cycle*. The tasks performed in this repeating cycle call for three general categories of skills: (*a*) accurately receiving information, which depends upon skills in listening, observing, and remembering, (*b*) critically evaluating

FIGURE 26-2   Steps in improving your interviewing skills

These steps assume that (a) you are to be the interviewer, (b) the respondent type has already been determined, and (c) the general purpose of the interview has already been set.

Planning your interview

1. Clarify the general purpose by breaking it down into objectives, topics, subtopics, and specific items of information needed.
2. Try to anticipate potential facilitators and inhibitors that might come into play when you discuss these kinds of interview topics with the type of respondent selected.
3. Plan the strategy of the approach to your respondent.
4. Design a tentative interview guide or schedule aimed at maximizing potential facilitators and minimizing potential inhibitors by using appropriate techniques and tactics.

Doing your initial interview

5. Pretest the interview situation.
6. Use a tape recorder.
7. Use an interview guide or schedule.
8. Take probe notes.

Analyzing your interview

9. Listen to the tape to evaluate the adequacy of the information. Is it relevant, valid, and complete in view of the interview objectives?
10. Critically analyze your strategy, techniques, and tactics as tools for communicating relevant questions and for motivating the respondent to be willing and able to give relevant, complete, and valid responses.

---

the information received, which depends on skill in retaining the objectives clearly in mind and constantly assessing the gap between information received and that needed to fulfill the objectives, and (*c*) appropriately regulating one's own verbal and nonverbal behavior to direct the respondent toward needed information and to motivate the respondent to give needed information.

The development of interviewing skills depends upon a three-phase process. First, we must *plan* the interview, at least tentatively. Second, we *do* the interview, being sensitive to any need to deviate from the plan. Third, we must *analyze* the results both in terms of the amount of relevant information obtained and the strategies, techniques, and tactics used by the interviewer. To complete the cycle the results of the analysis phase must be fed into the planning of the next interview. Without the planning and analysis phases, practice will only tend to harden certain habit patterns.

Before going on to actually plan, do, and analyze your own interview there are two more problems at the end of this chapter which will help bridge some of the remaining gaps in connecting concepts with behavior in the interview. Enjoy the vicarious experience of the armchair critic while you can, because after the next two problems you will be launched into a stage performance for self-teaching.

Figure 26–2 summarizes the steps for improving your interviewing skills that have been laid down in this chapter.

DISCUSSION QUESTIONS

1. What are the principal phases of the Interviewing Performance Cycle?

2. What are some of the main skills involved in accurately receiving information from the respondent?

3. What are some of the causes of the interviewer's failure to accurately receive information from the respondent?

4. Is it more difficult to critically evaluate the information given by the respondent in a scheduled or a nonscheduled interview? Why?

5. What are some of the forms of the interviewer's own nonverbal behavior he can become aware of by listening to his tape-recorded interviews?

6. In order to improve our interviewing skills, what must we do besides more interviewing?

7. What are the major things to be done in preparing to do an interview?

8. What are the main points the interviewer should focus on while doing the interview?

9. What are some of the main aspects of analyzing one's own interviews for learning skills?

LABORATORY PROBLEM 10

An Interview Critique (Car-Buyer Motivation Study)

PURPOSE

In the preceding laboratory problems on techniques and tactics, you were asked only to *identify* each type as it occurred in the interview script. You did not have to *listen* to an ongoing interview, or to *record* the relevant information, or to take *probe* notes. All of these opportunities are provided in this laboratory problem in addition to critically *evaluating* the interviewer's techniques and tactics.

The verbatim transcription of this motivation research interview has been carefully selected despite its vintage because it illustrates many of the problems of obtaining another person's point of view through interviewing. Since it is the initial exploratory interview in the study, there is much room for improvement.

PROCEDURE

Your instructor may want to assign all four phases of the problem or only two or three. If more than one phase is to be done, they must be done in the order indicated.

Phase 1: Taking probe notes on live interview

1. Read the purpose of the interview as described below.

2. Two people may role-play the interview from the script or the instructor may make a tape-recording of the role-played interview. You will listen carefully and note words and phrases that

are relevant even though in some cases the information is not complete or clear. The point here is to indicate those responses which should be probed further.

3. Discuss why certain points need to be probed in view of the objectives of the interview.

Phase 2: Coding relevant content

4. If you have not done Phase 1, carefully read the purpose of the interview as described below.

5. Study the *content analysis sheet* provided by the instructor to review the categories of relevant information.

6. Read the interview script, taking notes in the appropriate cells of the content analysis sheet by entering only words and phrases identified by the number of the response as shown in the script.

7. Compare your content analysis sheet with another one done independently. Discuss the differences in your entries.

Phase 3: Critique of interviewer's techniques and tactics

8. Read the script a second time *stopping* at each of the twenty interviewer's probes having the serial number in parentheses. Do *not* judge a probe by its immediate effect or anything which comes after, but view it in the context of what has gone on before it. Indicate on the *diagnosis-treatment sheet* supplied by the instructor:
    a. What is wrong, if anything, with the interviewer's probe or question, and
    b. What the interviewer should have said instead. If in a particular instance there is no room for improvement, say so.

Phase 4: Multiple-Choice problems

9. Answer the twenty multiple-choice problems while referring to the interview script in the textbook. The instructor will furnish the problems and a special answer sheet.

10. Submit your answers to the instructor who will summarize the group's responses as a basis for discussion.

Phase 5: Comparison and discussion

The instructor will supply you with materials for comparing your critique and/or multiple-choice Problem answers with the suggestions furnished by the author.

THE INTERVIEW

Purpose. This is the first interview in a series of exploratory interviews aimed at discovering why the sales of Brand X automobiles had dropped off 50 percent the previous year. The interviewer had expected to do five or six exploratory interviews to develop a more detailed interview schedule which would be used with a larger sample of car buyers; but he had sharpened the problem and planned the approach to some extent before this first interview. Generally, the interviewer wanted to know why the respondent bought his Brand X car which he currently owns and how these motivations compare with the reasons for buying previous cars and with his ideas about buying any future car. The relevant information would fall into three basic categories.

1. *Rational values:* such as efficiency, price, safety factors, gasoline economy, mechanical dependability, parking efficiency, etc. These could only be fulfilled by possible changes in the product.

2. *Nonrational values:* such as feeling of youth, power, social status, aesthetic appeal, feeling of escape, etc. These could be fulfilled by suggestive advertising copy.

3. *Social pressures:* such as pressures by friends, relatives, work associates and others with whom the buyer interacted. Only those influences which ran counter to the buyer's own private desires are to be considered pressure. This information could be used to suggest different channels of advertising or sales influence.

Strategy and tactics. The interviewer planned to first select current owners of Brand X cars and focus mainly on the person's values and pressures that influenced him *at the time* he purchased his Brand X. In addition he wanted to use a chronological approach to the respondent's car-buying history beginning from the first car he owned. This would put the Brand X buying situation in a more meaningful context by allowing some logical cross-checks upon the buyer's own statements of motivation. For example, if he said that he bought Brand X for a reason that is different from or conflicts with the reasons given for buying other cars in the past or his expected reasons for buying a particular brand in the future, then the interviewer would have to probe to check whether the respondent is confused, or fabricating, or whether his motivations are changing through time. If it could be established that motives typically change as a person goes through the life-cycle, this would be useful information.

As a guide in this exploratory set of interviews, the interviewer devised the "Guide for Probe-Notes or Content Analysis," reprinted here as Exhibit A–1, which could be used in two ways. During the interview it reminded the interviewer of the areas to be covered as represented by the column headings. He filled in the row headings according to which brands of cars the respondent had bought previously. After the interview was completed, since it was tape-recorded, the interviewer listened to it and did a content analysis of the relevant information on a

EXHIBIT A–1

Guide for Probe-Notes or Content Analysis (car buyer motivation study)			
Cars driven	Rational values	Nonrational values	Social pressure
Chevy Jeep Ambulance			
Kaiser (1947)			
Kaiser (1949)			
Brand X			
Future cars			
Changes in motivation			

second copy of the same form. This allowed a quick comparison of the information from one respondent with that given by another.

INTERVIEW SCRIPT: CAR-BUYER MOTIVATION RESEARCH

I–1: What I'd like to have you tell me is, can you remember when you first bought or drove a car? Tell me something about. . .

R–1: Well, when I first drove a car, it was a jeep in the army.

I–2: Oh, uh huh.

R–2: And (2)[9] I'll have to go back before that, I drove a 1934 Chevy that belonged to a high school friend of mine and he gave me a free driving lesson in that and then next I drove in the army I drove this jeep I got into the motor pool in the army and drove a jeep for a while that was my next driving experience (2) Then also while I was in service I was . . . it was necessary for me to drive other vehicles, including an ambulance across the Alps in a blizzard one time. So (3) then when I got out of the service I bought my own car. I bought a '47 Kaiser, the first Kaiser that came out. (2) (STOP 1)

I–3: That was your own car that you bought after you got out of the army?

R–3: That was my own first car. And (2) let's see my wife and I uh bought that and then we traded that in for a '49 (3) as soon as we could. (2)

I–4: '49 Kaiser?

R–4: '49 Kaiser and then we got divorced and she took the car with her and I was without a car for a couple of years (3) Is this what you want, you want the history of my automobile owning? (STOP 2)

I–5: Well, we might as well proceed along that line up to the present.

R–5: Right up to the present. Then I felt the need for an automobile, but I couldn't afford one until I moved from Park Forest into Chicago. Of course there was a great span of time in here. By this time I was divorced and living with my parents and my parents moved away. So I was out in Park Forest and I needed a car out there but I couldn't afford one so I moved into Chicago, sold the furniture and all that stuff and that gave me a little cash ahead and I started working at this motor club and then I needed a car definitely, I needed one in my work so I shopped around, and (2) my idea was to get (3) a postwar or rather . . . yeah a

---

[9]Numbers in parentheses represent seconds of silence.

postwar car that (2) would be initially reasonable to purchase and would still be dependable and in shopping around I saw this '47 Brand X and (3) . . . well, because it's a Brand X it didn't cost me much, I bought it in '51, (2) I bought it in '52 and it cost me $400 (4) . . . And so that way I at that time it was a (4) fairly late model car for me so and the initial outlay was very small so I got into a car that I could use for my business. (STOP 3)

I-6:   That's very good. Now I'd like to go back little bit. Can you remember, putting yourself back in time, can you remember how you felt about some of your earliest experiences with a car like when you shared the Chevy with or when your high school buddy gave you the lesson in driving or in the jeep in the army. Can you remember how you felt about this?

R-6:   Well, I remember this (3) that I was very pleased that my high school buddy had a car and of course that gave us an opportunity to get around a little bit and I was tickled pink that he would let me drive now and then, or rather give me a lesson because I wasn't capable of driving and of course that was a brand new experience, a feeling of importance being able to drive a car. That's about what my feelings were then as I remember now. And in service (2) driving a jeep was quite a big thing, I mean (4) to learn . . . the jeep was very new and it was an exciting thing to think that you would be permitted to drive it (2) and I remember the first driving lesson I had I think was up the side of a mountain. It scared the living hell out of me. That's an emotion I definitely remember. (Interrupting)

I-7:   Where was this?

R-7:   In Colorado, Camp Carson, Colorado.

I-8:   Oh unhuh! (2)

R-8:   They showed us how to put it in four-wheel drive and so on (4) . . . And run it up the side of this mountain (2) . . . I guess, thrill and excitement again was the idea, in that case. And, (2) well from then on I just kinda became, I felt I could drive and drive capably, and it became a normal chore driving.

I-9:   I see.

R-9:   What else, is that about what you want? (STOP 4)

I-10:   Yes that's fine I'm just trying to get a general background here and then pretty soon maybe I'll find something I want to go a little deeper into.

R-10:   Can you shut it off for just a moment I've got to put the waffle on. (Tape-recorder is off for a few minutes while waffles are put on.)

I-11: You say there was a lot of publicity for what the jeep could do! (Referring to respondent's remark while putting on the waffles.)

R-11: Yeh, it got a good deal of promotion you know secret weapon of the American army and all that, and as a result (3) to be able to drive one was a special thrill. (2) (STOP 5)

I-12: How would you compare the experience of driving a jeep with your later experience when you got the Kaiser?

R-12: Well . . . (9) the thrill of ownership I think can be described, can accurately describe (3) owning the Kaiser. It was the first car I ever had (2) . . . that really belonged to me. The thrill of driving was over, you know, the thrill of being able to maneuver a car was over (2) and how to own one on your own (3) and to have the feeling of importance you get with owning a $2,500 piece of equipment.

I-13: You bought this new, the '47?

R-13: Yes (Uh huh) and that was part of it too, of course at that time it was a very abnormal market you know you couldn't get cars easily, (2) and if you did or if you could find one you felt was in good condition that you'd like to buy, it was $200 or $300 under the table and all that stuff (2) so we, this Kaiser was available as a demonstrator and we got some of the price knocked off of it, and we were real thrilled that (2) we could that we'd found a car that was within our price range and also a new one (2) uh, my wife and my father were skeptical about it, but I felt that this was the thing, this was the car for us, that we could afford the money and so on, and it was initially my decision that we bought it (2) which we regretted later on because the first Kaiser wasn't too much of an automobile in comparison with the other makes (2). (STOP 6)

I-14: Well, forgetting about the fact that you were disappointed later on can you remember some of the things that made you use the phrase, "this is the car for me" can you remember why you'd say that? (2)

R-14: I think it was purely an emotional thing, Ray, I really do. I think the whole idea, (3), I'd suddenly found (4) a car that was available. (3) Now of course you realize I was quite young then . . . I was still (4) I think I was twenty-four years old and it was I think primarily an emotional thing that decided it the car was shiny and it seemed to be reasonable far more reasonable than anything else we could buy with the market the way it was then (2) and just being thrilled to think we could have it that is was available decided my mind. It wouldn't today, (3) I mean I realize that when you spend that amount of money you're making a real decision but at that time it was purely emotional. (3) (STOP 7)

I-15: Would you say that a Kaiser had any different significance for you than some other car? I mean, after all other cars are shiny too.

R–15:   Probably if I'd seen any other car and it had been in the price range that we were ready to pay (2) and you put the two together, I probably would have taken (3) . . . now wait, that does bring up, that does bring something to mind. (6) . . . I don't know, ah (2) I think there was an appeal there for this new automobile manufacturer I think I felt like I'd like to give him a break. (Pauses to put dishes on table.) Not many people owned Kaisers, and I felt if I could be one of them, now what do you call that (2) that's wanting to be different I suppose.

I–16:   Distinctive.

R–16:   Unhuh, I think that was a great part of the appeal in that case. Now put it up against another car, a Buick or Pontiac or an Olds, (2), I may have been less emotional about it and made a hard-headed decision that it's better to get into a well established brand of automobile rather than a Kaiser however, that being distinctive still had a very strong appeal.

I–17:   Well, you said your father was skeptical of this (R: Here's cream if you want it.   I: No, thanks.)   R: Yes.   I: What was the basis of his skepticism?

R–17:   That it's a brand new make of automobile. You're going to put $2,000 into an automobile that (2) you don't know how long it's going to hold out, it's a brand new car on the market, wait a couple of years before you buy one you're a fool (3).

I–18:   Well, in a sense you—

R–18:   (Interrupting) That was his objection. (STOP 8)

I–19:   (Interrupting) Unhuh, in a sense you would say that your motivation for doing it was quite the opposite point of view, because it was new this was one, at least it didn't deter you because it was a new manufacture you sort of. . . .

R–19:   No, as a matter of fact that has appeal to me. (5)

I–20:   Oh, now you've mentioned this idea, that buying a Kaiser is something distinctive not everybody has one.

R–20:   Unhuh.

I–21:   Well, is there any other kind of a car which might fulfill this same function if it were equal in other respects? (2)

R–21:   At that time or do you mean today?

I–22:   Either at that time or today.

R–22:   I don't think so, available on the market at that time. Today yes, foreign cars on the market (5) And I think that my next car will be a

British Consul or a Hillman Minx or (3) some car like that, small economical to run, and incidentally well maybe not incidentally it may be above all, it's different. (2) (STOP 9)

I–23: Now what do you mean?

R–23: I'll repeat that. At first it's small, easy to park, economical to run and so on and incidentally is also distinctive it may be above all it's distinctive, and secondly, however . . . no I can't say that . . . these buying factors I think will be about equal that I have a car that is easy to run. It's important that I have a car that's easy to park in small spaces because I'm going around the city constantly and I just might buy a Rambler too, or a . . . maybe one of the Nash Metropolitans because they're small, easy to run but probably because of this other thing, this being distinctive I think I'd like to have a British Consul or a Hillman Minx. (4) (STOP 10)

I–24: As you look back as you've gone through time in this area, would you say that your general attitude toward cars, towards the ownership and driving of cars, that you've gone through any process of change?

R–24: Oh yes, like anything (3) . . . maturing I think and feeling or rather understanding the value of a dollar bill changed my ideas about buying a car personally (2) in working for the Motor Club I am in a position to see the people that buy automobiles, how they buy them and where they buy them and so on, and personally I cannot understand or agree with people that buy a new car year after year when they can't afford it. And I've seen so many people like that (2). They're a thousand dollars behind on their . . . or rather they still owe a thousand dollars on their '53 car and they're shopping for a '54. They've gotta get out of the old one and into a new one and still they don't have the television set paid for. Why they ever bought a television set in the first place, when they were extended so far on the car, and they need new furniture they need new rugs they're not putting any money away, but still they're shopping for a '54 automobile. So far from that I do not feel that it's necessary for me to have a new car every year or even every two or three years. I'll run this one until I feel that it's in a mechanical shape where it's going to be more expensive to fix it than to get a new one or some other logical reason for getting out of it not because I feel . . . now I think that perhaps I'm different from the regular car-buying public in this respect (2) because I do not feel any urge now to get into shiny things and drive around flashy, I would like to be distinctive, yes, but I'm not going to get a *new* Hillman and I'm not going to get a *new* Consul. I'll get a *used* one . . . (3) so those are ways that my attitudes have changed about. . .

I–25: (Interrupting) That's very interesting.

R-25: (Continuing) buying cars in the years since I bought my first one.

I-26: Sort of a growing realism with regard to expense and the longer range outlook on this.

R-26: Unhuh. (2) (STOP 11)

I-27: Now would you say that you're still able to get (4) . . . well let's put it this way, how does pleasure fit in, now you were talking mostly about the economics of it. How does the pleasure element and satisfactions, other deeper satisfactions fit in? Has that changed in any way?

R-27: Pleasure?

I-28: Yeh, connected with ownership and driving a car. (3)

R-28: Well, the pleasure to me now I could call convenience, and that's what it is, being able to step out of doors get into the car and go where I want to at any time . . . And other than *that* pleasure I . . . I can't think of any. I will add this (2) I would like to get a convertible the next car I buy . . . I've never owned one and I think that maybe I could add to the element of pleasure by getting one. (STOP 12)

I-29: Could you tell me a little more about this, I mean. . . .

R-29: Well, (12) . . . uh . . . this perhaps too is, (4) I don't know, I just feel that I could probably have more fun. I could just take the top down in summer and buzz around I may find as I say never having owned one, that it's going to be a hell of a bother. It may be colder, it's gonna leak and do things that a hard top doesn't do, but I'm willing to try it; I just think it would be fun having a convertible, and if I find that this is so, the next one the following one I get won't be a convertible. I haven't tried it yet, so I think I'll try to get one. (2) (STOP 13)

I-30: Could you . . . is there any, could you give me an idea by giving sort of a picture of a . . . what you could consider an ideal situation which you're using this car in the way in which it would give you the most pleasure. . .

R-30: Yes I think. . .

I-31: (Continuing) by virtue of the fact that it's a convertible?

R-31: Yes, I think weekend trips, maybe going off to Michigan or something with the top down and with a girl friend. I think it would be more fun . . . because (4) on a lovely sunny day just to drive along with the top down and the breeze blowing over you and you'd be able to see the landscape and so on, completely unrestricted view. And just the idea of an open car rather than a closed car. (2) I think there's an association there with pleasure. (STOP 14)

I-32:   Could you a . . . is there anything you can put your finger on there about the difference between open and closed? Can you describe any feeling or imagery this gives you?

R-32:   Uh, yeh, I think there's kind of a carefree feeling, about sitting in an open car . . . ah, (2) ah (2) you can push on the pedal, that is push on the accelerator and off you go. You're breathing fresh air and you feel like you could stretch out your arm above you, and all is open and you can just fly if you want to; and I think the difference is feeling of confinement in a closed car. I don't think you get that carefree, happy gayness that you can have in a convertible. If this helps you I don't know, it's difficult to explain.

I-33:   Well, you're doing very well (4) so any vague, no matter how vague an idea you may have it may be difficult to express, but it's very significant to us.

R-33:   I think that's about it. I think it's probably a feeling of youth and freedom and associations like that. (4) (STOP 15)

I-34:   That's very interesting, I think you've expressed it very well (3) now with your Brand X which is the car you have now, (3) let's see . . . you told me a little bit about how you came to buy it, but could you elaborate on it a little bit. Was there anybody around trying to influence you like your father or father-in-law? Anybody in this case? Did you buy it new?

R-34:   (Interrupting) By golly I wanted to buy a Packard convertible for $900 and it was a lovely car, it was in excellent condition and it had electric windows you know was just it was a '49. And I asked my dad to lend me $600, my stepfather the same one as it was before (3) and he re-fused. (2) So then I had to get something much cheaper, so I shopped around, and I felt that if I got an older, or rather if I got an off-brand car, and I'd buy a big car I'd be able to get into a later model for $400 than if I got into a, if I bought a late car of a well-known brand, they're much more in demand.

I-35:   Oh, in other words the resale value was lower on the Brand X for the same year and for that size of a car.

R-35:   Unhuh. The bigger a car is the less in demand it will be on a used car market and of course then when it's an off brand, well, then it'll be less in demand. And so I saw this Brand X, the biggest one they made in '47 and it just seemed to get the bill perfectly. And it was in good condi-tion too when I bought it and so that's what made up my mind. (STOP 16)

I-36:   Was there anything else you'd say which entered into this be-sides the economic factor, so far you've been stressing the fact that you could get it cheaply, is there any other psychological factor involved do you think? Any satisfaction you might get out of this particular car? (3)

R–36:   Well, it was well appointed, that . . . that . . . that's one reason that . . . I probably decided, well this is probably the car I'm going to buy I mean I decided this is probably the car I am going to buy and I looked it over, I mean this is what I want, this fits in all ways it seems up to now. Of course if I found out the back seat was all burned out I wouldn't buy it, but otherwise it fit. So I looked at it and it seemed well appointed. It had all the equipment in it that makes owning a car a little more fun. (STOP 17)

I–37:   Like what?

R–37:   Radio and a heater and (3) this one had an automatic drive too but it didn't work, but it was in there and I hoped that maybe I could get it fixed up some day . . . (2) but it was well appointed and it had dividing (2) arm rest in the rear seat and the upholstery was clean and nice colors good fabrics (3) so that pleased me too and that helped make up my mind about buying it. (3)

I–38:   You think if you . . . let's see if just the strictly economic factors, and you got an equally good buy say in a Mercury for example, how would this comparison impress you?

R–38:   I think that I probably would have bought the Mercury . . . all things being equal, mileage and tires and all, (2) because I realize that (3) now did you say Mercury because you feel it's the same size of automobile or because you feel it's a, or for what other reasons. (STOP 18)

I–39:   Well, the Mercury I feel is comparable in some ways . . .

I–40:   (Continuing) I just don't know enough about different models of the Brand X for example there's such a wide, wide range in different models to know what's comparable.

R–40:   Well, Mercury of course has a better resale value and it seems like a somewhat smaller car because the wheelbase on this thing that I'm driving is very big, very big so I think that I would have bought the Mercury for these reasons . . .

I–41:   You think . . . which do you think is the more distinctive car, the Mercury or the Brand X? . . . in the same sense as you used it in reference to the Kaiser for example. . .

R–41:   Today or at that time? (STOP 19)

I–42:   At that time. (4)

R–42:   I think the Brand X is the most distinctive car because it was the homeliest car in the streets in 1947 (both laugh) it had this wide gaping grill and still had the prewar dies, and it was like a box and stood way up high, and I still think it had the homeliest lines of any car on the street so for that reason I think it was distinctive. (Laugh together) (STOP 20)

I–43:   I see. Did this sort of enter in, was this a negative factor in your decision, this homeliness?

R–43:   No, not at all. My idea was to get (3) a good car reasonable, and with that I didn't care much how it looked and I (3) that's the reason I bought it. I think today (2) that I'm somewhat changed. I think I'd like a little better-looking automobile. If I put myself today in that same situation I may not have selected the Brand X. I'd shop some more.

FIELD PROBLEM

Images and Feelings on the American Way of Life

Up to this point all of the problems have been *laboratory* problems in which you were asked to analyze or criticize someone else's interview. In this *field problem* you are to plan and do a series of three interviews, so you must shift from the role of critic to performer!

PURPOSE

The central purpose of this problem is to give you an opportunity to put into practice the general procedure for learning interviewing skills through planning, doing, and analyzing your own interview. The topic and specifications of the interview you are to do have been chosen because they demand a wide range of skills, yet all of the problems are soluble to some degree even in the first attempt.

To provide ample opportunity for improving through critical experience, this assignment is to do a *series of three interviews* on the same topic. To apply the procedure for development of skills, each of the three interviews will be carefully planned in advance, performed, and analyzed before going on to plan the next interview. If possible all three interviews should be tape-recorded. If only two of the three can be recorded, it should be the last two. In any case the last one must be tape-recorded.

OBJECTIVES

The objectives can be divided into the informational objectives specifying the type of information to be collected and the methodological objectives in terms of the development of the strategies, techniques, and tactics expected at the end of the series of three interviews.

Informational objectives. There are four dimensions of the meaning of "The American Way of Life" which must be explored:

a. What is the American way of life in the mind of the respondent? What are the most salient *ideas* and *images* associated with the term?

b. What about the American way of life is *changing* for the better? For the worse?

c. What are the *sources* of the respondent's most salient ideas, images, or feelings?

d. What is the *feeling tone,* attitude, or value attached to the most salient ideas or images? What is good or bad about the American way of life?

Methodological objectives. You are to use the three interviews to develop strategy, tactics, and techniques for achieving the informational objectives. Your final report after the third interview will contain your latest revision of the methods.

FORM OF YOUR FINAL REPORT

Your final report should be written after analyzing the results of your third interview and should include the following parts in sequence. The estimated number of pages (typed, double-spaced) for each part is given in parentheses. If you try to be concise, the total report should have fewer than ten pages.

1. *Revised strategy plan.* (1 page) Describe the strategy you would use if you were to do more interviews. How does it differ from what you had done before?

2. *Revised guide or schedule.* (3 pages) Revise the interview guide or schedule used in your third interview to improve it as much as you can on the basis of your experience to this point.

3. *Coded information.* (2 pages) Code *all* of the relevant information *verbatim* in some organized manner from your third interview only.

4. *Revised hypotheses.* (½ page) State your revised hypotheses which are *post hoc* answers to the four topical questions of the interview. Show what you would expect the answers to these four questions to be if you were to do a hundred more interviews. If any different categories of data would be needed than those used in Part 3 above, show how they would differ.

5. *Experience report.* (2 pages) Show what you learned by doing
    the series of three interviews. What were the main problems en-
    countered? What surprised you about the project? What would
    you need to work on most in the future to develop skills in inter-
    view planning and performance?

PROCEDURES

This is not a laboratory project assignment to be done in a couple of
hours but a field assignment requiring from ten to fourteen days elapsed
time and from twenty to thirty-five hours work time, depending on the
circumstances, how thoroughly each step is done, and how the group
works together. The extent to which each of the steps below shall be
done independently and how much in group discussion in or out of the
regular group sessions will be determined by the instructor.

1. Review and refine objectives. Look at the four dimensions of the
meaning of "The American Way of Life" as given above and think of different possible interpretations of the kind of information required by
each dimension. For example, in probing for the most salient images
and ideas associated with "the American way of life," should the interviewer define the phrase for the respondent at the onset or only if the respondent asks for a definition; or should the interviewer insist that the
respondent use his or her own definition by giving whatever the respondent associates with the verbal phrase?

2. Develop hypotheses. By hypothesis we mean a tentative answer,
on the basis of theory or an intuitive hunch, to each of the four topical
questions. For example, for dimension *a* a hypothesis would be a tentative answer (in advance of the interview) to the question: What are the
most salient ideas and images the respondents in general will associate
with "the American way of life"? The hypothetical answer may be given
at any level of abstraction, depending on what you feel to be the most
appropriate. For example, a very concrete answer might be that the
most salient image will be the American flag or the Statue of Liberty. In
contrast, it could be a very abstract; for example, "Most respondents
will associate images of physical objects rather than social institutions,"
or "Most respondents will associate individual rights and freedoms
more frequently than obligations or duties."

In any case you should *not* restrict your interview to testing your
hypothesis but always leave it open enough to allow for a full range of
unanticipated responses in addition to testing your hypotheses. After
each interview you should revise your hypotheses in light of the information collected.

3. Prepare interview guide or schedule. Plan an interview guide or schedule to perform both functions: (*a*) to *explore* for better hypotheses and (*b*) to *test* the hypothesis. Remember, for exploration and discovery you must use broad-scope questions and have a lot of neutral probes on hand to keep the conversation going. Both for the exploratory function and testing the hypotheses you must be careful that you do not suggest answers by the wording of a question, by the structuring of the answers, by the chronological order of questions, or by verbal or nonverbal statements. Put this in a form you will actually use in the interview!

4. Anticipate main inhibitors and facilitators. In view of the general types of questions represented by the four subtopics of the interview, and in view of some of the possible answers as expressed in your hypotheses, try to anticipate some of the *potential* inhibitors and facilitators in the situation. Keep these in mind for your next steps of planning your strategy, techniques, and tactics.

5. Plan the strategy. You will have to accept as a given the fact that *you* are to be the interviewer and that someone in your organization (college, university, plant, agency, office, etc.) is to be the respondent. You are to decide within the limitations of the local situation *who* to interview, *when*, and *where*, and what you will say or do to locate the respondent, to get the respondent's cooperation, and to define the interview situation. This should be done keeping in mind the specific objectives of the interview, the nature of the situation, and the potential inhibitors and facilitators. Some of the important facts about the nature of the situation are that you will be doing three interviews, others will also be interviewing on the same topic, and you must proceed in an ethical manner.

6. Do the interview. The interviews should be *tape-recorded* in a place where there is privacy and quiet. Do not forget to pretest the situation so that you can be sure to obtain a clearly audible recording. Even though you use a tape recorder you should also take *probe notes* as an aid to pursuing the informational objectives.

7. Type relevant content. Listen to your tape-recording, keeping in mind your informational objectives, and type (if possible) the words, phrases, or sentences constituting the relevant data. In cases where the meaning of the response is not clear, out of context, supply the context in parentheses. For example, often the response is meaningless without seeing the question or probe that prompted it. Do not try to rearrange the order of the relevant information; type it in the order it appears on the tape. Only a portion of the information will be relevant. Don't try to get perfect copy—strike over or x-out errors and barge on ahead. Make a carbon copy, and type double-spaced lines.

8. Code relevant content. Construct a code sheet for your interview showing the categories of information needed to test your specific hypotheses related to topics *a* (images or ideas), *b* (changes), and *c* (sources). Topic *d* (feeling tone) will be considered as a separate dimension applicable to all of the three preceding topics. For example, assume that your hypothesis for topic *a*, on images and ideas, is that *more abstract ideas than concrete images will be given.* Then your code would look like this:

a–1	Abstract idea	(freedom, individualism, idealistic).
a–2	Concrete image	(Statue of Liberty, traffic jam, smog).
a–X	Other	(Any idea or image not classifiable in the two hypothesized categories either because an additional category was needed or the meaning is not clearly abstract or concrete).

Note that the "*a*" indicates that the information deals with topic *a* and the numbers 1 and 2 indicate hypothesized categories of responses to topic *a*, and the X indicates information which is relevant to topic *a* but does not fall into the categories.

After you build a code for the first three topics, each relevant image, idea, change, or source can be cross-classified according to whether the feeling toward the particular item of information is positive, negative, or neutral. The content of one interview could be represented, then, on a coding sheet as shown in Exhibit A–2.

After you have constructed your code sheet (make a duplicate if you are going to have a coding partner also code your interview), go through one copy of the *typed relevant data*, and code each element of

EXHIBIT A–2

TOPICS		Code	SUB-TOPICS	FEELING TONE - TOPIC d		
				Positive (+)	Neutral (?)	Negative (–)
a	Ideas Images	a-1	Abstract			
		a-2	Concrete			
		a-x	Other			
b	Changes	b-1				
		b-2				
		b-3				
		b-4				
		b-x	Other			
c	Sources	c-1				
		c-2				
		c-3				
		c-x	Other			

information which is relevant. Remember that relevant data includes all data which fall into a category needed to test a hypothesis or into the X category under each topic, indicating that it is relevant to the topic but not specifically to your hypothesis about that topic. Each bit of relevant data must be designated with a *serial number*, followed by the code (the *topic letter* and the *answer-category number*) in parentheses, followed by the feeling-tone symbol, all written immediately above the underlined words (see Exhibit B).

Once the transcription of relevant data has been coded as in the example above, the data can be summarized by merely putting the *serial numbers* in the appropriate cells in the code sheet. It will be noted that, on the feeling-tone dimension, the coder assumed that he could classify smog and pollution as negative, but was not sure that any of the others was clearly positive or negative in the mind of the respondent, and he had failed to probe the feeling dimension. Sometimes the feeling tone is clear from the context or tone of voice, but in other cases it is necessary for the interviewer to probe. Otherwise the interviewer is merely indicating his or her own rather than the respondent's evaluation of the particular idea or image.

The attempt to code such material from the first interview will alert the interviewer to the need to probe for feeling tone, using something like the following:

> When you mentioned personal mobility just now, was that a good or bad aspect of the American way of life?

or

> Would you classify personal mobility as a good, neutral or bad part of the American way of life?

EXHIBIT B

```
        1(a-2)-      2(a-2)-
I think of smog and pollution as well as the
        3(a-2)?           4(a-2)?
Star-Spangled Banner and apple pie. The
        5(a-2)?              6(a-2)?
Washington Monument, the Statue of Liberty,
              7(a-2)?
or the Empire State Building is what most

people would think of. But (what distinguishes

America from most countries) is amount and
        8(a-1)?          9(a-1)?
type of residential and personal mobility.
```

The interviewer might avoid having to probe every image or idea for its position on the feeling dimension by asking broad questions such as "What are some of the best things about the American Way of Life?" "What are some of the worst things about the American Way of Life?" or "What are some of the most typical things of the American Way of Life? Which of these are good and which are bad?"

9. Criticize strategies, techniques, and tactics. Your self-critique should keep in mind the informational objectives of the interview as you ask yourself the following questions:

Accurately receiving information

1. Did you hear all of the relevant points during the interview or did you notice some of the information for the first time when you listened to the tape-recording?

2. Did you observe anything about the respondent's nonverbal reactions to the interview? If so, what?

3. Did you have any trouble remembering the relevant things the respondent said during the interview, so that you could know what had been covered and what had not?

Critically evaluating the information

1. What about the informational objectives, if anything, do you need to clarify before you go on to the next interview?

2. Where in the interview did you fail to probe when you should? Why do you suppose this was?

3. Did your probe notes indicate many points that needed further clarification or elaboration?

Controlling techniques and tactics

1. Did you have a plan regarding where to use broad-scope questions versus narrow-scope questions?

2. Had you planned several potential broad-scope questions to cover the same topic area in case the first one was not fruitful?

3. How often did you use low-topic-control encouragement probes?

4. How often did you use a silent probe and how often did you interrupt the respondent?

5. Did you ever directly praise the respondent for his efforts during the interview?

6. What should you do differently next time in strategy, techniques, or tactics? Consider a few of the most important possibilities.

10. Revise strategy, techniques, and tactics. On the basis of your analysis of relevant content in step 8 and your analysis of your strategy, tactics, and techniques in step 9, revise only the methods you feel most clearly need to be changed. After the first interview it may be necessary to make only minor changes, or it may be advisable to change the whole plan radically, depending upon the amount of work, insight, and luck involved in your preplanning of the first interview. After two interviews the plan for the third may take a clearer shape.

Steps 1 through 10 are done three times, once in connection with each interview, and do not require you to write any formal report. The five parts to your formal report have been specified earlier and can be done only after the completion of the third interview.

If you proceed in a creative, sensitive, and disciplined manner without undue rush, you will develop an invaluable pattern of self-instruction you can use in the future to review and improve your skill and insight into the total interview process, including clarifying the objectives, designing the interview strategy, constructing the interview guide, doing the interview, and finally analyzing the relevant data and criticizing the field methods used. This is the creative process which is the major portion of any small-scale, high-quality research; and it is the crucial preliminary phase in large-scale projects using a number of interviewers who are given a field-developed and pretested interview schedule and strategy instructions.

By following the basic formula of planning, doing, and analyzing, you will discover that much depends upon preplanning and postanalysis as well as upon an alert, sensitive impromptu performance in the interview. Through this three-phase cycle of learning activity you will improve your ability to transform the informational objectives, the conceptual model of facilitators and inhibitors, the tools of strategy, techniques, and tactics into specific behaviors of the interviewer. Only when this creative and insightful connection is made can we expect results in terms of information that is more relevant, more valid, and more complete. Good luck in your field venture!

Epilogue

After dealing with the complexities of interviewing method and the procedures for learning to interview, it is time to reaffirm the essential spirit and purpose of this book and renew its perspectives.

AIMS

This book does not aim to convert the reader into a highly skilled and polished interviewer in a few weeks. A more realistic expectation is that the interested student will have (a) gained a conceptual frame of reference that will sensitize him or her to the potential inhibitors and facilitators of communication in the interview, (b) become acquainted with a broad spectrum of tools (strategies, techniques, and tactics) that can be used to minimize the inhibitors and to maximize the facilitators, and (c) gained some meaningful experience in developing the basic skills needed to apply the relevant concepts and tools in a real interview situation.

These gains do not make a person into a skilled interviewer, but they do provide the basis for autonomous learning so that steady improvement can be made with further interviewing experience. Without this basis there is no assurance that a person will automatically improve with repeated interviews. In the author's experience, some of the worst interviewers have had hundreds of hours of interviewing. However, they lack both a sensitizing frame of reference to guide them and specific procedures for self-criticism and improvement; so they simply become less sensitive, more mechanical, less flexible in their methods, and more restricted in their options.

In short, this book aims at providing you with a canoe, a paddle, and a launch in the right direction, but it does not claim to have delivered you at your destination.

PERSPECTIVES ON INTERVIEWING

The direct empirical study of human behavior includes interviewing, empathy, participation, and observation. Each of these approaches could be dealt with at length separately, but interviewing involves certain aspects of the other three general methods.

Interviewing, unlike any of the basic methods in the physical sciences, depends upon an empathic relationship between the observer and the observed. There is nothing to be gained by lamenting or ignoring the fact that there are dangers of misempathizing or overempathizing, since empathy is a necessary element in human communication.

On the contrary, one of the advantages the social sciences have over the physical sciences is the fact that under certain conditions the human observer may successfully empathize with the object of his or her observation. The study of human behavior not only depends upon but also helps to develop empathy. Thus, we assume a complementary rather than an antithetical relationship between empathy as a common human characteristic and social science as a specialized, abstract, objective analysis of human behavior. Qualitatively valid observations must always precede any quantitative observation or analysis. This complementary relationship is further emphasized in the fact that the application of the results of any social science study depends upon an empathic relationship between the social engineer and the people in the community where the results are to be applied.

Thus, the whole social science enterprise may be viewed as a systematic extension of the range and quality of human empathy. The ability of the human being to invent and build the social structures needed to support cooperation over ever widening circles, from familial and tribal to national and international, depends upon this progressive extension of empathy.

The foregoing assumptions may at first glance seem to have little connection with learning to interview. Actually, these ideas regarding the relationship between human empathy, social science, and the general welfare of society have been some of the silent assumptions underlying this particular approach to interviewing. Instead of perceiving empathy and objectivity as antithetical, we see the problem as being one of developing an "informed empathy" that gives the observer of human phenomena an advantage over, for example, the psychologist studying the motivation of rats.

The successful application of the theoretical framework of inhibitors and facilitators of communication rests upon the interviewer's ability to empathize in the planning, execution, and analysis phases of the interviewing enterprise. This is not to say that we blindly trust empathy but that, since we cannot avoid using it, we must try to use its positive aspects and avoid its pitfalls. Methods of analyzing both the interviewing process and the resulting data can help correct empathic error.

The author has been considering interviewing as including the total process of planning, executing, and analyzing the interview, rather than taking the narrower view that interviewing properly includes only that portion of the process which is performed vis-á-vis the respondent.

This perspective does not conceal the vital interdependence between the strategy planning and the methods used by the interviewer when facing the respondent. If the strategy is designed without benefit of exploratory participation, observation, or interviewing in the field, there is the grave danger that the conceptualization of the problem may be inappropriate, the questions may be beside the point, or the contexts, wording, and sequence of questions may all work to inhibit rather than facilitate communication. Only in rare cases can the skilled interviewer completely overcome the initial disadvantages of a poorly planned strategy or an ill-conceived interview guide.

The selection from among the many tools of strategy, techniques, and tactics is the essence of the creative process of interviewing, and like all creative processes it is not a fixed mechanical sequence. For this reason no set of "do's" or "don'ts" can realistically be offered as a guide. Instead we have offered the general principle that the tools should be selected to maximize the facilitators and minimize the inhibitors. These eight inhibitors and eight facilitators of communication viewed in this social context are not proposed as an elegant theoretical model fitting neatly within one discipline; the variables are related to several disciplines bearing on human behavior. Two values of this eclectic frame of reference are that each concept clearly represents a real factor found in face-to-face communication situations and that each concept is relatable to basic theory and empirical findings in the social sciences.

ADVICE ON INTERVIEWING

Adapt and Invent Interviewing Methods, Not Adopt Them

Even though this book has offered a variety of strategies, techniques, and tactics to be used in minimizing inhibitors and maximizing facilitators, there are no rigid formulas to determine when each tool is appropriate. Each information-gathering situation must be approached with an open mind, and the initial plans for the interviewing method should be considered highly tentative and open to modification on closer acquaintance with the situation. Sometimes it is even premature to assume that interviewing should be used instead of consulting public records, case histories, diaries, letters, registration data, census data, questionnaires or essays written by the respondents. Only after it is clear that interviewing is the best method for collecting at least some of the information, must we make a tentative strategy design which specifies who should interview whom, where, when, and how to define the situation to the respondent. All this planning must be done in considerable detail with all the empathy that the planner can muster, even though it is tentative and subject to modification after the first field test.

To be fruitful, the strategy planning must begin with the broadest view of the total situation. There is a danger of beginning a field study with a bundle of restrictive assumptions, often unconscious, regarding the range of strategies to be considered. Often, these assumptions are built upon previous experience, direct or vicarious, with strategies for collecting data in a particular situation. Even the professional researcher may be caught in the net of habit and try to solve a new problem with only old formulas. For example, a person accustomed to doing public opinion polls or census-type surveys may unintentionally cripple a study of the local community power structure by assuming that all of the respondents should be randomly selected. This strategy of selecting respondents would make it impossible to trace the informal chain of command or to cross-check the account of one witness with that of another person participating in the same situation.

Just as strategy planning must be approached with a combination of empathic anticipation and reality testing in the field, so must our use of interviewing techniques. Such considerations as the vocabulary used in wording a question, whether or not to preface the question with a contextual statement, and whether to use an open-ended or multiple-choice answer structure must be tentatively answered in constructing the first draft of the interview guide or interview schedule in order to have something concrete to use in the exploratory field testing. The value of the field testing depends both on the amount of thought and insight that went into the tentative interview design and the skill and experience of the persons doing the field test. Usually, a field tester should be a much more highly qualified person than the interviewers who will ultimately use the finished interview guide.

When considering nonverbal techniques, the same careful approach should be used if we are to maximize the flow of relevant, clear, and complete information. The nonverbal part of the interviewer's behavior cannot be controlled by the written wording of the question. To a great extent nonverbal techniques consist of different ways of manifesting certain attitudes toward the respondent, toward the topic of discussion, or toward a particular response. These attitudes cannot be turned on and off at will. The problem can be solved partly by training interviewers to have positive attitudes toward their own task and to have nonjudgmental attitudes toward their respondents. Rather than trying to hide any negative attitudes, the interviewer can learn to show interest in the information received, appreciation of the respondent's efforts in giving it, and a critical assessment of the relevance of the information.

All this does not mean that the interviewer must have no values or beliefs contrary to those of the respondent. The interviewer does not need to be a sociopsychological chameleon but must perceive that in the role as interviewer the task is to see the world through the eyes of the respondent, not to approve or disapprove of what is seen. In the role as citizen the interviewer is free to judge whether or not the purposes of the particular proposed study are in agreement with personal values. If they are not, the interviewer should not participate in the study. Maintaining an operational distinction between the role as interviewer and the role as citizen is one of the disciplines a successful interviewer must learn.

The adequacy of an interviewer's experience and of his or her own personal values and background may be judged tentatively in the selection of the interviewer for a particular type of information gathering, but the final screening should be done in the actual field testing. It is often helpful for the interviewer to realize in advance that not everyone is cut out to do a particular type of interviewing and that those who feel most uncomfortable with the initial field experience may elect to withdraw and save their talents for another type of interviewing.

The same tentativeness and field testing should be applied to the tactics of the interview. Since tactics deal with the sequence of events in the give-and-take of the interview, some portion of this sequence can be planned, field-tested, and revised to effectively control much of the interview; but there may be portions of an interview which vary so much from respondent to respondent that the sequence cannot all be frozen into the interview schedule. The specific probe needed to clarify the answer to a question often must be invented on the spot. There is no substitute for general interviewing experience and specific experience with the particular interview at hand to improve the proficiency in meeting the tactical demands in the give-and-take of a particular interview.

After all the most empathic preplanning and the best field testing and revisions, the quality of the interview then depends completely upon the skill of the interviewer in delivering the question; in listening to the answer, in judging the relevance, validity, clarity, and completeness of the answer; and in formulating an appropriate follow-up probe to improve the quality of the information.

Plan for the Worst and Expect the Best

If we were to list all of the strategies, techniques, and tactics that could be used to minimize each of the eight potential inhibitors and to maximize each of the eight potential facilitators, we would clearly see that we cannot possibly apply all of the methods to a particular interview plan. First, we have to pool our knowledge, experience, and empathy to predict which inhibitors might be most salient in a particular type of interview. Then we plan to reduce the effects of these potential inhibitors as much as possible at the strategy level, then at the level of techniques and tactics. Second, we build into the interview schedule as many of the strategies, techniques, and tactics as we can to minimize these anticipated inhibitors. Third, by field-testing the interview we may find that certain precautions were advisable, others can be discarded or used only in special cases, and still others that had not been anticipated must be added.

In this whole process it is important for the interviewer not to be so affected by "negative" thinking involved in trying to anticipate inhibitors that a timid or apologetic attitude is developed and communicated to the respondent. This is most easily avoided by stressing the methods which tend to maximize the facilitators, one of which is to communicate the expectation of the respondent's full cooperation.

SUBJECTIVE ASPECTS OF LEARNING TO INTERVIEW

In training interviewers with widely differing backgrounds, the author has encountered many subjective reactions to learning to interview. Often these are curiously parallel to the culture shock felt when one must change linguistic and other habit patterns to adjust to a new way of life. Of course, this jolt is not so keenly felt when we simply read *about* an exotic culture or *about* interviewing. The experience is more profound when we must learn to *act* in a new way, when old habit patterns are no longer appropriate under the new circumstances, when we have an opportunity to see ourselves in a new perspective. In the cross-cultural experience, this new perspective is attained when we are able to communicate with the foreigner well enough to understand that his or her perception of us does not agree with our own image of ourselves. In learning to interview we can more quickly attain this new perspective by hearing ourselves interviewing on tape.

The shock of self-recognition can be both depressing and refreshing at different phases of the learning process. The author has observed a tendency for an initial euphoria to develop as the person plays with some of the new concepts, sees a broader horizon before him or her, and accepts the challenge to expand his or her repertoire of basic skills. Then comes a phase in which morale may drop as the learner increases awareness of the complexities of the task, of the type and amount of skill needed, and of some of his or her own shortcomings in controlling personal behavior in accordance with an intellectual understanding of the problem.

In this curiously contradictory situation the learner's self-esteem as an interviewer may drop as actual performance is making dramatic improvement. For example, in cases where the learner does a tape-recorded interview at the beginning and at the end of a training period and is asked to discuss each interview with the instructor immediately after each recording session, there is a clear tendency for the learner to be much more critical of the learner's performance in the posttest interview than he was of his pretest interview earlier. Yet, the posttest interview is usually far superior to the pretest. The remedy for this drop in morale was simple and dramatic. When the learner was allowed to hear a portion of both the pretest and posttest in the same session, the learner was impressed and often surprised by the substantial improvement. Often, however, in order to demonstrate increased awareness of the problems and solutions in interviewing, the learner would use the more modest approach of remarking about how gullible or insensitive he or she had been in the pretest, rather than directly saying how perceptive and sensitive he or she was in the posttest.

The learner must avoid allowing his or her desirably increased appreciation of the tasks of interviewing and greater ability to self-criticize own behavior to dampen an appreciation of the progress he or she has made or the faith in continued improvement.

Also, to avoid being overwhelmed by the intellectual complexity of the interviewing task, the reader should remember that, although many interviewing problems have been illustrated in a relatively short space, only a small proportion of them would normally occur in any series of interviews in a particular field study. The sheer number of strategies, techniques, and tactics need not lead to despair since only a few of them may be legitimately used in any one study. Furthermore, it is not necessary to retain the whole inventory of interviewing tools in one's mind since most of these decisions are made in the planning and evaluation stage in which we can use references. Although some of these interviewing tools may be rarely used, it is important to be familiar with them because we cannot predict when the situation will arise in which they are sorely needed.

The areas which the interviewer must master as his or her own are the performance skills of listening, manifesting positive attitudes, critically evaluating the information received, probing for elaboration and clarification of the responses, taking notes, and dealing with symptoms of resistance in the respondent. This is enough for anyone to concentrate on at one time!

One way the neophyte can convert an early euphoria into a depression is to jump into a practice interview unprepared and expect inspiration to guide the way to success. This is not to say an interviewer should never go into an interview unprepared; it might help jolt the interviewer out of old habits and leave him or her free to experiment. It is more likely, however, to show the interviewer the need for advance planning.

In the early stages of learning to interview, it is best to avoid attempting long and highly complex interviews with many topics and subtopics. The basic skills can be developed just as well in a short, simple interview. Fatigue and confusion do not enhance the learning value of the experience for the beginner. He or she can build endurance later.

The person learning to interview should not select a friend or acquaintance as the respondent. This creates a confusion of roles in which both the interviewer and the respondent may be tense, confused, or amused by the sudden change in the friend's behavior. This creates an artificial relationship incompatible with both friendship and interviewing. For the initial experience, it is easier and more fruitful to interview a stranger, but the stranger should be someone in the same social class and subculture as the interviewer to avoid possible communication problems that could unnecessarily complicate the interview.

It is sometimes essential to morale for the interviewer to realize that the best of strategies, techniques, and tactics will sometimes be relatively unproductive for reasons that are not the interviewer's fault. For example, the respondent may simply not have the relevant information. In this case, good interviewing may appear to be unproductive since no useful information is obtained. Actually, this is a positive rather than a negative outcome since the insensitive interviewer with a "bull in the china shop" approach might obtain a large quantity of fiction worse than useless. Also, a respondent who has relevant information may be fatigued, irritable, or sick. Sometimes the physical environment may be uncomfortable or lack privacy. It is even possible in rare cases that a personal characteristic of the interviewer may have some special meaning to the respondent who simply "can't talk to that type of person." These idiosyncratic circumstances do not arise often and should not be allowed to lower the interviewer's morale. The experienced interviewer will quickly diagnose such an interview situation as impossible and simply find a graceful way out.

The intelligent interviewer realizes that interviewing can never be a magical process by which the "truth, the whole truth, and nothing but the truth" can be efficiently extracted from every respondent. All of the present-day knowledge combined with the most intelligent and skillful application will not completely avoid some distortion or incompleteness in the information obtained from some respondents. But when we consider the contrast between the conditions and methods that can be used in much social science interviewing with the conditions and methods of communication between a prosecuting lawyer and a hostile witness, between an employer and potential employee, or between an applicant for admission to a university and the admission officer of that university, we see that many serious decisions are based upon information received under conditions not nearly so favorable to obtaining truth as can usually be attained in the social science interview.

If the reader will consider the ideas in this book as something to act upon, to verify and modify in active interviewing practice, the rewards will be much greater than if the reader views the book merely as a collection of theoretical concepts seasoned with interesting illustrative cases. It is hoped that this book will not be accepted on faith as gospel nor rejected because some of the ideas do not form an elegant theoretical or literary model that pleases the esthetic senses.

The book should be accepted for what it is. It is the author's sincere attempt to organize his insights, based upon his own and others' experiences in interviewing and upon ideas assimilated from systematic studies of the interviewing process, into a meaningful progression of conceptual and experiential steps. The author has attempted to share his discoveries in a way designed to launch the interviewer into a period of self-sustained development rather than to limit his or her potential growth by presenting a set of rules on interviewing. Insofar as the author has been able to share this voyage of discovery, the reader will have a broader grasp of the nature of the interviewing task, an expanded repertory of interviewing tools, and crescent insight into the appropriate use of these tools in a variety of interviewing settings. The continued development of interviewing skills will depend upon practice that combines thoughtful planning and disciplined interviewing with a critical evaluation of one's own performance and of the concepts presented here.

Index

ABOUT THE AUTHOR

RAYMOND L. GORDEN, Ph.D. with honors from the University of Chicago, became fascinated with interviewing problems while Field Supervisor at the National Opinion Research Center. He has acted as trainer and/or interviewer for such diverse organizations as the Illinois Bell Telephone Company, the IDET Project on Cross-Cultural Communication in Bogota, the Naval Instructional Technology Development Center, The Fund for the Republic, and the Michigan Office of Economic Opportunity. For twenty-five years he has been teaching interviewing to students in the work-study program at Antioch College where he is Professor of Sociology.

A NOTE ON THE TYPE

The text of this book was set in 10/12 Palatino using a film version of the face designed by Hermann Zapf that was first released in 1950 by Germany's Stempel Foundry. The face is named after Giovanni Battista Palatino, a famous penman of the 16th century. In its calligraphic quality, Palatino is reminiscent of the Italian Renaissance type designs, yet with its wide, open letters and unique proportions it still retains a modern feel. Palatino is considered one of the most important faces from one of Europe's most influential type designers.

Composition by Carlisle Graphics, Dubuque, Iowa

Printed and bound by Kingsport Press, Kingsport, Tennessee